Magic, Witchcraft, and Religion
A Reader in the Anthropology of Religion
Eighth Edition

Pamela A. Moro
Willamette University

James E. Myers
Emeritus, California State University, Chico

The McGraw·Hill Companies

Connect
Learn
Succeed™

A Division of The McGraw-Hill Companies

ISBN: 978-0-07-814001-3
MHID: 0-07-814001-3

Vice President and Editor in Chief: *Michael Ryan*
Publisher: *Frank Mortimer*
Senior Sponsoring Editor: *Gina Boedeker*
Managing Editor: *Nicole Bridge*
Executive Marketing Manager: *Pamela Cooper*
Developmental Editor: *Phillip Butcher*
Senior Production Editor: *Karol Jurado*
Project Management: *Aptara®, Inc.*
Manuscript Editor: *Susan Norton*
Design Manager: *Allister Fein*
Cover Designer: *Kay Lieberherr*
Senior Production Supervisor: *Louis Swaim*
Composition: *10/12 Sabon by Aptara®, Inc.*
Printing: *45# New Era Matte Plus, R.R. Donnelley & Sons*
Cover images: © *Purestock / PunchStock* (left); © *Brand X Pictures / PunchStock* (middle); © *Mark Downey / Lucid Images* (right)

Library of Congress Cataloging-in-Publication Data

Magic, witchcraft, and religion: a reader in the anthropology of religion / [compiled
   by] Pamela A. Moro, James E. Myers.—8th ed.
      p. cm.
   Includes bibliographical references and index.
   ISBN-13: 978-0-07-814001-3 (pbk. : alk. paper)
   ISBN-10: 0-07-814001-3 (pbk. : alk. paper)
   1. Religion. 2. Occultism. I. Myers-Moro, Pamela. II. Myers, James E. (James
Edward)
   BL50.M26 2010
   218—dc22   2009030622

To our Families and Students

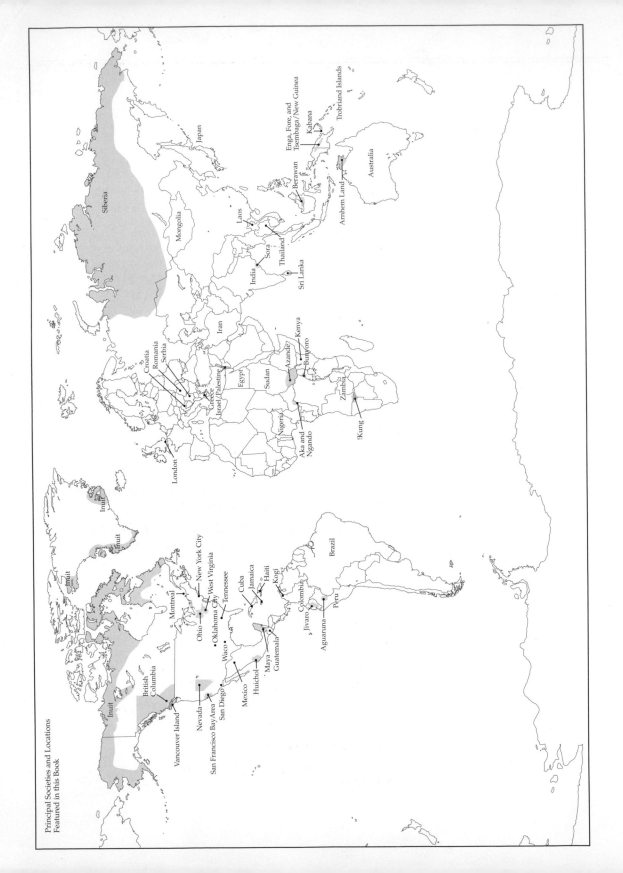

Principal Societies and Locations
Featured in this Book

Inuit

British Columbia

Vancouver Island

Nevada

San Francisco Bay Area
San Diego

Mexico

Huichol

Maya
Guatemala

Montreal

Ohio
Oklahoma City
Waco

New York City
West Virginia
Tennessee

Cuba
Jamaica
Haiti
Kogi

Colombia

Jivaro
Aguaruna

Peru

Brazil

Inuit
Inuit
Inuit

London

Croatia
Romania
Serbia
Greece
Israel/Palestine

Iran

Egypt
Sudan

Nigeria

Aka and
Ngando

Azande
Bunyoro
Kenya

Zambia

!Kung

Siberia

Mongolia

Japan

Laos

Sora
Thailand
India

Sri Lanka

Enga, Fore, and
Tsembaga/New Guinea
Kabana

Berawan

Arnhem Land

Australia

Trobriand Islands

Contents

3
Ritual   83

4
Shamans, Priests, and Prophets   139

5
Altered States of Consciousness and the Religious Use of Drugs   184

10
Religion as Global Culture: Migration, Media, and Other Transnational Forces 408

Preface

The Story of This Book

This volume was initially inspired by our desire to assemble a book of readings that would captivate and engage students in undergraduate courses on the anthropology of religion. At the time of the first edition, the other available texts—though of high scholarly standards—failed to communicate the excitement of anthropology in a form accessible to undergraduate students with relatively little background in the field. In our view, the cross-cultural study of religion and the supernatural is one of the most compelling subfields of anthropology, a topic guaranteed to motivate students if presented in the right manner. The title *Magic, Witchcraft, and Religion: A Reader in the Anthropology of Religion* was selected to highlight the broad realm of religious expression addressed by anthropologists, far beyond what many students might initially think of as "religion" or "church."

Informed by our own experiences as classroom teachers, we continue to feel that the best way to teach this subject is to present a range of scholarly voices in anthology format, from both classic and contemporary authors, with ethnographic materials from North America as well as the rest of the world. The original co-editors—Arthur Lehmann and James Myers—held decades of experience teaching at a state university with students of widely varying motivations and academic backgrounds, at graduate and undergraduate levels. Co-editor Pamela Moro's teaching experience has been at liberal arts colleges, where instructors are likely to emphasize classroom discussion and the critical reading of texts.

Together we share the goal of conveying our excitement about anthropology and providing students with a solid grounding in the issues, theories, and fundamental ethnographic content of the discipline. We want to help students apply anthropological perspectives to issues that are relevant both in their own lives and in the world at large.

The Approach of the Text

As editors, our thinking about the content and scope of this book has also, of course, been shaped by our own experiences as ethnographers. One of the original editors, Arthur Lehmann, held a career-long fascination with religion, medicine, and healing in Central Africa and the Caribbean, as his numerous trips to the field attested. James's research in the United States, initially with Native American communities in California and later on nonmainstream forms of body modification, led him to issues of identity, resistance, and, perhaps most simply, what it's like to be a minority in a complex, rapidly changing society. Pamela's research on music in Thailand has brought her to consider the interplay of music, ritual, festival, and the sacred worldview associated with Buddhism. Long hours watching dance processions at temples in northern Thailand, sitting with musicians at cremation services in Bangkok, and observing altars honoring the deities associated with music have inspired her consideration of religion as an integral part of human experience. Much of the thinking behind the recent editions of this book springs from these experiences as well as our observations of changes within the anthropological study of religion itself. Our inclusion of a chapter on globalization is a response to the inescapable fact of global change and its preeminent place in current anthropological scholarship. Our combined research experiences on three continents leave us profoundly aware of the significance of religious change in our world today.

The study of religion is historically significant within the discipline of anthropology. Some of the earliest questions asked by 19th-century anthropologists had to do with the development of religion and the pan-human concern with the ultimate. Throughout the 20th century, all major anthropological theorists addressed religion in one way or another. In the more recent eras of feminist, postmodern, and critical anthropology, religion and the supernatural have remained key concerns—grounds for experimental ethnographic writing and grist for new ways of thinking about culture. The study of religion has been amenable to the four-fields approach of anthropology, most evident in studies of altered states of consciousness (including the religious use of drugs), ethnomedicine, and questions about the relationship between science and religion. Inquiry into this subject brings us to many of the issues facing humanity today—such as ethnic, political, and economic conflicts expressed in terms of religion; controversies regarding religious autonomy versus state authority, in the United States and elsewhere; religion as a force for emancipation as well as a way to maintain the status quo, for local agency and globalization. In our own multicultural society, religion is one of the most salient features of difference, and, for many of us, brushing up against individuals of different faiths is one of the main ways we encounter cultural contrast on a local level. We sincerely feel that the anthropological approach to understanding religion (assisted by contributions from related fields, such as religious studies, sociology, and psychology) offers sound hope for a just and tolerant humanity.

Content and Organization

As in earlier editions of this book, in our selection of content we have chosen not to emphasize any particular ideological angle within the anthropology of religion. The multiple authors included in each chapter represent a range of interests, geographic foci, and ways of looking at each subject. Discipline-based vocabulary and style of scholarly writing varies from author to author, often reflecting the time period of each article's original publication. Our hope is that the contrasts and continuities among the various articles within each chapter will help readers begin to compare and evaluate not only content but also the approaches of different anthropologists.

The book is divided into ten chapters, beginning with a broad view of anthropological ways of looking at religion and moving on to some of the core topics within the subject, such as myth, ritual, and the various types of religious specialists. Although instructors may choose to utilize articles in any order they wish, there is a loose continuity to the chapters: thinking about certain types of specialists (for example, shamans) leads us to consider altered states of consciousness, which in turn takes us to religion and healing and then to the related topics of magic, divination, and witchcraft. The scope of the book widens again in the concluding chapters, as we present materials on religious change, from small-scale movements of protest to contemporary flows of culture, transcending the boundaries of nations.

Key Features

- *Chapter-Opening Essays:* These succinct, informative essays introduce the reader to the central concepts that unify each chapter.

- *Article Introductions:* Each article is prefaced with a brief introduction, drawing attention to the key themes and arguments of the work. In some cases, we have used these article introductions to make connections between selections in the volume or to recommend related scholarly works. Students may wish to use these short editorial introductions not only as preparation for reading each article but also as a review.

- *Breadth of Coverage:* As in previous editions, we have retained our commitment to integrating the analysis of religion in the West with ethnographic studies of less familiar examples. In most chapters, one or two articles deal specifically with contemporary North America.

- *Classic and Modern Selections:* Although the majority of the articles are contemporary pieces, we have also included classic readings by Mary Douglas, E. E. Evans-Pritchard, Clifford Geertz,

Horace Miner, Bronislaw Malinowski, Victor Turner, Anthony F. C. Wallace, and Eric Wolf.

Features of the Eighth Edition

• Chapter 5 is significantly widened to address forms of altered consciousness, including trance and possession, while retaining fascinating articles on the religious use of drugs.

• Continue commitment to classical anthropological literature by including works from the mid 20th century by Claude Lévi-Strauss, John Beattie, Eric R. Wolf, Barbara Myerhoff, Roy Rappaport, and Gerardo Reichel-Dolmatoff.

• Increased attention to charismatic, evangelical, and fundamentalist Christianity in articles by Thomas J. Csordas and Susan Friend Harding.

• Coverage of anthropological approaches is broadened to include embodiment theory and the analysis of language and culture.

• New articles on Islam, Buddhism, and Shamanism offer accessible introductions to world religions as studied by anthropologists.

• Timely issues are addressed in new articles on abortion rituals, raves, terror and violence, Santeria, and Hmong shamanism in America.

• A list of suggested readings concludes each chapter. These lists may be of assistance to the instructor, but they are also intended to provide a foundation for students pursuing independent research on topics related to the chapter.

• A comprehensive glossary, with terms new to the present edition, as well as an extensive index of subjects, authors, and titles and a bibliography of references from the volume's articles, offer students further help.

Supplements

Visit our companion Web site at www.mhhe.com/moro8 for instructor resources. (The password-protected instructor center contains an indispensable instructor's manual and comprehensive test bank.)

Acknowledgments

We would like to express our thanks to the scholars, teachers, and students who have shaped our understanding of anthropology and inspired our thinking about the anthropology of religion. We acknowledge with thanks the following reviewers, whose suggestions and comments guided our preparation of the eighth edition: Hex Kleinmartin, Buffalo State University; Derek Milne, Pasadena City College; Wendy Fonarow, Glendale College; Joseph Eisenlauer, Pierce College; Susan Johnston, George Washington University; Jacque Swartout, Cypress College; Vance Geiger, University of Central Florida; Tamara Cheshire, California State University, Sacramento; David Knowlton, Utah Valley State College. We also thank Pam's students at Willamette University for their critical evaluation of articles and their inspiring enthusiasm for anthropology. Pam owes thanks to colleagues Rebecca Dobkins, Joyce Millen, and Peter Wogan for their friendly support and bibliographic tips, as well as to Saad Moro for assistance with the hands-on aspects of manuscript preparation. We are grateful to Elaine Cha for her studious preparation of the instructional supplements. We extend a very special thank you to Sandra Booth for her cheerful and capable work on copyright permissions, including extensive correspondence with publishers. Finally, we would like to thank our families and friends for their patience and good humor throughout this project.

P.A.M.
J.E.M.

CHAPTER ONE

The Anthropological Study of Religion

Buffalo mask of the Bobo, Upper Volta.

Anthropologists have always been interested in the origins of religion, although the lack of both written records and archaeological evidence has made the subject speculative. It is reasonable to assume, however, that religion, like material culture, has a prehistory. Surely, uncertainty and change have always existed, exposing people in all ages to real and imagined threats and anxieties. The human animal alone senses a pattern behind the facts of existence and worries about life here and in the hereafter. We are born, we live, and we die. And although this is true of other animals, only humans are aware of the precariousness of life and the inevitability of death. As William Howells has observed, "Man's life is hard, very hard. And he knows it, poor soul; that is the vital thing. He knows that he is forever confronted with the Four Horsemen—death, famine, disease, and the malice of other men" (1962. 16).

Paleoanthropological evidence shows that Neanderthals buried their dead, often in a flexed position. Such deliberate burials, many feel, indicate the beginnings of religion and the conception of an afterlife. Interpretations of other items at Neanderthal sites, such as flower pollen, bear skulls, and red and black pigments, are more controversial. Such items may tell us something about the origins of religious behavior, but they may also simply be present accidentally.

In contrast, the era of *Homo sapiens sapiens* (modern humans in the biological sense) yields tremendous evidence of religious beliefs—more elaborate burials, carved figurines ("Venuses"), and magnificent cave art. And during the Neolithic period, which began about ten thousand years ago, burials indicate a deep respect for the power of the dead. It is likely that during this period, which is marked by the cultivation of crops and the domestication of animals, cycles of nature became an important feature of magic and religious beliefs. Drought, storms, and other natural perils of the farmer could have created a growing dependence on supernatural powers.

The antiquity of religion indirectly testifies to its utility; however, the usefulness of supernaturalism to contemporary societies is a clearer, more provable demonstration of its functions. The many forms of adversity facing individuals and groups require explanation and action; we are unwilling to let challenges to health, safety, and salvation go unchecked. Just as adversity is universal, so, too, is the use of religion as an explanation for and solution to adversity. Although the form religion takes is as diverse as its practitioners, all religions seek to answer questions that cannot be explained in terms of objective knowledge—to permit people reasonable explanations for often unreasonable events and phenomena by demonstrating a cause-and-effect relationship between the supernatural and the human condition. This may be its most important function.

In his article "Religion: Problems of Definition and Explanation" (1966: 109–17), Melford E. Spiro has distinguished three sets of basic desires (cognitive, substantive, and expressive), each of which is satisfied by a corresponding function of religion (adjustive, adaptive, and integrative). Spiro's first and second functions are basically those of explanation and solution: the adjustive function of religion, as he defines it, is to satisfy the cognitive desires we experience as we attempt to understand what goes on around us (illness, natural phenomena); the adaptive function seeks to satisfy substantive desires (the desire for rain or for victory in war). In his third category, however, Spiro moves to different territory: the often unconscious, expressive desires made up of what Spiro calls painful drives and painful motives.

According to Spiro, painful drives are anxieties concerning infantile and primitive fears (fears of destruction or of one's own destructiveness). Painful motives are culturally forbidden—for example, types of aggressive or sexual behavior that result in feelings of shame, inadequacy, and moral anxiety. Because of the pain they create in an individual, these drives and motives are usually relegated to the unconscious, where, "in the absence of other, or of more efficient means," religion becomes the vehicle "by which, symbolically, they can be handled and expressed." Thus, in what Spiro calls the integrative function of supernaturalism, "religious belief and ritual provide the content for culturally constituted projective mechanisms by which unconscious fears and anxieties may be reduced and repressed motives may be satisfied" (1966: 115).

Over the years, scholars have taken several approaches in their attempts to understand the reasons for the existence of religious behavior. The most prominent of these approaches are psychological, sociological, and anthropological. Spiro's belief that religious behavior reduces unconscious fears typifies the psychological approach, which, briefly stated, sees religion as functioning to reduce anxiety. For example, the famous British social anthropologist Bronislaw Malinowski held that the proper use of religious rites reduced anxieties brought on by crisis. (Like all theorists who apply the psychological approach, Freud also believed that religion and ritual functioned to reduce anxieties, but, unlike others, he saw religion as a neurotic need that humans would eventually outgrow.) In contrast, the sociological viewpoint stresses the societal origins of religion. The French sociologist Emile Durkheim, for example, viewed religion as a manifestation of social solidarity and collective beliefs. According to Durkheim, members of society create religious objects, rituals, beliefs, and symbols in order to integrate their cultures. A. R. Radcliffe-Brown, a British social anthropologist, agreed with Durkheim that participation in annual religious rites functioned to increase social solidarity.

Although their functional analyses of religious behavior and phenomena do explain, in part, the universality of religion, neither the psychological nor the sociological theorists adequately provide answers to the origin of religion. Both approaches are too limited in focus, centered as they are on human emotions and social structure respectively; neither explores the wide variety of cultural expressions of religion. Because religious experience, wherever it is observed, displays such great variation of cognitive and phenomenal expression, anything less than a wide-ranging holistic approach would not allow true comparisons; as a result, generalizations about the nature of religious systems would be incomplete as well as inaccurate.

The third, the anthropological approach to the study of religion, is by its very nature holistic, combining not only sociological and psychological but historical, semantic, and evolutionary perspectives as well. Anthropologists today attempt to go beyond the observable to the analysis of symbolic forms. In order to make generalizations on pan-human religious behavior, symbology, and ideology, however, anthropologists must work from the common basis of a definition of religion. Without an acceptable and accurate definition, anthropologists would be unable to establish a common basis for comparison of religions cross-culturally.

Many definitions of religion have been generated by anthropologists. Edward B. Tylor, the father of modern anthropology, described religion as the belief in spiritual beings, what he called "animism," the most primitive form of religion. At the opposite extreme from Tylor's open-ended definition, which set no limits as to what the study of spiritual beings would embrace, are a majority of contemporary anthropologists who, like Spiro, define religion more narrowly as "an institution consisting of culturally postulated superhuman beings" (1966: 96). At first glance, Tylor's and Spiro's definitions appear similar, but Spiro's use of the term *superhuman*, unlike Tylor's *spiritual beings*, emphasizes an aura of omnipotence unknown to the living. Further, Spiro's position that religion is an institution places it in the realm of phenomena that can be empirically studied, as any other cultural institution can be. Still, similarities in Tylor's and Spiro's definitions are apparent: both show, for example, that religion is the study of the nature of the unnatural. Spirits are not of this world, nor are superhumans; indeed, both are "supernatural," which has been defined by the anthropologist Edward Norbeck "to include all that is not natural, that which is regarded as extraordinary, not of the ordinary world, mysterious or unexplainable in ordinary terms" (1961: 11).

Expanding the definition of religion beyond spiritual and superhuman beings to include the extraordinary, the mysterious, and unexplainable allows a more comprehensive view of religious behaviors among the peoples of the world and permits the anthropological investigation of phenomena such as magic, sorcery, curses, and other practices that hold meaning for both preliterate and literate societies. For this reason, this book focuses on the concept of the supernatural and incorporates a wide variety of contemporary examples of religious beliefs and practices that demonstrate the breadth of human ideology.

Through their comparative research, anthropologists have shown that religious practices and beliefs vary in part as a result of the level of social structure in a given society. In *The Birth of the Gods* (1960), Guy Swanson applied a statistical approach to support the argument that religious forms are related to social development, and in *Religion: An Anthropological View* (1966: 84–101), Anthony F. C. Wallace presented a provocative typology of religious behavior based on the concept of the cult institution—"a set of rituals all having the same general goal, all explicitly rationalized by a set of similar or related beliefs, and all supported by the same social group" (p. 75). Ranging from the simplest to the most complex, Wallace describes individualistic, shamanic, communal, and ecclesiastical cult institutions. Each succeeding or more complex level contains all components of those preceding it. The ecclesiastical, for example, contains all the elements of the less complex individualistic, shamanistic, and communal cult institutions.

According to Wallace, in the simplest, *individualistic* cult institution, each person functions as his or her own specialist without need for such intermediaries as shamans or priests. Examples occur in both modern and primitive societies (the dream cult among the Iroquois, sealing magic among the Trobriand Islanders, and various cults among the Americans). The next level, the *shamanic*, also found in cultures around the world, marks the beginning of a religious division of labor. Individual part-time practitioners are designated by experience, birth, or training to help lay clients enlist the aid of the supernatural. The *communal* cult institution is even more complex, with laypeople handling important religious rituals for people in such special categories as secret societies, kinship groups, and age groups. (Examples include the ancestor ceremonies of the Chinese and some African tribal groups, Iroquois agricultural rituals, and Australian puberty rituals.) Although specialists such as shamans, skilled speakers, and dancers may participate, the lay group assumes the primary responsibility for conducting the sacred performance; an extensive religious hierarchy is still not in evidence. It is in the fourth, *ecclesiastical* cult institution that a professional religious clergy is formally elected or appointed and the division of labor is sharply drawn, with the laypeople usually passive participants instead of active performers. Ecclesiastical cult institutions have characteristically worshipped either an Olympian pantheon of gods (as among the ancient Greeks and Romans) or a monotheistic deity (as among the Judeo-Christian and Muslim religions).

The differences between religious behavior and belief in so-called primitive and modern cultures has been of great interest to anthropologists over the years. Howells (1962: 5) observed several characteristics that he believed distinguished the major world religions from the belief systems of more primitive cultures. First, the "great faiths" are messianic, their origins stemming from such charismatic figures as Jesus, Buddha, and Muhammad. Second, they have a rigid ethical form. Third, each has a missionary, imperialistic aspect, seeing itself as the one and only religion. Finally, each displays an exclusiveness in its belief system to the degree of being intolerant of other faiths. Howells is quick to point out that he has been generalizing, reminding the reader that the varied nature and heterogeneity of native cults may make an understanding of their nature arduous, especially for anyone aware only of the differences among Christian sects (1962: 6). His concluding remark is important to an understanding of all the articles in this book; referring to the "perfect legitimacy" of native cults, he states that the

> primitive devotees are not people of another planet, but are essentially exactly like us, and are engaged with precisely the same kind of religious appetite as the civilized. And that appetite is fed and stilled by their own religions. This is very important; it is why we are taking those religions seriously. They are not toys. They are what we might be doing ourselves; and they are what most of our ancestors were indeed doing, two thousand years ago today. (1962: 7)

Tomes have been written on the universality and tenacity of religion, even when they were faced with harsh repression by governments, modernization, and economic globalization. Vernon Reynolds and Ralph Tanner maintain that

> there is more to life, it seems, than the secular state can encompass. People want religion and faith; many of them could hardly imagine life without these things. . . . Religions are also down to earth, and we believe that it is this contact with the material world that explains the continued existence of religions in all countries, why they have survived and multiplied during history, and why they are a real force in the world today. (1995: 4, 9)

The five articles in this chapter have been selected to provide a basic understanding of the anthropological approach to the study of the supernatural. Each stresses the use of the comparative method, the very anchor for anthropological thought.

In the first article, Clifford Geertz demonstrates the importance of a historical, psychological, sociological, and semantic approach to the study of religion.

Next, Marvin Harris discusses the fascinating possibility of religion among nonhuman species. In addition, he advances the notion that spiritual beings are found also in the religions of prestate societies.

In the third article, Dorothy Lee shows how religion is part and parcel of a preliterate people's total way of life. Lee tells us about preliterate societies in which ceremonies and their preparation occupy most of a year.

In the fourth selection, Claude E. Stipe suggests possible explanations of why anthropologists traditionally have regarded missionaries as "the enemy."

Finally, in an article written for the present volume, Pamela Moro considers how anthropological concerns have shaped the study of Buddhism in Southeast Asia. The article includes an extended look at the recent popularity of amulets in Thailand, during a time of social unease.

References

Howells, William
    1962 *The Heathens: Primitive Man and His Religions.* Garden City, N.Y.: Doubleday.

Norbeck, Edward
    1961 *Religion in Primitive Society.* New York: Harper and Brothers.

Reynolds, Vernon, and Ralph Tanner
    1995 *The Social Ecology of Religion.* New York: Oxford University Press.

Spiro, Melford E.
    1966 "Religion: Problems of Definition and Explanation." In Michael Banton, ed., *Anthropological Approaches to the Study of Religion,* pp. 85–126. London: Tavistock Publications Limited for the Association of Social Anthropologists of the Commonwealth.

Swanson, Guy
    1960 *The Birth of the Gods: The Origin of Primitive Beliefs.* Ann Arbor: University of Michigan Press.

Wallace, Anthony F. C.
    1966 *Religion: An Anthropological View.* New York: Random House.

I

Religion

Clifford Geertz

In his classic work "Religion as a Cultural System" (1966), Clifford Geertz argued for a broadened analysis of religion. This argument, aimed primarily at the narrowness of the British sociological approach to the study of comparative religion, was accepted by American ethnologists and reflected in their contemporary research. In the following article, Geertz pursues his goal, demonstrating the importance of his historical, psychological, sociological, and semantic approaches to the study of religion and concluding that a mature theory of religion will integrate these approaches into a conceptual system whose exact form remains to be discovered. Geertz also explores the view of scholars who regard "primitive thought" as a distinctive mode of reasoning and/or a special body of knowledge, noting that their work persists as a minor but important theme in anthropological studies of religion.

Geertz's own work epitomizes the symbolic and interpretive approaches within anthropology. The most acclaimed response to Geertz, questioning the entire category of "religion" and urging alternatives to the symbolic approach, comes from Talal Asad, in his 1983 article, "The Construction of Religion as an Anthropological Category" (reprinted in Asad's Geneaologies of Religion. *Baltimore: The Johns Hopkins University Press, 1993). Throughout his long and influential career, Clifford Geertz carried out fieldwork in Java, Bali, and Morocco. He passed away in 2006.*

The anthropological study of religion has been highly sensitive to changes in the general intellectual and moral climate of the day; at the same time, it has been a powerful factor in the creation of that climate. Since the early discussion by Edward Tylor, interest in the beliefs and rituals of distant, ancient, or simpler peoples has been shaped by an awareness of contemporary issues. The questions that anthropologists have pursued among exotic religions have arisen from the workings—or the misworkings—of modern Western society, and particularly from its restless quest for self-discovery. In turn, their findings have profoundly affected the course that quest has taken and the perspective at which it has arrived.

Reprinted by permission of the publisher from INTERNATIONAL ENCYCLOPEDIA OF THE SOCIAL SCIENCES, David L. Sills, Editor. Vol. 13, pp. 398–406. Copyright 1972 by Crowell Collier and Macmillan.

Perhaps the chief reason for the rather special role of comparative religious studies is that issues which, when raised within the context of Western culture, led to extreme social resistance and personal turmoil could be freely and even comfortably handled in terms of bizarre, presumably primitive, and thus—also presumably—fanciful materials from long ago or far away. The study of "primitive religions" could pass as the study of superstition, supposedly unrelated to the serious religious and moral concerns of advanced civilization, at best either a sort of vague foreshadowing of them or a grotesque parody upon them. This made it possible to approach all sorts of touchy subjects, such as polytheism, value relativism, possession, and faith healing, from a frank and detached point of view. One could ask searching questions about the historicity of myth among Polynesians; when asked in relation to Christianity, these same questions were, until quite recently, deeply threatening. One could discuss the projection of erotic wishes found in the "totemic" rites of Australian aborigines, the social roots and functions of African "ancestor worship," or the protoscientific quality of Melanesian "magical thought," without involving oneself in polemical debate and emotional distress. The application of the comparative method—the essence of anthropological thought—to religion permitted the growth of a resolutely scientific approach to the spiritual dimensions of human life.

Through the thin disguise of comparative method the revolutionary implications of the work of such men as Tylor, Durkheim, Robertson Smith, Freud, Malinowski, and Radcliffe-Brown soon became apparent—at first mainly to philosophers, theologians, and literary figures, but eventually to the educated public in general. The meticulous descriptions of tribal curiosities such as soul loss, shamanism, circumcision, blood sacrifice, sorcery, tree burial, garden magic, symbolic cannibalism, and animal worship have been caught up in some of the grander intellectual battles of the last hundred years—from those over evolutionism and historicism in the late nineteenth century to those over positivism and existentialism today. Psychoanalysts and phenomenologists, Marxists and Kantians, racists and egalitarians, absolutists and relativists, empiricists and rationalists, believers and skeptics have all had recourse to the record—partial, inconsistent, and shot through with simple error as it is—of the spiritual life of tribal peoples to support their positions and belabor those of their opponents. If interest in "primitive religion" among savants of all sorts has been remarkably high, consensus concerning its nature and significance has not.

At least three major intellectual developments have exercised a critical influence on the anthropological study of religion: (1) the emergence, in the latter half of the nineteenth century, of history as the sovereign science of man; (2) the positivist reaction against this sovereignty in the first decades of the twentieth century and the radical split of the social sciences into resolutely psychological approaches, on the one hand, and resolutely sociological ones, on the other; and (3) the growth, in the interwar period, of a concern with the role of ideational factors in the regulation of social life. With the first of these came an emphasis on the nature of primitive reasoning and the stages of its evolution into civilized thought.

With the second came an investigation of the emotional basis of religious ritual and belief and the separate examination of the role of ritual and belief in social integration. The concern with value systems and other features of the ideational realm led to an exploration of the philosophical dimensions of religious ideas, particularly the symbolic vehicles in terms of which those ideas are expressed.

Evolutionism and Its Enemies

Like so much else in anthropology, the study of the religious notions of primitive peoples arose within the context of evolutionary theory. In the nineteenth century, to think systematically about human affairs was to think historically—to seek out survivals of the most elementary forms and to trace the steps by which these forms subsequently developed. And though, in fact, Tylor, Morgan, Frazer, and the rest drew more on the synthetic social-stage theories of such men as Comte and Hegel than on the analytic random-variation and natural-selection ideas of Darwin, the grand concept of evolution was shared by both streams of thought: namely, that the complex, heterogeneous present has arisen, more or less gradually, out of a simpler, more uniform past. The relics of this past are still to be found scattered, like Galápagos turtles, in out-of-the-way places around us. Tylor, an armchair scholar, made no "voyage of the *Beagle.*" But in combing and organizing the reports of missionaries, soldiers, and explorers, he proceeded from the same general premise as did Darwin, and indeed most of the leading minds of the day. For them a comprehensive, historically oriented comparison of all forms of a phenomenon, from the most primitive to the most advanced, was the royal road to understanding the nature of the phenomenon itself.

In Tylor's view, the elementary form out of which all else developed was spirit worship—*animism*. The minimal definition of religion was "a belief in spiritual beings." The understanding of religion thus came down to an understanding of the basis upon which such a belief arose at its most primitive level. Tylor's theory was intellectualistic. Belief in spirits began as an uncritical but nonetheless rational effort to explain such puzzling empirical phenomena as death, dreams, and possession. The notion of a separable soul rendered these phenomena intelligible in terms of soul departure, soul wandering, and soul invasion. Tylor believed that the idea of a soul was used to explain more and more remote and hitherto inexplicable natural occurrences, until virtually every tree and rock was haunted by some sort of gossamer presence. The higher, more developed forms of "belief in spiritual beings," first polytheism, ultimately monotheism, were founded upon this animistic basis, the urphilosophy of all mankind, and were refined through a process of critical questioning by more advanced thinkers. For this earnest Quaker the religious history of the world was a history of progressive, even inevitable, enlightenment.

This intellectualistic, "up from darkness" strain has run through most evolutionist thought about religion. For Frazer, a nineteenth-century figure who lived for forty years into the twentieth century without finding it necessary to alter either his views or his methods, the mental progress involved was from magic to religion to science. Magic was the primordial form of human thought; it consisted in mistaking either spatiotemporal connection ("sympathetic magic," as when drinking the blood of an ox transfers its strength to the drinker) or phenomenal similarity ("imitative magic," as when the sound of drumming induces thunderheads to form) for true scientific causality. For Durkheim, evolutionary advance consisted in the emergence of specific, analytic, *profane* ideas about "cause" or "category" or "relationship" from diffuse, global, *sacred* images. These "collective representations," as he called them, of the social order and its moral force included such sacra as "mana," "totem," and "god." For Max Weber, the process was one of "rationalization": the progressive organization of religious concern into certain more precisely defined, more specifically focused, and more systematically conceived cultural forms. The level of sophistication of such theories (and, hence, their present relevance) varies very widely. But, like Tylor's, they all conceive of the evolution of religion as a process of cultural differentiation: the diffuse, all-embracing, but rather unsystematic and uncritical religious practices of primitive peoples are transformed into the more specifically focused, more regularized, less comprehensively authoritative practices of the more advanced civilizations. Weber, in whom both intellectualism and optimism were rather severely tempered by a chronic apprehensiveness, called this transformation the "disenchantment (*Entzauberung*) of the world."

On the heels of evolutionism came, of course, anti-evolutionism. This took two quite different forms. On one side there was a defense, mainly by Roman Catholic scholars, of the so-called degradation theory. According to this theory, the original revelation of a high god to primitive peoples was later corrupted by human frailty into the idol worship of present-day tribal peoples. On the other side there was an attack, mainly by American scholars of the Boas school, upon the "armchair speculation" of evolutionary thinkers and a call for its replacement by more phenomenological approaches to the study of tribal custom.

The first of these reactions led, logically enough, to a search among the most primitive of existing peoples for traces of belief in a supreme being. The resulting dispute, protracted, often bitter, and stubbornly inconclusive as to the existence of such "primitive monotheism," turned out to be unproductive—aside from some interesting discussions by Lang (1898) concerning culture heroes and by Eliade (1949) concerning sky gods—and both the issue and the theory that gave rise to it have now receded from the center of scholarly attention. The second reaction has had a longer life and great impact on ethnographic methodology, but it too is now in partial eclipse. Its main contributions—aside from some devastating empirical demolitions of evolutionist generalization—came in the field of cultural diffusion. Leslie Spier's study of the spread of the Sun Dance through the Great Plains and A. L. Kroeber's application of the age-area approach to aboriginal religion in California are good examples of productive diffusion studies. However, apart from their importance for culture history, the contribution of such distributional studies to our understanding of religious ideas, attitudes, and practices as such has not been great, and few students now pursue these studies. The call of the Boas school for thorough field research and disciplined inductive analysis has been heeded; but its fruits, insofar as religious studies are concerned, have been reaped by others less inhibited theoretically.

Psychological Approaches

The major reaction against the intellectual tradition of the cultural evolutionists took place not within anthropology, however, but in the general context of the positivist revolt against the domination of historicist modes of thought in the social sciences. In the years before World War I the rise of the systematic psychologism of psychoanalysis and of the equally systematic sociologism of the *Année sociologique* forced evolutionist theorizing into the background, even though the leaders of both movements—Freud and Durkheim—were themselves still very strongly influenced by it. Perhaps even more relevant, it introduced a sharp split into anthropological studies of religion which has resolved into the militantly psychodynamic and the militantly social-structural approaches.

Freud's major work in this field is, of course, *Totem and Taboo,* a book anthropologists in general have had great difficulty in evaluating—as Kroeber's two reviews of it, the first facilely negative, the second, two decades later, ambivalently positive, demonstrate. The source of the difficulty has been an inability or an unwillingness to disentangle Freud's basic thesis—that religious rituals and beliefs are homologous with neurotic symptoms—from the chimerical ethnology and obsolete biology within which he insisted upon setting it. Thus, the easy demolition of what Kroeber called Freud's "just so story" concerning primal incest, parricide, and guilt within some protohuman horde ("in the beginning was the deed") was all too often mistaken for total rejection of the rather more penetrating proposition that the obsessions, dreams, and fantasies of collective life spring from the same intrapsychic sources as do those of the isolated individual.

For those who read further in Freud's writings, however—especially in "Mourning and Melancholia" and "Obsessive Acts and Religious Practices"—it became apparent that what was at issue was the applicability of theories concerning the forms and causes of individual psychopathology to the explanation of the forms and causes of public myth and group ritual. Róheim (1950) analyzed Australian circumcision rites against the background of orthodox Freudian theories of psychosexual development, especially those clustered around the Oedipal predicament. However, he explicitly avoided recourse to speculations about buried memories of primordial occurrences. Bettelheim (1954) adopted a similar, though more systematic and less orthodox, approach to initiation practices generally, seeing them as socially instituted symbolic mechanisms for the definition and stabilization of sexual identity. Kardiner (1945), taking a neo-Freudian position, sought to demonstrate that the religious institutions of tribal peoples were projections of a "basic personality structure," formed not by the action of an unconsciously remembered historical trauma but by the more observable traumas produced by child-training practices, an approach later extended and cast into quantitative form by Whiting (Whiting and Child 1953). Erikson (1950), drawing upon developments in ego psychology which conceived the emergence of the adult personality to be a joint product of psychobiological maturation, cultural context, and historical experience, interpreted the religious notions of the Yurok and the Sioux in terms of certain basic modes of relating to the world. These relationships gradually developed during the whole course of childhood and adolescence. Others—notably Devereux (1951)—have attempted to use the autobiographical, case-history approach to determine the relations between personality dynamics and religious orientation in particular individuals; still others—notably Hallowell (1937–1954)—have employed projective tests, questionnaires, reports of dreams, or systematic interviews toward similar ends.

In all such studies, even when individual authors have dissented from many of Freud's specific views, the basic premise has been Freudian: that religious practices can be usefully interpreted as expressions of unconscious psychological forces—and this has become, amid much polemic, an established tradition of inquiry. In recent years, however, responsible work of this type has come to question the degree to which one is justified in subjecting historically created and socially institutionalized cultural forms to a system of analysis founded on the treatment of the mental illnesses of individuals. For this reason, the future of this approach depends perhaps more upon developments within psychoanalysis, now in a somewhat uncertain state, than within anthropology. So far, perhaps only Kluckhohn's pioneering *Navaho Witchcraft* (1944) has attempted to systematically relate psychological factors to social and cultural aspects of primitive religion. The great majority of psychoanalytic studies of tribal beliefs and rites remain willfully parochial.

In any case, not all psychological approaches to religion have been Freudian. Jungian influences have had a certain impact, especially on studies of myth. Campbell (1949), for example, has stressed the continuity of certain themes both cross-culturally and temporally. These themes have been interpreted as expressions of transpersonal constancies in unconscious mental functioning which are at the same time expressions of fundamental cosmic realities.

Simple emotionalist theories have also been extremely popular. There have been two main varieties of these: awe theories and confidence theories. Awe theories have been based on some usually rather vague notion of "religious thrill" experienced by human beings when brought face to face with cosmic forces. A wide range of ethnologists, from Max Müller through Lang and Marett to Lowie and Goldenweiser, have accepted such theories in one form or another. However, awe theories remain mere notations of the obvious—that religious experience is, in the nature of the case, touched with intense feelings of the grandeur of the universe in relation to the self and of the vulnerability of the self in relation to the universe. This is not explanation, but circular reasoning.

Confidence theories also begin with a notion of man's inward sense of weakness, and especially of his fears—of disease, of death, of ill fortune of all kinds—and they see religious practices as designed to quiet such fears, either by explaining them away, as in doctrines of the afterlife, or by claiming to link the individual to external sources of strength, as in prayer. The best-known confidence theory was that set forth by Malinowski. He regarded magic as enabling man to pursue uncertain but essential endeavors by assuring him of their ultimate success. Confidence, or anxiety-reduction, theories, like awe theories, clearly have empirical foundation but do not adequately explore the complex relationship between fear and religious activity. They are not rooted in any systematic conceptualization of mental functioning and so merely point to matters desperately in need of clarification, without in fact clarifying them.

Sociological Approaches

The sociological approach to the analysis of the religions of nonliterate peoples proceeded independent of, and even at variance with, the psychoanalytic approach, but it shared a concern with the same phenomenon: the peculiar "otherness," the extraordinary, momentous, "set apart" quality of sacred (or "taboo") acts and objects, as contrasted with the profane. The intense aura of high seriousness was traced by Freud to the projection of unacceptable wishes repressed from consciousness onto external objects. The dramatic ambivalence of the sacred—its paradoxical unification of the commanded and the forbidden, the pure and the polluted, the salutary and the dangerous—was a symbolic expression of the underlying ambivalence of human desires. For Durkheim, too, the extraordinary atmosphere surrounding sacred acts and objects was symbolic of a hidden reality, but a social, not a psychological one: the moral force of the human community.

Durkheim believed that the integrity of the social order was the primary requisite for human survival, and the means by which that integrity superseded individual egocentricity was the primary problem of sociological analysis. He saw Australian totemism (which he, like Freud, made the empirical focus of his work) as a mechanism to this end. For example, the collective rituals involving the emblems of the totemic beings—the so-called bull roarers—aroused the heightened emotions of mass behavior and evoked a deep sense of moral identification among the participants. The creation of social solidarity was the result of the common public veneration, by specific groups of persons, of certain carefully designated symbolic objects. These objects had no intrinsic value except as perceptible representations of the social identity of the individuals. Collective worship of consecrated bits of painted wood or stone created a moral community, a "church," upon which rested the viability of the major social units. These sanctified objects thus represented the system of rights and obligations implicit in the social order and the individual's unformulated sense of its overriding significance in his life. All sacred objects, beliefs, and acts, and the extraordinary emotions attending them, were outward expressions of inward social necessities, and, in a famous phrase, God was the "symbol of society." Few anthropologists have been able to swallow Durkheim's thesis whole, when put this baldly. But the more moderate proposition that religious rituals and beliefs both reflect and act to support the moral framework underlying social arrangements (and are in turn animated by it) has given rise to what has become perhaps the most popular form of analysis in the anthropological study of religion. Usually called "functionalism"—or sometimes, to distinguish it from certain variants deemed objectionable, "structuralism"—this approach found its champion in Radcliffe-Brown and its major development in Great Britain, though its influence has now spread very much more widely.

Radcliffe-Brown (1952) agreed with Durkheim's postulate that the main role (or "function") of religion was to celebrate and sustain the norms upon which the integration of society depends. But unlike Durkheim (and like Freud), Radcliffe-Brown was concerned with the content of sacred symbols, and particularly with the reasons why one object rather than another was absorbed into rite or woven into myth. Why here stones, there water holes, here camp circles, there personified winds?

Durkheim had held this to be an arbitrary matter, contingent upon historical accident or psychological proclivity, beyond the reach of and irrelevant to sociological analysis. Radcliffe-Brown considered, however, that man's need for a concrete expression of social solidarity was not sufficient explanation of the structure of a people's religious system. Something was needed to tie the particular objects awarded sacred status (or, in his terminology, "ritual value") to the particular social interests they presumably served and reflected. Radcliffe-Brown, resolute empiricist that he was, chose a solution Durkheim had already magisterially demolished: the utilitarian. The objects selected for religious veneration by a given people were either directly or indirectly connected to factors critical to their collective well-being. Things that had real, that is, practical, "social value" were elevated to having spiritual, or symbolic, "ritual value," thus fusing the social and the natural into one overarching order. For primitives at least (and Radcliffe-Brown attempted to establish his theory with regard to the sanctified turtles and palm leaves of the pre-agricultural Andaman Islanders and, later on, with regard to Australian totemism), there is no discontinuity, no difference even, between moral and physical, spiritual and practical relationships and processes. These people regard both men and things as parts of a single normative system. Within that system those elements which are critical to its effective functioning (or, sometimes, phenomena empirically associated with such elements, such as the Andaman cicada cycle and the shifting monsoons) are made the objects of that special sort of respect and attention which we call religious but which the people themselves regard as merely prudential.

Radcliffe-Brown focused upon the content of sacred symbols and emphasized the relation between conceptions of the moral order of existence and conceptions of its natural order. However, the claim that the sanctity of religious objects derives from their practical social importance is one of those theories which works when it works and doesn't when it doesn't. Not only has it proved impossible to find even an indirect practical significance in most of the enormous variety of things tribal peoples have regarded as sacred (certain Australian tribes worship vomit), but the view that religious concerns are mere ritualizations of real-life concerns leaves the phenomenon of sacredness itself—its aura of mystery, power, fascination—totally unexplained.

More recent structuralist studies have tended to evade both these questions and to concentrate on the role played by religion in maintaining social equilibrium. They attempt to show how given sets of religious practices (ancestor worship, animal sacrifice, witchcraft and sorcery, regeneration rites) do in fact express and reinforce the moral values underlying crucial processes (lineage segmentation, marriage, conflict adjudication, political succession) in the particular society under investigation. Arnold van Gennep's study of crisis rites was perhaps the most important forerunner of the many analyses of this type. Although valuable in their own right as ethnography and as sociology, these structural formulations have been severely limited by their rigid avoidance on the one side, of the kind of psychological considerations that could account for the peculiar emotions which permeate religious belief and practice, and, on the other, of the philosophical considerations that could render their equally peculiar content intelligible.

The Analysis of Symbolic Forms

In contrast to other approaches—evolutionary, psychological, sociological—the field of what we may loosely call "semantic studies" of religion is extremely jumbled. There is, as yet, no well-established central trend to analysis, no central figure around whom to order debate, and no readily apparent system of interconnections relating the various competing trends to one another.

Perhaps the most straightforward strategy—certainly the most disarming—is merely to *accept* the myriad expressions of the sacred in primitive societies, to consider them as actual ingressions of the divine into the world, and to trace the forms these expressions have taken across the earth and through time. The result would be a sort of natural history of revelation, whose aim would be to isolate the major classes of religious phenomena considered as authentic manifestations of the sacred—what Eliade, the chief proponent of this approach, calls hierophanies—and to trace the rise, dominance, decline, and disappearance of these classes within the changing contexts of human life. The meaning of religious activity, the burden of its content, is discovered through a meticulous, wholly inductive investigation of the natural modalities of such behavior (sun worship, water symbolism, fertility cults, renewal myths, etc.) and of the vicissitudes these modalities undergo when projected, like the Son of God himself, into the flux of history.

Metaphysical questions (here uncommonly obtrusive) aside, the weaknesses of this approach derive from the same source as its strengths: a drastic limiting of the interpretations of religion to the sort that a resolutely Baconian methodology can produce. On the one hand, this approach has led, especially in the case of a scholar as erudite and indefatigable as Eliade, to the uncovering of some highly suggestive clusterings of certain religious patterns with particular historical conditions—for example, the frequent association of sun worship, activist conceptions of divine power, cultic veneration of deified heroes, elitist doctrines of political sovereignty, and imperialist ideologies of national expansion. But, on the other hand, it has placed beyond the range of scientific analysis everything but the history and morphology of the phenomenal forms of religious expression. The study of tribal beliefs and practices is reduced to a kind of cultural paleontology whose sole aim is the reconstruction, from scattered and corrupted fragments, of the "mental universe of archaic man."

Primitive Thought

Other scholars who are interested in the meaningful content of primitive religion but who are incapable of so thoroughgoing a suspension of disbelief as Eliade, or are repelled by the cultic overtones of this somewhat mystagogic line of thought, have directed their attention instead toward logical and epistemological considerations. This has produced a long series of studies that view "primitive thought" as a distinctive mode of reasoning and/or a special body of knowledge. From Lévy-Bruhl through Lévi-Strauss, and with important contributions from members of the evolutionary, psychoanalytic, and sociological schools as well, this line of exploration has persisted as a minor theme in anthropological studies of religion. With the recent advances in linguistics, information theory, the analysis of cognition, semantic philosophy, modern logic, and certain sorts of literary investigation, the systematic study of symbolic activity bids fair to become, in a rather thoroughly revised form, the major theme for investigation. The "new key" Susanne K. Langer heard being struck in philosophy in the early 1940s—"the concern with the concept of meaning in all its forms"—has, like the historicist and positivist "keys" before it, begun to have its echo in the anthropological study of religion. Anthropologists are increasingly interested in ideational expression, increasingly concerned with the vehicles, processes, and practical applications of human conceptualization.

The development of this approach has come in two fairly distinct phases, one before and one after World War II. In the first phase there was a concern with "the mind of primitive man" and in particular with its capacity for rational thought. In a sense, this concern represented the evolutionists' interest in primitive reasoning processes detached from the historicist context. In the second phase, which is still in process, there has been a move away from, and in part a reaction against, the subjectivist emphasis of the earlier work. Ideational expression is thought of as a public activity, rather like speech, and the structure of the symbolic materials, the "language," in whose terms the activity is conducted becomes the subject of investigation.

The first, subjectivist, phase was animated by a protracted wrangle between those who used the religious beliefs and practices of tribal peoples as evidence to prove that there was a qualitative difference between the thought processes of primitives and those of civilized men and the anthropologists who considered such religious activity as evidence for the lack of any such differences. The great protagonist of the first school was the French philosopher Lévy-Bruhl whose theories of "prelogical mentality" were as controversial within anthropology as they were popular outside it. According to Lévy-Bruhl, the thought of primitives, as reflected in their religious ideas, is not governed by the immanent laws of Aristotelian logical reasoning, but by affectivity—by the vagrant flow of emotion and the dialectical principles of "mystical participation" and "mystical exclusion."

The two most effective antagonists of Lévy-Bruhl's theories concerning primitive religion were Radin and Malinowski. Radin, influenced by Boas's more general attacks on theories of "primitive mentality," sought to demonstrate that primitive religious thought reaches, on occasion, very high levels of logical articulation and philosophical sophistication and that tribal society contains, alongside the common run of unreflective doers ("men of action"), contemplative intellectuals ("men of thought") of boldness, subtlety, and originality. Malinowski attacked the problem on an even broader front. Using his ethnographic knowledge of the Trobriand Islanders, Malinowski argued that alongside their religious and magical notions (which he, too, regarded as mainly emotionally determined) the "savages" also had a rather well-developed and, as far as it went, accurate empirical knowledge of gardening, navigation, housebuilding, canoe construction, and other useful arts. He further claimed that they were absolutely clear as to the distinction between these two sorts of reasoning, between mystical-magical and empirical-pragmatic thinking, and never confused them in actual practice. Of these two arguments, the former seems to be today nearly universally accepted and was perhaps never in fact really questioned. But with respect to the latter, serious doubts have arisen concerning whether the lines between "science," "magic," and "religion" are as simple and clear-cut in the minds of tribal peoples (or any peoples) as Malinowski, never one for shaded judgments, portrayed them. Nevertheless, between them, Radin and Malinowski rather definitively demolished the notion of a radical qualitative gap between the thought processes of primitive and civilized men. Indeed, toward the end of his life even Lévy-Bruhl admitted that his arguments had been badly cast and might better have been phrased in terms of different modes of thinking common to all men. (In fact, Freud, with his contrast between primary and secondary thinking processes, had already made this distinction.)

Thus, the debate about what does or does not go on in the heads of savages exhausted itself in generalities, and recent writers have turned to a concern with the symbolic forms, the conceptual resources, in terms of which primitives (and nonprimitives) think. The major figure in this work has been Claude Lévi-Strauss, although this line of attack dates back to Durkheim and Mauss's influential 1903 essay in sociological Kantianism, *Primitive Classification*. The writings of E. E. Evans-Pritchard on Zande witchcraft, Benjamin Whorf on Hopi semantics, and Gregory Bateson on Iatmul ritual and, among nonanthropologists, works by Granet, Cassirer, and Piaget have directed attention to the study of symbolic formulation.

Symbolic Systems

Lévi-Strauss, whose rather highly wrought work is still very much in progress, is concerned with the systems of classification, the "homemade" taxonomies, employed by tribal peoples to order the objects and events of their world (see Lévi-Strauss 1958; 1962). In this, he follows in the footsteps of Durkheim and Mauss. But rather than looking, as they did, to social forms for the origins and explanations of such categorical systems, he looks to the symbolic structures in terms of which they are formulated, expressed, and applied. Myth and, in a slightly different way, rite are systems of signs that fix and organize abstract conceptual relationships in terms of concrete images and thus make speculative thought possible. They permit the construction of a "science of the concrete"—the intellectual comprehension of the sensible world in terms of sensible phenomena—which is no less rational, no less logical, no more affect-driven than the abstract science of the modern world. The objects rendered sacred are selected not because of their utilitarian qualities, nor because they are projections of repressed emotions, nor yet because they reflect the moral force of social organization ritualistically impressed upon the mind. Rather, they are selected because they permit the embodiment of general ideas in terms of the immediately perceptible realities—the turtles, trees, springs, and caves—of everyday experience; not, as Lévi-Strauss says, apropos of Radcliffe-Brown's view of totems, because they are "good to eat," but because they are "good to think."

This "goodness" exists inherently in sacred objects because they provide the raw materials for analogical reasoning. The relationships perceived among certain classes of natural objects or events can be analogized, taken as models of relationships—physical, social, psychological, or moral—obtaining between persons, groups, or other natural objects and events. Thus, for example, the natural distinctions perceived among totemic beings, their species differentiation, can serve as a conceptual framework for the comprehension, expression, and communication of social distinctions among exogamous clans—their structural differentiation. Thus, the sharp contrast between the wet and dry seasons (and the radical zoological and botanical changes associated with it) in certain regions of Australia is employed in the mythology of the native peoples. They have woven an elaborate origin myth around this natural phenomenon, one that involves a rainmaking python who drowned some incestuous sisters and their children because the women polluted his water hole with menstrual blood. This model expresses and economizes the contrasts between moral purity and impurity, maleness and femaleness, social superiority and inferiority, fertilizing agent (rain) and that which is fertilized (land), and even the distinction between "high" (initiate) and "low" (noninitiate) levels of cultural achievement.

Lévi-Strauss contends that primitive religious systems are, like all symbolic systems, fundamentally communications systems. They are carriers of information in the technical Shannon-Weaver sense, and as such, the theory of information can be applied to them with the same validity as when applied to any physical systems, mechanical or biological, in which the transfer of information plays a central regulative role. Primitives, as all men, are quintessentially multichanneled emitters and receivers of messages. It is merely in the nature of the code they employ—one resting on analogies between "natural" and "cultural" distinctions and relationships—that they differ from ourselves. Where there is a distinguishing difference, it lies in the technically specialized codes of modern abstract thought, in which semantic properties are radically and deliberately severed from physical ones. Religion, primitive or modern, can be understood only as an integrated system of thought, logically sound, epistemologically valid, and as flourishing in France as in Tahiti.

It is far too early to evaluate Lévi-Strauss's work with any assurance. It is frankly incomplete and explorative, and some parts of it (the celebration of information theory, for example) are wholly programmatic. But in focusing on symbol systems as conceptual models of social or other sorts of reality, he has clearly introduced into the anthropology of religion a line of inquiry which, having already become common in modern thought generally, can hardly fail to be productive when applied to tribal myth and ritual.

Whether his own particular formulation of this approach will prove to be the most enduring remains, however, rather more of a question. His rejection of emotional considerations and his neglect of normative or social factors in favor of an extreme intellectualism which cerebralizes religion and tends to reduce it yet again to a kind of undeveloped (or, as he puts it, "undomesticated") science are questionable. His nearly exclusive stress on those intellectual processes involved in classification, i.e., on taxonomic modes of thought (a reflex of his equally great reliance on totemic ideas as type cases of primitive beliefs), at the expense of other, perhaps more common, and certainly more powerful styles of reasoning, is also doubtful. His conception of the critical process of symbolic formulation itself remains almost entirely undeveloped—hardly more than a sort of associationism dressed up with some concepts from modern linguistics. Partly as a result of this weakness and partly as a result of a tendency to consider symbol systems as entities functioning independently of the contextual factor, many of his specific interpretations of particular myths and rites seem as strained, arbitrary, and oversystematized as those of the most undisciplined psychoanalyst.

But, for all this, Lévi-Strauss has without doubt opened a vast territory for research and begun to explore it with theoretical brilliance and profound scholarship. And he is not alone. As the recent work of such diverse students as Evans-Pritchard, R. G. Lienhardt, W. E. H. Stanner, Victor W. Turner, Germaine Dieterlen, Meyer Fortes, Edmund R. Leach, Charles O. Frake, Rodney Needham, and Susanne K. Langer demonstrates, the analysis of symbolic forms is becoming a major tradition in the study of primitive religion—in fact, of religion in general. Each of these writers has a somewhat different approach. But all seem to share the conviction that an attempt must be made to approach primitive religions for what they are: systems of ideas about the ultimate shape and substance of reality.

Whatever else religion does, it relates a view of the ultimate nature of reality to a set of ideas of how man is well advised, even obligated, to live. Religion tunes human actions to a view of the cosmic order and projects images of cosmic order onto the plane of human existence. In religious belief and practice a people's style of life, what Clyde Kluckhohn called their *design for living*, is rendered intellectually reasonable; it is shown to represent a way of life ideally adapted to the world "as it 'really' ('fundamentally,' 'ultimately') is." At the same time, the supposed basic structure of reality is rendered emotionally convincing because it is presented as an actual state of affairs uniquely accommodated to such a way of life and permitting it to flourish. Thus do received beliefs, essentially metaphysical, and established norms, essentially moral, confirm and support one another.

It is this mutual confirmation that religious symbols express and celebrate and that any scientific analysis of religion must somehow contrive to explain and clarify. In the development of such an analysis historical, psychological, sociological, and what has been called here semantic considerations are all necessary, but none is sufficient. A mature theory of religion will consist of an integration of them all into a conceptual system whose exact form remains to be discovered.

2

Why We Became Religious *and* The Evolution of the Spirit World

Marvin Harris

The following selection by anthropologist Marvin Harris originally appeared as two separate essays, one entitled "Why We Became Religious," the other "The Evolution of the Spirit World." In the first essay, Harris comments on the fascinating possibility of religion among nonhuman species. He also discusses the concept of mana *(an inherent force or power), noting that, although the concepts of superstition, luck, and charisma in Western cultures closely resemble* mana, *they are not really religious concepts. Rather, according to Harris, the basis of all religious thought is animism, the universal belief that we humans share the world with various extracorporeal, mostly invisible beings. Harris closes the first essay with some thoughts on the concept of an inner being—a soul—pointing out that in many cultures people believe a person may have more than one.*

In "The Evolution of the Spirit World," Harris advances the notion that spiritual beings found in modern religions are also found in the religions of prestate societies. Thus, he briefly examines religious thought and behavior pertaining to ancestor worship at varying levels of societal complexity, starting with band-and-village societies, the earliest of human cultures. Next, Harris notes the importance of recently deceased relatives in the religions of more complexly developed societies, such as those based on gardening and fishing. Chiefdoms represent an even higher level of development, one in which greater specialization arose, including a religious practitioner who paid special attention to the chief's ancestors. Finally, Harris observes that, with the development of early states and empires, dead ancestors assumed a place of great prominence alongside the gods.

Human social life cannot be understood apart from the deeply held beliefs and values that in the short run, at least, motivate and mobilize our transactions with each other and the world of nature. So let me . . . confront certain questions concerning our kind's religious beliefs and behavior.

First, are there any precedents for religion in nonhuman species? The answer is yes, only if one accepts a definition of religion broad enough to include "superstitious" responses. Behavioral psychologists have long been familiar with the fact that animals can acquire responses that are falsely associated with rewards. For example, a pigeon is placed in a cage into which food pellets are dropped by a mechanical feeder at irregular intervals. If the reward is delivered by chance while the bird is scratching, it begins to scratch faster. If the reward is delivered while a bird happens to be flapping its wings, it keeps flapping them as if wing-flapping controls the feeder. Among humans, one can find analogous superstitions in the little rituals that baseball players engage in as they come up to bat, such as touching their caps, spitting, or rubbing their hands. None of this has any real connection with getting a hit, although constant repetition assures that every time batters get hits, they have performed the ritual. Some minor phobic behavior among humans also might be attributed to associations based on coincidental rather than contingent circumstances. I know a heart surgeon who tolerates only popular music piped into his operating room ever since he lost a patient while classical compositions were being played.

Superstition raises the issue of causality. Just how do the activities and objects that are connected in superstitious beliefs influence one another? A reasonable, if evasive, answer is to say that the causal activity or object has an inherent force or power to achieve the observed effects. Abstracted and generalized, this inherent force or power can provide the explanation for many extraordinary events and for success or failure in life's endeavors. In Melanesia, people call it *mana*. Fishhooks that catch big fish, tools that make intricate carvings, canoes that sail safely through storm, or warriors who kill many enemies, all have *mana* in concentrated quantities. In Western cultures, the concepts of luck and charisma closely resemble the idea of mana. A horseshoe possesses a concentrated power that brings good luck. A charismatic leader is one who is suffused with great powers of persuasion.

But are superstitions, mana, luck, and charisma religious concepts? I think not. Because, if we define religion as a belief in any indwelling forces and powers, we shall soon find it difficult to separate religion from physics. After all, gravity and electricity are also unseen forces that are associated with observable effects. While it is true that physicists know much more about gravity than about mana, they cannot claim to have a complete understanding of how gravity achieves its results. At the same time, couldn't one argue that superstitions, mana, luck, and charisma are also merely theories of causality involving physical forces and powers about which we happen to have incomplete understanding as yet?

True, more scientific testing has gone into the study of gravity than into the study of *mana*, but the degree of scientific testing to which a theory has been subjected cannot make the difference between whether it is a religious or a scientific belief. If it did, then every untested or inadequately tested theory in science would be a religious belief (as well as every scientific theory that has been shown to be false during the time when scientists believed it to be true!). Some astronomers theorize that at the center of each galaxy there is a black hole. Shall we say that this is a religious belief because other astronomers reject such a theory or regard it as inadequately tested?

It is not the quality of belief that distinguishes religion from science. Rather, as Sir Edward Tylor was the first to propose, the basis of all that is distinctly religious in human thought is animism, the belief that humans share the world with a population of extraordinary, extracorporeal, and mostly invisible beings, ranging from souls and ghosts to saints and fairies, angels and cherubim, demons, jinni, devils, and gods.

Wherever people believe in the existence of one or more of these beings, that is where religion exists. Tylor claimed that animistic beliefs were to be found in every society, and a century of ethnological research has yet to turn up a single exception. The most problematic case is that of Buddhism, which Tylor's critics portrayed as a world religion that lacked belief in gods or souls. But ordinary believers outside of Buddhist monasteries never accepted the atheistic implications of Gautama's teachings. Mainstream Buddhism, even in the monasteries, quickly envisioned the Buddha as a supreme deity who had been successively reincarnated and who held sway over a pantheon of lower gods and demons. And it was as fully animistic creeds that the several varieties of Buddhism spread from India to Tibet, Southeast Asia, China, and Japan.

Why is animism universal? Tylor pondered the question at length. He reasoned that if a belief recurred again and again in virtually all times and places, it could not be a product of mere fantasy. Rather, it must have grounding in evidence and in experiences that were equally recurrent and universal. What were these experiences? Tylor pointed to dreams, trances, visions, shadows, reflections, and death. During dreams, the body stays in bed; yet another part of us gets up, talks to people, and travels to distant lands. Trances and drug-induced visions also bring vivid evidence of another self, distinct and separate from one's body. Shadows and mirror images reflected in still water point to the same conclusion, even in the full light of normal wakefulness. The concept of an inner being—a soul—makes sense of all this. It is the soul that wanders off when we sleep, that lies in the shadows, and that peers back at us from the surface of the pond. Most of all, the soul explains the mystery of death: a lifeless body is a body permanently deprived of its soul.

Incidentally, there is nothing in the concept of soul per se that constrains us to believe each person has only one. The ancient Egyptians had two, and so do many West African societies in which both patrilineal and matrilineal ancestors determine an individual's identity. The Jívaro of Ecuador have three souls. The first soul—the *mekas*—gives life to the body. The second soul—the *arutam*—has to be captured through a drug-induced visionary experience at a sacred waterfall. It confers bravery and immunity in battle to the possessor. The third soul—the *musiak*—forms inside the head of a dying warrior and attempts to avenge his death. The Dahomey say that women have three souls; men have four. Both sexes have an ancestor soul, a personal soul, and a mawn soul. The ancestor soul gives protection during life, the personal soul is accountable for what people do with their lives, the mawn soul is a bit of the creator god, Mawn, that supplies divine guidance. The exclusively male fourth soul guides men to positions of leadership in their households and lineages. But the record for plural souls seems to belong to the Fang of Gabon. They have seven: a sound inside the brain, a heart soul, a name soul, a life force soul, a body soul, a shadow soul, and a ghost soul.

Why do Westerners have only one soul? I cannot answer that. Perhaps the question is unanswerable. I accept the possibility that many details of religious beliefs and practices may arise from historically specific events and individual choices made only once and only in one culture and that have no discernible cost-benefit advantages or disadvantages. While a belief in souls does conform to the general principles of cultural selection, belief in one rather than two or more souls may not be comprehensible in terms of such principles. But let us not be too eager to declare any puzzling feature of human life forever beyond the pale of practical reason. For has it not been our experience that more research often leads to answers that were once thought unattainable?

The Evolution of the Spirit World

All varieties of spirit beings found in modern religions have their analogues or exact prototypes in the religions of prestate societies. Changes in animistic beliefs since Neolithic times involve matters of emphasis and elaboration. For example, band-and-village people widely believed in gods who lived on top of mountains or in the sky itself and who served as the models for later notions of supreme beings as well as other powerful sky gods. In Aboriginal Australia, the sky god created the earth and its natural features, showed humans how to hunt and make fire, gave people their social laws, and showed them how to make adults out of children by performing rites of initiation. The names of their quasi-supreme beings—Baiame, Daramulum, Nurunderi—could not be uttered by the uninitiated. Similarly, the Selk'-nam of Tierra del Fuego believed in "the one who is up there." The Yaruro of Venezuela spoke of a "great mother" who created the world. The Maidu of California believed in a great "slayer in the sky." Among the Semang of Malaysia, Kedah created everything, including the god who created the earth and humankind. The Andaman Islanders had Puluga whose house is the sky, and the Winnebago had "earthmaker."

Although prestate peoples occasionally prayed to these great spirits or even visited them during trances, the focus of animistic beliefs generally lay elsewhere. In fact, most of the early creator gods abstained from contact with human beings. Having created the universe, they withdraw from worldly affairs and let other lesser deities, animistic beings, and humans work out their own destinies. Ritually, the most important category of animistic beings was the ancestors of the band, village, and clan or other kinship groups whose members believed they were bonded by common descent.

People in band-and-village societies tend to have short memories concerning specific individuals who have died. Rather than honor the recent dead, or seek favors from them, egalitarian cultures often place a ban on the use of the dead person's name and try to banish or evade his or her ghost. Among the Washo, a native American foraging people who lived along the border of California and Nevada, souls of the dead were angry about being deprived of their bodies. They were dangerous and had to be avoided. So the Washo burned the dead person's hut, clothing, and other personal property and stealthily moved their camp to a place where they hoped the dead person's soul could not find them. The Dusun of North Borneo curse a dead person's soul and warn it to stay away from the village. Reluctantly, the soul gathers up belongings left at its grave site and sets off for the land of the dead.

But this distrust of the recent dead does not extend to the most ancient dead, not to the generality of ancestor spirits. In keeping with the ideology of descent, band-and-village people often memorialize and propitiate their communal ancestral spirits. Much of what is known as totemism is a form of diffuse ancestor worship. Taking the name of an animal such as kangaroo or beaver or a natural phenomenon such as clouds or rain in conformity with prevailing rules of descent, people express a communal obligation to the founders of their kinship group. Often this obligation includes rituals intended to nourish, protect, or assure the increase of the animal and natural totems and with it the health and well-being of their human counterparts. Aboriginal Australians, for example, believed that they were descended from animal ancestors who traveled around the country during the dream-time at the beginning of the world, leaving mementos of their journey strewn about before turning into people. Annually, the descendants of a particular totemic ancestor retraced the dream-time journey. As they walked from spot to spot, they sang, danced, and examined sacred stones, stored in secret hiding places along the path taken by the first kangaroo or the first witchetty grub. Returning to camp, they decorated themselves in the likeness of their totem and imitated its behavior. The Arunta witchetty-grub men, for instance, decorated themselves with strings, nose bones, rattails, and feathers, painted their bodies with the sacred design of the witchetty grub, and constructed a brush hut in the shape of the witchetty-grub chrysalis. They entered the hut and sang of the journey they had made. Then the head men came shuffling and gliding out, followed by all the rest, in imitation of adult witchetty grubs emerging from a chrysalis.

In most village societies an undifferentiated community of ancestral spirits keep a close watch on their descendants, ready to punish them if they commit incest or if they break the taboos against eating certain foods. Important endeavors—hunting, gardening,

pregnancy, warfare—need the blessings of a group's ancestors to be successful, and such blessings are usually obtained by holding feasts in the ancestors' honor according to the principle that a well-fed ancestor is a well-intentioned ancestor. Throughout highland New Guinea, for example, people believe that the ancestral spirits enjoy eating pork as much as living persons enjoy eating it. To please the ancestors, people slaughter whole herds of pigs before going to war or when celebrating important events in an individual's life such as marriage and death. But in keeping with a big-man redistributive level of political organization, no one claims that his or her ancestors merit special treatment.

Under conditions of increasing population, greater wealth to be inherited, and intrasocietal competition between different kin groups, people tend to pay more attention to specific and recently deceased relatives in order to validate claims to the inheritance of land and other resources. The Dobuans, South Pacific yam gardeners and fishermen of the Admiralty Islands, have what seems to be an incipient phase of a particularized ancestor religion. When the leader of a Dobuan household died, his children cleaned his skull, hung it from the rafters of their house, and provided it with food and drink. Addressing it as "Sir Ghost," they solicited protection against disease and misfortune, and through oracles, asked him for advice. If Sir Ghost did not cooperate, his heirs threatened to get rid of him. Actually, Sir Ghost could never win. The death of his children finally proved that he was no longer of any use. So when the grandchildren took charge, they threw Sir Ghost into the lagoon, substituting their own father's skull as the symbol of the household's new spiritual patron.

With the development of chiefdoms, ruling elites employed specialists whose job was to memorize the names of the chief's ancestors. To make sure that the remains of these dignitaries did not get thrown away like Sir Ghost's skull, paramount chiefs built elaborate tombs that preserved links between generations in a tangible form. Finally, with the emergence of states and empires, as the rulers' souls rose to take their places in the firmament alongside the high gods, their mummified mortal remains, surrounded by exquisite furniture, rare jewels, gold-encrusted chariots and other preciosities, were interred in gigantic crypts and pyramids that only a true god could have built.

3

Religious Perspectives in Anthropology

Dorothy Lee

At first glance, the study of the religion of non-Western cultures may appear somewhat esoteric, albeit interesting. In reality, however, religion is very much a part of everyday, practical activities in these cultures, and knowledge of a society's religion is essential for the successful introduction of social changes. In the following article, Dorothy Lee dramatically shows how religion is part and parcel of preliterate people's worldview, or Weltanschauung: the corpus of beliefs about the life and environment in which members of a society find themselves. Among preliterate societies, economic, political, and artistic behavior is permeated by religion. Lee points out that anthropologists make every attempt to understand the insiders' "emic" view of their universe, which they share with other members of their group, and demonstrates that an outsider's "etic" view is too limited a base of cultural knowledge on which to introduce innovations that do not violate the religious tenets of the society and meet with acceptance.

In primitive societies, we do not always find the worship of God or a god, nor the idea of the supernatural. Yet religion is always present in man's view of his place in the universe, in his relatedness to man and nonhuman nature, to reality and circumstance. His universe may include the divine or may itself be divine. And his patterned behavior often has a religious dimension, so that we find religion permeating daily life—agriculture and hunting, health measures, arts and crafts.

We do find societies where a Supreme Being is recognized; but this Being is frequently so far removed from mundane affairs that it is not present in the consciousness of the people except on the specific occasions of ceremonial or prayer. But in these same societies, we find communion with the unperceiv-

able and unknowable in nature, with an ultimate reality, whether spirit, or power, or intensified being, or personal worth, which evokes humility, respect, courtesy or sometimes fear, on man's part. This relationship to the ultimate reality is so pervasive that it may determine, for example, which hand a man will use in adjusting his loin cloth, or how much water he will drink at a time, or which way his head will point when he sleeps, or how he will butcher and utilize the carcass of a caribou. What anthropologists label "material culture," therefore, is never purely material. Often we would be at least as justified to call the operation involved religious.

All economic activities, such as hunting, gathering fuel, cultivating the land, storing food, assume a relatedness to the encompassing universe, and with many cultures, this is a religious relationship. In such cultures, men recognize a certain spiritual worth and dignity in the universe. They do not set out to control, or master, or exploit. Their ceremonials are often periods of intensified communion, even social affairs, in a broad sense, if the term may be

"Religious Perspectives in Anthropology" by Dorothy Lee from RELIGIOUS PERSPECTIVES IN COLLEGE TEACHING, Hoxie N. Fairchild (ed.), The Ronald Press Company, New York City, 1952, pp. 338–359.

extended to include the forces of the universe. They are not placating or bribing or even thanking; they are rather a formal period of concentrated, enjoyable association. In their relationships with nature, the people may see themselves as the offspring of a cherishing mother, or the guests of a generous hostess, or as members of a democratic society which proceeds on the principle of consent. So, when the Baiga in India were urged to change over to the use of an iron plow, they replied with horror that they could not tear the flesh of their mother with knives. And American Indians have hunted many animals with the consent of the generic essence of these—of which the particular animal was the carnal manifestation—only after establishing a relationship or reciprocity; with man furnishing the ceremonial, and Buffalo or Salmon or Caribou making a gift of the countless manifestations of his flesh.

The great care with which so many of the Indian groups utilized every portion of the carcass of a hunted animal was an expression, not of economic thrift, but of courtesy and respect; in fact, an aspect of the religious relationship to the slain. The Wintu Indians of California, who lived on land so wooded that it was difficult to find clear land for putting up a group of houses, nevertheless used only dead wood for fuel, out of respect for nature. An old Wintu woman, speaking in prophetic vein, expressed this: "The White people never cared for land or deer or bear. When we Indians kill meat, we eat it all up. When we dig roots we make little holes. When we build houses, we make little holes. When we burn grass for grasshoppers, we don't ruin things. We shake down acorns and pinenuts. We don't chop down the trees. We only use dead wood. But the White people plow up the ground, pull up the trees, kill everything. The tree says, 'Don't. I am sore. Don't hurt me.' But they chop it down and cut it up. The spirit of the land hates them. They blast out trees and stir it up to its depths. They saw up the trees. That hurts them. The Indians never hurt anything, but the White people destroy all. They blast rocks and scatter them on the ground. The rock says, 'Don't! You are hurting me.' But the White people pay no attention. When the Indians use rocks, they take little round ones for their cooking. . . . How can the spirit of the earth like the White man? . . . Everywhere the White man has touched it, it is sore."

Here we find people who do not so much *seek* communion with environing nature as *find themselves* in communion with it. In many of these societies, not even mysticism is to be found, in our sense of the word. For us, mysticism presupposes a prior separation of man from nature, and communion is achieved through loss of self and subsequent merging with that which is beyond; but for many cultures, there is no such distinct separation between self and other, which must be overcome. Here, man is *in* nature already, and we cannot speak properly of man *and* nature.

Take the Kaingang, for example, who chops out a wild beehive. He explains his act to the bees, as he would to a person whom he considered his coordinate. "Bee, produce! I chopped you out to make beer of you! Yukui's wife died, and I am making beer of you so that I can cut his hair." Or he may go up to a hive and say simply, "Bee, it is I." And the Arapesh of New Guinea, going to his yam garden, will first introduce to the spirit of the land the brother-in-law whom he has brought along to help him with the gardening. This is not achieved communication, brought about for definite ends. It implies an already present relatedness with the ultimate reality, with that which is accepted in faith, and which exists irrespective of man's cognition or perception or logic. If we were to abstract, out of this situation, merely the food getting or the operational techniques, we would be misrepresenting the reality.

The same present relatedness is to be found in some societies where the deity is more specifically defined. The Tikopia, in the Solomon Islands Protectorate, sit and eat their meals with their dead under the floor, and hand food and drink to them; the dead are all somewhat divine, progressively so as they come nearer to the original, fully divine ancestor of the clan. Whatever their degree of divinity, the Tikopia is at home with them; he is aware of their vague presence, though he requires the services of a medium whenever he wants to make this presence definite.

Firth describes an occasion when a chief, having instructed a medium to invite his dead nephew to come and chew betel with him, found himself occupied with something else when the dead arrived, and so asked the medium to tell the spirit—a minor deity—to chew betel by himself. At another time, during an important ceremonial, when this chief was receiving on his forehead the vertical stripe which was the symbol that he was now the incarnation of the highest god, he jokingly jerked his head aside, so that the stripe, the insignium of the presence of the god, went crooked. These are the acts of a man who feels accepted by his gods, and is at one with them. And, in fact, the Tikopia appear to live in a continuum which includes nature and the divine without defining bounds; where communion is present, not achieved; where merging is a matter of being, not of becoming.

In these societies, where religion is an everpresent dimension of experience, it is doubtful that religion as such is given a name; Kluckhohn reports that the Navaho have no such word, but most ethnographers never thought to inquire. Many of these cultures, however, recognized and named the spiritual ingredient or attribute, the special quality of the wonderful, the very, the beyondness, in nature. This was sometimes considered personal, sometimes not. We have from the American Indians terms such as *manitou*, or *wakan*, or *yapaitu*, often translated as power; and we have the well-known Melanesian term *mana*. But this is what they reach through faith, the other end of the relationship; the relationship itself is unnamed. Apparently, to behave and think religiously, is to behave and think. To describe a way of life in its totality is to describe a religious way of life.

When we speak of agricultural taboos and rites, therefore, we often introduce an analytical factor which violates the fact. For example, when preparing seed for planting, one of the several things a Navaho traditionally does is to mix ground "mirage stone" with the seed. And in the process of storing corn, a double-eared stalk is laid at the bottom of the storage pit. In actual life, these acts are a continuous part of a total activity.

The distinction between the religious and the secular elements may even separate an act from the manner of performance, a verb from its adverb. The direction in which a man is facing when performing a secular act, or the number of times he shakes his hand when spattering water, often have their religious implications. When the Navaho planted his corn sunwise, his act reflected a total world view, and it would be nonsense for us to separate the planting itself from the direction of the planting.

Those of us who present religion as separate from "everyday" living reflect moreover the distinctions of a culture which will identify six days with the secular in life and only the seventh with religion. In many primitive societies, religion is rarely absent from the details of everyday living, and the ceremonials represent a formalization and intensification of an everpresent attitude. We have societies such as that of the Hopi of Arizona, where ceremonials, and the preparation for them, cover most of the year. Some years ago, Crowwing, a Hopi, kept a journal for the period of a year, putting down all events of ceremonial import. Day after day, there are entries containing some casual reference to a religious activity, or describing a ritual, or the preparation for a ceremonial. After a few weeks of such entries, we come to a sequence of four days' entries which are devoted to a description of a ball game played by two opposing groups of children and enjoyed by a large number of spectators. But, in the end, this also turns out to have been ceremonial in nature, helping the corn to grow.

Among many groups, agriculture is an expression of man's religious relatedness to the universe. As Robert Redfield and W. Lloyd Warner have written: "The agriculture of the Maya Indians of southeastern Yucatan is not simply a way of securing food. It is also a way of worshipping the gods. Before a man plants, he builds an altar in the field and prays there. He must not speak boisterously in the cornfield; it is a sort of temple. The cornfield is planted as an incident in a perpetual sacred contract between supernatural beings and men. By this agreement, the supernaturals yield part of what is theirs—the riches of the natural environment—to men. In exchange, men are pious and perform the traditional ceremonies in which offerings are made to the supernaturals. . . . The world is seen as inhabited by the supernaturals; each has his appropriate place in the woods, the sky, or the wells from which the water is drawn. The village is seen as a reflection of the quadrilateral pattern of the cosmos; the cornfield too is oriented, laid out east, west, north, and south, with reference to the supernaturals that watch over the cardinal points; and the table altars erected for the ceremonies again remind the individual of this pattern. The stories that are told at the time when men wait to perform the ceremony before the planting of the corn or that children hear as they grow up are largely stories which explain and further sanction the traditional way of life."

Art also is often so permeated with religion that sometimes, as among the Navaho, what we classify as art is actually religion. To understand the rhythm of their chants, the "plot" of their tales, the making of their sand paintings, we have to understand Navaho religion: the concept of harmony between man and the universe as basic to health and well being; the concept of continuity, the religious significance of the groups of four, the door of contact opened through the fifth repetition, the need to have no completely enclosing frame around any of their works so that continuity can be maintained and the evil inside can have an opening through which to leave.

The sand paintings are no more art than they are ritual, myth, medical practice or religious belief. They are created as an integral aspect of a ceremonial which brings into harmony with the universal order one who finds himself in discord with it; or which intensifies and ensures the continuation of a harmony which is already present. Every line and shape and color, every interrelationship of form, is the visible manifestation of myth, ritual and religious belief. The making of the painting is accompanied with a series of sacred songs sung over a sick person, or over someone who, though healed of sickness by emergency measures has yet to be brought back into the universal harmony; or in enhancing and giving emphasis to the present harmony. What we would call purely medical practices may or may not be part of all this. When the ceremonial is over, the painting is over too; it is destroyed; it has fulfilled its function.

This is true also of the art of the neighboring Hopi, where the outstanding form of art is the drama. In this we find wonderfully humorous clowning, involving careful planning and preparation, creation of magnificent masks and costumes, rehearsals, organization. Everyone comes to see and responds with uproarious hilarity. But this is not mere art. It is an important way of helping nature in her work of growing the corn. Even the laughter of the audience helps in this.

More than dramatic rehearsal and creation of costumes has gone into the preparation. The actors have prepared themselves as whole persons. They have refrained from sexual activity, and from anything involving conflict. They have had good thoughts only. They have refrained from anger, worry and grief. Their preparations as well as their performance have had a religious dimension. Their drama is one act in the great process of the cyclical growing of corn, a divinity indispensable to man's well being, and to whose well being man is indispensable. Corn wants to grow, but cannot do so without the cooperation of the rest of nature and of man's acts and thoughts and will. And, to be happy, corn must be danced by man and participate in his ceremonials. To leave the religious dimension out of all this, and to speak of Hopi drama as merely a form of art, would be to present a fallacious picture. Art and agriculture and religion are part of the same totality for the Hopi.

In our own culture, an activity is considered to be economic when it deals with effective utilization or exploitation of resources. But this definition cannot be used when speaking of Hopi economics. To begin with, it assumes an aggressive attitude toward the environment. It describes the situation of the homesteader in Alaska, for example, who works against tremendous odds clearing land for a dairy farm, against the inexorable pressure of time, against hostile elements. By his sweat, and through ingenuity and know-how and the use of brutally effective tools, he tames nature; he subjugates the land and exploits its resources to the utmost.

The Hopi Talayesua, however, describing his work on the land, does not see himself in opposition to it. He works *with* the elements, not *against* them. He helps the corn to grow; he cooperates with the thunderstorm and the pollen and the sun. He is in harmony with the elements, not in conflict; and he does not set out to conquer an opponent. He depends on the corn, but this is part of a mutual interdependence; it is not exploitation. The corn depends on him too. It cannot grow without his help; it finds life dull and lonely without his company and his ceremonials. So it gives its body for his food gladly, and enjoys living with him in his granary. The Hopi has a personal relationship with it. He treats it with respect, and houses it with the care and courtesy accorded to an honored guest. Is this economics?

In a work on Hopi economics we are given an account of the Hopi Salt Journey, under the heading "Secondary Economic Activities." This expedition is also described in a Hopi autobiography, and here we discover that only those men who have achieved a certain degree of experience in the Hopi way can go on this journey, and then, only if their minds are pure and they are in a state of harmony with the universe. There is a period of religious preparation, followed by the long and perilous journey which is attended by a number of rituals along the way. Old men, lowering themselves from the overhanging ledge onto the salt deposits, tremble with fear, knowing that they may be unable to make the ascent. The occasion is solemnly religious. This is no utilization of resources, in the eyes of the Hopi who makes the journey. He goes to help the growing corn; the Salt Journey brings needed rain. Twelve adult men will spend days and court dangers to procure salt which they can buy for two dollars from the itinerant peddler. By our own economic standards, this is not an efficient use of human resources. But Hopi ends transcend our economic categories and our standards of efficiency are irrelevant to them.

In many societies, land tenure, or the transference of land, operations involved in hunting and agriculture, are often a part of a religious way of life. In our own culture, man conceives of his relationship to his physical environment, and even sometimes his human environment, as mechanistic and manipulative; in other cultures, we often find what Ruth Benedict has called the animistic attitude toward nature and man, underlying practices which are often classified miscellaneously together in ethnographics, under the heading of superstitions or taboos. The courteous speech to the bear about to be killed, the offering to the deer world before the hunter sets out, the introduction of the brother-in-law to the garden spirit, or the sacrifice to the rice field about to be sold, the refraining from intercourse, or from the eating of meat or from touching food with the hand, are expressive of such an attitude. They are the practices we find in a democratic society where there is consideration for the rights of everyone as opposed to the brutal efficiency of the dictator who feels free to exploit, considering the rights of none. They reflect the attitude of people who believe in conference and consent, not in coercion; of people who generally find personality or mana in nature and man, sometimes more, sometimes less. In this framework, taboo and superstitious act mean that man acts and refrains from acting in the name of a wider democracy which includes nature and the divine.

With such a conception of man's place in nature, what is for us land tenure, or ownership, or rights of use and disposal, is for other societies an intimate belongingness. So the Arapesh conceive of themselves as belonging to the land, in the way that flora and fauna belong to it. They cultivate the land by the grace of the immanent spirits, but they cannot dispose of it and cannot conceive of doing so.

This feeling of affinity between society and land is widespread and appears in various forms and varying degrees of intensity, and it is not found only among sedentary peoples. We have Australian tribes where the very spirit of the men is believed to reside in the land, where a bush or a rock or a peculiar formation is the present incarnation of myth, and contains security and religious value; where a social class, a structured group of relatives, will contain in addition to human beings, an animal and a feature of the landscape. Here, when a man moves away from the land of his group, he leaves the vital part of himself behind. When a magistrate put people from such societies in jail in a distant city, he had no idea of the terrifying severity of the punishment he was meting; he was cutting the tribesman off from the very source of his life and of his self, from the past, and the future which were incorporated and present in his land.

In the technology of such societies we are again dealing with material where the religious and secular are not distinct from each other. We have, for example, the description which Raymond Firth gives of the replacing of a wornout wash strake on a canoe, among the Tikopia. This operation is expertly and coherently carried out, with secular and religious acts performed without distinction in continuous succession or concurrently. A tree is cut down for the new wash strake, a libation is poured out to the deities of the canoe to announce this new timber, and a kava rite is performed to persuade the deities to step out of the canoe and on to a piece of bark cloth, where they can live undisturbed, while the canoe is being tampered with. Then comes the unlashing of the old wash strake, the expert examination of the body of the canoe in search of lurking defects, the discovery of signs indicating the work of a borer, the cutting of the body of the canoe with a swift stroke to discover whether the borer is there, accompanied by an appeal to the deities of the canoe by the expert, to witness what he is doing, and the necessity for doing it.

Now a kinsman of the original builder of the canoe, now dead and a tutelary deity, spontaneously drops his head on to the side of the canoe and wails over the wounding of the body of the canoe. The borer is discovered, in the meantime, to be still there; but only a specially consecrated adze can deal with him successfully. The adze is sent for, dedicated anew to the deity, invoked, and finally wielded with success by the expert.

All this is performed with remarkable expedition and economy of motion yet the Tikopia workers are not interested in saving time; they are concerned neither with time limits not with speed in itself. Their concern is with the dispossessed deities whose home must be made ready against their return; and the speed of their work is incidental to this religious concern. The end result is efficiency; but unlike our own efficiency, this is not rooted in the effort to utilize and exploit material and time resources to the utmost; it is rooted in that profound religious feeling which also gives rise to the time-consuming rites and the wailing procedures which, from the purely economic point of view, are wasteful and interfering.

The world view of a particular society includes that society's conception of man's own relation to the universe, human and non-human, organic and inorganic, secular and divine, to use our own dualisms. It expresses man's view of his own role in the maintenance of life, and of the forces of nature. His attitude toward responsibility and initiative is inextricable from his conception of nature as deity-controlled, man-controlled, regulated through a balanced cooperation between god and man, or perhaps maintained through some eternal homeostasis, independent of man and perhaps of any deity. The way a man acts, his feeling of guilt and achievement, and his very personality are affected by the way he envisions his place within the universe.

For example, there are the Tiv of Southern Nigeria who, as described by one of them in the thirties, people the universe with potentially hostile and harmful powers, the *akombo*. Man's function in the maintenance of his own life and the moderate well-being of the land and of his social unit is to prevent the manifestation of *akombo* evil, through performing rites and observing taboos. So his rites render safe through preventing, through expulsion and purging. His role is negative, defending the normal course against the interference. Vis-à-vis the universe, his

acts arise out of negative motives. Thus what corresponds to a gift of first fruits to a deity in other cultures is phrased as a rite for preventing the deities from making a man's food go bad or diminish too quickly; fertility rites for a field are actually rites preventing the evil-intentioned from robbing the fields of their normal fertility.

In the writings of R. F. Barton, who studied the Ifugao of Luzon in the early part of this century, these people also appear to see deities as ready to interfere and bring evil, but their conception of man's role within the structure of the universe is a different one from that of the Tiv. In Barton's descriptive accounts, the Ifugao either accept what comes as deity-given, or act without being themselves the agents; they believe that no act can come to a conclusive end without the agency of a specific deity. They have a specific deity often for every step within an operation and for every part of the implement to be used. R. F. Barton recorded the names of 1,240 deities and believed that even so he had not exhausted the list.

The Ifugao associate a deity with every structured performance and at least a large number of their deliberate acts. They cannot go hunting, for example, without enlisting the aid of the deity of each step of the chase, to render each effective, or to nullify any lurking dangers. There is a deity for the level spot where "the hunter stands watching and listening to the dogs"; one for when the dogs "are sicced on the game"; one for when "the hunter leans on his spear transfixing the quarry"; twelve are listed as the deities of specific ways of rendering harmless to the hunter's feet the snags and fangs of snakes which he encounters. If he is to be successful in the hunt, a man does not ask the blessing of a deity. He pays all the particular deities of every specific spot and act, getting them to transitivize each act individually.

Even so, in most cases an Ifugao remains nonagentive, since the function of many of the deities is to save man from encounter, rather than to give him success in his dealing with it. For example, in the area of interpersonal relations, we have Tupya who is invoked so that "the creditor comes for dun for what is owed, but on the way he forgets and goes about other business"; and Dulaiya, who is invoked so that "the enemies just don't think about us, so they don't attack." His tools, also, are ineffective of themselves; so that, when setting a deadfall, he invokes and bribes such deities as that for the Flat Stone of the Deadfall, the Main Posts of the Deadfall, the Fall of the Deadfall, the Trigger of the Deadfall. Most of the Ifugao economy is involved in providing sacrifices to the deities, big or little according to the magnitude of the operation and the importance of the deities. There is no warmth in the sacrifices; no expression of gratitude or appeal or belongingness. As the Ifugaos see it, the sacrifice is a bribe. With such bribes, they buy the miraculous intervention and transitivization which are essential for achievement, health, and good personal relations.

The Ifugao show no humility in the face of this ineffective role in the universe; they merely accept it as the state of things. They accept their own failures, the frequent deaths, the sudden and disastrous flaring up of tempers, as things that are bound to happen irrespective of their own desires and efforts. But they are neither passive nor helpless. They carry on great undertakings, and, even now they go on forbidden head hunts. They know when and how and whom to bribe so as to perfect their defective acts. When however, a deity states a decision, they accept it as immutable. A Catholic priest tells a story about the neighboring Iloko which illustrates this acceptance. A Christian Iloko was on his deathbed, and the priest, trying to persuade him to repent of his sin, painted to him vividly the horrors of hell; but the dying man merely answered, "If God wants me to go to hell, I am perfectly willing."

Among the Wintu Indians of California we find that man sees himself as effective but in a clearly limited way. An examination of the myths of the Wintu shows that the individual was conceived as having a limited agentive role, shaping, using, intervening, actualizing and temporalizing the given, but never creating; that man was viewed as needing skill for his operations, but that specific skill was useless without "luck" which a man received through communion and pleading with some universal power.

It is to this limited role of man, geared to the working of the universe, that I referred when I spoke earlier of Hopi drama and agriculture. Without an understanding of this role, no Hopi activity or attitude or relationship can be understood. The Hopi have developed the idea of man's limited effectiveness in their own fashion, and have elaborated it systematically in what they call the "Hopi Way." Laura Thompson says of the Hopi, "All phenomena relevant to the life of the tribe—including man, the animals, and plants, the earth, sun, moon, clouds, the ancestors, and the spirits—are believed to be interdependent. . . . In this system each individual— human and non-human—is believed to have . . . a definite role in the universal order." Traditionally, fulfillment of the law of nature—the growth of the corn, the movements of the sun—can come only with man's participation, only with man's performance of the established ceremonials. Here man was effective, but only in cooperation with the rest of the phenomena of nature.

The Indians of the Plains, such as the Crow and the Sioux, have given a somewhat different form to this conception of man's circumscribed agency. The aggressive behavior for which they have been known, their great personal autonomy, their self-assurance and assertiveness and in recent years, their great dependence and apathy, have been explained as an expression of this conception. These societies envisioned the universe as pervaded by an undifferentiated religious force on which they were dependent for success in their undertakings and in life generally. The specific formulation differed in the different tribes, but, essentially, in all it was believed that each individual and particularly each man, must tap this universal force if his undertakings were to be successful. Without this "power" a man could not achieve success in any of the valued activities, whether warfare or the hunt; and no leadership was possible without this power. This was a force enhancing and intensifying the being of the man who acted; it was not, as with the Ifugao, an effectiveness applied to specific details of activities. The individual himself prepared himself in the hardihood, self-control, skills and areas of knowledge necessary. Little boys of five or seven took pride in their ability to withstand pain, physical hardship, and the terrors of running errands alone in the night. The Sioux did not appeal for divine intervention; he did not want the enemy to forget to come. Yet neither was he fearless. He appealed for divine strength to overcome his own fears as well as the external enemy.

The relationship with the divine, in this case, is personal and intense. The Plains Indian Sioux did not, like the Hopi, inherit a specific relatedness when he was born in a specific clan. Each man, each preadolescent boy, had to achieve the relationship for himself. He had to go out into the wilderness and spend days and nights without food or drink, in the cold, among wild beasts, afraid and hungry and anxious, humbling himself and supplicating, sometimes inflicting excruciating pain upon himself, until some particular manifestation of the universal force took pity upon him and came to him to become his life-long guardian and power. The appeals to the universal force were made sometimes in a group, through the institution of the Sun Dance. But here also they were individual in nature. The relationship with the divine was an inner experience; and when the Dakota Black Elk recounted his autobiography, he spoke mainly of these intense, personal religious experiences. Within this range of variation in form and concept and world view, we find expressed by all the same immediate relatedness to the divine.

4

Anthropologists Versus Missionaries: The Influence of Presuppositions

Claude E. Stipe

In this article, Claude Stipe suggests that the general attitude of anthropologists toward mission-aries has been negative, even though the discipline stresses the importance of objectivity. Stipe notes that, although there appears to be little "systematic indoctrination" that would lead to this negative attitude, it is evident that, early in the study of anthropology, students develop the attitude that missionaries are the enemy. However, he asks, if no systematic indoctrination occurs, how does one explain this basically negative attitude? Noting that the idea of an "objective observer," a long-held tenet in anthropology, is now generally regarded as a myth, Stipe points out that certain presuppositions influence the way we view situations. He then discusses in depth two presuppositions that he believes may result in the negative attitude of anthropologists toward missionaries: that pre-literate cultures display an organic unity (that is, they are ideal societies and change produced in them by other cultures is harmful to them) and that religious beliefs are basically meaningless. Stipe also suggests another possible factor contributing to the negative attitude (as suggested by Salamone 1977: 409): that anthropologists and missionaries are actually similar, "both believing they have the truth, being protective of the people among whom they work, and opposing that which they define as evil."

Anthropologists in general have a negative attitude toward missionaries, especially when they conceive of missionaries as agents of culture change. Even though there seems to be little systematic indoctrination, early in their training anthropology students

Excerpts from C. E. Stipe, "Anthropologists Versus Missionaries: The Influence of Presuppositions," CURRENT ANTHROPOLOGY 21:2 (1980) pp. 165–179. Reprinted by permission of The University of Chicago Press.

learn that missionaries are to be regarded as "ene-mies." Powdermaker (1966) refers to discussions which she and fellow students at the London School of Economics had in 1925 about the necessity of keeping natives pure and undefiled by missionaries and civil servants. Missionaries were seen as ene-mies who wanted to change cultures. She comments that "now, with the sociological interest in social change and the knowledge of the significant roles played by missionaries and civil servants, our hostile attitude seems indeed biased."

Although the majority of anthropologists have probably come into contact with missionaries while doing field research, Salamone (1977: 408) has noted that the mention of missionaries in textbooks and ethnographies is "both brief and somewhat hidden in the text" and that "rarely is a straightforward hostile antimissionary statement found" (Salamone 1979: 54). According to Burridge (1978: 9), anthropologists and other academics who have contributed to the negative stereotype "would never dream of committing to paper as a considered opinion the things they actually said." My own survey of the literature has corroborated these statements. The term "missionary" does not appear in the index of many standard texts in cultural anthropology, and when missionaries are mentioned it is often in terms of their disapproving of certain cultural practices such as wife lending or gambling (cf. Richards 1977: 218, 335) or tending to destroy a society's culture and self-respect (cf. Ember and Ember 1977: 306). Examples of negative statements in ethnographies include the suggestions that the missionaries in question do poor translation work (Hogbin 1964), use force and cruelty (Jocano 1969), unsuspectingly carry diseases (Graburn 1969), interfere with native customs (Fortune 1963), and disapprove of dancing (Middleton 1970). Turnbull (1961) is very negative toward some Protestant missionaries who refused to pray for a non-Christian pygmy who had been gored but has high praise for a Catholic priest.

One textbook with an extended discussion of missionaries is Keesing's (1976) *Cultural Anthropology: A Contemporary Perspective,* which includes positive as well as negative aspects of missionary work. Keesing notes that anthropologists and missionaries (at least in stereotype) have been at odds with one another for decades: "The caricatured missionary is a strait-laced, repressed, and narrow-minded Bible thumper trying to get native women to cover their bosoms decently; the anthropologist is a bearded degenerate given to taking his clothes off and sampling wild rites" (p. 459). He decries the fact that Christianity was taken to Latin America and other areas as an instrument of conquest and subjugation and notes that in many regions the "wounds to peoples' self-conception and to the integrity of their cultures remain deep and unhealed" (p. 460). On the other hand, he recognizes the old and enduring tradition

of missionary scholarship and statesmanship, including, e.g., Sahagún, Lafitau, Codrington, and Schebesta as well as many present missionary ethnographers and linguists. Keesing concludes his treatment by stating (p. 462):

> Many Christian missionaries have devoted their lives in ways that have enriched the communities where they worked. Many, in immersing themselves in other languages and cultures, have produced important records of ways now vanishing. But more important, in valuing these old ways and seeing Christianization as a challenge to create syntheses of the old and new, the best missionaries have helped to enrich human lives and provide effective bridges to participation in a world community.

One ethnography with an extended negative evaluation of missionaries is Tonkinson's (1974) account of the Jigalong Mob in Australia. The situation is quite atypical, since the Apostolic Church missionaries are given no training for their work. They know nothing about linguistics, anthropology, desert survival, or the aboriginal culture (Tonkinson 1974: 119). Most devote two or more years to missionary work to fulfill what they consider to be a religious duty.

Chagnon (1974: 181–82) seems to show an antimissionary bias when commenting on a group of Yanomamö who had accepted the missionaries' teaching that tobacco, drugs, and polygyny were sin:

> They were going to stay there in that swamp and be fed and clothed by the people from God's village until their gardens began producing; they were going to learn to sing and be happy. . . . [They were] swatting incessantly at the mosquitos with which they had chosen to live, free from sin. They were a mere shadow of the people who had greeted me boisterously in their magnificent, airy and mosquito-free *shabono* deep in the jungle a few years earlier, a sovereign people, strong and confident.

It is instructive to compare this comment with his earlier report (1967: 24) from a jungle village that "everybody in the village is swatting vigorously at the voracious biting gnats, and here and there groups of people delouse each other's heads and eat the vermin." He also seems to evaluate the people's actions differently in these two publications. In the earlier (1967: 26–30) he describes their graded system of violence, which includes duels, club fights, spear fights, raids, and tricks (in which they have killed visitors). Despite their extreme aggressiveness, they show at least two qualities he admires: "they are kind and indulgent with children and can quickly forget personal angers" (p. 31). It seems valid to infer that Chagnon's negative response to the condition of the Yanomamö involved with missionaries is based on the fact of that involvement as well as on their actual condition. A comment by Keesing (1976: 459) seems appropriate here:

> Anthropologists who have battled missionaries through the years have often bolstered their position with a cultural relativism and romanticism about the "primitive" that seems increasingly anachronistic. The anthropologist who finds himself in defense of infanticide, head-hunting, or the segregation and subordination of women, and in opposition to missionization, can well be uncomfortable about the premises from which he argues.

If no systematic indoctrination takes place, how can the basically negative attitude of anthropologists toward missionaries be explained? It is now generally accepted that the concept of an "objective observer" who does not let personal values influence observations and conclusions is a myth. We realize that experiences shape attitudes and values, which in turn affect our evaluations. Presuppositions influence the way in which we look at situations. I suggest that two common presuppositions may contribute to the negative attitude of anthropologists toward missionaries: that primitive cultures are characterized by an organic unity and that religious beliefs are essentially meaningless.

The Organic-Unity Concept

Many anthropologists have a penchant for seeing the culture they are studying (especially if it is sufficiently primitive) as a "work of art whose beauty [lies] in the way in which the parts [are] counterbalanced and interrelated" (Richardson 1975: 523). According to the teleological assumption of functionalism, which is

apparent in much of the ethnographic literature, the ideal society is in perfect equilibrium, and change, especially that produced by outside contacts, is harmful (Hughes 1978: 78).

Bennett (1946) has shown how the organic approach takes into account only certain facets of a culture. He contrasts Laura Thompson's "organic" approach with Esther Goldfrank's "repression" approach to Pueblo culture. Thompson sees the culture and society as "integrated to an unusual degree, all sectors being bound together by a consistent, harmonious set of values, which pervade and homogenize the categories of world view, ritual, art, social organization, economic activity, and social control" (Bennett 1946: 362–63). According to Thompson, such a culture develops an ideal personality type which fosters the virtues of gentleness, nonaggression, cooperation, modesty, and tranquility. She stresses the organic wholeness of preliterate life, contrasting it with the heterogeneity and diffuseness of modern civilization. On the other hand, Goldfrank characterizes Pueblo culture as marked by "considerable *covert* tension, suspicion, anxiety, hostility, fear, and ambition" (Bennett 1946: 363). Children are coerced subtly and sometimes brutally into behaving according to Pueblo norms. Authority is in the hands of the group and the chiefs, and the individual is suppressed and repressed. In contrasting the two positions, Bennett notes (p. 366) that "while the 'organic' approach tends to show a preference for homogeneous preliterate culture, the 'repressed' theory has a fairly clear bias in the direction of equalitarian democracy and non-neurotic 'free' behavior."

Since anthropologists have preached the integrity of each culture, change (unless it has been internally motivated) "has been seen as upsetting a delicate machine, a functioning organism, or an intricate symbolic or communication system—whichever metaphor we have used for organizing our ideas about society or culture" (Colson 1976: 267). Much has been written about the marginal person who is no longer at home in his or her own culture and is attempting to find a place of security in the larger social universe. We contrast the alienation we impute to such people with the contentment and emotional security we attribute to individuals in a closed community.

It is interesting that anthropologists for the most part have been reformers primarily with respect to other people in their *own* society. We are often uncomfortable with policies which endanger the customary ways of life of local communities, and when such communities are exposed to new, conflicting demands some of us even call those policies genocide or ethnocide. We seem to be saying that "options are bad for other people upon whom we do ethnography, but very good for ourselves, who use the teaching of social anthropology to free ourselves, and our peers, from constraining tradition" (Colson 1976: 267). As Lewis (1973: 584–85) has argued,

> The very qualities of primitive life which the anthropologist romanticizes and wants to see preserved are attributes which he finds unacceptable in his own culture. The personal freedom and self-determination he insists upon for himself he withholds from the "primitive" on the basis of cultural conditioning and the need for the accommodation of the individual within the community. He writes enthusiastically of the highly integrated life of the "primitive," of the lack of stress experienced when there is little freedom of choice and few alternatives from which to choose; yet he defends for himself the right to make his own decisions and his own choices.

A local point of view is often myopic, and anthropologists are no exception. We often do not realize that the seeming equilibrium of a tribe may have been largely created by the colonial situation. When one is concerned with a single society, it is often difficult to see how the populations of a given region are bound together in networks of trade, exchange, and the flow of ideas (Keesing 1976: 432). Although the present is a precipitate of history, attempts are often made to explain the present in terms of itself.

The organic view of cultures is due in part to the short time an anthropologist ordinarily spends in a given culture. Even though it may extend over several years, a single field trip encourages a description which emphasizes the homogeneity of a culture, the situation at a specific time being seen as the ideal condition (Colson 1976: 269). In too many cases the anthropologist does not observe a society long enough to see how the people grow dissatisfied with their condition and attempt to change it. What he/she may see as an ideal situation may be viewed by the people as an unsatisfactory compromise. As

Colson (1976: 264) notes:

> It is people who are the actors, attempting to adapt and use their institutions to attain their ends, always fiddling with the cultural inheritance and experimenting with its possibilities. They need to take thought of what they do. They lose sight of one end in pursuing another. Frequently they lose themselves in a dreadful muddle. There is no necessary feedback system that will automatically correct the state of affairs and return them to base one to start again having learned from their mistakes. And no shining model of an ideal society . . . is going to save them from their mistakes, though it may comfort them in their affliction. This is as true of those who live in African villages or the islands of the Pacific as it is of us in our cities and bureaucracies which we create and then decline to control. Ethnographers have usually presented each social group they study as a success story. We have no reason to believe this is true.

Although most people value their customary ways, they certainly are not reluctant to change when they anticipate that the changes will improve their situation. There is a sense, therefore, in which any given culture is always being tested, and this is no more true of our own than it is of others which are less complex.

O'Brien and Ploeg (1964: 291) discuss the fact that when a group of Dani met to plan for the burning of weapons, the throwing away of *jao,* and the abolition of in-law avoidances, no one questioned the desirability of these acts. "To account for this unanimity, one should realize that the motive underlying the movement—dissatisfaction with the original culture—applied with equal force to all Dani. Also, all concurred in thinking that the Europeans enjoyed a vastly superior way of life." The Dani appreciated the improvements in their standard of living which were due mainly to the cessation of warfare, availability of medical treatment, and improvement of the economic system. As Salamone (1976: 62) has noted, "Individuals will become converts to those religious systems which enable them to better adapt to their ecological niches."

Hippler (1974: 336) has argued that the introduction of Euro-American civilization to Alaskan native groups was more a blessing than a curse:

> It occurs to us that the introduction of modern medicine, freedom from the dangers and

uncertainties of the hunt, reduction in interpersonal violence and the like are positively accepted changes. The only Indians and Eskimos we know who wholly extoll the past are those too young to have experienced that untouched aboriginal culture. Mothers *do* prefer to have most of their children live; only fools wish to have unrestrained interpersonal violence. It is . . . very possible that much complaint about the "loss of one's culture" now expressed by young Eskimos and Indians is hyperbolic cant derived in part from a misreading or, unfortunately, a correct reading of some anthropological writings and the comments of local political ideologues.

Hippler concludes that the concept of the death of a culture, which is an analogy applied to an abstraction, may be less important in the scheme of individual human lives than many anthropologists make it seem.

Discussions of culture change often given the impression that indigenous peoples were passive spectators in the acculturation process and that missionization was a force which unilaterally impinged on passively recipient peoples. In actuality, there are usually "continuing interactions of Western and indigenous religious beliefs, structures, and institutional arrangements" (Tiffany 1978: 305; see also Lātūkefu 1978: 462).

From these examples, it is obvious that not all anthropologists take an idealistic view of the organic nature of a culture and therefore see culture change as necessarily bad for the indigenous peoples. However, one should not be surprised when those who do hold this position manifest a negative attitude toward missionaries who attempt to change cultures.

The Meaninglessness of Religious Beliefs

Although a missionary (Edwin Smith) was once president of the Royal Anthropological Institute, the majority of anthropologists are either atheistic or agnostic. According to Evans-Pritchard (1965, 1972), the early anthropological writers on religion (e.g., Tylor, Frazer, Malinowski, and Durkheim) had all had a relatively dreary religious upbringing which led to an animosity toward revealed religion. They were looking for a weapon which could be used with deadly effect against Christianity, for if they could explain away primitive religion as an intellectual aberration or by its social function they could discredit and explain away the higher religions as well (1965: 15). Evans-Pritchard concludes (1972: 205) that

social anthropology has been the product of minds which, with very few exceptions, regarded all religion as outmoded superstition, suited no doubt to a pre-scientific age and historically justified, like classes in the eyes of Marxists, for a given period, but now useless, and even without ethical value, and worse than useless because it stood in the way of a rational regeneration of mankind and social progress.

The basic approach of social anthropologists to religion can be characterized by Radcliffe-Brown's (1952: 155) dictum that in studying religion "it is on the rites rather than the beliefs that we should first concentrate our attention." Gluckman (1962: 14–15) elaborated on this position by asserting that modern minds are bored with the intellectualist approach of the 19th-century anthropologists and that contemporary anthropologists demonstrate that rituals "are in fact to be understood in terms of the social relations which are involved in the rituals." Leach (1954: 15) maintained that the structure which is symbolized in ritual is "the system of socially approved 'proper' relations between individuals and groups."

Lawrence (1970) and Horton (1971) trace this view to 18th-century rationalistic philosophy. God had ceased to be personal for many people by the end of the 17th century, and by the end of the 18th century many had decided that they could do without God completely. When religion no longer provides a theory for how the world really works, man's encounter with God can easily be relegated to the "supreme archetypal social relationship" (Horton 1971: 96).

In at least some cases, anthropologists seem to have had a type of "conversion experience" away from Christianity. At the 1974 meeting of the American Anthropological Association in Mexico City I gave a paper on the role of religion in culture change, in which I demonstrated that in many instances one cannot explain the occurrence or the direction of culture change without understanding the religious *beliefs* of the people. In the same session was a paper in which the author argued that *all* differences between Protestants and Catholics in a Guatemalan village could be explained by socioeconomic and political factors. He was disturbed by my approach and explained that he had been a seminary student and that his "conversion" to anthropology involved the rejection of the position that religious beliefs were meaningful. He therefore resented being subjected (especially by another anthropologist) to the very position from which he had been converted.

The only published statement I have seen is Richardson's (1975: 519), in which he attributes to anthropology his liberation from Christian beliefs:

> My freedom from the things that nearly destroyed me (and that continue to haunt me) would come from studying them, and wrestling with them in order to expose their secret. At that point, just short of stomping on them and destroying them, for some reason my private battle stops. Today, I have no love for the Southern Baptists, but I can almost say "Billy Graham" without sneering.

This comment seems incompatible with his statement (p. 523) that cultural relativism is a "moral justification for being an anthropologist." It seems incongruous that a cultural relativist would sneer at *anyone's* religion. From an anthropological perspective, Lowie's statement that it is the responsibility of the fieldworker to understand the "true inwardness" of the beliefs and practices is more appropriate. Lowie asserts (1963: 533),

> . . . I have known anthropologists who accorded a benevolent understanding to the Hopi but denied it to Catholics, Mormons, Buddhists, or Mohammedans. This dichotomy of viewpoint strikes me as ridiculous and completely unscientific. I will study as many religions as I can, but I will judge none of them. I doubt if any other attitude is scientifically defensible.

Burridge (1978: 10) mentions an anthropologist who was in the habit of smoking on the premises of a missionary organization that had strict regulations against the use of tobacco or alcohol within its compound. In fact, he even urged some of the people living there to accept free gifts of cigarettes. One wonders if he would just as inconsiderately have offered pork chops to the caretaker of a mosque or eaten hot dogs in a Hindu temple.

I suspect that, in at least some instances, the antipathy of anthropologists toward missionaries lies in the fact that missionaries take seriously and teach other people religious beliefs which the anthropologists have personally rejected. It would be difficult for most people to maintain a positive (or even neutral) attitude toward a position they had personally rejected as being either invalid or meaningless. As Burridge (1978: 8) suggests,

> Somehow, whether the person was a physician, an agricultural expert, a technician, a schoolteacher—whatever—the fact that he or she was also a missionary seemed to neutralize the expertise being proffered. One was left with the impression that it was the rarely articulated "Christian" in the general label "missionary" that was the prime target of objection.

Conclusion

Although early anthropologists relied heavily on missionary publications and there have been many missionary ethnographers, the general attitude of anthropologists toward missionaries has been negative. It would be simplistic to suggest that this attitude is entirely due to the acceptance of one (or both) of the presuppositions I have discussed. However, the positions that cultures are organic wholes which should not be disturbed and that religious beliefs are essentially meaningless would certainly contribute to such an attitude. Another contributing factor that has been suggested (Salamone 1977: 409) is that anthropologists and missionaries are actually similar, both believing they have the truth, being protective of the people among whom they work, and opposing that which they define as evil. Burridge (1978: 5) argues that Malinowski's diaries display an animus toward missionaries which has overtones of an unresolved Oedipus problem: "Missionaries had fathered the work to which he was dedicating himself with typical missionary zeal—on the other side of the fence."

Since the involvement of some anthropologists with missionaries will no doubt continue, we should be concerned with the bases of the negative attitude which many of us manifest and be candid in dealing with it. An unwillingness to do so can result in a failure to control for bias in field research (cf. Salamone 1979: 57). This is especially important in areas such as Oceania, where an analysis of missionary endeavor is crucial to an understanding of the process of culture change.

Thai Buddhism and the Popularity of Amulets in Anthropological Perspective

Pamela Moro

The following article begins by acknowledging the role of preconceptions in motivating the study of religions outside of one's own society, reflecting on the author's interest in Thailand. The article introduces some basic characteristics of the anthropological study of religion, with an emphasis on particular challenges in understanding Buddhism in Southeast Asia. The relationship between religion as articulated in authoritative texts and as lived in daily practice has been a key concern for ethnographers, including influential mid-20th century figures such as Melford E. Spiro and Robert Redfield. The second half of the article is an extended example of why religious beliefs and activities are fruitfully studied in social context. Everyday concerns in the lives of individuals, but also in society at large, can fuel short-lived responses only loosely connected to orthodox religion, such as the passionate collecting of amulets in Thailand.

When I began my training as an anthropologist with a specialization in Thailand, I knew from the start I would be studying an overwhelmingly Buddhist nation, which in the 2000 census was reported to be 94.6 percent Buddhist (CIA World Factbook). Even as I immersed myself in the sometimes dry volumes of reading necessary for graduate school, I half-consciously entertained distant childhood memories of *National Geographic* photographs of stunningly beautiful, lichen-covered Buddha sculptures, which I later learned were from Thailand's ancient capital, Sukhothai, now a UNESCO World Heritage Site. The photographs must have appeared during the time of the Vietnam War, and they provided counterpoint to the powerful war reportage I was accustomed to seeing in newspapers and on television. That made

even the name of the region—Southeast Asia—slightly scary and off-putting to me as an American child. I cannot discount the role such images played, both the sublime Buddha images and the now iconic photos of the Vietnam War, in motivating me—a white, middle-class female from a small university town in California—to eventually want to learn to speak Thai and write a dissertation about Thai musicians.

But what was this "Buddhism" that I vaguely expected to find in Thailand? Visiting *wats* (temples) with Thai friends in the United States, I began to get to know a louder, more sociable, more community-minded Buddhism than my earliest preconceptions had allowed, one with plenty of room for encountering and making sense of the supernatural. Once in Thailand, I found musicians intensely engaged with deities from the Hindu pantheon, deities that are manifested during performance and honored, along with esteemed teachers from the past, in elaborate

This selection was written especially for this volume.

rituals. In fact, contemporary scholarship on Thai Buddhism reveals a complex interplay between historical influences from India (both Hindu and Buddhist), Chinese religion, local spirit cults, astrology and fortune telling, political power and national identity, and today's globally mediated marketplace of religion (for example, Klima 2002, R. Morris 2000, Taylor 2008, Terwiel 1975.)

At any rate, thinking of Thailand as a "Buddhist nation," or any part of the world as a fill-in-the-religion-blank country, can foster misleading assumptions about how people engage in a day-to-day way with religious concerns. Anthropology offers a number of tools for understanding the relationship between a so-called world religion and the diverse ways of enacting it.

Anthropological studies of religion differ from those of other perspectives in goal, stance, and method. Our goal is to understand that wide assortment of difficult-to-define human experiences that Western intellectual traditions have led us to call religion (cf. Asad 1993), with particular concern for the specific cultural and historical circumstances that make each example meaningful. Depending on the anthropologist's training and theoretical inclinations, this may mean a focus on symbolism and ritual, or on the functions of religion for different groups in society, including the state, or on power and authority as shaped through historical processes. These approaches contrast strongly with those of the theologian or spiritual follower who seeks the truth, or correct teachings from the perspective of her own tradition—working from a perspective "within the faith." Instead, anthropologists adopt a stance that turns aside from questions of what is true, real, or correct. With its reliance upon ethnographic methods such as participant-observation, interviews, and immersion in primary sources, anthropology seeks multi-textured understandings of religious experience, with attention not only to religious authorities and specialists but also to the whole myriad of participants within a society. While scholars in other fields typically have strong interests in religion as it has been written down, such as scripture and other canonic texts—locating "the religion" in the normative version articulated by authorities throughout the ages—anthropologists are likely to be interested in how authoritative traditions are understood by, adapted, altered, used, or rejected by everyday participants as well as broadly influential leaders.

These characteristics are abundantly clear in the anthropological studies of Theravada Buddhism in Southeast Asia, the part of the world where my own research interests lie. Were one to read only historical and text-based accounts of Buddhism, one would be mightily surprised by the concerns and activities of actual Buddhists in Thailand, for example, whether ordained monks or lay people. The philosophical foundations expressed in the Diamond and Lotus Sutras seem a far cry from such everyday Thai concerns as donating food to monks on their morning alms-gathering walks and making offerings at household spirit shrines. As with many world religions, outsiders have developed particular preconceptions about Buddhism based on images circulated through popular culture, tourism, Western-authored interpretations of Buddhist philosophy and aesthetics, and well-intentioned encapsulations promoting multicultural tolerance. This discourse has long historical roots (cf. Lopez 1998). It comes as a shock to many non-Buddhist Westerners that, contrary to their expectations, most Thai, for example, do not meditate, and they do not eschew worldly possessions. The country has a high murder rate, and temples are only sometimes sites of quiet introspection. Even monks, visually distinctive in orange robes and shaved heads as they go about their highly disciplined daily routine, are motivated by a variety of goals, including entry into adulthood through temporary ordination for young men, fulfillment of parents' expectations, and the pursuit of power. Only some are concerned with systematic practices to seek enlightenment. It is the anthropologist's job to pay attention to such varieties of experiences within a society—as well as, of course, documenting cross-cultural similarities and contrasts discernable from a global level.

Not that anthropologists ignore canonic texts. In fact, one of the preeminent ethnographers of Theravada Buddhism in the mid 20th century, Melford E. Spiro, specialized precisely in the relationship between Buddhism as articulated in texts and Buddhism as lived experience, noting points of similarity, points of contrast, and how the two shaped one another. Spiro conducted fieldwork in village Burma in 1961–62, but as the work of other ethnographers has born out, the patterns identified by Spiro also apply to Thailand, Sri Lanka, and other places adhering to the Theravada tradition. (Theravada, or Hinayana, Buddhism is one of two majors sects in Buddhism, distinct from the Mahayana tradition which developed about two millennia ago.)

> Indeed, so far as Buddhist scholarship is concerned, one might say that the anthropologist takes off where the textual and historical scholar ends, for the anthropologist is not concerned with religious texts per se, but with the interaction between the doctrines found in these texts and conceptions found in the heads of religious devotees, and consequently, with the relation between these religious conceptions and the general ordering of social and cultural life (Spiro 1982:3).

To Spiro, text-focused studies tell an incomplete story of Buddhism, since "...many of its doctrines are only rarely internalized by the members of these societies, because they are either ignored or rejected by the faithful" (ibid: 10). While some of his contemporaries in anthropology deliberately ignored textual versions of Buddhism, Spiro's study of Burmese Buddhism was specifically concerned with the gap between textual scholarship—as normally carried out by historians of religion or religious studies specialists—and the field investigations of anthropologists. Around the time of Spiro's work on Burma—which was monumental in scope and published as three books—other anthropologists worked on the issue of how written, authoritative versions of culture, such as those of religious scripture, articulate with popular understandings, or as Spiro put it, how "the normative tradition and the social actors who have acquired it or been exposed to it" relate to one another (ibid:5). Robert Redfield (1956) coined the useful if somewhat evaluative-sounding terms Great Tradition and Little Tradition to describe the two spheres, and he urged the study of how the two shape each other. These terms were later taken up by Milton Singer (1970) and other anthropologists specifically interested in Asia, though they maintained that the terms were potentially misleading if applied too strictly or with the view that one completely derives from the other, or is a corruption or misunderstanding of the other.

Perhaps because of the lively interplay between the key ideas of Buddhism and the daily practices and attitudes of common people, both rural and urban, anthropologists have been fascinated by apparent paradoxes in the faith. In a recent overview, Brian Morris describes how Buddhism challenges the applicability of standard analytical categories in religion scholarship, by anthropologists or anyone (2006:44–76). Is Buddhism really "a religion"? To what extent are the Buddha and other significant figures, such as saintly monks, recognized as dead? What are the complex relationships between Buddhism and state power? Given that ordinary people do not live like monks, how do they attempt to live up to Buddhist values? As Spiro argued, the key ideals of Buddhism seem to be somehow separate from the daily practices and attitudes of the common people, whether in villages or urban communities. Yet despite the esoteric nature of the most intellectual Buddhist texts, to some degree even "the humblest villager" is familiar with basic principles of the faith.

> . . . [T]hroughout most of Thailand, Burma, and among the Sinhalese, Buddhism is a living tradition. The five basic precepts of Buddhism—not to kill, steal, engage in sexual misconduct, lie, or drink intoxicants—are upheld, and along with the famous "triple Jewel"—"I take refuge in the Buddha, I take refuge in the Dharma, I take my refuge in the Sangha"—are recited every day by almost every villager. Importantly, though such devotions are said before an image of the Buddha, the Buddha is not considered a god, though such images, as well as the famous relics, are often conceived as having spiritual power (B. Morris 2006:53).

Melford Spiro found his way around the paradoxes by inserting a decisive scholarly hand. He distinguished three orientations within Theravada Buddhism, related to different goals or instrumental needs and corresponding to some degree with an individual's status as either monk or layperson. The three categories are creations of the researcher, and the names given to them by Spiro are not household words that Southeast Asian people themselves would use, yet the general patterns alert us to the diversity of concerns and observances within the faith. Spiro's three orientations are:

• *nibbanic* Buddhism—concerned with reaching nirvana, the release from suffering and transcending of individuality. He also called this *soteriological* Buddhism because it is related to salvation;

• *kammic* Buddhism—concerned with karma or the accruing of spiritual merit to insure better rebirths;

• *apotropaic* Buddhism—concerned with relieving day-to-day problems, insuring luck and good fortune. Apotropaic means having the power to avert evil or ill fortune.

Nibbanic Buddhism tends to be the realm of only a few pious monks, while kammic Buddhism is the aim of the vast majority of lay people, and indeed many Theravada Buddhist ritual observances, whether enacted daily or at the time of holidays, are motivated by the accumulation of spiritual merit. Apotropaic concerns engage just about everyone at some point (1982:140ff).

It is in the realm of apotropaic Buddhism, to use Spiro's term, that the remainder of this article moves. We will see how Thai from all walks of life recently turned to a particular form of religious amulet in a time of social uncertainty. To unravel the amulet craze, we put to use the standard tools of anthropology: examination of historically situated cultural patterns as well as the immediate political and economic context, drawing on primary sources, field experiences, and related literature from scholars within as well as outside of Thailand.

Anthropologists have characterized the Thai worldview as concerned to the point of obsession with supernatural power (cf. Mulder 1985, Tambiah 1982). This power—to be feared, controlled, manipulated, and put to use—can collect in certain places and be imbued in particular objects. Among the countless such objects in Thailand are amulets, their trade long a vibrant informal economy, and their associated beliefs constituting a detailed realm of local knowledge and folk culture. The forms and functions of Thai amulets have varied across time, but the most common are molded clay or metal objects, most often featuring a Buddha image, and endowed with supernatural power to insure luck, safety, fertility, prosperity, or success, or to ward off undesirable conditions and fortunes. Some are in-the-round or three-dimensional—including special purpose amulets shaped like phalluses or animals—while others are flat lozenges; still others are swatches of printed fabric, bearing cabalistic writing and/or sacred images. Noted Thai folklorist

Phya Anuman Rajadhon contributed a detailed overview and classification of the many kinds, including categories of recitations, tattoos, and natural objects such as certain kinds of leaves. From Rajadhon's work it is clear that over time various styles of amulets have risen and fallen in popularity (1968).

Like all sacred objects in Thailand, especially all representations of the Lord Buddha (properly called Buddha images, never "Buddhas"), amulets are treated with respect and care. They are commonly worn on the body, most often under one's clothes on a neck chain, but they may also be placed on a home altar, the dashboard of a motor vehicle, or other special place. It is likely that nearly all Thai, whether urban or rural, possess at least a few amulets. While people in the West may wear a Christian cross or a Star of David on a neck chain as a sign of pride, to assert an identity, or as an intimately meaningful personal reminder of faith, Thai amulets (while they might serve the former roles as well) primarily function as objects of actual power. They do not stand for power but actually have power. Certain types are also offered as vow-fulfillment at sacred sites.

In the scholarly literature, amulets have also been referred to as talismans and charms. There is minimal consistency in definitions, and I have chosen to use the term "amulet" because it has been showcased in earlier studies of Thailand. Theodor H. Gaster, in the *Encyclopedia of Religion*, distinguishes amulets, as small objects charged with magical power to ward off undesirable things, from talismans, intended to enhance desirable qualities and fortunes. "Amulets and talismans are two sides of the same coin: the former are designed to repel what is baneful; the latter, to impel what is beneficial. The employment of both (which is universal) rests on the belief that the inherent quality of a thing can be transmitted to human beings by contact" (2005:297-98). Carolyn Morrow Long uses the generic European term "charm" to encompass both amulets and talismans: "A charm is any object, substance, or combination thereof believed to be capable of influencing physical, mental, and spiritual health; manipulating personal relationships and the actions of others; and invoking the aid of the deities, the dead, and the abstract concept of 'luck'" (2001:xvi).

Using concepts first introduced a century ago by James Frazer, in his massive cross-cultural compendium of religious beliefs, *The Golden Bough,* Long notes that charms work by the principle of sympathetic magic. They produce results because of a sympathetic connection between the charm and the person or events to be influenced (ibid:xvii). This sympathetic connection is articulated in imitative charms when the ingredients or appearance of the object is "like" its purpose—like produces like. In other cases the sympathetic connection operates because things that were once in contact continue to affect each other. Thai amulets generally fall in the imitative category. Though publications abound about amulets, talismans, and charms, most are of a non-scholarly or semi-scholarly nature (for example D. Morris 1999, Paine 2004). An early classic work is E.A. Wallis Budge's *Amulets and Talismans,* a comparative account tracing such items to ancient Egypt and Babylonia, first published in 1911 and reflecting the British antiquarian perspective of its day. However, all such classifications do little to deepen our understanding of what the amulets mean to the people who use them, or why their use becomes intense in particular times and places.

The methods for crafting amulets and imbuing them with sacred power are forms of specialized knowledge in Thailand, associated with lineages of participants who pass the knowledge along semi-secretly. Power can build or be proven, however, after the time of manufacture. What often happens is that a particular kind of amulet will be associated with a miraculous event, and legendary acclaim will follow. For example, when some small, bronze-colored metal amulets, bearing the image of a revered monk, were found to be carried by survivors in the horrific collapse of a hotel in 1992, that style of amulet suddenly grew in popularity. A dear friend's mother, concerned about our safety, gave a pair to my husband and me before a flight back to the United States.

As an anthropologist studying Thailand, while my central research interests were with music, I could not fail to be fascinated by amulets. Arriving in Bangkok for the first time in 1985, I quickly discovered neighborhoods known for the sale of amulets and other sacred objects and saw with my own eyes the ubiquity of amulet wearing. Grandmothers wore weighty strands of locket-encased charms and small babies were lovingly protected with tiny Buddha figurines on delicate chains. Despite having read the most important scholarly works on Thai amulets, I had somehow underestimated what must be one of the most immediate, everyday encounters with the supernatural for perhaps millions of Thai. I most definitely had underestimated the exchange value of amulets, evidenced not only in the lively streetside markets but also in glossy trade magazines for amulet dealers, collectors, and investors. Some enthusiasts put a great deal of effort into learning to distinguish real from fake or reproduction items. On the surface, the outsider might falsely compare such trade with coin or baseball card collecting, where scarcity, condition, and aesthetic appeal determine value. The value of amulets may well be partly shaped by such factors, and fair enough, coin and baseball card collectors may fetishize their objects of desire to a certain degree. Yet Thai sacred objects are fundamentally valuable because they contain power, and value will rise and fall with perceptions of the efficacy of that power.

Living in the northern city of Chiangmai for several months in 2007, as a guest at Chiangmai Rajabhat University, I was caught by surprise once again. A new style of amulet, *jatukham-rammathep,* had recently shot into prominence. Originally produced at a single monastery, Wat Mahathat, in the southern city of Nakhon Si Thammarat in the mid-1980s, they were just one among the many varieties of amulets until 2006 and especially 2007. They suddenly surged in popularity and monetary value, constituting a craze or what Thai slang refers to as a "hit." Their name refers to two Hindu deities, guardians to holy relics at Wat Mahathat and represented in images on doors at the temple. Jatukham-rammatheep amulets are distinctive visually. They are round, larger than most amulets (about 3" in diameter), embossed with Hindu images and astrological signs, and worn in eye-catching lockets on large gold chains—displayed openly for all to see, sometimes turned around to a person's back—especially by males. Though I have no proof, I have wondered if the lockets and chains are influenced by hip-hop fashion. There actually are countless different jatukham-rammathep amulets, with different images and manufactured from different substances. Compared to the subdued terra cotta or brass of most other amulets, they are colorful and, because they include herbal ingredients, are distinctively fragrant.

In 2007, the bazaar-style sale of the amulets in Chiangmai, and apparently throughout the nation, was striking. They just seemed to be everywhere, from sidewalk stalls to supermarket foyers. On weekends, the entire ground-level floor of a major shopping center turned into an amulet market with dozens of small-scale vendors offering jatukham-rammathep. 7-Eleven stores (incidentally, the largest chain store in the world in 2007, with massive numbers of outlets in Thailand (GreenwichMeanTime.com 2009; Japan News Review 2007), sold magazines and catalogs devoted to the amulets, displayed prominently near the cash registers, and even offered their own amulets via mail order. An entrepreneurial civil servant at my neighborhood post office sold, from behind the counter, shirts with jatukham-rammathep images. Some believe the shirts have the same potential power as the amulets. With so much buying, selling, and speculating, it is no wonder that the objects escalated in value precipitously. In 2007, their prices ranged from several hundred to several million *baht* (US$1 equals about 35–39 baht).

Unlike most amulets which are ready-to-go when acquired, in 2007 jatukham-rammathep required charging up: they needed to be consecrated by the user. This is commonly done in mass ceremonies officiated by monks (though most monks, by far, are not involved with the jatukham-rammathep craze). Especially desirable is blessing from the abbot of Wat Mahathat, the temple originally associated with their manufacture. A range of related commodities could also be used to enhance the power of the jatukham-rammathep, for example, candles ornamented with ritualistic writing. Such activities suggest a personal agency on the part of the users, a commitment to tending the artifact.

As with meteoric crazes in any part of the world, the phenomenon soon aroused controversy, and was documented in nearly daily, sometimes sensational, news stories. Thai economists became concerned by the wildly inflated prices of the amulets, and by how much of the Thai economy was tied up in them, like tulip mania in 16th and 17th century Holland. An Air Force pilot took a load of amulets up in a plane, to increase their power; a rural monastery created a special set containing ashes of cremated infants; other monasteries financed building and renovation projects through the sale of commissioned amulets; an outspoken monk, critical of the obsession, poked fun by marketing amulet-shaped cookies and dog treats. Yet by the time I was leaving Chiangmai in September 2007, prices were beginning to fall, and word on the street was that the craze was passing, the economic bubble burst.

Setting aside for the moment the purely economic aspects of the jatukham-rammathep phenomenon, with some participants undisputedly buying and selling in order to get rich, we might ask why the craze erupted when it did, and why this particular kind of amulet, out of all those available, became of such interest. A superficial answer to the question is the 2006 death of Major-General Phantarak Rajadej, the Nakhon Si Thammarat police chief who originally promoted the amulets (Head 2007). Tens of thousands of people attended his funeral, and copies of the amulets were distributed, stimulating interest in the older version (ibid.). However, there is no single miraculous event or crisis aversion associated with the police chief, or indeed with jatukham-rammathep as a whole. Instead, following the lead of Thai scholars who convened a 2007 conference devoted to the amulets, we must find our answer in the social, economic, and political circumstances of Thailand at the time.

Anthropologists frequently attribute belief in magic, and turns to religion in general, as ways to control the uncontrollable and to explain the unexplainable. Classic contributions from Bronislaw Malinowski on magic in the Trobriand Islands (see articles 36 and 37 in the present volume) and by E. E. Evans-Pritchard on witchcraft among the Azande (article 36) are in this vein. Humans are never without things that need to be controlled and explained, and hence—from a functionalist point of view—it is likely that the usual varied assortment of amulets has offered comfort and satisfaction to many Thai, in ways that the otherworldly philosophy of orthodox Buddhism might not. As Spiro pointed out, the apotropaic orientation within Southeast Asian Buddhism offers relief for daily problems, in its focus on "important matters in this existence" (1982:140).

However, around the time of the jatukham-rammathep phenomenon, a striking confluence of circumstances worried the nation and might account for why the public would be attracted to the promise of a new kind of supernatural assistance. The December 26, 2004, tsunami struck Thailand's southern peninsula, tragically killing both local people and foreigners, and temporarily devastating the region's tourist economy. A coup d'état on September 19, 2006, ousted controversial Prime Minister Thaksin Shinawatra and banned his party, and it led to leadership by a junta until elections in late 2007. During the period of junta leadership, Bangkok protests in support of the ousted prime minister frequently ended in mass arrests. For the first time ever, citizens approved a new constitution through referendum in August 2007. Under the leadership of Thaksin as well as the junta, long-simmering conflict between Thai-speaking Buddhists and Malay-speaking Muslims, all Thai citizens, in southern Thailand became violent. Hot spots erupted along Thailand's other, notoriously porous borders. During these same years concerns grew about avian influenza, contaminants in food, and the relocation of wage-paying jobs to China as multinational companies moved their factories to a cheaper source of labor. After years of robust economic growth that swelled the Thai middle class, the first inklings of global economic problems—stemming from the U.S. mortgage crisis—began to be reported in Thailand in 2007. Perhaps more than anything, however, there was concern for Thailand's revered king, approaching his 80th birthday in fragile health, arousing softly whispered anxiety about succession and stability. Public disquiet continued amidst political instability, public protests, and strong symbolic rallying around the king through 2008. In more ways than one, the symbolic body of the nation seemed to be under attack and destabilized.

It is eerie now to look back at Stanley Tambiah's detailed study of an earlier amulet craze (1982). Based on fieldwork in the 1970s in the nation's northeast as well as Bangkok, the work was published soon after Thailand's experimental democratic period, 1973–76, which ended tragically with a right-wing crackdown and the deaths of university student protestors (cf. Bowie 1997, Morell and Samudavanija 1981). Tambiah related the period's passion for amulets to what he called "street machismo," which he saw manifested in aggressive motor vehicle driving and urban crime. He was struck by a divide between the respectful etiquette governing interpersonal relations and the free-for-all of anonymous public behavior (ibid:228-29). "In a sense, then, the Thai craze for and insatiable collection of protective amulets and other fetishes should be viewed in relation to [Thai] propensities and preoccupations with the exercise of power, in which violence shows its dark face" (ibid:229).

Social tensions therefore help explain the timing of such crazes and account for why people who already accept the efficacy of amulets (as part of a cultural repertory of symbols) would become especially attracted to them in the years 2006 and 2007. We may still ask, however, given the variety of available sacred objects, many quite localized and supported by local legends and mystic figures, why the jatukham-rammathep would rise to prominence. Thai scholars who held a conference devoted to jatukham-rammathep (covered in a special issue of the journal *Sinlapawatthanatham* in June 2007) noted some significant factors. The amulets appear novel and are aesthetically pleasing in and of themselves. The interactiveness required, such as blessing and consecration, allow participants to do something actively, to take a psychologically reassuring step in uncertain circumstances. And, they were promoted ingeniously, at both grassroots and commercial levels. This included the marketing of sets or series which, as many consumers of "collectibles" around the world know, can motivate acquisition.

The specific connection between the growth in exchange value and the amulets' growth in supernatural efficacy and desirability remains somewhat unclear, and undoubtedly deserves further theorizing. What is clear is that jatukham-rammathep constitute a commodification of religious forms far beyond the scale to which most Thai were accustomed. The jatukham-rammathep craze generated internal cultural criticism, in part because Buddhist monks were involved in creating and selling the items. While monasteries have always raised funds to build and repair facilities, such practical necessities have usually been administered by lay people, often in festivities that encourage participation in dance, music, and local folkways. Monks are expected to model self-denial and the control of desires, and publicly visible business activity like promoting amulets draws certain condemnation, or at the very least gossip.

Of course, the buying and selling of small religious objects is far from limited to Thailand.

Cross-cultural examples demonstrate a widespread commercialization of religious forms in the last century, paralleling the spread of capitalism and its attendant commodification of many previously private spheres of life. Long's study of Africa-derived religions in North America traces a gradual commodification of traditional charms throughout the 20th century (2001:99-126). Long notes, however: "Despite the change from handmade charms to manufactured products, the intentions for which they are used remain the same: the state of one's own body and mind; relationships with others; and the control of external forces like luck, the saints, and the spirits" (p. 109). Inge Maria Daniels reaches a similar conclusion regarding household shrines in contemporary Japan, which entails the purchase of commercially available spiritual artifacts. Rather than viewing the mass production and commercial sale of such objects as a cultural ill, Daniels argues that commodification enables a democratic diffusion of spirituality. "Good luck charms are neither sacred nor secular; they challenge the supposed divide between the aesthetic value and utility of objects" (2003:619).

That amulets bridge the divide between sacred and secular, aesthetic and utilitarian, came home to me powerfully in Thailand in 2007, when my friend and language tutor, Gig, gave my family a jatukham-rammathep amulet. A black disc with white bas-relief figures, the amulet had been in her possession for years—since long before the craze, kept lovingly in a red-cushioned box. Gig said she had been collecting jatukham-rammathep since she was a teen in the 1980s, attracted to them for their beauty alone. She demurely denied any knowledge of what the amulet might be worth monetarily. "I don't care—now I just give them to my friends as gifts," she explained.

To conclude, amulets in Thailand are a local manifestation of global phenomena. They share features with similar charms that can be traced to antiquity, and that serve similar functions despite being found in diverse societies, in association with a variety of religions. As efficacious sacred objects, they increase in value when associated with propitious circumstances, and as commodities exchanged in the contemporary marketplace, they increase in value when there is consumer demand. As meaning-laden artifacts, they are part of Thailand's symbolic repertory, drawn into play during social crises. They are a superb example of the apotropaic orientation in Buddhism, in dialogue with orthodox religious expression but responding to immediate needs, and tied to a cultural concern with power.

Suggested Readings

Bowie, Fiona
    2006   *The Anthropology of Religion: An Introduction*. 2nd ed. Oxford: Blackwell.

deWaal Malefijt, Annemarie
    1968   *Religion and Culture:An Introduction to Anthropology of Religion*. New York: Macmillan.

Glazier, Stephen, D., ed.
    1999   *Anthropology of Religion: A Handbook*. Westport, Conn.: Praeger.

Klass, Morton, and Maxine Weisgrau, eds.
    1999   *Across the Boundaries of Belief: Contemporary Issues in the Anthropology of Religion*. Boulder, Colo.: Westview Press.

Lambek, Michael, ed.
    2002   *A Reader in the Anthropology of Religion*. Malden, Mass.: Blackwell.

Morris, Brian
    2006   *Religion and Anthropology: A Critical Introduction*. Cambridge: Cambridge University Press.

CHAPTER TWO

Myth, Symbolism, and Taboo

Indian mask of painted wood, northwest coast, North America.

Tales, legends, proverbs, riddles, adages, and myths make up what anthropologists call *folklore*, an important subject for the study of culture. Because of its sacred nature, myth is especially significant in the analysis of comparative religion. Fundamental to the definition of myths are the community's attitudes toward them. Myths are narratives that are held to be sacred and true; thus, they often are core parts of larger ideological systems (Oring 1986: 124). Myths are set outside of historical time, usually at the beginning of time up to the point of human creation, and they frequently account for how the world came to be in its present form. Many of the principal characters are divine or semi-divine; most are not human beings but animals or cultural heroes with human attributes. The place, time, and manner in which a myth is performed may be special, and even the language in which it is expressed may be out of the ordinary. Elliott Oring considers the familiar story of Adam and Eve as an example:

> For those who hold the story to be both sacred and true, the activities of this primordial couple, in concert with beguiling serpent and deity, explain fundamental aspects of world order: why the serpent is reviled, why a woman is ruled by her husband and suffers in childbirth, why man must toil to live—and most importantly—how sin entered the world and why man must die. (Ibid.)

To the anthropologist or folklorist, it is of no consequence whether the myth is objectively or scientifically true. What matters is its validity in its own cultural context. All of these characteristics distinguish myth from other forms of folk narrative, such as legend and folktale (Bascom 1965).

Beyond shaping worldview and explaining the origins of human existence, myths also serve as authoritative precedents that validate social norms. One of the founding figures of anthropology, Bronislaw Malinowski, described myth as a social "charter"—a model for behavior:

> [Myth] is a statement of primeval reality which lives in the institutions and pursuits of a community. It justifies by precedent the existing order and it supplies a retrospective pattern

of moral values, of sociological discriminations and burdens and of magical belief. . . . The function of myth is to strengthen tradition and to endow it with a greater value and prestige by tracing it back to a higher, better, more supernatural, and more effective reality of initial events (1931: 640–41).

Some anthropologists apply a psychological approach to myth analysis and see myths as symbolic expressions of sibling rivalry, male-female tensions, and other themes. Others—structural anthropologists such as Claude Lévi-Strauss—view myths as cultural means of resolving critical binary oppositions (life-death, matrilineal-patrilineal, nature-culture) that serve as models for members of a society (Hunter and Whitten 1976: 280–81). Whether in Judeo-Christian and Muslim cultures, where myths have been transcribed to form the Torah, Bible, and Koran, or in other, less familiar cultures, these sacred narratives still serve their time-honored function for the bulk of humanity as the basis of religious belief. What is important to remember is that myths are considered to be truthful accounts of the past, whether transmitted orally in traditional societies or through the scriptural writings of the so-called great religions.

The scholarly study of myth has been important in the West since the time of the ancient Greeks. To Plato we owe the confusion over the meaning of the word *myth*, as he felt it was synonymous with *falsehood* or *lie*. Indeed, the use of *myth* to mean "fallacy" continues today, in clear contrast to the way anthropologists and other scholars of religion use the term. We can credit the anthropologists of the early 20th century with drawing attention to how myth functions in actual societies, rather than regarding myths as texts from the past. Distinctive to the anthropological approach to myth is an emphasis upon culture-specific meanings. This perspective differs from that of popular myth theorist Joseph Campbell, whose compelling books and television appearances have inspired many in the United States. Influenced greatly by psychologist Carl Jung, Campbell's goal was to uncover common symbols and themes that lie beneath the mythic traditions of all the world's cultures. Today, the study of myth remains multidisciplinary, with important contributions continuing in the fields of anthropology, folklore, literary studies, psychology, and religion.

The study of symbolism, too, is vital to the study of religion. In fact, "the human beings who perform the rituals . . . , and those who are ostensibly a ritual's objects, are themselves representations of concepts and ideas, and therefore symbolic" (La Fontaine 1985: 13). Anthropology has been less than clear in its attempt to define the meaning of this important concept. Minimally, a symbol may be thought of as something that represents something else. The development of culture, for example, was dependent on human beings having the ability to assign symbolic meanings of words—to create and use a language. Religion is also a prime example of humanity's proclivity to attach symbolic meanings to a variety of behavior and objects. "The object of symbolism," according to Alfred North Whitehead, "is the enhancement of the importance of what is symbolized" (1927: 63).

That anthropological interest in the topic of symbolism had its start with the study of religious behavior is not surprising, especially in light of the plethora of symbols present in religious objects and ceremonies. Reflect for a moment on any religious service. Immediately on entering the building, be it a church, synagogue, or mosque, one is overwhelmed by symbolic objects—the Christian cross, the Star of David, paintings, statues, tapestries, and assorted ceremonial paraphernalia—each representing a religious principle. Fittingly, Clifford Geertz has noted that a religious system may be viewed as a "cluster of sacred symbols" (1957: 424). Unlike the well-defined symbols in mathematics and the physical sciences, these religious symbols assume many different forms and meanings: witness Turner's concept of the multivocalic nature of symbols (their capacity to have many meanings).

More than a simple reminder of some remote aspect of a religion's history, religious symbols are often considered to possess a power or force (*mana*) emanating from the spiritual world itself. The symbols provide people with an emotional and intellectual commitment to their particular belief system, telling them what is important to their society, collectively and individually, and helping them conform to the group's value system. Durkheim accounted for the universality of symbols by arguing that a society kept its value system through their use; that is, the symbols stood for the revered values. Without the symbols, the values and, by extension, the society's existence would be threatened.

Whereas symbols, like myths, prescribe thoughts and behaviors of people, taboos restrict actions. Because the term *taboo* (also known as *tabu* and *kapu*) originated in the Pacific Islands, beginning anthropology students often associate it with images of "savage" Polynesians observing mystical prohibitions. It is true that Pacific Islanders did cautiously regard these restrictions, being careful to avoid the supernatural retribution that was certain to follow violations. Taboos are not limited to the Pacific, however; every society has restrictions that limit behavior in one respect or another, usually in association with sex, food, rites of passage, sacred objects, and sacred people. The incest taboo is unique in that it is found in all societies. Although anthropologists have yet to explain adequately why the incest taboo exists everywhere, they have demonstrated that most taboos are reinforced by the threat of punishments meted out by supernatural forces.

As anthropologists have pointed out, taboos are adaptive human mechanisms: they function to counter dangers of both the phenomenal and ideational world. It is possible to theorize that the existence of fewer real or imagined dangers would result in fewer taboos, but it is equally safe to argue that all societies will continue to establish new taboos as new threats to existence or social stability arise. Certainly taboos function at an ecological level—for example, to preserve plants, animals, and resources of the sea. Taboos also function to distinguish between and control social groups, threatening violators with supernatural punishments as severe as the denial of salvation. Depending on the culture, sacred authority is often as compelling as the civil codes to which people are required to comply. Simply stated, the breaking of a sacred taboo, as opposed to a civil sanction, is a sin. The impersonal power of mana made certain objects and people in Pacific cultures taboo. Although the concept of mana does not exist in contemporary Western cultures, certain symbols and objects are similarly imbued with such an aura of power or sacredness that they, too, are considered taboo.

Using a variety of approaches to the study of myth, symbol, and taboo, the articles selected for this chapter clearly show the importance of these topics to the study of comparative religion. We begin with Leonard and McClure's exploration of myth, which introduces several ways of defining and studying myth in cross-cultural perspective. The authors consider the insights of key theorists in psychology, literary studies, and religious studies, as well as anthropology.

Leonard and McClure's overview is followed by examples of two contrasting approaches to myth within the field of anthropology. The excerpt by John Beattie illustrates the functionalist approach, with its attention to the close relationship between myth and social organization. "Harelips and Twins: The Splitting of a Myth" is an example of the structuralist approach of Claude Lévi-Strauss, one of the 20th century's most original scholars of myth.

In the fourth article, Eric Wolf explores a single, multifaceted, and historically significant symbol from Mexico.

In her examination of the concept of taboo, Mary Douglas defines and shows the significance of taboo in reducing ambiguity and injecting order into cultural systems, stressing commonalities in taboos, whether found in Polynesia or the West.

Mary Lee Daugherty's case study of snake-handling congregations in West Virginia, originally written in 1976, shows the integration of myth and symbol in religious practice. Daugherty argues that snake handling is a form of sacrament, a religious ceremony that symbolically expresses the relationship between believers and Christ.

References

Bascom, William
   1965   "The Forms of Folklore: Prose Narratives." *Journal of American Folklore* 78: 3–20.

Geertz, Clifford
   1957   "Ethos, World-View and the Analysis of Sacred Symbols." *Antioch Review* 17: 421–37.

Hunter, David E., and Phillip Whitten
   1976   *Encyclopaedia of Anthropology.* New York: Harper and Row.

La Fontaine, Joan S.
   1985   *Initiation.* Harmondsworth, England: Penguin Books.

Malinowski, Bronislaw
   1931   "Culture." In *Encyclopaedia of the Social Sciences,* Edwin R. A. Seligman, editor-in-chief, vol. 4, pp. 621–46. New York: The Macmillan Company.

Oring, Elliott
   1986   *Folk Groups and Folklore Genres: An Introduction.* Logan: Utah State University Press.

Whitehead, Alfred N.
   1927   *Symbolism.* New York: G. P. Putnam's Sons.

6

The Study of Mythology

Scott Leonard and Michael McClure

In this selection, authors Leonard and McClure help us understand the meaning and importance of myths. Myths, the authors tell us, are ancient narratives that help us understand such fundamental human questions as how the world came to be, how we came to be here, who we are, what our values should be, how we should behave or not behave, and what the consequences of such behavior are. They state that the meaning of myth has always been contested:

> *For two and a half millennia, debates over the importance and meaning of myth have been struggles over matters of truth, religious belief, politics, social custom, cultural identity, and history. The history of mythology is a tale told by idiots—but also by sages, religious fundamentalists and agnostic theologians, idealists and cynics, racists and fascists, philosophers and scholars. Myth has been understood as containing the secrets of God, as the cultural DNA responsible for a people's identity, as a means of reorganizing all human knowledge, and a justification for European and American efforts to colonize and police the world.*

In discussing the study of mythology, Leonard and McClure pay special attention to the 20th century, examining the various approaches to myth in such academic disciplines as anthropology, psychology, literary criticism, and the history of religions. They end the article with a look at the study of mythology today, suggesting that, despite intensive study over the years, we still have no single, all-encompassing explanation of myth.

Why Study Myths?

The study of myths—mythology—has a long, rich, and highly contested history of debate about exactly what myths *are*, what they *do*, and why they are worthy of systematic study. Because of the complexity of such considerations about myths, any short answer to the question "Why study myths?" will be, at best,

From PURPOSES AND DEFINITIONS, MYTH AND KNOWING: AN INTRODUCTION TO WORLD MYTHOLOGY by Scott Leonard and Michael McClure, pp. 1–31. Copyright © 2004. Reprinted by permission of The McGraw-Hill Companies.

only a starting place. Yet this very complexity is one of the reasons why such study can be so exciting. The study of myth is a field of inquiry that ranges from the earliest known history of humanity up to and including contemporary cultures and societies and even our own individual senses of self in the world.

Every part of this [inquiry] should serve more as a direction for further investigation than as a fully satisfactory explanation of settled facts. In our view, (1) the intertwined nature of the uses of myths in diverse cultures; (2) the myriad ways in which myths can be seen to embody cultural attitudes, values, and behaviors; and (3) the rich rewards awaiting questioners willing to approach myths from numerous points of view are all open-ended fields of inquiry. We see this [work] as an invitation to enter into these fields, whether briefly or as a lifelong interest. The study of myth entails discovering a way of making meaning that has been part of every human society.

What Are Myths?

Myths are ancient narratives that attempt to answer the enduring and fundamental human questions: How did the universe and the world come to be? How did we come to be here? Who are we? What are our proper, necessary, or inescapable roles as we relate to one another and to the world at large? What should our values be? How should we behave? How should we *not* behave? What are the consequences of behaving and not behaving in such ways?

Of course, any short definition, however carefully wrought, must oversimplify in order to be clear and short, so accept this definition as a starting point only. If this definition holds up under more extensive examination of myths across the world and in our own backyards, then what a promise with which to start a book, what an answer to the opening question, "Why study myths?"

Engaging thoughtfully with the myths in this book and with research projects that go far beyond what space constraints allow us to present in this book will deepen and complicate the elements of our starting definition. For example, myths are *ancient* narratives. But they are not static artifacts. They are not potsherds and weathered bone fragments. In many cases, they are living texts with which living people continue to write or narrate or perform their unique answers to basic human questions. This never-ending quality to myth is one reason we have included in this book not only ancient or "primary" versions of myths but also more contemporary tales, such as "Out of the Blue" by Paula Gunn Allen, which take up ancient myths and refashion their constituent elements in order to update answers to perennial questions and participate in ongoing cultural self-definitions.

Modern Native Americans, for example, who take up myths from their varied heritages and retell them do so in a context that includes the whole history of their people, from their ancient roots and primordial self-definitions to their contacts with European-American culture and modern self-definitions that search for meaning in a world forever changed by that contact. Today's Irish poets, for another example, who use Celtic myths as source material and inspiration and who write in Irish, a language which came perilously close to extinction, are engaged in cultural reclamation on a number of levels, and Irish myths, ancient and modern, are an important part of that effort. Looking at examples of ancient and more contemporary uses of myths introduces their varied cultural values and behaviors to us, and, at the same time, such study helps us develop intellectual tools with which to look at and question our own ancient and contemporary mythic self-understandings. In this sense, studying myths introduces other cultures to us and, at the same time, provides us with different lenses through which to view our own.

. . .

. . . Toward the end of the 19th century, . . . early anthropology's view of myth emphasized function above all else. Interest in this functional approach to mythology led to the breakup of the largely bookish and tendentious study of literary myth. What emerged were various approaches toward myth driven by disciplinary concerns within anthropology, psychology, literary criticism, and the history of religions.

Mythology in the 20th Century

Early Anthropology

The Golden Bough The first of these disciplines, anthropology, came to view myth as primarily a living, oral, culture-preserving phenomenon. Led by such pioneers as Edward B. Tylor, Andrew Lang, Franz Boas, Sir James George Frazer, and Emile Durkheim, emphasis switched from textual comparisons and blood-and-soil interpretive theories to discovering the ways in which myths *function* in living societies. Sir James Frazer's *The Golden Bough* is the best known and remains the most widely read example of the early versions of this anthropological work. *The Golden Bough,* which grew to 12 volumes, depicts the widely dispersed stories of dying and resurrecting gods as literary transformations of primitive, magical-religious rituals in which "sacred kings" were slaughtered in hopes of ensuring agricultural fertility. Frazer approached myth and culture from an evolutionary perspective, assuming, not unlike Vico, a progression from the "mute signs" of primitive magic (e.g., rituals believed to create desired effects) to the largely allegorical use of ritual in primitive religion (e.g., the substitutionary death of a "scapegoat") to the abstract symbolism of civilized religion (e.g., the doctrine of transubstantiation).

Frazer also assumed that myth was "primitive science," which attributed to the will of deities, people, or animals that which modern science attributes to the impersonal functioning of various physical laws and biological processes. While Frazer shared the new anthropological science's interests in myth's function in living cultures, he nevertheless did not completely break with comparative mythology's armchair approach.

The "Myth-and-Ritual" School Frazer's quasi-anthropological work had wide influence and inspired, at least in part, the also quasi-anthropological "myth-and-ritual" school. This relatively short-lived branch of mythological research was intensely functionalist in its approach, caring little for the origins of myth and looking at content only as a means of demonstrating the contention that myth is a script from which early religious rituals were performed. As Fontenrose puts it in the preface to *The Ritual Theory of Myth:* "Some . . . are finding myth everywhere, especially those who follow the banner of the 'myth-ritual' school—or perhaps I should say banners of the schools, since ritualists do not form a single school or follow a single doctrine. But most of them are agreed that all myths are derived from rituals and that they were in origin the spoken part of ritual performance" (1971, n.p.).

Modern Anthropology

Another of Frazer's admirers was Bronislaw Malinowski, whose fieldwork in the Trobriand Islands contributed much to the evolving methods of modern anthropology. In a 1925 lecture given in Frazer's honor, Malinowski lavishly praised the elder writer and then proceeded to outline what has been taken, until recently, as field anthropology's gospel:

> Studied alive, myth . . . is not symbolic, but a direct expression of its subject-matter; it is not an explanation in satisfaction of a scientific interest, but a narrative resurrection of a primeval reality, told in satisfaction of deep religious wants, moral

cravings, social submissions, assertion, even practical requirements. Myth fulfills in primitive culture an indispensable function: it expresses, enhances, and codifies belief; it safeguards and enforces morality; it vouches for the efficiency of ritual and contains practical rules for the guidance of man. Myth is thus a vital ingredient of human civilization; it is not an idle tale, but a hard-worked active force; it is not an intellectual explanation or an artistic imagery, but a pragmatic charter of primitive faith and moral wisdom (1926/1971, 79).

Malinowski's outline of anthropology's view of myth contains several crucial remarks. First, the anthropologist states emphatically that myth is not an "explanation in satisfaction of a scientific interest." This view contrasts sharply with the euhemerism of Frazer, Tylor, and the comparatists, who believed to one degree or another that myths are little more than primitive or mistaken science. Second, Malinowski saw myth as profoundly "true" in the sense that it had a visible role as "pragmatic charter of primitive faith and moral wisdom." He also saw myth as real in the sense that it could be observed by the field researcher in the form of oral performance, rituals, and ceremonies, and that it visibly influenced a living people's sociopolitical behavior. As his later fieldwork makes clear, Malinowski's views are considerably broader than those of the myth-ritualists, who would have limited myth's functionality to religious ritual only.

But we can also see from Malinowski's remarks that he did not entirely part ways with his mentor. Even though the younger man claimed to have also disputed the older's evolutionary theory of culture, it is significant that he nevertheless discusses myth's role in the "primitive faith" and in the "primitive psychology" of his research subjects. It can be argued that Malinowski and his contemporaries were not explicitly dismissive of "primitive" societies, that they were even respectful of the "face-to-face" nature of such societies when compared with more institutional and "impersonal" developed ones. Yet the effects of ethnocentric assumptions make it extremely difficult to avoid such hierarchical valuations, even if there is some question about the motives or intentions of the researchers.

Nevertheless, folkloric and anthropological methodologies profoundly influenced 20th-century mythology. For example, anthropological and folklorist approaches to myth emphasize field research and have thus underscored the importance of the real-world conditions in which myths perform their functions. As a result, those working in other disciplines have come to respect myth's functions as cultural charter and socializing agent. In addition, anthropology's correlation of myths to the material, social, political, and economic facts of living cultures helps those interested in the myths of extinct cultures to understand some of the obscure references and actions in the stories they study. Moreover, the insistence of anthropologists and folklorists on examining the function of myths in *living* societies demonstrates how ignorant the 19th century's armchair mythologists had been of what so-called primitives actually *do* understand about the physical world and the degree to which they are and are not naive about the truth-value of these narratives. In short, anthropology and folklore have encouraged all mythologists to relate their theories about myth to the lived experience of human beings.

The Rise of Psychology

About the time that Frazer and the early anthropologists were beginning to turn the focus of mythology away from questions of racial identity and to replace the comparative method of the Nature School with theories of social functionalism, psychiatric pioneers Sigmund Freud and Carl Jung had begun to investigate the relationship between myth and the unconscious. Freud and Jung believed that mythic symbols—both as they are encountered in religion and as they manifest themselves in dreams and works of the imagination—emerge from the deepest wells of the psyche. Although their conclusions about the landscape of the human mind differed, both men shared a belief that our gods and other mythic characters, as well as our dreams and works of fiction, are projections of that which the unconscious contains. For Freud, "the unconscious is the true psychical reality" (*Complete Works* 1953–1966, 612–13), but our conscious minds censor our impulses, desires, fantasies, and preconscious thoughts because they are too raw and dangerous to face unmediated. Freud saw the images that appear to us in dreams and in such imaginative works as novels and myths as tamed projections of the unconscious's ungovernable terrors. From this point of view, myths are the conscious mind's strategy for

making visible and comprehensible the internal forces and conflicts that impel our actions and shape our thoughts.

Jung's view is similar to but not identical with Freud's. Jung viewed the unconscious not as the individual's personal repository "of repressed or forgotten [psychic] contents" (1959/1980, 3). Rather, he argued, "the unconscious is not individual but universal [collective]; unlike the personal psyche, it has contents and modes of behavior that are more or less the same everywhere and in all individuals" (3–4). Jung defined "the contents of the collective unconscious . . . as archetypes" (4). Just exactly what an archetype is psychologically is far too complex to discuss here, but, briefly, Jung defined them as "those psychic contents which have not yet been submitted to conscious elaboration" (5). Indeed, Jung and Freud believed that we never see the unconscious and its contents; rather, we see only projected and therefore refined images that symbolize the things it contains.

Jung and his followers argued that such mythic archetypes as the Wise Woman, the Hero, the Great Mother, the Father, the Miraculous Child, and the Shadow are aspects of every individual psyche, regardless of gender, culture, or personal history. The healthy mind, they reasoned, learns to view the contradictory impulses represented by these archetypes in a balanced pattern, or "mandala." Those with various neuroses and psychoses, however, can't balance these impulses and are overwhelmed by the unconscious's self-contradictory forces. Jung saw the universalized symbols and images that appear in myth, religion, and art as highly polished versions of the archetypes lurking in the collective unconscious. Therefore, Zeus, Yahweh, Kali, and Cybele are their respective cultures' elaborations of universally available psychic material. Jung called these elaborations "eternal images" that

> are meant to attract, to convince, to fascinate, and to overpower. [These images] are created out of the primal stuff of revelation and reflect the ever-unique experience of divinity. That is why they always give man a premonition of the divine while at the same time safeguarding him from immediate experience of it. Thanks to the labors of the human spirit over the centuries, these images have become embedded in a comprehensive system of thought that ascribes an order to the world, and are at the same time

represented by . . . mighty, far-spread, and venerable institution[s like] the Church (1959/1980, 8).

Joseph Campbell: Literary and Cultural Critic

Whereas in the 19th century what passed for literary criticism of myth was largely a matter of antiquarians, classicists, biblicists, and specialists in dead languages reading myths and theorizing the linguistic and cultural events that explained and connected them, in the 20th century literary approaches to myth grew more sophisticated. Important literary critics interested in reading myths include Robert Graves, author of *The White Goddess* and *Greek Myths*, and Northrop Frye, whose *Anatomy of Criticism* makes the case that four basic motifs corresponding to the seasons (spring–comedy, summer–romance, autumn–tragedy, and winter–satire) give shape to all literature. Many scholars wrote extensively about myth and were influential in their disciplines, but Joseph Campbell achieved a much broader popular following.

Campbell was the best-known mythologist of the 20th century if for no other reason than because he was able to present his ideas on television. His six-part series in the 1980s with Bill Moyers, *The Power of Myth*, reached a wide audience eager to hear about "universal human truths" in an age of increasing social fragmentation. At first glance it might seem odd to highlight Campbell's television success here, but in terms of general awareness of myth in America today and in terms of the argument that myth has powerful resonance even in today's modern world, Campbell's television success is precisely to the point. His first book, *The Hero with a Thousand Faces*, continues to be widely read, and, according to Ellwood, "George Lucas freely acknowledges the influence of reading . . . [it] and [Campbell's] *The Masks of God*" (1999, 127–28) on his science fiction epic, *Star Wars*. Campbell wrote voluminously throughout his life, but the ideas he lays out in *Hero* form a core that changed little during his career—even when criticism and discoveries in other fields urged the necessity to revisit them.

Campbell openly acknowledged the influence of Jung and Freud on his work. Yet he never seems quite at home with Jung's *collective* unconscious. Rather, the American mythologist always saw myth as the story of the rugged *individual* who realizes his true nature through heroic struggle. Archetypal symbols and universals there may be, Campbell seems to say, but mythology is ultimately and always the vehicle through which the individual finds a sense of identity and place in the world. Like Jung and Frazer, Campbell sought to present *the* master theory through which all myths could be understood. In his view, there was a single "monomyth" organizing all such narratives. Ellwood summarizes Campbell's *Hero with a Thousand Faces* in this way:

> The basic monomyth informs us that the mythological hero, setting out from an everyday home, is lured or is carried away or proceeds to the threshold of adventure. He defeats a shadowy presence that guards the gateway, enters a dark passageway or even death, meets many unfamiliar forces, some of which give him threatening "tests," some of which offer magical aid. At the climax of the quest he undergoes a supreme ordeal and gains his reward: sacred marriage or sexual union with the goddess of the world, reconciliation with the father, his own divinization, or a mighty gift to bring back to the world. He then undertakes the final work of return, in which, transformed, he reenters the place from whence he set out (1999, 144).

Campbell arrived at his theory of the monomyth by synthesizing insights from psychoanalysis, methods from 19th-century comparative mythology, and analyses typical of literary and cultural criticism. He was *not* a member of the new wave of anthropology and folklore that searched myths for references to material, political, and social culture. Nor did he seem particularly interested in questions of translation, of variants, or in the possible social, religious, and ritual contexts of the myths he used. Rather, Campbell promoted what he called "living mythology," a nonsectarian spiritual path through which the individual might gain a sense of spiritual and social purpose and through which society might be returned to simplicity and moral virtue.

Claude Lévi-Strauss and Structuralism

At the other end of the spectrum from Campbell's individual-centered mythology is the work of French anthropologist Claude Lévi-Strauss, whose search for "deep structure" in myth had a profound influence on anthropologists and literary critics alike. Lévi-Strauss's search for the skeletal core of myth—and the related searches for organizing principles in literature carried out most famously by Vladimir Propp, Tzetvan Todorov, and Jonathan Culler—came to be known as structuralism. The influence of structuralism on the mythologies of the 20th century would be difficult to overstate, and structuralism as a critical model can be applied far beyond the boundaries of mythology or literature. It is the search for the undergirding steel that holds up the buildings of all human artifacts and endeavors, including those of meaning-making through myth and literature.

As Robert Scholes discusses the application of these ideas to literature (and, in fact, to any written text), structuralism sought "to establish a model of the system of literature itself as the external reference for the individual works it considers" (1974, 10). As such, structuralism can be seen as a reaction against 19th-century comparatist and literary approaches to myth and classical literature, especially to their subjective, even idiosyncratic, interpretations of these stories. What Lévi-Strauss and others sought was an objective way of discussing literary meaning. By borrowing from linguistics such structural notions as syntax, grammar, phonemes, and morphemes, the French anthropologist attempted to develop a model that would describe how all myths worked—and do so in a way that any literature specialist could duplicate without resorting to his or her personal impressions and imagination. With its focus on discovering an unchanging core of patterned relations giving shape to narratives of all kinds, structuralism promised to put literary criticism and anthropological investigations of myth on the firm ground of empirical science.

A quick way into the issues that structuralism wanted to raise would be to look at the work of one of Lévi-Strauss's contemporaries, Vladimir Propp, who worked almost exclusively on the Russian folktale, attempting to distinguish between constant and variable elements in that genre. After studying more than a thousand stories, he concluded that the characters in fairy tales change but their functions within the plot do not. Propp argued that fairy tales have 31 functions. For examples, Propp's folktale structures begin with (1) the hero leaves home, (2) an interdiction is addressed to the hero, and (3) the interdiction is violated. The 31 total possible plot functions include (12) the hero is tested, interrogated, attacked, which prepares the way for his receiving either a magical agent or helper, (17) the hero is branded,

(24) a false hero presents unfounded claims, (30) the villain is punished, and (31) the hero marries and ascends the throne (Scholes 1974, 63–64).

Lévi-Strauss, like Propp, gathered and analyzed as many versions of certain myths as he could find, hoping to penetrate their myriad surface elements and see into a basic grammar of meaning. Working among the natives of South America, Lévi-Strauss took inventory of the various references found in each myth. Ultimately, he determined that mythic structure reveals itself through a limited number of codes. For example, "among South American myths he [distinguished] a sociological, a culinary (or techno-economic), an acoustic, a cosmological, and an astronomical code" (Kirk 1970, 43). Lévi-Strauss further determined that these codes embodied polar opposites, or "binary oppositions." Thus, within the culinary code, as the title of one of his most famous books puts it, one finds the binary of the "raw and the cooked." Within the sociological code, one would find such binaries as married versus unmarried, family versus nonfamily, and the people versus the other.

Lévi-Strauss concluded that myths mediate the tension created by these always-present oppositions, whether individuals within a society are aware of it or not. Indeed, Lévi-Strauss discusses the codes and structures that manifest themselves in myths in much the same way that Freud and Jung discuss the unconscious. Whereas the psychologists described the unconscious as the hidden source from which individual consciousness arises, Lévi-Strauss viewed the structures of myth and language as the hidden bedrock upon which narratives are built. In fact, he sounds more like a metaphysician than a scientist when he claims that the deep structures of narrative exist—like Plato's ideal forms or St. John's *logos*—in a realm beyond and untouched by actual stories and storytellers. As Lévi-Strauss writes in *The Raw and the Cooked* (1964), "we cannot therefore grasp [in our analysis of myth] how men think, but how myths think themselves in men, and without their awareness" (1990, 20). In other words, people don't think myths into existence; mythic structures inherent in language do a people's thinking for them, expressing themselves when people use language. Ultimately, he reduced the codes and the patterned relations he discovered among South American Indian myths to a kind of algebra, a symbol system intended to express that which was always true of these stories, regardless of such surface details as plot, character, and setting.

Mircea Eliade's Time Machine

Mircea Eliade has been described as "the preeminent historian of religion of his time" (Ellwood 1999, 79), and his ideas about the essential connection between myth and religion remain influential among students of myth. As a young man Eliade invested himself in nationalist politics. Believing in the power of myth to give a downtrodden people the courage and vision necessary to stage a spiritually motivated political revolution, Eliade became involved with a proto-fascist group called the Legion of the Archangel Michael.

Recent criticism of Eliade's political associations has begun to erode his reputation as a mythologist to some extent. However, it is important to contextualize his sympathy with a political ideology that fused, in its early days, a Christian commitment to charity for the poor and outrage at injustice with a myth of a Romania that had a special destiny to fulfill. Like so many of the 19th- and early 20th-century mythologists who explored the connection between myth and *Volk*, Eliade looked to his people's Indo-European heritage for stories that would impart a spiritual authority to a people's revolution.

In his *Cosmos and History: The Myth of the Eternal Return; The Sacred and the Profane; Myths, Dreams, and Mysteries;* and *Myth and Reality*, Eliade demonstrates his own brand of structuralism. Space, time, and objects are perceived by the religious imagination, he argues, in binary terms, as either sacred or profane. Thus such objects as icons and religious utensils, such places as temples and special groves, and such times as religious festivals are designated as *sacred*. Only certain limited activities can properly be performed with or within them. The *profane*, on the contrary, are those things, places, and times available to people without special ceremony or ritual.

Another important binary in Eliade's mythology is the distinction he makes between "archaic" and modern man. In his view, archaic peoples are more attuned than modern, history-obsessed peoples to the sacred and express this understanding more clearly in their relationships to nature and in their myths. Eliade's mythology proposes yet another opposition—that which exists between cosmic time, or the time of origins, and human history. From his perspective, moderns live in unhappy exile from the Paradise of cosmic time in which a vital connection to the sacred is natural. Myth, for Eliade, provides moderns with a vehicle through which they can periodically return to the time of origins and thus begin their lives anew. This time-machine function resembles the myth-ritualists' view that sacred narratives facilitate the putting to death of stale, profane consciousness, restoring the participants to the virgin possibilities of creation. Thus we can see that from the perspective of religious studies—at least insofar as Eliade still represents that discipline—myth has a religious function. Like going to confession, fasting on Yom Kippur, making animal sacrifice, or doing penance, myth permits human beings, who are continually contaminated by exposure to the profane, to wipe the slate clean and make a fresh start.

Considering 20th-Century Mythology Critically

Our overview of 20th-century mythology has so far described the lenses through which myth has been studied in the past 100 years. One could easily imagine that the history of mythology presented here has been leading up to a happy ending: at last, we come to the end of the 20th century and the curtains will part to reveal state-of-the-art mythology. After millennia of deprecating myths as child's prattle and the fevered dreams of savages, after centuries of romanticizing the simplicity of our premodern past, after decades of trying to make the square peg of literature fit into the round hole of science, we have finally gotten it right. Surely we have a mythology that fairly and objectively examines the object of its study, that is methodologically but not blindly rigorous, and that duly considers history, custom, material culture, and sociopolitical and religious institutions without turning a story into a code to be cracked or a "to-do" list. But the fact is that no such mythology exists.

None of the mythologies of the past century has had it quite right—and it is instructive to see why not. Clearly, 19th-century comparative mythology was deeply flawed in its search for irrecoverable Ur-languages and highly dubious speculations about *the* German or Italian or Indian or Jewish character. The nature, ethnological, and myth-ritual schools, like Procrustes, made theoretical beds and then stretched or lopped off evidential limbs in order to achieve a perfect fit. While we owe the comparatists and their literary descendants gratitude for the thousands of myths they collected, and while we should not deny that natural environment and ritual, for example, are an important part of mythic content, we should also learn the lesson that no universal theory "explains" myth.

And we ought to ask ourselves what is to be gained from reducing all myth to a single "pattern." If we read all myths as allegories of the seasonal cycles of fertility and infertility as, for example, Frazer and Graves did, what is to be gained? Are we content to read the story of Jesus' birth, ministry, and death as one of many instantiations of the "year spirit"? Here's death and resurrection! A seasonal pattern! Is this label enough to satisfy our desire to understand mythic meanings and functions? Similarly, are we content to read all myths, as Campbell does, as yet another version of the hero's passage from home, through trial, through apotheosis, and back home again? Surely this plot line accounts for some significant events in myth, but are we content to reduce even myths of creation, fertility, and apocalypse to the story of an individual's separation, initiation, and return? What do we say after we identify, as Eliade does, the basic alienation that exists in myth between human beings and the sacred? A one-trick pony, even when the trick is pretty good, is still a one-trick pony.

But anthropology and folklore, despite the fact that they have done mythology an inestimable service by grounding it in observation-based science, are not quite the answer either. Following Malinowski, anthropologists have, to greater and lesser degrees, illuminated the relationships among myths, religion, custom, sociopolitical behaviors, and material culture. Working within this discipline, Lévi-Strauss and Propp attempted to create a completely objective typology of narrative functions through which all myths could be analyzed. To some degree, particularly in Propp's work on the morphology of the folktale, structuralism succeeded. Any student of myth can examine any number of fairy tales using Propp's model and will find that the Russian folklorist's functions are indeed present and in the described order.

Yet, for all that anthropologists and folklorists have contributed to the study of myth, their disciplined focus on the function of myths within a nexus of material, social, political, and economic phenomena has come at a considerable cost. Such concerns, as important as they are, are only partial, and they

ignore the pleasures and power of narrative per se for us here and now as well as for the myth tellers and their more immediate audiences. And structuralist anthropology does not and really cannot answer one of the most important questions: So what? Once we have learned Propp's 31 elements of the folk tale, the various codes in creation myths, and the binary oppositions Lévi-Strauss claims they suggest, what do we really have? From our point of view as professors of English, anthropology's tight focus on the functionality of and within myth diverts attention away from the fundamental fact that myths are stories. We need only think of Lévi-Strauss's algebra of mythic functions or Malinowski's search for references to food, clothing, shelter, and political relationships in the myths of the Trobriand islanders to realize that something vital is lost when myth is cannibalized for its references to the "real" world. We can ask anthropologists, as we asked literary theorists, whether reducing myths to lists of material culture items or to a set of narrative functions isn't as distorting as reducing all myths to allegories of nature, the year spirit, or the hero's quest.

While anthropology and folklore focused on myth's functions and 19th- and early 20th-century literary criticism preoccupied itself largely with myth's contents, psychological approaches have contemplated those dimensions of myth and suggested a theory of psychic origins as well. Psychological approaches to myth, therefore, have been generally more holistic than others. After all, whatever else can be said about them, myths proceed from the human mind if for no other reason than the mind needs to understand "the self" in relation to the larger cosmos. For this reason, many in the latter half of the 20th century assumed that Freud's or Jung's views about myth are fundamentally sound. And the psychological approach to myth has been powerfully suggestive. Jung's archetypes, for example, offer a potent interpretation of widely distributed symbols, images, and plot lines. There's a satisfying symmetry to the notion that each individual contains and balances oppositions such as elder and child, male and female, sinner and saint. Innumerable mythic characters embody these and other human qualities. And although Freud overstates his case when he claims that myths are *nothing other* than the working out of the complex interrelationships among identity, sexuality, and family relationships, a great many myths *do* feature incest, rape, infanticide, and parricide. Myths are about relationships among the irrational, the rational, and the individual's responsibility to society, or, in Freud's terms, among the id, the ego, and the superego.

However, a principal weakness of literary, psychological, and structuralist approaches is that they are ahistorical; they don't consider the specific material and social conditions that shape myth. Indeed, most of the major mythologists of the 20th century cared little for the cultural specifics of how living myths function in the day-to-day lives of the people who told them. They cared little for cultural distinctions that might explain why one version of a myth differs from another; and, in the cases of Jung, Campbell, and Eliade, they seemed interested in myth only as far as familiarity with its presumed "core" might provide the modern individual with a return to Paradise lost—to a sense of self closely connected to the soil and fully at home in a homogeneous sociopolitical order. Thus, while the mythologies of the early- and mid-20th century demonstrated considerable genius, their lack of concern for historical and cultural context and their insistence on reading myths through analytical schema that dispensed with all but a story's most rudimentary plot structure perpetuated most of the significant shortcomings of their 18th- and 19th-century predecessors. Now, at the beginning of the 21st century, awareness of these shortcomings has bred approaches to myth that insist on the importance of context, particularly where gender, cultural norms, and the specifics of the performance events are concerned. Moreover, much like this chapter, modern scholarship has increasingly focused on mythology rather than on myth itself. We conclude with a brief survey of several of the most recent and important contributions to the study of myth and consider, even more briefly, what uses these new ideas might have for the classroom.

Mythology Today

William Doty's "Toolkit"

Doty's *Mythography* concludes with a number of appendixes for "furbishing the creative mythographer's toolkit." Among these tools are "questions to address to mythic texts." Embedded in these questions is a comprehensive methodology that urges students of myth not to choose a single approach to myth but to use as many of the questions and concerns of various mythological schools as possible. Doty's questions arise from five central concerns: (1) the social, (2) the psychological, (3) the literary, textual, and performative, (4) the structural, and (5) the political (2000, 466–67). As the term "mythographer's toolkit" implies, Doty's approach to the subject is profoundly practical. Above all he is concerned with methodology and principles of analysis, and he has distilled the concerns of many fields, including sociology, anthropology, psychology, and literary criticism into a systematic series of exploratory questions and research procedures that are well within reach of most non-specialists. The questions that Doty poses for each of the five areas of concern just mentioned are particularly congenial to the kinds of thinking, discussion, and research performed in the classroom.

Bruce Lincoln's Ideological Narratives

As suggestive as Doty's questions are, other approaches to myth have been advocated recently. Lincoln, whose *Theorizing Myth* is an important contribution to the current study of myth, would define myth and mythology as "ideology in narrative form" because, as he says, all human communication is "interested, perspectival, and partial and . . . its ideological dimensions must be acknowledged, ferreted out where necessary, and critically cross-examined" (1999, 207, 208).

Ultimately, Lincoln advocates making modern mythology the study of previous mythologies. This scholarly endeavor would revolve around "excavating the texts within which that discourse [mythology] took shape and continues to thrive . . . [explicating] their content by placing them in their proper contexts, establishing the connections among them, probing their ideological and other dimensions, explicit and subtextual" (1999, 216). How students should approach myths other than those told by scholars about myth Lincoln doesn't say—though it seems plausible that his approach would be approximately the same for myth as for mythology.

Wendy Doniger's Telescopes and Microscopes

Wendy Doniger, in her *The Implied Spider: Politics and Theology in Myth*, argues for an updated and recalibrated version of the kind of comparative mythology that the Grimm brothers and Sir James Frazer practiced. Among the ways Doniger suggests improving the comparative mythology of the 19th century is, "whenever possible . . . to note the context: who is telling the story and why"; and, she argues, that context could also include—indeed would have to include—"other myths, other related ideas, as Lévi-Strauss argued long ago" (1998, 44, 45). Doniger advocates stripping individual myths to their "naked" narrative outlines—to symbols, themes, and similarities in plot—in order to manage the amount of detail that the comparatist will have to analyze. Unlike Lévi-Strauss, Doniger wouldn't reduce myth to a level where all myths look alike. Context would still matter. Accordingly, she says, we could include in our comparison the contexts of myths. Attention to the sociopolitical and performative contexts in which myths occur would, in Doniger's method, "take account of differences between men and women as storytellers, and also between rich and poor, dominant and oppressed" (46). Doniger would also have students of myth learn how to switch back and forth between the "microscope" of a single telling to the "telescope" of the world's numerous variations on a mythological theme.

Thus Doniger's comparative mythology respects the integrity of a single myth as a unique story and, at the same time, enriches our understanding of that story through comparisons with other stories with similar plots, characters, and symbolic imagery as well as through comparisons with other mythic stories with similar contexts of telling. For one example of this last sense of comparison, we might be enriched by considering myths specifically *told by* women even as we would likely be rewarded by comparing myths with women or goddesses as central characters.

Robert Ellwood's "Real Myths"

Robert Ellwood, who, like Lincoln, was one of Eliade's students at the University of Chicago in the 1960s, suggests yet another approach in *The Politics of Myth: A Study of C. G. Jung, Mircea Eliade, and Joseph Campbell* (1999). Ellwood argues that what we call "myth" does not exist. Or, to put it more precisely, modern students of myth do not study *mythos*, in Hesiod's sense of a poet "breathing" the divinely inspired utterance. Rather, what we call myth "is

always received from an already distant past, literary (even if only oral literature), hence a step away from primal simplicity" (174). This is an important point for Ellwood and other modern mythologists because "official" myths like the *Iliad* and the *Odyssey*, the *Theogony*—or the Bhagavad Gita or the Bible— "are inevitably reconstructions from snatches of folklore and legend, artistically put together with an eye for drama and meaning" (175). But "real" myths are, like one's own dreams, "so fresh they are not yet recognized as 'myth' or 'scripture,' [and] are fragmentary, imagistic rather than verbal, emergent, capable of forming many different stories at once" (175).

What students of myth study in mythology classes, then, are usually the *literary* product of many hands over the course of many generations. Even if a name like Homer or Hesiod gets attached to myths when they finally achieve their final form, they begin as folktales and campfire stories, as religious precepts, images, and rituals, as mystical revelations, and as entertaining fictional and speculative explorations of how the cosmos came into being and continues to operate. Over the generations, in the hands of gifted storytellers, a narrative capable of combining and artistically organizing these fragments and themes emerges. By the time a society officially authorizes a story as scripture or myth, the events it describes have slipped so far into the past that they can be believed—anything could have happened in the beginning—or disbelieved. Myth represents human truths in a variety of ways, few if any of which depend on mere plausibility of character or event. "To put it another way," as Ellwood says, "myth is really a meaning category on the part of hearers, not intrinsic in any story in its own right. Myth in this sense is itself a myth" (1999, 175).

Reading Mythology

Ellwood, like Lincoln, doesn't explicitly articulate a methodology by which students can analyze myths for themselves, but his suggestion that myths, like those contained in this book, come down to us in *literary* form suggests a well-established methodology: close reading and a consideration of how literary conventions inform and enable various levels of meaning.

Doty, when speaking of Müller's and Frazer's euhemerism, remarked that not only these two but "many other 19th-century [and 20th-century] scholars regarded myth almost exclusively as *a problem* for modern rationality" (2000, 11). Müller and Frazer, the myth-ritualists, the sociofunctionalist anthropologists, and the psychoanalysts have all attempted to "solve" the problem of the mythic irrational and to articulate in authoritative terms what myths "really" mean. Their efforts were not entirely wasted; they were simply too one-dimensional, too unable to engage with myth in a holistic sense. Our book takes the view that myths are *not* codes to be cracked or naive and mistaken perceptions that must be corrected. Rather, myths are literary truths told about the mysteries and necessities that always have and always will condition the human experience. These truths, these *mythoi,* have made sophisticated use of symbolic imagery and narrative strategy, have created unforgettable characters that continue to typify for us abstract realities such as love, bravery, wisdom, and treachery, and have enacted as compellingly as any modern novel the humor and horror, the ecstasy and anguish, and the fear and hope of the human drama.

One of the great strengths of the literary approach to myth is that one needn't dispense with the methods, concerns, and insights developed through other mythologies in order to pay appropriate attention to such features of narrative as plot, point of view, characterization, setting, symbols, and theme. Indeed, our understanding and enjoyment of myths is enhanced if, as Doty would say, we furnish our mythographer's toolkit with as many tools as possible. For example, by using such structural approaches as those developed by Campbell, Lévi-Strauss, and Propp we can sharpen our focus on such basic plotting issues as the events that constitute the rising action of the story, the precise moment at which the turning point is reached, and the events of the falling action that resolve the conflict or tension that gives the story its narrative energy. Yet, literary analysis offers students of myth more than charts and formulas because it also equips us with a conceptual vocabulary and specific language to understand and describe how the arrangement of a story's action and its setting affect our emotions and intellects. How, for example, are we affected by the opening lines that introduce the action in the Maya's *Popul Vuh?*

Here follow the first words, the first eloquence:
There is not yet one person, one animal, bird, fish, crab, tree, rock, hollow, canyon, meadow, forest.

Only the sky alone is there; the face of the earth is not clear. Only the sea alone is pooled under all the sky; there is nothing whatever gathered together. It is at rest; not a single thing stirs. It is held back, kept at rest under the sky. Whatever there is that might be is simply not there: only the pooled water, only the calm sea, only it alone is pooled (see Chapter 2, page 93).

How do we feel about the difficulty the narrator seems to have expressing a state of existence that is simultaneously nothing and yet contains a primordial sea with sleeping gods shining in its depths? What questions does this paragraph raise for us? What expectations are created and what words and phrases create them? Literary analysis of such details invites us to consider the personal connections we develop to a story and encourages us to reflect upon how a gifted storyteller (or generations of gifted storytellers) can utilize and refine language to create thought-shaping, life-defining images, ideas, and feelings within their hearers and/or readers.

Similarly, consulting the methods and insights of the comparative and psychological approaches to myth can increase our sensitivity to the universality of certain character types and to a deeper appreciation of the motives, values, and actions of the various protagonists and antagonists that people the world's sacred narratives. Through close reading of myth, we can make the crucial distinction between characterization and the more ambiguous notion of character. The characterization of Heracles (Hercules in Latin), for example, utilizes certain stock phrases that emphasize his strength, resilience, and resourcefulness. While pinpointing precisely the language through which storytellers have depicted characters has rewards, it can be even more rewarding to articulate and debate the psychological makeup of this Greek hero's character. For instance, does Heracles's alienation from his divine father, with all the rejection and confusion that such a separation implies, create in him the determination necessary to accomplish his famous twelve labors? Are Heracles's many mighty deeds motivated by an obsessive need to prove his worth to a distant father whose fame and influence far outmatch his own? While these questions are clearly speculative and center upon a fictional entity, they nevertheless take us to the heart of literature's mysterious power over us. How fascinating that people, places, and things that may never have had a literal existence off the page, can nevertheless live in our minds as vividly as any of our flesh-and-blood acquaintances!

Likewise, we can borrow from early anthropology its insights and raw data about the prevalence of certain themes in myth. Preoccupations with such matters as the seasons, fertility, and disastrous consequences of intimate union between gods and mortals abound in myth and some anthropological studies supply us with a vast wealth of cases in point. We can also follow the lead of more recent anthropological study and generate lists of material culture items, social strata, customs, and technologies and our understanding of some of myth's most obscure references can be illuminated by this discipline's focus on the ritual and performance contexts as well as the socio-political functions of myth in living cultures.

Literary analysis, however, urges us also to consider how a narrative's uses of various material goods, social arrangements, and technologies work as symbols and icons. Returning to the *Popul Vuh,* we notice that the creation of human beings is the culmination of four successive attempts, a creative process that is successful only after the correct material—maize—is used. While the scientist might view this reference as evidence that the Maya cultivated corn from earliest times, making similar observations about the tortilla griddles, domesticated dogs and turkeys, pots and grinding implements the story also mentions, the literary critic would likely emphasize the symbolic value of corn to the story. The gods' spoken word vibrating in the air, mud, and wood all prove inadequate materials for producing beings capable of intelligible speech and rational thought. However, the premier product of settled living and scientific observations about soil conditions, seeding, and the seasons is the perfect medium.

> And then the yellow corn and white corn were ground, and Xmucane [Grandmother of Light] did the grinding nine times. Corn was used, along with the water she rinsed her hands with, for the creation of grease; it became human fat when it was worked by the Bearer, Begetter, Sovereign Plumed Serpent, as they are called. After that, they put it into words: the making, the modeling of our first mother-father, with yellow corn, white corn alone for the flesh, food alone for the human legs and arms, for our first fathers, the four human works. It was staples alone that made up their flesh (see Chapter 2, page 98).

When the narrator places maize at the pivotal moment in the story when the gods at last perfect their creation, it suggests not only were human beings the pinnacle of the creation (the fourth time is the charm!) but that the Maya viewed themselves as literal children of the corn. While such archaeological evidence as carvings of corn stalks, farming implements, and the ruins of granaries and farms are sufficient to indicate that the mastery of agrarian technology supplied the nourishment and wealth necessary to build and sustain the Maya empire, those attending to the symbolic value of corn in their mythic charter know the degree to which the Maya themselves were aware of this fact.

Like an onion, a myth has many layers. Thus we urge students of myth to familiarize themselves with the methods and assumptions of each mythology and to combine them with the methods and assumptions of literary study. Euhemerism permits us to remove one layer of the myth-onion, the comparative method another, the structuralist and functionalist approaches further layers, and psychological and literary analyses still others. We should resign ourselves to the fact that, after all our efforts, we will find at the core, quite literally, no-thing, no *single* all-encompassing explanation of myth. But, those who exert the disciplined effort to peel away and examine the social, political, historical, psychological, cultural, functional, and literary layers of the myth-onion will certainly become permeated with its distinct essence. Given the fascinating subject we study, that is reward enough.

7

Nyoro Myth

John Beattie

Although numerous scholars emphasize the symbolic and structural aspects of myth, an important strand of anthropology has viewed myth instead as an explanation of the behavior and practices of present-day society. Because myth provides a sacred account of why the world is in its present form, it can authorize and underscore the legitimacy of sociopolitical arrangements. This functionalist view is associated strongly with the mid-20th-century anthropologist Bronislaw Malinowski, who considered myth to be a pragmatic set of rules, a social charter.

Malinowski's idea of myth as charter is exemplified in the following excerpt, drawn from a classic ethnography by one of Britain's best-known anthropological specialists on Africa. John Beattie initially studied the Nyoro, who live in Uganda, between 1951 and 1955. Using examples of Nyoro myths, Beattie shows how the narratives—divine and indisputable—account for such features of Nyoro life as hierarchical, descent-based social categories; respect for the wisdom of the old; inheritance customs; and the legitimacy of the current king. If a ruler's credentials are based on mythological antecedents, then his power is valid. Beattie ends by warning that myth should not be taken at face value as a literal account of history but, rather, as Malinowski suggests, as a justification for present structures of authority.

What interests us most about myths is the way in which they may express attitudes and beliefs current at the present time. Mythologies always embody systems of values, judgments about what is considered good and proper by the people who have the myth. Especially, myth tends to sustain some system of authority, and the distinctions of power and status which this implies. Thus Nyoro myths tend to validate the kinds of social and political stratification which I have said are characteristic of the culture, and to support the kingship around which the traditional political system revolved. In Malinowski's phrase, Nyoro legend provides a "mythical charter" for the social and political order.

From BUNYORO, AN AFRICAN KINGDOM, by John Beattie. © 1960. Reprinted with permission of Wadsworth, a division of Thomson Learning: www.thomsonrights.com. Fax 800 730-2215.

For Nyoro, human history begins with a first family, whose head is sometimes called Kintu, "the created thing." There are three children in this family, all boys. At first these are not distinguished from one another by name; all are called "Kana," which means "little child." This is of course confusing, and Kintu asks God if they may be given separate names. God agrees, and the boys are submitted to two tests. First, six things are placed on a path by which the boys will pass. These are an ox's head, a cowhide thong, a bundle of cooked millet and potatoes, a grass head-ring (for carrying loads on the head), an axe, and a knife. When the boys come upon these things, the eldest at once picks up the bundle of food and starts to eat. What he cannot eat he carries away, using the head-ring for this purpose. He also takes the axe and the knife. The second son takes the leather thong, and the youngest takes the ox's head, which is all that is left. In the next test the boys have to sit on the ground in the evening, with their legs stretched out, each holding on his lap a wooden milk-pot full of milk. They are told that they must hold their pots safely until morning. At midnight the youngest boy begins to nod, and he spills a little of his milk. He wakes up with a start, and begs his brothers for some of theirs. Each gives him a little, so that his pot is full again. Just before dawn the eldest brother suddenly spills all his milk. He, too, asks his brothers to help fill his pot from theirs, but they refuse, saying that it would take too much of their milk to fill his empty pot. In the morning their father finds the youngest son's pot full, the second son's nearly full, and the eldest's quite empty.

He gives his decision, and names the three boys. The eldest, and his descendants after him, is always to be a servant and a cultivator, and to carry loads for his younger brothers, and their descendants. For he chose the millet and potatoes, peasants' food, and he lost all the milk entrusted to him, so showing himself unfit to have anything to do with cattle. Thus he was named "Kairu," which means little Iru or peasant. The second son and his descendants would have the respected status of cattlemen. For he had chosen the leather thong for tying cattle, and he had spilt none of his milk, only providing some for his younger brother. So he was called "Kahuma," little cowherd or Huma, and ever since the cattle-herding people of this part of the inter-lacustrine region have been called Huma or Hima. But the third and youngest son would be his father's heir, for he had taken the ox's head, a sign that he would be at the head of all men, and he alone had a full bowl of milk when morning came, because of the help given him by his brothers. So he was named "Kakama," little Mukama or ruler. He and his descendants became the kings of Bunyoro, or Kitara, as the country was then called. When the three brothers had been named, their father told the two elder that they should never leave their young brother, but should stay with him and serve him always. And he told Kakama to rule wisely and well.

This myth explains and justifies the traditional division of Nyoro society into distinct social categories based on descent. At the beginning, people were undifferentiated—this is symbolized by the three boys having no separate names or identities—but this was confusing, and the only orderly solution was to grade them in three hierarchically ordered categories. It is true that in Bunyoro the distinction

between Hima and Iru is of decreasing social importance, but the distinctions of status implied by the myth and especially the differential allocation of authority are still strongly marked in social life. What is validated is basically the "givenness" of differences of status and authority based on birth and, in general, the preeminence of ascribed status over personal achievement. Subordinates may find subordination less irksome, and superordinates may rule more calmly and confidently, when everyone acknowledges the difference between them and the divine origin of that difference.

Many stories, all of which point a moral, are told of the very first kings, Kakama's earliest descendants. The following is one of the best known. King Isaza came to the throne as a very young man; he was disrespectful toward the elders whom his father had left to advise him, and he drove them away from the palace, replacing them by gay youngsters with whom he used to go hunting, which was his favorite pastime. One day he killed a zebra, and he was so pleased with its gaily striped hide that he determined to dress himself in it at once. So his young companions sewed the skin on him. But as the day wore on, the hot sun dried the skin, and it quickly shrank and began to squeeze Isaza until he was nearly dead. He begged his friends for help, but they just laughed at him and did nothing. When he had driven the old men away, two had stayed nearby, and now Isaza sent to them for help. First they refused, but after a while they relented, and told Isaza's young men to throw the king into a pond. They did so, and the moisture loosened the hide so that it could be removed. Isaza was so grateful to the old men that he called them all back to the palace, gave them a feast and reinstated them. At the same time he reprimanded his young associates, telling them that they should always respect the old.

This Nyoro "cautionary tale" points the familiar moral that a person in authority neglects at his peril the advice of those older and wiser than he, and that old men are likely to be better informed than callow youths. But it also stresses another important feature of Nyoro ideas about authority—namely, that it is not inappropriate for young persons to have power. It will be remembered that in the previous myth it was the youngest son, not the eldest, who succeeded to his father's authority; in fact, succession by the youngest, or a younger, son is a characteristic feature of Nyoro inheritance. The role of the older brother is to act as guardian until the heir is old enough to assume full authority. Nyoro say that a first son should not inherit; we shall see that the Mukama may not be succeeded by his eldest son. But the Isaza myth also stresses the wisdom of the old, and the respect due to them. Age is a qualification for advisory, not executive, authority; it is right that the aged should be spared the arduousness of decision making, but right that they should guide and advise those in power. The legend of Isaza and the zebra skin is a popular one, for it expresses values important to Nyoro and which we shall meet again.

It is important also to examine the cycle of dynastic myths which merge into traditional history and link up (if the series be regarded chronologically) with the "real" history which we shall go on to consider. Nyoro believe that there have been three royal dynasties; first, the shadowy Tembuzi, of whom Kakama was the first and Isaza the last; second, the Chwezi, part-legendary hero-gods whose marvelous exploits are still spoken of; and third, the Bito, the line to which the present king belongs. We shall see that part of the significance of the myths which we now discuss lies in the way in which they link these three dynasties together into a single line of descent, so creating an unbroken chain between the present ruler and the very first king of Bunyoro.

The story is rich in descriptive detail, but here we can only give an outline account. It begins by telling how the king of the world of ghosts, called Nyamiyonga, sent a message to king Isaza (whose hunting exploit has just been recounted) asking him to enter into a blood pact with him. Isaza's councilors advised against this, so Isaza had the pact made on Nyamiyonga's behalf with his chief minister, a commoner called Bukuku. When Nyamiyonga discovered that he had been united in the blood pact with an Iru or commoner, he was angry, and he determined to get Isaza into his power. So he sent his beautiful daughter Nyamata to Isaza's court, where she so attracted the king that he married her, not knowing who she was. But he resisted all her efforts to persuade him to visit her home, for he could not bear to be parted from his cattle, which he loved more than anything else. So Nyamiyonga thought of another plan. He caused two of his most handsome cattle to be discovered near Isaza's kraal, and these were taken to the king, who soon loved them most of

all his herd. One day they disappeared, and the distracted Mukama went in search of them, leaving Bukuku to rule the kingdom in his absence. After much wandering, Isaza arrived in the country of ghosts, where he found his two cattle and also his wife Nyamata, who had gone home some time previously to bear him a child. Nyamiyonga welcomed the Nyoro king, but he had not forgiven him, and he never allowed him to return to the world of men.

In due course Nyamata's child was born and was named Isimbwa. When Isimbwa grew up he married in the world of ghosts and had a son called Kyomya, of whom we shall hear more later. Isimbwa, unlike his father, could visit the world of living men, and on a hunting expedition he came to the capital where Bukuku still reigned in Isaza's place. Bukuku was unpopular because he was a commoner and had no real right to rule, but there was no one else to do so. He had a daughter called Nyinamwiru, and at Nyinamwiru's birth diviners had told Bukuku that he would have reason to fear any child that she might bear. So he kept her in a special enclosure which could only be entered through his own well-guarded palace. When Isimbwa reached Bukuku's capital he was intrigued by this state of affairs, and after making clandestine advances to Nyinamwiru through her maid, he managed to climb into her enclosure and, unknown to Bukuku, he stayed there for three months. He then left the kingdom and was not seen again for many years.

In due course Nyinamwiru bore a son, to the consternation of Bukuku, who gave orders for the child to be drowned. So the baby was thrown in a river, but by chance its umbilical cord caught in a bush, and the child was discovered by a potter, Rubumbi, who took it home and brought it up as a member of his family. He knew that it was Nyinamwiru's child, and he told her that it was safe. Bukuku, of course, believed it to be dead. The boy grew up strong and spirited, and was constantly in trouble with Bukuku's herdsmen, for when the king's cattle were being watered he would drive them away, so that he could water Rubumbi's cattle first. This angered Bukuku, who one day came to the drinking trough himself to punish the unruly potter's son. But before Bukuku's men could carry out his orders to seize and beat him, he rushed round to the back of Bukuku's royal stool and stabbed him mortally with his spear. He then sat down on the king's stool. The herdsmen were aghast, and ran at once to tell Nyinamwiru what had happened. The story tells that she was both glad and sorry; glad because her son had taken the throne, sorry because of her father's death. So Ndahura, which is what the young man was called, came to his grandfather Isaza's throne, and he is reckoned as the first of the Chwezi kings.

There were only three—some say two—Chwezi kings; Ndahura, his half-brother Mulindwa, and his son Wamara. Many wonderful things are told of their wisdom and achievements, but during Wamara's reign things began to go badly for them. So they called their diviners and an ox was cut open so that its entrails could be examined. The diviners were astonished to find no trace of the intestines, and they did not know what to say. At that moment a stranger from north of the Nile appeared, and said that he was a diviner and would solve the riddle for them. But first he insisted (wisely, as it turned out) on making a blood pact with one of the Chwezi, so that he could be safe from their anger if his findings were unfavorable. Then he took an axe and cut open the head and hooves of the ox. At once the missing intestines fell out of these members, and as they did so a black smut from the fire settled on them, and could not be removed.

The Nilotic diviner then said that the absence of the intestines from their proper place meant that the rule of the Chwezi in Bunyoro was over. Their presence in the hoofs meant that they would wander far away; in the head, that they would, nonetheless, continue to rule over men (a reference to the possession cult, centered on the Chwezi spirits). And the black smut meant that the kingdom would be taken over by dark-skinned strangers from the north. So the Chwezi departed from Bunyoro, no one knows whither.

Meantime the diviner went back to his own country in the north, and there he met the sons of Kyomya, who was, it will be remembered, Isimbwa's son by his first wife. Kyomya had married in the country to the north of the Nile, and had settled down there. The diviner told Kyomya's sons that they should go south and take over the abandoned Nyoro kingdom of their Tembuzi grandfathers. There were four brothers altogether: Nyarwa, the eldest; the twins Rukidi Mpuga and Kato Kimera; and Kiiza, the youngest. They were the first Bito. Nyarwa (as we might expect) did not become a ruler, though some

say that he remained as adviser to his second brother Rukidi, who became the first Bito king of Bunyoro. Kato was allotted Buganda, then a dependency of the great Nyoro empire (Ganda, of course, have a rather different version of these events), and Kiiza was given a part of what is now Busoga, a country many miles to the east of present-day Bunyoro.

When the Bito first arrived in Bunyoro, they seemed strange and uncouth to the inhabitants. It is said that half of Rukidi's body was black and half white, a reference to his mixed descent. They had to be instructed in the manners appropriate to rulers; at first, they were ignorant of such important matters as cattle keeping and milk drinking. But gradually Rukidi assumed the values and manners proper to the heir of the pastoral rulers of the earlier dynasties. So began the reign of the powerful Bito dynasty, which has lasted up to the present.

This series of myths establishes a genealogical link between the three recognized dynasties of Nyoro rulers. Having noted the importance in Bunyoro of hereditarily determined status, we can see that a major function is served by the genealogical linking of the present ruling line with the wonderful Chwezi, whose exploits are still talked of throughout the region, and, through them, with the even more remote Tembuzi and so with the very beginnings of human existence. The connection enables the present ruling line to claim descent of an honor and antiquity not exceeded even by that of the pastoral Huma (who are said in some contexts to look down upon the Bito as "commoners"). The marking off of the ruling Bito from all other Nyoro contributes to their unity and exclusiveness, and so lends validity to their claims to special respect, prestige, and authority. And not only the rulers, but all Nyoro, share in the glory of their ruling line and the wonderful feats of its progenitors. The exploits and conquests of Isaza and the Chwezi rulers are known to every Nyoro. When people think of themselves, as Nyoro sometimes do (for reasons which will become plain later), as being in decline, there may be compensation in the thought of past in default of present greatness. And we may suppose that historically the genealogical link was important for the immigrant Bito, who lacked the prestige of the already existing Huma aristocracy, and needed the enhancement of status which this "genealogical charter" provided. So the main social function of Nyoro mythical history is the establishment of Bito credentials to govern, by emphasizing the distinction and antiquity of their genealogical antecedents.

According to the myth, the present Mukama is descended in an unbroken patrilineal line from the very beginning of things, and it may well be asked (as indeed it has been) why in this case there are said to have been three dynasties in Nyoro history, and not only one. But the question implies a too literal interpretation of the myth. The fact is that for Nyoro there *are* three dynasties, and whatever the truth about their real relationship to one another, if any (or even, in the case of the earlier ones, their very existence), Nyoro believe them to have been three quite different kinds of people. In other contexts the Chwezi are spoken of as a strange and wonderful people who came from far away, took over the kingdom from the Tembuzi, remained in the country for a generation or two, and then mysteriously disappeared. There is linguistic and other evidence to support the view that the Bito are of quite different racial and cultural stock from the people whose country and kingship they took over. The myth is not to be understood as an attempt to reconstruct a history that has been lost forever; it is rather to be seen as providing a genealogical charter for a structure of authority whose existence is contemporaneous with the myth itself.

Harelips and Twins:
The Splitting of a Myth

Claude Lévi-Strauss

Claude Lévi-Strauss (born 1908) has been one of the most provocative and prolific anthropologists of the second half of the 20th century. He fostered a school of thought known as structuralism, which seeks to identify the underlying patterns of human thought that are common to all humans despite variations in culture. Lévi-Strauss looked especially for patterns in myth, ritual, and kinship in order to understand the unconscious structures that shape human cognition. His work often involved identifying binary oppositions—to Lévi-Strauss, a fundamental characteristic of human thought—as well as factors that mediate or resolve those oppositions. His studies of myth emphasized the cultures of South and North America.

Originally part of a radio series delivered in 1977, in this article Lévi-Strauss analyzes a related set of myths and mythological motifs that suggest an underlying similarity among twins, people with harelips, and people born feet first. Although unusually concise, this piece nonetheless encapsulates the most important features of the author's approach to myth. The analysis mixes together texts from several indigenous peoples of the Western Hemisphere. He seeks patterns or structures that, unseen at first, lie beneath the narrative sequence of events in the individual texts. In keeping with the structural study of myth, Lévi-Strauss here searches for binary pairs (in this case, human twins) as well as factors that mediate between binary oppositions. The hare, with its split lip and hence "incipient twinhood," is such an intermediary.

Because Lévi-Strauss's original works are in French, and are rich with literary allusions and double entendres, when translated into English they often prove to be challenging reading. For readers who would like a broader introduction to his work, we recommend Anthropology and Myth: Lectures 1951–1982 *(translated by Roy Willis, Oxford: Basil Blackwell, 1987). This collection of succinct summaries was originally delivered in annual lectures at his home university, Collège de France, over a period of three decades. They provide accessible introductions to all the major works published by this influential author, including his numerous volumes on myth.*

Our starting point here will be a puzzling observation recorded by a Spanish missionary in Peru,

Father P. J. de Arriaga, at the end of the sixteenth century, and published in his *Extirpacion de la Idolatria del Peru* (Lima 1621). He noted that in a certain part of Peru of his time, in times of bitter cold the priest called in all the inhabitants who were known to have been born feet first, or who had a harelip, or who were twins. They were accused of being responsible for the cold because, it was said, they had eaten salt and peppers, and they were ordered to repent and to confess their sins.

Now, that twins are correlated with atmospheric disorder is something very commonly accepted throughout the world, including Canada. It is well known that on the coast of British Columbia, among the Indians, twins were endowed with special powers to bring good weather, to dispel storms, and the like. This is not, however, the part of the problem which I wish to consider here. What strikes me is that all the mythographers—for instance, Sir James Frazer who quotes Arriaga in several instances—never asked the question why people with harelips and twins are considered to be similar in some respect. It seems to me that the crux of the problem is to find out: why harelips? why twins? and why are harelips and twins put together?

In order to solve the problem, we have, as sometimes happens, to make a jump from South America to North America, because it will be a North American myth which will give us the clue to the South American one. Many people have reproached me for this kind of procedure, claiming that myths of a given population can only be interpreted and understood in the framework of the culture of that given population. There are several things which I can say by way of an answer to that objection.

In the first place, it seems to me pretty obvious that, as was ascertained during recent years by the so-called Berkeley school, the population of the Americas before Columbus was much larger than it had been supposed to be. And since it was much larger, it is obvious that these large populations were to some extent in contact with one another, and that beliefs, practices, and customs were, if I may say so, seeping through. Any neighbouring population was always, to some extent, aware of what was going on in the other population. The second point in the case that we are considering here is that these myths do not exist isolated in Peru on the one hand and in Canada on the other, but that in between we find them over and over again. Really, they are pan-American myths, rather than scattered myths in different parts of the continent.

Now, among the Tupinambas, the ancient coastal Indians of Brazil at the time of the discovery, as also among the Indians of Peru, there was a myth concerning a woman, whom a very poor individual succeeded in seducing in a devious way. The best known version, recorded by the French monk André Thevet in the sixteenth century, explained that the seduced woman gave birth to twins, one of them born from the legitimate husband, and the other from the seducer, who is the Trickster. The woman was going to meet the god who would be her husband, and while on her way the Trickster intervenes and makes her believe that *he* is the god; so, she conceives from the Trickster. When she later finds the legitimate husband-to-be, she conceives from him also and later gives birth to twins. And since these false twins had different fathers, they have antithetical features: one is brave, the other a coward; one is the protector of the Indians, the other of the white people; one gives goods to the Indians, while the other one, on the contrary, is responsible for a lot of unfortunate happenings.

It so happens that in North America, we find exactly the same myth, especially in the northwest of the United States and Canada. However, in comparison with South American versions, those coming from the Canadian area show two important differences. For instance, among the Kootenay, who live in the Rocky Mountains, there is only one fecundation which has as a consequence the birth of twins, who later on become, one the sun, and the other the moon. And, among some other Indians of British Columbia of the Salish linguistic stock—the Thompson Indians and the Okanagan—there are two sisters who are tricked by apparently two distinct individuals, and they give birth, each one to a son; they are not really twins because they were born from different mothers. But since they were born in exactly the same kind of circumstances, at least from a moral and a psychological point of view, they are to that extent similar to twins.

Those versions are, from the point of view of what I am trying to show, the more important. The Salish version weakens the twin character of the hero because the twins are not brothers—they are cousins; and it is only the circumstances of their births which are closely parallel—they are both born thanks to a trick. Nevertheless, the basic intention remains the same because nowhere are the two heroes really twins; they are born from distinct fathers, even in the South American version, and they have opposed characters, features which will be shown in their conduct and in the behaviour of their descendants.

So we may say that in all cases children who are said to be twins or believed to be twins, as in the Kootenay verison, will have different adventures later on which will, if I may say so, untwin them. And this division between two individuals who are at the beginning presented as twins, either real twins or equivalents to twins, is a basic characteristic of all the myths in South America or North America.

In the Salish versions of the myth, there is a very curious detail, and it is very important. You remember that in this version we have no twins whatsoever, because there are two sisters who are travelling in order to find, each one, a husband. They were told by a grandmother that they would recognize their husbands by such and such characteristics, and they are then each deluded by the Tricksters they meet on their way into believing that they are the husband whom each is supposed to marry. They spend the night with him, and each of the women will later give birth to a son.

Now, after this unfortunate night spent in the hut of the Trickster, the elder sister leaves her younger sister and goes visiting her grandmother, who is a mountain goat and also a kind of magician; for she knows in advance that her granddaughter is coming, and she sends the hare to welcome her on the road. The hare hides under a log which has fallen in the middle of the road, and when the girl lifts her leg to cross the log, the hare can have a look at her genital parts and make a very inappropriate joke. The girl is furious, and strikes him with her cane and splits his nose. This is why the animals of the leporine family now have a split nose and upper lip, which we call a harelip in people precisely on account of this anatomical peculiarity in rabbits and hares.

In other words, the elder sister starts to split the body of the animal; if this split were carried out to the end—if it did not stop at the nose but continued through the body and to the tail—she would turn an individual into twins, that is, two individuals which are exactly similar or identical because they are both a part of a whole. In this respect, it is very important to find out what conception the American Indians all over America entertained about the origin of twins. And what we find is a general belief that twins result from an internal splitting of the body fluids which will later solidify and become the child. For instance, among some North American Indians, the pregnant woman is forbidden to turn around too fast when she is lying asleep, because if she did, the body fluids would divide in two parts, and she would give birth to twins.

There is also a myth from the Kwakiutl Indians of Vancouver Island which should be mentioned here. It tells of a small girl whom everybody hates because she has a harelip. An ogress, a supernatural cannibal woman, appears and steals all the children including the small girl with the harelip. She puts them all in her basket in order to take them home to eat them. The small girl who was taken first is at the bottom of the basket and she succeeds in splitting it open with a seashell she had picked up on the beach. The basket is on the back of the ogress, and the girl is able to drop out and run away first. She drops out *feet first.*

This position of the harelipped girl is quite symmetrical to the position of the hare in the myth which I previously mentioned: crouching beneath the heroine when he hides under the log across her path, he is in respect to her exactly in the same position as if he had been born from her and delivered feet first. So we see that there is in all this mythology an actual relationship between twins on the one hand and delivery feet first or positions which are, metaphorically speaking, identical to it on the other. This obviously clears up the connection from which we started in Father Arriaga's Peruvian relations between twins, people born feet first, and people with harelips.

The fact that the harelip is conceived as an incipient twinhood can help us to solve a problem which is quite fundamental for anthropologists working especially in Canada: why have the Ojibwa Indians and other groups of the Algonkian-speaking family selected the hare as the highest deity in which they believed? Several explanations have been brought forward: the hare was an important if not essential part of their diet; the hare runs very fast, and so was an example of the talents which the Indians should have; and so on. Nothing of that is very convincing. But if my previous interpretations were right, it seems much more convincing to say: 1, among the rodent family the hare is the larger, the more conspicuous, the more important, so it can be taken as a representative of the rodent family; 2, all rodents exhibit an anatomical peculiarity which makes out of them incipient twins, because they are partly split up.

When there are twins, or even more children, in the womb of the mother, there is usually in the myth a very serious consequence because, even if there are only two, the children start to fight and compete in order to find out who will have the honour of being born first. And, one of them, the bad one, does not hesitate to find a short cut, if I may say so, in order to be born earlier; instead of following the natural road, he splits up the body of the mother to escape from it.

This, I think, is an explanation of why the fact of being born feet first is assimilated to twinhood, because it is in the case of twinhood that the competitive hurry of one child will make him destroy the mother in order to be the first one born. Both twinhood and delivery feet first are forerunners of a dangerous delivery, or I could even call it a heroic delivery, for the child will take the initiative and become a kind of hero, a murderous hero in some cases; but he completes a very important feat. This explains why, in several tribes, twins were killed as well as children born feet first.

The really important point is that in all American mythology, and I could say in mythology the world over, we have deities or supernaturals, who play the roles of intermediaries between the powers above and humanity below. They can be represented in different ways: we have, for instance, characters of the type of a Messiah; we have heavenly twins. And we can see that the place of the hare in Algonkian mythology is exactly between the Messiah—that is, the unique intermediary—and the heavenly twins. He is not twins, but he is incipient twins. He is still a complete individual, but he has a harelip, he is half way to becoming a twin.

This explains why, in this mythology, the hare as a god has an ambiguous character which has worried commentators and anthropologists: sometimes he is a very wise deity who is in charge of putting the universe in order, and sometimes he is a ridiculous clown who goes from mishap to mishap. And this also is best understood if we explain the choice of the hare by the Algonkian Indians as an individual who is between the two conditions of (a) a single deity beneficent to mankind and (b) twins, one of whom is good and the other bad. Being not yet entirely divided in two, being not yet twins, the two opposite characteristics can remain merged in one and the same person.

The Virgin of Guadalupe:
A Mexican National Symbol

Eric R. Wolf

While anthropologists have long recognized the symbolic nature of culture, the following classic article identifies a single "master symbol" that sums up the central focus and worldview of a particular people. Eric Wolf traces the Virgin of Guadalupe to her origins in 16th-century legend and Aztec goddess worship and examines how the symbol expresses the major social relationships in Mexican society. As a mother figure, the Virgin is an emotionally rich symbol for life, hope, and health, yet her image also embodies political and religious aspirations. Wolf concludes that the symbol links family, politics and religion; the past and present; indigenous and Mexican identities.

Eric Wolf (1923–99) conducted fieldwork with agrarian peoples in Latin America and Europe and was keenly interested in the nature of power and the effects of European expansion. His influential book Europe and the People Without History *(University of California Press, 1982) argues that the peoples colonized by Europeans were not isolated and unchanging but had long been significant parts of global economic processes.*

Occasionally, we encounter a symbol which seems to enshrine the major hopes and aspirations of an entire society.[1] Such a master symbol is represented by the Virgin of Guadalupe, Mexico's patron saint. During the Mexican War of Independence against Spain, her image preceded the insurgents into battle.[2] Emiliano Zapata and his agrarian rebels fought under her emblem in the Great Revolution of 1910.[3] Today, her image adorns house fronts and interiors, churches and home altars, bull rings and gambling dens, taxis and buses, restaurants and houses of ill repute. She is celebrated in popular song and verse. Her shrine at Tepeyac, immediately north of Mexico City, is visited each year by hundreds of thousands of pilgrims, ranging from the inhabitants of far-off Indian villages to the members of socialist trade union locals. "Nothing to be seen in Canada or Europe," says F. S. C. Northrop, "equals it in the volume or the vitality of its moving quality or in the depth of its spirit of religious devotion."[4]

In this paper, I should like to discuss this Mexican master symbol, and the ideology which surrounds it. In making use of the term "master symbol," I do not wish to imply that belief in the symbol is common to all Mexicans. We are not dealing here with an element of a putative national character, defined as a common denominator of all Mexican nationals. It is no longer legitimate to assume "that any member of the [national] group will exhibit certain regularities of behavior which are common in high degree among the other members of the society."[5] Nations,

Journal of American Folklore, *Vol. 71, No. 279 (1958), pp. 34–39. Used by permission of the American Folklore Society (www.afsnet.org)*

* Parts of this paper were presented to the Symposium on Ethnic and National Ideologies, Annual Spring Meeting of the American Ethnological Society in conjunction with the Philadelphia Anthropological Society, on 12 May 1956.

like other complex societies, must, however, "possess cultural forms or mechanisms which groups involved in the same over-all web of relationships can use in their formal and informal dealings with each other."[6] Such forms develop historically, hand in hand with other processes which lead to the formation of nations, and social groups which are caught up in these processes must become "acculturated" to their usage.[7] Only where such forms exist can communication and coördinated behavior be established among the constituent groups of such a society. They provide the cultural idiom of behavior and ideal representations through which different groups of the same society can pursue and manipulate their different fates within a coördinated framework. This paper, then, deals with one such cultural form, operating on the symbolic level. The study of this symbol seems particularly rewarding, since it is not restricted to one set of social ties, but refers to a very wide range of social relationships.

The image of the Guadalupe and her shrine at Tepeyac are surrounded by an origin myth.[8] According to this myth, the Virgin Mary appeared to Juan Diego, a Christianized Indian of commoner status, and addressed him in Nahuatl. The encounter took place on the Hill of Tepeyac in the year 1531, ten years after the Spanish Conquest of Tenochtitlan. The Virgin commanded Juan Diego to seek out the archbishop of Mexico and to inform him of her desire to see a church built in her honor on Tepeyac Hill. After Juan Diego was twice unsuccessful in his efforts to carry out her order, the Virgin wrought a miracle. She bade Juan Diego pick roses in a sterile spot where normally only desert plants could grow, gathered the roses into the Indian's cloak, and told him to present cloak and roses to the incredulous archbishop. When Juan Diego unfolded his cloak before the bishop, the image of the Virgin was miraculously stamped upon it. The bishop acknowledged the miracle, and ordered a shrine built where Mary had appeared to her humble servant.

The shrine, rebuilt several times in centuries to follow, is today a basilica, the third highest kind of church in Western Christendom. Above the central altar hangs Juan Diego's cloak with the miraculous image. It shows a young woman without child, her head lowered demurely in her shawl. She wears an open crown and flowing gown, and stands upon a half moon symbolizing the Immaculate Conception.

The shrine of Guadalupe was, however, not the first religious structure built on Tepeyac; nor was Guadalupe the first female supernatural associated with the hill. In pre-Hispanic times, Tepeyac had housed a temple to the earth and fertility goddess Tonantzin, Our Lady Mother, who—like the Guadalupe—was associated with the moon. Temple, like basilica, was the center of large scale pilgrimages. That the veneration accorded the Guadalupe drew inspiration from the earlier worship of Tonantzin is attested by several Spanish friars. F. Bernardino de Sahagún, writing fifty years after the Conquest, says: "Now that the Church of Our Lady of Guadalupe has been built there, they call her Tonantzin too. . . . The term refers . . . to that ancient Tonantzin and this state of affairs should be remedied, because the proper name of the Mother of God is not Tonantzin, but Dios and Nantzin. It seems to be a satanic device to mask idolatry . . . and they come from far away to visit that Tonantzin, as much as before; a devotion which is also suspect because there are many churches of Our Lady everywhere and they do not go to them; and they come from faraway lands to this Tonantzin as of old."[9] F. Martín de León wrote in a similar vein: "On the hill where Our Lady of Guadalupe is they adored the idol of a goddess they called Tonantzin, which means Our Mother, and this is also the name they give Our Lady and they always say they are going to Tonantzin or they are celebrating Tonantzin and many of them understand this in the old way and not in the modern way. . . ."[10] The syncretism was still alive in the seventeenth century. F. Jacinto de la Serna, in discussing the pilgrimages to the Guadalupe at Tepeyac, noted: ". . . it is the purpose of the wicked to [worship] the goddess and not the Most Holy Virgin, or both together."[11]

Increasingly popular during the sixteenth century, the Guadalupe cult gathered emotional impetus during the seventeenth. During this century appear the first known pictorial representations of the Guadalupe, apart from the miraculous original; the first poems are written in her honor; and the first sermons announce the transcendental implications of her supernatural appearance in Mexico and among Mexicans.[12] Historians have long tended to neglect the seventeenth century which seemed "a kind of Dark Age in Mexico." Yet "this quiet time was of the utmost importance in the development of Mexican

Society."[13] During this century, the institution of the hacienda comes to dominate Mexican life.[14] During this century, also, "New Spain is ceasing to be 'new' and to be 'Spain.'"[15] These new experiences require a new cultural idiom, and in the Guadalupe cult, the component segments of Mexican colonial society encountered cultural forms in which they could express their parallel interests and longings.

The primary purpose of this paper is not, however, to trace the history of the Guadalupe symbol. It is concerned rather with its functional aspects, its roots and reference to the major social relationships of Mexican society.

The first set of relationships which I would like to single out for consideration are the ties of kinship, and the emotions generated in the play of relationships within families. I want to suggest that some of the meanings of the Virgin symbol in general, and of the Guadalupe symbol in particular, derive from these emotions. I say "some meanings" and I use the term "derive" rather than "originate," because the form and function of the family in any given society are themselves determined by other social factors: technology, economy, residence, political power. The family is but one relay in the circuit within which symbols are generated in complex societies. Also, I used the plural "families" rather than "family," because there are demonstrably more than one kind of family in Mexico.[16] I shall simplify the available information on Mexican family life, and discuss the material in terms of two major types of families.[17] The first kind of family is congruent with the closed and static life of the Indian village. It may be called the Indian family. In this kind of family, the husband is ideally dominant, but in reality labor and authority are shared equally among both marriage partners. Exploitation of one sex by the other is atypical; sexual feats do not add to a person's status in the eyes of others. Physical punishment and authoritarian treatment of children are rare. The second kind of family is congruent with the much more open, mobile, manipulative life in communities which are actively geared to the life of the nation, a life in which power relationships between individuals and groups are of great moment. This kind of family may be called the Mexican family. Here, the father's authority is unquestioned on both the real and the ideal plane. Double sex standards prevail, and male sexuality is charged with a desire to exercise domination.

Children are ruled with a heavy hand; physical punishment is frequent.

The Indian family pattern is consistent with the behavior towards the Guadalupe noted by John Bushnell in the Matlazinca-speaking community of San Juan Atzingo in the Valley of Toluca.[18] There, the image of the Virgin is addressed in passionate terms as a source of warmth and love, and the *pulque* or century plant beer drunk on ceremonial occasions is identified with her milk. Bushnell postulates that here the Guadalupe is identified with the mother as a source of early satisfactions, never again experienced after separation from the mother and emergence into social adulthood. As such, the Guadalupe embodies a longing to return to the pristine state in which hunger and unsatisfactory social relations are minimized. The second family pattern is also consistent with a symbolic identification of Virgin and mother, yet this time within a context of adult male dominance and sexual assertion, discharged against submissive females and children. In this second context, the Guadalupe symbol is charged with the energy of rebellion against the father. Her image is the embodiment of hope in a victorious outcome of the struggle between generations.

This struggle leads to a further extension of the symbolism. Successful rebellion against power figures is equated with the promise of life; defeat with the promise of death. As John A. Mackay has suggested, there thus takes place a further symbolic identification of the Virgin with life; of defeat and death with the crucified Christ. In Mexican artistic tradition, as in Hispanic artistic tradition in general,[19] Christ is never depicted as an adult man, but always either as a helpless child, or more often as a figure beaten, tortured, defeated and killed. In this symbolic equation we are touching upon some of the roots both of the passionate affirmation of faith in the Virgin, and of the fascination with death which characterizes Baroque Christianity in general, and Mexican Catholicism in particular. The Guadalupe stands for life, for hope, for health; Christ on the cross, for despair and for death.

Supernatural mother and natural mother are thus equated symbolically, as are earthly and otherworldly hopes and desires. These hopes center on the provision of food and emotional warmth in the first case, in the successful waging of the Oedipal struggle in the other.

Family relations are, however, only one element in the formation of the Guadalupe symbol. Their analysis does little to explain the Guadalupe as such. They merely illuminate the female and maternal attributes of the more widespread Virgin symbol. The Guadalupe is important to Mexicans not only because she is a supernatural mother, but also because she embodies their major political and religious aspirations.

To the Indian groups, the symbol is more than an embodiment of life and hope; it restores to them the hopes of salvation. We must not forget that the Spanish Conquest signified not only military defeat, but the defeat also of the old gods and the decline of the old ritual. The apparition of the Guadalupe to an Indian commoner thus represents on one level the return of Tonantzin. As Tannenbaum has well said, "The Church . . . gave the Indian an opportunity not merely to save his life, but also to save his faith in his own gods."[20] On another level, the myth of the apparition served as a symbolic testimony that the Indian, as much as the Spaniard, was capable of being saved, capable of receiving Christianity. This must be understood against the background of the bitter theological and political argument which followed the Conquest and divided churchmen, officials, and conquerors into those who held that the Indian was incapable of conversion, thus inhuman, and therefore a fit subject of political and economic exploitation; and those who held that the Indian was human, capable of conversion and that this exploitation had to be tempered by the demands of the Catholic faith and of orderly civil processes of government.[21] The myth of the Guadalupe thus validates the Indian's right to legal defense, orderly government, to citizenship; to supernatural salvation, but also to salvation from random oppression.

But if the Guadalupe guaranteed a rightful place to the Indians in the new social system of New Spain, the myth also held appeal to the large group of disinherited who arose in New Spain as illegitimate offspring of Spanish fathers and Indian mothers, or through impoverishment, acculturation or loss of status within the Indian or Spanish group.[22] For such people, there was for a long time no proper place in the social order. Their very right to exist was questioned in their inability to command the full rights of citizenship and legal protection. Where Spaniard and Indian stood squarely within the law, they inhabited the interstices and margins of constituted society. These groups acquired influence and wealth in the seventeenth and eighteenth centuries, but were yet barred from social recognition and power by the prevailing economic, social and political order.[23] To them, the Guadalupe myth came to represent not merely the guarantee of their assured place in heaven, but the guarantee of their place in society here and now. On the political plane, the wish for a return to a paradise of early satisfactions of food and warmth, a life without defeat, sickness or death, gave rise to a political wish for a Mexican paradise, in which the illegitimate sons would possess the country, and the irresponsible Spanish overlords, who never acknowledged the social responsibilities of their paternity, would be driven from the land.

In the writings of seventeenth century ecclesiastics, the Guadalupe becomes the harbinger of this new order. In the book by Miguel Sánchez, published in 1648, the Spanish Conquest of New Spain is justified solely on the grounds that it allowed the Virgin to become manifest in her chosen country, and to found in Mexico a new paradise. Just as Israel had been chosen to produce Christ, so Mexico had been chosen to produce Guadalupe. Sánchez equates her with the apocalyptic woman of the Revelation of John (12: 1), "arrayed with the sun, and the moon under her feet, and upon her head a crown of twelve stars" who is to realize the prophecy of Deuteronomy 8: 7-10 and lead the Mexicans into the Promised Land. Colonial Mexico thus becomes the desert of Sinai; Independent Mexico the land of milk and honey. F. Francisco de Florencia, writing in 1688, coined the slogan which made Mexico not merely another chosen nation, but the Chosen Nation: *non fecit taliter omni nationi*,[24] words which still adorn the portals of the basilica, and shine forth in electric light bulbs at night. And on the eve of Mexican independence, Servando Teresa de Mier elaborates still further the Guadalupan myth by claiming that Mexico had been converted to Christianity long before the Spanish Conquest. The apostle Saint Thomas had brought the image of Guadalupe-Tonantzin to the New World as a symbol of his mission, just as Saint James had converted Spain with the image of the Virgin of the Pillar. The Spanish Conquest was therefore historically unnecessary, and should be erased from the annals of history.[25] In this perspective, the Mexican War of Independence marks the final realization of the apocalyptic promise. The banner of the Guadalupe leads the insurgents; and their cause is referred to as "her law."[26] In this ultimate extension of the symbol, the promise of life held out by the supernatural mother has become the promise of an independent Mexico, liberated from the irrational authority of the Spanish father-oppressors and restored to the Chosen Nation whose election had been manifest in the apparition of the Virgin on Tepeyac. The land of the supernatural mother is finally possessed by her rightful heirs. The symbolic circuit is closed. Mother; food, hope, health, life; supernatural salvation and salvation from oppression; Chosen People and national independence—all find expression in a single master symbol.

The Guadalupe symbol thus links together family, politics and religion; colonial past and independent present; Indian and Mexican. It reflects the salient social relationships of Mexican life, and embodies the emotions which they generate. It provides a cultural idiom through which the tenor and emotions of these relationships can be expressed. It is, ultimately, a way of talking about Mexico: a "collective representation" of Mexican society.

10

Taboo

Mary Douglas

To an outside observer, a taboo or religious prohibition might seem irrational; to the believer, it simply seems right. Identifying where that sense of rightness comes from, and why it is so important, is Mary Douglas's task in the following article. Douglas's functional analysis of taboos shows that they underpin social structure everywhere. Anthropologists, studying taboos over extensive periods of time, have learned that taboo systems are not static and forever inviolate; on the contrary, they are dynamic elements of learned behavior that each generation absorbs. Taboos, as rules of behavior, are always part of a whole system and cannot be understood outside their social context. Douglas's explanation of taboos holds as much meaning for us in the understanding of ourselves as it does for our understanding of rules of conduct in the non-Western world. Whether considering the taboos surrounding a Polynesian chief's mana or the changing sexual taboos in the Western world, it is apparent that taboo systems maintain cultural systems.

A taboo (sometimes spelled tabu) is a ban or prohibition; the word comes from the Polynesian languages where it means a religious restriction, to break which would entail some automatic punishment. As it is used in English, taboo has little to do with religion. In essence it generally implies a rule which has no meaning, or one which cannot be explained. Captain Cook noted in his log-book that in Tahiti the women were never allowed to eat with the men, and as the men nevertheless enjoyed female company he asked the reason for this taboo. They always replied that they observed it because it was right. To the outsider the taboo is irrational, to the believer its rightness needs no explaining. Though supernatural punishments may not be expected to follow, the rules of any religion rate as taboos to outsiders. For example, the strict Jewish observance forbids the faithful to make and refuel the fire, or light lamps or put them out

during the Sabbath, and it also forbids them to ask a Gentile to perform any of these acts. In his book *A Soho Address,* Chaim Lewis, the son of poor Russian Jewish immigrants in London's Soho at the beginning of this century, describes his father's quandary every winter Sabbath: he did not want to let the fire go out and he could not ask any favor outright. Somehow he had to call in a passerby and drop oblique hints until the stranger understood what service was required. Taboos always tend to land their observers in just such a ridiculous situation, whether it is a Catholic peasant of the Landes who abstains from meat on Friday, but eats teal (a bird whose fishy diet entitles it in their custom to be counted as fish), or a Maori hairdresser who after he had cut the chief's hair was not allowed to use his own hands even for feeding himself and had to be fed for a time like a baby.

In the last century, when the word gained currency in European languages, taboo was understood to arise from an inferior mentality. It was argued that primitive tribes observed countless taboos as part of their general ignorance about the physical world. These rules, which seemed so peculiar to Europeans,

"Taboo" by Mary Douglas reprinted from Richard Cavendish, ed., MAN, MYTH, AND MAGIC (London, 1979), vol. 20, pp. 2767–71, by permission of the author and BPCC/Phoebus Publishing.

were the result of false science, leading to mistaken hygiene, and faulty medicine. Essentially the taboo is a ban on touching or eating or speaking or seeing. Its breach will unleash dangers, while keeping the rules would amount to avoiding dangers and sickness. Since the native theory of taboo was concerned to keep certain classes of people and things apart lest misfortune befall, it was a theory about contagion. Our scholars of the last century contrasted this false, primitive fear of contagion with our modern knowledge of disease. Our hygiene protects from a real danger of contagion, their taboos from imaginary danger. This was a comfortably complacent distinction to draw, but hygiene does not correspond to all the rules which are called taboo. Some are as obviously part of primitive religion in the same sense as Friday abstinence and Sabbath rest. European scholars therefore took care to distinguish on the one hand between primitive taboo with a mainly secular reference, and on the other hand rules of magic which infused the practice of primitive religion. They made it even more difficult to understand the meaning of foreign taboos by importing a classification between true religion and primitive magic, and modern medicine and primitive hygiene; and a very complicated web of definitions was based on this misconception.

In the Eye of the Beholder

The difficulty in understanding primitive taboo arose from the difficulty of understanding our own taboos of hygiene and religion. The first mistake was to suppose that our idea of dirt connotes an objectively real class from which real dangers to health may issue, and whose control depends on valid rules of hygiene. It is better to start by realizing that dirt, like beauty, resides in the eye of the beholder. We must be prepared to put our own behavior under the same microscope we apply to primitive tribes. If we find that they are busy hedging off this area from that, stopping X from touching Y, preventing women from eating with men, and creating elaborate scales of edibility and inedibility among the vegetable and animal worlds, we should realize that we too are given to this ordering and classifying activity. No taboo can ever make sense by itself. A taboo is always part of a whole system of rules. It makes sense as part of a classification whose meaning is so basic to those who live by it

that no piecemeal explanation can be given. A native cannot explain the meaning of a taboo because it forms part of his own machinery of learning. The separate compartments which a taboo system constructs are the framework or instrument of understanding. To turn around and inspect that instrument may seem to be an advanced philosophic exercise, but it is necessary if we are to understand the subject.

The nineteenth-century scholars could not understand taboo because they worked within the separate compartments of their own taboo system. For them religion, magic, hygiene, and medicine were as distinct as civilized and primitive; the problem of taboo for them was only a problem about native thought. But put in that form it was insoluble. We approach it nowadays as a problem in human learning.

First, discard the idea that we have anything like a true, complete view of the world. Between what the scientists know and what we make of their knowledge there is a synthesis which is our own rough-and-ready approximation of rules about how we need to behave in the physical world. Second, discard the idea that there can ever be a final and correct world view. A gain in knowledge in one direction does not guarantee there will be no loss or distortion in another; the fullness of reality will always evade our comprehension. The reasons for this will become clear. Learning is a filtering and organizing process. Faced with the same events, two people will not necessarily register two identical patterns, and faced with a similar environment, two cultures will construe two different sets of natural constraints and regular sequences. Understanding is largely a classifying job in which the classifying human mind is much freer than it supposes itself to be. The events to be understood are unconsciously trimmed and filtered to fit the classification being used. In this sense every culture constructs its own universe. It attributes to its own world a set of powers to be harnessed and dangers to be avoided. Each primitive culture, because of its isolation, has a unique world view. Modern industrial nations, because and insofar as they share a common experience, share the same rules about the powers and dangers aroused. This is a valid difference between "Us" and "Them," their primitive taboos and ours.

For all humans, primitive or not, the universe is a system of imputed rules. Using our own distinctions, we can distinguish firstly, physical Nature, inorganic (including rocks, stars, rivers) and organic (vegetable and animal bodies, with rules governing their growth, lifespan and death); secondly, human behavior; thirdly, the interaction between these two groups; fourthly, other intelligent beings whether incorporeal like gods, devils and ghosts or mixtures of human and divine or human and animal; and lastly, the interaction between this fourth group and the rest.

The use of the word supernatural has been avoided. Even a small amount of reading in anthropology shows how very local and peculiar to our own civilization is the distinction between natural and supernatural. The same applies even to such a classification as the one just given. The fact that it is our own local classification is not important for this argument as the present object is to make clear how taboos should be understood. Taboos are rules about our behavior which restrict the human uses of things and people. Some of the taboos are said to avoid punishment or vengeance from gods, ghosts and other spirits. Some of them are supposed to produce automatically their dreaded effects. Crop failures, sickness, hunting accidents, famine, drought, epidemic (events in the physical realm), they may all result from breach of taboos.

The Seat of *Mana*

Taboos can have the effect of expressing political ideas. For example, the idea of the state as a hierarchy of which the chief is the undisputed head and his officials higher than the ordinary populace easily lends itself to taboo behavior. Gradings of power in the political body tend to be expressed as gradings of freedom to approach the physical body of the person at the top of the system. As Franz Steiner says, in *Taboo* (1956):

> In Polynesian belief the parts of the body formed a fixed hierarchy which had some analogy with the rank system of society. . . . Now the backbone was the most important part of the body, and the limbs that could be regarded as continuations of the backbone derived importance from it. Above the body was, of course, the head, and it was the seat of *mana*. When we say this, we must realize that by *"mana"* are meant both the soul aspect, the life force, and a man's ritual status. This grading of the limbs concerned people of all ranks and both sexes. It could, for example, be so important to avoid

stepping over people's heads that the very architecture was involved: the arrangements of the sleeping rooms show such an adaptation in the Marquesas. The commoner's back or head is thus not without its importance in certain contexts. But the real significance of this grading seems to have been in the possibilities it provided for cumulative effects in association with the rank system. The head of a chief was the most concentrated mana object of Polynesian society, and was hedged around with the most terrifying taboos which operated when things were to enter the head or when the head was being diminished; in other words when the chief ate or had his hair cut. . . . The hands of some great chiefs were so dangerous that they could not be put close to the head.

Since the Polynesian political systems was very competitive and chiefs had their ups and downs, great triumphs or total failures, the system of taboo was a kind of public vote of confidence and register of current distributions of power. This is important to correct our tendency to think of taboo as a rigidly fixed system of respect.

We will never understand a taboo system unless we understand the kind of interaction between the different spheres of existence which is assumed in it. Any child growing up learns the different spheres and interactions between them simultaneously. When the anthropologist arrives on the scene, he finds the system of knowledge a going concern. It is difficult for him to observe the changes being made, so he gets the wrong impression that a given set of taboos is something hard-and-fast handed down the generations.

In fact, the classifying process is always active and changing. New classifications are being pushed by some and rejected by others. No political innovation takes place without some basic reclassification. To take a currently live issue, in a stratified society, if it is taboo for lower classes or Negroes to sit down at table or to join sporting events with upper classes or whites, those who assert the rule can make it stronger if they find a basis in Nature to support the behavior they regard as right. If women in Tahiti are forbidden to eat with men, or in Europe to enter certain male occupations, some ultimate justification for the rule needs to be found. Usually it is traced back to their physical nature. Women are said to be constitutionally feeble, nervous or flighty; Negroes to smell; lower classes to be hereditarily less intelligent.

Rules of the Game

Perhaps the easiest approach is to try to imagine what social life would be like without any classification. It would be like playing a game without any rules; no one would know which way to run, who is on his side or against him. There would be no game. It is no exaggeration to describe social life as the process of building classification systems. Everyone is trying to make sense of what is happening. He is trying to make sense of his own behavior, past and present, so as to capture and hold some sense of identity. He is trying to hold other people to their promises and ensure some kind of regular future. He is explaining continually, to himself and to everyone else. In the process of explaining, classifications are developed and more and more meanings successfully added to them, as other people are persuaded to interpret events in the same way. Gradually even the points of the compass get loaded with social meanings. For example, the west room in an Irish farmer's house used to be the room where the old couple retired to, when the eldest son married and brought his wife to the farm. West meant retirement as well as sundown. In the Buddhist religion, east is the high status point; Buddha's statue is on a shelf on the east wall of the east room; the husband always sleeps to the east of his wife. So east means male and social superior. Up and down, right and left, sun and moon, hot and cold, all the physical antitheses are able to carry meanings from social life, and in a rich and steady culture there is a steady core of such agreed classifications. Anyone who is prepared to support the social system finds himself impelled to uphold the classification system which gets meaning from it. Anyone who wants to challenge the social system finds himself up against a set of manifold classifications which will have to be rethought. This is why breach of taboo arouses such strong feeling. It is not because the minor classification is threatened, but because the whole social system (in which a great investment has been made) looks like tottering, if someone can get away with challenging a taboo.

Classification involves definition; definition involves reducing ambiguity; ambiguity arises in several ways and it is wrong to think it can ever be excluded. To take the classification of animal species, they can be classified according to their obvious features, and according to the habitat they live in, and according to how they behave. This gives three ways of classifying animals which could each place the same beasts in different classes. Classed by behavior, using walking, swimming or flying as basic types, penguins would be nearer to fish; classed by bone structure and egg laying, penguins would count more clearly as birds than would flying fish, which would be birds in the other classification. Animal life is much more untidy and difficult to fit into a regular system of classification than at first appears. Human social life is even more untidy. Girls behave like boys, there are adults who refuse to grow up, every year a few are born whose physical make-up is not clearly male or female. The rules of marriage and inheritance require clear-cut categories but always there will be some cases which do not fit the regularities of the system. For human classifications are always too crude for reality. A system of taboos covers up this weakness of the classification system. It points in advance to defects and insists that no one shall give recognition to the inconvenient facts or behave in such a way as to undermine the acceptability and clarity of the system as a whole. It stops awkward questions and prevents awkward developments.

Sometimes the taboo ban appears in ways that seem a long way from their point of origin. For example, among the Lele tribe, in the Kasai district of the Congo, it was taboo to bring fishing equipment direct into the village from the streams or lakes where it had been in use. All round the village fishing traps and baskets would be hung in trees overnight. Ask the Lele why they did this and they replied that coughs and disease would enter the village if the fishing things were not left out one night. No other answer could be got from them except elaboration of the danger and how sorcerers could enter the village if this barrier were not kept up. But another kind of answer lay in the mass of other rules and regulations which separated the village and its human social life from the forest and streams and animal life. This was the basic classification at stake; one which never needed to be explained because it was too fundamental to mention.

Injecting Order into Life

The novelist William Burroughs describes the final experiences of disgust and depression of some forms of drug addiction. What he calls the "Naked Lunch" is the point where all illusions are stripped away and every thing is seen as it really is. When everyone can see what is on everyone's fork, nothing is classed as edible. Meat can be animal or human flesh, caterpillars, worms, or bugs; soup is equally urine, lentils, scotch broth, or excreta; other people are neither friends nor enemies, nor is oneself different from other people since neither has any very clear definition. Identities and classifications are merged into a seething, shapeless experience. This is the potential disorder of the mind which taboo breaks up into classes and rules and so judges some activities as right and proper and others as horrifying.

This kind of rationality is the justification for the taboos which we ourselves observe when we separate the lavatory from the living room and the bed from the kitchen, injecting order into the house. But the order is not arbitrary; it derives from social categories. When a set of social distinctions weakens, the taboos that expressed it weaken too. For this reason sex taboos used to be sacred in England but are no longer so strong. It seems ridiculous that women should not be allowed in some clubs or professions, whereas not so long ago it seemed obviously right. The same for the sense of privacy, the same for hierarchy. The less we ourselves are forced to adopt unthinking taboo attitudes to breaches of these boundaries, the easier it becomes to look dispassionately at the taboos of other societies and find plenty of meaning in them.

In some tribal societies it is thought that the shedding of blood will cause droughts and other environmental disasters. Elsewhere any contact with death is dangerously polluting, and burials are followed by elaborate washing and fumigation. In other places they fear neither homicide nor death pollution but menstrual blood is thought to be very dangerous to touch. And in other places again, adultery is liable to cause illness. Some people are thickly beset with taboos so that everything they do is charged with social symbolism. Others observe only one or two rules. Those who are most taboo-minded have the most complex set of social boundaries to preserve. Hence their investment of so much energy into the control of behavior.

A taboo system upholds a cultural system and a culture is a pattern of values and norms; social life is impossible without such a pattern. This is the dilemma of individual freedom. Ideally we would like to feel free to make every choice from scratch and judge each case on its merits. Such a freedom would slow us down, for every choice would have to be consciously deliberated. On the one hand, education tries to equip a person with means for exercising private judgment, and on the other hand, the techniques of education provide a kind of mechanical decision-making, along well-oiled grooves. They teach strong reactions of anxiety about anything which threatens to go off the track. As education transmits culture, taboos and all, it is a kind of brainwashing. It only allows a certain way of seeing reality and so limits the scope for private judgment. Without the taboos, which turn basic classifications into automatic psychological reflexes, no thinking could be effective, because if every system of classification was up for revision at every moment, there would be no stability of thought. Hence there would be no scope for experience to accumulate into knowledge. Taboos bar the way for the mind to visualize reality differently. But the barriers they set up are not arbitrary, for taboos flow from social boundaries and support the social structure. This accounts for their seeming irrational to the outsider and beyond challenge to the person living in the society.

II

Serpent-Handling as Sacrament

Mary Lee Daugherty

Raised in West Virginia, author Mary Lee Daugherty was a clergywoman, theologian, and scholar who devoted herself to the study of religion in Appalachia until her death in 2004. In her films and writings about small Holiness/Pentecostal churches in the region, she maintains that the handling of snakes as a religious act reflects the social and economic challenges of the community. Here Daugherty argues that snake handling is similar to other Christian rituals, such as communion. Religious behavior that includes the handling of poisonous snakes and the drinking of such poisons as strychnine and lye has met with legal opposition in the United States. Several states specifically outlaw the handling of poisonous snakes in religious settings; West Virginia is not among them.

Other works on snake handling and Holiness churches include Thomas Burton's Serpent-Handling Believers *(University of Tennessee Press, 1993), Dennis Covington's* Salvation on Sand Mountain: Snake Handling and Redemption in Southern Appalachia *(Addison-Wesley, 1995), and the anthropological classic by Weston La Barre,* They Shall Take Up Serpents: Psychology of the Southern Snake-Handling Cult *(University of Minnesota Press, 1962).*

And he [Jesus] said unto them, Go ye into all the world, and preach the gospel to every creature. He that believeth and is baptized shall be saved; but he that believeth not shall be damned. And these signs shall follow them that believe; In my name shall they cast out devils; they shall speak with new tongues; they shall take up serpents; and if they drink any deadly thing, it shall not hurt them; they shall lay hands on the sick, and they shall recover.

—Mark 16:15–18 (AV)

The serpent-handlers of West Virginia were originally simple, poor, white people who formed a group of small, independent Holiness-type churches. Serpent-handlers base their particular religious practices on the familiar passage from the "long-conclusion" of the Gospel of Mark. (They are unaware of the disputed nature of this text as the biblical scholars know it.)

"Serpent-Handling as Sacrament" by Mary Lee Daugherty from THEOLOGY TODAY, Vol. 33, No. 3, October 1976, pp. 232–243. Reprinted by permission of Theology Today.

The handling of serpents as a supreme act of faith reflects, as in a mirror, the danger and harshness of the environment in which most of these people have lived. The land is rugged and uncompromisingly grim. It produces little except for coal dug from the earth. Unemployment and welfare have been constant companions. The dark holes of the deep mines into which men went to work every day have maimed and killed them for years. The copperhead and rattlesnake are the most commonly found serpents in the rocky terrain. For many years mountain people have suffered terrible pain and many have died from snake bite. Small wonder that it is considered the ultimate fact of faith to reach out and take up the serpent when one is filled with the Holy Ghost. Old timers here in the mountains, before the days of modern medicine, could only explain that those who lived were somehow chosen by God's special mercy and favor.

Today serpent-handlers are experiencing, as are other West Virginians, great economic improvement. Many now live in expensive mobile homes that dot the mountain countryside. They purchase and own among their possessions brand new cars and modern appliances. Many of the men now earn from twelve to eighteen thousand dollars a year, working in the revitalized mining industry. Most of the young people are now going to and graduating from high school. I know of one young man with two years of college who is very active in his church. He handles serpents and is looked upon as the one who will take over the pastor's position sometime in the future. What the effect of middle-class prosperity and higher education will be among serpent-handlers remains to be seen. It may be another generation before the effects can be adequately determined.

Knowing serpent-handlers to be biblical literalists, one might surmise that they, like other sects, have picked a certain passage of Scripture and built a whole ritual around a few cryptic verses. While this is true, I am persuaded, after years of observation, that serpent-handling holds for them the significance of a sacrament.

Tapestry paintings of the Lord's Supper hang in most of their churches. Leonardo da Vinci's *Last Supper* is the one picture I have seen over and over again in their churches and in their homes. But in West Virginia, the serpent-handlers whom I know personally do not celebrate the Lord's Supper in their worship services. It is my observation and hypothesis that the ritual of serpent-handling is their way of celebrating life, death, and resurrection. Time and again they prove to themselves that Jesus has the power to deliver them from death here and now.

Another clue to the sacramental nature of lifting up the serpents as the symbol of victory over death is to be observed at their funerals. At the request of the family of one who has died of snake bite, serpents may be handled at a funeral. Even as a Catholic priest may lift up the host at a mass for the dead, indicating belief that in the life and death of Jesus there is victory over death, so the serpent-handlers, I believe, lift up the serpent. Of course, none of this is formalized, for all is very spontaneous. But I am convinced that they celebrate their belief that "in the name of Jesus" there is power over death, and this is what the serpent-handling ritual has proved to them over and over again. This is why I believe they will not give up this ritual because it is at the center of their Christian faith, and in West Virginia, unlike all the other States, it is not illegal.

Many handlers have been bitten numerous times, but, contrary to popular belief, few have died. Their continued life, and their sometimes deformed hands, bear witness to the fact that Jesus still has power over illness and death. Even those who have not been bitten know many who have, and the living witness is ever present in the lives of their friends. If one of the members should die, it is believed that God allowed it to happen to remind the living that the risk they take is totally real. Never have I heard any one of them say that a brother or sister who died lacked faith.

The cultural isolation of these people is still very real. Few have traveled more than a few miles from home. Little more than the Bible is ever read. Television is frowned upon; movies are seldom attended. The Bible is communicated primarily through oral tradition in the church or read at home. There is little awareness of other world religions. Even contacts with Roman Catholics and Jews are rare. Most of their lives revolve around the local church where they gather for meetings two or three times a week.

When one sees the people handling serpents in their services, the Garden of Eden story immediately comes to mind. In the Genesis story, the serpent represents evil that tempts Adam and Eve and must be conquered by their descendants. But the serpent means something far different to West Virginia mountain people; it means life over death. There is never any attempt to kill the snake in Appalachian serpent-handling services. Practitioners seldom kill snakes even in the out of doors. They let them go at the end of the summer months so that they may return to their natural environment to hibernate for the winter. They catch different snakes each spring to use in their worship services. When you ask them why, they tell you quite simply that they do not want to make any of God's creatures suffer. The serpent is always handled with both love and fear in their services, but it is never harmed or killed. Handlers may be killed from bites, but they will not kill the snake. Neither do they force the handling of serpents on any who do not wish to do so.

The snake is seldom handled in private, but usually in the community of believers during a church service. Members may encourage each other to take the risk, symbolically taking on life and testing faith. Their willingness to die for their beliefs gives to their lives a vitality of faith. Handlers usually refuse medicine or hospital treatment for snake bite. But they do go to hospital for other illnesses or if surgery is needed. In the past, they usually refused welfare. They revere and care for their elderly who have usually survived numerous snake bites. Each time they handle the serpents they struggle with life once more and survive again the forces that traditionally oppressed mountain people. The poverty, the unemployment, the yawning strip mines, death in the deep mines have all been harsh, uncontrollable forces for simple people. The handling of serpents is their way of confronting and coping with their very real fears about life and the harshness of reality as experienced in the mountains in years gone by and, for many, even today.

Yet in the face of all this, they seek to live in harmony with nature, not to destroy it or any of its creatures, even the deadly serpent. It is only with the Holy Ghost, however, that they find the sustenance to survive. They live close to the earth, surrounded by woods, streams, and sky. Most live in communities of only a few hundred people or less.

The deep longing for holiness of these Appalachian people stands out in bold relief in the serpent-handling ritual of worship. The search for holiness is dramatized in their willingness to suffer terrible pain from snake bite, or even death itself, to get the feeling of God in their lives. The support of their fellow Christians is still with them. In their experience, God may not come if you don't really pray or ask only once. The person in the group who has been bitten most often and who has suffered the most pain or sickness is usually the leader. While it is the Holy Ghost who gives the power, those who have survived snake bite do get recognition and praise for their courage and their faith from the group. They have learned to cope with their anxieties by calling upon the names of Jesus and the power which he freely offers. Support is given to each member through the laying on of hands in healing ceremonies, through group prayers, and through verbal affirmations, such as: "Help her Jesus," "Bless him, Lord," "That's right, Lord." Through group support, anxiety about life is relieved. They feel ennobled as God becomes manifest in their midst.

The person of the Holy Ghost (they prefer this to Holy Spirit) enables them not only to pick up serpents, but to speak in tongues, to preach, to testify, to cure diseases, to cast out demons, and even to drink strychnine and lye, or to use fire on their skin when the snakes are in hibernation during the winter months. In these dramatic ways, the mountain folk pursue holiness above all else. They find through their faith both meaning and encouragement. Psychological tests indicate that in many ways they are more emotionally healthy than members of mainline Protestant churches.

Having internalized my own feelings of insecurity and worthlessness for many years because I was "no count" having been born from poor white trash on one side of my family, I have in my own being a deep appreciation and understanding of the need of these people to ask God for miracles accompanied with spectacular demonstrations. Thus they are assured of their own worth, even if only to God. They have never gotten this message from the outside world. They know they have been, and many still are, the undesirable poor, the uneducated mountain folk, locked into their little pockets of poverty in a rough, hostile land. So the Holy Ghost is the great equalizer in the church meeting. One's age, sex, years of schooling are all of less value. Being filled with the Holy Ghost is the only credential one needs in this unique society.

The Holy Ghost creates a mood of openness and spontaneity in the serpent-handling service that is beautiful to behold. Even though there is not much freedom in the personal lives of these people, there is a sense of power in their church lives. Their religion does seem to heal them inwardly of aches and pains and in many instances even of major illnesses. One often sees expressions of dependence as men and women fall down before the picture of Jesus, calling aloud over and over again, "Jesus . . . Jesus . . . Jesus . . ." The simple carpenter of Nazareth is obviously a person with whom mountain people can identify. Jesus worked with his hands, and so do they; Jesus was essentially, by our standards, uneducated, and so are they; Jesus came from a small place, he lived much of his life out of doors, he went fishing, he suffered and was finally done in by the "power structure," and so have they been in the past and often are today.

As I think about the mountain women as they fall down before the picture of Jesus, I wonder what he means to them. Here is a simple man who treated women with great love and tenderness. In this sense, he is unlike some of the men they must live with. Jesus healed the bodies of women, taught them the Bible, never told jokes about their bodies, and even forgave them their sexual sins. In the mountains, adultery is usually punished with beatings. Maybe it should not surprise us that in a State where the strip miners have raped the earth that the rape of the people has also taken place, and the rape of women is often deeply felt and experienced. Things are now changing, and for this we can be grateful.

In the serpent-handlers' churches, the Bible usually remains closed on the pulpit. Since most older members cannot read very well and have usually felt shy about their meager education, they did not read the Bible aloud in public, especially if some more educated people were present. They obviously read the Bible at home, but most remember it from stories they have heard. The Bible is the final authority for everything, even the picking up of serpents and the drinking of poison. It is all literally true, but the New Testament is read more often than the Old Testament.

In former years, their churches have given these poor and powerless people the arena in which they could act out their frustrations and powerless feelings. For a short time, while in church, they could experience being powerful when filled with the Holy Ghost. Frustrated by all the things in the outside world that they could not change, frustrated by the way the powerful people of the world were running things, they could nevertheless run their own show in their own churches. So they gathered three or four times a week, in their modest church buildings, and they stayed for three to five hours for each service. On these occasions, they can feel important, loved, and powerful. They can experience God directly.

I am always struck by the healing love that emerges at the end of each service when they all seem to love each other, embrace each other, and give each other the holy kiss. They are free from restrictions and conventions to love everyone. Sometimes I have the feeling that I get a glimmer of what the Kingdom of God will be like as we kiss each other, old and young, with or without teeth, rich and poor, educated and uneducated, male and female. So I have learned much and have been loved in turn by the serpent-handlers of West Virginia. As they leave the church and go back to their daily work, all the frustrations of the real world return, but they know they can meet again tomorrow night or in a few days. So they have faith, hope, and love, but the greatest message they have given to me is their love.

There are thousands of small Holiness churches in the rural areas of West Virginia. While four-fifths of all Protestants are members of mainstream denominations, no one knows just how many attend Holiness churches. Membership records are not considered important to these people, and although I personally know of about twenty-five serpent-handling churches, there may be others, for those in one church often do not know those in another. They laugh and make jokes about churches that give you a piece of paper as you enter the door, telling you when to pray and what to sing. They find it difficult to believe that you can "order around" the worship of the Holy Ghost on a piece of paper.

Those who make up the membership of the serpent-handling churches are often former members of other Holiness churches or are former Baptists or Methodists. In the Holiness churches, the attainment of personal holiness and being filled with the Spirit is the purpose and goal of life. Members view the secular world as evil and beyond hope. Hence they do not take part in any community activities or social programs.

Fifty-four percent of all persons in the state of West Virginia still live in communities of 1,000 people or less. Freedom of worship is the heritage of the Scotch-Irish, who settled these mountains 200 years ago. In more recent times, among Holiness groups there were no trained ministers. So oral tradition, spontaneous worship, and shared leadership are important.

Holiness church members live by a very strict personal code of morality. A large sign in the church at Jolo, W. Va., indicates that dresses must be worn below the knees, arms must be covered, no lipstick or jewelry is to be worn. No smoking, drinking, or other worldly pleasures are to be indulged in by "true believers." Some women do not cut their hair, others do not even buy chewing gum or soft drinks. For years, in the mountains, people have practiced divine healing, since medical facilities are scarce. Four counties in West Virginia still do not have a doctor, nurse, clinic, dentist, or ambulance service.

In a typical serpent-handling church service, the "true believers" usually sit on the platform of the church together. They are the members who have demonstrated that they have received the Holy Ghost. This is known to them and to others because they have manifested certain physical signs in their own bodies. If they have been bitten from snakes, as many have, and have not died, they have proved that they have the Holy Ghost. And those who have been bitten many times, and survived, are the "real saints." The "true believers" also demonstrate that they have the Holy Ghost by speaking in tongues, by the jerking of their bodies, and by their various trance-like states. They may dance for long periods of time or fall on the floor without being hurt. They may drink the "salvation cocktail," a mixture of strychnine or lye and water. They may also speak in tongues or in ecstatic utterances. Usually this is an utterance between themselves and God. But sometimes members seek to interpret the language of tongues. They lay their hands upon each other to heal hurts or even serious illnesses such as cancer. They sometimes pass their hands through fire. I have witnessed this activity and no burn effects are visible, even though a hand may remain in the flame for some time. A few years ago, they picked up hot coals from the pot bellied stoves and yet were not burned. They apparently can block out pain totally, when in a trance or deep into the Spirit of God.

One woman who attended church at Scrabble Creek, W. Va., experienced, on two occasions, the stigmata as blood came out of her hands, feet, side and forehead. This was witnessed by all present in the church. When asked about this startling experience, she said that she had prayed that God would allow people to see though her body how much Jesus suffered for them by his death and resurrection.

A local church in the rural areas may be known as "Brother So and So's" or "Sister So and So's" church to those who live nearby, but the sign over the door will usually indicate that the church belongs to Jesus. Such names as "The Jesus Church," "The Jesus Only Church," "The Jesus Saves Church," and "The Lord Jesus Christ's Church" are all common names. The churches do not belong to any denomination, and they have no written doctrines or creeds. The order of the service is spontaneous and different every night. Everyone is welcome and people travel around to each other's churches, bringing with them their musical instruments, snakes, fire equipment, poison mixtures, and other gifts.

Often the service begins with singing which may last thirty to forty-five minutes. Next, they may all pray out loud together for the Holy Ghost to fall upon them during the service. Singing, testifying, and preaching by anyone who feels God's spirit may follow. Serpents then will be handled while others are singing. It is possible that serpents will be handled two or three times in one service, but usually it is only once. Serpents are only handled when they feel God's spirit within them. After dancing ecstatically, a brother or sister will open the box and pull out a serpent. Others will follow if there are other snakes available. If only one or two serpents are present, then they may be passed around from believer to believer. Sometimes a circle may be made and the snakes passed. I have only once seen them throw snakes to each other. Children are kept far away.

There is much calling on the name of Jesus while the serpents are being handled, and once the "sacrament" is over, there is a great prayer of rejoicing and often a dance of thanksgiving that no one was hurt. If someone is bitten, there is prayer for his or her healing and great care is taken. If the person becomes too ill to stay in the church, he or she may be taken home and believers will pray for the person for days, if necessary. Even if the person does not die, and usually he or she doesn't, the person is usually very sick. Vomiting of blood and swelling are very painful. Some persons in the churches have lost the use of a finger or suffered some other deformity. But in many years of serpent-handling, I believe there are only about twenty recorded deaths.

The symbolism of the serpent is found in almost all cultures and religions, everywhere, and in all ages. It suggests the ambiguity of good and evil, sickness and health, life and death, mortality and immortality, chaos and wisdom. Because the serpent lives in the ground but is often found in trees, it conveys the notion of transcendence, a creature that lives between earth and heaven. And because it sheds its skin, it seems to know the secret of eternal life.

In the Bible, the serpent is most obviously associated with the Adam and Eve temptation (Gen. 3:1–13), but we also read of the sticks that Moses and Aaron turned into snakes (Ex. 7:8–12), and of Moses' bronze serpent standard (Num. 21:6–9). The two entwined snakes in the ancient figure of the caduceus, symbolizing sickness and health, has been widely adopted as the emblem of the medical profession. And sometimes in early Christian art, the crucifixion is represented with a serpent wound around the cross or lying at the foot of the cross (cf. John 3:14). Here again good and evil, life over death, are symbolized.

In early liturgical art, John the Evangelist was often identified with a chalice from which a serpent was departing, a reference to the legend that when he was forced to drink poison, it was drained away in the snake. Among the early Gnostics, there was a group known as Ophites who were said to worship the serpent because it brought "knowledge" to Adam and Eve and so to all humanity. They were said to free a serpent from a box and that it then entwined itself around the bread and wine of the Eucharist.

But, of course, this ancient history and symbolic lore are unknown to the mountain serpent-handlers of West Virginia, and even if they were told, they probably would not be interested. Their own tradition is rooted in their literal acceptance of what they regard as Jesus' commandment at the conclusion of Mark's Gospel. The problems of biblical textual criticism, relating to the fact that these verses on which they depend are not found in the best manuscript evidence, does not bother them. Their Bible is the English King James Version, and they know through their own experience that their faith in the healing and saving power of Jesus has been tested and proven without question. In any case, their ritual is unique in church history.

What the future holds for the serpent-handlers, no one can tell. Although the young people have tended to stay in their local communities, the temptation in the past to move out and away to find work has been very great. Now many of the young people are returning home as the mining industry offers new, high-paying jobs. And a new era of relative economic prosperity is emerging as the energy problem makes coal-mining more important for the whole Appalachian area. In the meantime, serpent-handling for many mountain people remains a Jesus-commanded "sacrament" whereby physical signs communicate spiritual reality.

Suggested Readings

Babcock, Barbara, ed.
   1978   *The Reversible World: Symbolic Inversion in Art and Society.* Ithaca, N.Y.: Cornell University Press.

Douglas, Mary
   1966   *Purity and Danger: An Analysis of Concepts of Pollution and Taboo.* New York: Praeger.
   1999   *Leviticus as Literature.* Oxford: Oxford University Press.

Dundes, Alan, ed.
   1984   *Sacred Narrative: Readings in the Theory of Myth.* Berkeley: University of California Press.
   1988   *The Flood Myth.* Berkeley: University of California Press

Georges, Robert A., ed.
   1968   *Studies on Mythology.* Homewood, Ill.: Dorsey Press.

Holden, Lynn, ed.
   2000   *Encyclopedia of Taboos.* Santa Barbara, Calif.: ABC-CLIO.

Lambek, Michael
   1992   "Taboo as Cultural Practice Among Malagasy Speakers." *Man* 27: 245–66.

Ortner, Sherry B.
   1973   "On Key Symbols." *American Anthropologist* 75: 1338–46.

Segal, Robert
   2004   *Myth: A Very Short Introduction.* Oxford: Oxford University Press.

CHAPTER THREE

Ritual

Tshan mask from Tibet.

Ritual is of crucial significance to all human societies, and since the nineteenth century it has been a major focus for anthropologists interested in the study of religion. There are numerous definitions of ritual, but nearly all emphasize repetition, formality, the reliance upon symbols, and the capacity to intensify bonds within a community. Ritual is action. Anthony Wallace highlights the elevated role of ritual when he labels it the primary phenomenon of religion: "Ritual is religion in action; it is the cutting edge of the tool. Belief, although its recitation may be part of the ritual, or a ritual in its own right, serves to explain, to rationalize, to interpret and direct the energy of the ritual performance. . . . It is ritual which accomplishes what religion sets out to do" (1966: 102). While rituals encapsulate ideas central to a culture and are often closely tied to myths, they are intended to bring about specific ends.

Through ritual, religion is able to impress on people a commitment to their system of religious beliefs. Participants in a religious ritual are able to express group solidarity and loyalty. History abounds with examples of the importance of the individual experience in religion, yet there is no denying the overwhelming effect of group participation. As William Howells has pointed out, ritual helps individuals but does so by treating them as a whole group: "They are like a tangled head of hair, and ritual is the comb" (1962: 243).

Some anthropologists believe, along with Malinowski and other early functionalists, that ritual helps allay anxiety. Through the shared performance of group dances and ceremonies, humans are able to reduce the fears that often come when life's events threaten their security and sense of well-being. Other scholars, such as A. R. Radcliffe-Brown, have taken the opposite tack, claiming that ritual may actually create rather than allay anxiety and fears.

Are all rituals religious? Early anthropological theorists assumed that all ritual was sacred in nature, most likely because they dealt with societies in which many aspects of daily life held sacred significance. More-contemporary writers have noted, however, the ritual nature of ceremonies and actions that do not clearly invoke spirits or deities yet still express the fundamental beliefs, values, and social foundations of a group. Sally F. Moore and Barbara G. Myerhoff call such actions *secular rituals*, highlighting their nonsacred status yet also drawing attention to their powerful, multifaceted meanings (1977). One example is a birthday party celebrated at a senior citizen center, as documented by Elizabeth Colson. Although the party was clearly secular, it transformed participants into a community honoring their common characteristic, age (1977).

Most introductory textbooks in anthropology divide religious ritual into rites of passage and rites of intensification. Rites of passage mark transition points in the lives of individuals—for example, birth, puberty, marriage, and death. Rites of intensification occur during a crisis for a group and are thus more important in maintaining group equilibrium and solidarity. They are typically associated with natural phenomena, such as seasonal changes or a lack of rain, but other events, such as impending warfare, could also trigger a rite of intensification. Whatever precipitates the crisis, there is need of a ritual to lessen the anxiety that is felt by the group.

Although the division of rituals into this twofold scheme is useful, it does not adequately represent the variety of ritual occurring in the world's cultures. Wallace, for example, has outlined five major categories of ritual (1966: 107–66):

1. *Technological rituals*, designed to control nature for the purpose of human exploitation, comprise three subdivisions:

   a. Divination rites, which help predict the future and gain hidden information

   b. Rites of intensification, designed to help obtain food and alcohol

   c. Protective rites, aimed at coping with the uncertainty of nature (for example, stormy seas, floods, crop disease, and bad luck)

2. *Therapy and antitherapy rituals* are designed to control human health. Curative rites exemplify therapy rituals; witchcraft and sorcery, antitherapy.

3. *Ideological rituals*, according to Wallace, are "intended to control, in a conservative way, the behavior, the mood, the sentiments and values of groups for the sake of the community as a whole." They consist of four subcategories:

   a. Rites of passage, which deal with role change and geographic movement (for example, marriages)

   b. Rites of intensification, to ensure that people adhere to values and customs (for example, Sunday church service)

   c. Taboos (ritual avoidances), courtesies (positive actions), and other arbitrary ceremonial obligations, which regulate human behavior

   d. Rites of rebellion, which provide a form of "ritualized catharsis" that contributes to order and stability by allowing people to vent their frustrations

4. *Salvation rituals* aim at repairing damaged self-esteem and other forms of impaired identity. Wallace sees three common subdivisions in this category:

   a. Possession, in which an individual's identity is altered by the presence of an alien spirit that occupies the body (exorcism is the usual treatment)

   b. Ritual encouragement of an individual to accept an alternate identity, a process similar to the ritual procedure shamans undergo upon assuming a shamanic role

   c. The mystic experience—loss of personal identity by abandoning the old self and achieving salvation by identifying with a sacred being

5. *Revitalization rituals* are aimed at what can be described as an identity crisis of an entire community. The revitalization movement may be seen as a religious movement (a ritual) that, through the help of a prophet, strives to create a better culture.

Regardless of the typological system used (and anthropologists have proposed others in addition to Wallace's), in practice the various types of ritual frequently overlap and may change over time.

It is similarly difficult to pinpoint the meaning or significance of ritual, particularly for all participants. This may vary between cultures, over time, and even between individuals in a given setting. Fiona Bowie writes (2000: 154–55):

> Reactions to ritual acts cannot be predetermined. Regular attendance at a place of worship, for instance, may reveal a wide range of possible individual responses to a liturgy, from boredom, anger, and frustration to elevation, joy, the intensity of mystical communion, and a sense of unity with fellow worshipers. The individual may inwardly assent to or dissent from the ritual process. Commentators often stress the formulaic aspect of ritual—a ritual is not simply a spontaneous event created by an individual on the spur of the moment. What, however, about the family burial of a pet rabbit? Spontaneous prayers and actions, and accumulation of symbols (a flower, a memorial, a tree planted), may dignify the committal of the deceased animal.

There is no reason to assume that the multiple experiences of ritual felt by people in the industrialized West are any less a part of ritual participation than those of people in less developed parts of the world.

Some contemporary anthropologists have found it fruitful to compare ritual to theater or drama and to interpret ritual as a kind of cultural performance. It is intriguing to consider the possible parallels between ritual and other forms of enactment, including prescribed physical movements and actions, scripted communication, the use of special costumes or props, and the demarcation of sacred space as a kind of stage. Outwardly, the similarities between ritual and theater may appear strong, but the differences become clearer if one considers the goals and internal experiences of participants. "Participants in ritual may be 'acting,' but they are not necessarily 'just pretending'" (Ibid.: 159). Taking part in a ritual can have consequences for participants. For example, some rites of passage deliver an individual into a new stage of life, with new rights, responsibilities, and privileges.

Like other aspects of culture, ritual changes over time. In the contemporary West, there are myriad examples of new and revised ritual traditions, including national commemorations intended to intensify patriotism. The African-based holiday observance Kwanzaa was invented in 1966 by Maulana Karenga, a professor of black studies. Originally intended as a substitute for the European-based customs of the Christmas season, Kwanzaa has grown in acceptance and popularity among diverse communities of Americans. Feminist and New Age movements have experimented with the creation of new forms of ritual expression, often drawing upon participants' own interpretations of non-Western religions and myths. These experiments have resulted in various self-help guides to creating one's own rituals, as well as programs such as those designed to take high school students on rites of passage modeled after the vision quests of Native North Americans. Such borrowing has been controversial, and some Native American groups have begun to protest the use of their myths and rituals by outsiders, however well intentioned. Catherine Bell writes,

> The ubiquitous dynamics of ritual appropriation are historically complex and politically charged, especially when socially or politically dominant groups appear to be mining the cultural traditions of the less powerful, taking the images they want and, by placing them in very new contexts, altering their meanings in ways that may sever these images from their own people. (1997: 240)

Whether we consider long-standing, highly formalized sacred rituals or the more inventive attempts to enact values in a ritual way, it is clear that ritual serves two functions. Ritual teaches participants—as well as anthropological observers—about the social arrangements and values of a community yet also helps construct and create those very arrangements and values.

In the six articles in this chapter, we encounter a range of rituals and possible interpretations. Building upon the seminal work of early-twentieth-century anthropologist Arnold van Gennep, Victor W. Turner scrutinizes one phase of rites of passage as they are practiced around the world. The works of both Van Gennep and Turner have been highly influential in anthropology, and their focus upon rites of passage has undoubtedly contributed to the popularity of that phrase among the general public.

While Van Gennep and Turner emphasized the structure and process of rituals, Michael Atwood Mason's article documents a Santería initiation with an emphasis on bodily experience.

Continuing in the intellectual vein of Victor Turner, Barbara G. Myerhoff's analysis of Huichol rituals explores how myth and symbolism create a sacred realm distant from everyday reality.

In the fourth article, Roy A. Rappaport takes a very different approach, emphasizing material and environmental explanations for ritual.

Thomas J. Csordas's article compares rituals that respond to abortions, as carried out in the Charismatic Renewal movement in North America and in Japan. Csordas is particularly interested in how ritual "works" and in the construction of culture-specific emotions and disorders.

In the final article, Horace Miner examines the body rituals of the Nacirema, a North American group that devotes a considerable portion of the day to ritual activity.

References

Bell, Catherine
   1997   *Ritual: Perspectives and Dimensions.* Oxford: Oxford University Press.

Bowie, Fiona
   2000   *The Anthropology of Religion: An Introduction.* Oxford: Blackwell.

Colson, Elizabeth
   1977   "The Least Common Denominator." In S. F. Moore and B. G. Myerhoff, eds., *Secular Ritual.* Assen, Netherlands: Van Gorcum, pp. 189–98.

Howells, William
   1962   *The Heathens.* Garden City, N.Y.: Doubleday.

Karenga, Maulana
   1988   *The African-American Holiday of Kwanzaa: A Celebration of Family, Community, and Culture.* Los Angeles: University of Sankore Press.

Moore, Sally F., and Barbara G. Myerhoff, eds.
   1977   *Secular Ritual.* Assen, Netherlands: Van Gorcum.

Wallace, Anthony F. C.
   1966   *Religion: An Anthropological View.* New York: Random House.

12

Betwixt and Between: The Liminal Period in *Rites de Passage*

Victor W. Turner

The following selection could not have been written were it not for the seminal writing on ritual by the French anthropologist Arnold van Gennep (1873–1957). Van Gennep is recognized by scholars as the first anthropologist to study the significance of rituals accompanying the transitional stages in a person's life—birth, puberty, marriage, and death. Ever since the publication of Les Rites de Passage *in 1909, the phrase "rites of passage" has become part and parcel of anthropological literature. Van Gennep saw in human rituals three successive but separate stages: separation, margin, and aggregation. In the following selection, Victor Turner singles out the marginal, or liminal, period for examination. The liminal stage in rites of passage is when the initiates are removed and typically secluded from the rest of society—in effect, they become invisible, or, as in the title of this article, "betwixt and between." It is Turner's belief that the neophyte at the liminal stage has nothing—no status, property rank, or kinship position. He describes this condition as one of "sacred poverty." Turner concludes his article with an invitation to researchers of ritual to concentrate their efforts on the marginal stage, believing that this is where the basic building blocks of culture are exposed and therefore open for cross-cultural comparison. Victor Turner taught at Cornell and the University of Chicago. His major field research was done in Uganda, Zambia, and Mexico.*

In this paper, I wish to consider some of the sociocultural properties of the "liminal period" in that class of rituals which Arnold van Gennep has definitively characterized as *"rites de passage."* If our basic model of society is that of a "structure of positions," we must regard the period of margin or "liminality" as an interstructural situation. I shall consider, notably in the case of initiation rites, some of the main features of instruction among the simpler societies. I shall also take note of certain symbolic themes that concretely express indigenous concepts about the nature of "interstructural" human beings.

Rites de passage are found in all societies but tend to reach their maximal expression in small-scale, relatively stable and cyclical societies, where change is bound up with biological and meteorological rhythms and recurrences rather than with technological innovations. Such rites indicate and constitute transitions between states. By "state" I mean here "a relatively fixed or stable condition" and would include in its

Reprinted from Victor W. Turner, "Betwixt and Between: The Liminal Period in Rites de Passages," *The Proceedings of the New American Ethnological Society (1964), Symposium on New Approaches to the Study of Religion, pp. 4–20.*

meaning such social constancies as legal status, profession, office or calling, rank or degree. I hold it to designate also the condition of a person as determined by his culturally recognized degree of maturation as when one speaks of "the married or single state" or the "state of infancy." The term "state" may also be applied to ecological conditions, or to the physical, mental or emotional condition in which a person or group may be found at a particular time. A man may thus be in a state of good or bad health; a society in a state of war or peace or a state of famine or of plenty. State, in short, is a more inclusive concept than status or office and refers to any type of stable or recurrent condition that is culturally recognized. One may, I suppose, also talk about "a state of transition," since J. S. Mill has, after all, written of "a state of progressive movement," but I prefer to regard transition as a process, a becoming, and in the case of *rites de passage* even a transformation—here an apt analogy would be water in process of being heated to boiling point, or a pupa changing from grub to moth. In any case, a transition has different cultural properties from those of a state, as I hope to show presently.

Van Gennep himself defined *"rites de passage"* as "rites which accompany every change of place, state, social position and age." To point up the contrast between "state" and "transition," I employ "state" to include all his other terms. Van Gennep has shown that all rites of transition are marked by three phases: separation, margin (or *limen*), and aggregation. The first phase of separation comprises symbolic behavior signifying the detachment of the individual or group either from an earlier fixed point in the social structure or a set of cultural conditions (a "state"); during the intervening liminal period, the state of the ritual subject (the "passenger") is ambiguous; he passes through a realm that has few or none of the attributes of the past or coming state; in the third phase the passage is consummated. The ritual subject, individual or corporate, is in a stable state once more and, by virtue of this, has rights and obligations of a clearly defined and "structural" type, and is expected to behave in accordance with certain customary norms and ethical standards. The most prominent type of *rites de passage* tends to accompany what Lloyd Warner (1959, 303) has called "the movement of a man through his lifetime, from a fixed placental placement within his mother's womb

to his death and ultimate fixed point of his tombstone and final containment in his grave as a dead organism—punctuated by a number of critical moments of transition which all societies ritualize and publicly mark with suitable observances to impress the significance of the individual and the group on living members of the community. These are the important times of birth, puberty, marriage, and death." However, as Van Gennep, Henri Junod, and others have shown, *rites de passage* are not confined to culturally defined life-crises but may accompany any change from one state to another, as when a whole tribe goes to war, or when it attests to the passage from scarcity to plenty by performing a first-fruits or a harvest festival. *Rites de passage*, too, are not restricted, sociologically speaking, to movements between ascribed statuses. They also concern entry into a new achieved status, whether this be a political office or membership of an exclusive club or secret society. They may admit persons into membership of a religious group where such a group does not include the whole society, or qualify them for the official duties of the cult, sometimes in a graded series of rites.

Since the main problem of this study is the nature and characteristics of transition in relatively stable societies, I shall focus attention on *rites de passage* that tend to have well-developed liminal periods. On the whole, initiation rites, whether into social maturity or cult membership, best exemplify transition, since they have well-marked and protracted marginal or liminal phases. I shall pay only brief heed here to rites of separation and aggregation, since these are more closely implicated in social structure than rites of liminality. Liminality during initiation is, therefore, the primary datum of this study, though I will draw on other aspects of passage ritual where the argument demands this. I may state here, partly as an aside, that I consider the term "ritual" to be more fittingly applied to forms of religious behavior associated with social transitions, while the term "ceremony" has a closer bearing on religious behavior associated with social states, where politico-legal institutions also have greater importance. Ritual is transformative, ceremony confirmatory.

The subject of passage ritual is, in the liminal period, structurally, if not physically, "invisible." As members of society, most of us see only what we expect to see, and what we expect to see is what we are conditioned to see when we have learned the definitions and classifications of our culture. A society's secular definitions do not allow for the existence of a not-boy-not-man, which is what a novice in a male puberty rite is (if he can be said to be anything). A set of essentially religious definitions co-exist with these which do set out to define the structurally indefinable "transitional-being." The transitional-being or "liminal *persona*" is defined by a name and by a set of symbols. The same name is very frequently employed to designate those who are being initiated into very different states of life. For example, among the Ndembu of Zambia the name *mwadi* may mean various things: it may stand for "a boy novice in circumcision rites," or "a chief-designate undergoing his installation rites," or, yet again, "the first or ritual wife" who has important ritual duties in the domestic family. Our own terms "initiate" and "neophyte" have a similar breadth of reference. It would seem from this that emphasis tends to be laid on the transition itself, rather than on the particular states between which it is taking place.

The symbolism attached to and surrounding the liminal *persona* is complex and bizarre. Much of it is modeled on human biological processes, which are conceived to be what Lévi-Strauss might call "isomorphic" with structural and cultural processes. They give an outward and visible form to an inward and conceptual process. The structural "invisibility" of liminal *personae* has a twofold character. They are at once no longer classified and not yet classified. In so far as they are no longer classified, the symbols that represent them are, in many societies, drawn from the biology of death, decomposition, catabolism, and other physical processes that have a negative tinge, such as menstruation (frequently regarded as the absence or loss of a fetus). Thus, in some boys' initiations, newly circumcised boys are explicitly likened to menstruating women. Insofar as a neophyte is structurally "dead," he or she may be treated, for a long or short period, as a corpse is customarily treated in his or her society. See Stobaeus's quotation, probably from a lost work of Plutarch, "initiation and death correspond word for word and thing for thing." The neophyte may be buried, forced to lie motionless in the posture and direction of customary burial, may be stained black, or may be forced to live for a while in the company of masked and monstrous mummers representing, *inter alia*, the dead, or

worse still, the un-dead. The metaphor of dissolution is often applied to neophytes; they are allowed to go filthy and identified with the earth, the generalized matter into which every specific individual is rendered down. Particular form here becomes general matter; often their very names are taken from them and each is called solely by the generic term for "neophyte" or "initiand." (This useful neologism is employed by many modern anthropologists.)

The other aspect, that they are not yet classified, is often expressed in symbols modeled on processes of gestation and parturition. The neophytes are likened to or treated as embryos, newborn infants, or sucklings by symbolic means which vary from culture to culture. I shall return to this theme presently.

The essential feature of these symbolizations is that the neophytes are neither living nor dead from one aspect, and both living and dead from another. Their condition is one of ambiguity and paradox, a confusion of all the customary categories. Jakob Boehme, the German mystic whose obscure writings gave Hegel his celebrated dialectical "triad," liked to say that "In Yea and Nay all things consist." Liminality may perhaps be regarded as the Nay to all positive structural assertions, but as in some sense the source of them all, and, more than that, as a realm of pure possibility whence novel configurations of ideas and relations may arise. I will not pursue this point here but, after all, Plato, a speculative philosopher, if there ever was one, did acknowledge his philosophical debt to the teachings of the Eleusinian and Orphic initiations of Attica. We have no way of knowing whether primitive initiations merely conserved lore. Perhaps they also generated new thought and new custom.

Dr. Mary Douglas, of University College, London, has recently advanced (in a magnificent book *Purity and Danger* [1966]) the very interesting and illuminating view that the concept of pollution "is a reaction to protect cherished principles and categories from contradiction." She holds that, in effect, what is unclear and contradictory (from the perspective of social definition) tends to be regarded as (ritually) unclean. The unclear is the unclean: e.g., she examines the prohibitions on eating certain animals and crustaceans in Leviticus in the light of this hypothesis (these being creatures that cannot be unambiguously classified in terms of traditional criteria). From this standpoint, one would expect to find that transitional beings are particularly polluting, since they are neither one thing nor another; or may be both; or neither here nor there; or may even be nowhere (in terms of any recognized cultural topography), and are at the very least "betwixt and between" all the recognized fixed points in space-time of structural classification. In fact, in confirmation of Dr. Douglas's hypothesis, liminal *personae* nearly always and everywhere are regarded as polluting to those who have never been, so to speak, "inoculated" against them, through having been themselves initiated into the same state. I think that we may perhaps usefully discriminate here between the statics and dynamics of pollution situations. In other words, we may have to distinguish between pollution notions which concern states that have been ambiguously or contradictorily defined, and those which derive from ritualized transitions between states. In the first case, we are dealing with what has been defectively defined or ordered, in the second with what cannot be defined in static terms. We are not dealing with structural contradictions when we discuss liminality, but with the essentially unstructured (which is at once destructured and prestructured) and often the people themselves see this in terms of bringing neophytes into close connection with deity or with superhuman power, with what is, in fact, often regarded as the unbounded, the infinite, the limitless. Since neophytes are not only structurally "invisible" (though physically visible) and ritually polluting, they are very commonly secluded, partially or completely, from the realm of culturally defined and ordered states and statuses. Often the indigenous term for the liminal period is, as among Ndembu, the locative form of a noun meaning "seclusion site" *(kunkunka, kung'ula)*. The neophytes are sometimes said to "be in another place." They have physical but not social "reality," hence they have to be hidden, since it is a paradox, a scandal, to see what ought not to be there! Where they are not removed to a sacred place of concealment they are often disguised, in masks or grotesque costumes or striped with white, red, or black clay, and the like.

In societies dominantly structured by kinship institutions, sex distinctions have great structural importance. Patrilineal and matrilineal moieties and clans, rules of exogamy, and the like, rest and are built up on these distinctions. It is consistent with this to find that in liminal situations (in kinship-dominated societies) neophytes are sometimes treated or symbolically represented as being neither male nor female. Alternatively, they may be symbolically assigned characteristics of both sexes, irrespective of their biological sex. (Bruno Bettelheim [1954] has collected much illustrative material on this point from initiation rites.) They are symbolically either sexless or bisexual and may be regarded as a kind of human *prima materia*—as undifferentiated raw material. It was perhaps from the rites of the Hellenic mystery religions that Plato derived his notion expressed in his *Symposium* that the first humans were androgynes. If the liminal period is seen as an interstructural phase in social dynamics, the symbolism both of androgyny and sexlessness immediately becomes intelligible in sociological terms without the need to import psychological (and especially depth-psychological) explanations. Since sex distinctions are important components of structural status, in a structureless realm they do not apply.

A further structurally negative characteristic of transitional beings is that they *have* nothing. They have no status, property, insignia, secular clothing, rank, kinship position, nothing to demarcate them structurally from their fellows. Their condition is indeed the very prototype of sacred poverty. Rights over property, goods, and services inhere in positions in the politico-jural structure. Since they do not occupy such positions, neophytes exercise no such rights. In the words of King Lear they represent "naked unaccommodated man."

I have no time to analyze other symbolic themes that express these attributes of "structural invisibility," ambiguity and neutrality. I want now to draw attention to certain positive aspects of liminality. Already we have noted how certain liminal processes are regarded as analogous to those of gestation, parturition, and suckling. Undoing, dissolution, decomposition are accompanied by processes of growth, transformation, and the reformulation of old elements in new patterns. It is interesting to note how, by the principle of the economy (or parsimony) of symbolic reference, logically antithetical processes of death and growth may be represented by the same tokens, for example, by huts and tunnels that are at once tombs and wombs, by lunar symbolism (for the same moon waxes and wanes), by snake symbolism (for the snake appears to die, but only to shed its old skin and appear in a new one), by bear symbolism (for the bear "dies" in autumn and is "reborn" in spring), by nakedness (which is at once the mark of a newborn infant and a corpse prepared for burial), and by innumerable other symbolic formations and actions. This coincidence of opposite processes and notions in a single representation characterizes the peculiar unity of the liminal: that which is neither this nor that, and yet is both.

I have spoken of the interstructural character of the liminal. However, between neophytes and their instructors (where these exist), and in connecting neophytes with one another, there exists a set of relations that compose a "social structure" of highly specific type. It is a structure of a very simple kind: between instructors and neophytes there is often complete authority and complete submission; among neophytes there is often complete equality. Between incumbents of positions in secular politico-jural systems there exist intricate and situationally shifting networks of rights and duties proportioned to their rank, status, and corporate affiliation. There are many different kinds of privileges and obligations, many degrees of superordination and subordination. In the liminal period such distinctions and gradations tend to be eliminated. Nevertheless, it must be understood that the authority of the elders over the neophytes is not based on legal sanctions; it is in a sense the personification of the self-evident authority of tradition. The authority of the elders is absolute, because it represents the absolute, the axiomatic values of society in which are expressed the "common good" and the common interest. The essence of the complete obedience of the neophytes is to submit to the elders but only in so far as they are in charge, so to speak, of the common good and represent in their persons the total community. That the authority in question is really quintessential tradition emerges clearly in societies where initiations are not collective but individual and where there are no instructors or *gurus*. For example, Omaha boys, like other North American Indians, go alone into the wilderness to fast and pray (Hocart, 1952: 160). This solitude is liminal between boyhood and manhood. If they dream that they receive a woman's burden-strap, they feel compelled to dress and live henceforth in every way as women. Such men are known as *mixuga*. The authority of such a dream in such a situation is absolute. Alice Cummingham Fletcher tells of one Omaha who had been forced in this way

to live as a woman, but whose natural inclinations led him to rear a family and to go on the warpath. Here the *mixuga* was not an invert but a man bound by the authority of tribal beliefs and values. Among many Plains Indians, boys on their lonely Vision Quest inflicted ordeals and tests on themselves that amounted to tortures. These again were not basically self-tortures inflicted by a masochistic temperament but due to obedience to the authority of tradition in the liminal situation—a type of situation in which there is no room for secular compromise, evasion, manipulation, casuistry, and maneuver in the field of custom, rule, and norm. Here again a cultural explanation seems preferable to a psychological one. A normal man acts abnormally because he is obedient to tribal tradition, not out of disobedience to it. He does not evade but fulfills his duties as a citizen.

If complete obedience characterizes the relationship of neophyte to elder, complete equality usually characterizes the relationship of neophyte to neophyte, where the rites are collective. This comradeship must be distinguished from brotherhood or sibling relationship, since in the latter there is always the inequality of older and younger, which often achieves linguistic representation and may be maintained by legal sanctions. The liminal group is a community or comity of comrades and not a structure of hierarchically arrayed positions. This comradeship transcends distinctions of rank, age, kinship position, and, in some kinds of cultic group, even of sex. Much of the behavior recorded by ethnographers in seclusion situations falls under the principle: "Each for all, and all for each." Among the Ndembu of Zambia, for example, all food brought for novices in circumcision seclusion by their mothers is shared equally among them. No special favors are bestowed on the sons of chiefs or headmen. Any food acquired by novices in the bush is taken by the elders and apportioned among the group. Deep friendships between novices are encouraged, and they sleep around lodge fires in clusters of four or five particular comrades. However, all are supposed to be linked by special ties which persist after the rites are over, even into old age. This friendship, known as *wubwambu* (from a term meaning "breast") or *wulunda*, enables a man to claim privileges of hospitality of a far-reaching kind. I have no need here to dwell on the lifelong ties that are held to bind in close friendship those initiated into the same age-set in East African Nilo-Hamitic and Bantu societies, into the same fraternity or sorority on an American campus, or into the same class in a naval or military academy in Western Europe.

This comradeship, with its familiarity, ease and, I would add, mutual outspokenness, is once more the product of interstructural liminality, with its scarcity of jurally sanctioned relationships and its emphasis on axiomatic values expressive of the common weal. People can "be themselves," it is frequently said, when they are not acting institutionalized roles. Roles, too, carry responsibilities and in the liminal situation the main burden of responsibility is borne by the elders, leaving the neophytes free to develop interpersonal relationships as they will. They confront one another, as it were, integrally and not in compartmentalized fashion as actors of roles.

The passivity of neophytes to their instructors, their malleability, which is increased by submission to ordeal, their reduction to a uniform condition, are signs of the process whereby they are ground down to be fashioned anew and endowed with additional powers to cope with their new station in life. Dr. Richards, in her superb study of Bemba girls' puberty rites, *Chisungu*, has told us that Bemba speak of "growing a girl" when they mean initiating her (1956: 121). This term "to grow" well expresses how many peoples think of transition rites. We are inclined, as sociologists, to reify our abstractions (it is indeed a device which helps us to understand many kinds of social interconnection) and to talk about persons "moving through structural positions in a hierarchical frame" and the like. Not so the Bemba and the Shilluk of the Sudan who see the status or condition embodied or incarnate, if you like, *in* the person. To "grow" a girl into a woman is to effect an ontological transformation; it is not merely to convey an unchanging substance from one position to another by a quasi-mechanical force. Howitt saw Kuringals in Australia and I have seen Ndembu in Africa drive away grown-up men before a circumcision ceremony because they had not been initiated. Among Ndembu, men were also chased off because they had only been circumcised at the Mission Hospital and had not undergone the full bush seclusion according to the orthodox Ndembu rite. These biologically mature men had not been "made men" by the proper ritual procedures. It is the ritual and the esoteric teaching which grows girls and makes men. It is the ritual, too, which among Shilluk makes a

prince into a king, or, among Luvale, a cultivator into a hunter. The arcane knowledge or "*gnosis*" obtained in the liminal period is felt to change the inmost nature of the neophyte, impressing him, as a seal impresses wax, with the characteristics of his new state. It is not a mere acquisition of knowledge, but a change in being. His apparent passivity is revealed as an absorption of powers which will become active after his social status has been redefined in the aggregation rites.

The structural simplicity of the liminal situation in many initiations is offset by its cultural complexity. I can touch on only one aspect of this vast subject matter here and raise three problems in connection with it. This aspect is the vital one of the communication of the *sacra*, the heart of the liminal matter.

Jane Harrison has shown that in the Greek Eleusinian and Orphic mysteries this communication of the *sacra* has three main components (1903: 144–60). By and large, this threefold classification holds good for initiation rites all over the world. *Sacra* may be communicated as: (1) exhibitions, "what is shown"; (2) actions, "what is done"; and (3) instructions, "what is said."

"Exhibitions" would include evocatory instruments or sacred articles, such as relics of deities, heroes or ancestors, aboriginal *churingas*, sacred drums or other musical instruments, the contents of Amerindian medicine bundles, and the fan, cist and tympanum of Greek and Near Eastern mystery cults. In the Lesser Eleusinian Mysteries of Athens, *sacra* consisted of a bone, top, ball, tambourine, apples, mirror, fan, and woolly fleece. Other *sacra* include masks, images, figurines, and effigies; the pottery emblem (*mbusa*) of the Bemba would belong to this class. In some kinds of initiation, as for example the initiation into the shaman-diviner's profession among the Saora of Middle India, described by Verrier Elwin (1955), pictures and icons representing the journeys of the dead or the adventures of supernatural beings may be shown to the initiands. A striking feature of such sacred articles is often their formal simplicity. It is their interpretation which is complex, not their outward form.

Among the "instructions" received by neophytes may be reckoned such matters as the revelation of the real, but secularly secret, names of the deities or spirits believed to preside over the rites—a very frequent procedure in African cultic or secret associations

(Turner, 1962: 36). They are also taught the main outlines of the theogony, cosmogony, and mythical history of their societies or cult, usually with reference to the *sacra* exhibited. Great importance is attached to keeping secret the nature of the *sacra*, the formulas chanted and instructions given about them. These constitute the crux of liminality, for while instruction is also given in ethical and social obligations, in law and in kinship rules, and in technology to fit neophytes for the duties of future office, no interdiction is placed on knowledge thus imparted since it tends to be current among uninitiated persons also.

I want to take up three problems in considering the communication of *sacra*. The first concerns their frequent disproportion, the second their monstrousness, and the third their mystery.

When one examines the masks, costumes, figurines, and such displayed in initiation situations, one is often struck, as I have been when observing Ndembu masks in circumcision and funerary rites, by the way in which certain natural and cultural features are represented as disproportionately large or small. A head, nose, or phallus, a hoe, bow, or meal mortar are represented as huge or tiny by comparison with other features of their context which retain their normal size. (For a good example of this, see "The Man Without Arms" in *Chisungu* [Richards, 1956: 211], a figurine of a lazy man with an enormous penis but no arms.) Sometimes things retain their customary shapes but are portrayed in unusual colors. What is the point of this exaggeration amounting sometimes to caricature? It seems to me that to enlarge or diminish or discolor in this way is a primordial mode of abstraction. The outstandingly exaggerated feature is made into an object of reflection. Usually it is not a univocal symbol that is thus represented but a multivocal one, a semantic molecule with many components. One example is the Bemba pottery emblem *Coshi wa ng'oma*, "The Nursing Mother," described by Audrey Richards in *Chisungu*. This is a clay figurine, nine inches high, of an exaggeratedly pregnant mother shown carrying four babies at the same time, one at her breast and three at her back. To this figurine is attached a riddling song:

My mother deceived me!
Coshi wa ng'oma!
So you have deceived me;
I have become pregnant again.

Bemba women interpreted this to Richards as follows:

Coshi wa ng'oma was a midwife of legendary fame and is merely addressed in this song. The girl complains because her mother told her to wean her first child too soon so that it died; or alternatively, told her that she would take the first child if her daughter had a second one. But she was tricking her and now the girl has two babies to look after. The moral stressed is the duty of refusing intercourse with the husband before the baby is weaned, i.e., at the second or third year. This is a common Bemba practice.

In the figurine the exaggerated features are the number of children carried at once by the woman and her enormously distended belly. Coupled with the song, it encourages the novice to ponder upon two relationships vital to her, those with her mother and her husband. Unless the novice observes the Bemba weaning custom, her mother's desire for grandchildren to increase her matrilineage and her husband's desire for renewed sexual intercourse will between them actually destroy and not increase her offspring. Underlying this is the deeper moral that to abide by tribal custom and not to sin against it either by excess or defect is to live satisfactorily. Even to please those one loves may be to invite calamity, if such compliance defies the immemorial wisdom of the elders embodied in the *mbusa*. This wisdom is vouched for by the mythical and archetypal midwife *Coshi wa ng'oma*.

If the exaggeration of single features is not irrational but thought-provoking, the same may also be said about the representation of monsters. Earlier writers—such as J. A. McCulloch (1913) in his article on "Monsters" in *Hastings Encyclopaedia of Religion and Ethics*—are inclined to regard bizarre and monstrous masks and figures, such as frequently appear in the liminal period of initiations, as the product of "hallucinations, night-terrors and dreams." McCulloch goes on to argue that "as man drew little distinction (in primitive society) between himself and animals, as he thought that transformation from one to the other was possible, so he easily ran human and animal together. This in part accounts for animal-headed gods or animal-gods with human heads." My own view is the opposite one: that monsters are manufactured precisely to teach neophytes to distinguish clearly between the different factors of reality, as it is conceived in their culture. Here, I think, William James's so-called law of dissociation may help us to clarify the problem of monsters. It may be stated as follows: when *a* and *b* occurred together as parts of the same total object, without being discriminated, the occurrence of one of these, *a*, in a new combination *ax*, favors the discrimination of *a*, *b*, and *x* from one another. As James himself put it, "What is associated now with one thing and now with another, tends to become dissociated from either, and to grow into an object of abstract contemplation by the mind. One might call this the law of dissociation by varying concomitants" (1918: 506).

From this standpoint, much of the grotesqueness and monstrosity of liminal *sacra* may be seen to be aimed not so much at terrorizing or bemusing neophytes into submission or out of their wits as at making them vividly and rapidly aware of what may be called the "factors" of their culture. I have myself seen Ndembu and Luvale masks that combine features of both sexes, have both animal and human attributes, and unite in a single representation human characteristics with those of the natural landscape. One *ikishi* mask is partly human and partly represents a grassy plain. Elements are withdrawn from their usual settings and combined with one another in a totally unique configuration, the monster or dragon. Monsters startle neophytes into thinking about objects, persons, relationships, and features of their environment they have hitherto taken for granted.

In discussing the structural aspect of liminality, I mentioned how neophytes are withdrawn from their structural positions and consequently from the values, norms, sentiments, and techniques associated with those positions. They are also divested of their previous habits of thought, feeling, and action. During the liminal period, neophytes are alternately forced and encouraged to think about their society, their cosmos, and the powers that generate and sustain them. Liminality may be partly described as a stage of reflection. In it those ideas, sentiments, and facts that had been hitherto for the neophytes bound up in configurations and accepted unthinkingly are, as it were, resolved into their constituents. These constituents are isolated and made into objects of reflection for the neophytes by such processes as componental exaggeration and dissociation by varying concomitants. The communication of *sacra* and other

forms of esoteric instruction really involves three processes, though these should not be regarded as in series but as in parallel. The first is the reduction of culture into recognized components or factors; the second is their recombination in fantastic or monstrous patterns and shapes; and the third is their recombination in ways that make sense with regard to the new state and status that the neophytes will enter.

The second process, monster- or fantasy-making, focuses attention on the components of the masks and effigies, which are so radically ill-assorted that they stand out and can be thought about. The monstrosity of the configuration throws its elements into relief. Put a man's head on a lion's body and you think about the human head in the abstract. Perhaps it becomes for you, as a member of a given culture and with the appropriate guidance, an emblem of chieftainship; or it may be explained as representing the soul as against the body; or intellect as contrasted with brute force, or innumerable other things. There could be less encouragement to reflect on heads and headship if that same head were firmly ensconced on its familiar, its all too familiar, human body. The man-lion monster also encourages the observer to think about lions, their habits, qualities, metaphorical properties, religious significance, and so on. More important than these, the relation between man and lion, empirical and metaphorical, may be speculated upon, and new ideas developed on this topic. Liminality here breaks, as it were, the cake of custom and enfranchises speculation. That is why I earlier mentioned Plato's self-confessed debt to the Greek mysteries. Liminality is the realm of primitive hypothesis, where there is a certain freedom to juggle with the factors of existence. As in the works of Rabelais, there is a promiscuous intermingling and juxtaposing of the categories of event, experience, and knowledge, with a pedagogic intention.

But this liberty has fairly narrow limits. The neophytes return to secular society with more alert faculties perhaps and enhanced knowledge of how things work, but they have to become once more subject to custom and law. Like the Bemba girl I mentioned earlier, they are shown that ways of acting and thinking alternative to those laid down by the deities or ancestors are ultimately unworkable and may have disastrous consequences.

Moreover, in initiation, there are usually held to be certain axiomatic principles of construction, and certain basic building blocks that make up the cosmos and into whose nature no neophyte may inquire. Certain *sacra*, usually exhibited in the most arcane episodes of the liminal period, represent or may be interpreted in terms of these axiomatic principles and primordial constituents. Perhaps we may call these *sacerrima*, "most sacred things." Sometimes they are interpreted by a myth about the world-making activities of supernatural beings "at the beginning of things." Myths may be completely absent, however, as in the case of the Ndembu "mystery of the three rivers." . . . This mystery (*mpang'u*) is exhibited at circumcision and funerary cult association rites. Three trenches are dug in a consecrated site and filled respectively with white, red, and black water. These "rivers" are said to "flow from Nzambi," the High God. The instructors tell the neophytes, partly in riddling songs and partly in direct terms, what each river signifies. Each "river" is a multivocal symbol with a fan of referents ranging from life values, ethical ideas, and social norms, to grossly physiological processes and phenomena. They seem to be regarded as powers which, in varying combination, underlie or even constitute what Ndembu conceive to be reality. In no other context is the interpretation of whiteness, redness, and blackness so full; and nowhere else is such a close analogy drawn, even identity made, between these rivers and bodily fluids and emissions: whiteness = semen, milk; redness = menstrual blood, the blood of birth, blood shed by a weapon, etc.; blackness = feces, certain products of bodily decay, etc. This use of an aspect of human physiology as a model for social, cosmic, and religious ideas and processes is a variant of a widely distributed initiation theme: that the human body is a microcosm of the universe. The body may be pictured as androgynous, as male or female, or in terms of one or other of its developmental stages, as child, mature adult, and elder. On the other hand, as in the Ndembu case, certain of its properties may be abstracted. Whatever the mode of representation, the body is regarded as a sort of symbolic template for the communication of *gnosis*, mystical knowledge about the nature of things and how they came to be what they are. The cosmos may in some cases be regarded as a vast human body; in other belief systems, visible parts of the body may be taken to portray invisible faculties such as reason, passion, wisdom and so on; in others again, the different parts of the social order are arrayed in terms of a human anatomical paradigm.

Whatever the precise mode of explaining reality by the body's attributes, *sacra* which illustrates this are always regarded as absolutely sacrosanct, as ultimate mysteries. We are here in the realm of what Warner (1959: 3–4) would call "nonrational or nonlogical symbols" which

> arise out of the basic individual and cultural assumptions, more often unconscious than not, from which most social action springs. They supply the solid core of mental and emotional life of each individual and group. This does not mean that they are irrational or maladaptive, or that man cannot often think in a reasonable way about them, but rather that they do not have their source in his rational processes. When they come into play, such factors as data, evidence, proof, and the facts and procedures of rational thought in action are apt to be secondary or unimportant.

The central cluster of nonlogical *sacra* is then the symbolic template of the whole system of beliefs and values in a given culture, its archetypal paradigm and ultimate measure. Neophytes shown these are often told that they are in the presence of forms established from the beginning of things. . . . I have used the metaphor of a seal or stamp in connection with the ontological character ascribed in many initiations to arcane knowledge. The term "archetype" denotes in Greek a master stamp or impress, and these *sacra*, presented with a numinous simplicity, stamp into the neophytes the basic assumptions of their culture. The neophytes are told also that they are being filled with mystical power by what they see and what they are told about it. According to the purpose of the initiation, this power confers on them capacities to undertake successfully the tasks of their new office, in this world or the next.

Thus, the communication of *sacra* both teaches the neophytes how to think with some degree of abstraction about their cultural milieu and gives them ultimate standards of reference. At the same time, it is believed to change their nature, transform them from one kind of human being into another. It intimately unites man and office. But for a variable while, there was an uncommitted man, an individual rather than a social *persona*, in a sacred community of individuals.

It is not only in the liminal period of initiations that the nakedness and vulnerability of the ritual subject receive symbolic stress. Let me quote from Hilda Kuper's description of the seclusion of the Swazi chief during the great *Incwala* ceremony. The *Incwala* is a national First-Fruits ritual, performed in the height of summer when the early crops ripen. The regiments of the Swazi nation assemble at the capital to celebrate its rites, "whereby the nation receives strength for the new year." The *Incwala* is at the same time "a play of kingship." The king's well-being is identified with that of the nation. Both require periodic ritual strengthening. Lunar symbolism is prominent in the rites, as we shall see, and the king, personifying the nation, during his seclusion represents the moon in transition between phases, neither waning nor waxing. Dr. Kuper, Professor Gluckman, and Professor Wilson have discussed the structural aspects of the *Incwala* which are clearly present in its rites of separation and aggregation. What we are about to examine are the interstructural aspects.

During his night and day of seclusion, the king, painted black, remains, says Dr. Kuper, "painted in blackness" and "in darkness"; he is unapproachable, dangerous to himself and others. He must cohabit that night with his first ritual wife (in a kind of "mystical marriage"—this ritual wife is, as it were, consecrated for such liminal situations).

> The entire population is also temporarily in a state of taboo and seclusion. Ordinary activities and behavior are suspended; sexual intercourse is prohibited, no one may sleep late the following morning, and when they get up they are not allowed to touch each other, to wash the body, to sit on mats, to poke anything into the ground, or even to scratch their hair. The children are scolded if they play and make merry. The sound of songs that has stirred the capital for nearly a month is abruptly stilled; it is the day of *bacisa* (cause to *hide*). The king remains secluded; . . . all day he sits naked on a lion skin in the ritual hut of the harem or in the sacred enclosure in the royal cattle byre. Men of his inner circle see that he breaks none of the taboos . . . on this day the identification of the people with the king is very marked. The spies (who see to it that the people respect the taboos) do not say, "You are sleeping late" or "You are scratching," but "You cause the king to sleep," "You scratch him (the king)"; etc. (Kuper, 1947: 219–220).

Other symbolic acts are performed which exemplify the "darkness" and "waxing and waning moon" themes, for example, the slaughtering of a black ox, the painting of the queen mother with a black mixture—she is compared again to a half-moon, while the king is a full moon, and both are in eclipse until the paint is washed off finally with doctored water, and the ritual subject "comes once again into lightness and normality."

In this short passage we have an embarrassment of symbolic riches. I will mention only a few themes that bear on the argument of this paper. Let us look at the king's position first. He is symbolically invisible, "black," a moon between phases. He is also under obedience to traditional rules, and "men of his inner circle" see that he keeps them. He is also "naked," divested of the trappings of his office. He remains apart from the scenes of his political action in a sanctuary or ritual hut. He is also, it would seem, identified with the earth which the people are forbidden to stab, lest the king be affected. He is "hidden." The king, in short, has been divested of all the outward attributes, the "accidents," of his kingship and is reduced to its substance, the "earth" and "darkness" from which the normal, structured order of the Swazi kingdom will be regenerated "in lightness."

In this betwixt-and-between period, in this fruitful darkness, king and people are closely identified. There is a mystical solidarity between them, which contrasts sharply with the hierarchical rank-dominated structure of ordinary Swazi life. It is only in darkness, silence, celibacy, in the absence of merriment and movement that the king and people can thus be one. For every normal action is involved in the rights and obligations of a structure that defines status and establishes social distance between men. Only in their Trappist sabbath of transition may the Swazi regenerate the social tissues torn by conflicts arising from distinctions of status and discrepant structural norms.

I end this study with an invitation to investigators of ritual to focus their attention on the phenomena and processes of mid-transition. It is these, I hold, that paradoxically expose the basic building blocks of culture just when we pass out of and before we re-enter the structural realm. In *sacerrima* and their interpretations we have categories of data that may usefully be handled by the new sophisticated techniques of cross-cultural comparison.

13

"I bow my head to the ground": Creating Bodily Experience Through Initiation

Michael Atwood Mason

According to Michael Atwood Mason, the author of the following selection, the religious system known as Santería is rooted in West African beliefs and practices, as brought to Cuba through the Atlantic slave trade. Since the 1940s, Cuban immigrants have introduced the religion to the United States, where it has flourished in large cities among Latinos, as well as some African- and Euro-Americans. Because of the historical experience of slavery and repression, African-derived religion in Cuba was long protected through secrecy, a practice continued in the United States today by some immigrants who want to assimilate into American society (Mason 2002:8–9). Santería recognizes a creator god or High God, who has placed the everyday workings of the universe and humans in the hands of divinities called orichas. *The rituals of Santería involve worshipping and making sacrifices to orichas. Practitioners may be involved at a variety of levels, from neophyte to priestess or priest.*

Mason's richly descriptive ethnographic study, extracted from a book-length work on Santería rituals, focuses on an American man as he goes through his first rites of initiation. The author is especially interested in the bodily experience of ritual, which in this case involves washing the head, taking part in an animal sacrifice, and bowing to the ground in respect. How does the initiate perceive, experience, and learn through the non-verbal enactment of the ritual? By using his body in specific ways, Mason argues, the initiate learns to be a part of the community. Mason's emphasis on bodily experience—what anthropologists call embodiment—is a significant addition to structural analyses of ritual, such as Van Gennep's tripartite model of rites of passage (see preceding article by Turner).

The author identifies vocabulary from Lucumí, the ritual dialect of the West-African language Yoruba, as (Lu.), and from Spanish as (Sp.). Fieldwork for the study was conducted in the 1990s.

Bright light shines from the next room, and music pours into the dark living room where a young Euro-American sits alone. As he waits, he watches the pattern of the blinking Christmas lights in his godmother's suburban Maryland home. A 1990 calendar advertises Botánica San Lázaro, which his godmother, Idaberta, owns and manages. George Carter knows that the songs honor the orichas that

From LIVING SANTERÍA: RITUALS AND EXPERIENCES IN AN AFRO-CUBAN RELIGION, *2002, pp. 27–42. Smithsonian Institution, Washington, D.C.*

constitute the pantheon of Santería;[1] his *padrinos* (Sp. godparents) are creating the sacred herbal water, *osain* (Lu.). Soon they will use it to cleanse him and baptize the divinities that he is to receive. He is separated because only the fully initiated can witness the making of the osain. As a new godchild of the same house, I sit with him and wait.

He is called into the room and kneels over a large basin in the middle of the floor. I too am called in and watch as the ceremony unfolds. He hangs his neck on the edge of the basin and water pours over his head. "Get his neck," says a voice from behind him; his godfather, José, splashes the liquid onto the man's neck and rubs vigorously. "Good." The osain flows through his hair and across his closed eyes. He is lifted up and sent into a nearby bathroom. Again he kneels; this time he is next to the bathtub. Again he closes his eyes, and again the osain is poured over his head; his godfather washes the back of his neck with soap and sings to the seat of his being, his head. The man is told to wash himself from head to toe with the osain and is left alone.

When he returns to the room, a cluster of objects stands in the middle of the floor. A cement head with cowrie shells for eyes, nose, and mouth sits in a small terracotta saucer, and next to it sits a smaller image that resembles it; these are Elegguá, the trickster, the lord of the crossroads and the ruler of destiny. Behind these stand a small, black iron cauldron; here is Ogún, the fierce and independent oricha of iron and warfare. With Ogún lives his brother Ochosi, the archer and god of the hunt; his power resides in the metal bow and arrow inside the cauldron. Next to the cauldron stands a metal cup that is closed and topped with a small rooster. This is Osun, a guardian who represents the neophyte's head; in it are the herbs used to make the osain. Osain pools in the saucers and in the cauldron, and drips down the metal shaft that elevates Osun. These orichas, the Guerreros, are the beginning of a person's "road in the saint." The man has come to "receive" them.[2]

Boxes are brought in from the patio. The godfather reaches into a box and pulls out a black rooster. He washes its underwings, the bottom of its feet, and its beak with clear water. He holds it by the legs, and its wings flap. The aleyo is told to turn slowly in a circle; as he rotates, he is brushed with the rooster in long sweeping motions from his head toward his feet. This is repeated until he has rotated completely. His hands are turned palm up and brushed with the bird's wings, then turned over and brushed again, and finally turned palm up and brushed a third time. The bird is stretched out and its neck cut. The blood flows onto Elegguá. Its head is placed next to Elegguá and its neck touches his saucers; the bird kicks, and the padrino pushes down hard to squeeze the air from the bird's lungs in order to quiet the animal. It kicks again and squeals; this time, the aleyo reaches down and forces the air from the bird and silences it. The slaughtering process is repeated with three doves, one each for Ogún, Ochosi, and Osun, and then again with a Guinea hen.

Following the *matanza* (Sp. slaughter), the aleyo is told to "do *moforibale*" (Lu. prostration). A mat is spread out in front of the orichas; his godfather stands next to them. The man lies down on the mat, first on his left side and then on his right. His knees are bent and his arm curls beneath his head as he "goes to the ground." "*¿Bueno?*" he asks. "Is this all right?" "Yes." He does moforibale to show his respect to the orichas that he has just received and to the oricha that "lives" in his godfather's head. His godfather touches his shoulders with his fingers and helps him up. The aleyo crosses his arms across his chest and is drawn to his elder's cheek, first on one side and then on the other. His padrino says softly, "*Santo. Ocha. Alafia*" (Lu. and Sp. saint, oricha, and peace, respectively). This gesture is repeated as he greets all of his elders and receives their blessings. George now belongs to their ritual family.

In an eastern city of the United States, this young man enters a new religious community; he is receiving

---

1. I witnessed the ritual described here in December 1990. Since 1988 I have worked extensively with the community that performed the ceremony. This group of practitioners is led by Cuban priests and priestesses but includes people of various social, economic, and cultural backgrounds. Because of this diversity I have limited my analysis to the religious system. I have also limited the detailed personal information about the participants. Santería is still not widely accepted, and so these people have asked that I not make their identities public or recognizable. I created a pseudonym for each person and used it consistently throughout the book.

2. "The road in the saint" is a common expression in Santería that refers to a person's destiny in the religion. This initiation is referred to as "receiving the Warriors."

a group of important deities and entering into ritual kin relationships with his initiators. He must have his head washed, his body cleaned by animals, and must perform the moforibale; to enter this tradition, he uses his body in ways that are new to him. As he receives the gods, he learns new patterns of body use. The creation of these new bodily patterns in the Guerreros initiation ritual presents an interesting case: the signs used in the ritual have meanings that can be communicated verbally, but here the signs are experientially apprehended through the body; they are not simply understood but also enacted. As he uses his body in new ways, his subjectivity is transformed.

In recent years, studies of cultural performances have demonstrated clearly that meaning is not latent in ritual signs and awaiting discovery; instead people involved in ritual performances engage signs and activate them (Schieffelin 1985:707). Through performance, people communicate cultural meanings; by employing the various culturally relevant and available communicative resources, including specific generic and gestural forms, people produce their culture. This production takes place in all cultured behavior, and ritual—any ritual—effectively opens the door to understanding the entire culture (V. Turner 1967).[3] Cultural performances "are occasions in which as a culture or society we reflect upon and define ourselves, dramatize our collective myths and history . . ." (MacAloon 1984a:1). Although communicative resources such as ritual do carry specific expectations for all involved, only through enactment and negotiation can meaning be established and understood. As Richard Bauman (1986:3) has written, "Performance, like all human activity, is situated, its form, meaning, and functions rooted in culturally defined scenes or events—bounded segments of the flow of behavior and experience that constitute meaningful contexts for action, interpretation, and evaluation." Cultural performances—performances of cultural forms—can have meaning and functions only when enacted (Abrahams 1977:95), and enactments often produce heightened experiences for participants.

Because this initiate, George, was not born into Santería, these experiences are new to him. These new bodily activities, quite common to the tradition, represent a change for George. To enter the tradition fully he must learn to use his body in new ways; he must master certain gestures and series of actions. As he experiences himself enacting new gestures and cultural forms of behavior, he realizes that his body is both a sign communicating meanings in a new way and simultaneously a locus of new experiences (Cowan 1990:4; cf. B. Turner 1984:1). His body is not simply a constructed sign that links him to the group (Douglas 1978:87); instead, the individual's body mediates all of the ritual signs, for he can only act by employing his body (cf. Ekman 1977). The enacting of these forms by the body represents the "modes of construction" of a culturally specific and useful body (Feher 1989:11). George needs to be able to enact each of the three gestures that I will explore in order to enter the religion more fully. He must understand *and* experience the importance of his head, he must learn the detailed gestures of sacrifice, and he must enact respect by prostrating himself in front of his elders. George learns to be a part of the community by using his body in specific ways.

The initiation ritual begins the establishment of new "habitual body sets, patterns of practical activity, and forms of consciousness" (Jackson 1989:119–120). The activities of the ritual and the meanings therein are inseparable. In social action, an essential communicative form in Santería, pragmatic and semantic dimensions fuse; ideology is not an explicit discourse but an embodied, lived experience (Comaroff 1985:5). Because meaning merges with actions, the ritual represents the creation of a new *habitus* in the initiate; it is an enactment of some of the "principles of the generation and structuring of practices and representations" (Bourdieu 1989:72). Practitioners rarely provide detailed evaluations of social actions or of ceremonies, but they do refer to certain rituals as *bien hecha* (Sp. well done) or *linda* (Sp. beautiful). This choice of language suggests that the sought-after quality is aesthetic and nonanalytical— a kind of satisfaction or well-being. The manipulation of physical objects, those used on altars and in sacrifices as well as bodies, produces the elusive but desirable beautiful ceremony.[4]

---

3. Certainly ritual does not simply "reflect" the entire culture (cf. Benedict 1935), but it does provide a useful and edifying entry point for cultural analysis.

4. I plan to explore these valuative, aesthetic categories in future work.

This habitus represents a new social position for the neophyte in the case described earlier. This ritual is an important initiation on the road to the priesthood; it creates new bodily patterns for the initiate and thus inscribes the body into the new discourse. Previously abstract, verbal knowledge is enacted and incorporated. Never before has he had his head washed in osain; never before has he been cleaned by the sweepings of birds' wings; nor has he performed the moforibale. The giving and receiving of the Guerreros, repeated many times and in many places each year, assimilates people more fully into the community and gives them limited access to the supernatural world, and this example is no different. Here, however, the medium for assimilation is George. He must enact respect and embody the tradition.

This embodiment of tradition in the ritual context structures George's experience. As he uses his body in new ways and places it in new positions, he makes physical certain relationships and experiences them bodily; the initiation, then, regulates experience "through its capacity to reorganize the actor's experience of the situation" (Munn 1973:605). Although initiations vary according to the performers involved and these variations affect the structure of the ritual (Hanks 1984:131), the aleyo's body always structures the experience.

In Santería, the teaching of ritual skills and moral behavior happens informally and nonverbally, and thus embodiment is especially important. Ritual elders tire quickly of answering questions and suggest that the best method of learning is involvement. By paying attention and attending many rituals, an aleyo becomes known as "serio" (Sp. a serious [student of the religion]; see Friedman 1982). People do learn this religion through the exegesis of important concepts, but they learn primarily through observation and enactment. Because learning centers on practice and entering actively into this tradition, the body naturally emerges as central to any analysis of this kind of ritual (cf. Wafer 1991 on the body). This learning takes place slowly, so it is extremely difficult to document. The body exists in a complex relationship with social knowledge and interpretation. The informal learning style of Santería makes social knowledge a kind of esoteric power. People who know certain ceremonies exercise power in the community. My analysis reflects the social realities of this community. Ritual focuses on the body and its manipulation, and personal experience represents the primary method for understanding; when a practitioner integrates experience with more commonly held, culturally produced expressive forms such as divination stories, social knowledge is expanded. "The essential part of the *modus operandi* which defines practical mastery is transmitted in practice . . . without attaining the level of discourse" (Bourdieu 1989:87). The aleyo here clearly grasps this emphasis on practice and the use of the body; as George Carter remarks, "Although I had never done too much in Santería before, I, I guess I wanted to be part of the community which I was joining, to act like they do. I wanted to be involved and do what they did so I could learn the religion" (1990). Involvement must be physical to be complete; although George knows a great deal about the beliefs and sacred stories of Santería, he greatly values entering the habitus of the community and expects to learn from his experience.

It is important to note that neophytes who undergo rituals are not somehow miraculously transformed by some inexplicable and awesome power. Rather, ritualizations in Santería frequently place the individual in a series of ceremonies that engage many aspects of the individual's subjectivity. Virtually all initiations—including receiving the Warriors—result from divination rituals; as the previous chapter explains, these ceremonies evoke the specific aspects of the multiplex subjectivity of the client and then recontextualize them within the religious system. Divination almost always results in the prescription of additional ceremonies to address specific needs in the client's life; these rituals often overwhelm the human subject with repeated gestures, unfamiliar smells, alien sights, and unusual songs and other sounds. The sensory force of the ritual augments the emotional investment in the ceremony that results from the divination. After the ceremonies are completed, practitioners routinely socialize their experiences of transformation through narratives that focus on particular but patterned aspects of the process and on the role of the spirits and orichas in their lives. These narratives represent an important but uninvestigated area of mythological information within the religion, an area that is constantly renewing itself through social action and lived experience.

Washing the Head

Because no expressive bodily activity happens without real bodies and no meanings can be assigned to gestures without reference to a specific event (Poole 1975:101), the specific example at hand best reveals George's bodily practice. The community of ritual specialists washes George's head as he prepares to enter the community. He leans over with eyes closed to receive their attention and blessings. The herbal mixture "cools" his head and "refreshes" him. His head is washed over the basin and then again in the bathtub. Each time the priest rubs the osain and the herbs floating in it into his skin and scalp.

In the bathroom cleansing, which I have witnessed many times, the gestures of the ritual are highly stylized. The aleyo leans over the tub and places the chest on the edge; the hands rest on the bottom, one on top of the other. I have seen this priest, whom I will call José, demonstrate to people how they should position themselves as they receive the *despojo* (Sp. cleaning). Through this instruction in how properly to perform the gesture, José shows that he has an aesthetic by which he evaluates it. Similarly, José washes the head with a specific pattern of movements. He takes the osain from its basin in a small gourd and pours it first over the crown of the head and then over the neck. Again starting at the crown, he lathers the soap by moving it around the head in growing circles until he reaches the neck, which he scrubs vigorously. He then rinses the head with more osain and squeezes the water from the hair with a motion similar to the one with which he lathers it. These highly stylized gestures reveal a culturally structured pattern of bodily movement, and, although they are performed by the padrino, they suggest that the despojo does contain gestures that the aleyo learns and experiences through his body.

The head, which receives most of the attention in the cleaning, carries complex and multiple symbolic meanings in Santería. First, the head, called either orí or eledá, is the spiritual faculty and central locus of a human being (Murphy 1981:287). Before birth, each orí goes before the Creator and receives its essential character. This character, which people closely associate with an individual's destiny, can be either "hot" or "cool" (Cabrera 1980:121). Although practitioners disagree about how mutable the head's character is, the ritual washing here in refreshing herbs and water helps to cool a hot head. The head also idiomatically refers to the oricha that rules a person; an individual and the deity also establish this relationship in front of the Creator before birth (see Bascom 1991:115).

This central deity, often called "the owner of the head," represents an important part of the individual's character. For example, the white, calm, and generous oricha Obatalá rules the head of George's padrino, and so people assume that José is slow to anger, relatively intellectual, benevolent, and, others might add, "big-headed." In fact, at times practitioners confuse the "owner of the head" and the individual; "an Obatalá" refers to a child of Obatalá who in ritual may act in the role of that oricha. The eledá can be identified through various divination systems, and a growing relationship between an individual and the eledá often leads to initiations, after which the aché of the oricha literally resides inside the initiate's head; after a full initiation, the oricha can "mount" the initiate in trance possession and thus take control of the body that they share.[5]

In the Guerreros initiation, the aleyo, with the help of the oloricha, cleans and refreshes his head. Thus, the ritual attention to the head marks it as socially and religiously important. The osain is both an empowering and a cleaning agent; when applied to the head, it strengthens the spirit that dwells there. By cleaning the head, the ritual cools and refreshes the whole person. As the night goes on, after the aleyo departs from the site of the initiation, the leaves of the mixture, entwined in his hair, often begin to scratch and cause itching. George Carter recalls, "I felt a little strange scratching my head after José [his godfather] had spent so much time attending to it. He prayed and I scratched; it, it seemed so, so strange to treat what had been made sacred as something annoying, but my scalp really itched. Later, I said a prayer to my head [ruling oricha] in thanksgiving and slept with a white cloth over it"[6] (1990). This attention to the head, moreover, represents

---

5. For an extended discussion of the sexual implications of mounting in Brazil, see Wafer 1991.
6. Carter has been involved in this ritual house since before I started studying it. He, like most new American practitioners, has a mixture of book learning and practical experience within the religion. I am not certain where he learned the prayer to which he refers here.

the beginning of a new cultural pattern. Many of the religion's rituals and customs underscore the centrality of the head. People entering Santería often start their affiliation when they need healing, and frequently the first ritual they undergo is the *rogación de la cabeza* (Sp. prayers for the head), where coconut, water, and cotton are applied to the head to "feed" it. Similarly, most practitioners cover their heads with hats (Sp. *gorros*) or handkerchiefs (Sp. *pañuelos*) during ritual activities. If their destinies include initiation, and they often do (Rogers 1973:28–29), their heads will receive still more attention.

Through various initiatory rites, the head is a focal point. Santería must be understood as an initiatory religion; initiations punctuate the changes and elevation of a person in the tradition. In one of the first initiations that a person receives, a priestess places necklaces (Lu. *eleke*, Sp. *collares*), consecrated, like the Guerreros, with herbal waters and the blood of sacrificial animals, over the neophyte's head and onto the shoulders. Each necklace has a different pattern of colored beads and conveys the power of one of the deities. An initiate most often receives the necklaces of the five most powerful and popular orichas; the necklaces, spiritually powerful and ritually charged, reflect the aché of each of them. The necklaces are both manifestations of the particular power of each deity and a channel for communication between the neophyte and the deities (Brandon 1983:355–356). They rest on the shoulders and reinforce the spiritual agent living in the head. Their form reflects the belief that the deities reside in the head. When the necklaces are received, the aleyo must again bow over a bathtub and have the head washed by the oloricha; all initiations include this bodily action of submission and reception of blessings.

The initiation of a full priest, capable of being mounted by an oricha, reiterates the attention on the head, that centralized idiom of spiritual power and life. In this ritual, the initiators wash the head of the neophyte and then shave it completely. The elders then mark the neophyte again, cutting a small cross into the top of the head; into this incision the initiators rub the most sacred herbs that contain the aché of the principal oricha. The head is covered with cloth, which will be worn for many hours to come. Finally the primary initiator crowns the neophyte with the tureens that contain the sacred stones that

are the "spirit of the orichas" (Brandon 1983:397–401; see Ecún 1985 for examples of the variations within different initiations); the head, again, is the focus of the ritual.

During the ritual of receiving the Warriors, George receives Osun, an equivalent of his head. As I mentioned earlier, Osun contains the same herbs that are used to make the osain. When he receives Osun, he learns a simple ritual to call upon the oricha; thus he now has a simple but effective method of communication with a central part of himself.[7] If the aleyo continues in the religion and undergoes the full initiation, if he "makes the saint" (Sp. *hacer santo*), the practitioners will place an herbal mixture, called *aché de santo* (Lu. power of the saint), in the head and also place it within the Osun, which has a cup to receive this mixture. Thus, the Guerreros initiation, too, emphasizes the head beyond the cleansings. After this ritual the neophyte has an image of his head with which he can communicate. If the Osun falls, for example, the aleyo knows that danger is at hand.

The head, then, represents the bodily center of the spiritual life in Santería. Its import reveals itself throughout a variety of initiation ceremonies. Moreover, because other initiations repeat the cultural forms of this ritual, the Guerreros initiation anticipates a whole social and religious commitment to the Santería community. The head receives respect because "the head carries the body."[8] As the seat of spiritual power and possibility, as the place that the ruling oricha dwells, people associate the head with destiny or "the road of life." Elder priests and priestesses clean the head, feed it, and sing to it. While George experiences these things he is literally incorporating important values in Santería. Although he may reflect upon them as the actions happen through his physical involvement and the attention

---

7. I have not described the Osun ritual because in the house that I am studying I was asked not to divulge it; for a similar ritual, see Murphy 1988. There are interesting correlations between Ocha's emphasis on the head and Vodou ritual practice; see K. Brown 1991:67, 350–351.

8. "The head carries the body" is an often quoted proverb (Sp. *refrán*) that is associated with the divination figure called Eyeunle, which is ruled by the white deity Obatalá, the owner of all heads.

to his head, he joins a wider practice that is common to all people involved in Santería. Similarly, it anticipates other cleanings, sacrifices, and initiations that are socially constituted and bodily enacted and learned.

The social actions that focus on the head do not reveal the meanings of the initiation. The meanings, communicated through signs, do not lie in a separate plane outside the immediate domain of actions (Jackson 1989:122). The actions of these people as they enact the ritual bespeak a commonality.

> It is because actions speak louder *and* more ambiguously than words that they are more likely to lead us to common truths; not semantic truths, established by others at other times, but experiential truths which seem to issue from within our own Being [sic] when we break the momentum of the discursive mind or throw ourselves into some collective activity in which we each find our own meaning yet at the same time sustain the impression of having a common cause and giving common consent (Jackson 1989:133).

This passage argues the extreme importance and power of signs and their messages for the *participants* of ritual; participants, by both framing events personally and conforming to the larger social and cosmological order that the ritual communicates, come to embody the very contrast of structure and agency. By enacting the ritual, the initiate accepts socially and publicly the order that the ritual signifies (Rappaport 1989:469). George and his padrinos act together and, regardless of any other conflicts that they have, they serve his head and thus care for his essence. George expresses that attention as he leans over the basins to make his head available, and his padrinos show it in gestures of washing. Here, through these actions, as George accepts this cultural emphasis on the head, he begins to accept the new habitus of the religion.

"Making Sacrifice"

By receiving the Guerreros, George Carter "opens the roads" for himself by "making sacrifice" (Lu. *rubó*, Sp. *hacer ebó*). He is committing himself not simply to the members of ritual house, nor is he simply attending to his head; he is also committing himself to a life-long relationship with the Warriors themselves, and this relationship will include, at a minimum, a regular weekly offering to the orichas. However, it is likely that he will have to sacrifice other animals in the future. The initiation is the first time that George has witnessed the sacrifice of birds, and he now is religiously bound to make regular sacrifices himself. Thus, sacrifice represents another form of behavior in which George participates at his initiation but that he must also learn to enact himself.

In the sacrifice, the birds are washed. Holding them by the feet, José brushes each animal across the aleyo to sweep off any negative influences that may be lingering on George. Slowly José sweeps from the head down toward the feet. An oloricha draws back the birds' wings and holds their feet; with the Guinea hen and the rooster, José pulls the neck to extend it, then pierces it with a knife, and the blood runs down the knife and onto the awaiting orichas. The doves receive similar treatment; however, instead of cutting their necks, José bends their necks to the side and then plucks them off. Because a special initiation confers the right to use a sacrificial knife, the aleyo will have to pull the heads off any birds he sacrifices to feed his Warriors. These formal processes, which George is witnessing and learning, will represent an essential aspect of his religious life in the future.

Whenever divination suggests the need, George will feed his Warriors. He will gather the necessary birds and perform this ceremony, which is central to the religion. Just as he has witnessed at his initiation, he will wash the birds' underwings, their heads, and their feet. He will say the prayers and sing the *cantos* (Sp. chants) that he has heard and learned. Although he may not understand the Lucumí words that he uses, he will stretch out the birds and pull their heads off to slaughter them. He will mimic the way he has seen matanzas performed and thus will constitute his own tradition within the tradition. Because he has never before witnessed sacrifice, the initiation represents a crucial moment of learning for George. He watches, and he learns new behaviors. As he said of the experience, "I was anxious because I had never seen a matanza before, but I guess, well, I was also, I think I wanted to see how to do it so I could feed my Elegguá and give him the blood and do works. I had read the songs and the prayers in different places, and I had read about sacrifices, but I knew that seeing one would teach me even more. Only if I saw a sacrifice would I know how to do one" (1990). By watching, George learns what he cannot learn elsewhere; he understands what gestures to perform in a sacrifice.

Perhaps the most striking example of this learning lies not in the future sacrifices that George will make but in the event itself. When the rooster continues to move and make noise after its head is severed, José leans on it to force the air from its lungs. When the bird again kicks and squeals, George, imitating what he has just seen, quiets the bird. "I wanted to try and see how to do it. I wanted to quiet that bird *with my own two hands*" (Carter 1990). This moment represents the essence of the initiation process. Here George is observing the "techniques of the body" that Santería employs (Mauss 1973), but he goes beyond simple observation and uses his body in ways that are new to him: he enacts culturally specific behavior and practices his performance.

By forcing the air from the rooster, he shows the community around him not only that he wants to be a member but also that he will act in appropriate ways. He begins to assert his competence (Bauman 1977:11), although, as a person with the status of a child, he risks failing. But he has successfully acquired an understanding of how this gesture is used (see Hymes 1974:75) and thus begins to act socially within this religious community. Because social action has a kind of power in the community, George asserts himself as a serio. By mimicking his padrino, George performs a relatively unimportant ritual task; the ritual in no way revolves around quieting the rooster, but is a bit more pleasant for everyone because of it. Quieting the bird also demonstrates that George is willing and capable of entering the tradition. Here he performs his membership in the group; the tradition diffuses as people enact specific gestures, and the aleyo follows the lead of his godfather:[9] "Carter is a serious guy and he is not afraid to jump into things. If I do something in a ritual, he repeats. . . . He will be a good santero when the

time comes. He will be a good santero because he puts himself into a ceremony and doesn't hesitate" (González 1992).

Just as the sacrifice itself is an important practice that George learns in the initiation, the sweeping of the body by animals for cleansing purposes represents another traditional behavior that he begins to enact. Rubbing rituals use animals or fruit to remove negative influences, and they represent an entire subclass of ritual offerings to the deities. Diviners frequently suggest these "works" (Lu. *ebó*, Sp. *trabajos*). Here George is learning the correct speed to turn and the gestures that are done with the hands. As he goes through these acts, he again learns culturally specific behavior. As he turns and is swept by the wings, George is again acquiring the practical and bodily patterns of Santería ritual.

Moforibale: I Bow My Head to the Ground

Although previous work on cultural performances has focused on the role of individuals as signs (see Stoeltje 1988) and the presentation of social structure for reflection (for example, see Stoeltje and Bauman 1989), authors have not embraced an ongoing examination of the process of learning a social and cosmological order through performance. Performance studies must account for the production and maintenance of social relationships by actors in the social field (McArthur 1989:115); "ritual action effects social transitions or spiritual transformations; it does not merely mark or accompany them" (MacAloon 1984b:250). The ritual causes change simply by its occurrence; it expresses and communicates its meanings with or without the participants' consent or knowledge (Myerhoff 1984:170).

The moforibale represents an important religious behavior that George acquires during his initiation and through which he performs his social obligations.[10] After the washing and after the divinities eat,

---

9. It is worth noting that a priestess present at the ritual also squeezed the air from the rooster when it squealed. Thus, this particular instance does not represent the acquisition of gendered behavior. It seems probable that an investigation of Santería and gender would be helped by this rich ethnographic example where a man gives "*macho*" (Sp. masculine, male) divinities to another man. It should be noted that women also receive the Guerreros, and always from a man.

---

10. The word *moforibale* is Lucumí, and its translation is revealing: It is an elision of the phrase *mo fi orí ba ilé. Mo* is the first person pronoun "I"; *fi* is an operative marking indicating the use of something, in this case *orí*, "the head." *Ba* is the verb "to touch," and *ilé* is "the ground" or "the earth." Thus, a more literal translation would be "I use my head to touch the ground."

he must "put his head to the ground" in front of his padrino and the other members of his ritual family. Because the oricha that "owns his head" is female, he must go down on each side with his head facing the direction of the oricha he is honoring. If the aleyo's head were male, the moforibale would have a different form; instead of reclining on each side, a person ruled by a male oricha must prostrate with the forehead on the floor and the arms and legs extended straight out. Here the body gesture marks the gender of the ruling oricha and not the person; the gender of the oricha defines the way the person must bow. Again, as in the previous discussion of the despojo, the stylization of these gestures reiterates their cultural significance. José explains how to go down, and then George lies down; he asks if he is doing it correctly. His padrino raises him and blesses him. This series of gestures is central to the kinship that the ritual creates.

> I had seen people do the moforibale before, and I knew that it was an important form of respect. Respect is important in Santería. We have to respect the elders because we receive the orichas from their hands. The dead gave birth to the orichas. That's a proverb that means we have to show respect. . . . My head doesn't have a saint in it so I have to put it on the floor in front of my padrino, whose head does have an oricha in it (Carter 1990).

Here George articulates the complexity of the moforibale, which indexes a series of important relationships. One head honors another by going to the floor. A new initiate shows respect to a ritual elder. By going to the floor, George enacts spatial, social, and cosmic relationships.

By receiving the Guerreros, the aleyo becomes attached to the initiator's ritual family and begins a serious commitment to the religious community. By receiving the Warriors, neophytes commit themselves to a life-long relationship with not only the oloricha but also the ritual house, the wider religious community that congregates at important festivals. Inside this community exists a complex family of ritual kin (Brandon 1983:480; cf. D. Brown 1989:162–186). The initiating priest, after the ritual, becomes the padrino and the neophyte the *ahijado* or *ahijada* (Sp. godson, goddaughter). This relationship entails mutual commitment, and both parties are expected to treat the other as a family member (Murphy 1988:83; cf. D. Brown 1989:174–186). Just as parents raise a child, so too will the godparents enculturate the aleyo; they demonstrate the proper behavior, and the aleyo learns by following their example; they "speak without a voice" (Flores 1990:49).

Ritual kinship is construed in terms of *casas* or *ilé* (Sp., Lu. houses) and *ramas* (Sp. branches, lineages). A house is a single oloricha and the people initiated by that person. Filial relationships occur at every initiation, and thus a person can have many ahijados and many padrinos simultaneously. Those previously initiated by José become George's brothers and sisters "in the saint." To differentiate between different kinds of godchildren, José refers to individuals by the initiations that they have received from him; for example, after this initiation George becomes his ahijado de Guerreros (Sp. godson of the Warriors). These lines of relationship are traced through generations of living and dead ritual forebears. Thus, José's godmother *de asiento* (Sp. of the full initiation) becomes George's grandmother in the saint (Sp. *abuela de santo*).[11] These larger groups are the ramas that connect people across time. Just as an aleyo descends from a godparent and ritual ancestors, the orichas are also "born" from each other. George's Warriors are born from José's. Ritual elders (Sp. *mayores*) expect respect, and moforibale expresses that honor concretely and directly (D. Brown 1989:170).

The moforibale reiterates social order as it exists and as sanctioned by the morality of Santería tradition. For example, an aleyo, when needing help from the orichas, employs a godparent as intermediary or, at the very least, as a guide. This relationship subordinates the uninitiated to those with experience within the religion. The godparents have knowledge, spiritual power, and, according to Santería morality, a social responsibility. In the Guerreros initiation, George must approach the orichas with the aid of his ritual family.

By working the orichas—that is, being initiated, attending as many rituals as possible, and serving the community—the aleyo gains knowledge; however, that knowledge remains, by definition, social (Gregory 1986:141). Increased skill with the orichas increases his responsibility both to the orichas and to

---

11. Ritual kin, relatives *de santo*, are usually contrasted by practitioners with blood kin, relatives *de sangre* (Sp. of blood).

his ritual house. Initiation creates access to ritual knowledge; it attaches the neophyte to the house's members, both living and dead. Although the hierarchical system of initiations limits and regulates the access to ritual skill, people learn the skills themselves in social interaction within the ritual house. Degree and seniority of initiation determine the ritual status and social responsibility of a practitioner; to act within these boundaries is to act "coolly."

In the moforibale, the touching of the head to the floor, a ritually younger person salutes the "head" of the elder. Thus, George honors José's oricha; he physically submits his oricha to the oricha of his elder. By enacting this social and religious hierarchy, George publicly shows his acceptance of his new relationship with José and the submission that it implies. This public display makes the body a focus of interaction, and so it becomes an important locus of self-definition in the social context (see Glassner 1990:222; Mead 1938:292). Although he will "have" the Warriors after this initiation, he still needs his godparents to help him solve problems and teach him how to interact with the orichas. The moforibale is a bodily performance of this relationship.[12]

After "going down," George is raised by his padrino and blessed. The reciprocal relationship is complete. George honors José's head and receives a blessing: "The raising is a blessing which elevates, strengthens, and honors the junior . . . a sign of ritual recognition: symbolically conveying, affirming and supporting membership in a relationship" (Yvette Burgess-Polcyn, quoted in D. Brown 1989:171). The body physically learns and enacts this ritual greeting and display of honor. The body and its position communicate the respect, and the raising changes the relationship. But this relationship is not just projected onto the body; the body's gesture constructs and communicates it. George conceives of the moforibale as an important act: "I was glad and excited to [mo]foribale in front of José and my Guerreros. It felt strange to be, to be on the floor in the middle of a room with people all around, but . . . I just felt that I had to do it to show my respect and fit into the ilé. It seemed even weirder to go down for the other olorichas that I didn't even know" (Carter 1990). George must perform the moforibale repeatedly to show his respect for all who are his elders in the saint; despite its distinct and foreign feel, he goes down because he wants to show his respect to the people who have brought him into the religion.[13] What is perhaps more important, he goes down to act as other people in the ilé act, "to fit in." By reproducing an important cultural form in a noticeable social space, he embodies a social position and continues to maintain the status relationships.

Embodied Meanings and Living Traditions

This initiation is, indeed, a rite of passage. But an approach that relies on such a structural analysis, which isolates form and social function from more personal meaning, ignores an entire aspect of the ritual. Rather than focus on the patterns in the ritual structure, highlighting the forms the aleyo must enact alters the emphasis of interpretation. If we are to understand how transformations of subjectivity and social status are accomplished and experienced, the initiate's body must remain central to the analysis. The experience of transformation in rites of passage surely includes something more complicated and more delicate than the tripartite structure as put forth (see Van Gennep 1909; V. Turner 1969:94–130). People and their experiences always overflow the concepts and categories that social scientists use to comprehend them. I am advocating a more individual approach to this kind of material. How does the

---

12. In fact, the moforibale is performed in many other contexts as a form of respect. Most important, it is done in front of elaborate altars called *tronos* (Sp. thrones) that are offered to the orichas. See Friedman 1982:198–214 for a lengthy discussion of mutual respect in Santería. See D. Brown 1989, especially chapters 5 and 7, for excellent and extended discussions of tronos and the attendant rituals of respect. See also D. Brown 2003.

---

13. It is important to note that George is not thoroughly separating the orichas and his ritual elders. When he does moforibale, he is technically honoring the physical orichas as well as the orichas that are crowned in the heads of the elders. David Brown (1989:170–171) quotes Melba Carrillo, an oloricha in New Jersey, as reiterating that the moforibale salutes the "*oricha* crowned on the head of the person, not the person." George's experience of the ritual does not include this highly differentiated semantic meaning for the moforibale.

initiate use the body before and after the ritual? What effect does the change have on other aspects of life? Is the new habitus limited to one context, or does it spill into other parts of the person's life? (For excellent examples of body-focused analyses of rites of passage, see V. Turner 1967, 1969:1–93.)

The meaning of this initiation cannot be understood without reference to the bodily practices of the initiate. It is by using his body in new ways and performing specific gestures that George enters into the religion. Through performing these specific cultural forms, through attending to his head in various ways, through sacrificing and all its gestures, through going to the floor in the moforibale, he enacts his membership in his new religious context and venerates the gods. Under the guidance of his initiators, he transforms his subjectivity. The bodily reproduction of socially prescribed behaviors keys the emergent meanings of the initiation; through enactment practitioners display their relationships with each other and the forces of the universe. Moreover, the meaning of the signs in these rituals lies not so much in their abstract meanings but in how they are experienced through the body of the aleyo. The meanings of the signs are only accessible and sensible through the use of the body. As Pierre Bourdieu observes, "Rites, more than any other type of practice, serve to underline the mistake of enclosing them in concepts a logic made to dispense with concepts; of treating movements of the *body* and practical manipulations as purely logical operations" (1989:116, italics mine).

People learn the bodily and social practice of Santería through initiation; by experiencing a new habitus, the aleyo joins his new tradition. Although he has understood the tradition in an intellectual way and has studied a great deal, by joining a ritual family and offering a sacrifice, he places himself into the practical life of the religion. He knows the tradition in a different way now, and he feels different as well. Now he understands the worship of the orichas and some of their stories, and he also knows how to worship them. In Santería, personal identity, social relationships, and ritual knowledge are performed by people as they bow their heads to the ground.

14

Return to Wirikuta: Ritual Reversal and Symbolic Continuity on the Peyote Hunt of the Huichol Indians

Barbara G. Myerhoff

*P*ersuasively illustrating the close integration of myth and symbolism within ritual, the following article by Barbara G. Myerhoff explores symbolic reversals and oppositions within the annual peyote hunt of the Huichol, an indigenous population of north-central Mexico. Based on fieldwork in 1965 and 1966, Myerhoff's work exemplifies the anthropological analysis of symbolism within a ritual context. A shaman leads small groups to Wirikuta, which is both an actual geographic location and a myth-based spiritual state, where everything ordinary is inverted. These reversals occur in naming, interpersonal behavior, ritual behavior, and emotional states. Through such ritual reversals, the author argues, a number of functions are served. Everyday existence is set apart from the sacred. The ordinary is turned into something extraordinary yet continuous. Peyote-seekers become supernatural deities and, in the dramatization that is ritual, act and behave within the realm of the sacred.*

Although Barbara Myerhoff's early field research took place in Mexico, later in her career she documented Jewish communities in southern California. She paid special attention to rituals in the lives of elderly Jews. Her research is highlighted in two documentary films, both of which are excellent illustrations of a skilled ethnographer at work: "Number Our Days" (1983) and "In Her Own Time" (1985), both produced by Direct Cinema Ltd.

God is day and night, winter summer, war peace, satiety hunger—all opposites, this is the meaning.

—Heraclitus

The Peyote Hunt of the Huichol Indians

Rituals of opposition and reversal constitute a critical part of a lengthy religious ceremony, the peyote hunt, practiced by the Huichol Indians of north-central Mexico.[1] In order to understand the function

1. The Huichol Indians are a quasi-tribe of about 10,000 living in dispersed communities in north-central Mexico. They are among the least acculturated Mexican Indians and

of these rituals it is necessary to adumbrate the major features and purposes of the peyote hunt. Annually, small groups of Huichols, led by a shaman-priest or *mara'akáme*, return to Wirikuta to hunt the peyote. Wirikuta is a high desert several hundred miles from the Huichols' present abode in the Sierra Madre Occidentál. Mythically and in all likelihood historically, it is their original homeland, the place once inhabited by the First People, the quasi-deified ancestors. But Wirikuta is much more than a geographical location; it is *illud tempus,* the paradisical condition that existed before the creation of the world and mankind, and the condition that will prevail at the end of time.

In Wirikuta, as in the paradise envisioned in many creation myths, all is unity, a cosmic totality without barriers of any kind, without the differentiations that characterize the mundane mortal world. In Wirikuta, separations are obliterated—between sexes, between leader and led, young and old, animals and man, plants and animals, and man and the deities. The social order and the natural and supernatural realms are rejoined into their original state of seamless continuity. Wirikuta is the center of the four directions where, as the Huichol describe it, "All is unity, all is one, all is ourselves."

In Wirikuta, the three major symbols of Huichol world view are likewise fused. These are the Deer, representing the Huichols' past life as nomadic hunters; the Maize, representing their present life as sedentary agriculturalists; and peyote, signifying the private, spiritual vision of each individual. To reenter Wirikuta, the peyote pilgrims must be transformed into the First People. They assume the identity of particular deities and literally hunt the peyote which grows in Wirikuta, tracking and following it in the form of deer footprints, stalking and shooting it with bow and arrow, consuming it in a climactic ceremony of total communion. Once the peyote has been hunted, consumed, and sufficient supplies have been gathered for use in the ceremonies of the coming year, the pilgrims hastily leave and return to their homes and to their mortal condition. The entire

---

in part their resistance to outside influence is attributable to the complex and extraordinarily rich ritual and symbolic life they lead. A detailed presentation of the peyote hunt is presented in Myerhoff 1974. The fieldwork on which the present paper was based took place in 1965 and 1966.

peyote hunt is very complex, consisting of many rituals and symbols; here I will only concentrate on one set of rituals, those which concern reversal and opposition, and the part they play in enabling the pilgrims to experience the sense of totality and cosmic unity that is their overarching religious goal.

Mythological and Ritual Aspects of Reversals

"In Wirikuta, we change the names of everything . . . everything is backwards." Ramón Medina Silva, the officiating mara'akáme, who led the Peyote Hunt of 1966 in which I participated, thus explained the reversals that obtain during the pilgrimage. "The mara'akáme tells [the pilgrims], 'Now we will change everything, all the meanings, because that is the way it must be with the *hikuritámete* [peyote pilgrims]. As it was in Ancient Times, so that all can be united.' "

The reversals to which he refers occur on four distinct levels: naming, interpersonal behavior, ritual behavior, and emotional states. The reversals in naming are very specific. Ideally, everything is its opposite and everything is newly named each year. But in fact, for many things there are often no clear opposites, and substitutions are made, chosen for reasons that are not always clear. Frequently the substitutions seem dictated by simple visual association—thus the head is a pot, the nose a penis, hair is cactus fiber. A great many of these substitutions recur each year and are standardized. Nevertheless, they are defined as opposites in this context and are treated as if they were spontaneous rather than patterned.

On the interpersonal-behavioral level, direct oppositions are more straightforward. One says yes when he or she means no. A person proffers a foot instead of a hand. Conversations are conducted with conversants standing back to back, and so forth. Behavior is also altered to correspond with the ritual identity of the participant. Thus the oldest man, transformed into a *nunutsi* or little child for the journey, is not permitted to gather firewood because "this work is too heavy and strenuous for one so young."

The deities are portrayed as the opposite of mortals in that the former have no physiological needs. Thus the pilgrims, as the First People, disguise, minimize, and forego their human physiological activities as much as possible. Sexual abstinence is practiced. Washing is forsworn. Eating, sleeping, and drinking are kept to an absolute minimum. Defecation and urination are said not to occur and are practiced covertly. All forms of social distinction and organization are minimized, and even the mara'akáme's leadership and direction are extremely oblique. The ordinary division of labor is suspended and altered in various ways. All forms of discord are strictly forbidden, and disruptive emotions such as jealousy and deceit, usually tolerated as part of the human condition, are completely proscribed for the pilgrims. No special treatment is afforded to children; no behavioral distinctions between the sexes are allowed. Even the separateness of the mara'akáme from his group is minimized, and his assistant immediately performs for him all rituals that the mara'akáme has just performed for the rest of the party.

In terms of ritual actions, reversals are quite clear. The cardinal directions, and up and down, are switched in behaviors which involve offering sacred water and food to the four corners and the center of the world. The fire is circled in a counterclockwise direction instead of clockwise as on normal ceremonial occasions. In Wirikuta, the mara'akáme's assistant sits to the latter's left instead of to his right.

Emotions as well as behaviors are altered on the basis of the pilgrims' transformation into deities. Since mortals would be jubilant, presumably, on returning to their pre-creation, mythical homeland, and grief-stricken on departing from it, the pilgrims weep as they reenter Wirikuta and are exultant on departing. This reflects the fact that they are deities leaving paradise, not mortals returning from it.

I should note also some of the attitudes and values toward the reversals that I observed. For example, there seems to be an aesthetic dimension since they regard some reversals as more satisfying than others. Humorous and ironic changes are a source of much laughter and delight. Thus the name of the wife of the mara'akáme was changed to "ugly *gringa*." The mara'akáme himself was the pope. The anthropologists' camper was a burro that drank much tequila. They also delight in compounding the reversals: "Ah what a pity that we have caught no peyote. Here we sit, sad, surrounded by baskets of flowers under a cold sun." Thus said one pilgrim after a successful day of gathering baskets full of peyote, while standing in the moonlight. Mistakes and humorous improvisations are also the source of new reversals. When in a careless moment Los Angeles was referred to as "home," everyone was very pleased and amused; from then on home was Los Angeles and even in sacred chants and prayers this reversal was maintained. Accidental reversals such as this are just as obligatory as the conventional ones and the new ones "dreamed" by the mara'akáme. Mistakes are corrected with good will but firmly, and everyone shares in the responsibility for keeping track of the changes, reminding each other repeatedly of the changes that have been instituted. The more changes the better, and each day, as more are established, more attention by all is required to keep things straight. Normal conversation and behavior become more difficult with each new day's accumulation of changes. Sunsets are ugly. No one is tired. Peyote is sweet. The pilgrimage is a failure. There is too much food to eat, and so forth.

The reversals were not instituted or removed by any formal rituals, although it is said that there are such. It became apparent that the reversals were in effect at the periphery of Wirikuta when someone sneezed. This was received by uproarious laughter, for, the nose had become a penis and a sneeze, accordingly, was an off-color joke. After the peyote hunt, the reversals were set aside gradually as the group moved away from Wirikuta. On returning home, the pilgrims regaled those who had remained behind with descriptions of the reversals and the confusions they had engendered.

The Functions and Symbolism of the Reversals

How should these ideas and actions concerning reversal and opposition be understood? In the Huichol context, they achieve several purposes simultaneously. Perhaps most familiar and straightforward is their function in transforming the mundane into the sacred by disguising the everyday features of environment, society, and behavior, and in the Durkeimian sense "setting it apart." As Ramón Medina Silva explained, "One changes everything . . . when [we] cross over there to the Peyote Country . . .

because it is a very sacred thing, it is the most sacred. It is our life, as one says. That is why nowadays one gives things other names. One changes everything. Only when they return home, then they call everything again what it is." Here the totality and scope of the reversals are important—actions, names, ritual, and everyday behaviors are altered so that participants are conscious at all times of the extraordinary nature of their undertaking. Nothing is natural, habitual, or taken for granted. The boundaries between the ordinary and the sacred are sharply defined and attention to this extraordinary state of affairs cannot lag when one has to be perpetually self-conscious and vigilant against lapses. Reversals promote the essential attitude of the sacred, the *mysterium tremendum et fascinans*.

The transformation of mortals into deities is related to this purpose. Again and again in theological, mythological, and ethnographic literature one encounters the impossibility of mortals entering a supernatural realm in their normal condition. The shaman transforms himself into a spirit in order to perform his duties as soul guide or psychopomp. This is the essence of the Symplegades motif in shamanism—the passage into the other world through the crashing gates, as Eliade (1964) points out. The "paradoxical passage" to the supernatural domain is open only to those who have been transformed from their human state into pure spirit. An apotheosis is required of those who would "cross over" and achieve the "breakthrough in planes." The peyote hunt opens Wirikuta to all proper pilgrims, but they, like the shaman, cannot enter in mortal form. To enter Wirikuta, the Huichol peyote-seekers do not merely impersonate the deities by assuming their names and garb. Ritually and symbolically, they *become* supernatural, disguising the mortal coil, abrogating human functions and forms.

This "backwardness" operates on two levels: as the deities, they are the obverse of mortals; as deities, they are going back, going backwards, and signifying this by doing everything backwards. Backwardness is found frequently in connection with supernatural states, and with the denial of humanity. Lugbara witches are inverted beings who walk on their heads (Middleton 1960). And in Genesis we find that "the inhabitants of paradise stand on their heads and walk on their hands; as do all the dead" (Graves and Patai 1966:73, citing Gen. 24:65). The

examples could be expanded indefinitely. Eliade suggests this widespread association of backwardness and the supernatural when he comments, "Consequently to do away with this state of [humanity] even if only provisionally, is equivalent to reestablishing the primordial condition of man, in other words, to banish time, to go backwards, to recover the 'paradisial' *illud tempus*" (1960:72).

A third function of these reversals is their provision of mnemonic, or aid to the imagination and memory, for conception and action. For a time the peyote pilgrims in the Huichol religion live in the supernatural. They go beyond invoking and discussing it, for Wirikuta exists in ritual as well as mythical terms. Ritual, unlike myth, requires action. Ritual is a dramatization. Pilgrims must not only imagine the unimaginable, they must behave within it. It is through its action dimension that ritual makes religious values "really real," and fuses the "lived-in" and the "dreamed-of order," as Geertz puts it. Full staging is necessary. The unfathomable—*illud tempus*, the primordial state before time—is the setting. Props, costumes, etiquette, vocabulary, emotions—all must be conceived and specified. The theme of opposition provides the details that are needed to make the drama credible and convincing; the metaphor of backwardness makes for a concretization and amplification of the ineffable. Again Eliade's writings offer an insight along these lines. He points out that the theme of *coincidentia oppositorum* is an "eschatological symbol par excellence, which denotes that Time and History have come to an end—in the lion lying down with the lamb" (1962:121). It is in the Garden of Eden that "opposites lie down together," it is there that conflicts and divisions are ultimately abolished and man's original innocence and wholeness are regained.

Separation, transformation, and concretization then are three purposes achieved by the reversals in Wirikuta. There is a fourth, perhaps the most important and common function of rituals of this nature. That is the capacity of reversals to invoke continuity through emphasis on opposition. How this operates in the Huichol case was explained in very precise terms by Ramón Medina Silva in a text he dictated about the 1966 peyote hunt five years later. He was elaborating on the beauties of Wirikuta and for the first time indicated that it was the state that would prevail at the end of time as well as that which characterized the beginning. When the world ends, the First People would return. "All will be in unity, all will be one, all will be as you have seen it there, in Wirikuta." The present world, it became clear, was but a shallow and misleading interlude, a transient period characterized by difference and separations, bracketed by an enduring condition of totality and continuity.

> When the world ends it will be like when the names of things are changed during the Peyote Hunt. All will be different, the opposite of what it is now. Now there are two eyes in the heavens, the Sun and the Moon. Then, the Moon will open his eye and become brighter. The sun will become dimmer. There will be no more difference between them. Then, no more men and no more women. No more child and no more adult. All will change places. Even the mara'akáme will no longer be separate. That is why there must always be a *nunutsi* when we go to Wirikuta. Because the old man and the tiny baby, they are the same.
> —Personal communication, Los Angeles, 1971

Polarity reaffirms continuity. The baby and the adult ultimately are joined, ends of a single continuum. Watts states it as follows: "What exactly is polarity? It is something much more than simple duality or opposition. For to say that opposites are polar is to say much more than that they are joined . . . , that they are the terms, ends, or extremities of a single whole. Polar opposites are therefore inseparable opposites, like the poles of the earth or of a magnet, or the ends of a stick or the faces of a coin" (1970:45).

Surely the vision of an original condition of unity, before the world and mankind began, is one of the most common themes in religions of every nature and place. Again to draw on Eliade, "Among the 'primitive' peoples, just as among the Saints and the Christian theologians, mystic ecstasy is a return to Paradise, expressed by the overcoming of Time and History . . . , and [represents] a recovery of the primordial state of Man" (1960:72).

The theme of nostalgia for lost paradise recurs so often as to be counted by some as panhuman. Theories attribute this yearning to various causes: a lingering memory of the undifferentiated state in the womb, the unfilled wish for a happy childhood, a fantasy of premortal blessedness and purity, a form

of what the Jungians call uroboric incest, a fatal desire for nonbeing, and so forth (see Neumann 1954). Many theologians have viewed this vision of cosmic oneness as the essence of the mystical experience and of religious ecstasy. The particulars vary from one religion to the next but the ingredients are stable: paradise is that which existed before the beginning of time, before life and death, before light and darkness. Here animals and man lived in a state of easy companionship, speaking the same language, untroubled by thirst, hunger, pain, weariness, loneliness, struggle, or appetite. Humans knew neither discord nor distinction among themselves— they were sexless, without self-awareness, and indeed undifferentiated from the very gods. Then an irreversible and cataclysmic sundering took place and instead of wholeness there was separation, the separation that was Creation. Henceforth, the human organism was no longer indistinguishable from the cosmos. The primordial splitting left mankind as we know it now, forever haunted by remembrance of and attraction for an original condition of wholeness.

The reversals, then, express the most lamentable features of the human condition by emphasizing the loss of the paradisical state of oneness. Humans are fragmented, incomplete, and isolated from the deities; they are vulnerable and literally mortal, which is to say helpless before the ravages of pain, time, and death. At the same time, the reversals remind mankind of the primordial wholeness that will again prevail when paradise is regained. Here is the theme expressed in a cultural form familiar to most of us, the Gospel according to Thomas:

> They said to Him: Shall we then, being children enter the Kingdom? Jesus said to them:
> When you make the two one, and
> when you make the inner as the outer
> and the outer as the inner and the above
> as the below, and when
> you make the male and the female into a single one,
> so that the male will not be male and
> the female [not] be female, when you make
> eyes in the place of an eye, a hand
> in the place of a hand, and a foot in the place
> of a foot, an image in the place of an image,
> then shall you enter [the Kingdom].
> —Logia 23–35, cited in Guillaumont et al.
> 1959:17–19

Conclusions

The theme of reversal, in all its permutations and combinations—opposition (complementary and binary), inversion, and dualism—has always been of great interest to anthropologists, mythographers, theologians, psychologists, linguists, and artists. The subject seems inexhaustible. In anthropology alone, we continue to unravel additional layers of meaning, to discover more and more functions fulfilled by reversals in various contexts. Recent studies especially have shown how reversals can be used to make statements about the social order—to affirm it, attack it, suspend it, redefine it, oppose it, buttress it, emphasize one part of it at the cost of another, and so forth. We see a magnificently fruitful image put to diverse purposes, capable of an overwhelming range of expression. Obviously there is no question of looking for the true or correct meaning in the use of reversals. We are dealing with a symbolic referent that has new meanings in every new context and within a single context embraces multiple and contradictory meanings simultaneously. In Wirikuta, the reversals accomplish many purposes and contain a major paradox. They emphasize the difference between Wirikuta and the mundane life, and the differentiated nature of the human condition. Also they stress the nondifferentiated nature of Wirikuta. The reversals thus portray differentiation and continuity at the same time. Both are true, separation and oneness, though this is contradictory and paradoxical. But this should come as no surprise, for paradox is the very quick of ritual. In ritual, as in the Garden, opposites are made to lie down together.

Appendix: How the Names Are Changed on the Peyote Journey

Text dictated by Ramón Medina Silva, mara'akáme of San Sebastián, Mexico, to explain the reversals used on the peyote hunt.

Well, let's see now. I shall speak about how we do things when we go and seek the peyote, how we change the names of everything. How we call the things we see and do by another name for all those

days. Until we return. Because all must be done as it must be done. As it was laid down in the beginning. How it was when the mara'akáme who is Tatewarí[2] led all those great ones to Wirikuta. When they crossed over there, to the peyote country. Because that is a very sacred thing, it is the most sacred. It is our life, as one says. That is why nowadays one gives things other names. One changes everything. Only when they return home, then they call everything again that it is.

When everything is ready, when all the symbols which we take with us, the gourd bowls, the yarn discs, the arrows, everything has been made, when all have prayed together we set out. Then we must change everything, all the meanings. For instance: a pot which is black and round, it is called a head. It is the mara'akáme who directs everything. He is the one who listens in his dream, with his power and his knowledge. He speaks to Tatewarí, he speaks to Kauyumari.[3] Kauyumari tells him everything, how it must be. Then he says to his companions, if he is the leader of the journey to the peyote, look, this thing is this way, and this is how it must be done. He tells them, look, now we will change everything, all the meanings, because that is the way it must be with the *hikuritámete* (peyote pilgrims). As it was in ancient times, so that all can be united. As it was long ago, before the time of my grandfather, even before the time of his grandfather. So the mara'akáme has to see to everything, so that as much as possible all the words are changed. Only when one comes home, then everything can be changed back again to the way it was.

"Look," the mara'akáma says to them, "it is when you say 'good morning,' you mean 'good evening,' everything is backwards. You say 'goodbye, I am leaving you,' but you are really coming. You do not shake hands, you shake feet. You hold out your right foot to be shaken by the foot of your companion. You say 'good afternoon,' yet it is only morning."

So the mara'akáme tells them, as he has dreamed it. He dreams it differently each time. Every year they

---

2. Huichol name for the deity with whom the shaman has a special affinity, roughly translatable as Our Grandfather Fire.

3. Kauyumari is a trickster hero, quasi-deified and roughly translatable as Sacred Deer Person.

change the names of things differently because every year the mara'akáme dreams new names. Even if it is the same mara'akáme who leads the journey, he still changes the names each time differently.

And he watches who makes mistakes because there must be no error. One must use the names the mara'akáme has dreamed. Because if one makes an error it is not right. That is how it is. It is a beautiful thing because it is right. Daily, daily, the mara'akáme goes explaining everything to them so that they do not make mistakes. The mara'akáme says to a companion, "Look, why does that man over there watch us, why does he stare at us?" And then he says, "Look, what is it he has to stare at us?" "His eyes," says his companion. "No," the mara'akáme answers, "they are not his eyes, they are tomatoes." That is how he goes explaining how everything should be called.

When one makes cigarettes for the journey, one uses the dried husks of maize for the wrappings. And the tobacco, it is called the droppings of ants. Tortillas one calls bread. Beans one calls fruit from a tree. Maize is wheat. Water is tequila. Instead of saying, "Let us go and get water to drink," you say, "Ah, let us take tequila to eat." *Atole* [maize broth], that is brains. Sandals are cactus. Fingers are sticks. Hair, that is cactus fiber. The moon, that is a cold sun.

On all the trails on which we travel to the peyote country, as we see different things we make this change. That is because the peyote is very sacred, very sacred. That is why it is reversed. Therefore, when we see a dog, it is a cat, or it is a coyote. Ordinarily, when we see a dog, it is just a dog, but when we walk for the peyote it is a cat or a coyote or even something else, as the mara'akáme dreams it. When we see a burro, it is not a burro, it is a cow, or a horse. And when we see a horse, it is something else. When we see a dove or a small bird of some kind, is it a small bird? No, the mara'akáme says, it is an eagle, it is a hawk. Or a piglet, it is not a piglet, it is an armadillo. When we hunt the deer, which is very sacred, it is not a deer, on this journey. It is a lamb, or a cat. And the nets for catching deer? They are called sewing thread.

When we say come, it means go away. When we say "shh, quiet," it means to shout, and when we whistle or call to the front we are really calling to a person behind us. We speak in this direction here.

That one over there turns because he already knows how it is, how everything is reversed. To say, "Let us stay here," means to go, "let us go," and when we say "sit down," we mean, "stand up." It is also so when we have crossed over, when we are in the country of the peyote. Even the peyote is called by another name, as the mara'akáme dreamed. Then the peyote is flower or something else.

It is so with Tatewarí, with Tayaupa.[4] The mara'akáme, we call him Tatewarí. He is Tatewarí, he who leads us. But there in Wirikuta, one says something else. One calls him "the red one." And Tayaupa, he is "the shining one." So all is changed. Our companion who is old, he is called the child. Our companion who is young, he is the old one. When we want to speak of the machete, we say "hook." When one speaks of wood, one really means fish. Begging your pardon, instead of saying "to eat," we say "to defecate." And, begging your pardon, "I am going to urinate" means "I am going to drink water." When speaking of blowing one's nose, one says "give me the honey." "He is deaf" means "how well he hears." So everything is changed, everything is different or backwards.

The mara'akáme goes explaining how everything should be said, everything, many times, or his companions would forget and make errors. In the late afternoon, when all are gathered around Tatewarí, we all pray there, and the mara'akáme tells how it should be. So for instance he says, "Do not speak of this one or that one as serious. Say he is a jaguar. You see an old woman and her face is all wrinkled, coming from afar, do not say, 'Ah, there is a man,' say 'Ah, here comes a wooden image.' You say, 'Here comes the image of Santo Cristo.' Or if it is a woman coming, say 'Ah, here comes the image of Guadalupe.'"

Women, you call flowers. For the woman's skirts, you say, "bush," and for her blouse you say "palm roots." And a man's clothing, that too is changed. His clothing, you call his fur. His hat, that is a mushroom. Or it is his sandal. Begging your pardon, but what we carry down here, the testicles, they are called avocados. And the penis, that is his nose. That is how it is.

---

4. Our Father Sun.

When we come back with the peyote, the peyote which has been hunted, they make a ceremony and everything is changed back again. And those who are at home, when one returns they grab one and ask, "What is it you called things? How is it that now you call the hands hands but when you left you called them feet?" Well, it is because they have changed the names back again. And they all want to know what they called things. One tells them, and there is laughter. That is how it is. Because it must be as it was said in the beginning, in ancient times [Adapted from Myerhoff 1974].

15

Ritual Regulation of Environmental Relations Among a New Guinea People

Roy A. Rappaport

In this article, originally published in 1967, Roy A. Rappaport takes issue with anthropologists who emphasize only the symbolic and emotional aspects of ritual. To Rappaport, ritual may have observable, measurable, practical results, even if those results are not recognizable to the participants. By expanding his focus of study to include the ecosystem of which humans are a part, the author argues that the true functions of ritual may be understood.

Rappaport documents the Tsembaga, a small, politically egalitarian population in one of the interior valleys of New Guinea. The author presents a detailed description of the Tsembaga ecosystem and subsistence methods, emphasizing the place of pigs. Tsembaga carefully control the size of their pig herds, limiting reproduction and slaughtering pigs only for ritual purposes. After considering the cycle of rituals involving pig slaughter—which relates to warfare and maintaining relationships with allies—Rappaport concludes that the size of a pig herd actually determines the timing of some rituals, especially the kaiko, *or "pig festival," which redistributes pork to a large number of people in the territory. When the cost of maintaining a large number of pigs becomes too great, social forces call for the ritual. Therefore, the timing of Tsembaga rituals is connected to the natural environment, including other humans in the region. In clear opposition to such anthropologists as Mary Douglas, Clifford Geertz, and Victor Turner, Rappaport concludes that "[r]eligious ritual may do much more than symbolize, validate, and intensify relationships."*

A key feature of Rappaport's argument is his distinction between the "operational environment," which can be observed by the anthropologist, and the "cognized environment," or the Tsembaga's perceived environment—including their reasons for rituals and beliefs about their effects. Rappaport maintains that the Tsembaga, like other peoples, do not see all the empirical effects of their rituals.

Most functional studies of religious behavior in anthropology have as an analytic goal the elucidation of events, processes, or relationships occurring within a

"Ritual Regulation of Environmental Relations among a New Guinea People," ETHNOLOGY 6:17–30, 1967. Reprinted by permission.

social unit of some sort. The social unit is not always well defined, but in some cases it appears to be a church, that is, a group of people who entertain similar beliefs about the universe, or a congregation, a group of people who participate together in the performance of religious rituals. There have been exceptions. Thus Vayda, Leeds, and Smith (1961) and

O. K. Moore (1957) have clearly perceived that the functions of religious ritual are not necessarily confined within the boundaries of a congregation or even a church. By and large, however, I believe that the following statement by Homans (1941: 172) represents fairly the dominant line of anthropological thought concerning the functions of religious ritual:

> Ritual actions do not produce a practical result on the external world—that is one of the reasons why we call them ritual. But to make this statement is not to say that ritual has no function. Its function is not related to the world external to the society but to the internal constitution of the society. It gives the members of the society confidence, it dispels their anxieties, it disciplines their social organization.

No argument will be raised here against the sociological and psychological functions imputed by Homans, and many others before him, to ritual. They seem to me to be plausible. Nevertheless, in some cases at least, ritual does produce, in Homans' terms, "a practical result on the world" external not only to the social unit composed of those who participate together in ritual performances but also to the larger unit composed of those who entertain similar beliefs concerning the universe. The material presented here will show that the ritual cycles of the Tsembaga, and of other local territorial groups of Maring speakers living in the New Guinea interior, play an important part in regulating the relationships of these groups with both the nonhuman components of their immediate environments and the human components of their less immediate environments, that is, with other similar territorial groups. To be more specific, this regulation helps to maintain the biotic communities existing within their territories, redistributes land among people and people over land, and limits the frequency of fighting. In the absence of authoritative political statuses or offices, the ritual cycle likewise provides a means for mobilizing allies when warfare may be undertaken. It also provides a mechanism for redistributing local pig surpluses in the form of pork throughout a large regional population while helping to assure the local population of a supply of pork when its members are most in need of high quality protein.

Religious ritual may be defined, for the purposes of this paper, as the prescribed performance of conventionalized acts manifestly directed toward the involvement of nonempirical or supernatural agencies in the affairs of the actors. While this definition relies upon the formal characteristics of the performances and upon the motives for undertaking them, attention will be focused upon the empirical effects of ritual performances and sequences of ritual performances. The religious rituals to be discussed are regarded as neither more nor less than part of the behavioral repertoire employed by an aggregate of organisms in adjusting to its environment.

The data upon which this paper is based were collected during fourteen months of field work among the Tsembaga, one of about twenty local groups of Maring speakers living in the Simbai and Jimi Valleys of the Bismarck Range in the Territory of New Guinea. The size of Maring local groups varies from a little over 100 to 900. The Tsembaga, who in 1963 numbered 204 persons, are located on the south wall of the Simbai Valley. The country in which they live differs from the true highlands in being lower, generally more rugged, and more heavily forested. Tsembaga territory rises, within a total surface area of 3.2 square miles, from an elevation of 2,200 feet at the Simbai river to 7,200 feet at the ridge crest. Gardens are cut in the secondary forests up to between 5,000 and 5,400 feet, above which the area remains in primary forest. Rainfall reaches 150 inches per year.

The Tsembaga have come into contact with the outside world only recently; the first government patrol to penetrate their territory arrived in 1954. They were considered uncontrolled by the Australian government until 1962, and they remain unmissionized to this day.

The 204 Tsembaga are distributed among five putatively patrilineal clans, which are, in turn, organized into more inclusive groupings on two hierarchical levels below that of the total local group. Internal political structure is highly egalitarian. There are no hereditary or elected chiefs, nor are there even "big men" who can regularly coerce or command the support of their clansmen or co-residents in economic or forceful enterprises.

It is convenient to regard the Tsembaga as a population in the ecological sense, that is, as one of the components of a system of trophic exchanges taking place within a bounded area. Tsembaga territory and the biotic community existing upon it may be conveniently viewed as an ecosystem. While it would be permissible arbitrarily to designate the Tsembaga as a population and their territory with its biota as an ecosystem, there are also nonarbitrary reasons for doing so. An ecosystem is a system of material exchanges, and the Tsembaga maintain against other human groups exclusive access to the resources within their territorial borders. Conversely, it is from this territory alone that the Tsembaga ordinarily derive all of their foodstuffs and most of the other materials they require for survival. Less anthropocentrically, it may be justified to regard Tsembaga territory with its biota as an ecosystem in view of the rather localized nature of cyclical material exchanges in tropical rainforests.

As they are involved with the nonhuman biotic community within their territory in a set of trophic exchanges, so do they participate in other material relationships with other human groups external to their territory. Genetic materials are exchanged with other groups, and certain crucial items, such as stone axes, were in the past obtained from the outside. Furthermore, in the area occupied by the Maring speakers, more than one local group is usually involved in any process, either peaceful or warlike, through which people are redistributed over land and land redistributed among people.

The concept of the ecosystem, though it provides a convenient frame for the analysis of interspecific trophic exchanges taking place within limited geographical areas, does not comfortably accommodate intraspecific exchanges taking place over wider geographic areas. Some sort of geographic population model would be more useful for the analysis of the relationship of the local ecological population to the larger regional population of which it is a part, but we lack even a set of appropriate terms for such a model. Suffice it here to note that the relations of the Tsembaga to the total of other local human populations in their vicinity are similar to the relations of local aggregates of other animals to the totality of their species occupying broader and more or less continuous regions. This larger, more inclusive aggregate may resemble what geneticists mean by the term population, that is, an aggregate of interbreeding organisms persisting through an indefinite number of generations and either living or capable of living in isolation from similar aggregates of the same species. This is the unit which survives through long periods of time while its local ecological (*sensu stricto*) subunits, the units more or less independently involved in interspecific trophic exchanges such as the Tsembaga, are ephemeral.

Since it has been asserted that the ritual cycles of the Tsembaga regulate relationships within what may be regarded as a complex system, it is necessary, before proceeding to the ritual cycle itself, to describe briefly, and where possible in quantitative terms, some aspects of the place of the Tsembaga in this system.

The Tsembaga are bush-following horticulturalists. Staples include a range of root crops, taro (*Colocasia*) and sweet potatoes being most important, yams and manioc less so. In addition, a great variety of greens are raised, some of which are rich in protein. Sugar cane and some tree crops, particularly *Pandanus conoideus*, are also important.

All gardens are mixed, many of them containing all of the major root crops and many greens. Two named garden types are, however, distinguished by the crops which predominate in them. "Taro-yam gardens" were found to produce, on the basis of daily harvest records kept on entire gardens for close to one year, about 5,300,000 calories[1] per acre during their harvesting lives of 18 to 24 months; 85 percent of their yield is harvested between 24 and 76 weeks after planting. "Sugar–sweet potato gardens" produce about 4,600,000 calories per acre during their harvesting lives, 91 percent being taken between 24 and 76 weeks after planting. I estimated that approximately 310,000 calories per acre is expended on cutting, fencing, planting, maintaining, harvesting, and walking to and from taro-yam gardens. Sugar–sweet potato gardens required an expenditure of approximately 290,000 calories per acre.[2] These energy ratios, approximately 17:1 on taro-yam

1. Because the length of time in the field precluded the possibility of maintaining harvest records on single gardens from planting through abandonment, figures were based, in the case of both "taro-yam" and "sugar–sweet potato" gardens, on three separate gardens planted in successive years. Conversions from the gross weight to the caloric value of the yield were made by reference to the literature. The sources used are listed in Rappaport (1966: Appendix VIII).
2. Rough time and motion studies of each of the tasks involved in making, maintaining, harvesting, and walking to and from gardens were undertaken. Conversion to energy expenditure values was accomplished by reference to energy expenditure tables prepared by Hipsley and Kirk (1965: 43) on the basis of gas exchange measurements made during the performance of garden tasks by the Chimbu people of the New Guinea highlands.

gardens and 16:1 on sugar–sweet potato gardens, compare favorably with figures reported for swidden cultivation in other regions.[3]

Intake is high in comparison with the reported dietaries of other New Guinea populations. On the basis of daily consumption records kept for ten months on four households numbering in total sixteen persons, I estimated the average daily intake of adult males to be approximately 2,600 calories, and that of adult females to be around 2,200 calories. It may be mentioned here that the Tsembaga are small and short-statured. Adult males average 101 pounds in weight and approximately 58.5 inches in height; the corresponding averages for adult females are 85 pounds and 54.5 inches.[4]

Although 99 percent by weight of the food consumed is vegetable, the protein intake is high by New Guinea standards. The daily protein consumption of adult males from vegetable sources was estimated to be between 43 and 55 grams, of adult females 36 to 48 grams. Even with an adjustment for vegetable sources, these values are slightly in excess of the recently published WHO/FAO daily requirements (Food and Agriculture Organization of the United Nations 1964). The same is true of the younger age categories, although soft and discolored hair, a symptom of protein deficiency, was noted in a few children. The WHO/FAO protein requirements do not include a large "margin for safety" or allowance for stress; and, although no clinical assessments were undertaken, it may be suggested that the Tsembaga achieve nitrogen balance at a low level. In other words, their protein intake is probably marginal.

Measurements of all gardens made during 1962 and of some gardens made during 1963 indicate that, to support the human population, between .15 and .19 acres are put into cultivation per capita per year. Fallows range from 8 to 45 years. The area in secondary forest comprises approximately 1,000 acres, only 30 to 50 of which are in cultivation at any time. Assuming calories to be the limiting factor, and assuming an unchanging population structure, the territory could support—with no reduction in lengths of fallow and without cutting into the virgin forest from which the Tsembaga extract many important items—between 290 and 397 people if the pig population remained minimal. The size of the pig herd, however, fluctuates widely. Taking Maring pig husbandry procedures into consideration, I have estimated the human carrying capacity of the Tsembaga territory at between 270 and 320 people.

Because the timing of the ritual cycle is bound up with the demography of the pig herd, the place of the pig in Tsembaga adaptation must be examined.

First, being omnivorous, pigs keep residential areas free of garbage and human feces. Second, limited numbers of pigs rooting in secondary growth may help to hasten the development of that growth. The Tsembaga usually permit pigs to enter their gardens one and a half to two years after planting, by which time second-growth trees are well established there. The Tsembaga practice selective weeding; from the time the garden is planted, herbaceous species are removed, but tree species are allowed to remain. By the time cropping is discontinued and the pigs are let in, some of the trees in the garden are already ten to fifteen feet tall. These well-established trees are relatively impervious to damage by the pigs, which, in rooting for seeds and remaining tubers, eliminate many seeds and seedlings that, if allowed to develop, would provide some competition for the established trees. Moreover, in some Maring-speaking areas swiddens are planted twice, although this is not the case with the Tsembaga. After the first crop is almost exhausted, pigs are penned in the garden, where their rooting eliminates weeds and softens the ground, making the task of planting for a second time easier. The pigs, in other words, are used as cultivating machines.

Small numbers of pigs are easy to keep. They run free during the day and return home at night to receive their ration of garbage and substandard tubers, particularly sweet potatoes. Supplying the latter requires little extra work, for the substandard tubers are taken from the ground in the course of harvesting the daily ration for humans. Daily consumption records kept over a period of some months show

---

3. Marvin Harris, in an unpublished paper, estimates the ratio of energy return to energy input on Dyak (Borneo) rice swiddens at 10:1. His estimates of energy ratios on Tepotzlan (Meso-America) swiddens range from 13:1 on poor land to 29:1 on the best land.

4. Heights may be inaccurate. Many men wear their hair in large coiffures hardened with pandanus grease, and it was necessary in some instances to estimate the location of the top of the skull.

that the ration of tubers received by the pigs approximates in weight that consumed by adult humans, i.e., a little less than three pounds per day per pig.

If the pig herd grows large, however, the substandard tubers incidentally obtained in the course of harvesting for human needs become insufficient, and it becomes necessary to harvest especially for the pigs. In other words, people must work for the pigs and perhaps even supply them with food fit for human consumption. Thus, as Vayda, Leeds, and Smith (1961: 71) have pointed out, there can be too many pigs for a given community.

This also holds true of the sanitary and cultivating services rendered by pigs. A small number of pigs is sufficient to keep residential areas clean, to suppress superfluous seedlings in abandoned gardens, and to soften the soil in gardens scheduled for second plantings. A larger herd, on the other hand, may be troublesome; the larger the number of pigs, the greater the possibility of their invasion of producing gardens, with concomitant damage not only to crops and young secondary growth but also to the relations between the pig owners and garden owners.

All male pigs are castrated at approximately three months of age, for boars, people say, are dangerous and do not grow as large as barrows. Pregnancies, therefore, are always the result of unions of domestic sows with feral males. Fecundity is thus only a fraction of its potential. During one twelve-month period only fourteen litters resulted out of a potential 99 or more pregnancies. Farrowing generally takes place in the forest, and mortality of the young is high. Only 32 of the offspring of the above-mentioned fourteen pregnancies were alive six months after birth. This number is barely sufficient to replace the number of adult animals which would have died or been killed during most years without pig festivals.

The Tsembaga almost never kill domestic pigs outside of ritual contexts. In ordinary times, when there is no pig festival in progress, these rituals are almost always associated with misfortunes or emergencies, notably warfare, illness, injury, or death. Rules state not only the contexts in which pigs are to be ritually slaughtered, but also who may partake of the flesh of the sacrificial animals. During warfare it is only the men participating in the fighting who eat the pork. In cases of illness or injury, it is only the victim and certain near relatives, particularly his co-resident agnates and spouses, who do so.

It is reasonable to assume that misfortune and emergency are likely to induce in the organisms experiencing them a complex of physiological changes known collectively as "stress." Physiological stress reactions occur not only in organisms which are infected with disease or traumatized, but also in those experiencing rage or fear (Houssay et al. 1955: 1096), or even prolonged anxiety (National Research Council 1963: 53). One important aspect of stress is the increased catabolization of protein (Houssay et al. 1955: 451; National Research Council 1963: 49), with a net loss of nitrogen from the tissues (Houssay et al. 1955: 450). This is a serious matter for organisms with a marginal protein intake. Antibody production is low (Berg 1948: 311), healing is slow (Large and Johnston 1948: 352), and a variety of symptoms of a serious nature are likely to develop (Lund and Levenson 1948: 349; Zintel 1964: 1043). The status of a protein-depleted animal, however, may be significantly improved in a relatively short period of time by the intake of high quality protein, and high protein diets are therefore routinely prescribed for surgical patients and those suffering from infectious diseases (Burton 1959: 231; Lund and Levenson 1948: 350; Elman 1951: 85ff.; Zintel 1964: 1043ff.).

It is precisely when they are undergoing physiological stress that the Tsembaga kill and consume their pigs, and it should be noted that they limit the consumption to those likely to be experiencing stress most profoundly. The Tsembaga, of course, know nothing of physiological stress. Native theories of the etiology and treatment of disease and injury implicate various categories of spirits to whom sacrifices must be made. Nevertheless, the behavior which is appropriate in terms of native understandings is also appropriate to the actual situation confronting the actors.

We may now outline in the barest of terms the Tsembaga ritual cycle. Space does not permit a description of its ideological correlates. It must suffice to note that the Tsembaga do not necessarily perceive all of the empirical effects which the anthropologist sees to flow from their ritual behavior. Such empirical consequences as they may perceive, moreover, are not central to their rationalizations of the performances. The Tsembaga say that they perform the rituals in order to rearrange their relationships with the supernatural world. We may only reiterate here that behavior undertaken in reference to their "cognized environment"—an environment which includes as very important elements the spirits of ancestors—seems appropriate in their "operational environment," the material environment specified by the anthropologist through operations of observation, including measurement.

Since the rituals are arranged in a cycle, description may commence at any point. The operation of the cycle becomes clearest if we begin with the rituals performed during warfare. Opponents in all cases occupy adjacent territories, in almost all cases on the same valley wall. After hostilities have broken out, each side performs certain rituals which place the opposing side in the formal category of "enemy." A number of taboos prevail while hostilities continue. These include prohibitions on sexual intercourse and on the ingestion of certain things—food prepared by women, food grown on the lower portion of the territory, marsupials, eels, and while actually on the fighting ground, any liquid whatsoever.

One ritual practice associated with fighting which may have some physiological consequences deserves mention. Immediately before proceeding to the fighting ground, the warriors eat heavily salted pig fat. The ingestion of salt, coupled with the taboo on drinking, has the effect of shortening the fighting day, particularly since the Maring prefer to fight only on bright sunny days. When everyone gets unbearably thirsty, according to informants, fighting is broken off.

There may formerly have been other effects if the native salt contained sodium (the production of salt was discontinued some years previous to the field work, and no samples were obtained). The Maring diet seems to be deficient in sodium. The ingestion of large amounts of sodium just prior to fighting would have permitted the warriors to sweat normally without a lowering of blood volume and consequent weakness during the course of the fighting. The pork belly ingested with the salt would have provided them with a new burst of energy two hours or so after the commencement of the engagement. After fighting was finished for the day, lean pork was consumed, offsetting, at least to some extent, the nitrogen loss associated with the stressful fighting (personal communications from F. Dunn, W. McFarlane, and J. Sabine, 1965).

Fighting could continue sporadically for weeks. Occasionally it terminated in the rout of one of the antagonistic groups, whose survivors would take refuge with kinsmen elsewhere. In such instances, the victors would lay waste their opponents' groves and gardens, slaughter their pigs, and burn their houses. They would not, however, immediately annex the territory of the vanquished. The Maring say that they never take over the territory of an enemy for, even if it has been abandoned, the spirits of their ancestors remain to guard it against interlopers. Most fights, however, terminated in truces between the antagonists.

With the termination of hostilities a group which has not been driven off its territory performs a ritual called "planting the *rumbim*." Every man puts his hand on the ritual plant, *rumbim* (*Cordyline fruticosa* (L.), A. Chev; *C. terminalis*, Kunth), as it is planted in the ground. The ancestors are addressed, in effect, as follows:

> We thank you for helping us in the fight and permitting us to remain on our territory. We place our souls in this *rumbim* as we plant it on our ground. We ask you to care for this *rumbim*. We will kill pigs for you now, but they are few. In the future, when we have many pigs, we shall again give you pork and uproot the *rumbim* and stage a *kaiko* (pig festival). But until there are sufficient pigs to repay you the *rumbim* will remain in the ground.

This ritual is accompanied by the wholesale slaughter of pigs. Only juveniles remain alive. All adult and adolescent animals are killed, cooked, and dedicated to the ancestors. Some are consumed by the local group, but most are distributed to allies who assisted in the fight.

Some of the taboos which the group suffered during the time of fighting are abrogated by this ritual. Sexual intercourse is now permitted, liquids may be taken at any time, and food from any part of the territory may be eaten. But the group is still in debt to its allies and ancestors. People say it is still the time of the *bamp ku*, or "fighting stones," which are actual objects used in the rituals associated with warfare. Although the fighting ceases when *rumbim* is planted, the concomitant obligations, debts to allies and ancestors, remain outstanding; and the fighting stones may not be put away until these obligations are fulfilled. The time of the fighting stones is a time of debt and danger which lasts until the *rumbim* is uprooted and a pig festival (*kaiko*) is staged.

Certain taboos persist during the time of the fighting stones. Marsupials, regarded as the pigs of the ancestors of the high ground, may not be trapped until the debt to their masters has been repaid. Eels, the "pigs of the ancestors of the low ground," may neither be caught nor consumed. Prohibitions on all intercourse with the enemy come into force. One may not touch, talk to, or even look at a member of the enemy group, nor set foot on enemy ground. Even more important, a group may not attack another group while its ritual plant remains in the ground, for it has not yet fully rewarded its ancestors and allies for their assistance in the last fight. Until the debts to them have been paid, further assistance from them will not be forthcoming. A kind of "truce of god" thus prevails until the *rumbim* is uprooted and a *kaiko* completed.

To uproot the *rumbim* requires sufficient pigs. How many pigs are sufficient, and how long does it take to acquire them? The Tsembaga say that, if a place is "good," this can take as little as five years; but if a place is "bad," it may require ten years or longer. A bad place is one in which misfortunes are frequent and where, therefore, ritual demands for the killing of pigs arise frequently. A good place is one where such demands are infrequent. In a good place, the increase of the pig herd exceeds the ongoing ritual demands, and the herd grows rapidly. Sooner or later the substandard tubers incidentally obtained while harvesting become insufficient to feed the herd, and additional acreage must be put into production specifically for the pigs.

The work involved in caring for a large pig herd can be extremely burdensome. The Tsembaga herd just prior to the pig festival of 1962–63, when it numbered 169 animals, was receiving 54 percent of all the sweet potatoes and 82 percent of all the manioc harvested. These comprised 35.9 percent by weight of all root crops harvested. This figure is consistent with the difference between the amount of land under cultivation just previous to the pig festival, when the herd was at maximum size, and that immediately afterwards, when the pig herd was at minimum size. The former was 36.1 percent in excess of the latter.

I have estimated, on the basis of acreage yield and energy expenditure figures, that about 45,000 calories per year are expended in caring for one pig 120–150 pounds in size. It is upon women that most of the burden of pig keeping falls. If, from a woman's daily intake of about 2,200 calories, 950 calories are allowed for basal metabolism, a woman has only 1,250 calories a day available for all her activities, which include gardening for her family, child care, and cooking, as well as tending pigs. It is clear that no woman can feed many pigs; only a few had as many as four in their care at the commencement of the festival; and it is not surprising that agitation to uproot the *rumbim* and stage the *kaiko* starts with the wives of the owners of large numbers of pigs.

A large herd is not only burdensome as far as energy expenditure is concerned; it becomes increasingly a nuisance as it expands. The more numerous pigs become, the more frequently are gardens invaded by them. Such events result in serious disturbances of local tranquillity. The garden owner often shoots, or attempts to shoot, the offending pig; and the pig owner commonly retorts by shooting, or attempting to shoot, either the garden owner, his wife, or one of his pigs. As more and more such events occur, the settlement, nucleated when the herd was small, disperses as people try to put as much distance as possible between their pigs and other people's gardens and between their gardens and other people's pigs. Occasionally this reaches its logical conclusion, and people begin to leave the territory, taking up residence with kinsmen in other local populations.

The number of pigs sufficient to become intolerable to the Tsembaga was below the capacity of the territory to carry pigs. I have estimated that, if the size and structure of the human population remained constant at the 1962–1963 level, a pig population of 140 to 240 animals averaging 100 to 150 pounds in size could be maintained perpetually by the Tsembaga without necessarily inducing environmental degradation. Since the size of the herd fluctuates, even higher cyclical maxima could be achieved. The level of toleration, however, is likely always to be below the carrying capacity, since the destructive capacity of the pigs is dependent upon the population density of both people and pigs, rather than upon population size. The denser the human population, the fewer pigs will be required to disrupt social life. If the carrying capacity is exceeded, it is likely to be exceeded by people and not by pigs.

The *kaiko* or pig festival, which commences with the planting of stakes at the boundary and the uprooting of the *rumbim*, is thus triggered by either the additional work attendant upon feeding pigs or the destructive capacity of the pigs themselves. It may be said, then, that there are sufficient pigs to stage the *kaiko* when the relationship of pigs to people changes from one of mutualism to one of parasitism or competition.

A short time prior to the uprooting of the *rumbim*, stakes are planted at the boundary. If the enemy has continued to occupy its territory, the stakes are planted at the boundary which existed before the fight. If, on the other hand, the enemy has abandoned its territory, the victors may plant their stakes at a new boundary which encompasses areas previously occupied by the enemy. The Maring say, to be sure, that they never take land belonging to an enemy, but this land is regarded as vacant, since no *rumbim* was planted on it after the last fight. We may state here a rule of land redistribution in terms of the ritual cycle: *If one of a pair of antagonistic groups is able to uproot its* rumbim *before its opponents can plant their* rumbim, *it may occupy the latter's territory.*

Not only have the vanquished abandoned their territory; it is assumed that it has also been abandoned by their ancestors as well. The surviving members of the erstwhile enemy group have by this time resided with other groups for a number of years, and most if not all of them have already had occasion to sacrifice pigs to their ancestors at their new residences. In so doing they have invited these spirits to settle at the new locations of the living, where they will in the future receive sacrifices. Ancestors of vanquished groups thus relinquish their guardianship over the territory, making it available to victorious groups. Meanwhile, the *de facto* membership of the living in the groups with which they have taken refuge is converted eventually into *de jure* membership. Sooner or later the groups with which they have taken up residence will have occasion to plant *rumbim*, and the refugees, as co-residents, will participate, thus ritually validating their connection to the new territory and the new group. A rule of population redistribution may thus be stated in terms of ritual cycles: *A man becomes a member of a territorial group by participating with it in the planting of* rumbim.

The uprooting of the *rumbim* follows shortly after the planting of stakes at the boundary. On this particular occasion the Tsembaga killed 32 pigs out of their herd of 169. Much of the pork was distributed to allies and affines outside of the local group.

The taboo on trapping marsupials was also terminated at this time. Information is lacking concerning the population dynamics of the local marsupials, but it may well be that the taboo which had prevailed since the last fight—that against taking them in traps—had conserved a fauna which might otherwise have become extinct.

The *kaiko* continues for about a year, during which period friendly groups are entertained from time to time. The guests receive presents of vegetable foods, and the hosts and male guests dance together throughout the night.

These events may be regarded as analogous to aspects of the social behavior of many nonhuman animals. First of all, they include massed epigamic, or courtship, displays (Wynne-Edwards 1962: 17). Young women are presented with samples of the eligible males of local groups with which they may not otherwise have had the opportunity to become familiar. The context, moreover, permits the young women to discriminate amongst this sample in terms of both endurance (signaled by how vigorously and how long a man dances) and wealth (signaled by the richness of a man's shell and feather finery).

More importantly, the massed dancing at these events may be regarded as epideictic display, communicating to the participants information concerning the size or density of the group (Wynne-Edwards 1962: 16). In many species such displays take place as a prelude to actions which adjust group size or density, and such is the case among the Maring. The massed dancing of the visitors at a *kaiko* entertainment communicates to the hosts, while the *rumbim* truce is still in force, information concerning the amount of support they may expect from the visitors in the bellicose enterprises that they are likely to embark upon soon after the termination of the pig festival.

Among the Maring there are no chiefs or other political authorities capable of commanding the support of a body of followers, and the decision to assist another group in warfare rests with each individual male. Allies are not recruited by appealing for help to other local groups as such. Rather, each member of the groups primarily involved in the hostilities appeals to his cognatic and affinal kinsmen in other local groups. These men, in turn, urge other of their co-residents and kinsmen to "help them fight." The channels through which invitations to dance are extended are precisely those through which appeals for military support are issued. The invitations go not from group to group, but from kinsman to kinsman, the recipients of invitations urging their co-residents to "help them dance."

Invitations to dance do more than exercise the channels through which allies are recruited; they provide a means for judging their effectiveness. Dancing and fighting are regarded as in some sense equivalent. This equivalence is expressed in the similarity of some pre-fight and pre-dance rituals, and the Maring say that those who come to dance come to fight. The size of a visiting dancing contingent is consequently taken as a measure of the size of the contingent of warriors whose assistance may be expected in the next round of warfare.

In the morning the dancing ground turns into a trading ground. The items most frequently exchanged include axes, bird plumes, shell ornaments, an occasional baby pig, and, in former times, native salt. The *kaiko* thus facilitates trade by providing a market-like setting in which large numbers of traders can assemble. It likewise facilitates the movement of two critical items, salt and axes, by creating a demand for the bird plumes which may be exchanged for them.

The *kaiko* concludes with major pig sacrifices. On this particular occasion the Tsembaga butchered 105 adult and adolescent pigs, leaving only 60 juveniles and neonates alive. The survival of an additional fifteen adolescents and adults was only temporary, for they were scheduled as imminent victims. The pork yielded by the Tsembaga slaughter was estimated to weigh between 7,000 and 8,500 pounds, of which between 4,500 and 6,000 pounds were distributed to members of other local groups in 163 separate presentations. An estimated 2,000 to 3,000 people in seventeen local groups were the beneficiaries of the redistribution. The presentations, it should be mentioned, were not confined to pork. Sixteen Tsembaga men presented bridewealth or child-wealth, consisting largely of axes and shells, to their affines at this time.

The *kaiko* terminates on the day of the pig slaughter with the public presentation of salted pig belly to allies of the last fight. Presentations are made through the window in a high ceremonial fence built specially for the occasion at one end of the dance ground. The name of each honored man is announced to the assembled multitude as he charges to the window to receive his hero's portion. The fence is then ritually torn down, and the fighting stones are put away. The pig festival and the ritual cycle have been completed, demonstrating, it may be suggested, the ecological and economic competence of the local population. The local population would now be free, if it were not for the presence of the government, to attack its enemy again, secure in the knowledge that the assistance of allies and ancestors would be forthcoming because they have received pork and the obligations to them have been fulfilled.

Usually fighting did break out again very soon after the completion of the ritual cycle. If peace still prevailed when the ceremonial fence had rotted completely—a process said to take about three years, a little longer than the length of time required to raise a pig to maximum size—*rumbim* was planted as if there had been a fight, and all adult and adolescent pigs were killed. When the pig herd was large enough so that the *rumbim* could be uprooted, peace could be made with former enemies if they were also able to dig out their *rumbim*. To put this in formal terms: *If a pair of antagonistic groups proceeds through two ritual cycles without resumption of hostilities their enmity may be terminated.*

The relations of the Tsembaga with their environment have been analyzed as a complex system composed of two subsystems. What may be called the "local subsystem" has been derived from the relations of the Tsembaga with the nonhuman components of their immediate or territorial environment. It corresponds to the ecosystem in which the Tsembaga participate. A second subsystem, one which corresponds to the larger regional population of which the Tsembaga are one of the constituent units and which may be designated as the "regional subsystem," has been derived from the relations of the Tsembaga with neighboring local populations similar to themselves.

It has been argued that rituals, arranged in repetitive sequences, regulate relations both within each of the subsystems and within the larger complex system as a whole. The timing of the ritual cycle is largely dependent upon changes in the states of the components of the local subsystem. But the *kaiko*, which is the culmination of the ritual cycle, does more than reverse changes which have taken place within the local subsystem. Its occurrence also affects relations among the components of the regional subsystem. During its performance, obligations to other local populations are fulfilled, support for future military enterprises is rallied, and land from which enemies have earlier been driven is occupied. Its completion, furthermore, permits the local population to initiate warfare again. Conversely, warfare is terminated by rituals which preclude the reinitiation of warfare until the state of the local subsystem is again such that a *kaiko* may be staged and completed. Ritual among the Tsembaga and other Maring, in short, operates as both transducer, "translating" changes in the state of one subsystem into information which can effect changes in a second subsystem, and homeostat, maintaining a number of variables which in sum comprise the total system within ranges of viability. To repeat an earlier assertion, the operation of ritual among the Tsembaga and other Maring helps to maintain an undegraded environment, limits fighting to frequencies which do not endanger the existence of the regional population, adjusts man-land ratios, facilitates trade, distributes local surpluses of pig throughout the regional population in the form of pork, and assures people of high quality protein when they are most in need of it.

Religious rituals and the supernatural orders toward which they are directed cannot be assumed *a priori* to be mere epiphenomena. Ritual may, and doubtless frequently does, do nothing more than validate and intensify the relationships which integrate the social unit, or symbolize the relationships which bind the social unit to its environment. But the interpretation of such presumably *sapiens*-specific phenomena as religious ritual within a framework which will also accommodate the behavior of other species shows, I think, that religious ritual may do much more than symbolize, validate, and intensify relationships. Indeed, it would not be improper to refer to the Tsembaga and the other entities with which they share their territory as a "ritually regulated ecosystem," and to the Tsembaga and their human neighbors as a "ritually regulated population."

16

A Handmaid's Tale: The Rhetoric of Personhood in American and Japanese Healing of Abortions

Thomas J. Csordas

Thomas J. Csordas is an influential cultural and psychological anthropologist whose interests include the relationships between religion, mental health, emotions, and the body. Much of his research has been with the Charismatic Renewal movement, a non-mainstream group within Roman Catholicism that incorporates features of charismatic or Pentecostal Protestant worship. Reflecting his interest in both the therapeutic efficacy of ritual and the construction of emotions and disorders unique to particular cultures, Csordas here examines religious rituals for women who have undergone abortions. The author utilizes a comparative approach to consider the Charismatic Renewal post-abortion rituals and similar rituals in Japan.

Given the different ideological contexts of abortion in the North America and Japan, what do these superficially similar rituals tell us about how their respective cultures perceive the fetus? Cross-cultural evidence indicates that societies around the world have profoundly different ideas about when a fetus becomes a person (despite various confident answers in the United States about "when life begins"), what a "person" is, and about the relationship between fetuses and the divine.

Csordas focuses his analysis on the rituals themselves, and how they accomplish the emotional healing that their particular cultures call for. The Charismatic Renewal movement carries out workshops and retreats in which, through guided visualization, participants aim to heal painful memories. Women who have undergone abortions envision the aborted fetus as a person who can be named, baptized, and entrusted to Jesus; in a sense, they undo the abortion, and maintain the gender ideology of their religious community. A very different ritual response occurs in Japan, where abortion is not the contentiously political public issue that it is in the United States. Fetuses lost through miscarriage, stillbirth, or abortion are propitiated through prayer and the offering of child-shaped statues. These rituals, mizuko kuyo, *are Buddhist in nature but—like the post-abortion rituals of Charismatic Catholics—developed in the last decades of the 20th century.*

Like many present-day anthropologists, Csordas does not hide his own position behind a façade of neutrality. Early in the article, he discloses his discomfort with some aspects of the community under study. Abortion is a controversial issue in contemporary North America, and as Csordas points out, responses to it stretch the limits of cultural relativism. He provocatively concludes: ". . .cultures can create and define the very problems to which they then develop therapeutic solutions," and this includes the possibility of oppression.

This chapter has to do with religious rituals directed at the experience of women in North America and Japan who have undergone abortions. In each case, they are rituals aimed at the healing of a particular cultural construction of grief and guilt predicated upon a particular ethnopsychology of the person. I will first present the North American ritual and then contrast it with a parallel ritual in contemporary Japan.

The North American ritual, or more precisely the ritual technique, is disturbing in the way it taps into one of the most emotionally, ethically, and politically provocative issues in contemporary society. It is disturbing in the same sense as is Margaret Atwood's powerful novel, *A Handmaid's Tale*, from which I've borrowed my title. Atwood describes a North American society in the very near and almost-present future in which fundamentalist Christianity has acceded to political power and created a totalitarian state. In this psychic, the act of performing abortion is punishable by death and the public exhibition of one's humiliated corpse. Because environmental pollution has decreased the population's fertility to a dangerously low level, the Commanders who constitute a ruling elite are assigned Handmaids. These fertile young women complement the Commanders' privileged Wives as reproductive servants within their sanctified households.

When I first encountered Atwood's work, I was frankly jolted by the similarity of terminology to that prevalent in some of the Catholic Charismatic "covenant communities" I had been studying. "Household" was indeed a specialized term for a Christian living arrangement that included more members than a nuclear family. There was an office of "handmaid," admittedly without reproductive function, but understood as a role in which some women had additional responsibilities for community service, particularly regarding the well-being of other women, but always under direct male "headship" or authority. Somewhat ominously, in the leading covenant community, the office of handmaid

was itself suspended for a period of several years, presumably because those who held it were arrogating more authority than was regarded as biblically warranted by the male ruling elite. The ruling elite of these communities, which considered themselves vanguard outposts of a coming kingdom of God (the logical extension of which seemed to me to be Atwood's Republic of Gilead), styled themselves not as Commanders within a religious police state, but in a slightly more bureaucratic vein, as "Coordinators" (Csordas 1997).

The possibility of seeing the Charismatics as "proto-Gileadean" was entranced during my study of their system of ritual healing when I discovered the rite I will describe below. Let me note from the outset that some Catholic Charismatics are quite active in the political opposition to abortion, prompted by the double influence of embracing the conservative position of the Roman Catholic hierarchy and embracing the fundamentalist conservatism of neo-Pentecostalism. Some are additionally active in a campaign to achieve medical recognition of what they call "post-abortion syndrome," a fabricated psychiatric syndrome modeled very closely on the definition of "post-traumatic stress disorder" found in the American Psychiatric Association's Diagnostic and Statistical Manual. Such a disorder is, strictly speaking, a culture-bound disorder in the sense that it is relevant only within a Charismatic culture that defines the experience of abortion as necessarily traumatic.

Leaving that point aside for the present, note that the healing practices we have been discussing among Catholic Charismatics show a remarkable uniformity across regions and locales, at least within North America. This is in part due to a highly developed distribution system for movement publications including books, magazines, and audiotapes, as well as the existence of a class of teachers and healers who travel to workshops, conferences, retreats, and "days of renewal" at which such practices and their rationales are disseminated. Again, the three principal forms of healing are prayer for healing of physical or medical problems, Deliverance or casting out of evil spirits, and inner healing or Healing of Memories.[1] The Healing of Memories is the ritual transformation of the consequences of emotional trauma or

Originally appeared in GENDER AND HEALTH: AN INTERNATIONAL PERSPECTIVE, eds. Carolyn Sargent and Caroline Brettell. Englewood Cliffs: Prentice-Hall (1996), pp. 227–41. Article also appears in Csordas's book, BODY/ MEANING/HEALING. Palgrave/Macmillan (2002), as Chapter 3.

1. For comprehensive treatments of Catholic Charismatic healing, see Csordas (1994a) and McGuire (1982, 1983).

"woundedness" by means of prayer. This prayer often includes imaginal processes in the form of guided imagery initiated by the healer or the spontaneous enactment of a scenario by the patient. At times the memory identified as in need of transformation is that of having had an abortion. In Charismatic culture, undergoing an abortion is presumed traumatic to the pregnant woman, entailing the emotional consequences of guilt and the grief of bereavement, and is also presumed to produce a death trauma for the aborted fetus.[2]

Healing of memories for the mother and fetus is described in a book by the highly popular Charismatic Jesuit priests Dennis and Matthew Linn and their collaborator Sheila Fabricant (1985:105–139). Their book treats miscarriages, stillbirths, and abortions as a single class, beginning with a theological discussion emphasizing that while these unbaptized do not necessarily end up in the "limbo" of Catholic lore and can go to heaven, they are in need of healing. The authors go on to a psychological discussion of prenatal research, arguing for the emotional viability, and hence vulnerability of these beings. Then follows a discussion of grief among mothers, which quickly turns to focus on abortion and argues for the commonality of grief and guilt among women who choose abortions.

The authors narrate two cases of praying for such women. The first was a woman who had had one abortion, and had also attempted to abort her now-18-year-old daughter who was having frequent violent outbursts against family members. During a mass offered for the aborted fetus and for "any part of" the living daughter that had died during the abortion attempt, the adult woman collapsed on the floor and experienced all the pains and contractions of labor, following which the healers initiated her symbolically "to give her baby to Jesus and Mary to be cared for." Subsequently the woman claimed that her chronic back pain improved, as did her daughter's violent outbursts, both changes interpreted by the healers as evidence of relief of "the trauma of the abortion." The second case was a woman for whom healing hurt and self-hatred from having an abortion

nine years previously caused a variety of other hurts to emerge, including the perinatal effects of grief experienced by her own mother over the death of her father and anger at her relatives who refused to allow the pregnant woman a deathbed visit, as well as the effects of being born with her umbilical cord wrapped around her neck, and of having been physically and sexually abused during childhood.

These examples exhibit an ethnopsychology in which abortion (in a degree greater than miscarriage or stillbirth) is a powerful pathogenic agent, and in which ritual healing is a powerful and occasionally dramatic antidote. The rite often includes specific imaginal techniques. Linn, Linn, and Fabricant describe four steps: (1) the patient visualizes Jesus and Mary holding the child, and the patient holds it with them, asking forgiveness from the deity and the child for any way in which he or she hurt the child, and is instructed to imaginally "see what Jesus or the child says or does in response to you," and with them to forgive anyone else who may have hurt the child; (2) the patient chooses a name for the dead fetus and symbolically baptizes it, with the instruction to "feel the water cleansing and making all things anew," thus granting the fetus the cultural status of a person and, in effect, ritually "undoing" the abortion; (3) the patient prays that the fetus receive divine love, and is instructed to imaginally "place it in the arms of Jesus and Mary and see them do all the things you can't do," and to ask the fetus to become an intercessor for the patient and the patient's family; (4) the patient has a mass offered for the child, and while receiving the Eucharist is instructed to "let Jesus' love and forgiving blood flow through you to the child and to all other deceased members of your family tree" (1985:138–139).

Person, Gender, and Efficacy

The degree of multisensory vividness that can be attained in what we can call this embodied imaginal performance (see also Csordas 1994a) is evident in the following case narrated by a team of two Charismatic healers (G and H):

G: . . . one lady that we had prayed over for an abortion [was so upset that] she turned purple at one point. . . . Anyway, we asked the Lord if she could have the vision of her baby, aborted baby.

---

2. For a cultural analysis of the loss of wanted pregnancy that includes religious and symbolic responses see Layne (1992).

And she physically cupped her hands, arms and hands, as if she was holding a baby. And if you saw her, if you saw any of us, [you'd] probably think we were all nuts. But if you saw her, it looked like she was holding a baby. I mean she was there like this. And talking to it. Of course there was nothing there that anyone could see. But we had just asked the Lord if He would allow her to hold the baby. And the next moment she was holding her baby.

TC: You asked aloud with her or you asked [God] silently whether she could . . .

G: No, we asked her first, out loud. And she said she wanted to. Then she wouldn't give it up. So we were quite a while until she was able to let the baby go.

H: And we would just remain silent and just keep praying silently and with our hands on her. So that He [God] would go into her . . .

G: Real physical manifestation . . .

H: And you could just feel it all around, in the air, of the Lord just loving her.

C: Did she have the physical experience of holding the baby?

G: Oh, yeah.

TC: And what did the purple in her face mean?

G: Well that was before [the imagery sequence]. I just think it was the guilt and the mourning over it.

H: See the thing is she didn't want to come to the acceptance that she had anything to do with the abortion. It was "all her husband's fault." And when she finally came to realize that she had to take a responsibility to . . .

G: She started screaming.

H: Then it was kind of scary, ya know. But [we] just loved her through that. And He was there with us. So it was a beautiful experience.

G: And something very interesting on that was, when we deal with the healing for an abortion, we always ask them if they have a sense of what gender the baby is, and if they have any sense of a name . . . if they even hear a name or see a name or the Lord places a name in their heart. And I forgot what the name was, but it was a girl. And both . . . we dealt with them separately. Both had a sense it was a girl and both came up with the same name. Husband and wife. And they did not consult with each other. Because we saw her first, and then we ushered her out of the room. There was no

communication between the two. And both sensed that it was a girl, and both came up with the exact same name. And neither one had talked about this since the day that the abortion occurred. Never brought it up again. So I mean there was no possible way that they could have named it . . . that before the abortion they had even thought it.

I will organize my analysis of this text around the four elements that I identified [. . .] as essential to therapeutic process in ritual healing. Regarding *disposition*, it is evident that the supplicant must be culturally disposed not only to accept the possibility of divine healing but also to regard having undergone an abortion as a problem in need of healing. The healer's presumption that the supplicant's "turning purple" indicated states of guilt and mourning are part of the taken-for-granted nature of the latter disposition, apparently never challenged by participants. The presence of both dispositions is suggested by the apparent fact that the healing was directed specifically toward the abortion experience and that the woman's husband was included in a systematic way, separate from his wife. The disposition to maternal attachment enacted in the woman's refusal to relinquish her imaginal baby is consistent with participation in the healing system.

Nevertheless it is necessary to recognize that the presumption of guilt as an emotion in the supplicant can, through performance, act as an induction of guilt. This is especially the case when guilt is regarded not only as an emotional but an objective state—that is, a state of sin. Characteristically for Charismatics, there is no explicit discussion of sin and repentance, which remain implicit in the reference to "taking responsibility for" the action. In no way does this phrase mean that healing is constituted by "coming to terms with having made a responsible, though difficult, decision." Instead, it means that emotional healing requires "acknowledging that by consenting to your husband's demand you too are responsible for a sin," and accepting divine forgiveness.

Experience of the sacred is actualized by multisensory imagery in several cultural forms. Gendering and naming the fetus is achieved through revelatory imagery, and the conviction of divine empowerment is reinforced by the concurrence of husband's and wife's images in the absence of consultation. Divinely granted haptic, kinesthetic, and visual imagery of an exceedingly vivid, eidetic quality is evident in the woman's holding the imaginal baby and talking to it. The experience of divine presence as a phenomenon of embodiment is attested by the healers' account that, for their own part, they could "feel it all around, in the air," and that the supplicant's imagery sequence was a "real physical manifestation" of divine power entering her. Finally, although not specifically recounted in this text, it is likely that the supplicant with her child was led through a complete imaginal performance of baptizing the baby and finally letting it go into the hands of Jesus.

While the imaginal form and eidetic quality of these experiences define them as sacred, their content achieves the third therapeutic function of *elaboration of alternatives.* Two such alternatives are implicit in this episode. First is that of actually having a baby, elaborated in the imaginal holding of the baby and its cultural thematic of maternal-child intimacy. Second is that of having the fetus die in a culturally appropriate way, that is, as a baby with definite gender, name, and Christian baptism.

It is the latter alternative that is taken up as part of the *actualization of change,* for part of the efficacy of ritual performance is precisely transforming the fetus into a person. A person in this sense is a cultural representation, or more precisely an objectification of indeterminate self processes [. . .] While both a fetus and a baby are biological entities, whether, and at what point, they are objectified as "persons" varies across cultures. The current North American debate is based on whether the person begins at conception, at birth, or in one of the culturally established "trimesters" between the two. In cross-cultural perspective we see that the issue of personhood extends even beyond birth, however. Among the Northern Cheyenne, children are not participants in the moral community because they lack knowledge or responsibility for their actions, and are therefore considered only "potential" persons (Fogelson 1982; Ann Straus 1977). Among the Mande peoples of Africa, a newborn is not yet a member of the worldly family, remaining unnamed till eight days after birth. The shape of the placenta is examined to determine whether the newborn is in fact not a human person but a *saa* or spirit child (R. Whittemore, personal communication). Among the Dogon, a fetus is conceived as a kind of fish until it has received a se-

ries of names and has been circumcised or excised, at which time only it is recognized as truly a boy or girl (Dieterlin 1971:226). For the Tallensi, "it is not until an infant is weaned and has a following sibling (*nyeer*) that it can be said to be on the road to full personhood," a status that is in fact "only attained by degrees over the whole course of a life" (Fortes 1987:261). Among the poorest of Brazil, children are often neither baptized nor named till they are toddlers, and the infant that dies is considered neither a human child nor yet a blessed angel. Instead, "the infant's humanness, its personhood, and its claims on the mother's attention and affections grow over time, slowly, tentatively, and anxiously" (Scheper-Hughes 1990:560).

Such examples could be multiplied, and indeed a paper by Lynn Morgan (1989) does a masterful job of synthesizing the cross-cultural data on the personhood of neonate humans. However in all of these examples, the contrast with the Charismatic practice could not be more striking: Whereas in these instances an already-born infant is *not yet* a person, in Charismatic healing a never-to-be-born fetus is *still* a person. The difference is doubtless grounded in the circumstance that in the former cases, where infant mortality is high, no infant can necessarily be expected to survive, whereas in the middle-class North America of the Charismatics, no infant is ever expected to die. Nevertheless, in all the cases it is the ritual action of naming (and baptizing or its equivalent) that bestows the cultural status of person. Phenomenologically reinforced by imaginal performance, part of the actualization of change in the healing of abortion is creation of a person that can subsequently be prayed for and regarded as being "with Jesus."

This is not all, however, for in this instance actualization of change includes the dual movement of "accepting responsibility" and "letting go." In the healers' account the supplicant's screaming must be categorized as a kind of therapeutic breakthrough that was buffered as they "loved her through that in collaboration with the divine presence." The rather peculiar juxtaposition of "scary" and "beautiful" to describe the situation carries a dual message related both to efficacy to situational dynamics. To redefine a scary situation as a beautiful one is at once to say that what was potentially negative and dangerous was, in fact, highly successful—beauty is synonymous with efficacy. At the same time, it is an acknowledgment that the dynamics of the situation nearly got out of hand but didn't and here, beauty is synonymous with control. Finally, the actualization of "letting go" is the epitome of the Charismatic surrender of control to the deity in exchange for emotional freedom. Here again is a dual meaning. On the one hand, the supplicant "lets go of" the guilt expressed in her cathartic scream, and on the other she "lets go of" her cherished maternal intimacy and the associated grief over its absence by relinquishing the imaginal baby.

In brief summary, in the Charismatic rite for healing abortions we see the rhetorical power of multisensory imaginal performance to create a proto-Gileadean cultural reality for women who participate in the ritual healing system of the Charismatic Renewal. A clear ideological choice is made not to make them feel alright about what they have done but to presume their guilt and absolve them of it through divine forgiveness; not to affirm the pre-personhood of the fetus, but to create a person and bestow upon it an identity by naming/baptizing it and specifying its gender; not to emphasize the termination of the woman's pregnancy but the death trauma of the fetus and to resolve it by commending the unborn soul to the care of the deity.

In her important cultural analysis of the abortion debate in the contemporary United States, Faye Ginsburg (1989) identifies a series of what she calls "interpretive battlegrounds" in the struggle between prochoice and prolife forces. The Charismatic ritual is not a public battleground, but an internal ideological exercise where what is at stake is to intensify the world view that binds the ranks of antiabortion warriors by ritually enacting that world view in a way that displays its doxic qualities. The spontaneous entrainment of multisensory imagery is a product of deeply inculcated dispositions of a patriarchal habitue, and by its spontaneity is a rhetorically powerful display of an ethnopsychological reality. In this capacity the healing ritual goes beyond addressing the issue of fetal personhood to play a powerful role in what Ginsburg calls the "re-negotiation of pregnancy, childbirth, and nurturance . . . in the construction of female gender identity in American culture" (1989:110). Since the legalization of abortion, motherhood can no longer be presumed to be an ascribed status, the inevitable result of pregnancy conceived as an inevitable process in women's lives. Instead it becomes an achieved status, the result of a decision that

"comes to signify an assertion of a particular construction of female identity," in the face of necessity for rhetorical strategies for reproducing the culture in the absence of its formerly taken-for-granted self-reproduction (1989:109). The ritual undoing of the abortion is just such a strategy, restoring through imaginal performance the inevitability of pregnancy, childbirth, and nurturance. Ginsburg argues that an essential aspect of prolife political action is "the refiguring of a gendered landscape through prayer, demonstration, and efforts to convert others, particularly women in the vulnerable and liminal position of carrying an unwanted pregnancy" (1989:110). The Charismatic healing of abortions extends this refiguring from women who choose to carry an unwanted pregnancy to women who once chose not to carry a pregnancy.

In the example recounted above, the patient was chastised for blaming her husband, an escape from responsibility by citing lack of accountability in the face of the patriarchal authority of the husband. On the one hand, the healer's insistence that she take a share of responsibility for the decision to abort may seem to proffer a degree of empowerment, and the inclusion of the husband in the ritual carries the message that the woman is not abandoned to the emotional consequences of the abortion. On the other hand, insofar as the notions of sin and guilt are inevitably contained within this acceptance of responsibility, the patriarchal logic is enforced wherein the woman is obligated to bear children at all costs, even if her husband abdicates his procreative conscience.

Japanese *Mizukoo Kuyo*: Notes Toward a Comparison

In the above discussion of efficacy I situated the Charismatic ritual ethnologically by surveying definitions of the objectification, or coming into being, of persons across a variety of cultures. In this final section I want to return to the same theme with a more precise comparison in mind. (Contemporary Japanese society is the site of a more public ritual practice of postabortion healing.)[3] It is a ritual in which the spirits of aborted fetuses are propitiated through

---

3. I am grateful to Susan Sered for drawing my attention to the Japanese case.

prayer and through representation by stylized statues or tablets. These rites are called *mizuko kuyo,* where *mizuko* refers to fetuses miscarried, stillborn, and aborted, as well as the already-born who succumb to infanticide (LaFleur 1992:16) and *kuyo* is a type ritual based on an offering of simple gifts in thanks to objects or beings that have been in some sense used up, ranging from domestic objects like sewing need to deceased humans (LaFleur 1992:143–146). The *mizuko kuyo* rites appear to be essentially Buddhist in nature, but originated in the social context of the Japanese New Religions since the 1970s (Blacker 1989), and are cited as evidence of the commercialization of contemporary Japanese religion since they are often highly profitable to the temples and organizations that perform them (Picone 1986). In what follows, I will briefly discuss the Japanese Buddhist *mizuko kuyo* in relation to the North American Catholic Charismatic healing of abortions in order to begin to point to the place these overtly similar practices occupy in the cultural configurations of their respective societies.[4]

First let us take care to contextualize the relative social space occupied by these two practices. The American practice is largely a private one that takes place within the membership of a discrete religious movement within Christianity and is a specific instance of the healing system elaborated within that movement. The Japanese practice has a relatively public profile not limited to a particular social group and is an instance of a type of ritual common to a variety of forms of Buddhism. Historically, the Charismatic Renewal and the *mizuko* cult are contemporaneous, products of the post-1960s cultural ferment that spawned the New Age Christian fundamentalism, a renewed interest in Eastern spiritualities in the United States, and the various New Religions and a fluorescence of interest in spirit possession in Japan. Just as the Charismatic Renewal and other forms of neo-Pentecostalism have been associated with the neoconservative Christian right in America, some of the Japanese *mizuko* have been observed to have right-wing fundamentalist, naturalist, or Shinto connections.

In the United States, abortion was legalized for the first time in the early 1970s as a result of the Supreme Court decision in *Roe v. Wade,* while in Japan abortion has a deeper history. Both abortion and infanticide were common from the early 1700s to the mid-1800s, when an abortion debate ensued among Buddhist, neo-Shinto, and neo-Confucian positions in the context of a nationalism that demanded population growth and condemned such practices. Only following World War II in 1948 was abortion again legalized. Since that time, it has become the most popular form of birth control in Japan. Just as in the context of the American abortion debate the Charismatic prayer for healing tends to emphasize the aborted rather than the stillborn or miscarried fetus, in the context of the postwar commonality of abortion the aborted fetus has taken precedence as the primary referent of the Japanese term *mizuko.*

In both societies the affective issue addressed by the ritual is guilt, whereas in the United States this is a guilt occurring under the sign of sin, in Japan it is guilt under the sign of necessity. For the Americans abortion is an un-Christian act, and both perpetrator and victim must be ritually brought back into the Christian moral and emotional universe; for the Japanese both the acceptance of abortion as necessary and the acknowledgment of guilt are circumscribed within the Buddhist moral and emotional universe. Both rites are intended to heal the distress experienced by the woman, but the etiology of the illness is somewhat differently construed in the two cases. For Charismatics, any symptoms displayed by the woman are the result of the abortion as psychological trauma compounded by guilt, along with the more or less indirect effects of the restive fetal spirit "crying out" for love and comfort. In Japan such symptoms are attributed to vengeance and resentment on the part of the aborted fetal spirit that is the pained victim of an unnatural, albeit necessary, act.[5] Finally, not only the etiology but the emotional work accomplished by the two rituals is construed differently. As we have seen, for the Charismatics

---

4. My discussion of *mizuko kuyo* and abortion in Japan relies heavily on the excellent account provided by LaFleur (1992).

5. Necessity is sometimes conceived under the metaphor of "culling of seedlings," is performed in order to enhance the viability of those that survive (LaFleur 1992:99) The notion of *tatari,* that spirits of those who die untimely, unnatural, or unjust deaths may seek revenge on the living, is an old one in Japan, and is currently rather controversial with respect to the practice of *mizuko kuyo* (LaFleur 1992:55, 163–172).

this is a work of forgiveness and of letting go. For the Japanese it is a work of thanks and apology to the fetus, where m cultural context gratitude and guilt are not sharply differentiated. Thus, "[t]here is no great need to determine precisely whether one is addressing a guilt—pre-supposing 'apology' to a *mizuko* or merely expressing 'thanks' to it for having vacated its place in the body of a woman and having moved on, leaving her—and her family—relatively free of its physical presence" (LaFleur 1992:147).

We can now compare the two postabortion healing practices with respect to what they assume and what they produce with regard to the ethno-ontology of the person. The American Charismatic ritual is largely an "imaginal performance" (confer Csordas 1994a) in which the woman may vividly experience holding the imaginal fetus/baby, while the Japanese ritual typically includes the concrete representation of the fetus/baby in the form of a statue. For the Americans, the fetus is a distinct little being that at a certain point is given over to Jesus who is its savior and protector. The Japanese statue (*mizuko jizo*), on the other hand, assimilates the infant and savior in the same representation, a bald and diminutive monklike entity with infantile features sometimes described as "the Bodhisattva who wears a bib." This contrast in the ontological status of the fetus is recapitulated in the respective cultural notions of the coming into being of persons. American Charismatics regard personhood to be definitive at the moment of conception, whereas for Japanese becoming a person is neither a matter of conception nor of birth, but a gradual ontological process wherein "in coming bit by bit into the social world of human beings there is a thickening or densification of being," the inverse of a thinning of being as a person ages into ancestorhood and Buddhahood (LaFleur 1992:33). Thus, for the Charismatics, abortion is the definitive termination of a human life, while in the Japanese vies the aborted fetus can as easily be thought of as returning to a state of prebeing where it may be held till a later date as to a state comparable to that of deceased ancestors.

Given these differences, the intent of the Charismatic ritual is to move rhetorically the dead fetus ahead into a secure post-life union with the deity, whereas the intent of the Japanese ritual is to secure the fetus' good will either as it slips back into its pre-life state or as it advances to the realm of the Buddhas.

Charismatics tend to eschew the old Catholic folk notion of a limbo where unbaptized infants must remain separated from the deity (Linn, Linn, and Fabricant 1985), whereas Japanese may embrace a kind of limbo from whence the fetus may return at a later date. In this respect it is instructive to consider the difference in meaning of the ritual symbolism of water and of naming. In the Charismatic ritual imaginal water is used to baptize the fetus, an act that ensures the reunion of the fetus with Jesus. In the Japanese case, water is an essential element in the very definition of the fetus: The term *mizuko* means literally "children of the waters," which in a literal sense refers to the amniotic fluids, while in an ontological sense refers to the ambiguous status of the fetus we have been discussing. Whereas for Charismatics water baptism and return to Jesus is the cultural constitution of the fetus as person, the use of water symbolism in Japan highlights the fluidity of being that characterizes the ontological status of the fetus. Given that in Buddhism impermanence, suffering, and the absence of self are fundamental characteristics of all things, "the fetus as a *mizuko* in the process of sliding from its relative formedness as a human into a state of progressive liquidization is doing no other than following the most basic law of experience" (LaFleur 1992:28). A similar point can be made with respect to naming the aborted fetus. For the American Charismatics, naming is an aspect of baptism that contributes to the objectification of the fetus as person. For the Japanese, while the process of bestowing a posthumous ancestral name (*kaimyo*) is often a part of the ritual, it is often controversial whether it is more appropriate to allow an unnamed fetus to "slip back" into pre-being or to be named and thereby advanced into a state comparable to ancestorhood.

Contemporary civilization has advanced too far into the process of globalization to allow us to presume that the two rituals we have been discussing are necessarily isolated one from the other. Werblowsky (1991) critically refers to claims that there is a movement in the United States that is learning from Japan to fill the lacunae within Christianity, and sarcastically asks whether "in addition to their belief in souls they also believe (in good Japanese fashion) in family trees of souls, in which the souls of even unborn children remain closely related to the ancestors" (1991:327, 328). In this Werblowsky appears to confuse the movement associated with the label of "Zen Catholicism" among progressive Catholic monks with the quite separate and markedly more conservative Catholic Charismatic Renewal. The former is doubtless connected in some degree with the Japan-based Catholic journal of religious studies in which Werblowsky's own article appears. In his own text, however, he implicitly refers to the Catholic Charismatic Renewal, even citing the work by Linn, Linn, and Fabricant. While in addition to Zen Catholicism there is some proselytizing with respect to *mizuko kuyo* on the part of Japanese Buddhists in the West (confer LaFleur 1992:150, 172), if such an influence is present among Charismatics it is certainly less direct than Werblowsky presumes. Charismatic healers Linn, Linn, and Fabricant in passing acknowledge awareness of *mizuko kuyo*, citing another Charismatic author who in turn cites an article in *The Wall Street Journal*, of the practice of Japanese women "increasingly going to Buddhist temples where they pay $115 for a ritualized service to get rid of their guilt for the abortion, experienced in recurring bad dreams" (1985:128).

On the other hand, to answer Werblowsky's comment about family trees, in the 1980s many Charismatics adopted a form of healing called, variously, healing of ancestry or healing the family tree. Along with their more psychological interpretations of guilt and grief, Linn, Linn, and Fabricant (1985) favorably cite this notion, popularized by the British Charismatic psychiatrist Kenneth McCall (1982). They write that the fetus that has not been lovingly accepted by its family and committed to God "will cry out for love and prayer to a living family member," with subsequent psychological impact on parents, on parents' abilities to relate to older children or children yet to be born, and on such children themselves. What is noteworthy here is that McAll's practice was inspired by observing Chinese practices with regard to ancestors and ghosts, implicitly assimilating them to souls in purgatory or limbo, while living and practicing abroad. More significant than whether the Charismatic practice is an instance of either classic cultural diffusion or spurious cultural borrowing, what this suggests is that despite its overt fundamentalist tendencies, the Catholic Charismatic Renewal and contemporary New Religion/Buddhism are mutually participant in the globally prevailing postmodern condition of culture.

Conclusion

For a society in the throes of moral debate about abortion, where claims are made in terms of moral absolutes, the limits of cultural relativism are tested with the mere observation that "ritual performance creates a cultural reality." In this chapter I have attempted to give an account of the creation of meaning and the nature of therapeutic efficacy in a ritual that rhetorically partakes in this serious cultural debate in contemporary American society, and to contrast it with a parallel ritual in contemporary Japan. The account and the cross-cultural comparison point beyond relativism to the observation that within the limits posed by their own configuration, cultures can create and define the very problems to which they then develop therapeutic solutions. In the end, to cultivate guilt in order to relieve it is doubtless a form of creativity, but this cannot be said without also acknowledging that one of the products of human creativity can be human oppression.

17

Body Ritual Among the Nacirema

Horace Miner

This article is a classic of anthropological literature. In it, Horace Miner gives readers a thorough and exciting ethnographic account of the myriad of taboos and ceremonial behaviors that permeate the everyday activities of the members of a magic-ridden society. Focusing on secret rituals that are believed to prevent disease while beautifying the body, Miner demonstrates the importance of ceremonial specialists, such as the "holy-mouth-men" and the "listeners," in directing even the most routine aspects of daily life among the Nacirema. Miner finds it difficult to understand how the Nacirema have managed to exist so long under the burdens that they have imposed on themselves.

The anthropologist has become so familiar with the diversity of ways in which different peoples behave in similar situations that he is not apt to be surprised by even the most exotic customs. In fact, if all of the logically possible combinations of behavior have not been found somewhere in the world, he is apt to suspect that they must be present in some yet undescribed tribe. This point has, in fact, been expressed with respect to clan organization by Murdock (1949: 71). In this light, the magical beliefs and practices of the Nacirema present such unusual aspects that it seems desirable to describe them as an example of the extremes to which human behavior can go.

Professor Linton first brought the ritual of the Nacirema to the attention of anthropologists twenty years ago (1936: 326), but the culture of this people is still very poorly understood. They are a North American group living in the territory between the Canadian Cree, the Yaqui and Tarahumare of Mexico, and the Carib and Arawak of the Antilles.

Reprinted by permission of the American Anthropological Association from AMERICAN ANTHROPOLOGIST, vol. 58 (1956), pp. 503–507. Not for further reproduction.

Little is known of their origin, though tradition states that they came from the east. According to Nacirema mythology, their nation was originated by a culture hero, Notgnishaw, who is otherwise known for two great feats of strength—the throwing of a piece of wampum across the river Pa-To-Mac and the chopping down of the cherry tree in which the Spirit of Truth resided.

Nacirema culture is characterized by a highly developed market economy which has evolved in a rich natural habitat. While much of the people's time is devoted to economic pursuits, a large part of the fruits of these labors and a considerable portion of the day are spent in ritual activity. The focus of this activity is the human body, the appearance and health of which loom as a dominant concern in the ethos of the people. While such a concern is certainly not unusual, its ceremonial aspects and associated philosophy are unique.

The fundamental belief underlying the whole system appears to be that the human body is ugly and that its natural tendency is to debility and disease. Incarcerated in such a body, man's only hope is to avert these characteristics through the use of the powerful influences of ritual and ceremony. Every household has one or more shrines devoted to this purpose. The more powerful individuals in the society have several shrines in their houses and, in fact, the opulence of a house is often referred to in terms of the number of such ritual centers it possesses. Most houses are of wattle and daub construction, but the shrine rooms of the more wealthy are walled with stone. Poorer families imitate the rich by applying pottery plaques to their shrine walls.

While each family has at least one such shrine, the rituals associated with it are not family ceremonies but are private and secret. The rites are normally only discussed with children, and then only during the period when they are being initiated into these mysteries. I was able, however, to establish sufficient rapport with the natives to examine these shrines and to have the rituals described to me.

The focal point of the shrine is a box or chest which is built into the wall. In this chest are kept the many charms and magical potions without which no native believes he could live. These preparations are secured from a variety of specialized practitioners. The most powerful of these are the medicine men, whose assistance must be rewarded with substantial gifts. However, the medicine men do not provide the curative potions for their clients, but decide what the ingredients should be and then write them down in an ancient and secret language. This writing is understood only by the medicine men and by the herbalists who, for another gift, provide the required charm.

The charm is not disposed of after it has served its purpose, but is placed in the charm-box of the household shrine. As these magical materials are specific for certain ills, and the real or imagined maladies of the people are many, the charm-box is usually full to overflowing. The magical packets are so numerous that people forget what their purposes were and fear to use them again. While the natives are very vague on this point, we can only assume that the idea in retaining all the old magical materials is that their presence in the charm-box, before which the body rituals are conducted, will in some way protect the worshipper.

Beneath the charm-box is a small font. Each day every member of the family, in succession, enters the shrine room, bows his head before the charm-box, mingles different sorts of holy water in the font, and proceeds with a brief rite of ablution. The holy waters are secured from the Water Temple of the community, where the priests conduct elaborate ceremonies to make the liquid ritually pure.

In the hierarchy of magical practitioners, and below the medicine men in prestige, are specialists whose designation is best translated "holy-mouth-men." The Nacirema have an almost pathological horror and fascination with the mouth, the condition of which is believed to have supernatural influence on all social relationships. Were it not for the rituals of the mouth, they believe that their teeth would fall out, their gums bleed, their jaws shrink, their friends desert them, and their lovers reject them. (They also believe that a strong relationship exists between oral and moral characteristics. For example, there is a ritual ablution of the mouth for children which is supposed to improve their moral fiber.)

The daily body ritual performed by everyone includes a mouth-rite. Despite the fact that these people are so punctilious about care of the mouth, this rite involves a practice which strikes the uninitiated stranger as revolting. It was reported to me that the ritual consists of inserting a small bundle of hog hairs into the mouth, along with certain magical powders, and then moving the bundle in a highly formalized series of gestures.

In addition to the private mouth-rite, the people seek out a holy-mouth-man once or twice a year. These practitioners have an impressive set of paraphernalia, consisting of a variety of augers, awls, probes, and prods. The use of these objects in the exorcism of the evils of the mouth involves almost unbelievable ritual torture of the client. The holy-mouth-man opens the client's mouth and, using the above-mentioned tools, enlarges any holes which decay may have created in the teeth. Magical materials are put into these holes. If there are no naturally occurring holes in the teeth, large sections of one or more teeth are gouged out so that the supernatural substance can be applied. In the client's view, the purpose of these ministrations is to arrest decay and to draw friends. The extremely sacred and traditional character of the rite is evident in the fact that the natives return to the holy-mouth-men year after year, despite the fact that their teeth continue to decay.

It is to be hoped that, when a thorough study of the Nacirema is made, there will be a careful inquiry into the personality structure of these people. One has but to watch the gleam in the eye of a holy-mouth-man, as he jabs an awl into an exposed nerve, to suspect that a certain amount of sadism is involved. If this can be established, a very interesting pattern emerges, for most of the population shows definite masochistic tendencies. It was to these that Professor Linton referred in discussing a distinctive part of the daily body ritual which is performed only by men. This part of the rite involves scraping and lacerating the surface of the face with a sharp instrument. Special women's rites are performed only four times during each lunar month, but what they lack in frequency is made up in barbarity. As part of this ceremony, women bake their heads in small ovens for about an hour. The theoretically interesting point is that what seems to be a preponderantly masochistic people have developed sadistic specialists.

The medicine men have an imposing temple, or *latipso*, in every community of any size. The more elaborate ceremonies required to treat very sick patients can only be performed at this temple. These ceremonies involve not only the thaumaturge but a permanent group of vestal maidens who move sedately about the temple chambers in distinctive costume and headdress.

The *latipso* ceremonies are so harsh that it is phenomenal that a fair proportion of the really sick natives who enter the temple ever recover. Small children whose indoctrination is still incomplete have been known to resist attempts to take them to the temple because "that is where you go to die." Despite this fact, sick adults are not only willing but eager to undergo the protracted ritual purification, if they can afford to do so. No matter how ill the supplicant or how grave the emergency, the guardians of many temples will not admit a client if he cannot give a rich gift to the custodian. Even after one has gained admission and survived the ceremonies, the guardians will not permit the neophyte to leave until he makes still another gift.

The supplicant entering the temple is first stripped of all his or her clothes. In every-day life the Nacirema avoids exposure of his body and its natural functions. Bathing and excretory acts are performed only in the secrecy of the household shrine, where they are ritualized as part of the body-rites. Psychological shock results from the fact that body secrecy is suddenly lost upon entry into the *latipso*. A man, whose own wife has never seen him in an excretory act, suddenly finds himself naked and assisted by a vestal maiden while he performs his natural functions into a sacred vessel. This sort of ceremonial treatment is necessitated by the fact that the excreta are used by a diviner to ascertain the course and nature of the client's sickness. Female clients, on the other hand, find their naked bodies are subjected to the scrutiny, manipulation, and prodding of the medicine men.

Few supplicants in the temples are well enough to do anything but lie on their hard beds. The daily ceremonies, like the rites of the holy-mouth-men, involve discomfort and torture. With ritual precision, the vestals awaken their miserable charges each dawn and roll them about on their beds of pain while performing ablutions, in the formal movements of which the maidens are highly trained. At other times they insert magic wands in the supplicant's mouth or force him to eat substances which are supposed to be healing. From time to time the medicine men come to their clients and jab magically treated needles into their flesh. The fact that these temple ceremonies may not cure, and may even kill the neophyte, in no way decreases the people's faith in the medicine men.

There remains one other kind of practitioner, known as a "listener." This witch-doctor has the power to exorcise the devils that lodge in the heads of people who have been bewitched. The Nacirema believe that parents bewitch their own children. Mothers are particularly suspected of putting a curse on children while teaching them the secret body rituals. The counter-magic of the witch-doctor is unusual in its lack of ritual. The patient simply tells the "listener" all his troubles and fears, beginning with the earliest difficulties he can remember. The memory displayed by the Nacirema in these exorcism sessions is truly remarkable. It is not uncommon for the patient to bemoan the rejection he felt upon being weaned as a babe, and a few individuals even see their troubles going back to the traumatic effects of their own birth.

In conclusion, mention must be made of certain practices which have their base in native esthetics but which depend upon the pervasive aversion to the natural body and its functions. There are ritual fasts to make fat people thin and ceremonial feasts to make thin people fat. Still other rites are used to make women's breasts large if they are small, and smaller if they are large. General dissatisfaction with breast shape is symbolized in the fact that the ideal form is virtually outside the range of human variation. A few women afflicted with almost inhuman hyper-mammary development are so idolized that they make a handsome living by simply going from village to village and permitting the natives to stare at them for a fee.

Reference has already been made to the fact that excretory functions are ritualized, routinized, and relegated to secrecy. Natural reproductive functions are similarly distorted. Intercourse is taboo as a topic and scheduled as an act. Efforts are made to avoid pregnancy by the use of magical materials or by limiting intercourse to certain phases of the moon. Conception is actually very infrequent. When pregnant, women dress so as to hide their condition. Parturition takes place in secret, without friends or relatives to assist, and the majority of women do not nurse their infants.

Our review of the ritual life of the Nacirema has certainly shown them to be a magic-ridden people. It is hard to understand how they have managed to exist so long under the burdens which they have imposed upon themselves. But even such exotic customs as these take on real meaning when they are viewed with the insight provided by Malinowski when he wrote (1948: 70):

> Looking from far and above, from our high places of safety in the developed civilization, it is easy to see all the crudity and irrelevance of magic. But without its power and guidance early man could not have mastered his practical difficulties as he has done, nor could man have advanced to the higher stages of civilization.

Suggested Readings

Beattie, John
    1970   "On Understanding Ritual." In Bryan R. Wilson, ed. *Rationality*. Oxford: Blackwell.

Bell, Catherine
    1997   *Ritual: Perspectives and Dimensions*. New York: Oxford University Press.

Moore, Sally Falk, and Barbara, Myerhoff, eds.
    1977   *Secular Ritual*. Assen, Netherlands: Van Gorcum.

Turner, Victor
    1967   *The Forest of Symbols: Aspects of Ndembu Ritual*. Ithaca, N.Y.: Cornell University Press.

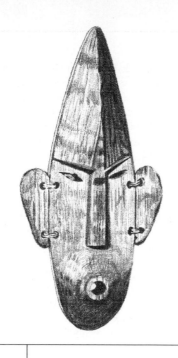

CHAPTER FOUR

Shamans, Priests, and Prophets

Where and how do religious leaders get their power? What is the distinction between a shaman and a priest, or a prophet and a priest? How do sorcerers, diviners, and magicians differ? This chapter introduces the topic of religious specialists.

Any member of society may approach the supernatural on an individual basis; for example, a person may kneel to the ground, all alone, and recite a prayer for help from the spiritual world. But the religions of the world, whether small, animistic cults or the "great faiths," also have intermediaries: religious people who, acting as part-time or full-time specialists, intervene on behalf of an individual client or an entire community. Paul Radin (1937: 107) argued that the development of religion can be traced to the social roles undertaken by each of these "priest-thinkers"—at once, a philosopher of religion, a theologian of beliefs, a person who is the recognized master of worship.

If all religions appear to have specialists, anthropologists have also found that some societies place more emphasis on these religious experts than others do. Robert Textor has noted, for example, that the societies that are more likely to have religious specialists tend to produce food rather than collect it, use money as a medium of exchange, and display different social classes and a complex political system (1967). In other words, the more complex the society, the greater is the likelihood of having religious intermediaries.

Early anthropologists were drawn to the view of unilineal evolution: how institutions progressed from savagery to barbarism, finally achieving a civilized state. As societies advance, all institutions become more complex and specialized. In this classic work *Primitive Culture* (1871), E. B. Tylor posited an early definition of religion that prompted his colleagues to concern themselves with religious specialization. Describing religion as the belief in spiritual beings, what he called "animism," Tylor implied that a society's degree of religious specialization was directly related to its position on the evolutionary scale. Unilineal evolutionary theory was pockmarked with faulty premises, of course: although cultures do evolve, they do not necessarily follow a prescribed series of stages. What is important to note here, however, is that Tylor and his contemporaries began to look carefully at religious specialization and categories of religious phenomena. J. G. Frazer, in *The Golden Bough* (1890), distinguished between magic and religion and described the role of specialists. And Herbert Spencer's approach, in the *Principles of Sociology* (1896), that religious stages could be comprehended only if the functions of religion and the interrelationships of religion with other institutions were known, demanded that religious specialization be studied in terms of its functions in society—an approach that anthropologists still adhere to today. Anthropological data have shown the importance of shamans, priests, prophets, and other specialists to the maintenance of economic, political, social, and educational institutions of their societies.

The anthropological literature devoted to religious specialists is extensive; much work remains, however, to define and distinguish adequately between the actual functions they perform for members of their societies. Because of limitations on the application of biomedical (Western) therapy in the Third World, traditional doctors play a crucial role in healing (Hepburn 1988: 68). Shamans, for example, have duties and religious obligations that differ from society to society, although their basic duty of curing through the use of the supernatural is accepted by anthropologists. J. M. Atkinson's review article, "Shamanisms Today" (1992), demonstrates the continuing importance of shamanic practices in the contemporary non-Western world. The same kinds of differences exist in the tasks performed by prophets, priests, sorcerers, and others designated as "intermediaries" with the supernatural. Without a clear understanding of these distinctions, systematic cross-cultural comparisons would be impossible.

In addition to the definitional problem associated with specialists, anthropologists must also determine whether to place the tasks performed by these experts under the rubric of "the religious" or to create other categories for such activities. Is the performance of magic, witchcraft, and sorcery "religious" behavior, or are these examples of nonreligious, indeed antireligious acts? If those who practice these acts are outside the religious realm, then what, if any, connection do they have with the sacred? The real question becomes, What is religion? In Western culture, witchcraft, magic, and sorcery are assigned to the occult and are considered outside of and, ordinarily, counter to religion. In the non-Western world, however, specialists who take part in these kinds of activities are often considered to be important parts of the total religious belief system. It is a common view in Africa south of the Sahara that people are often designated witches by God, and that sorcerers and magicians receive their power from the spirit world—that is, from supernatural agencies controlled by God. In these terms, is drawing upon supernatural aid from shamans, priests, or prophets more "religious" than turning to magicians, sorcerers, and other specialists who also call upon supernatural agents but for different ends? In light of these questions, anthropologists have found it necessary to consider all specialists whose power emanates from supernatural agents to be in the realm of the religious, although some specialists serve, whereas others harm society through their actions.

Because not all societies contain identical religious specialists, determining why certain specialists exist and others do not is important to our understanding of the structure of a society and its supernatural world, as well as of the causal forces behind good and bad fortune. In societies where witches do not exist, for example, it is frequently malicious ghosts or ancestors who are believed to bring misfortune and illness. In such cases, elders may play an important role as diviners, in contrast to the diviner specialists that exist in other groups. Such data not only aid our understanding of supernatural causation and specialization but also demonstrate the connection between the social structure of the living—the position of the elder in society—and that of the ancestor or ghost in the afterworld.

The difficulty in making distinctions among non-Western specialists may be further realized by considering the position of the religious layleader in the United States. Although not a specialist in the traditional sense, this individual is nevertheless more involved and usually more knowledgeable than the typical church member. Is the layleader significantly different from one of the more traditional part-time specialists? The problem of the degree of participation comes to mind—part-time versus full-time—accompanied by the complicating factor of training—formal versus on-the-job learning. Making distinctions such as these is an important part of analytic accounts of religious functionaries.

The five excellent articles that follow tell us much about the religious specialist. Victor W. Turner's lead-off essay provides a broad-spectrum account of the various specialists who appear in ethnographic descriptions of religions around the world.

Piers Vitebsky provides an overview of shamanism as understood by anthropologists, focusing on the Inuit and Sora, and with attention to intellectual disagreements over definitions.

Reflecting on research in Peru, Michael Fobes Brown rejects romanticized views of shamanism, reminding readers of the anxiety and violence that may accompany the phenomenon.

The fourth article, by Gerardo Reichel-Dolmatoff, provides a detailed account of priesthood among the Kogi of Colombia. The author focuses on the lengthy and elaborate training young men must undergo to become priests.

Michael Barkun concludes the chapter with an in-depth look into the minds of the Branch Davidians and their prophetic leader, David Koresh, as well as the FBI and ATF authorities and the tragic clash at Waco, Texas.

References

Atkinson, J. M.
   1992 "Shamanisms Today." *Annual Reviews in Anthropology* 21: 307–30.

Frazer, J. G.
   1890 *The Golden Bough.* London: MacMillan.

Hepburn, Sharon J.
   1988 "Western Minds, Foreign Bodies." *Medical Anthropology Quarterly* 2 (New Series): 59–74.

Radin, Paul
   1937 *Primitive Religion: Its Nature and Origin.* New York: Dover.

Spencer, H.
   1896 *Principles of Sociology.* New York: D. Appleton.

Textor, Robert
   1967 *A Cross-Cultural Summary.* New Haven, Conn.: HRAF Press.

Tylor, E. B.
   1871 *Primitive Culture: Researches into the Development of Mythology, Philosophy, Religion, Language, Art and Custom.* London: J. Murray.

18

Religious Specialists

Victor W. Turner

*N*oted for his contributions to the study of symbolism and the structure of rituals, Victor W. Turner here introduces the basic terms for different types of religious specialists, as conventionally used by anthropologists. Turner focuses upon the most commonly used terms such as shaman, priest, and prophet, but includes other, less prominent but often equally important religious specialists as well—diviners, seers, mediums, witches, sorcerers, and magicians—and discusses how each type of specialist is likely to appear in societies with particular levels of social complexity and political specialization. While these terms appear throughout the anthropological literature with a fair degree of consistency, in some cases (for example, the term "shaman"), anthropologists disagree about how widely or narrowly the term should be applied. Turner's overview lays the groundwork for the articles to follow, which deal specifically with shamans, priests, and prophets.

A religious specialist is one who devotes himself to a particular branch of religion or, viewed organizationally, of a religious system. "Religion" is a multivocal term whose range of meanings varies in different social and historical contexts. Nevertheless, most definitions of religion refer to the recognition of a transhuman controlling power that may be either personal or impersonal. A religious specialist has a culturally defined status relevant to this recognition. In societies or contexts where such power is regarded as impersonal, anthropologists customarily describe it as *magic,* and those who manipulate the power are magicians. Wherever power is personalized, as deity, gods, spirits, daemons, genii, ancestral shades, ghosts, or the like, anthropologists speak of *religion.* In reality, religious systems contain both magical and religious beliefs and procedures: in many of them the impersonal transhuman (or mystical, or non-empirical, or supernatural) power is considered to be a devolution of personal power, as in

the case of the mystical efficacy of rites established *in illo tempore* by a deity or divinized ancestor.

Priest and Prophet

Scholars have tended to distinguish between two polarities of religious specialization. Max Weber, for example, although well aware of numerous historical instances of their overlap and interpenetration, contrasts the roles of priest and prophet. He begins by making a preliminary distinction between priest and magician. A priest, he writes, is always associated with "the functioning of a regularly organized and permanent enterprise concerned with influencing the gods—in contrast with the individual and occasional efforts of magicians." Accordingly, the crucial feature of priesthood is that it represents the "specialization of a particular group of persons in the continuous operation of a cultic enterprise, permanently associated with particular norms, places and times, and related to specific social groups." In Weber's view, the prophet is distinguished from the priest by "personal call." The priest's claim to religious authority derives from his service in a sacred tradition; the authority of the prophet is founded on revelation and personal "charisma." This latter term has been variously defined by Weber (in some contexts it seems almost to represent the *Führerprinzip*), but it may broadly be held to designate extraordinary powers. These include, according to Weber, "the capacity to achieve the ecstatic states which are viewed, in accordance with primitive experience, as the preconditions for producing certain effects in meteorology, healing, divination and telepathy." But charisma may be either ascribed or achieved. It may be an inherent faculty ("primary charisma") or it may be "produced artificially in an object or person through some extraordinary means." Charisma may thus be "merited" by fastings, austerities, or other ordeals. Even in such cases, Weber asserts, there must be some dormant capacity in the persons or objects, some "germ" of extraordinary power, already vested in them. The prophet, then, is a "purely individual bearer of charisma," rather than the representative of a sacred tradition. He produces discontinuity in that cultic enterprise which it is the priest's major role to keep "in continuous operation." Weber's prophet feels that he has a "mission" by virtue of which he "proclaims religious doctrine or divine commandment." Weber refuses to distinguish sharply between a "renewer of religion" who preaches "an older revelation, actual or supposititious" and a "founder of religion" who claims to bring completely new "deliverances," for, he says, "the two types merge into one another." In Weber's view, the charisma of a prophet appears to contain, in addition to ecstatic and visionary components, a rational component, for he proclaims "a systematic and distinctively religious ethic based upon a consistent and stable doctrine which purports to be a revelation" [(1922)].

Weber's distinction between priest and prophet has its main relevance in an analytical frame of reference constructed to consider the relationship between religion as "a force for dynamic social change" and religion as "a reinforcement of the stability of societies" (Parsons 1963). It has been found effective by such anthropologists as Evans-Pritchard ([1956] 1962) and Worsley (1957a; 1957b) who are dealing directly with social transitions and "the prophetic break," or what Parsons calls "the primary decision point [between] a direction which makes for a source of evolutionary change in the . . . established or traditional order, and a direction which tends either to reinforce the established order

or at least not to change it drastically" (1963; p. xxix in 1964 edition).

Priest and Shaman

Anthropologists who are less concerned than Weber with the genesis of religions and with internal developments in complex societies or their impact on the "primitive" world are inclined to contrast priest not with prophet but with shaman or spirit medium and to examine the relationship between these statuses as part of the normal working of the religious system in the simpler societies. In their excellently representative *Reader in Comparative Religion* (1958), the editors W. A. Lessa and E. Z. Vogt devote a whole section to this distinction.

Often, where there is a priest the shaman is absent, and vice versa, although both these roles may be found in the same religion, as among the Plains Indians. According to Lowie (1954), a Plains Indian shaman is a ritual practitioner whose status is acquired through a personal communication from a supernatural being, whereas a priest does not necessarily have a face-to-face relationship with the spirit world but must have competence in conducting ritual. Lessa and Vogt ([1958] 1965: 410) expand these differences: a shaman's powers come by "divine stroke," a priest's power is inherited or is derived from the body of codified and standardized ritual knowledge that he learns from older priests and later transmits to successors. They find that shamanism tends to predominate in food-gathering cultures, where the shaman most frequently performs a curing rite for the benefit of one or more patients and within the context of an extended family group. Shamanistic rites are "non-calendrical," or contingent upon occasions of mishap and illness. The priest and priestly cult organization are characteristically found in the more structurally elaborated food-producing—usually agricultural—societies, where the more common ceremonial is a public rite performed for the benefit of a whole village or community. Such rites are often calendrical, or performed at critical points in the ecological cycle.

Shaman and Medium

Raymond Firth (1964a: 638) regards shamanism as itself "that particular form of spirit mediumship in which a specialist (the *shaman*) normally himself a medium, is deemed to exercise developed techniques of control over spirits, sometimes including mastery of spirits believed to be possessing another medium." This definition, like that of Howells (1948), stresses the *control* exercised over spirits. Howells describes the shaman as "bullyragging" gods or spirits and emphasizes his intellectual qualities as a leader. This element of mastery makes the shaman a distinctive type of spirit medium, one who is believed to be "possessed by a spirit (or closely controlled by a spirit) [and who] can serve as a means of communication between other human beings and the spirit world" (Firth 1964b: 689). The spirit medium per se need not exert mastery; he is rather the vessel or vehicle of the transhuman entity.

Thus, although we sometimes find the two functions of priest and shaman combined in the same individual (Piddington 1950), mediums, shamans, and prophets clearly constitute subtypes of a single type of religious functionary. The priest communicates with transhuman entities through ritual that involves cultural objects and activities. The medium, shaman, and prophet communicate in a person-to-person manner: they are in what Buber (1936) would describe as an I-thou relationship with the deities or spirits. The priest, on the other hand, is in what may be called an I-it relationship with the transhuman. Between the priest and the deity intervenes the institution. Priests may therefore be classified as institutional functionaries in the religious domain, while medium, shaman, and prophet may be regarded as subtypes of inspirational functionaries. This distinction is reflected in characteristically different modes of operation. The priest presides over a rite; the shaman or medium conducts a seance. Symbolic forms associated with these occasions differ correlatively: the symbols of a rite are sensorily perceptible to a congregation and have permanence in that they are culturally transmissible, while those of a seance are mostly in the mind of the entranced functionary as elements of his visions or fantasies and are often generated by and limited to the unique occasion. The inspirational functionary may describe what he has clairvoyantly perceived (or "been shown" as he might put it), but the institutional functionary manipulates symbolic objects with prescribed gestures in full view of this congregation.

Sociocultural Correlates

Since the priest is an actor in a culturally "scripted" drama, it is but rarely that priests become innovators, or "dramatists." If they do assume this role it is mainly as legislative reformers—by altering the details of liturgical procedure—that they do so. If a priest becomes a radical innovator in religion, he is likely to become a prophet to his followers and a heretic to his former superiors. From the priestly viewpoint it is the office, role, and script that are sacred and "charismatic" and not the incumbent of priestly office. The priest is concerned with the conservation and maintenance of a deposit of beliefs and practices handed down as a sacred trust from the founders of the social or religious system. Since its symbols at the semantic level tend to condense the critical values, norms, and principles of the total cultural system into a few sensorily perceptible representations, the sanctification of these symbols is tantamount to a preservative of the entire culture. What the priest is and does keeps cultural change and individual deviation within narrow limits. But the energy and time of the inspirational functionary is less bound up with the maintenance of the total cultural system. His practice has more of an ad hoc flavor; he is more sensitive and responsive than the priest to the private and personal, to the mutable and idiosyncratic. This type of functionary thrives in loosely structured food-gathering cultures, where he deals individually with specific occasions of trouble, or during periods of social turbulence and change, when societal consensus about values is sharply declining and numerically significant classes of persons and social groups are becoming alienated from the orthodox social order. The shaman subtype is completely a part of the cultural system of the food-gatherers; the prophet may well stand outside the cultural system during such a period of decomposition and propose new doctrines, ethics, and even economic values.

The shaman is not a radical or a reformer, since the society he services is traditionally flexible and mobile; the prophet is an innovator and reformer, for he confronts a tightly structured order that is moribund and points the way to religious forms that will either provide an intensified cognitive dynamic for sociocultural change or codify the new moral, ideational, and social structures that have been inarticulately developing.

There are of course significant differences in the scale of the societies in which shaman and prophet operate. The shaman enacts his roles in small-scale, multifunctional communities whose religious life incorporates beliefs in a multitude of deities, daemons, nature spirits, or ancestral shades—societies that Durkheim might have described as possessing mechanical solidarity, low moral density, and segmental organization. The prophet tends to come into his own when the division of labor is critically replacing "mechanical" by "organic" solidarity, when class antagonisms are sharpened, or when small-scale societies are decisively invaded by the powerful personnel, ideas, techniques, and cultural apparatus (including military skills and armaments) of large-scale societies. The shaman deals in a personal and specific way with spirits and lesser deities; the prophet enters into dialogue, on behalf of his whole community, with the Supreme Being or with the major deities of a traditional pantheon, whose tutelary scope embraces large numbers of persons and groups, transcending and transecting their traditional divisions and animosities. Alternatively he communicates with the generalized ancestors or *genii loci,* conceived to be a single anonymous and homogeneous collectivity rather than a structure of known and named shades, each representing a specific segment of society. Whereas the shaman's function is associated with looseness of structure in small-scale societies, the prophet's is linked with loosening of structure in large-scale societies or with incompatibilities of scale in culture-contact situations.

Divination and Religious Specialists

In its strict etymological sense the term "divination" denotes inquiry about future events or matters, hidden or obscure, directed to a deity who, it is believed, will reply through significant tokens. It usually refers to the process of obtaining knowledge of secret or future things by mechanical means or manipulative techniques—a process which may or may not include invoking the aid of non-empirical (transhuman) persons or powers but does not include the empirical methods of science.

In the analysis of preliterate societies divination often is concerned with the immediate problems and interests of individuals and subgroups and but seldom with the destinies of tribes and nations. It is this specificity and narrowness of reference that primarily distinguishes divination from prophecy. Nadel (1954: 64) has called the kind of guidance it offers "mechanical and of a case-to-case kind." The diviner "can discover and disentangle some of the hidden influences which are at work always and everywhere. . . . He cannot uncover any more embracing design. . . . Yet within the limits set to it divination has a part to play, providing some of the certainty and guidance required for provident action." Thus, although its range and scope are more circumscribed than those of prophecy, divination is believed to reveal what is hidden and in many cases to forecast events, auspicious and inauspicious.

Divination further refers to the analysis of past events, especially untoward events; this analysis often includes the detection and ascription of guilt with regard to their perpetrators, real or alleged. Where such untoward events are attributed to sorcerers and witches the diviner has great freedom of judgment in detecting and determining guilt. Diviners are frequently consulted by victims' relatives and show intuitive and deductive virtuosity in discovering quarrels and grudges in their clients' kin groups and local communities. Social anthropologists find important clues to areas and sources of social strain and to the character and strength of supportive social norms and values in the diviners' diagnoses.

There is evidence that mediums, shamans, and priests in various cultures have practiced divination. The medium and shaman often divine without mechanical means but with the assistance of a tutelary spirit. In the work of Lessa and Vogt there is a translation of a vivid first-person account by a Zulu informant of a diviner's seance. This mediumistic female diviner

> dramatically utilizes some standard procedures of her art—ventriloquism, prior knowledge of the clients, the overhearing of the client's unguarded conversation, and shrewd common sense—to enable her spirits to provide the clients with advice. In this example, . . . a boy is suffering from a convulsive ailment. The spirits discover that an ancestral spirit is spitefully causing the boy's illness: the spirits decree that the location of the family's village must be moved; a goat must be sacrificed to the ancestor and the goat's bile poured over the boy; the boy must drink *Itongo* medicine.

The treatment thus ranges from physical to social actions—from propitiation of wrathful ancestors to prescription of a medicinal potion (Lessa & Vogt [1958] 1965: 340).

Similar accounts of shamanistic divinatory seances have been recorded by anthropologists working among North and South American Indians, Eskimos, and Siberian tribes, in many parts of Africa, and among Afro-Americans.

Divination was a function of members of the priesthood in many of the complex religious systems of Polynesia, west Africa, and ancient Mexico; in the religions of Israel, Greece, Etruria, and Rome; in Babylonia, India, China, Japan, and among the Celts. According to Wach,

> The Etruscans made these practices so much a part of their culture that the discipline has been named after them (*disciplina Etrusca* or *auguralis*). Different phenomena and objects were used as media to ascertain the desires of the gods (regular and irregular celestial events, lightning, fire, and earthquakes, the shape or utterances of animals, flights of birds, movements of serpents, barking of dogs, forms of liver or entrails). Both in Etruria and Rome a numerous and well-organized hierarchy of functionaries existed for practice of the sacred arts (1958, p. 111 in 1961 edition).

Indeed, diffused through the Roman world, many of these techniques passed into medieval and modern culture.

Diviner and Doctor

Callaway's account (1868–1870) of the combined divinatory and curative seance in Zululand emphasizes the close relationship believed to hold in many preliterate societies between the functions of divination and therapy. Sometimes, as in the case cited, the diviner and "doctor" are the same person, but more often the roles are specialized and performed by different individuals. Modern therapy is taking increasingly into account the psychosomatic character of many maladies and the importance of sociological factors in their etiology. In most preliterate societies bodily symptoms are regarded as signs that the soul or life principle of the patient is under attack or has been abstracted by spiritual forces or beings. Furthermore, it is widely held that these attacks are motivated by animosities provoked by breaches of cultural, mainly religious, prescriptions and/or breaches of social norms regarded as binding on members of kin groups or local communities. Thus, to acquire a comprehensive understanding of why and how a patient was afflicted with certain symptoms by a spirit or witch, primitives seek out a diviner who will disclose the secret antagonisms in social relations or the perhaps unconscious neglect of ritual rules (always a threat to the cultural order) that incited mystical retribution or malice. The diviner is a "diagnostician" who refers his clients to his colleague, the doctor or "therapist." The doctor in question has both shamanistic and priestly attributes. The division of labor which in more complex societies segregates and institutionalizes the functions of priest and medical man has hardly begun to make its influence felt. The diviner-doctor dichotomy does not depend, as does the priest-shaman dichotomy, upon contrasting roles in regard to the transhuman realm but upon different phases in a social process which involves *total* human phenomena—integral personalities, many psychosomatic complexes, multiple social relationships, and multiform communities.

Modes of Religious Specialization

As the scale and complexity of society increase and the division of labor develops, so too does the degree of religious specialization. This process accompanies a contraction in the domain of religion in social life. As Durkheim stated with typical creative exaggeration in his *Division of Labor in Society* ([1893] 1960: 169): "Originally [religion] pervades everything; everything social is religious; the two words are synonymous. Then, little by little, political, economic, scientific functions free themselves from the religious function, constitute themselves apart and take on a more and more acknowledged temporal character."

Simple Societies

In the simplest societies every adult has some religious functions and the elders have most; as their capacity to hunt or garden wanes, their priestlike role comes into ever greater prominence. Women tend to receive more recognition and scope as religious functionaries than in more developed societies. There is some tendency toward religious specialization in such societies, based on a variety of attributes, such as knowledge of herbalistic lore, skill in leechcraft, the capacity to enter a state of trance or dissociation, and sometimes physical handicap that compels a man or woman to find an alternative means of support to subsistence activities. (I have met several diviners in central Africa with maimed hands or amputated limbs.) But such specialization can hardly be defined, in the majority of cases, as more than part-time or even spare-time specialization. Michael Gelfand's description of the Shona *nganga,* variously translated in the ethnographic literature as "medicine man," "doctor," or "witch doctor," exemplifies the sociocultural situation of similar practitioners in very many preliterate societies (1964). The Shona *nganga* is at once a herbalist, a medium, and also a diviner who, possessed by a spirit of a dead relative, diagnoses both the cause of illness and of death. Yet, reports Gelfand,

> when he is not engaged in his medical practice he leads exactly the same life as the other men of his village. He cultivates his land, looks after his cattle, repairs his huts, makes blankets or other equipment needed by his family. And the same applies to a woman *nganga,* who busies herself with the tasks expected of every Shona woman. . . . The amount the *nganga* does in his village depends, of course, on the demands of his patients, but on the average he has a fair amount of spare time. . . . A fair guess would be [that there is a *nganga*] to every 800 to 1,000 persons. . . . The *nganga* is given no special status in his village, his chances of being appointed headman are the same as anyone else's (1964: 22–23).

Complex Societies

To bring out best the effects of increase in scale and the division of labor it is necessary to examine religious systems at the opposite end of the gradient of complexity. Religion no longer pervades all social domains; it is limited to its own domain. Furthermore, it has acquired a contractual and associational character; people may choose both the form and extent of their religious participation or may opt out of any affiliation. On the other hand, within each religious group a considerable amount of specialization has taken place. Much of this has been on the organizational level. Processes of bureaucratization, involving rationality in decision making, relative impersonality in social relations, routinization of tasks, and a hierarchy of authority and function, have produced a large number of types, grades, and ranks of religious specialists in all the major religious systems.

For example, the Catholic clerical hierarchy may be considered as (1) the hierarchy of order, whose powers are exercised in worship and in the administration of the sacraments, and (2) as the hierarchy of jurisdiction, whose power is over the members of the church. Within the hierarchy of jurisdiction alone we find such manifold statuses as pope and bishop (which are held to be of divine institution); cardinal, patriarch, exarch, and primate (whose powers are derived by delegation expressed or implied from the holy see); metropolitan and archbishop (who derive their powers from their patriarch, exarch, or primate); archdeacon, vicar general, vicar forane, rural dean, pastor, and rector (who derive their powers from their diocesan bishop).

In addition to the clerical hierarchy there are in the Catholic church numerous institutes of the religious, that is, societies of men and women approved by ecclesiastical superiors, in which the members in conformity with the special laws of their association take vows, perpetual or temporary, and by this means aspire to religious perfection. This is defined as "the heroic exercise of the virtue of supernatural charity" and is pursued by voluntary maintenance of the vows of poverty, chastity, and obedience, by ascetical practices, through charitable works, such as care of the poor, sick, aged, and mentally handicapped, and by contemplative techniques, such as prayer. Within each religious institution or congregation there is a marked division of function and gradation of office.

Thus there are many differences of religious status, rank, and function in a developed religious system such as the Catholic church. Differences in charismata are also recognized in such terms as "contemplative," "ascetic," "mystic," "preacher," "teacher," "administrator." These gifts may appear in any of the major divisions of the church: among clergy or laity, among hermits, monks, or friars, among female as well as male religious. Certain of these charismata are institutionalized and constitute the devotional pattern particular to certain religious institutions: thus there are "contemplative orders," "friars preachers," and the like.

Medium-Scale Societies

Other developed religions, churches, sects, cults, and religious movements exhibit degrees of bureaucratic organization and specialization of role and function. Between the situational specialization of religious activities found in small-scale societies and the full-time and manifold specialization in large-scale societies falls a wide variety of intermediate types. A characteristic religious dichotomy is found in many of the larger, politically centralized societies of west and east Africa, Asia, Polynesia, and pre-Columbian Central and South America. National and tribal gods are worshiped in the larger towns, and minor deities, daemons, and ancestral shades are venerated in the villages. At the village level we find once more the multifunctional religious practitioner. But where there are national gods there are usually national priests, their official servants, and worship tends to take place in temples or at fixed and elaborate shrines. Parrinder writes:

> In the cults of the West African gods [for example, in Dahomey, Yoruba, and Ashanti] there are priests who are highly trained to do their work. These priests are often set aside from birth, or they may be called to the service of the god by being possessed by his spirit. They will then retire from their families and public life, and submit to the training of an older priest. The training normally lasts several years, during which time the novice has to apply himself to learn all the secrets of consulting and serving the god. The training of a priest is an arduous matter. . . . [He] has to observe chastity and strict taboos of food and actions. He frequently has to sleep on a hard floor, have insufficient food, and learn to bear hardship. He is regarded as married to the god, though later he may take a wife. Like an Indian devotee, he seeks by self-discipline to train himself to hear the voice of his god. He learns the ritual and dances appropriate to the cult, receives instruction in the laws and taboos of the god, and gains some knowledge of magical medicines (1954: 100–101).

In these west African cults of deities there is a formal division of function between priests and mediums. In general, priests control mediums and carefully regulate their experience of possession. This situation is one solution to the perennial problem posed for priesthoods by what Ronald Knox (1950) has termed "enthusiasm," that is, the notion that one can become possessed by or identified with a god or God and that one's consequent acts and words are divinely inspired, even if they transgress religious or secular laws. In Dahomey, for example (Herskovits 1938), there are communal training centers, called cult houses or "convents," for mediums and assistants to priests. Here the novices are secluded for considerable periods of time. Part of their training involves the attempt to induce the return of the initial spirit possession that marked their calling. They learn later to produce coherent messages in a state of trance. During this period they are under the surveillance of priests. The Catholic church has similarly brought under its control as members of contemplative orders mystics and visionaries who claim "experimental knowledge of God's presence."

Religious and Political Specialization

In many primitive societies an intimate connection exists between religion and politics. If by politics we denote those behavioral processes of resolution of conflict between the common good and the interests of groups by the use of or struggle for power, then religion in such societies is pragmatically connected with the maintenance of those values and norms expressing the common good and preventing the undue exercise of power. In centralized political systems that have kings and chiefs, these dignitaries themselves have priestly functions; in many parts of Africa, for example, they take charge of observances which safeguard many of the basic needs of existence, such as rainmaking, sowing, and harvest rites, rituals to promote the fertility of men, domestic and wild animals, and so on. On the other hand, even where this is the case, there are frequently other specialized religious functionaries whose duties are bound up with the office of kingship. An illustration of this occurs among the Bemba of Zambia, where the *Bakabilo*

> are in charge of ceremonies at the sacred relic shrines and take possession of the *babenye* when the chief dies. They alone can purify the chief from the defilement of sex intercourse so that he is able to enter his relic shrine and perform the necessary rites there. They are in complete charge of the accession ceremonies of the paramount and the bigger territorial chiefs, and some of their number are described as *bafingo,* or hereditary buriers of the chief. Besides this, each individual *mukabilo* has his

own small ritual duty or privilege, such as lighting the sacred fire, or forging the blade of the hoe that is to dig the foundations of the new capital (Richards 1940, p. 109 in 1955 edition).

The *Bakabilo* constitute a council that exerts a check on the paramount's power, since the members are hereditary officials and cannot be removed at will. They are immune to the paramount's anger and can block the implementation of decisions that they consider to be detrimental to the interests of the Bemba people by refusing to perform the ritual functions that are necessary to the exercise of his office. A priesthood of this type thus forms a constituent part of the interior structure of the government of a primitive state.

In stateless societies in Africa and elsewhere, incumbents of certain ritual positions have similar functions in the maintenance of order and the resolution of conflict. The "leopard-skin chief" or "priest of the earth" (as this specialist has been variously called) among the Nuer of the Nilotic Sudan is a person whose ritual relationship with the earth gives him power to bless or curse, to cleanse a killer from the pollution of bloodshed, and, most important, to perform the rites of reconciliation between persons who are ready to terminate a blood feud. A similar role is performed by the "masters of the fishing spear" among the Dinka and the *tendaanas,* or earth priests, among the Tallensi and their congeners in the northern territories of Ghana. Similar religious functionaries are found in many other regions of Africa. They serve to reduce, if not to resolve, conflict within the society. As against sectional and factional interests they posit the commonweal. In these contexts, moreover, the commonweal is regarded as part of the cosmic order; breach, therefore, is mystically punished. The religious specialists are accorded the function of restoring the right relation that should obtain between society, the cosmos, and the deities or ancestral shades.

19

Shamanism

Piers Vitebsky

The religious systems loosely grouped under the term "shamanism" generally involve a specialist whose soul is perceived to leave the body during trance and, on behalf of clients, travel to other realms and encounter spirits or ancestors. As author Piers Vitebsky explains, the term "shaman" derives from the Tungus of Siberia, but was applied by early researchers—and later the general public—to perhaps thousands of religions thought to have something in common. In truth, there is no "-ism" to shamanism, and the breadth of the word's applicability is somewhat controversial in anthropology today. Nonetheless, many researchers find the term useful and can point to consistent basic features shared by practitioners.

Piers Vitebsky has conducted fieldwork among the Sora of Eastern India and has published numerous works on shamanism. In this article, he introduces the most important features of the shaman's role, with attention to the various intellectual concerns about definitions. He explains how the shaman is distinct from other forms of religious specialist, such as spirit mediums, and argues that the shaman must be understood in the context of such local cultural features as social structure, concepts of nature and personhood, and the economy. Vitebsky cautiously compares shamans to social workers and psychotherapists, as illustrated in extended examples from the Inuit and the Sora.

The article ends with examination of shamanic revival or neo-shamanic practices. In the urbanized West, these adaptations reconfigure shamanism as something that can be taught and learned, to be used as a form of therapy or spiritual enhancement. A different form of shamanic revival is occurring today among some of the peoples who lost their indigenous shamanic practices under colonialism.

The Terms "Shamanism" and "Shaman"

From the Stone Age to the New Age, the figure of the shaman has continued to grip the human imagination. Being chosen by the spirits, taught by them to enter a trance and fly with one's soul to other worlds in the sky or clamber through dangerous crevasses into terrifying subterranean worlds; being stripped of one's flesh, reduced to a skeleton and then re-

assembled and reborn; gaining the power to combat spiritual enemies and heal their victims, to kill enemies and save one's own people from disease and starvation—these are features of shamanic religions in many parts of the world. And yet they are generally regarded by the communities in which they occur, not as part of some extraordinary sort of mystical practice, but as a specialized development of the relationship which every person has with the world around them.

"Shamanism" is probably the world's oldest form of religion. It is a name generally given to many hundreds, perhaps thousands, of religions around the world. These are thought to have something in

From: Indigenous Religions: A Companion, *ed. Graham Harvey. London and NY: Cassell (2000), pp. 55–67.*

common with the religion of the Tungus hunters and reindeer herders in Siberia from whom the word "shamán" or "hamán" was taken. (In English the word is widely pronounced "sháy-man." The ending has nothing to do with the English word "man." Whichever way one pronounces it, the plural is "shamans.") It could thus be said that there are many shamanisms (Atkinson 1992), just as there are many monotheisms.

Among the Tungus peoples such as the Evenki and the Even, a shaman is a man or woman whose soul is said to be able to leave their body during trance and travel to other realms of the cosmos. The term is thus named after a central figure and refers, not to a single religion, but rather to a style of religious activity and a kind of understanding of the world. The term was not traditionally used in any indigenous culture, for two reasons: first, every language has its own words for figures who correspond to the shaman, such as the female *udaghan* and the male *oyuun* among the Sakha (Yakut) of Siberia, the *kuran* among the Sora of tribal India, the *angakkoq* of the Greenlandic Kalaallit (Eskimo) or the *Payé* in various languages of the upper Amazon. Second, the ending "-ism" carries an implication of formal doctrine which belongs to more systematized religions and ideologies from the "western" world and is inappropriate for the fluidity and flexibility of these uncodified religions from largely non-literate societies. The word's usefulness therefore depends on our ability, and our need, to perceive parallels between these many different religions. Even if we accept these parallels, it has been suggested that, rather than shamanism as a systematic form of religion, we should speak of "shamanship" as a skill or personal disposition which is manifested to a greater or lesser degree in various cultures and persons (Atkinson 1989; Vitebsky 1993, 21–2).

By a strict definition, "shamanism" should perhaps be used only for religions of the non-European peoples of the circumpolar north, and especially of Siberia, where many other peoples have similar religions to those of the Tungus peoples. This view is taken by some scholars specializing in the religions and cultures of this region (for good overviews, see Siikala 1978; Hoppál 1984; Balzer 1990). A broader and more common approach (Eliade 1964; Lewis 1989; Atkinson 1992; Vitebsky 1995a) recognizes shamanic kinds of religion around the world, partic-

ularly among the Inuit (Eskimo) peoples,[1] in Amazonia, in Arctic and sub-Arctic North America, and underlying other more mainstream or "world religions" in Mongolia, Tibet, Central Asia, Nepal, China, Japan, Korea, aboriginal India and Indonesia.

There is less agreement about how far the term should be applied to indigenous religions in Africa, Australia, the Pacific, North America south of the sub-Arctic, or ancient Europe. Such controversies generally concern the nature of the relationship between religious practitioner and spirits, and particularly the frequent absence of soul travel. In African religions, for example, with some exceptions (e.g. the !Kung Bushmen, see Katz 1982) the souls of specialists do not generally travel to the world of spirits. Rather, spirits more commonly visit this world and possess people here (de Heusch 1981). This is a reminder that, even if we believe that all early religions were based on direct relationships between humans and spirits, these can take many different forms.

In industrial or "western" society today, people interested in spiritual revival sometimes use the word "shaman" for anyone who is thought to have a special relationship with spirits. In this chapter I shall keep to the criterion of soul flight, since this constitutes a distinctive form of human religiosity with its own particular theological, psychological and sociological implications. This already contains enough diversity to make generalization difficult, but I shall try to highlight some widespread features which such religions have in common.

Prehistory and Hunting

Broadly speaking, shamanic kinds of religion have tended to be marginalized or persecuted with the growth of urban civilizations, centralized states (Thomas and Humphrey 1994), and institutionalized priest-based religions (though their legacy can be seen, for example, in mystical experiences of ascent in Christianity and Islam). Their scattered distribution

---

1. Each of the different peoples of this family in Greenland, Canada, Russia, and Alaska has their own name for themselves. The name "Eskimo" is now considered insulting among some groups such as the Inuit ("Real People") of Canada. However, other groups reject the name Inuit and there is currently no name which is universally acceptable for the peoples of this family.

worldwide, mostly in small-scale societies outside the main orbit of these structures, raises the question of whether these religions could be relics of some pan-human form of early religion.

Prehistoric paintings and petroglyphs, some dating to the paleolithic era, have been found in Europe, South Africa, Australia, Siberia and elsewhere, portraying figures which are part-human, part-animal. Though this is impossible to prove, some scholars have interpreted these as shamans undergoing transformation into animals. Less controversially, rock carvings in Siberia which are several thousand years old show recognizable modern Siberian shaman's costumes, complete with reindeer-antler helmets and drums stretched over a distinctive style of wooden framework. This at least suggests that, even if not unchanging, the religions of this region have a very ancient core.

Another possible link with prehistory is the close, though not exclusive, link between soul flight and hunting. In many societies the shaman's journey across the landscape or the sea echoes the movements and experiences of the hunter but also enlarges and intensifies them. Just as the hunter may try to share the mentality and being of his quarry by dressing in its skins and smelling, calling and moving like an animal, so the shaman may undertake a soul flight in order to locate game animals. But the shaman may also go further and experience turning into an animal, possibly even living for a while as a member of that animal's community and then using this knowledge to encourage members of the species to give themselves up to the community's hunters, or to become the shaman's own spirit helper. Such imagery is often quite male and contrasts with the more female shamanisms found in some agrarian societies in Asia (Kendall 1985).

Trance, Cosmology and Reality

Shamanic believers generally say that many features of the world, whether animals, trees, streams, mountains, heavenly bodies, even man-made objects like knives and drums, may be imbued with some form of spirit. These manifestations of spirit represent the very essence of these phenomena: the bearness of a bear, the treeness of a tree, the musical power of a drum. At the same time, they resemble human consciousness in that they are capable of experience and

volition. They notice how we treat them and can give or withhold from us. They also represent a principle of causality in human affairs. Just as bears, trees and knives interact with us physically according to their qualities and powers of growing and cutting, so their spirits may have effects and cause events in our lives in accordance with their own nature and desires.

The shaman's journeys allow him or her to perceive the true nature or essence of phenomena, to understand how this is implicated in the causation of events in this world, and to act upon this understanding in order to change undesirable situations and sustain desirable ones.

This dimension of reality is not accessible to ordinary people, or in an ordinary state of consciousness. The shaman's switch to an altered state of consciousness is expressed as a journey in space. This imagery conveys the otherness of the spirit realm, but it also opens up a whole topography of mental or spiritual states. This topography is elaborated by different cultures in very different ways. Though the shaman may also fly around the known local landscape, it is also very common to travel up and down through a many-layered cosmology in which our world occupies a position somewhere in the middle. For example, in various parts of Siberia there may be several lower worlds as well as seven, eleven or more upper worlds, of which the higher ones can be reached only by shamans with appropriate skills and training.

Though the shaman's journey to another world suggests a theology of transcendence, the fact that that other world also animates the phenomena of this world shows that this theology is also deeply immanentist. Rather than occasional theophanies, shamanic religions tend to emphasize concentrations or intensifications of a divine presence which is continuously in the world, while humans are not separated from the divine but shade into it, or partake of it, through forms of shared soulhood.

This emphasis on immanence can also be linked to what may be called a shamanic view of time. Unlike the linear historical time of Semitic religions, with their strong concern with eschatology, shamanic thinking tends to conceive time as cyclical or steady-state. The Inuit shaman's journey to the bottom of the sea and the Sora shamans' journeys to the Underworld described below are intended to ameliorate a situation, but they do not provide a permanent solution. The sea spirit may withhold whales from hunters again on another occasion, the Sora patient who gets better today may be ill again tomorrow and will eventually die. Similarly, the shamanic community's cosmos may contain a finite amount of soul-force, so that animals hunted must be paid for by trading in the lives of humans (the Tukano of Amazonia, see Reichel-Dolmatoff 1971) or parts of a seal must be honoured and thrown back into the sea to be reincarnated (some Inuit of the Arctic).

This is not because these religions are theologically undeveloped. Rather, it is because they regard the problematic nature of life as existentially given, rather than as a situation of ignorance or sin awaiting a historical redemption. Shamanic rites are based on an acknowledgement of the essences and processes of the world, combined with a willingness to use them to achieve one's goals.

Person, Powers and Initiatory Experience of the Shaman

In many societies there can be several kinds of shaman, who shade in turn into a range of other specialists such as midwives, diviners, exorcists, bonesetters or herbalists. Some shamans may use techniques of soul journey to fulfil any of these functions, as well as those of doctor, priest, mystic, social worker, psychoanalyst, hunting consultant, psychopomp, astronaut and many others. It often seems that a shaman has to encompass the totality of possibilities of being, transcending boundaries of gender, species and other categories. The ability to make a soul journey is linked to special skills at transformation. Shamans may be transvestite or sexually ambiguous, may speak languages of other peoples or other worlds, or may transform themselves into animals or other beings.

The trance of an experienced shaman is a technique of dissociation with a high degree of control, entered into more or less at will. It is often established with the aid of rhythmical drumming, chanting and dancing, or invocations describing the imminent journey, obstacles which will be encountered, and anticipated battles with hostile spirits and monsters. Other aids, especially in Amazonia, can include the ingestion of psychotropic plants which are said to teach the shaman by revealing what cannot be seen by other means (Reichel-Dolmatoof 1975; Schultes and Hofmann 1979).

The element of will and control in trance makes shamans very different from some other kinds of

spirit mediums who stay in this world and are possessed or dominated by spirits which come to visit them and take over their body. Eliade (1964) and Shirokogoroff (1935) have emphasized the shaman's "mastery" of spirits, but it should be remembered that the degree of this control is always precarious. The shaman's involvement with spirits is very dangerous and there is said to be a constant risk of insanity or death.

Though there is much variation across societies, shamanic power and practice are often inherited within a lineage or kin-group. But at the same time it is generally said that a future shaman does not choose his or her profession, but is chosen by the spirits themselves to serve them. The young candidate may be made aware of this through dreams or by other signs. Their first response is often to refuse to accept such a life of suffering and hardship. The spirits then torment them for months or years until they submit, threatening to kill them if they resist, driving them mad, dismembering them in visions, sending spirit animals to devour them, or forcing them to live up trees eating bark or rush crazily across mountains and snowfields.

The symbolism of transformation and rebirth is often very clear. The candidate comes to understand the true nature of things by being dismembered and reassembled as someone greater and more complete than before. These additional powers are represented by animal helpers whose properties of skill or strength the shaman acquires. Other power objects can include crystals, drums and costumes, melodies, spells, and parts of animals such as a deer's paw for swiftness or (in Nepal) porcupine quills to fire as darts at evil spirits.

Here is part of an account of his initiation in the lower world given by a Siberian shaman to a Russian anthropologist earlier this century (Popov 1936, 84ff., translated in Vitebsky 1995a, 58–61; for other shaman's narratives, see Halifax 1979):

> The Great Underground Master told me that I would have to travel the path of every illness. He gave me a stoat and a mouse as my guides and together with them I continued my journey further into the underworld. My companions led me to a high place where there stood seven tents. 'The people inside these tents are cannibals,' the mouse and stoat warned me. Nevertheless I went into the middle tent, and went crazy on the spot. These were the

Smallpox People. They cut out my heart and threw it into a cauldron to boil. Inside this tent I found the Master of my Madness, in another tent I saw the Master of Confusion, in another the Master of Stupidity. I went round all these tents and became acquainted with the paths of various human diseases.

Then I went through an opening in another rock. A naked man was sitting there fanning the fire with bellows. Above the fire hung an enormous cauldron as big as half the earth. When he saw me the naked man brought out a pair of tongs the size of a tent and took hold of me. He took my head and cut it off, and then sliced my body into little pieces and put them in the cauldron. There he boiled my body for three years. Then he placed me on an anvil and struck my head with a hammer and dipped it into ice-cold water to temper it.

He took the big cauldron off the fire and poured its contents into another container. Now all my muscles had been separated from the bones. Here I am now, I'm talking to you in an ordinary state of mind and I can't say how many pieces there are in my body. But we shamans have several extra bones and muscles. I turned out to have three such parts, two muscles and one bone. When all my bones had been separated from my flesh, the blacksmith said to me, "Your marrow has turned into a river" and inside the hut I really did see a river with my bones floating on it. "Look, there are your bones floating away!" said the blacksmith and started to pull them out of the water with his tongs.

When all my bones had been pulled out on to the shore the blacksmith put them together, they became covered with flesh and my body took on its previous appearance. The only thing that was still left unattached was my head. It just looked like a bare skull. The blacksmith covered my skull with flesh and joined it onto my torso. I took on my previous human form. Before he let me go the blacksmith pulled out my eyes and put in new ones. He pierced my ears with his iron finger and told me, 'You will be able to hear and understand the speech of plants.' After this I found myself on the summit of a mountain and soon afterwards woke up in my own tent. Near me sat my worried father and mother.

The Shaman in Practice

A shaman's practice will vary enormously across numerous diverse cultures. It may also cover a wide range of domanis which industrial society regards as very separate. In theological terms, it represents a communion with the divine; medically and psychiatrically, it can represent a movement from sickness to health; socially, it leads from a dysfunctional situation to one of communal harmony. So while it is reminiscent in some ways of mystical experience in the mainstream historical religions, shamanic journeying is at the same time extremely pragmatic and goal-oriented.

In many rites one can discern a re-enactment of the central experience of transformation from the shaman's initiation, but on a smaller and less drastic scale. Some rites, such as offerings, are performed regularly or seasonally to maintain order. Others are performed in response to a problem. When a person falls ill because their soul has been abducted by spirits, or the community begins to starve because animals refuse to give themselves to hunters, the shaman must go on a soul journey to visit the spirits concerned and persuade or coerce them to change their behaviour. This widespread format can be seen clearly in a classic example collected earlier this century from a community of Iglulik Inuit (Eskimo) in northern Canada (summarized from Rasmussen 1929, 123–29).

When there was an incurable sickness, a hunter was particularly unsuccessful, or an entire village was threatened by famine, this was thought to be due to the anger of the sea spirit Takanakapsaluk, who had become contaminated with the community's accumulated sins and breaches of taboos. She was a woman whose father had cruelly cut off her fingers, which then turned into the different species of sea creatures on which the Iglulik Eskimo depend and which she grants them or withholds from them at will. This immediately highlights a central dilemma of traditional Inuit life. Not only do they have to take the life of animals to live, so that those animals must be treated with respect and gratitude, but these animals are also part of the flesh of the sea spirit and humans are able to live only as a result of her suffering.

Anywhere in the world, a shaman's response to this kind of problem may be to enter a trance and go on a soul journey. In this case, the shaman prepares for a difficult journey to Takanakapsaluk's house on the sea-bed. The community gathers in a house and the shaman sits behind a curtain. After particularly elaborate preparations he calls his helpers, saying again and again, 'The way is made ready for me, the way opens before me!', while the audience reply "Let it be so!" Finally, from behind the curtain the shaman can be heard crying "Halala – he – he – he, halala – he – he!" Then as he drops down a tube which is said to lead straight to the bottom of the sea, his voice can be heard receding ever further into the distance: "Halele – he!," until it is lost altogether.

During the shaman's absence, the audience sits in the darkened house and hears the sighing and groaning of people who lived long ago. These can be heard puffing and splashing and coming up for air in the form of seals, whales and walruses. As soon as the shaman reaches the sea-bed, he follows a coast-line past a series of obstacles to the sea spirit's house. He has to dodge three deadly stones which churn around leaving hardly any room to pass. The entrance tunnel to the sea spirit's house is guarded by a fierce dog over which the shaman must step. He is also threatened by her father.

When the shaman finally enters the house he finds Takanakapsaluk with a great pool of sea creatures over the floor beside her, all puffing, blowing and snorting. As a sign of her anger, she is sitting with her back to this pool and to the blubber-oil lamp which is the only source of light. She is in a pitiful state. Her hair is filthy and uncombed and hangs over her eyes so that she cannot see. Her body is also filthy. This dirt represents the sins and misdeeds of the human community up above. The shaman must overcome her anger and slowly, gently turn her towards the lamp and the animals. He must comb her hair, for she has no fingers and is unable to do this for herself. When he has calmed her, he tells her, "Those above can no longer help the seals up by grasping their foreflippers," and she answers, "The secret miscarriages of the women and breaches of taboo bar the way for the animals." When the shaman has fully mollified her, Takanakapsaluk releases the animals one by one and they are carried out by a torrent through the entrance tunnel into the sea, to become available again to hunters.

Just as when a patient's soul has been kidnapped, a shaman will regain possession of it in preparation for restoring it to the patient's body, so here the shaman has moved the situation decisively towards a resolution. He has done this by precipitating, and winning, an encounter. Here, he achieves his goal by tender persuasion, though in other situations a shaman may have to beg a great

spirit lord for mercy, or lead serried ranks of helper spirits in a pitched battle against armies of hostile demons.

Now the shaman starts to return. He can be heard a long way off returning through the tube which his helper spirits have kept open for him. With one last "Plu – a – he – he," he shoots up into his place behind the curtain, gasping for breath. After an expectant silence, he says, "Words will arise." Then, one after another, poeple start to confess their misdeeds, often bringing out secrets which were quite unsuspected even in a small community living at close quarters. In particular, many women confess to a breach of taboo which the sea spirit finds particularly offensive, the concealment of miscarriages. (After a miscarriage, all soft skins and furs belonging to everyone inside the house must be thrown away. This is such a serious loss that a woman may try to conceal any miscarriage or irregular bleeding.) By the end of the seance there is such a mood of optimism about the next hunt that people may even feel grateful to the women whose behaviour caused the problem in the first place.

This example shows how intensely the community is involved, both in commissioning the shaman's soul journey and in participating in it from a complementary position as audience or congregation. The shaman's activities are intensely embedded in the local social structure. The entire practice of shamanism must therefore be understood with reference not only to indigenous theology, but also to local concepts of nature, humanity and the person, the meanings of life and death, and even the workings of the economy. Many writings about shamans ignore social context or even deny the shaman's social role, promoting an image of the shaman as some kind of solitary mystic (Eliade 1964, 8; Castaneda 1968). But as the earlier initiation narrative shows, a shaman may pass through eremitic or psychotic phases, but must always be re-socialized and psychologically reintegrated to serve a social function within the community. The mystic is also a social worker.

The public role of the shaman also emerges clearly among the Sora, an aboriginal tribe in eastern India (Vitebsky 1993). The Inuit shaman's trance, like that of the Siberian shaman, is a rare and highly dramatic occasion. But in every Sora village, almost every day, one of the many shamans will go into trance, allowing groups of living people to hold dialogues with the dead, who come one at a time to speak to them through the shaman's mouth. Here, instead of being called in for a crisis, the shaman is involved in a constant regulation of social relations.

The shaman (usually a woman) sits down and invokes her predecessors and helper spirits with a rhythmic chant. When she enters trance she experiences her soul clambering down terrifying precipices to the underworld like a monkey. This leaves her body vacant for the dead to use as their vehicle of communication and one by one, they begin to speak through her mouth. (Here, the technically distinct "shamanism" and "possession" are combined into one system.)

Every case of illness or death is thought to be caused by the dead. The living respond by staging dialogues in which they summon the dead persons responsible, interrogate them in an attempt to understand their state of mind, and negotiate with them. Closely related groups thus find themselves in constantly recurring contact: mourners crowd around the shaman arguing vehemently with the dead, laughing at their jokes, or weeping at their recriminations; family conversations and quarrels continue after some of their participants have crossed the dividing line between what are called life and death.

In this way, everyone engages in a continual fine-tuning of their mutual relationships and each dialogue is only a fleeting episode in an open-ended relationship which explores and ultimately resolves a range of emotional ambiguities in the lives of the participants.

After death, a person's consciousness becomes a form of spirit called *sonum*. Sonums are a powerful causal principle in the affairs of the living. But they are also a contradictory one. On the one hand, in certain moods or aspects, sonums nourish their living descendants through the soul-force they put into their growing crops, giving them their continued sustenance and their very existence; but on the other hand, they 'eat them up' and destroy them.

A person's susceptiblity to the effects of sonums depends on a subtle interplay between their own state of mind and that of the numerous other living and dead persons who are caught up in the ongoing dialogue. Different categories of sonum are located in different features of the landscape. As a living person moves around this landscape, he or she may encounter sonums and become involved with them. But this happens not at random, but as a develop-

ment of their long-term relationships with the various dead persons who now reside in those places. What seems at first sight like a person's medical history also turns out to be a comprehensive social and emotional biography.

Illness arises out of the playing out of an emotional attachment and healing consists in altering the nature of that attachment over time. When a dead Sora encounters a living one, it is said that the dead person's attachment can be so strong that, even without meaning to, they overwhelm and engulf the living. During the course of several years' dialogue, living and dead will discuss and develop their relationship to the point where the deceased is gradually persuaded to move into ever less unwholesome places on the landscape and less disturbed and threatening categories of sonum. Finally, the deceased becomes a pure ancestor, who is supposed to have no remaining aggressive impulses but to recycle his or her name into a new baby among their descendants and to watch over this baby. This is the final resolution of a range of ambivalences which can be emotional, sociological and even legal, concerning inheritance.

If the Inuit example directs us towards one aspect of shamanic way of thinking, namely the intimate and complex relationship between humans, animals and morality, the Sora show us something else: a system in which shamans use their trance to act as conduits for a shifting and constantly renegotiated concept of personhood. It would be hard to conceive the Sora person without these dialogues since the Sora person seems not to have a unitary core but to be composed almost entirely of the confluence of the person's relationship with other persons.

Shamans have often been compared to psychoanalysts and psychotherapists, and here we see how both Inuit and Sora shamans not only engage with spirits, but also use dramatic enactment to conduct a form of psychotherapy and sociotherapy. The Inuit shaman makes a shaper contrast between the roles of shaman and audience, while the Sora shaman bows out as the dead arrive and leaves the living clients to face them unaided. Either way, however, there is a profound theological contrast with psychoanalysis concerning the presumed reality of spirits. In the Sora view, the dead not only exist but are equal partners in their encounters with the living. In Freud's model of bereavement, the dead have ceased to exist and the mourner who continues to speak with them is suffering from a "hallucinatory wishful psychosis" (Vitebsky 1993, 238–47)—just as in zoology, marine mammals have no spirit keepers.

A Shamanic Revival?

In the West, there is a growing fascination with indigenous and synthetic forms of shamanism (see e.g. *Shaman's Drum: A Journal of Experiential Shamanism*). Forms of so-called "shamanism" flourish in popular magazines and weekend workshops, under the guidance of a new profession of "urban shamans." As organized religion retreats ever further from the lives of millions and as institutionalized medicine is subjected to unprecedented criticism, increasing numbers are wondering whether what they call shamanism may offer an appropriate new way of thinking and acting in the industrial and post-industrial world. The evaluation of shamans themselves has shifted from their earlier dismissal as crazy and deluded, to a respect and awe for these people who are said to go to the edge of psychosis, perceive reality and return to serve society (see Walsh 1990 for a survey of shamanic and related states of mind).

However, such movements do not deal easily with the embeddedness of shamanic beliefs in their social structures, and some neo-shamanic practitioners advocate a composite form of "shamanism" based on ideas of universal human spiritual poten-

tial (Harner 1982), arguing that shamanism is not religion but a technique which anyone can learn. This contrasts strikingly with the claim in many traditional societies that a shaman is a rare person who has been specially chosen by the spirits.

While shamanic revival is a major strand in Western life today, it is also appearing among the people who were the world's earlier shamanists but who abandoned shamanic religions under colonial pressure. But revival cannot mean a return to an old way of life. Modern indigenous "shamanisms" have become linked to ethnic identity, environmental protest, democratic ideals or a backlash against the militant atheism of communist regimes (Vitebsky 1995b). Moreover, even the remotest tribal shamans may now have relationships, not only with white people, but increasingly even with shamans from other, separate traditions of which they are only just becoming aware.

So, perhaps as in the paleolithic era, there is a possibility that shamanism may now become a sort of world religion. But this is most likely to come about only in a globalized form in which diverse shamanic ideas and practices are severed from their roots in numerous small-scale societies, largely at the hands of white outsiders. For the foreseeable future, the term "shamanism" will be the subject of intense controversy centering especially on questions of definition, authenticity and appropriation.

20

Dark Side of the Shaman

Michael Fobes Brown

Spiritual seekers in the United States have long turned to non-Western and indigenous cultures for inspiration, often adopting practices they perceive as superior or more natural than their Western biomedical and religious counterparts. Shamanism has been particularly attractive to some Americans in recent decades, including those in the therapeutic professions and self-improvement movement. Anthropologist Michael Fobes Brown, who spent two years with the Aguaruna of northeastern Peru, offers a contrasting point of view. His research yielded first-hand knowledge of the complexity of Aguaruna shamanism and its accompanying beliefs, including sorcery intended to cause harm. Individuals identified as sorcerers face execution, and shamans in turn are at risk for sorcery accusations or vengeance from a sorcerer's family. To Brown, shamanism and sorcery function well for the Aguaruna, providing rituals of community support, ethnomedical treatment, and rules and punishments in a society without a police force or written laws. However, Brown strongly dismisses the romantic attitude of U.S. enthusiasts who strip shamanism of its original cultural context and who seek an easily acquired set of techniques for personal development.

For another discussion of the distinction between Western neo-shamanism and shamanism as traditionally studied by anthropologists, see Fiona Bowie, The Anthropology of Religion: An Introduction *(Malden, Mass.: Blackwell, 2006, pp. 191–95).*

Santa Fe, New Mexico, is a stronghold of that eclectic mix of mysticism and folk medicine called "New Age" thought. The community bulletin board of the public library, just around the corner from the plaza and the venerable Palace of the Governors, serves as a central bazaar for spiritual guides advertising instruction in alternative healing methods. Many of these workshops—for example, classes in holistic massage and rebirthing—have their philosophical roots in the experiments of the 1960s. Others resist easy classification: What, I've wondered, is Etheric Body Healing and Light Body Work, designed to

"resonate the light forces within our being"? For thirty-five dollars an hour, another expert offers consultations in "defense and removal of psychic attack." Most of the classes, however, teach the healing arts of non-Western or tribal peoples. Of particular interest to the New Agers of Santa Fe is the tradition known as shamanism.

Shamans, who are found in societies all over the world, are believed to communicate directly with spirits to heal people struck down by illness. Anthropologists are fond of reminding their students that shamanism, not prostitution, is the world's oldest profession. When, in my role as curious ethnographer, I've asked Santa Feans about their interest in this exotic form of healing, they have expressed their admiration for the beauty of the shamanistic tradition, the ability of shamans to "get in touch with their inner healing powers," and the superiority of spiritual treatments over the impersonal medical practice of our own society. Fifteen years ago, I would have sympathized with these romantic ideas. Two years of fieldwork in an Amazonian society, however, taught me that there is peril in the shaman's craft.

A man I shall call Yankush is a prominent shaman among the Aguaruna, a native people who make their home in the tropical forest of northeastern Peru. Once feared headhunters, the Aguaruna now direct their considerable energies to cultivating cash crops and protecting their lands from encroachment by settlers fleeing the poverty of Peru's highland and coastal regions.

Yankush is a vigorous, middle-aged man known for his nimble wit and ready laugh. Like every other able-bodied man in his village, Yankush works hard to feed his family by hunting, fishing, and helping his wife cultivate their fields. But when his kinfolk or friends fall ill, he takes on the role of *iwishín*—shaman—diagnosing the cause of the affliction and then, if possible, removing the source of the ailment from the patient's body.

In common with most peoples who preserve a lively shamanistic heritage, the Aguaruna believe that life-threatening illness is caused by sorcerers. Sorcerers are ordinary people who, driven by spite or envy, secretly introduce spirit darts into the bodies of their victims. If the dart isn't soon removed by a shaman, the victim dies. Often the shaman describes the dart as a piece of bone, a tiny thorn, a spider, or a blade of grass.

The Aguaruna do not regard sorcery as a quaint and colorful bit of traditional lore. It is attempted homicide, plain and simple. That the evidence of sorcery can only be seen by a shaman does not diminish the ordinary person's belief in the reality of the sorcerer's work, any more than our inability to see viruses with the naked eye leads us to question their existence. The Aguaruna insist that sorcerers, when discovered, must be executed for the good of society.

Shaman and sorcerer might seem locked in a simple struggle of good against evil, order against chaos, but things are not so straightforward. Shamans and sorcerers gain their power from the same source, both receiving spirit darts from a trusted instructor. Because the darts attempt to return to their original owner, apprentice shamans and sorcerers must induce them to remain in their bodies

by purifying themselves. They spend months in jungle isolation, fasting and practicing sexual abstinence. By wrestling with the terrifying apparitions that come to plague their dreams, they steel themselves for a life of spiritual struggle.

There the paths of sorcerer and shaman divide. The sorcerer works in secret, using spirit darts to inflict suffering on his enemies. The shaman operates in the public eye and uses his own spirit darts to thwart the sorcerer's schemes of pain and untimely death. (I say "he" because to my knowledge all Aguaruna shamans are men. Occasionally, however, a woman is accused of sorcery.) Yet because shamans possess spirit darts, and with them the power to kill, the boundary between sorcerer and shaman is sometimes indistinct.

The ambiguities of the shaman's role were brought home to me during a healing session I attended in Yankush's house. The patients were two women: Yamanuanch, who complained of pains in her stomach and throat, and Chapaik, who suffered discomfort in her back and lower abdomen. Their illnesses did not seem life threatening, but they were persistent enough to raise fears that sorcery was at the root of the women's misery.

As darkness fell upon us, the patients and their kin waited for Yankush to enter into a trance induced by a bitter, hallucinogenic concoction he had taken just before sunset (it is made from a vine known as *ayahuasca*). While the visitors exchanged gossip and small talk, Yankush sat facing the wall of his house, whistling healing songs and waving a bundle of leaves that served as a fan and soft rattle. Abruptly, he told the two women to lie on banana leaves that had been spread on the floor, so that he could use his visionary powers to search their bodies for tiny points of light, the telltale signature of the sorcerer's darts. As Yankush's intoxication increased, his meditative singing gave way to violent retching. Gaining control of himself, he sucked noisily on the patients' bodies in an effort to remove the darts.

Family members of the patients shouted words of concern and support. "Others know you are curing. They can hurt you, be careful!" one of the spectators warned, referring to the sorcerers whose work the shaman hoped to undo. Torn by anxiety, Chapaik's husband addressed those present: "Who has done this bewitching? If my wife dies, I could kill any man out of anger!" In their cries of encouragement to

Yankush, the participants expressed their high regard for the difficult work of the shaman, who at this point in the proceedings was frequently doubled over with nausea caused by the drug he had taken.

Suddenly there was a marked change of atmosphere. A woman named Chimi called out excitedly, "If there are any darts there when she gets back home, they may say that Yankush put them there. So take them all out!" Chimi's statement was an unusually blunt rendering of an ambivalence implicit in all relations between Aguaruna shamans and their clients. Because shamans control spirit darts, people fear that a shaman may be tempted to use the cover of healing as an opportunity to bewitch his own clients for personal reasons. The clients therefore remind the shaman that they expect results—and if such results are not forthcoming, the shaman himself may be suspected of, and punished for, sorcery.

Yankush is such a skilled healer that this threat scarcely caused him to miss a step. He sucked noisily on Yamanuanch's neck to cure her sore throat and, after singing about the sorcery darts lodged in her body, announced she would recover. For good measure, he recommended injections of a commercial antibiotic. Yankush also took pains to emphasize the intensity of his intoxication. Willingness to endure the rigors of a large dose of *ayhausca* is a sign of his good faith as a healer. "Don't say I wasn't intoxicated enough," he reminded the participants.

As Yankush intensified his singing and rhythmic fanning of the leaf-bundle, he began to have visions of events taking place in distant villages. Suddenly he cried out, "In Achu they killed a person. A sorcerer was killed." "Who could it be?" the other participants asked one another, but before they could reflect on this too long, Yankush had moved on to other matters. "I'm concentrating to throw out sickness, like a tireless jaguar," he sang, referring to Chapaik, who complained of abdominal pains. "With my help she will become like the tapir, which doesn't know how to refuse any kind of food."

After two hours of arduous work, Yankush steered the healing session to its conclusion by reassuring the patients that they were well on their way to recovery. "In her body the sickness will end," he sang. "It's all right. She won't die. It's nothing," he added, returning to a normal speaking voice. Before departing, the patients and their kin discussed the particulars of Yankush's dietary recommendations and made plans for a final healing session to take place at a later date. As the sleepy participants left Yankush's house for their beds in other parts of the village, they expressed their contentment with the results of his efforts.

During the year I lived near Yankush, he conducted healing sessions like this one about twice a month. Eventually, I realized that his active practice was only partly a matter of choice. To allay suspicions and demonstrate his good faith as a healer, he felt compelled to take some cases he might otherwise have declined. Even so, when I traveled to other villages, people sometimes asked me how I could live in a community where a "sorcerer" practiced on a regular basis.

When a respected elder died suddenly of unknown causes in 1976, Yankush came under extraordinary pressure to identify the sorcerer responsible. From the images of his *ayahuasca* vision he drew the name of a young man from a distant region who happened to be visiting a nearby village. The man was put to death in a matter of days. Because Yankush was widely known to have fingered the sorcerer, he became the likely victim of a reprisal raid by members of the murdered man's family. Yankush's willingness to accept this risk in order to protect his community from future acts of sorcery was a source of his social prestige, but it was also a burden. I rarely saw him leave his house without a loaded shotgun.

In calling attention to the violent undercurrents of shamanism, my intention is not to disparage the healing traditions of the Aguaruna or of any other tribal people. I have no doubt that the cathartic drama I witnessed in Yankush's house made the two patients feel better. Medical anthropologists agree that rituals calling forth expressions of community support and concern for sick people often lead to a marked improvement in their sense of well-being. Shamans also serve their communities by administering herbal medications and other remedies and even, as in Yankush's case, helping to integrate traditional healing arts with the use of modern pharmaceuticals. At the same time, however, they help sustain a belief in sorcery that exacts a high price in anxiety and, from time to time, in human life.

In their attempts to understand this negative current, anthropologists have studied how shamanism and accusations of sorcery define local patterns of power and control. Belief in sorcery, for example, may provide a system of rules and punishments in societies that lack a police force, written laws, and a formal judicial system. It helps people assign a cause to their misfortunes. And it sustains religions that link human beings with the spirit world and with the tropical forest itself.

What I find unsettling, rather, is that New Age America seeks to embrace shamanism without any appreciation of its context. For my Santa Fe acquaintances, tribal lore is a supermarket from which they choose some tidbits while spurning others. They program computers or pursue other careers by day so that by night they can wrestle with spirit-jaguars

and search for their power spots. Yankush's lifetime of discipline is reduced to a set of techniques for personal development, stripped of links to a specific landscape and cultural tradition.

New Age enthusiasts are right to admire the shamanistic tradition, but while advancing it as an alternative to our own healing practices, they brush aside its stark truths. For throughout the world, shamans see themselves as warriors in a struggle against the shadows of the human heart. Shamanism affirms life but also spawns violence and death. The beauty of shamanism is matched by its power—and like all forms of power found in society, it inspires its share of discontent.

21

Training for the Priesthood Among the Kogi of Colombia

Gerardo Reichel-Dolmatoff

Gerardo Reichel-Dolmatoff's writings on the Kogi, published during the 1950s through 1970s, document one of the most fascinating examples of religious specialists to be found anywhere in anthropology. The Kogi are an indigenous people of Colombia, who sought refuge in the mountains to escape the brutality of Spanish conquerors. Relatively untouched by other cultures until recent times, and despite the hardship of their highland natural environment, they developed a worldview with what the author calls "profound spiritual satisfactions," supported by a highly formalized priesthood.

This article begins with an overview of the Kogi environment, subsistence methods, and social organization, as well as their elaborate cosmology, which includes a Mother-Goddess and distinctive, culturally specific ethical values. Reichel-Dolmatoff's chief concern here, however, is with the training of the mámas, men whose priestly functions require years of training and are carried out in solemn rituals. If selected to be trained as a máma, a young boy is separated from his family, segregated from females, kept indoors during the day, and fed a special diet. The author stresses how the training of the young máma, which normally takes eighteen years, shapes his later behavior as an adult priest. The priest's responsibilities include officiating at ceremonial centers and listening to the confession of misdeeds.

The Kogi claim to be elder brothers of humanity and to possess the only true religion. They are, therefore, deeply concerned for the education of future priests, who will maintain not only Kogi society but the entire world. Reichel-Dolmatoff warns us, however, not to think of the Kogi as noble savages living in harmony with nature but as people who have developed a spiritual means of accepting harsh reality and misfortune.

The Kogi of the Sierra Nevada de Santa Marta in northeastern Colombia are a small tribe of some 6,000 Chibcha-speaking Indians, descendants of the ancient Tairona who, at the time of the Spanish

Source: Gerardo Reichel-Dolmatoff, "Training for the Priesthood among the Kogi of Columbia," in ENCULTURATION IN LATIN AMERICA; AN ANTHOLOGY, edited by Johannes Wilbert (Los Angeles: UCLA Latin American Center Publications, 1976), 265–288. Reproduced with permission of The Regents of the University of California.

conquest, had reached a relatively high development among the aboriginal peoples of Colombia. The Sierra Nevada, with its barren, highly dissected slopes, steep and roadless, presents a difficult terrain for Creole settlement and, owing to the harshness and poor soils of their habitat, the Kogi have been able to preserve, to a quite remarkable degree, their traditional way of life.

The present tribal territory lies at an altitude of between 1,500 and 2,000 meters, where the Indians occupy several small villages of about ten to several dozen round huts, each of about 3 to 4 meters in diameter and built of wattle and daub covered with a conical thatched roof. Each house is inhabited by one nuclear family composed of four or five people who sleep, cook, and eat in this narrow, dark space that they share with their dogs and with most of their material belongings. The huts of a village cluster around a larger, well-built house, also round in its ground plan, but provided with a wall of densely plaited canes; this is the ceremonial house, the temple, access to which is restricted to the men, and where women and children are not allowed to enter. Kogi villages are not permanently occupied; most Indians live in isolated homesteads dispersed over the mountain slopes, and the villages are hardly more than convenient gathering places where the inhabitants of a valley or of a certain restricted area can come together occasionally to exchange news, discuss community matters, discharge themselves of some minor ritual obligations, or trade with the visiting Creole peasants. When staying in the village, the men usually spend the night in the ceremonial house where they talk, sing, or simply listen to the conversation of the older men. As traditional patterns of family life demand that men and women live in not too close an association and collaborate in rigidly prescribed ways in the daily task of making a living, most Kogi families, when staying in their fields, occupy two neighboring huts, one inhabited by the man while the other hut serves as a kitchen and storeroom, and is occupied by his wife and children.

The economic basis of Kogi culture consists of small garden plots where sweet manioc, maize, plantains, cucurbits, beans, and some fruit trees are grown. A few domestic animals such as chicken, pigs, or, rarely, some cattle, are kept only to be sold or exchanged to the Creoles for bush knives, iron pots, and salt. Some Kogi make cakes of raw sugar for trading. Because of the lack of adequate soils, the food resources of one altitudinal level are often insufficient, and many families own several small gardens and temporary shelters at different altitudes, moving between the cold highlands and the temperate valleys in a dreary continuous quest for some harvestable food. Although the starchy tubers provide a fairly permanent food supply, protein sources are few, and a chronic state of malnutrition seems to be the rule. Slash-and-burn agriculture is heavy

work, and the harsh, mountainous environment makes transportation a laborious task. Much agricultural work is done by women and children who collaborate with the men in clearing and burning the fields.

The objects of material culture are coarse and simple, and generally are quite devoid of ornamentation. Some heavy wooden benches, a pair of old string hammocks, smoke-blackened cooking vessels and gourd containers, and a few baskets and carrying bags are about all an average family owns. It is evident then that, to the casual observer, Kogi culture gives the impression of deject poverty, and the disheveled and sullen countenance of the Indian adds to this image of misery and neglect. Indeed, if judged by their external appearance and their austere and withdrawn manner, one would easily come to the conclusion that by all standards of cultural evolution these Indians are a sorry lot.

But nothing could be more misleading than appearances. Behind the drab façade of penury, the Kogi lead a rich spiritual life in which the ancient traditions are being kept alive and furnish the individual and his society with guiding values that not only make bearable the arduous conditions of physical survival, but make them appear almost unimportant if measured against the profound spiritual satisfactions offered by religion. After days and weeks of hunger and work, of ill health and the dreary round of daily tasks, one will suddenly be taken into the presence of a scene, maybe a dance, a song, or some private ritual action that, quite unexpectedly, offers a momentary glimpse into the depths of a very ancient, very elaborate culture. And stronger still becomes this impression in the presence of a priest or an elder who, when speaking of these spiritual dimensions, reveals before his listeners this coherent system of beliefs which is the Kogi world view.

Traditional Kogi religion is closely related to Kogi ideas about the structure and functioning of the Universe, and Kogi cosmology is, in essence, a model for survival in that it molds individual behavior into a plan of actions or avoidances that are oriented toward the maintenance of a viable equilibrium between Man's demands and Nature's resources. In this manner the individual and society at large must both carry the burden of great responsibilities which, in the Kogi view, extend not only to their own society but to the whole of mankind.

The central personification of Kogi religion is the Mother-Goddess. It was she who, in the beginning of time, created the cosmic egg, encompassed between the seven points of reference: North, South, East, West, Zenith, Nadir, and Center, and stratified into nine horizontal layers, the nine "worlds," the fifth and middlemost of which is ours. They embody the nine daughters of the Goddess, each one conceived as a certain type of agricultural land, ranging from pale, barren sand to the black and fertile soil that nourishes mankind. The seven points of reference within which the Cosmos is contained are associated or identified with innumerable mythical beings, animals, plants, minerals, colors, winds, and many highly abstract concepts, some of them arranged into a scale of values, while others are of a more ambivalent nature. The four cardinal directions are under the control of four mythical culture heroes who are also the ancestors of the four primary segments of Kogi society, all four of them Sons of the Mother-Goddess and, similarly, they are associated with certain pairs of animals that exemplify the basic marriage rules. The organizing concept of social structure consists of a system of patrilines and matrilines in which descent is reckoned from father to son and from mother to daughter, and a relationship of complementary opposites is modeled after the relationship between certain animal species. The North is associated with the marsupial and his spouse the armadillo; the South with the puma and his spouse the deer; the East with the jaguar and his spouse the peccary; and the West with the eagle and his spouse the snake. In other words, the ancestral couples form antagonistic pairs in which the "male" animal (marsupial, puma, jaguar, eagle) feeds on the "female" animal (armadillo, deer, peccary, snake) and marriage rules prescribe that the members of a certain patriline must marry women whose matriline is associated with an animal that is the natural prey of the man's animal. The equivalence of food and sex is very characteristic of Kogi thought and is essential for an understanding of religious symbolism in myth and ritual. Moreover, each patriline or matriline has many magical attributes and privileges that together with their respective mythical origins, genealogies, and precise ceremonial functions, form a very elaborate body of rules and relationships.

The macrocosmic structure repeats itself in innumerable aspects of Kogi culture. Each mountain peak of the Sierra Nevada is seen as a "world," a house, an abode, peopled by spirit-beings and enclosed within a fixed set of points of reference: a top, a center, a door. All ceremonial houses contain four circular, stepped, wooden shelves on the inside of their conical roofs, representing the different cosmic layers, and it is thought that this structure is repeated *in reverse* underground, the house being thus an exact reproduction of the Universe, up to the point where its center becomes the "center of the world." Moreover, the cosmic egg is conceived as a divine uterus, the womb of the Mother-Goddess, and so, in a descending scale, our earth is conceived as a uterus, the Sierra Nevada is a uterus, and so is every mountain, house, cave, carrying bag, and, indeed, every tomb. The land is conceived as a huge female body that nourishes and protects, and each topographic feature of it corresponds to an inclusive category of anatomical detail of this vast mother-image. The large roof apexes of the major ceremonial houses, constructed in the shape of an open, upturned umbrella, represent the sexual organ of the Mother-Goddess and offerings are deposited there representing a concept of fertilization.

The Kogi conceive the world in terms of a dualistic scheme that expresses itself on many different levels. On the level of the individual as a biological being, it is the human body that provides the model for one set of opposed but complementary principles, manifest in the apparent bilateral symmetry of the body and the distinction between male and female organisms. On the level of society, the existence of groups of opposed but complementary segments is postulated, based on the mythical precedency and controlled by the principles of exogamy. The villages themselves are often divided into two parts and a divisory line, invisible but known to all, separates the village into two sections. The ceremonial houses are imagined as being bisected into a "right side" and a "left side," by a line running diametrically between the two doors that are located at opposite points of the circular building, and each half of the structure has its own central post, one male and another female. On a cosmic level, the same principle divides the Universe into two sides, the division being marked by the tropical sun, which, going overhead, separates the world into a right and a left half. The dualistic elaborations of this type are innumerable: male/female, man/woman, right/left, heat/cold, light/dark, above/below, and the like, and they are furthermore associated with certain categories of animals, plants, and minerals; with colors, winds, diseases, and, of course, with the principles of Good and Evil. Many of these dualistic manifestations have the character of symbolic antagonists that share a common essence; just as the tribal deities who, in one divine being, combine benefic and malevolent aspects, thus man carries within himself this vital polarity of Good and Evil.

Apart from the Mother-Goddess, the principal divine personifications are her four sons and, next to them, a large number of spirit-owners, the masters of the different aspects of Nature, the rulers over rituals, and the beings that govern certain actions. That all these supernatural beings are the appointed guardians of certain aspects of human conduct—cultural or biological—has many ethical implications that provide the basis for the concept of sin. When the divine beings established the world order, however, they made provision for individual interpretation and thus confirmed a person's autonomy of moral choice. Life is a mixture of good and evil and, as the Kogi point out very frequently, there can be no morality without immorality. According to Kogi ethics one's life should be dedicated entirely to the acquisition of knowledge, a term by which are meant the myths and traditions, the songs and spells, and all the rules that regulate ritual. This body of esoteric knowledge is called by the Kogi the "Law of the Mother." Every object, action, or intention has a spirit-owner who jealously guards what is his own, his privilege, but who is willing to share it with mankind if compensated by an adequate offering. The concept of offerings, then, is closely connected with divinatory practices because it is necessary to determine the exact nature of the offerings that will most please a certain spirit-being. These details—some of them esoteric trivia but nonetheless functional units of a complex whole—can only be learned in the course of many years. Closely related to this body of knowledge, Kogi learning includes a wide range of information on phenomena that might be classified as belonging to tribal history, geography, and ecology, animal and plant categorization, and a fair knowledge of anatomy and physiology.

But all this knowledge has a single purpose: to find a balance between Good and Evil and to reach old age in a state of wisdom and tolerance. The process of establishing this balance is called *yulúka*, an expression that might be translated as "to be in agreement with" or "to be in harmony with." One should be careful, however, not to see in this concept a kind of romantic *Naturphilosophie*, of noble savages living in harmony with nature, but take it for what it is—a harsh sense of reality paired, at times, with a rather cynical outlook on human affairs. The concept of yulúka does not stand for blissful tranquillity, but means grudging acceptance of misfortune, be it sickness or hunger, the treachery of one's closest of kin, or the undeserved ill will of one's neighbor. A Kogi, when faced with hardships or high emotional tensions will rarely dramatize his situation, but will rather try to establish an "agreement" by a process of rationalization.

Another philosophical concept of importance is called *aluna*. There are many possible translations ranging from "spiritual" to "libidinous," and from "powerful" to "traditional" or "imaginary." Sometimes the word is used to designate the human soul. An approximate general translation would be "otherworldly," a term that would imply supernatural power with vision and strength, but otherwise the meaning of this concept has to be illustrated by examples, to convey its significance to the outsider. For example, to say that the world was created "in aluna" means that it was designed by a spiritual effort. The deities and the tribal ancestors exist in aluna, that is, in the Otherworld, and in an incorporeal state. Similarly, it is possible to deposit an offering in aluna at a certain spot, without really visiting that place. A man might sin in aluna, by harboring evil intentions. And to go further still: to the Kogi, concrete reality quite often is only appearance, a semblance that has only symbolic value, while the true essence of things exists only in aluna. According to the Kogi, one must therefore develop the spiritual faculty to see behind these appearances and to recognize the aluna of the Universe.

The divine personifications of the Kogi pantheon are not only continuously demanding offerings from men but, being guardians of the moral order, also watch any interaction between mortals, and punish the breaking of the rules that govern interpersonal relations. The Kogi put great emphasis on collaboration, the sharing of food, and the observance of respectful behavior toward elders and other persons of authority. Unfilial conduct, the refusal to work for one's father-in-law, or aggressive behavior of any kind are not only social sins, but are transgressions of the divine rules, and for this the offender is bound to incur the displeasure of the divine beings. Among the worst offenses are violations of certain sexual restrictions. Kogi attitudes toward sex are dominated by deep anxieties concerned with the constant fear of pollution, and prolonged sexual abstinence is demanded of all men who are engaged in any ritual activity. The great sin is incest, and the observation of the rules of exogamy is a frequent topic of conversations and admonitions in the ceremonial house.

Kogi culture contains many elements of sexual repression, and there is a marked antifeminist tendency. The men consider the acquisition of esoteric knowledge to be the only valid objective in life and claim that women are the prime obstacle on the way of achieving this goal. Although a Kogi husband is expected to be a dutiful provider and should produce sufficient food to keep his family in good health, it is also stated that a man should never work for material gain and should not make efforts to acquire more property than he needs in order to feed and house his family. All his energies should be spent on learning, on taking part in ritual, and on acquiring the necessary knowledge of procedure and moral precepts to contribute to the maintenance of the ordained world order. Now women have very few ritual functions and, except when quite old, show but little interest in metaphysical matters. To them the balance of the Universe is of small concern; they eat, they sleep, they chat and idle; in other words, to a Kogi man they personify all the elements of indulgence, of disruption, and of irresponsibility. "They are like cockroaches," the Kogi grumble, "always near the cooking place, and eating all the time!" Besides, Kogi women are not squeamish about sex and, being oblivious to the delicate details of ritual purity, appear to their men as eternal temptresses bent upon destroying the social order and, with it, the religious concepts that are so closely connected with it.

The Kogi are a deeply religious people and they are guided in their faith by a highly formalized priesthood. Although all villages have a headman who nominally represents civil authority, the true power of decision in personal and community matters is concentrated in the hands of the native priests, called *mámas*. These men, most of whom have a profound knowledge of tribal custom, are not simple curers or shamanistic practitioners, but fulfill priestly functions, taught during years of training and exercised in solemn rituals. The mámas are sun-priests who, high up in the mountains behind the villages, officiate in ceremonial centers where people gather at certain times of the year, and each ceremonial house in a village is under the charge of one or two priests who direct and supervise the nightlong meetings of the men when they gather in the settlement. The influence of this priesthood extends to every aspect of family and village life and completely overshadows the few attributes of the headmen.

To begin with, all people must periodically visit a priest for confession—in private or in public—of all their actions and intentions. An important mechanism of control is introduced here by the idea that sickness is, in the last analysis, the consequence of a state of sinfulness incurred by not living according to the "Law of the Mother." A man will therefore scrutinize his conscience in every detail and will try to be absolutely honest about his actions and intentions, to avoid falling ill or to cure an existing sickness. Confession takes place at night in the ceremonial house, the máma reclining in his hammock while the confessant sits next to him on a low bench. The other men must observe silence or, at least, converse in subdued voices, while between the priest and the confessant unfolds a slow, halting dialogue in which the máma formulates several searching questions about the confessant's family life, social relations, food intake, ritual obligations, dreams, and many other aspects of his daily life. People are supposed to confess not only the actual fault they have committed, but also their evil intentions, their sexual or aggressive fantasies, anything that might come to their minds under the questioning of the priest. The nagging fear of sickness, the hypochondriacal observation and discussion of the most insignificant symptoms, will make people completely unburden themselves. There can be no doubt that confession is a psychotherapeutic institution of the first order, within the general system of Kogi religion.

To act as a confessor to people as metaphysically preoccupied as the Kogi puts high demands upon a máma's intelligence and empathy; his role is never that of a passive listener but he must be an accomplished conversationalist, able to direct the confessant's discourse into channels that allow him to probe deeply into the troubled mind of his confidant.

But confession in the ceremonial house is not the only occasion when an individual can relieve himself of his intimate doubts and conflicts. At any time, any man, woman, or child can approach a máma and ask him for advice. It is natural then that a máma obtains, in this manner, much information on individual attitudes and community affairs which allows him to exercise control over many aspects of local sociopolitical development. I know of no case, however, where a máma would have taken advantage of this knowledge for his own ends. The mámas constitute a truly moralizing force and, as such, occupy a highly respected position.

Kogi priests are the products of a long and arduous training, under the strict guidance of one or several old and experienced mámas. In former times it was the custom that, as soon as a male child was born, the máma would consult in a trance the Mother-Goddess, to ascertain whether or not the newborn babe was to be a future priest. It is also said that a máma might dream the name of a certain family and thus would know that their newborn male child would become a priest. Immediately the máma would then "give notice" to the newborn during a visit to his family, and it is pointed out that, in those times, the parents would have felt greatly honored by the knowledge that their son would eventually become a priest. From several traditions it would appear that certain families or, rather, patrilines, may have had hereditary preeminence in priesthood, and even today priests belonging to a high-ranking exogamic group are likely to be more respected than others.

Ideally, a future priest should receive a special education since birth; the child would immediately be separated from his mother and given into the care of the máma's wife, or any other woman of childbearing age whom the máma might order to join his household as a wet nurse. But occasionally the mother herself would be allowed to keep the child, with the condition that he be weaned before reaching the age of three months. From then on the child would have to be fed a mash of ripe bananas and cooking plantains, and soon afterwards would have to be turned over to the máma's family. If, for some reason, a family refused to give up the child, the civil authorities might have to interfere and take the child away by force. It was always the custom that the

family should pay the máma for the education of the boy, by sending periodically some food to his house, or by working in his fields.

These ideal conditions, it might be said, probably never existed; under normal circumstances—and this refers also to the present situation—the training begins at about two or three years of age, but certainly not later than the fifth year, and then continues through childhood, adolescence, and young adulthood, until the novice, aged now perhaps twenty or twenty-two, has acquired his new status as máma by fulfilling all necessary requirements. The full training period should be eighteen years, divided into two cycles of nine years each, the novice reaching puberty by the end of the first cycle.

There exist about three or four places in the Sierra Nevada where young people are being trained for the priesthood. In each place, two, or at most, three boys of slightly different ages live in an isolated valley, far from the next village, where they are taken into the care of their master's family. The geographical setting may vary but, in most cases, the small settlement, consisting of a ceremonial house and two or three huts, is located at a spot that figures prominently in myth and tradition. It may be the place where a certain lineage had its origin, or where a culture hero accomplished a difficult task; or perhaps it is the spot where one of the many spirit-owners of Nature has his abode. In any case, the close association of a "school" with a place having certain religious-historical traditions is of importance because at such a spot there exists the likelihood of ready communication with the supernatural sphere; it is a "door," a threshold, a point of convergence, besides being a place that is sacred and lies under the protection of benevolent spirit-beings.

The institution of priestly training has a long and sacred tradition among the Kogi. Several lengthy myths tell of how the four sons of the Mother-Goddess created Mount Doanankuívi, at the headwaters of the Tucurinca River and, inside the mountain, built the first ceremonial house where novices were to be trained for the priesthood. The first legendary máma to teach such a group of disciples was Búnalyue, and once they had acquired the status of priests, they settled in the nearby valley of Mukuánauiaishi which, thereafter, became the center for the training of novices from all over the Sierra Nevada. According to several myths, it was

Búnkuasé, one of the sons of the Mother-Goddess, who established the rules according to which a future máma was to be chosen and educated. Búnkuasé, "the shining one," is the personification of the highest moral principles in Kogi ethics and is thus taken to be the patron and spiritual guardian of the priesthood. It is, however, characteristic of Kogi culture that there should exist several other traditions according to which it is Kashindúkua, the morally ambivalent jaguar-priest, who is the tutelary divine personification. Kashindúkua, also a son of the Mother-Goddess, had been destined by her to be a great curer of human ills, a thaumaturge able to extract sickness from the patient's body as if it were a concrete, tangible substance. But occasionally, and much to his brother's grief, he misused his powers and then did great harm to people. Kashindúkua came to personify sexual license and, above all, incest but, as an ancient priest-king, curer, and protector of all ceremonial houses, he continues to occupy a very important place in the Kogi pantheon.

A novice, training for the priesthood, is designated by the term *kuívi* (abstinent). This concept refers not only to temperance in food and drink, but also to sex, sleep, and any form of overindulgence. This attitude of ascetic self-denial is said to have been the prime virtue of the ancient mámas of mythical times. But, as always, the Kogi introduce an element of ambivalence, of man's difficult choice of action, and also tell of outstanding sages and miracle workers who, at the same time, were great sinners.

At the level of cultural development attained by the Kogi, the teacher position is well recognized and there is full agreement that all priests must undergo a long process of organized directed training, in the course of which the novice's education is functionally specialized. The ideal image of the great teacher and master, the ancient sage, is often elaborated in myths and tales, and in their context the máma is generally represented as a just but authoritarian father figure. In the great quest for knowledge and divine illumination, the teacher never demands from his pupils more than he himself is willing to give; he suffers patiently with them and is a model of self-control and wisdom. In other tales, the opposite is shown, the vicious hypocrite who stuffs himself with food while his disciples are fasting, or the lecherous old man who seduces nubile girls while publicly preaching chastity. These images of the saint and the sinner—patterned after those of the hero and the villain, in another type of tale—are always present in Kogi thought and, in many aspects, are statements of the importance society attributes to the role of the priesthood. Some of these tales are really quite simplistic in that they tend to measure a máma's stature merely in terms of his cunning, his reconciliatory abilities, rote memory, or miracle-working capacity, but other tales contain examples of true psychological insight, high moral principles, and readiness for self-sacrifice. The image of the teacher is thus well defined—though somewhat stereotyped—in Kogi culture and is also referred to in situations that lie quite outside the sphere of priestly training and that are connected—to give some examples—to the acquisition of skills, the tracing of genealogical ties, or the interpretation of natural phenomena. On the one hand, then, it is plain that not all mámas are thought to be adequate teachers and to be trusted with the education of a small child. On the other hand, not all mámas will accept disciples; some live in abject poverty, others are in ill health, and others still feel disinclined to carry the responsibilities that teaching entails. Old age is not of the essence if it is not accompanied by an alert mind and a manifestly "pure" behavior, and quite often a fairly young máma has great renown because of his high moral status, while older men are held in less esteem.

The novices should spend most of their waking hours inside the ceremonial house. In former times they used to live in a small enclosure (*hubi*) within the ceremonial structure, but at present they sleep in one of the neighboring huts. This hut, which is similar to the ceremonial house but smaller, has an elaborate roof apex and the walls of plaited canes have two doors at opposite points of the circumference, while the hut of the máma's family lacks the apex and has only one door. All during their long training the novices must lead an entirely nocturnal life and are strictly forbidden to leave the house in daylight. Sleeping during the day on low cots of canes placed against the walls, the novices rise after sunset and, as soon as darkness has set in, are allowed to take their first meal in the kitchen annex or outside the máma's house. A second meal is taken around midnight and a light third meal shortly before sunrise. Even during the night, the novices are not supposed to go outside except in the company of a máma and then only for a short walk. The principal interdictions, repeated most emphatically over and over again, refer to the sun and to women; a novice should be educated, after weaning, only by men and among men, and should never see a girl or a woman who is sexually active; and throughout his training period, he should never see the sun nor be exposed to his rays. "The sun is a máma," the Kogi say; "And this máma might cause harm to the child." When there is a moon, a novice should cover his head with a specially woven basketry tray (güíshi) when leaving the house at night.

During their training period the novices are supervised and strictly controlled by one or two attendant wardens (hánkua-kúkui), adult men who have joined the máma's household, generally after having spent some years as novices under his guidance. These wardens are mainly in charge of discipline, but may occasionally participate to some degree in the educational process, according to the máma's orders.

Apart from the little group of people who constitute the settlement—the máma and his family, the wardens, and some aged relatives of either—the novices should avoid any contact with other people; in fact, they should never even be *seen* by an outsider. The manifest danger of pollution consists in the presence of people who are in contact with women; should such a person see a novice or should he speak to him, the latter would immediately lose the spiritual power he has accumulated in the course of his apprenticeship. It is supposed, then, that the community consists only of "pure" people, that is, of persons who abstain from any sexual activity and who also observe very strict dietary rules.

As in many primitive educational systems, the observance of dietary restrictions is a very important point in priestly training. In general, a novice should soon learn to eat sparingly and, after puberty has been reached, should be able to go occasionally without food for several days. He should eat very little meat, but rather fowl such as curassow, and should avoid all foodstuffs that are of non-Indian origin such as bananas, sugar cane, onions, or citrus fruits. He should never, under any circumstances, consume salt, nor should he use any condiments such as peppers. A novice, it may be added here, should not touch his food with his left hand because this is the "female" hand and is polluted. During the first nine years the prescribed diet consists mainly of some

small river catfish and freshwater shrimp, certain yellow-green grasshoppers of nocturnal habits, land snails collected in the highlands, large black *túbi* beetles, and certain white mushrooms. Vitamin D appears to be sufficient to compensate for the lack of sunlight during these years. Three or four different classes of maize can also be eaten, as well as some sweet manioc, pumpkins, and certain beans. Some mámas insist that all food consumed by the novices should be predominantly of a white color: white beans, white potatoes, white manioc, white shrimps, white land snails, and so forth. Only after puberty are they allowed to eat, however sparingly, the meat of game animals such as peccary, agouti, and armadillo. These animals, it is said, "have great knowledge, and by eating their flesh the novices will partake in their wisdom." In preparing their daily food, only a clay pot made by the máma himself should be used and all food should be boiled, but never fried nor smoked. Shoe-shaped vessels (or, rather, breast-shaped ones) are used especially for the preparation of a ritual diet based on beans.

The boys are dressed in a white cotton cloth woven by the máma or, later on, by themselves, which is wrapped around the body, covering it from under the armpits to the ankles, and held in place by a wide woven belt. For adornment they wear bracelets, armlets, necklaces, and ear ornaments, all of ancient Tairona origin and made of gold, gilded copper, and semiprecious stones. There is emphasis on cleanliness and at night the boys go to bathe in the nearby mountain stream.

In former times, that is, perhaps until three or four generations ago, it was the custom to educate also some female children who, eventually, were to become the wives of the priests. The girls were chosen by divination and then were brought up by the wife of a máma. Aided by other old women, the girls were taught many ancient traditions primarily referring to the dangers of pollution. They were trained to prepare certain "pure" foods, to collect aromatic and medical herbs, and to assist in the preparation of minor rituals. At present, the education of girls under the guidance of a máma's wife is institutionalized in some parts, but the aim is not so much to prepare spouses for future priests than to educate certain intelligent girls "in the manner of the ancients" and send them back to their families after a few years of schooling, so they can teach the women-folk of their respective villages the traditions and precepts they have learned in the máma's household, and be thus living examples of moral conduct.

But I must return now to the boy who has been taken into a strange family and who is now undergoing a crucial period of adaptation.

The novice is exposed to the varied influences of a setting that differs notably from that of his own family. Although the child will find in the máma's household a certain well-accustomed set of familial behavioral patterns, he is made aware that he now lives in a context of nonkin. This is of special relevance where the novice was educated for the first three or four years by his own family and has thus acquired a certain cultural perspective that, in his new environment, is likely to differ from the demands made by the máma's kin. Between teacher and pupil, however, there generally develops a fairly close emotional tie; the novice addresses the máma with the term *hátei* (father), and he, in turn, refers to his disciples as his "children," or "sons." Only after the novice has reached puberty does the apprentice-master relationship usually acquire a more formal tone.

During the first two years of life, Kogi children are prodded and continuously encouraged to accelerate their sensory-motor development: creeping, walking, speaking. But in later years they are physically and vocally rather quiet. A Kogi mother does not encourage response and activity, but rather tries to soothe her child and to keep him silent and unobtrusive. Very strict sphincter training is instituted, and by the age of ten or twelve months the boy is expected to exercise complete control during the daytime hours. Play activity is discouraged by all adults and, indeed, to be accused of "playing" is a very serious reproach. There are practically no children's games in Kogi culture and for this reason a teacher's complaints refer rather to lack of attention or to overindulgence in eating or sleeping, than to any boisterous, playful, or aggressive attitudes.

Although older children are sometimes scolded for intellectual failures, the Kogi punish or reward children rather for behavioral matters. Punishment is often physical; a máma punishes an inattentive novice by depriving him of food or sleep, and quite often beats him sharply over the head with the thin hardwood rod he uses to extract lime from his gourd-container when he is chewing coca. For more serious misbehavior, children may be ordered to kneel on a handful of cotton seeds or on some small pieces of a broken pottery vessel. A very painful punishment consists in kneeling motionless with horizontally outstretched arms while carrying a heavy stone in each hand.

In practically all ceremonial houses one can see a large vertical loom leaning against the wall, with a half-finished piece of cloth upon it. The weaving of the coarse cotton cloth the Kogi use for the garments of both sexes is a male activity and has a certain ritual connotation. But to weave can also become a punishment. An inattentive novice—or a grown-up who has disregarded the moral order—can be made to weave for hours, sitting naked in the chill night and frantically working the loom, while behind him stands the máma who prods him with his lime rod, sometimes beating him over the ears and saying: "I shall yet make you respect the cloth you are wearing!"

Life in the ceremonial house is characterized by the regularized scheduling of all activities and thus expresses quite clearly a distinct learning theory. We must, first of all, look at the general outline of the aims of education. In doing so, it is necessary to use categories of formal knowledge in the way they are defined in *our* culture, a division that would make no sense to a Kogi, but which is useful here to give an order to the entire field of priestly instruction. The main fields of a máma's learning and competence are, thus, the following:

1. Cosmogony, cosmology, mythology

2. Mythical social origins, social structure, and organization

3. Natural history: geography, geology, meteorology, botany, zoology, astronomy, biology

4. Linguistics: ceremonial language, rhetoric

5. Sensory deprivations; abstinence from food, sleep, and sex

6. Ritual; dancing and singing

7. Curing of diseases

8. Interpretation of signs and symbols, dreams, animal behavior

9. Sensitivity to auditory, visual, and other hallucinations

The methods by which these aims of priestly education are pursued are many and depend to a high degree upon the recognition of a sequence of stages in the child's mental and physical development. During the early years of training, at about five or six years of age, the child is literally hand-reared, in that he is in very frequent physical contact with or, at least, proximity to, his teacher. While sitting on a low bench, the máma places both hands upon the hips of the boy who stands before him and rhythmically pushes and bends the child's body to the tune of his songs or recitals, or while marking the pace with a gourd-rattle. During this period, the Kogi say, the child "first learns to dance and only later learns to walk."

During the first two years of training, the teaching of dances is accompanied only by the humming of songs and by the sound of the rattle; only later on are the children taught to sing. During these practices the children always wear heavy wooden masks topped with feather crowns and are adorned with all the heavy ornaments mentioned above. The peculiar smell of the ancient mask, the pressure of its weight, and the overall restriction of body movements caused by the stiff ceremonial attire and the hands of the teacher produce a lasting impact on the child, and even decades later, people who have passed through this experience refer to it with a mixture of horror and pride. For hours on end, night after night, and illuminated only by torches and low-burning fires, the children are thus taught the dance steps, the cosmological recitals, and the tales relating to the principal personifications and events of the Creation story. Many of the songs and recitations are phrased in the ancient ceremonial language which is comprehensible only to an experienced máma, but which has to be learned by the novices by sheer memorization. During these early years, myths, songs, and dances become closely linked into a rigid structure that alone—at least, at that time—guarantees the correct form of presentation.

One of the main institutionalized teaching concepts consists in iterative behavior. This is emphasized especially during the first half of the curriculum, when the novices are made to repeat the myths, songs, or spells until they have memorized not only the text and the precise intonation, but also the body movements and minor gestures that accompany the performance. Rhythmic elements are important and the learning of songs and recitals is always combined with dancing or, at least, with swaying motions of the body. This is not a mere mechanistic approach to the learning process and does not represent a neurally based stimulus-response pattern, but the child is simultaneously provided with a large number of interpretative details that make him grasp the context and meaning of the texts.

Between the end of the first nine-year cycle of education and the onset of the second cycle, the novice reaches puberty. It is well recognized by the Kogi that during this period significant personality changes occur, and for this reason allowance is made for the eventual interruption of the training process or, as a matter of fact, for its termination. Having reached puberty, a boy who fails to display a truly promising attitude toward priesthood, demonstrated, above all, by his repressive attitude toward sexuality, is allowed to return to his family. At no time is such a boy forced to stay on, even if he should wish to do so; if his master believes that the youth does not have the calling to become a máma, he will insist on his returning to his people. But these cases seem to be the exception rather than the rule; more often puberty is reached as a normal transition, and a few years later, at the age of fourteen or fifteen years, the boy is initiated by the máma and receives from him the lime container and the little rod—a female and a male symbol—together with the permission to chew from now on the coca leaves the youth forthwith toasts in a special vessel.

Ideally, a Kogi priest should divest himself of all sensuality and should practice sexual abstinence, but this prohibition is contradicted in part by the rule that all nubile girls must be deflowered by the máma who, alone, has the power to neutralize the grave perils of pollution that according to the Kogi are inherent in this act. Similar considerations demand that, at puberty, a boy should be sexually initiated by the máma's wife or, in some cases, by an old woman specially designated by the máma. During the puberty ritual of a novice, the master's wife thus initiates the youth, an experience frought with great anxiety and which is often referred to in later years as a highly traumatic event.

During the second cycle, the teachings of the master concentrate upon divinatory practices, the preparation of offerings, the acquisition of power objects, and the rituals of the life cycle. During this period, education tends to become extremely formal because now it is much more closely associated with ritual and ceremony. The youth is taught many divinatory techniques, beginning with simple yes-or-no alternatives, and going on to deep meditation accompanied by exercises of muscular relaxation, controlled breathing, and the "listening" to sudden signs or voices from within. Power objects are acquired slowly over the years and consist of all kinds of "permits" (*sewá*) granted by the spirit-owners of Nature. Most of these permits consist of small archaeological necklace beads of stone, of different minerals, shapes, colors, and textures, that are given to the novice as soon as he has mastered the corresponding knowledge. At that age, a novice will need, for example, a permit to chew coca, to eat certain kinds of meat, to perform certain rituals, or to sing certain songs. During this period the novices are also taught the complex details of organization of the great yearly ceremonies that take place in the ceremonial centers, higher up in the mountains.

The novices have ample opportunity to watch their master perform ritual actions, a process during which a considerable body of knowledge is transmitted to them. The seasons of the year are paced with special ritual markings: equinoxes and solstices, planting and harvesting, the stages of the individual life cycle. Now that they themselves begin to perform minor rituals, the recurrent statements contained in the texts, together with the identical behavioral sequences, become linked into a body of highly patterned experiential units. The repetition of the formulas, "This is what happened! Thus spoke our forefathers! This is what the ancient said!" insists upon the rightness, the correctness of the actions and contents that constitute ritual.

During the education of a novice there is no skill training to speak of. Kogi material culture, it has been said already, is limited to an inventory of a few largely undifferentiated, coarse utilitarian objects, and the basic skills of weaving or pottery making—both male activities—are soon mastered by any child. There is hardly any specialization in the manufacture of implements and a máma is not expected to have any manual or artistic abilities. He is not a master-craftsman; as a matter of fact, he should avoid working with his hands because of the ever-present danger of pollution.

Language training, however, is a very different matter. In the first place, since early childhood the novice learns a very large denotative vocabulary. The Kogi are fully aware that any intellectual activity depends upon linguistic competence and that only a very detailed knowledge of the language will permit the precise naming of things, ideas, and events, as a fundamental step in establishing categories and values. In part, linguistic tutoring is concerned with correctness of speech, and children are discouraged from using expressions that are too readily associated with their particular age group. As most of the linguistic input comes from a máma, the novices soon demonstrate a very characteristic verbal behavior consisting of well-pronounced, rather short, sentences, with a rich vocabulary, and delivered in an even but very emphatic voice.

While in normal child-training techniques care is taken to transmit a set of simple behavioral rules that tend to advance the child's socialization process, in training for the priesthood socialization is not a desirable goal. An average child is taught to collaborate with certain categories of people and is expected to lend a helping hand, to share food, to be of service to others. Emphasis is placed on participation in communal labor projects such as road building, the construction of houses or bridges, or on attendance at meetings in which matters of community interest are being discussed. But priestly education does not concern itself with these social functions of the individual. On the contrary, it is evident that a máma is quite intentionally trained *not* to become a group member, but to stand apart, aloof and superior. To the Kogi, the image of the spiritual leader is that of a man whose ascetic hauteur makes him almost unapproachable. A máma should not be too readily accessible, but should keep away from the discussion of public affairs and the petty details of local power politics, because only by complete detachment and by the conscious elimination of all emotional considerations can he become a true leader of his people.

This aloofness, this standing alone, is, in part, the consequence of the narrow physical and social environment in which the novices spend their long formative years of schooling. They *are* socialized, of course, but they are socialized in a context of a very small and very select group of people associated into a unit that is not at all representative of the larger society. It is a fact that the novice learns very little about the practical aspects of the society of which he is eventually becoming a priest. Life in the ceremonial house or in the small group of the máma's family does not give the novices enough social contacts to enable them to obtain a clear picture of the wider society. It is a fact that, during the years of a priest's training period, he hardly becomes acquainted with the practical aspects of land tenure and land use, of seed selection and soil qualities, or of the ways in which gossip, prestige, envy, and the wiles of women are likely to affect society. A novice brought up quite apart from society forms an image of the wider scene, which, at best, is highly idealized, and at worst, is an exaggeration of its evils and dangers.

In Kogi culture, sickness and death are thought to be the direct consequences of sin, and sin is interpreted mainly in terms of sex. Even in those relationships that are culturally approved, that is, in marriage between partners belonging to complementary exogamic units, the Kogi always see an element of pollution, of contamination, because most men are periodically engaged in some ritual demanding purity, abstinence, fasting, attendance at nightly sessions in the ceremonial house, or prolonged travel to some sacred site. Kogi women are often, therefore, quite critical of male religious activities, being in turn accused by their husbands of exercising a "weakening" influence upon their minds, which are bent upon the delicate task of preserving the balance of the Universe. Kogi priests live in a world of myth, of heroic deeds and miraculous events of times past, in which the female characters appear cast in the role of evil temptresses. To a young priest who, after years of seclusion, finally returns to village life and community affairs, women constitute the main danger to cultural survival and are a direct threat to the moral order. Therefore, it again takes several years before the máma learns about life in society and acquires a practical understanding of the daily problems of life.

Moral education is, of course, at the core of a priest's training. Since childhood, a common method of transmitting a set of simple moral values consists in the telling and retelling of the "counsels," cautionary tales of varying length that contain a condensed social message. These tales are a mixture of myth, familial story, and recital, and often refer to specific interpersonal relations within the family setting: husband and wife, elder brother and younger brother, son-in-law and father-in-law, and so on. Other tales might refer to some famous máma of the past, to culture heroes and their exploits, or to animals that behave like humans. The stories are recited during the nightly sessions when a group of men has gathered or they are told to an individual who has come for advice. In all these stories, what is condemned is overindulgence in food, sleep, and sex; physical aggressiveness is proscribed; theft, disrespectful behavior, and cruelty to children and animals are disapproved of, and inquisitiveness by word or deed is severely censured, especially in women and children. Those qualities that receive praise are economic collaboration, the sharing of food, the willingness to lend household utensils, respectful attitudes towards one's elders, and active participation in ritual. The behavioral message is quite clear and there are no ambivalent solutions: the culprits are punished and the virtuous are rewarded. These counsels, then, do not explain the workings of the Universe and are not overburdened with esoteric trivia, but refer to matters of daily concern, to commonplace events and to average situations. They form a body of entertaining, moralizing stories that can be embroidered or condensed to fit the situation. It may be mentioned here that it is characteristic of the highly impersonal quality of social relations among the Kogi that friendship is not a desirable institution. It is too close, too emotional a relationship, and social rules quite definitely are against it.

It is evident that the counsels constitute a very simplistic level of moral teaching. These stories are useful in propagating some elementary rules among the common people; they are easy to remember and their anecdotal qualities and stereotyped characters have become household words. Everyone knows the story of Sekuishbúchi's wife or how Máma Shehá forfeited his beautiful dress. But it is also obvious that there is another, deeper level where the moral issues are far more complex.

According to the Kogi, our world exists and survives because it is animated by solar energy. This energy manifests itself by the yearly round of seasons that coincides with the position of the sun on the horizon at the time of the solstices and equinoxes. It is the máma's task to "turn back the sun" when he advances too far and threatens to "burn the world," or to "drown it with rain," and only by thus controlling the sun's movements with offerings, prayers, and dances can the principles of fertility be conserved. This control of the mámas, however, depends on the power and range of their esoteric knowledge and this knowledge, in turn, depends upon the purity of their minds. Only the pure, the morally untainted, can acquire the divine wisdom to control the course of the sun and, with it, the change of the seasons and the times for planting and harvesting. It is for this reason that the Kogi, both priests and laymen, are deeply concerned about the education of future generations of novices and about their requirements of purity. Their survival as well as that of all mankind depends on the moral stature of Kogi priests, now and in the future; and it is only natural, then, that the correct training of novices should be of profound concerns to all.

The Kogi claim to be the "elder brothers" of mankind and, as they believe they are the possessors of the only true religion, they feel responsible for the moral conduct of all men. There is great interest in foreign cultures, in the strange ways of other peoples, and the Kogi readily ask their divine beings to grant protection to the wayward "younger brothers" of other nations. The training of more novices is, therefore, a necessity not only for Kogi society, but also for the maintenance of the wider moral order.

From the preceding pages it would, perhaps, appear that, during all these years of priestly education, most knowledge is acquired by rote memory or by the endless repetition of certain actions meant to transmit a set of socioemotional messages that are not always fully understood by the novice, but have to be dealt with nevertheless. But it would be a mistake to think that training for the priesthood consists only, or mainly, of these repetitious, empty elements of a formalized ritual. The true goals of education are quite different and the iterative behavior described above is only a very small part of the working behavior of the novices.

First of all, the aim of priestly education is to discover and awaken those hidden faculties of the mind that, at a given moment, enable the novice to establish contact with the divine sphere. The mámas know that a controlled set or sequence of sensory privations eventually produces altered states of consciousness enabling the novice to perceive a wide range of visual, auditory, or haptic hallucinations. The novice sees images and hears voices that explain and extol the essence of being, the true sources of Nature, together with the manner of solving a great variety of common human conflict situations. In this way, he is able to receive instructions about offerings to be made, about collective ceremonies to be organized, or sickness to be cured. He acquires the faculty of seeing behind the exterior appearances of things and perceiving their true nature. The concept of aluna, translated here as "inner reality," tells him that the mountains are houses, that animals are people, that roots are snakes, and he learns that this manipulation of symbols and signs is not a simple matter of one-to-one translation, but that there exist different levels of interpretation and complex chains of associations. The Kogi say: "There are two ways of looking at things; you may, when seeing a snake, say: 'This is a snake,' but you may also say: 'This is a rope I am seeing, or a root, an arrow, a winding trail.'" Now, from the knowledge of these chains of associations that represent, in essence, equivalences, he acquires a sense of balance, and when he has achieved this balance he is ready to become a priest. He then will practice the concept of yulúka, of being in agreement, in harmony, with the unavoidable, with himself, and with his environment, and he will teach this knowledge to others, to those who are still torn by the doubts of polarity.

The entire teaching process is aimed at this slow, gradual building up to the sublime moment of the self-disclosure of god to man, of the moment when Sintána or Búnkuasé or one of their avatars reveals himself in a flash of light and says: "Do this! Go there!" Education, at this stage, is a technique of progressive illumination. The divine personification appears bathed in a heavenly light and, from then on teaches the novice at night. From out of the dark recesses of the house comes a voice and the novice listens to it and follows its instructions. A máma said: "These novices hear everything and know everything but they don't know who is teaching them."

To induce these visionary states the Kogi use certain hallucinogenic drugs the exact nature of which is still uncertain. Two kinds of mushrooms, one of them a bluish puffball, are consumed only by the mámas, and a strong psychotropic effect is attributed to several plants, among them to the chestnutlike fruits of a large tree (*Meteniusa edulis*). But hallucinatory states can, of course, be produced endogenously by sensory privations and other practices; most trancelike states during which the mámas officiate at certain rituals are produced, in all probability, by a combination of ingested drugs and strenuous body exercise. The Kogi say: "Because the mámas were educated in darkness, they have the gift of visions and of knowing all things, no matter how far away they might be. They even visit the Land of the Dead."

In the second place, an important aspect of priestly education consists of training the novice to work alone. Although a Kogi priest has many social functions, his true self can find expression only in the solitary meditation he practices in his hut when he is alone. In order to evaluate people or events, he must be alone; he may discuss occasionally some difficult matter with others, but to arrive at a decision, he must be quite alone. This ability to stand alone and still act on behalf of others is a highly valued behavioral category among the Kogi, and children, although they often learn by participation, are trained already at an early age to master their fears and doubts and to act alone. A máma's novice might be sent alone, at night, to accomplish a dangerous task, perhaps a visit to a spot where an evil spirit is said to dwell, or a place that is taken to be polluted by disease. A máma takes pride in climbing—alone—a steep rock, or in crossing a dangerous cleft, and he readily faces any situation that, in the eyes of others, might entail the danger of supernatural apparitions of a malevolent type.

But what really counts is his moral and intellectual integrity, his resolution when faced with a choice of alternative actions. The adequate evaluation of his followers' attitudes and needs requires a sense of tolerance and a depth of understanding of human nature, which can only be attained by a mind that is conscious of having received divine guidance.

The final test comes when the master asks the novice to escape from the tightly closed and watched ceremonial house. The novice, in his trance, roams freely, visiting faraway valleys, penetrating into mountains, or diving into lakes. And when telling then of the wanderings of his soul, the others will say: "You have learned to see through the mountains and through the hearts of men. Truly, you are a máma now!"

The education of a máma is, essentially, a model for the education of all men. Of course, not everyone can or should become a máma, but all men should follow a máma's example of frugality, moderation, and simple goodness. There are no evil mámas, no witch doctors or practitioners of aggressive magic; they only exist in myths and tales of imagination, as threatening examples of what *could be*. On the contrary, Kogi priests are men of high moral stature and acute intellectual ability, measured by any standards, who are deeply concerned about the ills that afflict mankind and who, in their way, do their utmost to alleviate the burdens all men have to carry. But they are also quite realistic in their outlook. An old máma once said to me: "You are asking me what is life; life is food, a woman—then, a house, a field—then, god."

Reflecting back on what was said at the beginning of this essay where I tried to trace an outline of Kogi culture, it is clear that priestly education constitutes a very coherent system that, as a model of conduct, obeys certain powerful adaptive needs.

Kogi culture is characterized by a marked lack of specificity in object relations. To a Kogi, people can exist only as categories, such as women, children, in-laws, but not as individuals among whom close emotional bonds might be established. The early weaning of the child is only the beginning of a series of mechanisms by which all affective attachments with others are severed. Sphincter training, accomplished at about ten months, reinforces this independence of affective rewards. A child's crying is never interpreted as an expression of loneliness and the need for affection, and a baby is always cared for by several mother-substitutes such as older siblings, aunts, or most any woman who might be willing to take charge of the child for a while. During the first two years of life, all sensory-motor development is optimized while, at the same time, all emotional bonds are inhibited. It is probable that the highly impersonal quality of all social relations among adults is owing in a large measure to these early child-training patterns.

That novices chosen for the priesthood must be exposed to a máma's teaching *before* they reach five years of age plainly refers to the observation that, at that precise stage of development, their cognitive functioning is beginning and that mental images of external events are being formed. If educated within the social context of their families, the child would develop a normative cognitive system, which has to be avoided because the cognitive system of a priest must be very specific and wholly different from that of an average member of society.

As has been said, there are no children's games, that is, there is no rehearsal for future adult behavior. Nothing is left to fantasy, can be solved in fantasy;

everything is stark reality and has to be faced as such. And as the child grows up into an adolescent, these precepts are continuously restated and reinforced. The youth must eradicate all emotional attitudes, because nothing must bias his judgment—neither sex, hunger, fear, nor friendship. A man once said categorically: "One never marries the woman one loves!" Moreover, most cultural mechanisms in Kogi behavior are accommodative. The individual has to adapt himself to the reality that surrounds him and cannot pretend to change the world, not even momentarily—not even in his fantasies. The concept of yulúka, too, becomes an accommodative tool because it represents an undifferentiated state of absolute unconsciousness.

To exercise spiritual leadership over his society, the priest must be completely detached from its daily give-and-take, and it is evident that separation, isolation, and emotional detachment are among the most important guiding principles of priestly education. This "otherness" of the Kogi priest is expressed in his training in many ways: from his nocturnal habits, which make him "see the world in a different light," to his isolation from society, which makes of him a lonely observer, devoid of all affection.

The Spartan touch in Kogi culture must be understood in its wider historical perspective. During almost one hundred years, from the time of the discovery of the mainland to the early years of the seventeenth century, the Indian population of the Sierra Nevada de Santa Marta was exposed to the worst aspects of the Spanish conquest. After long battles and persecutions, the chieftains and priests were drawn and quartered, the villages were destroyed, and the maize fields were burned by the invading troops. In few other parts of the Spanish Main did the Conquest take a more violent and destructive form than in the lands surrounding Santa Marta and in the foothills of the neighboring mountains. During the colonial period, the Indians lived in relative peace and isolation and were able to recuperate and reorganize higher up in the mountains. But modern times brought with them new pressures and new forms of violence. Political propaganda, misdirected missionary zeal, the greed of the Creole peasants, the ignorance of the authorities, and the irresponsible stupidity of foreign hippies have made of the Sierra Nevada a Calvary of tragic proportions on which one of the most highly developed aboriginal cultures of South America is being destroyed. So far the Kogi have withstood the onslaught, thanks mainly to the stature of their priests, but it is with a feeling of despair that one foresees the future of their lonely stand.

22

Reflections After Waco: Millennialists and the State

Michael Barkun

No question existed in the minds of the Branch Davidians that the predictions of their charismatic prophet, David Koresh, were correct; the apocalypse engineered by God and the millennia it promised were at hand. Their conscious attempt to change their culture under the direction of their messiah-like leader fit well the model of revitalization movements set out by Wallace (see Chapter 9). As Michael Barkun makes clear, parties in the Waco, Texas, tragedy accurately fulfilled the millennialists' prophecy of the battle between good and evil.

More than simply recounting the events at Waco, Barkun analyzes the characteristics of millenarianism and charismatic leadership and demonstrates that neither the Bureau of Alcohol, Tobacco, and Firearms (ATF) nor the Federal Bureau of Investigation (FBI) understood or took seriously the millenarian beliefs of the Branch Davidians. Falling victim to the "cult concept," the ATF and FBI perceived the activity of Koresh and his followers not as the manifestation of a religion but as that of a psychopathology to be dealt with as they would deal with hijackers or hostage takers. The direct assaults on the compound at Waco were, as Barkun points out, fulfillment of the millenarianists' prophecy. It is important to recall Reverend Jim Jones and the tragedy at Jonestown, Guyana, in November 1978 to put in proper perspective the reaction of the Branch Davidians to federal authority. But it appears that these types of movements may not be exclusively American. The reader is reminded of the mass immolations of fifty-two members of the Order of the Solar Temple in Quebec and Switzerland in 1994 and the murder-suicide ritual that took the lives of sixteen more members of the group in a woods near Grenoble, France, the day before Christmas, 1995, in what appears at this point to be a ritual timed for the winter solstice. At this writing, little is known of the Order of the Solar Temple or its deceased leader, Luc Jouret.

Barkun ends his article with two questions. First, will U.S. federal authorities come to understand the worldview of millennialists, particularly those who follow the "posttribulationist" approaches of some survivalists, and change their agencies' strategies of force? Second, and more important in the long run, will the First Amendment's guarantee of the free exercise of religion be shared equally by all groups in the future?

Not since Jonestown has the public been gripped by the conjunction of religion, violence and communal living as they have by the events at the Branch Davidians' compound. All that actually took place near Waco remains unknown or contested. Nonetheless, the information is sufficient to allow at least a preliminary examination of three questions: Why did it happen? Why didn't it happen earlier? Will it happen again?

As a *New York Times* editorialist put it, "The Koresh affair has been mishandled from beginning to end." The government's lapses, errors and misjudgments can be grouped into two main categories: issues of law-enforcement procedure and technique, with which I do not propose to deal; and larger issues of strategy and approach, which I will address.

The single most damaging mistake on the part of federal officials was their failure to take the Branch Davidians' religious beliefs seriously. Instead, David Koresh and his followers were viewed as being in the grip of delusions that prevented them from grasping reality. As bizarre and misguided as their beliefs might have seemed, it was necessary to grasp the role these beliefs played in their lives; these beliefs were the basis of *their* reality. The Branch Davidians clearly possessed an encompassing worldview to which they attached ultimate significance. That they did so carried three implications. First, they could entertain no other set of beliefs. Indeed, all other views of the world, including those held by government negotiators, could only be regarded as erroneous. The lengthy and fruitless conversations between the two sides were, in effect, an interchange between different cultures—they talked past one another.

Second, since these beliefs were the basis of the Branch Davidians' sense of personal identity and meaning, they were nonnegotiable. The conventional conception of negotiation as agreement about some exchange or compromise between the parties was meaningless in this context. How could anything of ultimate significance be surrendered to an adversary steeped in evil and error? Finally, such a belief system implies a link between ideas and actions. It requires that we take seriously—as apparently the authorities did not—the fact that actions might be based on something other than obvious self-interest.

Conventional negotiation assumes that the parties think in terms of costs and benefits and will calculate an outcome that minimizes the former and maximizes the latter. In Waco, however, the government faced a group seemingly impervious to appeals based upon interests, even where the interests involved were their own life and liberty. Instead, they showed a willingness to take ideas to their logical end-points, with whatever sacrifice that might entail.

The Branch Davidians did indeed operate with a structure of beliefs whose authoritative interpreter was David Koresh. However absurd the system might seem to us, it does no good to dismiss it. Ideas that may appear absurd, erroneous or morally repugnant in the eyes of outsiders continue to drive believers' actions. Indeed, outsiders' rejection may lead some believers to hold their views all the more tenaciously as the group defines itself as an island of enlightenment in a sea of error. Rejection validates their sense of mission and their belief that they alone have access to true knowledge of God's will.

These dynamics assumed particular force in the case of the Branch Davidians because their belief system was so clearly millenarian. They anticipated, as historian Norman Cohn would put it, total, immediate, collective, imminent, terrestrial salvation. Such commitments are even less subject than others to compromise, since the logic of the system insists that transcendent forces are moving inexorably toward the fulfillment of history.

Federal authorities were clearly unfamiliar and uncomfortable with religion's ability to drive human behavior to the point of sacrificing all other loyalties. Consequently, officials reacted by trying to assimilate the Waco situation to more familiar and less threatening stereotypes, treating the Branch Davidians as they would hijackers and hostage-takers. This tactic accorded with the very human inclination to screen out disturbing events by pretending they are simply variations of what we already know. Further, to pretend that the novel is really familiar is itself reassuring, especially when the familiar has already provided opportunities for law-enforcement officials to demonstrate their control and mastery. The FBI has an admirable record of dealing effectively with hijackers and hostage-takers; therefore, acting as if Waco were such a case encouraged the belief that here too traditional techniques would work.

The perpetuation of such stereotypes at Waco, as well as the failure to fully approach the religious dimension of the situation, resulted in large measure from the "cult" concept. Both the authorities and the media referred endlessly to the Branch Davidians as a "cult" and Koresh as a "cult leader." The term "cult" is virtually meaningless. It tells us far more about those who use it than about those to whom it is applied. It has become little more than a label slapped on religious groups regarded as too exotic, marginal or dangerous.

As soon as a group achieves respectability by numbers or longevity, the label drops away. Thus books on "cults" published in the 1940s routinely applied the term to Christian Scientists, Jehovah's Witnesses, Mormons and Seventh-Day Adventists, none of whom are referred to in comparable terms today. "Cult" has become so clearly pejorative that to dub a group a "cult" is to associate it with irrationality and authoritarianism. Its leaders practice "mind control," its members have been "brainwashed" and its beliefs are "delusions." To be called a "cult" is to be linked not to religion but to psychopathology.

In the Waco case, the "cult" concept had two dangerous effects. First, because the word supplies a label, not an explanation, it hindered efforts to understand the movement from the participants' perspectives. The very act of classification itself seems to make further investigation unnecessary. To compound the problem, in this instance the classification imposed upon the group resulted from a negative evaluation by what appear to have been basically hostile observers. Second, since the proliferation of new religious groups in the 1960s, a network of so-called "cult experts" has arisen, drawn from the ranks of the academy, apostates from such religious groups, and members' relatives who have become estranged from their kin because of the "cult" affiliations. Like many other law-enforcement agencies, the FBI has relied heavily on this questionable and highly partisan expertise—with tragic consequences. It was tempting to do so since the hostility of those in the "anti-cult" movement mirrored the authorities' own anger and frustration.

These cascading misunderstandings resulted in violence because they produced erroneous views of the role force plays in dealing with armed millenarians. In such confrontations, dramatic demonstrations of force by the authorities provoke instead of intimidate. It is important to understand that millenarians possess a "script"—a conception of the sequence of events that must play out at the end of history. The vast majority of contemporary millenarians are satisfied to leave the details of this script in God's hands. Confrontation can occur, however, because groups often conceive of the script in terms of a climactic struggle between forces of good and evil.

How religious prophecy is interpreted is inseparable from how a person or a group connects events with the millenarian narrative. Because these believers' script emphasizes battle and resistance, it requires two players: the millenarians as God's instruments or representatives, and a failed but still resisting temporal order. By using massive force the Bureau of Alcohol, Tobacco, and Firearms on February 28, and the FBI on April 19, unwittingly conformed to Koresh's millenarian script. He wanted and needed their opposition, which they obligingly provided in the form of the initial assault, the nationally publicized siege, and the final tank and gas attack. When viewed from a millenarian perspective, these actions, intended as pressure, were the fulfillment of prophecy.

The government's actions almost certainly increased the resolve of those in the compound, subdued the doubters and raised Koresh's stature by in effect validating his predictions. Attempts after the February 28 assault to "increase the pressure" through such tactics as floodlights and sound bombardment now seem as pathetic as they were counterproductive. They reflect the flawed premise that the Branch Davidians were more interested in calculating costs and benefits than in taking deeply held beliefs to their logical conclusions. Since the government's own actions seemed to support Koresh's teachings, followers had little incentive to question them.

The final conflagration is even now the subject of dispute between the FBI, which insists that the blazes were set, and survivors who maintain that a tank overturned a lantern. In any case, even if the FBI's account proves correct, "suicide" seems an inadequate label for the group's fiery demise. Unlike Jonestown, where community members took their own lives in an isolated setting, the Waco deaths occurred in the midst of a violent confrontation. If the fires were indeed set, they may have been seen as a further working through of the script's implications. It would not have been the first time that vastly outnumbered millenarians engaged in self-destructive behavior in the conviction that God's will required it. In 1525, during the German Peasants' Revolt, Thomas Münzer led his forces into a battle so hopeless that five thousand of his troops perished, compared to six fatalities among their opponents.

Just as the authorities in Waco failed to understand the connections between religion and violence, so they failed to grasp the nature of charismatic leadership. Charisma, in its classic sociological sense, transcends law and custom. When a Dallas reporter asked Koresh whether he thought he was above the law, he responded: "I *am* the law." Given such self-perception, charismatic figures can be maddeningly erratic; they feel no obligation to remain consistent with pre-existing rules. Koresh's swings of mood and attitude seemed to have been a major factor in the FBI's growing frustration, yet they were wholly consistent with a charismatic style.

Nevertheless, charismatic leaders do confront limits. One is the body of doctrine to which he or she is committed. This limit is often overcome by the charismatic interpreter's ingenuity combined with the texts' ambiguity (Koresh, like so many millennialists, was drawn to the vivid yet famously obscure language of the Book of Revelation).

The other and more significant limit is imposed by the charismatic leader's need to validate his claim to leadership by his performance. Charismatic leadership is less a matter of inherent talents than it is a complex relational and situational matter between leader and followers. Since much depends on followers' granting that a leader possesses extraordinary gifts, the leader's claim is usually subject to repeated testing. A leader acknowledged at one time may be rejected at another. Here too the Waco incident provided an opportunity for the authorities inadvertently to meet millennialist needs. The protracted discussions with Koresh and his ability to tie down government resources gave the impression of a single individual toying with a powerful state. While to the outer world Koresh may have seemed besieged, to those in the community he may well have provided ample evidence of his power by immobilizing a veritable army of law-enforcement personnel and dominating the media.

Given the government's flawed approach, what ought to have been done? Clearly, we will never know what might have resulted from another strategy. Nonetheless, taking note of two principles might have led to a very different and less violent outcome. First, the government benefited more than Koresh from the passage of time. However ample the Branch Davidians' material stockpiles, these supplies were finite and diminishing. While their resolve was extraordinary, we do not know how it might have been tested by privation, boredom and the eventual movement of public and official attention to other matters. Further, the longer the time that elapsed, the greater the possibility that Koresh in his doctrinal maneuvering might have constructed a theological rationalization that would have permitted surrender. Messianic figures, even those cut from seemingly fanatic cloth, have occasionally exhibited unpredictable moments of prudential calculation and submission (one thinks, for example, of the sudden conversion to Islam of the seventeenth century Jewish false messiah Sabbatai Zevi). Time was a commodity the government could afford, more so than Koresh, particularly since a significant proportion of the community's members were almost certainly innocent of directly violating the law.

As important as patience, however, would have been the government's willingness to use restraint in both the application and the appearance of force. The ATF raid, with its miscalculations and loss of life, immediately converted a difficult situation into one fraught with danger. Yet further bloodshed might have been averted had authorities been willing both to wait and to avoid a dramatic show of force. Federal forces should have been rapidly drawn down to the lowest level necessary to prevent individuals from leaving the compound undetected. Those forces that remained should have been as inconspicuous as possible. The combination of a barely visible federal presence, together with a willingness to wait, would have accomplished two things: it would have avoided government actions that confirmed apocalyptic prophecies, and it would have deprived Koresh of his opportunity to validate his charismatic authority through the marathon negotiations that played as well-rehearsed millenarian theater. While there is no guarantee that these measures would have succeeded (events within the compound might still have forced the issue), they held a far better chance of succeeding than the confrontational tactics that were employed.

The events in Waco were not the first time in recent years that a confrontation between a communal group and government forces has ended in violence. Several years ago the Philadelphia police accidentally burned down an entire city block in their attempt to evict the MOVE sect from an urban commune. In 1985 surrender narrowly averted a bloody confrontation at Zarephath-Horeb, the heavily armed Christian Identity community in Missouri organized by the Covenant, Sword and Arm of the Lord. In August 1992 a federal raid on the Idaho mountaintop cabin of a Christian Identity family resulted in an eleven-day armed standoff and the deaths of a U.S. marshal and two family members. In this case, too, the aim was the arrest of an alleged violator of firearms law, Randy Weaver, whose eventual trial, ironically, took place even as the FBI prepared its final assault on the Branch Davidians. In retrospect, the Weaver affair was Waco in microcosm—one from which, apparently, the ATF learned little.

These cases, which should have been seen to signal new forms of religion-state conflict, were untypical of the relationships with government enjoyed by earlier communal societies. While a few such groups, notably the Mormons, were objects of intense violence, most were able to arrive at some way of living with the established order. Many, like the Shakers, were pacifists who had a principled opposition to violence. Some, like the German pietist sects, were primarily interested in preserving their cultural and religious distinctiveness; they only wanted to be left alone. Still others, such as the Oneida perfectionists, saw themselves as models of an ideal social order—exemplars who might tempt the larger society to reform. In all cases, an implied social contract operated in which toleration was granted in exchange for the community's restraint in testing the limits of societal acceptance. When external pressure mounted (as it did in response to the Oneida Community's practice of "complex marriage"), communitarians almost always backed down. They did so not because they lacked religious commitment, but because these communities placed such a high value on maintaining their separate identities and on convincing fellow citizens that their novel social arrangements had merit.

The Branch Davidians clearly were not similarly motivated, and it is no defense of the government's policy to acknowledge that Koresh and his followers would have sorely tested the patience of any state.

Now that the events of Waco are over, can we say that the problem itself has disappeared? Are armed millenarians in America likely to be again drawn or provoked into violent conflict with the established order? The answer, unfortunately, is probably yes. For this reason Waco's lessons are more than merely historically interesting.

The universe of American communal groups is densely populated—they certainly number in the thousands—and it includes an enormous variety of ideological and religious persuasions. Some religious communities are millenarian, and of these some grow out of a "posttribulationist" theology. They believe, that is, that Armageddon and the Second Coming will be preceded by seven years of turmoil (the Tribulation), but they part company with the dominant strain of contemporary Protestant millennialism in the position they assign to the saved. The dominant millenarian current (dispensational premillennialism) assumes that a Rapture will lift the saved off the earth to join Christ before the tribulation begins, a position widely promulgated by such televangelists as Jerry Falwell. Posttribulationists, on the other hand, do not foresee such a rescue and insist that Christians must endure the tribulation's rigors, which include the reign of the Antichrist. Their emphasis upon chaos and persecution sometimes leads them toward a "survivalist" lifestyle—retreat into defendable, self-sufficient rural settlements where they can, they believe, wait out the coming upheavals.

Of all the posttribulationists, those most likely to ignite future Wacos are affiliated with the Christian Identity movement. These groups, on the outermost fringes of American religion, believe that white "Aryans" are the direct descendants of the tribes of Israel, while Jews are children of Satan. Not surprisingly, Identity has become highly influential in the white supremacist right. While its numbers are small (probably between 20,000 and 50,000), its penchant for survivalism and its hostility toward Jews and nonwhites renders the Christian Identity movement a likely candidate for future violent conflict with the state.

When millenarians retreat into communal settlements they create a complex tension between withdrawal and engagement. Many communal societies in the nineteenth century saw themselves as showcases for social experimentation—what historian Arthur Bestor has called "patent office models of society." But posttribulationist, survivalist groups are defensive communities designed to keep at bay a world they despise and fear. They often deny the legitimacy of government and other institutions. For some, the reign of Antichrist has already begun. To white supremacists, the state is ZOG—The Zionist Occupation Government. For them, no social contract can exist between themselves and the enemy—the state. Their sense of besiegement and their links to paramilitary subcultures virtually guarantee that, no matter how committed they may be to lives of isolation, they will inevitably run afoul of the law. The flash-point could involve firearms regulations, the tax system, or the treatment of children. . . .

If this prognosis is valid, what should government policy be toward millennial groups? As I have suggested, government must take religious beliefs seriously. It must seek to understand the groups that hold these beliefs, rather than lumping the more marginal among them in a residual category of "cults." As Waco has shown, violence is a product of interaction and therefore may be partially controlled by the state. The state may not be able to change a group's doctrinal propensities, but it can control its own reactions, and in doing so may exert significant leverage over the outcome. The overt behavior of some millenarian groups will undoubtedly force state action, but the potential for violence can be mitigated if law-enforcement personnel avoid dramatic presentations of force. If, on the other hand, they naively become co-participants in millenarians' end-time scripts, future Wacos will be not merely probable; they will be inevitable. The government's inability to learn from episodes such as the Weaver affair in Idaho provides little cause for short-term optimism. The lesson the ATF apparently took from that event was that if substantial force produced loss of life, then in the next case even more force must be used. Waco was the result.

Admittedly, to ask the government to be more sensitive to religious beliefs in such cases is to raise problems as well as to solve them. It raises the possibility of significant new constitutional questions connected with the First Amendment's guarantee of the free exercise of religion. If the state is not to consign all new and unusual religious groups to the realm of outcast "cults," how is it to differentiate among them? Should the state monitor doctrine to distinguish those religious organizations that require particularly close observation? News reports suggest that Islamic groups may already be the subjects of such surveillance—a chilling and disturbing prospect. Who decides that a group is dangerous? By what criteria? If beliefs can lead to actions, if those actions violate the law, how should order and security be balanced against religious freedom? Can belief be taken into account without fatally compromising free exercise?

These are difficult questions for which American political practice and constitutional adjudication provide little guidance. They need to be addressed, and soon. In an era of religious ferment and millennial excitation, the problems posed by the Branch Davidians can only multiply.

Suggested Readings

Fuller, C. J.
   1984   *Servants of the Goddess: The Priests of a South Indian Temple.* Cambridge: Cambridge
           University Press.

Johnson, Douglas, H.
   1994   *Nuer Prophets: A History of Prophecy from the Upper Nile in the Nineteenth and Twentieth
           Centuries.* Oxford: Clarendon Press; New York: Oxford University Press.

Kehoe, Alice Beck
   2000   *Shamans and Religion: An Anthropological Exploration in Critical Thinking.* Prospect Heights,
           Ill.: Waveland Press.

Kendall, Laurel
  1985   *Shamans, Housewives, and Other Restless Spirits: Women in Korean Ritual Life.* Honolulu: University of Hawaii Press.

Leavitt, John, ed.
  1997   *Poetry and Prophecy: The Anthropology of Inspiration.* Ann Arbor: University of Michigan Press.

Lewis, I. M.
  1971   *Ecstatic Religion: An Anthropological Study of Spirit Possession and Shamanism.* Harmondsworth, UK: Penguin. (Rev. ed. 1978.)

Spiro, Melford E.
  1971   *Buddhism and Society: A Great Tradition and Its Burmese Vicissitudes.* Berkeley: University of California Press.

Vitebsky, Piers
  1995   *The Shaman.* Boston: Little, Brown.

Walter, Mariko Namba, and Eva Jane Neumann Fridman
  2004   *Shamanism: An Encyclopedia of World Beliefs, Practices, and Culture,* vols. I and II. Santa Barbara, Calif.: ABC-CLIO.

Altered States of Consciousness and the Religious Use of Drugs

Zapotec mask representing life and death, from Oaxaca, Mexico.

Ordinary human consciousness includes a number of discrete, recognizable states, including different levels of alertness and relaxation, different forms of sleep and dreaming, and a wide gamut of experiences ranging from moments of creative inspiration and flow to drowsiness and boredom (Bourguignon 1996.) All states correspond to activities in the central nervous system and can be observed as psychobiological phenomena. The most dramatic forms of consciousness, which in some cases may be induced deliberately, can be grouped under the umbrella term *altered states of consciousness,* often referred to by the acronym ASC. Michael Winkelman and Philip M. Peek describe how what happens in the brain provides the potential for particular culturally shaped experiences:

> The altered state of consciousness is a natural response to many different conditions that result in the production of slow-wave brain discharges in the serotonergic connections between the limbic system and brain stem regions. . . . Altered states of consciousness integrate information from the lower levels of the brain into the processing capacity of the frontal cortex, particularly integrating nonverbal emotional and behavioral information into the frontal brain. This integration of information from preverbal brain structures into the language-mediated activities of the frontal cortex provides intuition, understanding, enlightenment, a sense of unity, and personal integration (2004:11).

Altered states are studied by scholars in a number of fields, including psychology and medicine, but it is when altered states are interpreted as religious phenomena that anthropologists become especially interested.

Altered states are particularly appropriate for anthropological consideration because they represent a biological capacity common to all humans, yet have been defined, interpreted, cultivated, and institutionalized differently, if at all, in different cultures and historical periods. One of the foremost anthropological authorities on ASC, Erika Bourguignon, compared ethnographic data from 488 societies and found that an astounding majority are reported to have one or more culturally patterned forms of altered states of consciousness (Bourguignon 1973:9–11.) She notes:

The presence of institutionalized forms of altered states of consciousness in 90% of our sample societies represents a striking finding and suggests that we are, indeed, dealing with a matter of major importance, not merely a bit of anthropological esoterica. It is clear that we are dealing with a psychobiological capacity available to all societies, and that, indeed, the vast majority of societies have used it in their own particular ways, and have done so primarily in a sacred context. Yet some societies have not done so, or had abandoned the practice before the time period [of the report.] (ibid.:11).

In the anthropological literature, works documenting trance, possession, ecstasy, visions, drug use, and shamanism can all be considered studies of altered states. Anthropologists have not always been consistent in their use of terminology related to ASC, though a good deal of scholarship has been devoted to clarifying and standardizing the relevant vocabulary. For example, Bourguignon offers a careful distinction between *possession* as an idea or concept used to interpret behavior within a culture, and *possession trance,* the experience of a person who is changed in some way through the presence of a spirit entity or power (1973:7–8). Working along slightly different lines, I.M. Lewis's article in the present volume argues that trance is a cover term that includes spirit possession, an integral component of shamanism.

Regardless of terminology, ASC vary in the their desirability, their means of induction, and their personnel. For example, throughout Christian history many forms of possession have been recognized, variously seen as demonic and requiring exorcism, or as a spiritual gift such as the ability to speak in tongues (glossolalia) or to prophesize. Similar distinctions can be found around the world, with spirit possession either being diagnosed as a problem to be solved, or as a valued and sought after state, depending on the cultural circumstances. These responses tend to fall into broad patterns around the world, in part related to the dominant religions of a region.

Most trance—whether or not it is interpreted as possession—must be induced in culturally patterned ways that people are accustomed to and which serve as triggers. These methods range from sensory deprivation (being alone, abstaining from food) to sensory overload (drumming, chanting, dance, or use of hallucinogenic drugs). In some contexts, specialists enter trance on behalf of clients and in order to assist their community, as in shamanism. In other cases, trance or possession offer participants opportunities for voicing dissent, social criticism, and personal reflection that would otherwise be impermissible. The ethnographic work of Janice Boddy, who studies the *zar* cult among women in Sudan, provides an outstanding example of the latter (1989). Boddy documents how, in the village in which she studied, women under the possession of spirits engage in behaviors forbidden to women in ordinary life, such as drinking alcohol, speaking loudly, dressing like men, wielding swords, and burping, all guided and interpreted by older women.

For many students of anthropology, a fascinating aspect of ASC is their induction through the use of hallucinogenic drugs. Humans on all continents, and likely since very ancient times, have utilized plant and animal substances to produce dramatically powerful altered states. In many examples, drug use for religious purposes has been carried out not by everyday participants but by specialists, usually placed by anthropologists into the category of shaman, who control the spirit world for the benefit of their community. Psychotropic substances provide the shamans with their visions of the supernatural realm. What one society considers real or unreal is not always shared by another society. Michael Harner's article in this chapter demonstrates, for example, that the Jívaro of the Ecuadorian Amazon consider reality to be what is found in the hallucinogenic state that results from drinking a tea made from the Banisteriopsis vine; the nonhallucinogenic, ordinary state is considered to be an illusion. Cultural variation occurs as well in the classification of substances as psychotropic; some drugs not considered hallucinogens in Western pharmacology are utilized elsewhere to bring about a visionary state, for example tobacco as used by shamans in South America (Wilbert 1987).

Anthropology, of course, never exists in a vacuum, and certain areas of inquiry can arguably be traced to a social environment or *zeitgeist* that supports their study. Such is the case with hallucinogens and culture, and with ASC in general. There was a heyday of sorts in their study, with researchers from numerous fields working actively in the 1960s and 1970s, inspired by and to some extent possibly enabling counter-cultural interest in mind-altering substances. Much of the anthropological and ethnobotanical work referenced here comes from that period, as does much laboratory research into ASC, sometimes sponsored by government agencies such as the Central Intelligence Agency (cf. Lee and Shlain 1985). In an attempt to better understand the role of drugs in religious life, some anthropologists have ingested hallucinogens themselves. Celebrated accounts include Michael Harner's description of using *ayahuasca* among the Conibo of Peru (1980), and Napoleon Chagnon's narratives of using *ebene* snuff while carrying out fieldwork in Venezuela (originally 1968). Nonetheless, cross-cultural comparison demonstrates not only that drugs are perceived differently but also that they may actually have different effects on the users from one society to the next, due to different culturally based expectations. Ayahuasca or peyote as taken in a ritual context, by a population with particular social tools for interpreting the experience, will in significant ways have a different effect than on an urban, middle-class tourist—or anthropologist—from abroad.

The articles selected for this chapter introduce a variety of examples and issues related to the study of altered states of consciousness, including the religious use of drugs. The opening article by I.M. Lewis considers numerous contrasting examples in order to clarify the definitions of trance, possession, and shamanism.

The second article by Sydney Greenfield draws attention to the trance experiences of patients undergoing surgery by Brazilian healer-mediums.

In the third article, Thomas J. Csordas introduces the reader to Mike Kiyaani, a Navajo leader of peyote rites. Kiyaani recounts his first introduction to peyote.

Furst and Coe's "Ritual Enemas" is an ethnohistorical reconstruction of Maya drug usage through an analysis of their pottery.

In "The Sound of Rushing Water," Michael Harner offers an insight into Jivaro reality, a state that can be achieved only through consumption of the hallucinogenic drink *natema*.

In the concluding article, our focus moves to altered states of consciousness intentionally sought by contemporary North Americans and Europeans. Scott Hutson argues that the rave—which for some participants may include drug use—can be interpreted as a form of spiritual healing.

References

Boddy, Janice
    1989 *Wombs and Alien Spirits: Women, Men, and the Zar Cult in Northern Sudan*. Madison, WI: University of Wisconsin Press.

Bourguignon, Erika
    1976 *Possession*. Prospect Heights, IL: Waveland Press.
    1996 Altered States of Consciousness in *Encyclopedia of Cultural Anthropology*, eds. David Levinson and Melvin Ember. NY: Henry Holt and Company, pp. 48–50.

Bourguignon, Erika, ed.
    1973 *Religion, Altered States of Consciousness, and Social Change*. Columbus: Ohio State University Press.

Chagnon, Napoleon
    1968 Yanomamo: *The Fierce People*. NY: Holt, Rinehart, and Winston.

Harner, Michael
    1980 *The Way of the Shaman*. NY: Harper and Row.

Lee, Martin A. and Bruce Shlain
    1985 *Acid Dreams: The CIA, LSD and the Sixties Rebellion*. NY: Grove Press, Inc.

Wilbert, Johannes
    1987 *Tobacco and Shamanism in South America*. New Haven and London: Yale University Press.

Winkelman, Michael and Philip M. Peek, eds.
    2004 *Divination and Healing:* Potent Vision. Tucson: University of Arizona Press.

23

Trance, Possession, Shamanism, and Sex

I. M. Lewis

Anthropologists confront altered states of consciousness when studying trance, possession, and shamanism. However, the definition and delimitation of these three terms has often been imprecise. In the following article, I. M. Lewis identifies the general characteristics of trance—as the core or most basic form of altered consciousness—and notes common features in examples from a variety of cultures and historical periods. Throughout the article, Lewis observes similarities between trance and sexual experiences, noting that both are simultaneously physiological, social, psychological, and deeply symbolic.

While trance can be measured and explained through neurochemistry, it conforms to and is understood through local cultural expectations. Therefore trance is interpreted in different ways by different cultures. The most common interpretation is that the human body has been invaded by a spirit, one that either has been invited or needs to be expelled through exorcism. Thus to Lewis, spirit possession is a form of trance activity. Most anthropologists separate spirit mediums from shamans (see article by Vitebsky in Chapter 4), yet Lewis notes that the trance experience involved for both is essentially the same. The difference between a spirit medium and a shaman lies with the social role and recognition of the religious specialist within the community.

I. M. Lewis is noted for his ethnographic work in the Horn of Africa and for his publications on trance, possession, and related phenomena. His Ecstatic Religion: An Anthropological Study of Spirit Possession and Shamanism *(1971) is considered a definitive source on the anthropological study of altered states of consciousness.*

Trance and Altered States of Consciousness

"Altered States of Consciousness" is an umbrella term, applied to psychological and sociological phenomena regularly encountered in the study of trance, possession, and shamanism—all of which have significant if problematic links with music. This article[1] reviews what is implied in relation to ASC by these terms, which have become common-place in the anthropological study of religion.

Altered States of Consciousness are most clearly exhibited externally in the form that we commonly call 'trance.' When I think of trance states, apart from my own private experience of rapturous moments and episodes (so-called "peak-experiences"), I think

From: Anthropology of Consciousness, *Vol. 14, No. 1, pp. 20–39, 2003.*

1. Paper given at Seminar on "Music and States of Altered Consciousness: A Still Open Question," Intercultural Studies Institute for Comparative Music, Fondazione Giorgio Cini, Venice, January 2002.

particularly of two dramatic examples, involving others, which I witnessed. The first was at a women's spirit possession séance in the Sudan which I attended with a female colleague who was carrying out anthropological research on the famous *zar* cult in Khartoum (see Constantinides 1977 and Lewis et al. 1991).

The séance took place in a large barn which had become a dancing hall regularly used for spirit ceremonies by the *zar* adherents. There was a large crowd of women, and a few male transvestite homosexuals, dressed in the costumes favored by their regular spirit partners. The air was heavy with incense and perfume and the women were dancing to the music, dedicated to the spirits, and beaten out on four drums in syncopation and with an increasing tempo. Led by a spirit cult leader (*sheikha*), the women were dancing round a large round stone regularly used for grinding corn. Suddenly one of the women, very obviously pregnant and as obviously, deeply in trance, began to pound her stomach violently against the grinding stone, thus endangering her baby. Other participants explained that the woman was possessed by a violent southern spirit (associated with the non-Islamic peoples of the southern Sudan). Immediately several other dancing women, with glazed eyes, who appeared also to be in trance, wordlessly sat down on the stone, and thus prevented the frenzied dancer from continuing to beat her body on the stone. It is obvious that these entranced women were not totally oblivious to what was going on round them. Their perception was concentrated on the ritual and the spirits for whom they were dancing, but this did not exclude peripheral attention to other movement in their surroundings.

My other example occurred in a very different and, from some points of view, a more exotic setting, at an international scientific conference on the paranormal held some years ago in a luxury hotel in London (the Hilton). Most of the eighteen participants, well-known figures in this field, were clearly believers, but there were a minority of equally obvious skeptics, including the English specialist on the paranormal, Eric J. Dingwall, the psychological anthropologist George Devereux and myself. As at a regular European séance, we sat round a large table. At one point in the discussion, as Devereux and I were expressing strongly skeptical views on the reality of ESP, one of the most credulous of the participants, a white South African who claimed to have

been initiated as a "witchdoctor" suddenly collapsed in his chair. Several of the participants with medical expertise, including a well-known Italian psychoanalyst who was also a believer in the paranormal, rushed to the witchdoctor's side to see if he required medical attention. This, however, soon appeared unnecessary since, in the trance-like state into which our colleague had fallen, he suddenly started speaking—not fully "in tongues"—but with a strange guttural muttering in which he could be heard saying: "They are knocking it out of us, they are knocking it all out of us . . . "

Devereux and I took this as a defensive reaction to our skeptical and ironical remarks. Everyone, including our psychiatrist colleagues, was embarrassed by this episode from which after about ten minutes our witchdoctor recovered to resume his normal demeanor, carrying on as if nothing had happened and making no reference to the little drama. In contrast to the Sudanese séance, trance here was an unexpected individual reaction and there was no musical stimulus, only the pressure of conflict and disbelief to which trance here seemed a significant reaction.

I was also myself recently involved in a much more banal and familiar incident, when someone crashed his car into mine while I was stationary. The driver apologized profusely for his negligence and simply said, rather strikingly in the present context, that "he was far away, and had not noticed my car." I took this to mean, and he certainly had a glazed facial expression, that his mind was elsewhere, almost as if he were in trance. While not all degrees of distraction from a person's immediate surroundings imply "trance" in a serious sense, they can be close to it as I think we all recognize.

As these examples, like most people's casual personal experience of exalted states of being illustrate, *trance* is appropriately defined as an altered state of consciousness, variable in its intensity, and at its height resembling hypnosis. Along these lines, psychologists define it as a condition of dissociation, characterized by the lack of voluntary movement, and frequently by automatisms in action and thought, illustrated by hypnotic and mediumistic conditions. As our séance examples illustrate, trance also typically involves "an enhanced internal or external focus of attention" (Overton 1998).

As such, while it is obviously felt as a private, individual experience, particularly in its intense forms, it is also a transpersonal, transcultural condition which can be externally observed and, with some technical difficulty, even measured in variations in brain rhythm as recorded by EEG tests. Such personal, psychological experiences may, of course, be shared and mutually intensified as in spirit cult séances, evangelical religious services, pop concerts, political rallies, football crowds, etc. The discovery of natural euphoriates (endorphins) in the blood stream in the early 1970s provided a plausible chemical explanation of trance and linked it with the effect of psychotropic drugs, thus giving a novel and unexpected meaning to Marx's famous definition of religion as "the opium of the people"—more accessible, and less mysterious than he ever imagined.

Trance Induction

That such neurochemistry is implicated in trance experiences does not invalidate its status as culturally conventionalized behavior, recognized cross-culturally, and readily observable to the anthropologist who has no means available to test endorphin levels or measure EEGs. Contrary to what the French Tungus specialist Hamayon (1995) appears to argue, nor does the ultimate involvement of such neuro-physical processes reduce the validity of trance as a sociological as well as psychological phenomenon. This is no more the case than it would be with sexual orgasm, which is obviously a psychological and social, as well as physiological, phenomenon with profound cultural coloring and meaning. If women's popular magazines are to be believed, like trance it is moreover subject to artifice and pretence. This does not reduce the value of sexual climax as a symbol of intimacy and transcendence.

More generally, in all known cultures and civilizations, we find essentially two, at first sight contradictory processes which induce trance. One involves sensory deprivation—trauma, stress, illness, isolation, fasting, and deliberate physical mortification as in many mystical religious traditions. The other equally common stimulus involves sensory overloading—with musical and other sonic bombardment (especially monotonous drumming), strobe lighting effects, the ingestion of hallucinogenic drugs, and more mundane procedures like over-breathing and even strenuous exercise such as jogging (which has been shown experimentally to increase endorphin levels) (Banyai 1984; Prince 1982).

As far as music's role is concerned, the French ethnomusicologist Gilbert Rouget concludes his magisterial study of music and trance by declaring that "music's great achievement is to be able to induce trance in the manner that an electric current can set a tuning fork vibrating with the same frequency." But at the same time, he questions those such as Neher who have claimed that drumming induces convulsive effects through its influence on the alpha rhythm of the brain. (More recently, Maxfield (1990), has reported that "monotonous drumming, characterized cross-culturally by a rhythm with 4–7 beats per second induces a corresponding increase in the so-called theta rhythm in the EEG.") I do not know whether Rouget would accept this. In any case, he says that music is: "less significant in triggering trance than in sustaining it. It is indispensable for providing the cult member with the means of manifesting identification (with the spirit) and hence externalizing trance." This is so, according to Rouget, because "music is the only language to speak at once to the head and legs, since it is through music that the group holds up to the individual the mirror in which to behold his borrowed identity." Following this, Rouget is led to pursue what he sees as an analogy between opera in modern culture and the possession séance in traditional cultures, indeed he calls opera "lyric possession." It seems to me, however, that a more obvious analogy is with ballet, and indeed it is significant to record here that in westernized circles in contemporary Egypt, a folkloristic version of the north-east African *zar* cult has been developed into a new "Oriental" form of ballet (see the ballet magazine *Arabesque* 1978, 1983).

We must remember, however, that such an embarrassment of riches in the wealth and variety of sensual stimulants headed by music is not the only route to trance: sensory deprivation may not be so alluring but it is equally effective. These contrasting eliciting forces are consistent with the contradictory experiences commonly reported in trance: overwhelming sensations of despair, often associated with images of death and birth, alternating with sensations of ineffable joy. Interestingly here, psychiatrists employing LSD and similar psychotropic drugs in clinical treatment report that drugged female patients often become confused as to whether they are being born or giving birth (see Grof 1977: more recently, Grof has launched 'Breath-work,' in which numbers of subjects lie on mattresses for up to a whole day engaging in deep breathing exercises to a background program of music culled from the cinema. Most of those involved seem to have trance experiences).

The opposition of these themes, and their resolution is, according to Reichel-Dolmatoff (1971), vividly expressed by the Amazonian Tukano shamans of Columbia. Tukano state that their creator deity, the Sun-father, committed incest with his own daughter at the time of creation. This act produced the hallucinogen (the bannisteriopsis caapi vine) regularly employed by them to achieve ecstatic visions. This trance experience is explicitly compared to incestuous sexual intercourse. Hallucination and sexual intercourse, according to Reichel-Dolmatoff, are viewed by the Tukano Indians as equivalent and full of anxiety because of their relation to the idea of incest. The Tukano declare that they take the drug in order to return to the uterus, source and origin of all things, where the individual confronts the tribal divinities, the creation of the universe and of humanity, the first human couple, the creation of the animals, and the establishment of social order with the laws of exogamy. With this example we have broached the question of the meaning of trance (here a transcendent religious experience), and the range of possible interpretations of it in different cultures and sometimes in different contexts in the same culture.

The Interpretation of Trance

Despite its range of sensory modalities and meanings, trance in my view is a universal phenomenon, theoretically and to a certain extent actually open, as we have seen to identification and description. Our naturalistic, scientist definition of trance and dissociation is not unique and is found in some traditional societies. Amongst the Samburu pastoralists of Northern Kenya, for example, trance states are associated with situations of tension and danger and regarded as a sign of machismo and self-assertion appropriate to members of the warrior age-grade in this gerontocratic society. Rather similarly, among the Abelan tribe of New Guinea, young bachelors sometimes exhibit similar symptoms which are described as "deafness." This is not ascribed to spiritual intervention. Again among the Tungus reindeer

herders of Siberia, who represent the *locus classicus* of shamanism to which we refer later, hysterical states, involving trembling and the compulsive imitation of words and gestures, do not always signify possession by a spirit. They may simply indicate that those who manifest this behavior, called *olon,* are in a state of involuntary fear, so that this represents a kind of "startle" reaction.

The well-known Italian culture complex of tarantism,[2] in its medieval, dancing mania manifestation, represents a more complex phenomenon involving non-mystical and mystical components. The ostensible naturalistic explanation for this compulsion to dance viewed it as a disease and traced it to the poisonous bite of the tarantula spider. Two cures were favored: dance therapy to the brisk rhythm of the tarantella played on fife, clarinets and drums when, it was believed the poison was expelled as perspiration; and religious exorcism at the shrines of particular saints. However, in his brilliant study, *La terra del rimorso* (1966), de Martino decisively demonstrated that the phenomenon was much more complicated and far from being a simple matter of "poisoning" as those afflicted appeared to believe. In fact it involved a form of spirit possession by a hybrid spider-saint (for more recent information on the cult's vestiges in southern Italy today and the continuing significance of its symbolism, see Pizza 1997).

Again, in some cultures, trance may be seen as a manifestation of "soul-loss," as for example among many of the North American Indians. To some extent this is also true of the !Kung bushmen, where in healing dance ceremonies, to a musical accompaniment of hand-clapping and singing, men work themselves up into trance states in which the intrinsic "boiling energy" (or soul) is released from their bodies to fight those evil powers causing illness in others.

But the most common explanation of trance across cultures is that it is a manifestation of the invasion of

---

2. In contemporary Apulia, tarantism and its *pizzicata* music has been folklorized and is now a familiar part of the local pop scene, with large scale festivals which attract throngs of tourists in the summer. Tarantism has become an important element in the construction of a new, neo-traditional local identity in Salento—a sub-Southern Italian local nationalism. This movement is also associated with the local Greek dialect which is increasingly taught in local schools.

the human body by an external spirit agent. This may, or may not, be coupled with the idea of soul-loss involving the displacement of the host's soul by the alien spirit. As classical tarantism illustrates, we regularly find naturalistic and spiritual explanations of trance competing in the same culture and invoked in different contexts. Possession by an external spiritual force is, of course, a culturally specific explanation of behavior or of a state of being. It does not necessarily coincide with trance. Indeed it is often invoked to explain minor maladies (even those as trivial as constipation!) where there is no evidence or expectation of trance. Nevertheless, the two phenomena do coincide at the peak of ecstatic activity, in possession rituals, for example, where members of a possession group are dancing in honor of their possessing spirits (as in our *zar* example), and when the spirit troubling a new victim is being interrogated to establish its identity so that it can be treated appropriately.

Here we must note that virtually universally, the initial diagnostic treatment of what is often presented as an illness or affliction leads to two opposed possible outcomes. One, aimed at expelling the spirit, is of course, exorcism, with which we are familiar from our own Christian culture and which is equally common in Islam. The other contrasting treatment, referred to usefully by Luc de Heusch as "adorcism," instead of seeking to expel the intrusive spirit, endeavors to come to terms with it, reaching an accommodation with it, by paying it cult. Possession then becomes the first step in initiation into a spirit cult. Trance is critical in both cases, since as has long been noted, it is most marked at the dramatic climax of exorcism as the exorcist wrestles with the intrusive spirit prior to successfully casting it out.

We should note that in male-dominated societies where such women's spirit possession cults flourish, men usually prefer their womenfolk to seek exorcism for their problems rather than induction into such a cult. Hence in this context exorcism becomes a further implement in the control and subjection of women—as I have argued elsewhere (Lewis 1996). This sociologically significant point is well-illustrated in the famous 11th-century Japanese literary classic, *The Tale of the Genji* where, as Doris Bargen (1997) has demonstrated, Japanese noblemen sought to control their rebellious "women's weapon" of spirit possession by insisting on exorcism as the proper treatment. Thus, although exorcism and spirit accommodation

(adorcism) have normally very different outcomes and social implications, they are equally signaled by the coincidence of trance and possession, in a "peak" experience, one marking an exit and the other the entrance to the routine cult of ecstasy. (In keeping with this common peak experience, it has at once to be acknowledged that this imparts an ambiguity to active (trance) possession which enables some possession cults to masquerade as exorcism: see, e.g., Davis 1980; Lewis 1996; de Heusch 1997; Hell 1997).

Trance and Shamanism

These ecstatic cults—secret religions for women and low-status males—have spirit-inspired leaders who graduate from the ranks of the possessed. These cult leaders are empowered by their special relationship (regularly represented explicitly as a marital union) with particular spirits who become their spirit partners and guides. In Haiti, such spiritual unions may even be formally solemnized in actual marriage certificates (Metraux 1959:215). As in the myths of ancient Greece and other cultures, such celestial marriages are regularly believed to be blessed with progeny. Thematically, there is an interesting analogy here between possession and pregnancy (cf. Graham 1977): but possession is not, as some have argued, inherently related to gender through the biological experience of sexual intercourse. Not surprisingly, such spirit unions are seen as standing in contrast to the human marriages of the female devotees concerned, creating rival loyalties and potential conflict. Amongst the Tamils of south India (Nabokov 1997), young brides may succumb to possession by lusty *pey* spirits which force their prey to elope with them, and "not only sexually enjoy their victims' but incite them to reject their lawful husbands by kicking and biting them" (Nabokov 1997: 301). Equally generally, such conjugal spirits are said to ride or "mount" their human hosts who, in their turn, in some African cultures, are described as the "Mares of the Gods."

On the human side, devotees demonstrate their intimacy with the spirits by going into trance when dancing to their tunes. Those cult members who graduate to become inspired priestesses behave and practice in the same way as shamans (who are predominantly male) in shamanic religions (Lewis 1982; cf. Hell 1995: 411ff.). Such possession cult leaders are often women past menopause and/or widows and are consequently ascribed male qualities.

Trance, which is sometimes referred to as "half death" or "little death," may involve actual sexual orgasm—both, where adorcism is practiced, or its opposite, exorcism. In the latter case, for instance, in Christian Sri Lanka, female pilgrims are reported to experience orgasm as they are exorcised at a local shrine where they rub their genitals on the holy cross and, at the climax, claim they are penetrated by Christ himself (Stirrat 1977; Gombrich and Obeyesekere 1988).

The same sexual aura shrouds adorcism in the Christian and Muslim traditions. In the former, Saint Marie of the Incarnation worshipped Jesus as her "Beloved." For her part, St. Teresa of Avila recorded that in her transports of mystical feeling she had achieved "spiritual marriage" with Christ. Her most sublime experiences she described as unfolding in three stages: "union," "rapture," and the climactic "wound of love." As has been recently pointed out (Fales 1996), St. Teresa was a member of a family which had been forced to convert from Judaism to Christianity during the religious persecution administered by the Inquisition in 15th-century Spain. As a woman, a spinster, and a member of a convert family, despite the latter's wealth, she was in several important respects a marginal figure and, like others in these circumstances in traditional cultures, a strong candidate for spiritual attention. In such a setting, St. Teresa appears to have very successfully employed her spiritual intimacy with Christ as a form of personal empowerment and even political criticism. In similar language if with less political ambition, the well-known 7th-century Muslim Sufi poet of Basra, Rabi'al-'Adawiyya, expressed her passionate devotion to the Prophet Mohammed in many ardent poems using this conjugal imagery. Similarly, in those North African saints' cults, associated with the former slave populations and known as "black brotherhoods," ecstatic female dancers explicitly compare their feelings after experiencing trance to those of sexual intercourse (Crapanzano 1973).

These lusty themes are familiar, of course, in the Dionysian cults of ancient Greece as presented in Euripides' drama the *Bakchai* and in other sources (Dodds 1951; Devereux 1974; Maffesoli 1993). Indeed, in a rather tortuous and not entirely convincing argument, Devereux even claims to distinguish between female followers of Dionysus who experienced true sexual climax in the orgiastic rites, and those whose ecstasy took the form of a "grand hysterical seizure," without actual orgasm (These he considers experienced trance as "a coitus and orgasm equivalent." Most women, he adds, "who have such attacks are vaginally frigid").

This sexual aspect was also strongly emphasized in the earlier tarantist cult and expressed in songs addressed to the hybrid figure of the Spider-Saint (Paul) as in this invocation sung by female devotees at St. Paul's chapel in Galatina (Apulia): "My St. Paul of the Tarantists who pricks the girls in their vaginas; My St. Paul of the Serpents who pricks the boys in their testicles" (de Martino 1966).

Trance, as I am arguing, is cross-culturally the most conclusive public demonstration that a human being has been seized by a spirit, and, in the case of those who develop ongoing relationships with spirits, the regular expression of that relationship. Consequently, it is hardly surprising that trance behavior should be conventionalized and culturally standardized. As a socio-cultural phenomenon, trance necessarily responds and conforms to local expectations: if it did not it could not be securely recognized as a signal of spiritual intervention in human affairs. Hence, while it is also a cross-culturally recognizable state, regularly induced and sustained by particular musical rhythms, it nevertheless respects the cultural form given it in a particular society. In this it clearly resembles the female sexual climax which, despite its physiological features, is also affected by cultural conventions—to which the vast literature, popular and learned, on the subject testifies.

We have so far been dealing with trance in the social context of marginal cults involving women and low-status categories of men where the cult leaders, in my view, exercise a shamanic role. We now come to shamanism proper where the social context shifts to the center of the stage and is concerned with public morality and order in the widest sense. Here in these "main morality" religions, shamans are typically males and it is their special relationship with the spirits that is the central issue. As we shall see, however, the same imagery and symbolism is used to describe and sanctify shaman-spirit relationships.

The importance of inspirational spirit possession in shamanism disproves the allegedly crucial distinction between these phenomena, promoted by Mircea Eliade (1951) who was himself, of course, not a primary source of ethnographic evidence. On the basis of an inaccurate and partial reading of the primary sources of other scholars, Eliade, as is well known, claimed that the defining feature of shamanism was the shaman's "mystical flight," in which he experienced "the ecstasy provoked by the ascension to the sky, or the descent to Hell" (Eliade 1951:434). This erroneous distinction between possession and shamanism, as essentially separate cultural phenomena, was given a sociological twist and further elaborated rather imaginatively by Luc de Heusch (1962; 1971).

Although the term *shaman* comes originally from the Tungus reindeer herders of Siberia and is obviously associated there with the local (but externally influenced) cosmology, I do not see the word as limited to that particular ethnological context, nor despite Eliade's advocacy, does it necessarily exclude possession. As I have argued elsewhere at length, we need a wider understanding of the term (Lewis 1971 etc.). Thus, I agree with the French Siberian specialist E. Lot-Falck (1973), who writes: "To be a shaman does not signify professing particular beliefs, but rather refers to a certain mode of communication with the supernatural."

Many lines of communication are open here, but contrary to Eliade and his eminent Belgian disciple de Heusch, the crucial one is possession by a spirit or spirits. Shirokogoroff (1935), a medical doctor and our brilliant first-hand source on Tungus shamanism, as it was before and at the beginning of the Russian Revolution, emphasizes how the shaman's ecstatic trance behavior, signifying the intimacy of his relations with the spirits, was central to his role. As he puts it himself: the shaman is a master of spirits, and his body is a "placing," or receptacle, for the invading spirits during the séance. Here, in his classic description, "The rhythmic music and singing, and later the dancing of the shaman, gradually involve every participant more and more in a collective action. When the audience begins to repeat the refrains together with his assistants, only those who are defective fail to join the chorus. The tempo of the action increases, the shaman with a spirit is no more an ordinary man or relative, but is a

"placing" (i.e. incarnation) of the spirit; the spirit acts together with the audience, and this is felt by everyone. The state of many participants is now near to that of the shaman himself, and only a strong belief that where the shaman is there the spirit may only enter him, restrains the participants from being possessed en masse by the spirit. This is a very important condition of shamanizing which does not, however, reduce mass susceptibility to the suggestion, hallucinations, and unconscious acts produced in a state of ecstasy. When the shaman feels that the audience is with him and follows him he becomes still more active and this effect is transmitted to the audience.

The contemporary French Tungus specialist Roberte Hamayon provides further detailed information on the nature of the shaman's relations with his spirit guides to whom, as elsewhere, he is bound by marriage. Indeed, here again, the centrality of the marriage alliance between shamans and spirits illuminates the sexual imagery which abounds in shamanic discourse, as is also emphasized by the Italian scholar Zolla (1986). The séance is of course a drama and the shaman's "play acting" in his animal costume, as Hamayon puts it, mimes the act of rutting or coupling with his animal spirit partner. The words employed to describe them clearly demonstrate the sexuality of these actions and gestures that collectively constitute sexual play. In harmony with this strong emphasis on the shaman's séance as a sexual encounter, even the shaman's drum and drum-stick, beaten vigorously while he leaps and bounds ritually, are representative of sexual intercourse. This is in keeping with the etymology of the word *shaman* itself, as expounded by Siberian specialists, who stress that the root *sam* signifies the idea of violent movement and of dancing exuberantly, throwing one's body about. Romano Mastromattei (1988) reports that orgasmic seizures occur in the parallel shamanic rituals in Nepal.

Our classical authority, Shirokogoroff, the medical doctor who was such a meticulous observer (in agreement with most other first-hand observers), insisted on the key role of trance as the sine qua non of the shaman's séance performance. "No one," Shirokogoroff reported, "can be accepted as a shaman unless he can demonstrably experience ecstasy—a half delirious condition 'abnormal' in European terms" (Shirokogoroff 1935: 274). Shirokogoroff also gives a vivid impression of the highly charged psychological atmosphere of the séance and of the emotionally intense interaction between the shaman and his audience as he works himself up into the state he describes as "ecstasy."

"After shamanizing, the audience recollects various moments of the performance, their great psycho-physiological emotion and the hallucinations of sight and hearing which they have experienced. They then have a deep satisfaction—much greater than that from emotions produced by theatrical and musical performances, literature and general artistic phenomena of the European complex, because in shamanizing the audience at the same time acts and participates." (These contrasts could not, of course, be sustained with reference to shamanism and modern Western theatre—nor, indeed, the theatre of Shakespeare's day.) Shirokogoroff also noted the physiological changes in the shaman's comportment during and after ecstasy. During the séance the shaman expended such tremendous energy that, at the end he was covered in perspiration and was unable to move, his pulse weak and slow, his breath-ing shallow.

The ritual drama of the Siberian séance has been elegantly confirmed by the distinguished Finnish specialist on shamanism, Anna-Leena Siikala (1978), who employs the term "counter roles" for the shaman's spirit guides which he enacts with such full ecstatic virtuosity.

In relation to this highly developed drama of the shamanic séance, which is so thoroughly documented, it seems perverse of Roberte Hamayon to claim that the psychological overlay of trance performances invalidates their key significance: all the more so in that she emphasizes the sexual imagery and symbolism of the shaman's relations with the spirits, which would imply that this trance represents a kind of spiritual sexual climax. Moreover, as

we have already noted earlier, sexual intercourse and sexual climax are not merely physiological acts but have also a complex psychological overlay, and are far from being immune from cultural influence and even fashion. Such considerations, however, certainly do not reduce their significance cross-culturally as defining particular relationships.

More generally, ritual sexual congress in a number of African cultures is used to signify religious blessing and fertility. In this vein to take a specific example, amongst the Kikuyu, as Bernardo Bernardi has shown, the traditional term for the sacred means more colloquially simply human sexual intercourse.

Why sexual images and symbolism are so widely utilized in expressing religious feeling is an old problem. I believe that Manning Nash suggests a plausible answer. "Erotic love," he argues, is frequently a template for religious meaning since this form of strenuous play provides a readily available expression of self-transcendence.

This seems to me to elucidate very well the pervasiveness of eroticism in describing the relations between humans and spirits. More directly to our purposes here, although every instance of trance cannot, of course, be considered an experience of actual orgasm, at their peak, both seem likely to overlap. In this regard it is suggestive that there are reports from Western ESP contexts of successful mediumistic performances involving actual orgasm on the part of the medium (see Devereux 1974: 50). Sexual congress seems thus to offer a rich store of psychological and physiological experience upon which trance draws, just as the conjugal relationship provides an armory of powerful symbols to describe and articulate intimate relations between humans and their spirit partners. In this sensual perspective, although the precise modalities of music and trance seem still imprecisely defined, music is nevertheless evidently the food of love.

24

Hypnosis and Trance Induction in the Surgeries of Brazilian Spiritist Healer-Mediums[1]

Sidney M. Greenfield

In what is surely one of the most fascinating long-running ethnographic studies in recent anthropology, Sidney M. Greenfield has documented the healing practices of Spiritist mediums in Brazil. Related psychic surgeries in the Philippines have received considerable attention from outsiders, including celebrities and professional magicians who claim that the techniques involve sleight-of-hand. Greenfield asserts that the dramatic examples in Brazil are different in that the actual flesh of the patient is cut open, and implements such as scalpels, tweezers, and even rotary saws are inserted; no anesthesia is used, and apparently few patients experience infections or complications. In the following article, Greenfield is not interested in evaluating efficacy or potential fraudulence, however, but asks how altered states of consciousness facilitate the surgeries.

He begins the article with a series of detailed descriptions of individual healers at work. Conforming to the beliefs of Spiritism, each healer serves as a medium for deceased medical physicians from the past and enters trance before beginning work. The altered states of healers are well-documented in the anthropological literature, but Greenfield shifts focus to the trance states of the patients, to determine how they are able to undergo surgery without anesthesia. Because the patients do not undergo any kind of deliberate trance induction, Greenfield looks to features in Brazilian culture that might account for the ability to enter a hypnotic state merely in response to a powerful patron, the healer.

While not discussed in Greenfield's article here, some Brazilian healer-mediums now have international clientele and have attracted media attention, both skeptical and affirming. Information on the healer John of God (João de Jesus), for example, is accessible on various web sites, some of which include video footage of surgeries, testimonials from clients, and offers for guided travel arrangements.

Sidney M. Greenfield is Professor of Anthropology Emeritus from the University of Wisconsin-Milwaukee and has recently published a book-length account of his study, Spirits with Scalpels: The Cultural Biology of Religious Healing in Brazil *(Left Coast Press, 2008).*

From: Anthropology of Consciousness, *Vol. 2, Issue 3–4, pp. 20–25, 1991.*

1. Revised version of a paper presented at a symposium on "Hypnosis, Trance and Healing in Cross-Cultural Perspective," at the 89th Annual Meeting of the American Anthropological Association, New Orleans, LA, November, 28–December 2, 1990.

Introduction

In Part I of this paper I describe several surgical procedures performed by José Carlos Ribeiro, Edson Queiroz and Antônio de Oliveira Rios, three of the many Brazilian Spiritist[2] healer-mediums I have observed and studied since the early 1980s. What is unusual, if not spectacular, about these surgeries, at least from the perspective of Western science and medicine, is that the healer-medium actually cuts into the flesh of the patients, extracting human tissue without either anesthesia or antisepsis.[3] In spite of this, most patients experience little if any pain, bleed but minimally if at all, and few if any cases of infections or other complications have been reported.[4]

While performing these surgeries the healer-mediums are in an altered state of consciousness (ASC) which they enter during a brief ritual usually participated in by their followers and supporters. The patients, I shall argue, also are in an ASC. However, there are no rituals in which they participate during which they can be seen to enter a trance state. Furthermore, the healer-mediums do not consciously induce them into ASCs, as for example do western surgeons, physicians, and other therapists who use hypnosis in treating patients. They participate in no formal rituals during which they can be seen to enter an ASC. In Part II of the paper, after briefly summarizing the results of studies of hypnosis that help at least in part to account for what is described in Part I, I outline, as an hypothesis, a model explaining how specific aspects of Brazilian culture and social structure combine to move individuals, when presented with appropriate cues in identifiable social contexts, from what may be considered their ordinary states of consciousness into ASCs.[5]

The Healers and the Surgeries

José Carlos Ribeiro

The first healer-medium whose surgeries I describe is José Carlos Ribeiro. When I first met him in 1982 I was living in the city of Fortaleza, capital of the northeastern Brazilian state of Ceará. I first learned of his presence in the city from an article in the newspaper. After reading the story, I went to the address given where I introduced myself, my wife and my daughter to him. I told him of my interest in his work and asked if I might observe him. His reply was that not only was I welcome to see what he did, but that I would assist him. Without another word he placed a tray in my hands on which there were a few scalpels, several pairs of surgical scissors, a few pairs of tweezers of assorted sizes, a syringe, some cotton, some gauze, adhesive tape and a glass of water. He then turned to a poorly dressed, dark skinned man who had been waiting with his wife.[6]

---

2. Spiritism of Kardecism is a possession-trance (or "mediumistic") religion that is widespread in Brazil.
3. This contrasts the practices of the Brazilian healer-mediums with those of the more celebrated healers from the Philippines who often do not cut but rather appear to open the bodies of their patients with their hands. The Philippine tradition often has been referred to as psychic surgery. The Brazilians discussed below do actual surgery, with instruments, as opposed to psychic surgery— although at times I have also seen bodies opened without the use of scalpels, scissors or other instruments. I have videotaped most of the Brazilian Spiritist healer-mediums I have observed and have shown the tapes to physicians, surgeons and others familiar with surgical procedures. They assured me unanimously that the bodies of the patients had been entered surgically. Any reader who doubts this is welcome to view my tapes.
4. This is not to say that pain is never experienced, excessive bleeding never occurs and there are never infections. Instead it is to say that over the period of a decade of observations I have noted few expressions of pain, even after deep incisions were made in tender areas, relatively little bleeding, and have been able to find very few complaints of infections caused by the procedures of healer-mediums.

---

5. The ASCs of the patients also are to be seen in the tapes.
6. Patients treated by Spiritist healer-mediums come from all sectors of the population. Although I have never examined their composition systematically, based on my informal observations over a 10 year period they appear to be representative of the general population of Brazil, except that they are considerably older. In contrast with the large number of Brazilians under the age of 18, most of the patients seeking help from healer-mediums are considerably older. But there are rich and poor, Black and white in numbers that roughly approximate the percentages of these categories in the general population. While some of the patients are Spiritist practitioners, and others admit to being interested in and/or knowing something about Spiritism, the majority claim they are not Spiritists, but rather Roman Catholics, Protestants, etc. Many patients, especially the more affluent ones, turn to healers only after unsuccessful attemps to obtain relief from conventional medical sources. The poor, however, most of whom cannot afford medical treatment, often turn to a healer-medium when they first develop symptoms.

The woman started to tell the healer about her mate's problem with his vision. As she did so José Carlos directed his eyes away from her towards the ceiling. He then mumbled some words I was not able to understand and began to shake. He was entering into a self-induced trance state. An instant later he interrupted the woman abruptly to ask a question and to issue a command. He did this with an authority not previously demonstrated, and he spoke in a sharp accent that contrasted with the soft tone he usually used. It sounded to me as if he were a native speaker of Spanish trying to communicate in Portuguese.

He asked the couple if they believed in God. Before they could answer, he picked up a scalpel from the tray in my hand and, while ordering them both to think of God, plunged it with his right hand into the man's left eye, under the lid. With a series of jabbing and twisting movements he slid the instrument down under the eye. As he did this he substituted the back of a pair of tweezers taken from the tray with his left hand for the scalpel. While doing this he eased the eye forward, tilting it out of its socket. He then scraped the lens of the protruding eye with the scalpel still held in his right hand.

More than twenty people—mostly friends, former patients, and patients to be seen by him later—had crowded into the small, hot, poorly ventilated room to watch the healer. Several of them gasped as the scalpel was thrust into the eye, and one woman was unable to stifle a scream. My wife, who had been placed directly behind the healer, felt faint. As the blood left her face, José Carlos, though unable to see her, moved his left hand quickly in her direction, leaving the tweezers dangling momentarily from its place under the protruding eye. As he did so he again mumbled something I could not understand. As the blood returned to her cheeks, the healer secured his grip on the dangling tweezers. After a few more scraping motions with the scalpel still held in his right hand he slid the tweezers, held securely again in his left hand, back to the top of the eye under the lid where he had first introduced the scalpel. As he covered the eye with gauze and some adhesive tape, he asked the man if he had felt any pain. To his negative reply the patient added that he had been aware of all that had happened. The procedure I estimated had lasted a little more than a minute.

José Carlos then wrote a prescription that seemingly flowed from the pen itself. He looked at neither the pen nor the pad but instead off into space as he wrote. As he handed it to the somewhat startled woman, he quickly listed things the patient was to do and not do, and foods he was to eat or avoid. He then dismissed the patient telling him that he would be well.

The healer then turned to the next patient on whom he also performed eye surgery, using the same scalpel and tweezers that had been returned to the tray in my hands without being cleaned. Diagnosis, surgery, bandaging, writing of a prescription for post-operative medication, and the dictation of a list of behavioral restrictions and a special diet took only a few minutes.

As the morning progressed, José Carlos alternated between the performance of other surgery—the removal of several cysts and tumors—and the writing of prescriptions that were to cure patients or prepare them for return visits and possible surgery at a later date.

Edson Cavalcante de Queiroz

The second healer whose surgeries I describe is Edson Cavalcante de Queiroz who when I met him was a resident of Recife, the capital of the neighboring northeastern state of Pernambuco. In contrast with José Carlos who had attended the university but never completed his course work and Antônio de Oliverira Rios, the third healer to be discussed below who has but a first grade education, Edson was a trained and licensed physician, a graduate of the medical school of the Federal University of Pernambuco.[7] He earned his livelihood by providing medical services for a fee at a private clinic specializing in gynecology and surgery. Away from the clinic, at a center he founded in honor of his spirit guide, he performed Spiritist healing and surgeries.

The first surgical procedure I present was done on a young woman who had a growth on her right shoulder. She had been brought to Edson by her mother who had heard stories about patients not

---

7. I use the past tense because Edson, as he was known to his patients and supporters, was killed in October [1991].

experiencing pain when he operated on them. Fatima became uncontrollably irrational at the thought of the possible pain she might experience should a doctor try to remove the growth on her shoulder surgically.[8]

As the healer approached her, the professional nurse who regularly assisted handed him a scalpel still wrapped in its sterile packaging. The patient, seated on a small operating table, did not move nor did she make a sound when he unwrapped the instrument and then thrust it into her shoulder. A small trickle of blood appeared that stopped after being patted with a piece of gauze. Fatima did not react when Edson next put down the scalpel and jabbed a pair of scissors into the opened wound. She did not flinch as he pulled at the growth first with the scissors and then with his unwashed fingers[9] which he inserted into the opening.

After tearing loose and removing the infected material Edson handed it to a pathologist who prepares a report on all of the healer's cases.

The patient meanwhile sat motionlessly on the surgical table. The healer then placed a piece of adhesive tape over the open wound saying that there was no need for suturing.[10] The nurse completed the

bandaging and then directed Fatima, assisted by her mother—who stood at her side throughout the procedure—to the other side of the room where she was given a glass of special water to drink. Edson then wrote a prescription which, as had been the case with José Carlos, appeared to flow from the pen. He looked at neither his hand nor the paper. The entire procedure had taken no more than a minute or two.[11]

A second patient seen by the healer the same evening had been suffering from sinus problems and a perennially stuffed nose. To treat her a pair of scissors were driven up each of her nostrils, deep into the sinus cavity.[12] To demonstrate that in spite of the apparent lack of asepsis there would be no infection, Edson asked a bystander to spit on the gauze he wrapped around one of the pairs of scissors before driving it into the sinus cavity. The healer regularly asked those observing him to introduce germs and other contaminants into open wounds.

Earlier that same evening he had jammed several syringe needles (about two to two and one-half inches in length) into the back of a woman who could scarcely walk. She had made the journey to the Center on crutches assisted by her relatives. Edson forcefully inserted the needles in a line about two to three inches apart, along her spinal column. As he placed the final one just above the base of the spine, he ordered the pathologist to bring him a test tube—to collect the spinal fluid that that was starting to flow. When the tube was about one-third full, he slapped the patient's back forcefully and rapidly removed the needles. As he dismissed the somewhat startled woman—telling her that she would be

---

8. Prior to seeing any patients Edson had entered a trance state to the reading of a passage from The Scriptures—as interpreted by Allan Kardec—by a close associate and remained in an ASC until the last patient left the Center several hours later.

9. Edson does not wear gloves when performing surgery and he does not wash his hands after each surgery. He will not wash his hands until he has attended all of the patients to be seen on a given night. To the best of our knowledge, however, no cases of infection, or other post-surgical complications have been reported thus far by any of his patients.

10. I am unable to generalize as to the use of suturing. At times I have seen wounds opened by healer-mediums sewn closed while at other times they were simply bandaged and left to heal. Some healers used sutures more often than others. Antônio, as we shall see below, had all surgeries sutured closed; but this was because he claimed not to be doing the healing. He simply opened up the patient so that the spirits could cure them. Then his assistants sutured closed the wounds he opened. Edson, José Carlos and others who claimed to heal when they operated, sutured at times and not at others independent of the size or depth of the incision.

11. Fatima was her usual outgoing, vivacious self when I saw her on Friday morning when she returned to the Spiritist Center to have the bandage changed by the nurse. She restated her fear of doctors and the pain they inflict and expressed her relief in no longer having to be concerned about the growth on her shoulder.

12. Inserting scissors, or more often needles, into the body of a patient is a treatment that Edson often uses. While in trance he explains that the procedure itself is not a cure; the needles and/or scissors instead direct energy from the spiritual plane that will dematerialize growths and other foreign objects in the patient's body thus effecting the cure.

fine—he handed the test tube to the pathologist and ordered a complete analysis.[13]

On another occasion Edson removed a growth of film from the eye of a poor, elderly diabetic woman. She said that she had come to him, rather than going to a conventional doctor, not only because he charges no fee,[14] but more importantly because she feared that she might not survive the chemical anesthesia used in hospitals by conventional surgeons.

As the nurse directed her to lie on the table, Edson told her to think of God. Then, as he secured the end of the growth with a pair of tweezers held in his left hand, the healer ordered her not to move the eye while he worked. Snipping at the film with a pair of scissors in his blood-stained right hand, he explained that this procedure takes between 30 and 40 minutes when done in the operating room of a hospital. It took him about 25 seconds.

Before starting the procedure, however, Edson invited a visitor to assist him by holding the patient's eye lids open while he cut out the growth. After handing the excised tissue to the pathologist, the healer ordered the stranger to spit into the eye. This was to show that in spite of the apparent absence of asepisis there would be no infection.[15]

As the nurse bandaged the eye the healer, looking elsewhere, wrote a prescription that he handed to the patient after she drank the special (fluidified) water given to each patient after treatment. As she left she told me that she had experienced no pain and was confident that she would be well.

The final surgery to be described was performed on a distinguished looking man in his sixties wearing a well-tailored three-piece suit. His card indicated that he was a physician with his own clinic in Copacabana, an elite section of Rio de Janeiro. He had a large bandage on the left side of his neck. When Edson removed it, he exposed an infected, festering growth. One of those assisting, who happened to be a physician, could not hold back the question on the mind of all present: "How could he (the patient), a trained doctor, permit something like this to go on so long without treating it?"

Unmoved, Edson ordered the patient to take off his jacket and lie down on the table. As he did, the healer picked up a scalpel and pierced the wound which he secured with a pair of tweezers. He lifted as he cut. When blood started to spurt, he put down the scalpel to place pieces of gauze, handed to him by the nurse, over the wound.

He then told those observing that he had permitted the bleeding in order to show that this was human blood and not a trick, as has been reported about "psychic" healers in the Philippines who use the blood of a chicken and do not actually open the skin of their patients.

When the bleeding subsided, Edson picked up the scalpel and started to cut again. Cutting and stopping to control the bleeding, the growth was about half removed when he paused for questions. During surgeries Edson often stopped for questions which he answered with short sermons on Spiritist themes.

When he finished speaking he turned back to the patient, cutting away at the growth with renewed vigor. Within minutes it was removed, leaving a raw, slightly concave wound. More gauze was applied to control the bleeding. The excised flesh was handed to the pathologist. The open wound then was covered with an ointment, although the healer said that it really was not necessary. A bandage, which the healer told the patient could be removed within a few days, was placed over the area. It will heal and there will be no scar, Edson promised.

Before he left the room I asked the patient to tell me what he had experienced. In a soft, dignified

---

13. In another patient, who had complained to me earlier of a problem with her adenoids, Edson thrust needles into her throat. As the young woman sat motionlessly and did not utter a sound, the healer jammed eight needles, one at at time, into her throat only to pull them out with equal force a few seconds later. When I asked the startled patient if she had felt any pain, she at first did not answer. The healer meanwhile kidded me, saying that she did not understand my Portuguese. When she realized what was happening, she apologized explaining that she could not hear in her right ear. Immediately the healer thrust two additional needles into the ear. When he removed them the shocked woman claimed that she could now hear the questions I was asking.

14. All healing is done by Spiritists as charity.

15. In similar surgeries he had others run their finger across the bottom of their shoe and then rub it into the open wound.

voice he said that he had felt the cutting, but had experienced no pain. Stating that he now felt fine, he added that he was relieved that it was over. I asked him why he, a doctor, had come to Edson and not gone to a conventional physician when the growth first developed. With his head erect and a straight look he responded, as would most believers in Spiritist doctrine, that it was because he wanted to get at the source of the problem. Conventional doctors we know, he said with conviction, only treat symptoms and work at the surface. If you want to get at the cause you go to a Spiritist healer; and since Edson is the best, he had waited until he was able to see him in Recife.

A year later I had the opportunity to visit the doctor at his penthouse home on Avenida Atlántica overlooking Copacabana beach in Rio de Janeiro. He appeared to be, and said that he was, in excellent health. He had had no reaction to the surgery and when he showed me his neck I could find no trace of a scar.

Antônio de Oliveira Rios

In contrast with Edson, José Carlos, and most Spiritist healers who work in large urban centers, Antônio de Oliveira Rios treated patients in the small town of Palmelo, about 100 kilometers from the national capital of Brasília in the interior state of Goias.[16] Semi-literate, with only a first-grade education, and a bricklayer by trade, Antônio diagnosed illnesses from photographs brought to him by patients. Each Saturday large crowds lined up outside the Center waiting to see him. Each brought with them a photograph of themselves, or a friend or relative—the sick person did not have to be present. When their turn came the healer would look at the picture and after a few seconds write, in an almost illegible, child-like script—that had to be rewritten for the patient (or his representative) by his wife who assisted him—a diagnosis and a course of treatment that often combined medications, diet, and a visit to the Center for surgery.

In one of the surgeries I witnessed, an educated, sophisticated, business man, who had traveled by plane from São Paulo, had his stomach opened by the healer.[17] The man was lying on a gurney outside the Center when Antônio, already in trance, approached him. Pushing a cart on which surgical instruments were laid out, the healer, wearing gloves, a white jacket, and a mask, picked up a scalpel that he brought towards the patient. Before he could begin to cut, however, the man engaged him in conversation, asking about the procedure and other matters. The healer responded and before long the two were deep in conversation. Antônio, however, did not stop the surgery. As he chatted with the man on the gurney, with a hundred or more observers watching him, he thrust the scalpel into the man's chest, below the ribs, sliding it down some six to eight inches. He then took a pair of scissors with which he spread the opening he had made apart. Blood flowed and an artery soon resembled a fountain. As Antônio placed gauze inside the opening, eventually stopping the flow of blood, the patient, seemingly oblivious to what was being done to him, continued his conversation with the healer. After a minute or so of cutting, Antônio left to work on another patient, leaving the business man with his stomach open on the table in the street. Not bothered in the least, the patient, after bending over to look at the open wound, put his head back and quietly closed his eyes.

A few minutes later Antônio's wife came out the door with a needle and surgical thread in her hands. As she sutured closed the opening, which was bleeding very little now, the patient opened his eyes and engaged her in conversation as he had Antônio. When she completed her task, covering the sutured

---

16. I also use the past tense because Antônio also was killed in 1990 after being attacked by bees while fishing.

17. In contrast with José Carlos, Edson, and the other Spiritist healers with whom I have worked, Antônio, as I observed in footnote 10, said that he did not actually operate on the patients. He claimed only to cut them open. The therapeutic procedure that benefited them was performed by one of the spirits (see below) who worked with him. His wife or an assistant then sutured the patient while Antônio went off, almost in assembly-line fashion, cutting open other patients.

For treatment patients were placed on surgical tables in the several small rooms of the center. Additional patients were placed on gurneys and rolled out under an extension of the roof on the concrete side walk that faced onto the dirt road that ran through the town. On an average Sunday and Monday, when Antônio operated, there were usually several hundred people standing in the road waiting to be treated or to observe the surgeries.

area with gauze and tape, she helped the patient, who still was chatting with her, to stand up. In front of the somewhat startled crowd she wrapped a bandage around his chest and stomach and instructed him to put on his shirt. As he did so, he informed me that had had felt no discomfort, as he had not the previous time Antônio had operated on him. He then took out his business card and invited me to visit him in São Paulo to follow his progress.

The final patient whose surgery I describe also was placed on a gurney outside the Center. He told me prior to being treated that he had been the victim of a bullet wound some ten years previously and still had no use of his legs.

Antônio started by injecting something into the upper part of his back.[18] He then took a scalpel from his instrument cart and made an incision some 10 to 12 inches in length and about one-half inch deep along the spinal column. He patted the small amount of blood that flowed with some gauze. He then took a pair of scissors and jammed them at an angle into the open wound. He took another pair of scissors and used them to hammer the first pair deeper so that they could be heard hitting against the bone. After a pause he repeated the procedure.

Antônio then took from the lower shelf of the instrument cart what appeared to be a rotary, or buzz saw. The people in the street moved closer to watch what was to come next when he connected the instrument to an extension cord handed to him through an open window at the side of the building. The patient meanwhile remained motionless, apparently unaware of the saw. Antônio turned on the instrument and inserted its churning blade into the open wound, running it along the spinal column. A small amount of blood spurted up as the opening in the patient's back was enlarged. The onlookers gasped. The patient, however, did not react.

After running the blade up and down the patient's back a few times, Antônio turned off the saw, disconnected it from the extension cord, removed the blade, and returned the parts to the shelf on the cart. Without stopping to look at the patient, he pushed the cart hurriedly through the door into the building, stopping it in front of what was to be his next patient. The man lying quietly on the gurney in the street with his back open was left unattended.

A few minutes later Antônio's wife exited the building with a needle and surgical thread in her hands. She sutured closed the patient's back and covered the area with a bandage. Before I could get to him several of the onlookers questioned him about what he had experienced. He had felt no pain and was only slightly uncomfortable when the saw blade entered his back. As he left with the friends who had helped him travel to the healer he gave me his address in São Paulo so that I could visit him on my next visit to that city.

The Patients and Trance States in Brazilian Culture

Having described a small sample of the somewhat unusual, if not spectacular, surgeries I have observed and video taped over the past decade, procedures that if for no other reason than that the patients survive, let alone get better, challenge some of the basic truths of Western science and medicine, I turn now to their explanation. The question I address in the second part of this paper is: How do we explain or account for the fact that patients on whom surgeries are performed by Brazilian Spiritist healer-mediums who do not use antisepsis or anesthesia, and who often not only do not wash their hands between procedures but deliberately introduce contaminants into open wounds, experience little or no pain, bleed but minimally and rarely if ever become infected or develop other complications?[19] The answer I propose starts from the assumption that the patients are in an ASC when surgery is performed on them.

During the nineteenth century, it must be remembered, after the Marquis de Puysegur's refinement and elaboration of Franz Anton Mesmer's hypnotic therapy, and before the introduction of chemical anesthesia, we have documentation of numerous successful surgeries by Elliotson (Hilgard and Hilgard 1975:4,63) and Esdaile (1975[1850]) that share at least some of the features of what has been described above. And today

---

18. I was unable to learn what was in the syringe.

19. This, of course, is an overgeneralization. Some patients, as we have seen above, do bleed, at times profusely. Others occasionally feel excruciating pain and still others develop post-surgical complications. Given the number of surgeries performed by the healer-mediums, hundreds at each session, those reacting negatively are such a tiny fraction of the total that the majority effect calls out for explanation.

we have documented cases of surgeries performed in hospitals on patients in a state of hypnotic trance that also show results comparable in part with what has been described above.[20]

Ernest L. Rossi (1986) has proposed what thus far is perhaps the most comprehensive, though controversial, theory of the psychophysiology of the relationship between trance states and healing. Using information theory as a metaphor, he has developed a communications model as a way around the Cartesian mind-body dualism. He proposes thinking of the human organism as a communication system in which by means of a series of translations (or transductions) information is conveyed from the mind to the several bodily systems—the autonomic nervous system, the endocrine system, the immune system, and the neuropeptide system—and back, with each system encoding what is received from the others. Information vital to its own functioning and to that of the total organism then is constantly flowing from one bodily system to the others.

Information, Rossi hypothesizes, is transmitted and then encoded in each system under specific conditions related to the unique experiences of the individual. This learned information, which itself at times may precipitate symptomatic conditions, may be accessed for treatment. Since the mind (and the cultural content to which it has been exposed) in this framework is a part of the communications network, it can be used to obtain information about illness, the conditions under which it was encoded, etc. It also can convey information that can be used to modify the situation resulting in the possible disappearance of the symptoms. Rossi proposes hypnosis, the ASC his associate Milton Erickson reintroduced into Western psychotherapy and used so effectively, as a means of accessing what he calls state dependent learning—the unique conditions under which the information associated with an illness (that may be causing it) first was encoded. In trance a patient often can access, through translations from the bodily system that is malfunctioning, information that can help in treatment. Accessing state dependent memory may be, as Rossi

(1986:55) proposes, "the common denominator between traditional Western medicine and the holistic, shamanistic, and spiritistic approaches to healing that depend upon highly specialized cultural belief systems, world views, and frames of reference."

According to Brazilian Spiritists, however, the surgeries described here were done not by the healers, but rather by the spirits of Ignatius of Loyola, Dr. Adolph Fritz, Dr. Ricardo Stams and others. Spiritism teaches that there are two worlds, or planes of reality, the one in which we live and another inhabited by spirits, the assumed vital force in the universe. In seeking moral advancement individual spirits are believed to return periodically to the material world, reincarnating as human beings to learn lessons (see Cavalcanti 1983; Greenfield 1987; Greenfield and Gray 1988; Kardec n.d.). Humans, according to this view, are spirits incarnate temporarily in a material body.

Spiritists also believe that communication and contact are possible between the material world and the world of the spirits. They further maintain that spirits in the other plane can return for short periods to this world through the bodies of special individuals who are called mediums. José Carlos Ribeiro, Edson Queiroz and Antônio de Oliveira Rios are mediums, special mediums able to receive and incorporate spirits who in previous incarnations were trained as and practiced as physicians, surgeons and healers. In Spiritist parlance they are known as healer-mediums. Using their bodies the spirits of disincarnate physicians and healers—wishing to advance spiritually without reincarnating—are able to return to the material world to do the good works (charity) of treating the sick (see Greenfield 1987; McGregor 1967; Renshaw 1969). Dr. Adolph Fritz, a German physician who is believed to have last been incarnate during the First World War, for example, works through Edson Queiroz. Dr. Ricardo Stams, another German of World War I vintage, treats patients through the healer-medium Antônio de Oliveira Rios,[21] while Ignatius of Loyola ministers

---

20. At the symposium in New Orleans when this paper was first presented a videotape was shown of a hysterectomy performed on a patient who had been induced into hypnotic trance. On the same videotape I showed some of the procedures described in Part I of this paper.

21. Drs. Fritz and Stams, in the tradition of modern medicine are said to be assisted by a team of disincarnate healers each of whom takes over the medium's body when their specialty is required. On each team there is said to be an anesthetist and someone providing asepses. This is the explanation for the absence of pain, infections and other complications.

to the ill through the mediumship of José Carlos Ribeiro.

To receive their spirit guides, José Carlos, Edson, Antônio and other healer-mediums go into trance at the beginning of each treatment session, usually in the presence of associates who assist them.[22]

Spiritist writers, and most observers, go into great detail describing and analyzing how mediums go into trance and the changes that take place in them when their spirits arrive. Writing about another part of the world Michele Stephen (1989:218) provides yet another example of what to me is misplaced attention. "In Western techniques, such as hypnotism . . . ," she writes,

> the patient is usually encouraged to experience an altered state of consciousness (told to relax, for example), while guided by the suggestions and instructions of the therapist. A contrast, which I think has so far gone unnoticed, is that in shamanism and other traditional healing techniques, it is the healer, not the patient, who induces an altered state in himself, wherein he experiences the healing imagery.

Focusing on the healer and not the patient may be appropriate for symbolic analysis; it is not if we wish to understand the psychophysiology of the healing process.

Most of the patients treated by Brazilian Spiritist healers also are in an ASC when being operated on or otherwise treated.[23] Spiritist healer-mediums and other believers, however, deny—often vehemently—that patients are in trance when being treated.[24] They say this, I believe, because no one is consciously aware of hypnotizing, or otherwise trying to induce patients into ASCs, and unlike the mediums, patients participate in no ritual during which they may be seen to enter a trance state.

If patients are in an ASC when being treated, however, and this helps to explain the unusual if not spectacular results achieved by the healers, how do they enter a trance state without an induction procedure? The answer, I suggest, is to be found in Brazilian culture which has patterned certain contexts in which individuals, in response to a range of cues, learn to enter trance states.[25] To understand how this works let me turn briefly first to some of the basic features of hypnosis and then to Brazilian culture and a hypothesized model of how it patterns trance induction.

Hypnosis, the ASC that has been best studied scientifically, refers to two interdependent features: 1) a state of heightened suggestibility said to resemble sleep; and 2) the procedure for its induction. "Hypnotic suggestibility" refers to both a trait or capacity and the state in which an individual accepts, as true, with varying degrees of intensity of receptivity, information, presented in a particular way and under particular conditions.

The procedure for an individual entering an hypnotic ASC centers on the establishment of a special relationship between the hypnotist and a subject or client—"hypnotic rapport." Two other traits also appear to be critical: 1) fantasy proneness of the subject—his or her capacity to imagine and believe what is imagined; and 2) the capacity for total attention (absorption).

Hypnotic induction then centers on the establishment of a special relationship between a person being hypnotized and a hypnotist and it works best on people who are fantasy prone and can concentrate (focus) their attention.

---

22. The medium himself, or some member of the group, will begin a brief ritual by first invoking God and asking His blessing and cooperation and then appealing to Jesus Christ—who is not seen as the son of God, but as a great healer and one of the most advanced spirits ever to appear on this planet. Someone then reads a passage from the scriptures—as interpreted by Allan Kardec. During the reading the healer-medium goes into trance incorporating the spirit who then takes over the session.

23. This first was brought to my attention by a group of stage magicians to whom I showed videotapes of the surgeries described above at a magician's convention. While confirming that the healers really were cutting into the flesh of the patients—and that there was no sleight of hand—they pointed out the signs that indicated that the patients also were in a trance state that in their words resembled hypnosis, not that induced during a formal procedure, but like what some of them were able to do with members of an audience.

---

24. The most common statement is that the patients have not been hypnotized, nor have they been magnetized. The use of the word magnetized is evidence of the historical connection between Spiritist beliefs and the thinking of Franz Anton Mesmer.

25. For the development of this insight I am deeply indebted to my friend and colleague Patric Giesler.

Let me begin with the importance of fantasy-prone subjects for hypnotic induction. Brazilian culture, in contrast with our own, for example, teaches, reinforces, and rewards fantasy. Children (and adults) who claim to see the Virgin Mary, Saint Francis, some other saint, or other supernatural being not only are not punished or taken to a therapist—as they would be in North America and Western Europe—but are rewarded and held up for praise. Those who claim to "receive" a spirit, whether a doctor from the past like Adolph Fritz or Ricardo Stams, or a deity from Africa such as Iemanja, Oxala, etc. as in Candomble, Xango or Batuque, or the spirit of a former slave (a *preto velho*) or an Indian (a *caboclo*) as in Umbanda (Brown 1986; Greenfield and Gray 1989; Greenfield and Prust 1990; Pressel, 1974), not only are believed, but their help is sought by others who treat them deferentially and with respect. Participants in the Spiritist tradition, or in one of the several Afro-Brazilian religions, learn to go into trance and to believe that they, or others around them, are possessed. And since most Brazilians, from just about all geographical regions, classes and segments of the population are exposed to and participate to some degree in these alternative religious (and healing traditions—including "Popular" Catholicism), we may conclude that Brazilians in general, like good hypnotic subjects in North America and Western Europe, are able to imagine and believe what they imagine.[26]

Besides creating a society composed of a large number of fantasy prone individuals, Brazilian culture also patterns social relationships in ways that share elements similar to that between hypnotist and client. I refer here to social relationships of patronage and clientage that have long characterized the society (see Greenfield 1968, 1972, 1977, 1979; Hutchinson 1966; Roniger 1981, 1987, 1990; Strickon and Greenfield 1972).

Many of the new urban religious leaders function as patrons to their client-followers (see Brown 1986; Greenfield 1990; Greenfield and Prust 1990).[27] They

fill a social and economic void, providing needed services, as the society has urbanized and modernized. The spirits—and/or deities—they receive have come to be viewed as supernatural patrons who validate and reinforce the social acceptance of their mediums. Desperate urban clients then willingly accept the help of the new patrons. They place their trust in the religious leaders and in return for the help given them are willing to do almost anything asked of them. They obey every suggestion, not to speak of command, made by their religious leader, healer-patron. The patron-client relationship in urban Brazil then shares many of the features of that between successful hypnotist and client.

Countless Brazilians then are fantasy prone and sincerely believe that the supernaturals and other entities they imagine both are real and will help them in their daily life. They learn to enter trance easily and ASCs are a part of their ordinary life. Furthermore, they have learned to trust their patron, who often is a medium for helping spirits and/or dieties. Like clients in a hypnotist-client relationship, dependents in a patron-client relationship trust their patron and willingly accept as true and act positively in response to what he or she tells them.

Therefore, although no formal induction procedures are used by religious leaders and healers, their client-dependents, who have been socialized to recognize and acknowledge ASCs, and to enter them, often go effortlessly into trance when they are in the presence of a José Carlos Ribeiro, an Edson Queiroz, an Antônio de Oliveira Rios or other healer who is known to be a medium for spirits who are believed to be able to heal them and perhaps also help them with a range of their other problems, problems they have no other way to resolve.

We may conclude from this that Brazilians, in the absence of formal induction procedures, tend to enter trance states easily, usually in response to cues not consciously intended, by a religious leader and/or healer. And although the latter may not be aware of what he or she is doing, the result may well be that patients become receptive to suggestions that enable them to access their bodily systems and processes in ways they could not do in an ordinary state of consciousness. They may be able, as are hypnotized subjects in the laboratory or clinic, to control pain, alter the flow of their blood—to slow down bleeding or speed it up to heal wounds more

---

26. It is interesting to add that the elaborate costumes made and worn for Carnival are called "fantasias."

27. Edson Queiroz, for example, had been elected to the legislature of the State of Pernambuco less than two years before he was killed. Other Spiritists, Umbandistas and leaders of alternative religious groups also have been elected to office or have been influential in electing other public officials.

rapidly—and probably also access state dependent memories that may enable them to communicate changes, as Rossi hypothesizes, that result in their being able to heal a variety of symptomatic conditions. Unaware of what they are doing or what is happening to them, I would propose that large numbers of fantasy prone clients of Brazilian religious leaders and/or healers are induced into trance states by the mere presence of a powerful patron who often also is the medium for a powerful supernatural. Once in trance the client-patient responds to suggestions as do hypnotized subjects. The difference is that in Brazil there is no need for a formal induction procedure. Given the cultural assumptions and the socialization process, relating to a patron in certain contexts induces the dependent into a trance state in which he or she accepts as real, and acts on, the suggestions of his (or her) patron. Where the patron is a healer, much of what happens during a successful hypnotic induction takes place with the patient demonstrating some of the extreme behavioral responses we are just beginning to understand.

25

On the Peyote Road

Mike Kiyaani and Thomas J. Csordas

The peyote religion—or "Peyote Way," as it is known by its members—is followed by some 250,000 American Indians. Peyote (the name is derived from the Aztec word peyotl) *was used by Indians in central and northern Mexico in pre-Columbian years, its use spreading north to the Indians in the United States and Canada around 1890. Since 1918, peyotists have been organized as the Native American Church, and, despite recurring legal issues (peyote contains the hallucinogenic agent mescaline and thus is classified as a controlled substance), it has become an important religious movement among North American Indians. Although there are tribal and community differences in the ceremonies and beliefs of Native American Church members, the practice of peyotism is decidedly similar across groups. The leader of a peyote rite is known as a road man because he leads the group along the peyote road to a life of dignity and respect for nature and for other people. In this brief selection, Thomas J. Csordas introduces the reader to one such road man, Mike Kiyaani. Kiyaani, a Navajo who first used peyote in the late 1940s, served in World War II as a marine "code talker." (Due to its complexity, the Navajo language proved to be an ideal way to communicate secret information.) Kiyaani recounts his first introduction to peyote and how it changed his life, then briefly describes a peyote ceremony and how ingestion of the peyote buttons affects the individual. Kiyaani ends the selection by expressing his worry about white people becoming involved with peyote, observing that Native Americans use the herb with more sincerity.*

Most Americans know peyote only as a cactus containing an illegal psychotropic substance, but to some 250,000 American Indian adherents of the peyote religion, it is a sacrament and a spirit. To live according to its inspiration is to follow the peyote road of personal dignity and respect for nature and for other people. Those recognized as having the ability to lead others along this path are known as "road men." Mike Kiyaani, who underwent his own long apprenticeship, is such a road man. Now seventy-seven, Kiyaani is a Navajo who first used peyote in the late 1940s, after returning to his native Arizona

as an honored veteran of military service. He had served in an elite Marine unit, along with other Navajos who used their complex native language to communicate sensitive information—a code that defied penetration.

The peyote religion, formally institutionalized as the Native American Church, was introduced to the Navajos in the 1930s by members of several Plains Indian tribes. Its practices and spirituality differ from those of the traditional Navajo religion, although both are fundamentally concerned with healing. Traditional Navajo medicine men—Kiyaani's own father was one—lead ceremonies known as chants. Lasting as long as nine consecutive nights, chants involve prayers in the form of songs, specific acts by the healer and patient, and the creation of potent visual symbols such as sand paintings. A peyote ceremony, in contrast, is a prayer meeting during which peyote is eaten by participants under the leadership of a road man. Combining singing, drumming, and prayers, the ceremony typically lasts one night, from dusk to dawn.

Assembled in a tepee or hogan, the participants focus their prayers on an altar or fire place. In the style learned by Mike Kiyaani, the centerpiece of the fire place is a crescent of heaped-up earth on which rests a special cactus button known as the chief peyote. The road man cherishes his chief peyote and may pass it down through several generations. Kiyaani concentrates on his chief peyote and the fire place to facilitate his dialogue with nature. He says that whereas white people talk directly to God, the humble prefer going through the intermediary of nature—the air and the sunshine, which are God's creations. Kiyaani is not a shaman who takes spirit flights to other worlds but a healer who prays through the elements of nature in which, for him, God already resides.

Mike Kiyaani's mentor was Truman Dailey, an Oto Indian who instructed him not to imitate Plains Indian ways but to take the medicine home and adapt its use to the Navajo culture and way of life. For Dailey, the elements of the altar represent parts of the eagle, which is sacred to his clan. Kiyaani stresses the Navajo understanding of corn as a symbol of growth and life. He performs the traditional corn pollen blessing, sprinkling some grains to make a path that corresponds to the peyote road. He also uses a song learned from his father that metaphorically connects the prayer meeting to the growth of the life-giving corn plant.

Navajo adherents of the peyote religion once faced opposition from their own tribal government, which decreed the religion illegal in 1940 and did not move for tolerance until 1966. Only in 1994 did the federal government adopt a law that guarantees the right of American Indians to practice the peyote religion. Mike Kiyaani remains deeply concerned that, against the background of a long struggle for freedom of religion, the use of peyote be protected for its importance in healing, spirituality, and identity. He has traveled widely to describe his work to audiences of health care professionals, and on the reservation his reputation as a road man keeps him in great demand by Navajos who travel considerable distances to seek his assistance.—T.J.C.

I'm a Navajo veteran—World War II, Navajo Code Talker, wounded in action. My clan is Salt Clan. I got my name from Kiyaani; that's my grandfather's clan. When I came back from the war, I was a sick man. There was something wrong with my mind, something wrong all over my body. No pain, but I felt kind of lousy. My father had died in 1944, and I guess that's what got into me. One man I got acquainted with took me to Oklahoma. I met this man Truman Dailey there, and he noticed my condition. He said, "You take this peyote," and gave me a twenty-five-pound flour sack filled with Mexican dry peyote. I took that back home.

During that time I was way up there where nobody lives, herding sheep, and I used peyote. Just a little bit during the day, every day. It seemed like it went all through my system. Then one particular day I felt like eating, and I had fifty buttons. In about another hour and a half, I ate another fifty buttons—maybe four times, fifty buttons. At midnight everything started coming. My life seemed to be coming to an end. That's the way the medicine showed me, but I still kept on eating until morning. Everything began coming out different. There was a lot of sagebrush out there, and everything was too beautiful. But every time I looked to the peyote, it wasn't pleasant to look at.

Then toward noon I looked for that peyote, and now I saw it was real pure, real white. It kind of talked to me, "Your body is like that, your body is pure. Now you don't need treatment, you're a well man. You wanted to get well, now you're well." I understood it to be that way. At that time I sure cried. I was all right then. After that I was pretty much on the go most of the time performing ceremonies for sick people. I kind of experimented with the peyote eating, how it works, how it can heal.

At the start of the ceremony, I don't know what's ailing the patient, but when you take some peyote into your system, the peyote affects you, and then you kind of know. A lot of people just say, "I'm sick," that's all. They don't know exactly what's bothering them. But peyote does wonderful things. My patient eats peyote. He has peyote in his system. Peyote is in my system, too. He's talking; then I kind of know. I kind of see things, what's wrong in that way. It's the peyote that shows me things. It's my patient talking his mind—the way he talks, the way he expresses himself. It might be his action in there that's kind of unusual; that tells me. But I don't watch him directly, I keep my eyes on the fire all the time.

I say, "You come to me, and I want you to help yourself; whatever it is that's bothering your mind, whatever it is you think that's bothering your health, get your mind off of it. You get on to this medicine, this fire place, this singing that you hear, the prayers that you are hearing in here, which are all for you. The people sitting here, they're talking for you. They're singing for you. Everybody wants you to get well. Whatever's bothering you—maybe it's an evil, maybe it's that lightning struck near you, maybe something else. Get your mind off of it." He might have a hard time [from nausea] through the peyote effect, but that's going to help him. That's the time he's going to figure out what's wrong, why he's sick.

I go outside for a special ceremony at midnight. I get my bone whistle out. Some medicine men take their flashlight out there or maybe take somebody with them out there. I don't do those things. I'd rather be in the dark, praying by myself. A lot of Navajos, while they're out there, they see something, visualize something. I don't look for those things. But I might be hearing that the patient's mind is bothered by witchcraft or maybe some lightning struck that might be affecting his body, his mind.

Peyote. You eat it and it goes through your body, your blood veins, your flesh, your bone, your brain, and we talk to this peyote. And this peyote goes through all the patient's blood veins, goes to his brain, brain vessel; it seems like we talk to the peyote like that. Talking with nature; that's all it is. Whatever you do, peyote knows it, nature knows it. Whatever is wrong inside here, nature knows it. The Almighty knows it, so there's no way you can get away from this peyote, from this Almighty, from nature. If at some place you get off the road, then you notice it. Then you come back and pray. You go back to the Almighty, back to peyote. You get back on the road.

The spirit peyote came up among the Navajo people on a very hard road. But peyote found its way here, and so you see it has some kind of power. It found its way into the Navajo people, into the Navajo hogan, into the heart. Where the heart is, this peyote goes in there. So I want this thing to go on, this peyote religion, peyote worship. It's something for Indians who are humble. Just like in the Bible—it says the meek shall inherit the earth.

Now I'm worried the white man is going to go for it. That's what they usually do. That's what we don't want to happen. I don't think it's for the white people. This natural herb peyote is used by Native Americans with more sincerity. Indian people are more serious in their mind, in their heart, in the way they worship. Just let the Indians have it, let the Indians use it the way they want it, just natural. Our identity is there.

26

Ritual Enemas

Peter T. Furst and Michael D. Coe

As we have seen in earlier articles, many of the world's cultures contain religious specialists and laypeople who routinely undergo, for ritual purposes, an altering of their normal state of consciousness. Although this state can be obtained by non-drug-related methods, it is not uncommon to find ethnographic accounts of drugs being used to enhance and quicken an altered state of consciousness. This article is about the religious use of various psychoactive substances among the Mayan Indians of central Mexico. The authors note that, although hallucinogenic mushrooms, morning glories, and other psychedelic plants were known and used by the Maya, yet another substance seems to have been employed—intoxicating enemas. This phenomenon quite clearly appears in Maya art as early as the first millennium A.D.; it is curious that it has not been described in the literature over the years. Ritual enemas were well known in South America, where rubber tree sap was used for bulbed syringes. Furst and Coe reason that a rectal infusion of intoxicants could result in a more quickly and more radically changed state of consciousness, with fewer negative side effects.

When the Spaniards conquered Mexico in the sixteenth century, they were at once fascinated and repelled by the Indians' widespread use not only of alcoholic beverages but also of numerous hallucinogenic plants.

From the Spaniards' point of view, however, both served the same purpose—to conjure up visions of demons and devils and to take imbibers from their daily life to supernatural realms.

Distillation was unknown in the New World before the conquest, but Mesoamerican Indians were making, as they still do, a variety of intoxicating ritual drinks, principally by fermenting cactus fruit; agave, or century plant, sap; or maize kernels. Among the Maya, the ritual beverage was balche, made from fermented honey mixed with a bark extract from the balche tree, *Lonchocarpus longistylus.* These concoctions were all taken orally.

"Ritual Enemas" by Peter T. Furst & Michael D. Coe reprinted from NATURAL HISTORY, March 1977, pp. 88–91; copyright © Natural History Magazine, Inc., 1977.

But according to a Spanish writer known only as the Anonymous Conqueror, the Huastec people of northern Veracruz and southern Tamaulipas had pulque (fermented agave sap) "squirted into their breech," meaning that they used intoxicating enemas. There are indications that the Aztecs, as well as several other Mesoamerican groups, also followed this practice.

Mesoamerican Indians generally used liquor only on sacred occasions, when, according to such sixteenth-century observers as Bishop Diego de Landa of Yucatán, the Indians often drank themselves into states approaching oblivion. Similarly, the use of many botanical hallucinogens, first described by Fray Bernardino de Sahagún and his contemporaries, was strictly limited to occasions when direct communication with the otherworld was required. Today, the best known of these is peyote, *Lophophora williamsii,* a small, spineless cactus native to the north-central desert of Mexico and southern Texas. The plant now serves as sacrament for 225,000 adherents of the Native American Church and also plays an important role in the religious life of the

Huichol Indians of western Mexico. Before the conquest, peyote was widely traded throughout Mexico, where the Aztec priests numbered it among their important magical and medicinal plants.

At the time of the conquest the seeds of the white-flowered morning glory *Turbina corymbosa* were a widely used hallucinogen. In 1960, Albert Hofmann, the Swiss discoverer of LSD (a synthetic hallucinogenic drug), isolated the active alkaloids in this morning glory species and a related species, the purple- or blue-flowered *Ipomoea violacea,* and found them to be lysergic acid derivatives closely resembling LSD-25. The latter species is often referred to as "heavenly blue" in the United States.

Mushrooms also played an important role in preconquest Mesoamerican Indian life. Certain species, most of them now known to belong to the genus *Psilocybe,* were perhaps the most extraordinary natural hallucinogens in use in Mexico. The Aztecs called them *teonanácatl,* or "God's flesh." Psychedelic fungi were widely employed in Mexico when the Spaniards came, and their use in divination and supernatural curing survives to this day in central Mexico, as well as in the state of Oaxaca (*see* "Drugs, Chants, and Magic Mushrooms," *Natural History,* December 1975). The Indians even used tobacco to induce ecstatic trance states, which the Spanish only saw as diabolic communication.

While Spanish writers of the sixteenth and seventeenth centuries left us relatively detailed accounts of the use of hallucinogens in central Mexico, there is little mention of this intriguing aspect of native religion among the Maya, who lived farther to the south. The silence is the more puzzling because we have circumstantial evidence of a very early cult of sacred mushrooms in the Maya highlands of Guatemala and the adjacent lowlands, in the form of more than 250 mushroom effigies made of carved stone, many dating to the first millennium B.C.

The Maya were an integral part of Mesoamerican civilization and shared many of its basic assumptions about the nature of the universe and the relationship of humans to the natural and supernatural environment. Like the central Mexicans, they divided the cosmos into upperworlds and underworlds with their respective gods, believed in the cyclical destruction and regeneration of the earth and its inhabitants, and followed the 260-day ritual calendar.

In view of these many similarities, as the Maya scholar J. Eric Thompson has written, it was hard to believe that the Maya did not use intoxicating plants. Thompson searched the pages of sacred traditional books of the Yucatec Maya, set down in the European alphabet in the colonial period, for hints of ecstatic visionary trances through which the priests made their prophecies. In the *Books of Chilam Balam* (jaguar-priest) of Tizimín and Maní, he found mention of trancelike states but no hint whatever of any hallucinogenic plants. He also discovered scattered scenes in Maya relief sculpture that suggested visionary experiences characteristic of hallucinogenic ritual.

This is slim evidence, however, compared with the data from central Mexico, and some Maya scholars are not convinced that the Maya practiced the kinds of ecstatic shamanistic rituals or vision quests with botanical hallucinogens that played so pervasive a role in central Mexico, or among the Zapotecs, Mixtecs, Mazatecs, and other peoples of Oaxaca.

The silence of Spanish colonial writers on the subject of hallucinogenic plants or rituals among the Maya accords well with the view, once widely held among scholars, that the Maya were quite unlike their Mexican contemporaries in temperament, being less preoccupied with warfare and the Dionysian excesses than with the contemplative interpretation of the heavens and the passage of time. But the discovery at Bonampak, Chiapas, of mural paintings that depict, among other events, a fierce battle among Maya warriors, indicate that this traditional view is very wide of the mark.

As specialists have more closely examined Maya art and iconography in recent years, they have accumulated increasing evidence that among the classic Maya, ecstatic ritual was important. One suggestion for this is that some of the major Mexican hallucinogens—among them the morning glories and the hallucinogenic mushroom *Stropharia cubensis*—occur in the Maya country. These and other psychedelic plants were undoubtedly known to the Maya.

Had Maya specialists looked more closely at the earliest dictionaries of the Quiché and Cakchiquel languages, compiled in the first centuries after the conquest of highland Guatemala, they would have discovered mention of several varieties of mushrooms with hallucinogenic properties. One is called *xibalbaj okox* (*xibalba* means "underworld," or "land of the dead," and *okox,* "mushroom"), said by the sixteenth-century compiler to give those who eat it visions of hell. If the association of this species with the Maya underworld left any doubt of its psychedelic nature, it is dispelled by a later reference to the same species in Fray Tomas Coto's dictionary of the Cakchiquel language. According to him, *xibalbaj okox* was also called *k'aizalah okox*, which translates as the "mushroom that makes one lose one's judgment." Still another fungus, *k'ekc'un*, had inebriating characteristics, and another, *muxan okox*, apparently brought on insanity or caused one to "fall into a swoon."

We have recently come across a wholly unexpected use of psychoactive substances among the Maya—the ritual use of intoxicating enemas, unmistakably depicted in classic Maya art of the first millennium A.D., but not mentioned either in the colonial or the modern literature. This practice is well documented among the inhabitants of South American tropical forests as well as among the Inca and their contemporaries in the Andes, where archeologists have discovered enema syringes.

Sixteenth-century sources describe the Incas as regularly intoxicating themselves with infusions of *willka*, now known to be the potent hallucinogenic seeds of the acacialike *Anadenanthera colubrina* tree. Lowland Indians also used tobacco enemas.

South American Indians were the first people known to use native rubber tree sap for bulbed enema syringes. While medical enemas had a long history in the Old World, having been used by ancient Sumerians and Egyptians, as well as by Hindus, Arabs, Chinese, Greeks, and Romans, the rubber bulb syringe was unknown in Europe until two centuries after the discovery of the New World.

The native Amerindian enema was distinguished from its Old World counterpart in that its primary purpose was to introduce medicines and intoxicants into the body, while the Old World enema was employed principally to clear the bowels. During the seventeenth and eighteenth centuries, the enema as a relief for constipation, real or imagined, became a craze in Europe—so much so, that Louis XIV had more than 2,000 enemas administered to him during his reign, sometimes even receiving court functionaries and foreign dignitaries during the procedure.

The wide dissemination of the intoxicating enema in South America suggests the discovery by Indians that the rectal administration of intoxicants could radically alter one's state of consciousness more rapidly, and with fewer undesirable side effects,

such as nausea, than oral administration. The physiological reason is simple: Substances injected into the rectum enter the colon, the last segment of the large intestine; the principal function of the large intestine is the reabsorption of liquids into the system and the storage of wastes until they can be evacuated. The absorbed liquid immediately enters the bloodstream, which carries it to the brain. An intoxicant or hallucinogen injected rectally closely resembles an intravenous injection in the rapidity of its effects.

The first evidence that not only the Huastecs, whose language is related to the Maya languages, but also the classic Maya knew of and employed the intoxicating enema came to light this past year through the examination of a painted vase in a private collection in New York. This polychrome jar, with a high, vertical neck and flaring rim, was probably painted in the heavily forested Petén district of northern Guatemala during the classic Maya phase, which dated from the third century A.D. to the first decades of the seventh century. Seven male-female pairs, the women easily distinguished by their robes and long hair, are depicted in two horizontal rows. That one woman is fondling a child suggests a familial setting. The activity being portrayed would have brought blushes to the cheeks of the traditional Maya specialist, for while one man is inserting a syringe into his rectum, this delicate task is being carried out for another male by his consort. One male also has a bulbed enema syringe tucked into his belt.

Nine vases, identical in shape to the actual vessel, are painted between the couples, and painted dots at the mouth of each represents a foaming, fermented liquid that is probably balche, the common alcoholic drink among the Maya at the time of the conquest. We must conclude that the people on the vase are taking intoxicating enemas, a practice previously unrecorded for this culture.

An understanding of the scenes depicted on the Maya vase was only the first link in a chain of iconographic discovery of the Mesoamerican enema phenomenon. Suddenly, several previously enigmatic scenes and objects in classic Maya art had new meaning. A small clay figurine from a burial excavated in 1964 by Mexican archeologists on the island of Jaina, in the Gulf of Campeche, depicts a male in squatting position, his hand reaching back to his rectum. For a long time Maya experts were puzzled because the figure's position seemed to represent defecation. But would the Maya have interred such a scene as an offering to their dead?

A small hole in the anus suggested that a piece was missing—that some small object previously inserted there had either become lost during excavation or had been made of some perishable material, long since decayed. The discovery of the enema vase from the Petén district seems to have solved the riddle. The little Maya was probably not defecating but was in the act of giving himself an enema.

The gods themselves were also depicted as indulging in the enema ritual. One Maya vase has the figures of thirty-one underworld deities painted on it. A naturalistically designed enema syringe dangles from the paw of one of the principal figures. Maya experts did not recognize the significance of the object until they had examined the enema vase in New York. As another example, a polychrome bowl from Yucatán, now in the National Museum of Anthropology in Mexico City, shows a naked being with a pointed head injecting himself with liquid.

The ritual importance of the intoxicating enema is highlighted by the involvement in the rite of one of the greatest underworld deities, an old lord associated with earth, water, and agricultural fertility. The Maya may have believed that this god—now identified by Mayanists only by the letter N, but very likely the same deity as the ancient Yucatecan god Pauhatun—consisted of four parts, each part living in the underworld and supporting the four corners of the earth.

The quadripartite god is depicted on a fine vase in a private collection in Chicago. Each of the four parts has a characteristically chapfallen face. Four young and fetching consorts are apparently preparing each of the god's representations for the enema rite. Enema pots with syringes on top are in front of two of the consorts. The female consorts may well represent the important Mother Goddess of the Maya, known as Ixchel, as several figurine examples of the god N embracing this goddess have been found.

The same association of the god N, females and enemas is depicted on another pottery vase, with a consort shown standing behind each god representation and untying his loincloth. Again, the same enema pots are in front of the consorts. So often are the pottery forms and syringes encountered together that we must conclude that they were commonly used in the enema rite.

The explicit depiction of enema rituals on Maya vases has led us to take a new look at a hitherto puzzling type of clay figurine from central Veracruz, which also dates from the classic Maya period. Some archeologists have interpreted these curious sculptures as representing human sacrifice. They are usually of males whose facial expressions suggest pleasure or ecstatic trance, not death. Their legs are raised, either draped over a high pillow or some other type of support of else slightly spread, with the feet up in the air. The posture—and the enraptured look—suggest the intoxicating enema. The reclining position also conforms to the Anonymous Conqueror's description of the method of enema intoxication among the Huastecs.

The hallucinogenic or intoxicating enema has apparently not disappeared altogether from Middle America. While conducting linguistic research in the Sierra Madre Occidental in western Mexico some years ago, ethnographer Tim Knab was shown a peyote apparatus reportedly used by an elderly woman curer. The bulb was made from a deer's bladder and the tube from the hollow femur of a small deer. The curer prepared peyote by grinding it to a fine pulp and diluting it with water. Instead of taking the peyote by mouth, as for example, the Huichols normally do, either whole or ground (see "An Indian Journey to Life's Source," *Natural History*, April 1973), she injected it rectally, experiencing its effects almost at once while avoiding its bitter and acrid taste and the nausea that even some experienced Indian *peyoteros* continue to feel as they chew the sacred plant.

We do not know what materials the ancient Maya used for their syringes. The deer was sacred to the Maya, as it still is to Indians in western Mexico. Still, to make the transition from contemporary western Mexico to the Maya requires an enormous jump in time and space. Fish bladders and the bones of birds, which are prominent in Maya art, might have served for the syringe, as might rubber from the latex tree, which is native to the Maya region. More important than the precise technology, however, is the discovery that, no less than the simpler folk of the South American tropical rain forests, the creators of the most flamboyant and intellectually advanced native civilization in the New World hit upon the enema as a technique of intoxication or ecstasy—a practical means of ritually altering or transforming the ordinary state of consciousness.

27

The Sound of Rushing Water

Michael Harner

Native peoples of the Amazon region, as in the case of forest dwellers everywhere, have a tremendous depth of understanding of the chemical properties of plants indigenous to their habitats. Extracts of plants are prepared as medicines that are used both in the Western pharmacological sense and in the supernatural sense. Preparations take a variety of forms and range from ebene, *the snuff used by the Yanomamo of Brazil and Venezuela, to the hallucinogenic drink* natema, *used by the Jívaro of Ecuador. Both contain hallucinogenic properties, provide the taker entry into the spirit world, and offer powers otherwise unattainable without ingestion of potent alkaloid compounds. However, elsewhere, as among the Warao of South America, nonhallucinogenic drugs, such as tobacco, are consumed by shamans to achieve a similar ecstatic state, which, as in the case of* ebene *and* natema, *provides visions of spirit helpers and other agents of the supernatural world (Wilbert 1972). Comparisons such as these give anthropologists insight into the importance of shared belief systems and suggestibility. Describing the use of the* Banisteriopsis *vine by Jívaro shamans, Michael Harner draws on his field data to illustrate the use of the hallucinogenic drink* natema. *Called by a variety of names in other Amazonian societies, this drug gives extraordinary powers to cure or bewitch, and shamans specialize in either one or the other.*

He had drunk, and now he softly sang. Gradually, faint lines and forms began to appear in the darkness, and the shrill music of the *tsentsak*, the spirit helpers, arose around him. The power of the drink fed them. He called, and they came. First, *pangi*, the anaconda, coiled about his head, transmuted into a crown of gold. Then *wampang*, the giant butterfly, hovered above his shoulder and sang to him with its wings. Snakes, spiders, birds, and bats danced in the air above him. On his arms appeared a thousand eyes as his demon helpers emerged to search the night for enemies.

The sound of rushing water filled his ears, and listening to its roar, he knew he possessed the power of *tsungi*, the first shaman. Now he could see. Now he could find the truth. He stared at the stomach of the sick man. Slowly, it became transparent like a shallow mountain stream, and he saw within it, coiling and uncoiling, *makanchi*, the poisonous serpent, who had been sent by the enemy shaman. The real cause of the illness had been found.

The Jívaro Indians of the Ecuadorian Amazon believe that witchcraft is the cause of the vast majority of illnesses and non-violent deaths. The normal waking life, for the Jívaro, is simply "a lie," or illusion, while the true forces that determine daily events are supernatural and can only be seen and manipulated with the aid of hallucinogenic drugs. A reality view of this kind creates a particularly strong demand for specialists who can cross over into the supernatural world at will to deal with the forces that influence and even determine the events of the waking life.

These specialists, called "shamans" by anthropologists, are recognized by the Jívaro as being of two types: bewitching shamans or curing shamans. Both kinds take a hallucinogenic drink, whose Jívaro name is *natema*, in order to enter the supernatural world. This brew, commonly called *yagé*, or *yajé*, in Colombia, *ayahuasca* (Inca "vine of the dead") in Ecuador and Peru, and *caapi* in Brazil, is prepared from segments of a species of the vine *Banisteriopsis*, a genus belonging to the Malpighiaceae. The Jívaro boil it with the leaves of a similar vine, which probably is also a species of *Banisteriopsis*, to produce a tea that contains the powerful hallucinogenic alkaloids harmaline, harmine, d-tetrahydroharmine, and quite possibly dimethyltryptamine (DMT). These compounds have chemical structures and effects similar, but not identical, to LSD, mescaline of the peyote cactus, and psilocybin of the psychotropic Mexican mushroom.

When I first undertook research among the Jívaro in 1956–57, I did not fully appreciate the psychological impact of the *Banisteriopsis* drink upon the native view of reality, but in 1961 I had occasion to drink the hallucinogen in the course of field work with another Upper Amazon Basin tribe. For several hours after drinking the brew, I found myself, although awake, in a world literally beyond my wildest dreams. I met bird-headed people, as well as dragon-like creatures who explained that they were the true gods of this world. I enlisted the services of other spirit helpers in attempting to fly through the far reaches of the Galaxy. Transported into a trance where the supernatural seemed natural, I realized that anthropologists, including myself, had profoundly underestimated the importance of the drug in affecting native ideology. Therefore, in 1964 I returned to the Jívaro to give particular attention to the drug's use by the Jívaro shaman.

The use of the hallucinogenic *natema* drink among the Jívaro makes it possible for almost anyone to achieve the trance state essential for the practice of shamanism. Given the presence of the drug and the felt need to contact the "real," or supernatural, world, it is not surprising that approximately one out of every four Jívaro men is a shaman. Any adult, male or female, who desires to become such a practitioner, simply presents a gift to an already practicing shaman, who administers the *Banisteriopsis* drink and gives some of his own supernatural power—in the form of spirit helpers, or *tsentsak*—to the apprentice. These spirit helpers, or "darts," are the main supernatural forces believed to cause illness and death

in daily life. To the non-shaman they are normally invisible, and even shamans can perceive them only under the influence of *natema*.

Shamans send these spirit helpers into the victims' bodies to make them ill or to kill them. At other times, they may suck spirits sent by enemy shamans from the bodies of tribesmen suffering from witchcraft-induced illness. The spirit helpers also form shields that protect their shaman masters from attacks. The following account presents the ideology of Jívaro witchcraft from the point of view of the Indians themselves.

To give the novice some *tsentsak*, the practicing shaman regurgitates what appears to be—to those who have taken *natema*—a brilliant substance in which the spirit helpers are contained. He cuts part of it off with a machete and gives it to the novice to swallow. The recipient experiences pain upon taking it into his stomach and stays on his bed for ten days, repeatedly drinking *natema*. The Jívaro believe they can keep magical darts in their stomachs indefinitely and regurgitate them at will. The shaman donating the *tsentsak* periodically blows and rubs all over the body of the novice, apparently to increase the power of the transfer.

The novice must remain inactive and not engage in sexual intercourse for at least three months. If he fails in self-discipline, as some do, he will not become a successful shaman. At the end of the first month, a *tsentsak* emerges from his mouth. With this magical dart at his disposal, the new shaman experiences a tremendous desire to bewitch. If he casts his *tsentsak* to fulfill this desire, he will become a bewitching shaman. If, on the other hand, the novice can control his impulse and reswallow the first *tsentsak*, he will become a curing shaman.

If the shaman who gave the *tsentsak* to the new man was primarily a bewitcher, rather than a curer, the novice likewise will tend to become a bewitcher. This is because a bewitcher's magical darts have such a desire to kill that their new owner will be strongly inclined to adopt their attitude. One informant said that the urge to kill felt by bewitching shamans came to them with a strength and frequency similar to that of hunger.

Only if the novice shaman is able to abstain from sexual intercourse for five months will he have the power to kill a man (if he is a bewitcher) or cure a victim (if he is a curer). A full year's abstinence is considered necessary to become a really effective bewitcher or curer.

During the period of sexual abstinence, the new shaman collects all kinds of insects, plants, and other objects, which he now has the power to convert into *tsentsak*. Almost any object, including living insects and worms, can become a *tsentsak* if it is small enough to be swallowed by a shaman. Different types of *tsentsak* are used to cause different kinds and degrees of illness. The greater the variety of these objects that a shaman has in his body, the greater is his ability.

According to Jívaro concepts, each *tsentsak* has a natural and supernatural aspect. The magical dart's natural aspect is that of an ordinary material object as seen without drinking the drug *natema*. But the supernatural and "true" aspect of the *tsentsak* is revealed to the shaman by taking *natema*. When he does this, the magical darts appear in new forms as demons and with new names. In their supernatural aspects, the *tsentsak* are not simply objects but spirit helpers in various forms, such as giant butterflies, jaguars, or monkeys, who actively assist the shaman in his tasks.

Bewitching is carried out against a specific, known individual and thus is almost always done to neighbors or, at the most, fellow tribesmen. Normally, as is the case with intratribal assassination, bewitching is done to avenge a particular offense committed against one's family or friends. Both bewitching and individual assassination contrast with the large-scale headhunting raids for which the Jívaro have become famous, and which were conducted against entire neighborhoods of enemy tribes.

To bewitch, the shaman takes *natema* and secretly approaches the house of his victim. Just out of sight in the forest, he drinks green tobacco juice, enabling him to regurgitate a *tsentsak*, which he throws at his victim as he comes out of his house. If the *tsentsak* is strong enough and is thrown with sufficient force, it will pass all the way through the victim's body causing death within a period of a few days to several weeks. More often, however, the magical dart simply lodges in the victim's body. If the shaman, in his hiding place, fails to see the intended victim, he may instead bewitch any member of the intended victim's family who appears, usually a wife or child. When the shaman's mission is accomplished, he returns secretly to his own home.

One of the distinguishing characteristics of the bewitching process among the Jívaro is that, as far as I could learn, the victim is given no specific indication that someone is bewitching him. The bewitcher does not want his victim to be aware that he is being supernaturally attacked, lest he take protective measures by immediately procuring the services of a curing shaman. Nonetheless, shamans and laymen alike with whom I talked noted that illness invariably follows the bewitchment although the degree of the illness can vary considerably.

A special kind of spirit helper, called a *pasuk,* can aid the bewitching shaman by remaining near the victim in the guise of an insect or animal of the forest after the bewitcher has left. This spirit helper has his own objects to shoot into the victim should a curing shaman succeed in sucking out the *tsentsak* sent earlier by the bewitcher who is the owner of the *pasuk.*

In addition, the bewitcher can enlist the aid of a *wakani* ("soul," or "spirit") bird. Shamans have the power to call these birds and use them as spirit helpers in bewitching victims. The shaman blows on the *wakani* birds and then sends them to the house of the victim to fly around and around the man, frightening him. This is believed to cause fever and insanity, with death resulting shortly thereafter.

After he returns home from bewitching, the shaman may send a *wakani* bird to perch near the house of the victim. Then if a curing shaman sucks out the intruding object, the bewitching shaman sends the *wakani* bird more *tsentsak* to throw from its beak into the victim. By continually resupplying the *wakani* bird with new *tsentsak,* the sorcerer makes it impossible for the curer to rid his patient permanently of the magical darts.

While the *wakani* birds are supernatural servants available to anyone who wishes to use them, the *pasuk,* chief among the spirit helpers, serves only a single shaman. Likewise a shaman possesses only one *pasuk.* The *pasuk,* being specialized for the service of bewitching, has a protective shield to guard it from counterattack by the curing shaman. The curing shaman, under the influence of *natema,* sees the *pasuk* of the bewitcher in human form and size, but "covered with iron except for its eyes." The curing shaman can kill this *pasuk* only by shooting a *tsentsak* into its eyes, the sole vulnerable area in the *pasuk*'s armor. To the person who has not taken the hallucinogenic drink, the *pasuk* usually appears to be simply a tarantula.

Shamans also may kill or injure a person by using magical darts, *anamuk*, to create supernatural animals that attack a victim. If a shaman has a small, pointed armadillo bone *tsentsak*, he can shoot this into a river while the victim is crossing it on a balsa raft or in a canoe. Under the water, this bone manifests itself in its supernatural aspect as an anaconda, which rises up and overturns the craft, causing the victim to drown. The shaman can similarly use a tooth from a killed snake as a *tsentsak,* creating a poisonous serpent to bite his victim. In more or less the same manner, shamans can create jaguars and pumas to kill their victims.

About five years after receiving his *tsentsak,* a bewitching shaman undergoes a test to see if he still retains enough *tsentsak* power to continue to kill successfully. This test involves bewitching a tree. The shaman, under the influence of *natema,* attempts to throw a *tsentsak* through the tree at the point where its two main branches join. If his strength and aim are adequate, the tree appears to split the moment the *tsentsak* is sent into it. The splitting, however, is invisible to an observer who is not under the influence of the hallucinogen. If the shaman fails, he knows that he is incapable of killing a human victim. This means that, as soon as possible, he must go to a strong shaman and purchase a new supply of *tsentsak.* Until he has the goods with which to pay for this new supply, he is in constant danger, in his proved weakened condition, of being seriously bewitched by other shamans. Therefore, each day, he drinks large quantities of *natema,* tobacco juice, and the extract of yet another drug, *pirípirí.* He also rests on his bed at home to conserve his strength, but tries to conceal his weakened condition from his enemies. When he purchases a new supply of *tsentsak,* he can safely cut down on his consumption of these other substances.

The degree of illness produced in a witchcraft victim is a function of both the force with which the *tsentsak* is shot into the body, and also of the character of the magical dart itself. If a *tsentsak* is shot all the way through the body of a victim, then "there is nothing for a curing shaman to suck out," and the patient dies. If the magical dart lodges within the body, however, it is theoretically possible to cure the victim by sucking. But in actual practice, the sucking is not always considered successful.

The work of the curing shaman is complementary to that of a bewitcher. When a curing shaman is called in to treat a patient, his first task is to see if the illness is due to witchcraft. The usual diagnosis and treatment begin with the curing shaman drinking *natema,* tobacco juice, and pirípirí in the late afternoon and early evening. These drugs permit him to see into the body of the patient as though it were glass. If the illness is due to sorcery, the curing shaman will see the intruding object within the patient's body clearly enough to determine whether or not he can cure the sickness.

A shaman sucks magical darts from a patient's body only at night, and in a dark area of the house, for it is only in the dark that he can perceive the drug-induced visions that are the supernatural reality. With the setting of the sun, he alerts his *tsentsak* by whistling the tune of the curing song; after about a quarter of an hour, he starts singing. When he is ready to suck, the shaman regurgitates two *tsentsak* into the sides of his throat and mouth. These must be identical to the one he has seen in the patient's body. He holds one of these in the front of the mouth and the other in the rear. They are expected to catch the supernatural aspect of the magical dart that the shaman sucks out of the patient's body. The *tsentsak* nearest the shaman's lips is supposed to incorporate the sucked-out *tsentsak* essence within itself. If, however, this supernatural essence should get past it, the second magical dart in the mouth blocks the throat so that the intruder cannot enter the interior of the shaman's body. If the curer's two *tsentsak* were to fail to catch the supernatural essence of the *tsentsak,* it would pass down into the shaman's stomach and kill him. Trapped thus within the mouth, this essence is shortly caught by, and incorporated into, the material substance of one of the curing shaman's *tsentsak.* He then "vomits" out this object and displays it to the patient and his family saying, "Now I have sucked it out. Here it is."

The non-shamans think that the material object itself is what has been sucked out, and the shaman does not disillusion them. At the same time, he is not lying, because he knows that the only important thing about a *tsentsak* is its supernatural aspect, or essence, which he sincerely believes he has removed from the patient's body. To explain to the layman that he already had these objects in his mouth would serve no fruitful purpose and would prevent him from displaying such an object as proof that he had effected the cure. Without incontrovertible evidence, he would not be able to convince the patient and his family that he had effected the cure and must be paid.

The ability of the shaman to suck depends largely upon the quantity and strength of his own *tsentsak*, of which he may have hundreds. His magical darts assume their supernatural aspect of spirit helpers when he is under the influence of *natema*, and he sees them as a variety of zoomorphic forms hovering over him, perching on his shoulders, and sticking out of his skin. He sees them helping to suck the patient's body. He must drink tobacco juice every few hours to "keep them fed" so that they will not leave him.

The curing shaman must also deal with any *pasuk* that may be in the patient's vicinity for the purpose of casting more darts. He drinks additional amounts of *natema* in order to see them and engages in *tsentsak* duels with them if they are present. While the *pasuk* is enclosed in iron armor, the shaman himself has his own armor composed of his many *tsentsak*. As long as he is under the influence of *netema*, these magical darts cover his body as a protective shield, and are on the lookout for any enemy *tsentsak* headed toward their master. When these *tsentsak* see such a missile coming, they immediately close up together at the point where the enemy dart is attempting to penetrate, and thereby repel it.

If the curer finds *tsentsak* entering the body of his patient after he has killed *pasuk*, he suspects the presence of a *wakani* bird. The shaman drinks *maikua* (*Datura*), an hallucinogen even more powerful than *natema*, as well as tobacco juice, and silently sneaks into the forest to hunt and kill the bird with *tsentsak*. When he succeeds, the curer returns to the patient's home, blows all over the house to get rid of the "atmosphere" created by the numerous *tsentsak* sent by the bird, and completes his sucking of the patient. Even after all the *tsentsak* are extracted, the shaman may remain another night at the house to suck out any "dirtiness" (*pahuri*) still inside. In the cures which I have witnessed, this sucking is a most noisy process, accompanied by deep, but dry, vomiting.

After sucking out a *tsentsak*, the shaman puts it into a little container. He does not swallow it because it is not his own magical dart and would therefore kill him. Later, he throws the *tsentsak* into the air, and it flies back to the shaman who sent it originally into the patient. *Tsentsak* also fly back to a shaman at the death of a former apprentice who had originally received them from him. Besides receiving "old" magical darts unexpectedly in this manner, the shaman may have *tsentsak* thrown at him by a bewitcher. Accordingly, shamans constantly drink tobacco juice at all hours of the day and night. Although the tobacco juice is not truly hallucinogenic, it produces a narcotized state, which is believed necessary to keep one's *tsentsak* ready to repel any other magical darts. A shaman does not even dare go for a walk without taking along the green tobacco leaves with which he prepares the juice that keeps his spirit helpers alert. Less frequently, but regularly, he must drink *natema* for the same purpose and to keep in touch with the supernatural reality.

While curing under the influence of *natema*, the curing shaman "sees" the shaman who bewitched his patient. Generally, he can recognize the person, unless it is a shaman who lives far away or in another tribe. The patient's family knows this, and demands to be told the identity of the bewitcher, particularly if the sick person dies. At one curing session I attended, the shaman could not identify the person he had seen in his vision. The brother of the dead man then accused the shaman himself of being responsible. Under such pressure, there is a strong tendency for the curing shaman to attribute each case to a particular bewitcher.

Shamans gradually become weak and must purchase *tsentsak* again and again. Curers tend to become weak in power, especially after curing a patient bewitched by a shaman who has recently received a new supply of magical darts. Thus, the most powerful shamans are those who can repeatedly purchase new supplies of *tsentsak* from other shamans.

Shamans can take back *tsentsak* from others to whom they have previously given them. To accomplish this, the shaman drinks *natema*, and, using his *tsentsak*, creates a "bridge" in the form of a rainbow between himself and the other shaman. Then he shoots a *tsentsak* along this rainbow. This strikes the ground beside the other shaman with an explosion and flash likened to a lightning bolt. The purpose of this is to surprise the other shaman so that he temporarily forgets to maintain his guard over his magical darts, thus permitting the other shaman to suck them back along the rainbow. A shaman who has had his *tsentsak* taken away in this manner will discover that "nothing happens" when he drinks *natema*. The sudden loss of his *tsentsak* will tend to make him ill, but ordinarily the illness is not fatal unless a bewitcher shoots a magical dart into him while he is in this weakened condition. If he has not become disillusioned by his experience, he can again purchase *tsentsak* from some other shaman and resume his calling. Fortunately for anthropology some of these men have chosen to give up shaman-ism and therefore can be persuaded to reveal their knowledge, no longer having a vested interest in the profession. This divulgence, however, does not serve as a significant threat to practitioners, for words alone can never adequately convey the realities of shamanism. These can only be approached with the aid of *natema*, the chemical door to the invisible world of the Jívaro shaman.

28

The Rave: Spiritual Healing in Modern Western Subcultures

Scott Hutson

Drawing upon anthropological understandings of altered states of consciousness, the ritual process, and shamanism, Scott Hutson argues that the youth subcultural events known as raves function as a form of spiritual healing. By focusing on what participants themselves say, Hutson finds that raves are therapeutic and comparable to ecstatic healing as documented cross-culturally. According to the author, the most distinctive characteristics of raves are techno dance music, long duration, and ecstatic experience. Raves began in London but spread internationally, flourishing in the late 1980s and 1990s, and in many places eventually blended into the general nightclub scene.

In this article, Hutson sketches ways in which raves are connected to religion: some are hosted by churches interested in youth outreach; some participants stimulate altered states through drug use; and even by participants, DJs are compared to "technoshamans." The author describes features likely to have physiological effects on participants, akin to trance induction in other cultures, such as flashing lights, repetitive percussive music, and dancing for long periods of time, as well as symbolic and ritual features that produce feelings of communality.

Scott Hutson is primarily an archaeologist with expertise in the Americas. His study of raves is notable in its use of anthropological theory, but raves have also attracted attention from scholars outside of anthropology. Two among the many works available are Rave Culture and Religion, *ed. Graham St. John (Routledge 2003) and* Trance Formation: the Spiritual and Religious Dimensions of Global Rave Culture, *by Robin Sylvan (Routledge 2005.)*

Ever had an experience that makes you sit up and re-evaluate all your ideas, thoughts and incidents in your life?[1]

From: Anthropological Quarterly 73(1):35–49, 2000.
Acknowledgments I would like to thank Byron Hamann, Megan Mooney, Michael Brown, Beth Conklin, and James Hutson for commenting on this paper. A preliminary version was read at the 97th Annual Meeting of the American Anthropological Association, December 2–6, 1998, Philadelphia.
1. David King, "Why 'Goa Trance?'" in www.thirdeye.org .uk/trip/why.html [Internet]. 7 May 1997 [cited 22 October 1997].

Introduction

The question above was voiced by a young man who had just returned from a rave: a dance party, usually all night long, featuring loud "techno"[2] music, also

2. Techno music includes various forms of pre-recorded dance music mixed by disc jockeys, though it can be produced live. Electronica is a more recent term coined by U.S. media and record companies. The various forms or sub-genres of techno change rapidly; many of the genres that were popular five years ago no longer exist or have evolved into new genres with their own names. Some of the genres of techno that were popular at the time of my research include house, trance, drum 'n bass, speed garage, trip hop, and big beat.

called electronica, in which participants often reach ecstatic states, occasionally with the help of drugs.[3] Initially, in the late 1980s, when they first appeared in Britian, raves were underground events, taking place in makeshift and occasionally secretive venues such as warehouses and outdoor fields. By the mid-1990s analysts could comment that "the scale is huge and ever increasing" (McRobbie 1994: 168). Fully licensed and often held in nightclubs, raves now penetrated to the center of British youth culture. Combined attendance at dance events in Great Britain in 1993 reached 50 million, which was substantially more than at "sporting events, cinemas, and all the 'live' arts combined" (Thornton 1995: 15). Commercially, the 1993 British rave market brought in approximately $2.7 billion (Thornton 1995: 15). In Germany nearly two million youngsters and post-adolescents united in the so-called "rave nation" of the mid-1990s (Richard and Kruger 1998). Following this initial north European florescence, rave hot spots emerged around the world at Rimini (Italy), Ko Phangan (Thailand), the Balearic Islands (Spain), Goa (India), and coastal Mozambique. Though they have never been as popular in the United States as in Great Britain, raves have been a fixture in San Francisco, Los Angeles, and New York since the early 1990s and some of techno music's strongest roots are in Detroit and Chicago.

Raves today are remarkably diversified. In fact, in places like London where raves have their deepest roots, the rave "scene" has fragmented into many successor sub-scenes, usually centered on divergent varieties of techno music, such as Big Beat or Drum $'n Bass. Raves in the traditional sense—semi-legal and located in factories and outdoors—are rare. Nevertheless, rave's various offshoots all feature what I believe are the critical elements of rave: dance music, long duration, and ecstatic experience. As in London, most all-night dance parties in U.S. cities with a long tradition of raves have blended into the regular nightclub scene and are no longer called raves. However, in smaller cities and especially in the Midwest (Champion 1998)

and the Southeast, raves in the traditional sense are alive and well.[4]

Demographically, most people who attend raves—often called "ravers"—are between the ages of 15 and 25, thus making rave a "youth" subculture (see Epstein 1998). The socioeconomic and ethnic backgrounds of ravers are not nearly so predictable as their ages. For example, early raves in Great Britain attracted people of various backgrounds, mostly from the working classes (Reynolds 1998a: 64). This socially mixed tradition continues today in most urban venues. At the other extreme, in the midwestern United States, for example, most ravers are white and middle class. Though slightly more males than females attend raves, the organizers, producers, and musicians behind the rave scene are predominantly male (McRobbie 1994: 168, Tomlinson 1998: 198, Reynolds 1998a: 274; Richard and Kruger 1998: 169).

Much of the academic discourse on raves focuses on the rave as a hedonistic, temporary escape from reality. Writers who support this position argue from a "neoconservative" (Foster 1985: 2), postmodern perspective that emphasizes the prominence of nostalgia and meaninglessness in modern amusements. Though I find this view of the rave both plausible and informative, I argue that it is incomplete because it ignores the poignant and meaningful spiritual experiences that ravers say they get from raves. In this article I attend to discourses in which ravers claim that raves are therapeutic. Based on these testimonials, the rave can be conceptualized as a form of healing comparable both to shamanic, ecstatic healing documented in ethnographies of small-scale non-western societies, and to spiritual experiences in modern western subcultures. Our understanding of the rave, previously approached from a cultural studies or communications studies perspective, might therefore benefit from a perspective attuned to anthropological discussions of shamanism and spirituality.

Notes on Method

The primary source materials for my interpretations come from testimonials posted on the internet from 1993 to 1997, e-mails contributed to listservs,

3. For an insider definition, see Brian Behlendorf, "The official alt.raveFAQ," in www.hyperreal.com/raves/altraveFAQ.html# [Internet]. May 8, 1994 [cited 3 November 1997]. Hyperreal is the largest and oldest internet resource for rave music and culture:.

4. Though similar to early 1990s raves, these late 1990s raves have many of their own peculiar features, as Champion (1998) elegantly documents.

participant-observation at raves and dance clubs in San Francisco and the southeastern United States, and interviews with informants. The use of web-based sources of information exposes my study to the considerations of how Internet or "cyber"-ethnography differs from traditional, real-time ethnography (Fischer 1999). The methodological issue most relevant to my study is the effect of computer-mediated communication on the construction of identity. In other words, the major issue to be addressed is whether people behave differently when corresponding on e-mail or posting messages to interactive web sites as opposed to when engaged in traditional face-to-face communication.

A number of authors suggest that advanced information technology can modify behavior in profound ways (Hakken 1999: 44). The anonymity of much computer-mediated communication removes inhibitions that govern normal social encounters. For example, social conventions such as courtesy and politeness may disappear, leading to what is referred to as "flame wars." According to Mark Dery (1994: 1),

> electronic communication accelerates the escalation of hostilities when tempers flare: disembodied, sometimes pseudonymous combatants tend to feel that they can hurl insults with impunity.

Gotcher and Kanervo (1997) note that people exhibit anger on-line more often than in person. In many cases the emotions embedded in on-line communication can be difficult to interpret due to the absence of paralinguistic vocal cues such as stress, pitch, intensity, and volume (Dery 1994: 2). Cues that identify race, gender, and sex may also be absent in online communication, allowing for the utopian possibility of interaction with others not on the potentially discriminatory bases of racialized, gendered real-life identities, but on what people choose to write (p. 3). Beyond concealing real-life identity, the anonymity of computer-mediated communication also enables people to enact fantasies and create any number of fictional identities (Turkle 1995: 12).

These considerations suggest that communication on line is affected by largely different norms than those governing face-to-face communication. However, David Hakken (1999) argues that identity formation on-line, though complex, is not qualitatively different from identity formation off-line. More precisely, Hakken avoids distinguishing sharply between

on-line and off-line and instead places computer-mediated communications like e-mail and Multiple User Domains (MUDs) along a continuum of cyborgic, machine-enhanced communications. Hakken makes the point that correspondence through e-mail might be quantitatively more cyborgic than correspondence through a telephone, but both forms of communication are machine-enhanced and not qualitatively different. Most importantly, identity formation in cyberspace, just like identity formation elsewhere, is semiotic rather than empirical, depends recursively on socializations produced through face-to-face experience, occurs within social hierarchies similar to those found in real-life, and derives from comparison with others (Hakken 1999: 89–91). Dibbell (1994) has noted that even in those cyberspaces where role-playing and fictional identities are most common, such as MUDs, people soon stop treating the Internet as a vast playpen for their disembodied fantasies and begin acting with the maturity characteristic of real life.

Hakken's and Dibbell's skepticism toward the revolutionary differences of computer-mediated communication leads me to think that my web informants do not act very different from my face-to-face informants. There is further justification for taking this position. None of the texts that inform my study is angry or hostile, as in flame wars. Authors often used common names that are likely to be actual names, which suggests that they were consciously accountable for what they wrote. There were no indications that authors of statements were role-playing, as in MUDs, and there were no patent incentives for dissimulation. Perhaps the form of writing most analogous to the sources I consulted is the travelogue, or, more appropriately, the "rave-log," in which ravers share their experiences and delights to kindred spirits. Such a form of writing, of course, does not escape all forms of distortion. Testifying about the power of raves on a listserv most often read by other ravers may lead to partisan hype and exaggeration—a sort of community-reinforced boosterism. On the other hand, there is no reason to believe that such exaggeration would not occur in face-to-face communication.

By subjecting "odd" behavior in our own society to the same type of anthropological analysis that is often reserved for religions of Asia, Africa, and elsewhere, this article joins a growing number of studies that give serious treatment to experiences of healing and empowerment that anthropologists once deemed "inauthentic." After confronting the "intrusion" of Western mass culture into "authentic" and "exotic" traditions of shamanism in coastal Peru, Donald Joralemon (1990: 112) stumbled upon anthropology's stubborn disposition to "celebrate the exotic and disparage the familiar." As Joralemon explains, anthropologists hesitate to apply to what is culturally nearest to them the same respectful yet detached perspective that they habitually reserve for the culturally distant. For example, when metaphors of healing are embedded in oral traditions of geographically localized cultures, they are seen as legitimate, yet when they come from diffuse, literate and economically empowered Westerners they are seen as ridiculous "psychobabble" (Joralemon 1990). In this article, I join Joralemon and others (Brown 1997; Danforth 1989) in challenging this assumption. Regardless of the authenticity of shamanic idioms used by Westerners, statements about healing at raves deserve serious study. As Joralemon points out, anthropologists who study modern "spiritual healing," rather then pretending superiority and ignoring it altogether, might stand to gain unforeseen insight on behavioral processes.

Approaching the rave with respectful detachment, however, does not preclude a critical analysis. When Michael Brown announced his intent to research New Age channels, his colleagues discouraged him from what they thought would be a "contaminating" research project, fearing that he would "go native" (1997: x). The solution, however, does not seem to be to avoid studying New Age channels, as Brown's colleagues implied, but to engage them in the hope of fashioning a robust cultural critique (Marcus and Fisher 1986). Brown's ethnography as well as other ethnographies, like that of Loring Danforth (1989), in which Greek firewalkers are compared to New Age firewalkers in the United States, show that "unusual" western practices can be successfully and critically engaged by anthropologists. The anthropology of raves is not yet thorough enough to formulate a "robust" cultural critique. Toward this end, however, I include brief comparisons between spiritual healing at raves with similar experiences among fundamentalist Christians, Grateful Dead fanatics, New Age channels, and other groups. Such lateral moves point to

areas of research that can be pursued more deeply in the future.

Academic and "Native" Perspectives on the Rave: Meaning, Spirituality, Healing

The postmodern approach views the rave as culture of abandonment, disengagement, and disappearance. To Fredric Jameson (1984: 60,64), postmodernism is typified by the disappearance of the subject. Lack of subjectivity at raves is said to be reflected in the style of dance (Rushkoff 1994: 121; McKay 1996: 110; Russell 1993:128–129), the relative anonymity of the DJ (disc jockey), the nature of the music (Tagg 1994; Reynolds 1998a: 254, Melechi 1993: 34), the ego-reducing effects of Ecstasy (the most prominent drug at raves, known chemically as "3, 4 methylene-dioxy-metamphetamine" [MDMA] [Saunders 1995][5]), and the occurrence of raves in out-of-the-way places at times when the rest of the population sleeps (Melechi 1993: 33–34; Rietveld 1993). Ravers fill the void of subjectivity with a collage of fragments, the archetypal form of postmodernist expression (Jameson 1984: 64). Fragmentation is seen in the DJ's sampling of various past and present styles of music (Connor 1997: 207, Reynolds 1998a: 41–45). Such bricolage of older styles exemplifies Jameson's idea that, with the decline of the high modernist ideology of style, the producers of culture have nowhere to turn but the past (1984: 65). Informed by this perspective, some argue that the first raves in London were simulacra of past all-night disco extravaganzas at tourist nightclubs in the Balearic Islands of the Mediterranean (Reynolds 1998a: 58–59; Melechi 1993: 30; Russell 1993: 119). Finally, the rave experience is said to be hyperreal in the sense that a multiplicity of surfaces replaces singularity of depth (Jameson 1984: 62). Due to the sensory overload of throbbing music, exotic lighting, exhaustive dance, and sensation-stimulating drugs, the rave becomes a mega-surface that gratifies a relentless and intense desire for pleasure.

Reynolds (1998b: 90), an authoritative rave journalist, summarizes the postmodern interpretation elegantly: rave culture is "geared towards fascination

---

5. See also Mike Brown, "Techno Music and Raves FAQ," in http://www.hyperreal.com/-mike/pub/altraveFAQ.html [Internet]. 1 December 1995 [cited 7 November 1996].

rather than meaning, sensation rather than sensibility; creating an appetite for impossible states of hyper-simulation." I find the postmodern approach deficient precisely because it fails to acknowledge meaning. Baudrillard believes that in the postmodern world of simulacra, meaning is exterminated (1988: 10): the joy of Disneyland, raves, and similar amusements lies not in their intellectual stimulation, but in their ability to satisfy, on a purely sensory level, our voracious appetite for surfaces. Once the surfaces are rendered meaningless, interpretation stops. As a result, such interpretations are not very deep (Bruner 1994) and certainly not "thick" (Geertz 1973). The studies cited above do not consider the complex ways in which symbols and surfaces connect, intersect, and/or conflict with the praxis of the real human beings who construct and consume them. Their lives are certainly not meaningless, yet those who write about the rave rarely solicit the voices and experiences of people who actually go to raves.

As an exemplar of the idea that the rave is indeed a very meaningful experience to many of those who attend, I quote a raver named Megan:

The rave is my church. It is a sritual to perform. I hold it sacred to my perpetuality . . . we in the rave are a congregation—it is up to us to help each other, to help people reach heaven. . . . After every rave, I walk out having seen my soul and its place in eternity.[6]

Megan's statement exemplifies the religiosity of the rave. The analogy between rave and religion manifests itself at various sites. In Nashville a club known as the Church hosted raves by the name of "Friday Night Mass." Thornton (1995: 90) reports on a rave in Great Britain that was held inside a church; the DJs operated from the altar. In an introduction to rave culture Brian Behlendorf refers to the DJ as "high priest."[7] Saunders' London informants refer to the drug Ecstasy as the holy sacrament (Saunders 1995). One raver, commenting on a rave in Orlando, said that the DJ did not just make him boogey, he made him "see God."[8]

Noticing the similarities between raves and Christian spirituality, Matthew Fox and Chris Brain, sponsored by the Episcopal church in Sheffield, UK, have fused traditional services with raves in an effort to increase youth church membership (Reynolds 1998a: 242). Brain's services, known colloquially as "Planetary Mass," feature ambient house music, nightclub-style lighting, and video screens with computer generated graphics.[9] In the United States a similar hybrid ceremony, also called Planetary Mass, takes place in the Grace Cathedral, San Francisco (p. 316).

Robin Green and other ravers disapprove of organized religion's attempts to co-opt the rave experience. According to Green,

raves should influence people metaphysically outside of the religious sphere. In actual effect, this is the creation of a . . . religion without theological foundation or unified expression.[10]

Another raver claimed

[On Sunday morning after the rave] I see people headed off to church dressed in their Sunday best and I just have to smile because I know that last night on the dance floor I felt closer to God than their church with all its doctrines and double standards will ever bring them.[11]

Rave is thus seen by some as a more "direct" form of spirituality than organized religion.

The ravers' own explanation of why they interpret their experiences in spiritual terms centers around the concept of "technoshamanism." The term was coined by Fraser Clark, who helped organize two prominent London dance clubs, UFO and Megatripolis, and edited *Evolution*, an underground magazine focusing on the culture of house music in London (Rushkoff 1994: 121). Technoshamanism refers to the DJ's role as "harmonic navigator," "in charge of the group mood/mind." The DJ "senses when it's time to lift the mood, take it down, etc., just as the shaman did in the good ol' tribal

6. Megan, "Coup d'Academe.html," in www.hyperreal.org/raves/spirit/ [internet]. [cited 16 November 1997].
7. Brian Behlendorf, "The official alt.raveFAQ," in www.hyperreal.com/raves/altraveFAQ.html# [Internet]. 8 May 1994 [cited 3 November 1997].
8. Anonymous, "DJ_Journeys.html," in www.hyperreal.org/raves/spirit/technoshamanism [Internet]. 29 February 1996 [cited 2 December 1997].

9. Bob, "Rave_Mass.html," in www.hyperreal.org/raves/spirit/culture [Internet]. 28 November 1955 [cited 10 December 1997].
10. Robin Green, No title. In www.hyperreal.org/raves/spirit/history [Internet]. [cited 4 January 1998].
11. "Beautiful_Visions.html," in www.hyperreal.org/spirit/vibes [Internet]. [cited 17 November 1997].

days."[12] In other words, through a tapestry of mind-bending music, the DJ is said to take the dancers on an overnight journey, with one finger on the pulse of the adventure and the other on the turntables[13] (Rushkoff 1994: 123; Thornton 1995: 65; McKay 1996: 111). Though such a description of the technoshaman does not match all of Eliade's criteria for the definition of shamanism (the technoshaman, for example does not appear to control "helper spirits"), the DJ's mastery of the techniques of ecstasy qualify him/her as a shaman in the more general sense of Eliade's definition (Eliade 1964: 4–6).

With the help of the DJ's ecstatic techniques, ravers like Edward Lantz claim to enter "areas of consciousness not necessarily related to everyday 'real' world experiences."[14] Though Ecstasy enables altered states of consciousness, drugs are not necessary (Reynolds 1998a: 9). In this sense, raves are similar to the trance dances of the Dobe Ju/'hoansi, which do not involve any mind-altering substances. In both cases, altered states of consciousness are stimulated by a combination of upbeat rhythmic drumming, exhaustive all night dancing, and flickering light (Lee 1967; Katz 1982). One raver remarked that techno music itself (especially genres like Goa and the suitably named "trance") is enough to cause an ecstatic experience without even dancing: "It's the only music that lifts you out of your body without putting something down your throat first."[15] According to another raver, techno music returns to you "the human ability to dream while awake."[16] The experiences recorded by ravers in ecstasy, specifically flying, also recall shamanic experiences documented ethnographically. In one particular trip San Francisco promoter Mark Heley claims to have visited the dead and transformed into a puma and then an eagle (Rushkoff 1994: 140), recalling the type of peregrinations that shamans all over the world experience as part of initiation (Eliade 1964).

Much more than a fantasy simulacrum, the altered states of consciousness that are part of the technoshamanistic journey are said to heal: according to an anonymous raver, "Our means of healing and growth is ritual celebration, where we gather once in a while to expand our consciousness and celebrate life with rhythm and dance."[17] Ravers most often attest to healing of a psychological sort, as the above quote on consciousness expansion implies. The technoshamanistic journey is said to bring calm: "After the trip, when we finally arrive back home, the inner peace and contentment we so deeply desired settles our restlessness."[18] Raves restore "general feelings of happiness and grooviness . . . raving brings me up when I'm down."[19] Themes of self-empowerment are also common in ravers' reflections on their journeys: according to raver Sean Case, "The goal of the techno journey is for people to see themselves without the crushing ego, to know the possibilities of the self."[20]

> It is through dance that I have found transcendence. Music has taught me to fly using wings I never knew I had. It is through music and dance that my soul is free to soar amongst the heavens . . . allowing a clearer vision of the world that I am creating.[21]

Because the rave experience is so often described in religious and spiritual terms, and because the type of healing is of the spirit as opposed to the body, I refer to the type of healing discussed above as "spiritual healing."

12. Fraser Clark, "Technoshamanism_Definitions.html," in www.hyperreal.org/raves/spirit/technoshamanism [Internet]. 24 May 1995 [cited 8 December 1997].

13. Brian Behlendorf, "The official alt.raveFAQ," in www.hyperreal.com/raves/altraveFAQ.html# [Internet]. 8 May 1994 [cited 3 November 1997], and Anonymous, "Perfect_Party.html," in www.hyperreal.org/raves/spirit/ hopeful [Internet]. [cited 16 November 1997].

14. Edward Lantz, "Otherworlds_Experience," in www.hyperreal.org/raves/spirit/technoshamanism [Internet]. [Cited 2 December 1997].

15. Zazgooeya, "Why 'Goa Trance?'" in www.thirdeye. org.uk/trip/why.html [Internet]. [cited 8 November 1997].

16. Jake Barnes, "Why 'Goa Trance?'" in www.thirdeye.org. uk/trip/why.html [Internet]. [cited 24 October 1997].

17. Omananda@geocities.com, "Goa trance," in www. hyperrreal.org/raves/spirit/technoshamanism [Internet]. 16 May 1993 [cited 22 November 1997].

18. Omananda@geocities.com, "Goa trance," in www. hyperrreal.org/raves/spirit/technoshamanism [Internet]. 16 May 1993 [cited 22 November 1997].

19. Noah Raford, "Dance_for_tomorrow.html," in www. hyperreal.org/raves/spirit/hopeful [Internet]. [cited 11 January 1998].

20. Sean Casey, "Techno_and raving.html," in www. hyperreal.org/raves/spirit/technoshamanism [Internet]. 28 December 1994 [cited 10 December 1997].

21. Glenn Fajardo, "Dance_to_Transcendence.html," in www.hyperreal.org/raves/spirit/hopeful [Internet]. 15 February 1997 [cited 11 January 1998].

Raver testimony of "spiritual healing" also bears a family resemblance to experiences of evangelical conversion. There is a long history of evangelical conversion in North America, of which the exemplary form appeared in the British colonies during the Great Awakening of the 1740s. The testimony of Nathan Cole of Connecticut serves as an early example of Great Awakening conversions (Cole 1970). After hearing itinerant preacher George Whitefield, Cole felt doomed to Hell and endured two years of misery and inner turmoil. Finally, God appeared to Cole, precipitating an unearthly disembodiment: "Now while my soul was viewing God, my fleshy part was working imaginations and saw many things which I will omit to tell." After the moment of conversion, Cole writes, "My heart and soul were filled as full as they could hold with joy and sorrow: now I perfectly felt truth . . . and all the air was love." Other accounts of conversion show that those in crisis were not as lonely as Cole, receiving support from small, like-minded congregations (Calhoon 1994). Though evangelical conversion since the eighteenth century has become much more peripheral and, according to Brushman (1970: xi), "commonly disdained," the structure of conversion remains approximately the same. Ethnographers of southern Baptist communities Susan Harding (1987) and Carol Greenhouse (1986) note that, similar to Cole's crisis, a period of questioning accompanied by a sense of being "lost" often precedes the conversion. Conversion, which may take years or minutes, replaces emptiness with a therapeutic sense of comfort, meaning, and purpose.

Three aspects of Evangelical conversions like that of Cole resemble raver testimony: 1) raw, personal emotions of a spiritual nature, unstructured by the norms of the church; 2) out-of-body experience, sometimes involving hallucinations that bring the convert close to God; and 3) healing and mental hygiene experienced after conversion. Despite such resemblances there are two major differences between spiritual healing at raves and evangelical conversion. The first of these differences has to do with context. Despite the raw, personal emotion associated with evangelical healing, the conversion takes place in an institutionalized context. In the Great Awakening a clergy devoted to the spiritual revival's advancement placed conversion in a commanding intellectual and theological structure

(Brushman 1970: 67). In Baptist communities of the 1980s conversion was contextualized through hell-fire-and-brimstone preaching (Harding 1987) and close attention to the scripture (Greenhouse 1987: 75). Furthermore, fundamentalists of the 1980s were part of a community that, by giving witness of God's grace to the unconverted, provided those in crisis with a normalizing structure. As I will demonstrate below, raves do have a doctrine, codified as "Peace, Love, Unity, Respect" (PLUR) which is reinforced by exemplary behavior at raves and testimonial witnessing on the Internet. Nevertheless, the institutional context of rave spirituality is not nearly as serious, perhaps because eternal salvation is not at stake. PLUR is a four-word slogan not nearly so well developed or thorough, as evangelical theology. Also, passive witnesses on the Internet cannot compare to ponderous, hell-fire-and-brimstone preaching nor the extended, face-to-face witnessing that characterizes evangelism.

The second difference has to do with the process of transformation. For evangelical Christians, a burdensome period of guilt and despair, characterized with deep intellectual questioning, precedes salvation and transformation and is triggered by a crisis. Though disillusionment with society often precedes the positive spiritual transformation at a rave, the process of transformation, which I will discuss below, is usually neither painful nor triggered by personal crisis. Also, conversion is such an important milestone for evangelicals that it is called a second birth. Though rave experiences are remarkable, they occur frequently and are not as biographically salient as birth itself.

Physiological and Symbolic Processes of Healing

The previous section provided native testimony on technoshamanism and how the technoshamanistic voyage releases anxieties, builds self-empowerment, and brings peace and contentment. In this section I discuss physiological and symbolic processes that, though not described by ravers themselves, might also contribute to the "spiritual healing" that ravers claim to undergo.

Flashing lights, dancing, and repetitive percussion, each of which are prominent features of the rave, may physiologically produce altered states of consciousness. Walter and Walter (1949: 63) note that rhythmic light can cause visual sensations (color, pattern, or movement) unrelated to the stimulus, non-visual sensations of kinaesthetic (swaying, spinning, jumping, vertigo) and cutaneous (prickling, tingling) varieties, emotional and physiological experiences (fear, anger, disgust, confusion, fatigue, pleasure), hallucinations, epileptic seizures and "clinical psychopathic states." Lights that flash to the rhythm of the music and other elaborate visual effects, such as spinning lasers and wall projections of fractals, are frequent components of raves in both areas of my participant observation.

Dancing is an important physiological factor because it is a motor activity. Extended rhythmic dancing and bodily movement brings on physical exhaustion, vertigo, hyperventilation, and other physiological conditions that may alter consciousness (Lee 1967: 33, Rouget 1985: 118). Csikszentmihalyi (1975: 43) argues that dancing and other forms of play are intrinsically stimulating because they produce a holistic sensation of total involvement—a sensation that he calls "flow." Dance as flow merges the act with the awareness of the act, producing self-forgetfulness, a loss of self-consciousness, transcendance of individuality, and fusion with the world (p. 49).

With regard to repetitive percussion, Andrew Neher argues that trance states and unusual behavior observed ethnographically in ceremonies involving drums result primarily from the effects of rhythmic drumming on the central nervous system. Neher found observations from laboratory studies on the effects of rhythmic stimulation and accounts of stimulation from anthropological drum ceremonies and found that the responses, which included unusual perceptions and hallucinations, were comparable. Neher believes that stimulation is the result of auditory driving: that the sensory and motor areas of the brain not normally affected are activated through the stimulation of the sensory area being stimulated—in this case the ear. Neher notes that drums are most successful as auditory stimulants because the sound of the drum contains many frequencies. Because "different sound frequencies are transmitted along different nerve pathways in the brain," the sound of a drum should stimulate a larger area in the brain. Furthermore, drum beats with main rhythms accompanied by slightly different reinforcing rhythms produce the strongest responses. Under Neher's criteria,

techno music would be extremely successful in promoting auditory driving because percussion is a major feature of techno and because techno tracks have at least three complementary rhythms.[22] In their own testimonies ravers state that music is a key to their journey.

Michael Harner (1990: 50–51) has seized upon Neher's study to support his claim that the drum and the rattle are the basic tool for evoking and maintaining altered states of consciousness. Other scholars question the universality of Neher's results. Gibert Rouget (1985), who reviewed an encyclopedic range of ethnographically documented ceremonies involving spirit possession, found that drums are not always used to initiate altered states of consciousness. This and the common observation that two people react very differently to the same music at the same event within the same culture lead Rouget to conclude that music does not have any straightforward physiological affect on consciousness. Rouget does not deny the importance of music; he simply cautions us not to generalize its specific effects. In considering Rouget's critique, it is important to remember that spirit possession is a specific altered state of consciousness not described by ravers. Nevertheless, none of the aspects discussed above—flashing light, dancing, music—is a necessary condition for altered states of consciousness. However, when combined, as at a rave, they are more likely to have an effect: "rhythmic stimulation in more than one sensory mode aids the response" (Neher 1962: 155).

The physiological interpretation does not explain the rave as a social event. If an altered state of consciousness is the only prerequisite to "spiritual healing," why do young people go to the trouble of attending raves when they could attain an ecstatic state more easily by staying at home and taking drugs? To begin to understand how raves might "heal"—how they create a framework for therapeutic spiritual transformations—requires close attention to the symbols surrounding the rave and embellishing ravers' descriptions of their voyages. Much of the symbolism has to do with idealized versions of small scale "primitive communities." One

---

22. Usually, snare drum, base drum, cymbal, and often keyboard and synthetic bass each contribute separate but aligned rhythms. Bass drum usually supplies the main rhythm.

rave website is decorated with pictures of people wearing loincloths, headdresses, and bodypaint, and holding spears.[23] The official Ibiza rave website is cluttered with images of Native American masks.[24] Music is often described as "tribal," and one genre of rave music is called "jungle." At some raves, like those sponsored by the New Moon collective or the Gateway collective, pagan altars are set up, sacred images from "primitive" cultures decorate the walls, and rituals of cleansing are performed over the turntables and the dance floor.[25]

A second theme at raves is futurism. Renegade Records, which feature drum 'n bass producers Future Forces, claims to market "future beats for future people." Eklectic, a weekly San Francisco drum 'n bass club, subtitles itself "San Francisco Futurism," and decorates its fliers with what its organizers call "neo-Tokyo" fashion: women enhanced with space-age graffiti. The name of the DJ/producer/artist responsible for the neo-Tokyo style, UFO!, highlights a prevalent motif of futurism—outer space. Among the most common outer space icons, which range from planets to fantasy space ships to actual satellites and satellite dishes, is the friendly extra-terrestrial. Anthropomorphic, neotonized, with massive forehead and long, slender eyes angled together in "V" formation, this friendly martian icon appears in a range of places—T-shirts, fliers, music videos, album cover art—and is the symbol of drum 'n bass record label Liquid Sky. The rave scene is also futuristic in that it embraces advanced technology. Production of techno music is an almost entirely digital affair, requiring thousands of dollars of synthesizers, samplers, mixers, and computers. It is no coincidence that the wide variety of rave musics are referred to collectively as "techno" or "electronica." Ravers are also savvy Internet users who design websites, who engineer webcasts of live events, and whose attentions have been targeted directly by Internet firms such as Gomo mail and Eradio. Futurism also shows

in the preference for sans seriph, machine-like fonts and abstract, geometric, digital imagery.

The juxtaposition of primitives and martians appears to exemplify the random, superficial play of postmodern cultural expression. However, I argue that the predominance of these two genres of symbolism—future and primitive—is neither random nor meaningless. Both genres share a sense of distance from and disdain for the present age and reveal an attraction to alternative possibilities. Fondness for distant societies is in fact an explicit feature of rave discourse. Raver Jason Parsons yearns for "a memory of a time before cement cages and aloof societies; a humanity that was part of the world, not apart from it."[26] For raver Chris Newhard the journey involves reuniting with "the ancestors."[27] For others, the rave is about going back to ancient history (Rushkoff 1994: 120). According to raver Sean Casey,

> techno [music] brings us back to our roots . . . [it] sings to a very visceral ancient part of us deep down inside. It draws from the "reptilian" brain, past our egos and beckons us to dance with abandon.[28]

For just about everybody, the return to tribal roots is characterized by total unity and harmony, a "vibe" of collectivization.

Together, idealization of the past and interest in the future creates the incendiary combination of 1) what is seen as a model society (the past), and 2) the prospect of such a society's reenactment (the future). This combination recalls what Eliade (1960) has termed the "myth of eternal return": the nostalgic desire to return to an original, primordial time and place—a paradise. The blend of characteristics that informs the ravers' conception of the primitive experience—the destination of the technoshamanistic voyage—resembles many features of this primordial paradise. A paradise is a timeless land of perfect and total joy, a pre-sexual age of innocence where there is no social discord, no differentiation between the self and

---

23. Glenn Fajardo, "Dance_to_Transcendence.htm," in www.hyperreal.org/raves/spirit/hopeful [Internet]. 15 February 1997 [cited 11 January 1998].

24. See the Ibiza website at www.the-tribe.com/main.html [Internet]. [cited 7 November 1997].

25. Ann, "The New Moon Altar," in www.hyperreal.org/ raves/newmoon/altar [Internet]. August 1997 [cited 22 October 1997].

26. Jason Parsons, "Vibe.Tribe.html," in www.hyperreal. org/raves/spirit/hopeful [Internet]. 23 August 1996 [cited 4 January 1997].

27. Niehls Mayer, "Burning Man 95-Nevada.html," in www.hyperreal.org/raves/spirit/testimonials [Internet]. 27 September 1995 [cited 17 November 1997].

28. Sean Casey, "Techno_and_raving.htm," in www. hyperreal.org/raves/spirit/technoshamanism [Internet]. 28 December 1994 [cited 10 December 1997].

other.[29] There is little doubt that raves are joyful, even hyperjoyful. Raves are timeless in the sense that they are long and that they occur in the interstices—the "carnivalesque inversion" (Reynolds 1998a: 66)—of normal time, in that dark void where most of the population is asleep. Ravers describe how time stops.[30]

Perhaps the most important element of the raver's paradise is non-differentiation. Non-differentiation, unity, solidarity, and similar themes figure prominently in raver discourse. Explaining Unity, the third pillar of the rave motto PLUR (Peace Love Unity Respect), the mission statement of Cloudfactory, a San Francisco rave collective, states that

> we all share a lot in common, regardless of age, gender, race, [sexual] orientation, whatevah. We all need other people. Though we may have differences, we all arise from the same source.[31]

According to raver Mike Brown, you could have dance music and laser lighting, but it is not a rave unless it is unified.[32] In short, "We rave because boundaries must be broken."[33]

> What matters is the inclusive gestures that recognize the groove across cultures, whether technologically literate or aboriginal.[34]

Further statements about inclusiveness at raves indicate that transcendence of individual identity brings ravers to a therapeutic, non-differentiated state of being, in unity with the gods and the world.

> Once purified, you can join in the dance of the celestial beings within the kingdom of the ultimate and enjoy the freedom of existing anywhere.[35]

According to raver Charlene Ma, if a rave is successful, it all "melds into one cosmic soup and everything is one and you can't separate the music or the moves or which came first."[36] Drawing on quantum physics, an anonymous raver states that "the dancing gives a sense of oneness as we all become part of the same uncertainty wave equation."[37] Raver Alice Braley claims that

> The effect is to align the physical, mental, and emotional bodies with the oneness of All That Is. This results in a downflow of force from above . . . [which] causes vivification and definite illumination.[38]

Rushkoff (1994: 120) writes enthusiastically that ravers are "phase locked": by being on the same drugs, on the same nocturnal schedule, and under the same music, they have reached complete synchronicity. Organic and familial metaphors are also used to express the sense of unity and reunification. The group of friends one makes at a rave is often referred to as a family.[39] To quote raver Jason Page,

> Throw yourself in the winds of transformation and sow the seeds for a new world—one where the family is together again, when people respect and care for each other as a community—an organism.

The sense of unity that ravers claim to attain resembles communitas (Turner 1967: 96): Raves blend

---

29. The rave might even compare to the primordial state of being in the womb, where maturity, individuation, and separation have not yet occurred. The rave also matches the sensory experience of being in the womb. Raves are dark, humid (due to mist makers), and warm (due to sweating dancers), while the dance beat replicates the mother's heartbeat.

30. Jason Parsons, "Vibe.Tribe.html," in www.hyperreal. org/raves/spirit/hopeful [Internet]. 23 August 1996 [cited 4 January 1997].

31. Brad Finley. 1995. "We are all connected," in www. cloudfactory.org [Internet]. 12 December 1995 [cited 2 December 1997].

32. Mike Brown. "Techno Music and Raves FAQ," in http://www.hyperreal.com/~mike/pub/altraveFAQ.html [Internet]. 1 December 1995 [cited 7 November 1996].

33. Salami and Komotion International, "Why you are here," in www.couldfactory.org [Internet]. 12 December 1995 [cited 2 December 1997].

34. A. Lopez. 1994. "Techno_Subculture.html, in www. hyperreal.org/raves/spirit/technoshamanism [Internet]. 27 December 1994 [cited 22 October 1997].

35. Omananda@geocities.com. 1993. "Goa trance," in www.hyperreal.org/raves/spirit/technoshamanism [Internet]. 16 May 1993 [cited 22 November 1997].

36. Charlene Ma, "Telepathic message," in www.hyperreal. org/raves/spirit/technoshamanism [Internet]. 19 September 1996 [cited 3 November 1997].

37. Lee, "Physics_and_raving.html," in www.hyperreal. org/raves/spirit/technoshamanism [Internet]. 12 May 1995 [cited 10 December 1997].

38. Alice Braley, "House Music and Planetary Healing," in www.cloudfactory.org [Internet]. 12 December 1995 [cited 2 December 1997].

39. Jason Page, Untitled, in DCRaves listserv [Listserv]. 17 November 1997 [cited 13 November 1997]. Available at DCRaves@American.edu.

homogeneity and comradeship in a moment in and out of time. Just as Turner wrote that communitas feeds the spirit, one raver claimed that raves nurture the soul.[40] The feeding of the spirit is what might make the rave so therapeutic. By crossing over into a communitas state, rave culture dissipates the tension of entering a world of wage slavery, underemployment, and shrinking opportunity. Thus, by manipulating symbols of tribalism, ravers enter communitas where they reaffirm what they say the world ought to be—liberation, freedom, union, communion, harmony, warmth, peace, love, family, euphoria, bliss, happiness, godliness, and health. They confront with renewed vigor what they say the world actually is— violence, fear, hatred, racism, poverty, injustice, hunger, greed, performance, achievement, competition, enterprise, judgment, division, comparison, differentiation, distinction, distraction, isolation, impotence, and alienation.[41] In other words, the rave, like most "authentic" rituals, successfully unifies the "ought" and the "is" through symbols and experience.

Communitas cannot be a permanent state, however, because structure and social differentiation are necessary to maintain the physical body. Without the allocation of roles and resources, the division of labor, the organized, restrained, rational considerations necessary to meet daily needs would not be met. (Turner 1967, cited by Myerhoff 1974: 246). This may explain why few permanent raver communities exist, despite the abundant chatter about forming a new world (see below). One raver/DJ even recognizes the inevitability of the return to structure: "raves are good because they don't happen all the time."[42]

To complete the description and explanation of rave transformation, I would like to contrast the experiences described above with the very similar phenomenon of group consciousness induced at Grateful Dead concerts. Citing Victor Turner, Robert Sardiello (1994: 129–131) states that Grateful Dead concerts are secular rituals which "symbolically separate individuals in both space and time from their ordinary social lives." Both Deadheads (loyal fans of the Grateful Dead) and ravers refer to their events as escapes from reality. According to Anthony Pearson (1987: 419),

> large numbers of Deadheads report a psychic connection with the band, often reporting Jungianlike synchronicities and other esoteric phenomena in the concert setting.

The altered states of consciousness recounted by Deadheads, referred to alternatively as hypnosis and catharsis, seem quite similar to transformations described by ravers. Grateful Dead drummer Mickey Hart acknowledges these ecstatic states induced at concerts, stating "we've got transformation going on here" (quoted in Pearson 1987: 419).

Pearson notes that drug use is high at Grateful Dead concerts, but, as I argue with regard to similar drugs at raves, Pearson (p. 426) argues that drug use cannot be simply viewed as the cause of the cognitive experiences reported by Deadheads. Rather, he believes that the Grateful Dead concert experience is triggered by feelings of psychic connection between band and audience (see also Sardiello 1994: 128). Audience members often feel that the band played a particular song because of the way it relates to a specific problem or situation in their lives. Or, a poignant Grateful Dead lyric may simultaneously coincide with a fan's own, unrelated thought, causing the fan to assume a causal connection between the two. The connection between Deadhead and band recalls the shamanic connection between raver and DJ. Sardiello (pp. 124–126) adds a symbolic interpretation to Pearson's psychic explanation. Omnipresent symbols such as tie-dyed T-shirts and colorful icons of skeletons, roses, and dancing bears work to unify the audience and create a shared text with mythical and philosophical meaning. Though neither Sardiello nor Pearson discusses the physiological mechanisms I propose for altered states of consciousness among ravers, the symbolic aspects and ritual nature of Grateful Dead concerts closely resemble raves and produce a similar ethos of communality.

Subcultural Capital

It is difficult to accept ravers' statements about non-differentiation, unity, and oneness because a certain "political economy" underlies the rave scene.

---

40. Omananda@geocities.com. "Goa trance," in www. hyperrreal.org/raves/spirit/technoshamanism [Internet]. 16 May 1993 [cited 22 November 1997].

41. All of these terms appear in raver characterizations of the two worlds.

42. Interview conducted November 1997.

Thornton (1995) points out in her ethnography of club cultures that, despite the mantras of unity and collectivity, there is noticeable selectivity and exclusivity in the rave scene, based on a scale of hipness. Unable to compete with adults for occupational status, but in many cases still supported by parents, young ravers derive self esteem by competing for what Thornton calls subcultural capital, a concept founded in Bourdieu's notions of cultural and symbolic capital (Bourdieu 1977, 1984). Hierarchies of prestige and standards of authenticity develop based on familiarity with the latest music, the latest slang, the latest fashions (Appadurai 1986: 44–45). Those who make a living from subcultures—connoisseurs of rave authenticity such as club owners, promoters, and professional DJs—must uphold such hierarchies of subcultural capital in order to be successful. For example, to attract the best crowd, a club owner must be selective about which DJs can perform and who can enter the club (Thornton 1995: 102–105). The resulting exclusivity conflicts with the language of unity. Even London's first raves, held at the club Shoom, were restricted to a small clique (including some celebrities), despite an ethos of love, peace, and unity (Reynolds 1998a: 61). Though Thornton's research might not apply to the many raves organized outside the club scene and its selective door policies, it certainly demonstrates the presence of difference and distinction within the rave.

This contradiction between the egalitarian unity claimed by ravers and the hierarchical divisions documented by Thornton can be reconciled by conceptualizing the rave as a temporal process. I believe that the rave process can be understood as a sort of journey, a term which ravers also use to characterize their events. The distinctions of hipness that Thornton observes best characterize the behavior behind the *organization* of a rave—when decisions are made as to which DJs are given the chance to spin, who gets on the guest list of a club, or who gets invited to secretive events—and possibly at the *beginning* of raves—when bouncers might be selective about who they let into a club and when egos may interfere with the proper vibe of Peace, Love, Unity, and Respect (PLUR). To repeat, many of these distinctions only pertain to raves held in nightclubs. After these distinctions have been made and the technoshamanistic journey progresses, remaining differences are slowly eliminated through dance, drugs, and other rituals

that transform structures of subcultural capital into antistructure. Specifically, egos can be shed and inhibitions erased by MDMA, which is renowned as a harmony inducing drug (Saunders 1995; McRobbie 1995; Redhead 1993). Also, ravers suggest that dancing to trance music can bind communities together.[43] Similarly, Rietveld states that you can lose yourself in "the anonymity of fellow ravers and in blinding music" (1993: 69). Dance, as a technique of ecstasy, becomes a portal to transformation.

Maintaining the hypothesis that the rave experience is much like Eliade's myth of the eternal return, I believe that the rave journey can be fruitfully compared with a classic journey in the anthropological literature. The pilgrimage to Wirikuta made by the Huichol of Mexico is interpreted by Barbara Myerhoff (1974) as an enactment of Eliade's myth. On their journeys the Huichol and the ravers become one with the world. Barriers between young and old, male and female, and leader and follower are broken. A specific Huichol ritual for achieving oneness in which pilgrims connect with each other by each tying a knot on a string and then burning the string has a parallel in a ritual performed at raves sponsored by the New Moon collective and Gateway collective. At these raves the organizers set up an altar on the dance floor and each raver contributes an item to the altar. The altar becomes an objectification of the community and in contributing to the altar, the raver disconnects from the self and connects to the whole. Also, Wirikuta is a primordial place of origins that is very similar to the primitive tribal village described by ravers. Both destinations are viewed as places where ancestors dwell and places of origins from which human history has diverged. In the case of the Huichol the distinction between human and divine is erased. The rave scene also contains references to identity with gods: the DJ is referred to as god[44] and ravers can become gods, as in the Keoki track "Caterpillar,"[45] the name of which appropriately

---

43. Erich Schneider, "Technoshamanism_Definitions.html: Why don't we start with a definition," in www.hyperreal. org/raves/spirit/technoshamanism [Internet]. 24 May 1995 [cited 8 December 1997].
44. See liner notes in Doc Martin. 1994. *UrbMix Volume 1: Flammable Liquid*. Planet Earth compact disk P50105-2.
45. Superstar DJ Keoki. 1995. *Caterpillar*. Moonshine Music compact disk MM 88419.

signifies the possibility of metamorphosis. Also, ravers claim to see the gods at the end of their journey and come closer to the gods than any other worldly experience could bring them. Finally, the journey to the lost homeland is said to bring positive spiritual transformations in both groups. Like those who return from raves with positive spiritual transformations, Huichol who endure the peyote hunt achieve unity and community, their highest religious goal, and are reassured through visions (Myerhoff 1974) that the world is a happy place. According to one raver, the "project" of the rave journey is also to visualize a world whose people are happy and healthy.[46] In sum, both ravers and the Huichol receive hopeful visions[47] of why life is good in the midst of disjointed times.

The Rave in Context

The rave subculture also resembles other North American subcultures that emphasize spiritual healing and alternative spirituality, such as followers of New Age Channels, the Rainbow People, and cults like the Divine Light Mission. A major point of social or academic commentary on therapeutic activities like channeling and attending raves is the dynamic between individual healing and social improvement. The consciousness movement, of which channeling is one of the most controversial offshoots, is said to have arisen "out of a pervasive dissatisfaction with the quality of personal relations" (Lasch 1979: 27). An individualist and privatist movement emphasizing personal improvement, the consciousness movement "advises people not to make too large an investment in love and friendship, to avoid excessive dependence on others" (p. 27). Channels, who use altered states of consciousness to contact spirits or to "experience spiritual energy from other times and dimensions" (Brown 1997: viii), are also intensely individualistic, sharing a deep mistrust of churches and society as a whole (p. 123). Channels, like the ravers quoted above, feel that

their spirituality is more authentic than the spirituality of organized religion. However, the channels' resistance to community organizations exists only on a local, pragmatic level. The concept of a global community, as abstract world universal enough to transcend race, class, and nationality, is a goal toward which many channels claim passionate commitment (p. 124). The Internet has become the primary locus for such community building among channels, and the sense of togetherness fostered by the net is deeply felt (p. 125). However, Brown adds a patent critique of this form of virtual community: channels do not "walk their talk." They fail to address any of the practical, day-to-day concerns of an actual community, such as who will supply water, run hospitals, capture criminals, and collect garbage.

Just like new age channels, many ravers appear to be committed to a global village blind to age, race, sex, and class. One raver desires "that through the rave ritual we can use technology to bring the people of the world together in peace by means of dance."[48] According to raver Robert Jesse, "during our shared moments of ecstatic joy, we explore who we are and we advance visions of our harmonious planet."[49] Despite the rhetoric of communal harmony, ravers, like channels, do not work toward creating such a community. Aside from

> a few disparate groups . . . [demonstrating] for the right to carry on getting out of their heads and dancing to weird music on weekends (McKay 1996: 104),

there is almost no political activism in the rave scene. Ravers do little more than attend late night and early morning parties in out-of-the-way places;[50] visions

---

46. Robert Jesse, "The Monk in Europe," in www.hyperreal. org/raves/spirit/testimonials/ [Internet]. 16 May 1993 [cited 22 October 1997].

47. Anonymous, "Hopeful visions," in www.hyperreal.org/ raves/spirit/hopeful [Internet]. [cited 16 November 1997].

48. *Cyberpun@wam.umd.edu* "Technopagan_Raveprayer. html," in www.hyperreal.org/raves/spirit/technoshaman ism [Internet]. 28 December 1994 [cited 3 November 3 1997].

49. Robert Jesse, "The Monk in Europe," in www.hyperreal. org/raves/spirit/testimonials/ [Internet]. 16 May 1993 [cited 22 October 1997].

50. Most collectives, such as the New Moon Collective, San Francisco (www.hyperreal.org/raves/newmoon), Daydream Collective, Eugene OR (www.hyperreal.org/ raves/daydream), Friends and Family collective, San Francisco (www.bass-station.com/fnf), and Catalyst Effusion, Toronto (announced on an email message posted to the DCRaves listserv, 18 November 1997), in fact do nothing more than organize parties.

of future unity and global communities remain visions (Hesmondhalgh 1995). When ravers say that "We can only improve the society if we improve ourselves first,"[51] or that "consciousness unfolds and expands itself slowly from the individual to a group awareness,"[52] they sound very much like the channel who said

> We have to have inner communication to figure out who we are first, then those communities that we want can really happen (Brown 1997: 124).

The Rainbow Family is also dedicated to the creation of a cooperative, egalitarian, and utopian community (Niman 1997). However, whereas rave and new age utopias remain virtual, the Rainbow Family creates real, though temporary, utopias at their various national and regional Gatherings. Usually over the course of a month the Rainbow Family works to transform park land into actual communities with fully functional infrastructures (kitchens, latrines, infirmaries, childcare). In such a "Temporary Autonomous Zone," everybody is welcome, from yuppies to the homeless, and no money is required. The Rainbow family enacts a working model of multiculturalism, a society whose differences are celebrated and unity achieved (Niman 1997: 99).

Perhaps at the far end of the spectrum of community building we find cults such as the Divine Light Mission, whose members completely renounce previous beliefs, communities (friends, family), and jobs and devote their lives to the preservation and outreach of their cult (Galanter 1989). Though these communities are often totalizing, raves and cults have some things in common. Cults involve spiritual highs and altered states of consciousness, and are highly popular among youths reacting against the uncertainties of the transition to adult society (Hexham and Poewe 1986). As in the rave, the experience of community is a cornerstone of the cult experience. In his study of the Divine Light Mission Galanter (1989: 10) noticed that the more people

affiliated themselves with the cult, the more relief they received. Relief reinforces the members' involvement in the group and attachment to the group's principles. However, Galanter (pp. 5–7) argues that psychological processes cause the cult members to affiliate with the cult community, whereas I have made an explicitly cultural case for the positive transformations ravers say they undergo. Furthermore, the process of group attachment in cults is circular and self-reinforcing, so that involvement in the cult grows to dominate the cult members' lives. In contrast, ravers detach from their "group" when the rave event comes to an end in the early morning. Though such regular detachment from raves might be expected to produce frustrated feelings of interruption, testimonies of ravers instead reveal satisfaction and excitement about reuniting under the same principles of PLUR the next weekend. Perhaps permanent utopias are not viable, as Turner and others suggest, and that the superficiality of rave "community" reflects that condition.

Niman's ethnography of the Rainbow Family highlights a second commentary. Like ravers, the Rainbow Family has conscious roots in the revival of primitivism, paganism, and tribalism (1997: 37). Those who attend Rainbow Gatherings often mimic and alter Native American culture and religious rituals, believing that what they contrive is the real thing. Teepees, sweat lodges, pipe ceremonies, medicine bags, and feathers are central features of the gathering. Rather than dismissing such "fakelore" as inauthentic Indian culture, it might be better, to call it simply Rainbow culture (Niman 1997). Such a move puts us in line with Bruner (1994), who argues with Baudrillard that scholars should not criticize authenticity in the sense of fidelity to an original model because all cultures are caught in a process of copying and reinventing themselves. Instead, scholars should attend to authenticity as it is constructed by informants, particularly when competing segments of society call it into question in the context of uneven power relations (p. 408). With regard to power relations, the Rainbow practice of borrowing Native American customs might reflect a form of cultural imperialism that has powerfully negative consequences, and it is on this basis that a critique of authenticity should be considered. As Niman cogently argues, Rainbow impersonations of Indians trivialize Native American practices such that

---

51. Salami and Komotion International, "Why you are here," in www.cloudfactory.org [Internet]. 12 December 1995 [cited 2 December 1997].

52. Omananda@geocities.com. "Goa trance," in www.hyperrreal.org/raves/spirit/technoshamanism [Internet]. 16 May 1993 [cited 22 November 1997].

these practices lose their force. The impersonations consequently undermine attempts by Native Americans to affirm their own identities and thwart legal battles to preserve religious freedom. Though ravers also use Native American symbols, I argue that they are not as complicit in the unintentional cannibalization and trivialization of Native American culture because fakelore is comparatively limited within rave culture and located in highly fragmented contexts. The spiritual aspect of raves does not include conscious mimicry of Native American ceremonies. Unlike some New Age healing procedures, for example, rave rituals do not imitate Native American ceremonies, dress, orations, or props. I am aware of no raves that use Native paraphernalia like sweat lodges or medicine bags. I know of no DJs who, like new age shamans, take Native American names. Fakelore is most often limited to the use of Native American-inspired icons in two-dimensional, decorative contexts, sometimes tongue-in-cheek, and often heavily diluted by other motifs, futuristic and otherwise.

Conclusion

The critique of fakelore foregrounds a key question of this article: whether or not the technoshaman is a real shaman or just a plastic medicine man. Some commentators see the rave as a meaningless simulacrum. For some young people, raves are a form of entertainment not taken as seriously as a religious experience. Nevertheless, this does not eliminate the fact that for many people, the rave is spiritual and highly meaningful (Reynolds 1998a: 9). Based on the testimonials presented here, raves increase self esteem, release fears and anxieties, bring inner peace, and improve consciousness, among other things. When an informant claims that "Last night a DJ saved my life," it is reasonable to accept that this is "spiritual healing." I have elucidated the ritual framework for this therapeutic effect by attending to physiological factors as well as symbols and metaphors that dominate rave discourse. With the help of the DJ, ravers embark on an overnight journey to a primitive paradise where individuality is left behind and communitas is achieved. At their destination ravers claim to find a world of harmony, equality, and communality; a place similar to humanity in its early tribal stage, according to ravers, but diametrically opposed to the modern world. Reynolds (1998b: 86) points out that the myth of unity is just a myth; indeed, as seen in the previous section, ravers can be criticized for not following through on their goals of community building. But as the Huichol example makes clear, myths are powerful. The enactment of the myth of eternal return—a symbolic return to the primordial place where life is as it should be—invigorates the ravers, allowing them to face the sobriety and tedium of daily life, at least until the next rave. The rave experience might be highly symbolic, but these symbols are fashioned and imbued with such meaning that they far surpass the empty, touristic simulacra that some academic commentators consider them to be.

Suggested Readings

Furst, Peter T.
    1976   *Hallucinogens and Culture*. Novato, CA: Chandler and Sharp.

Journal of Psychoactive Drugs
    1989   "Shamanism and Altered States of Consciousness." Special theme issue.

Lambek, Michael
    1981   *Human Spirits: A Cultural Account of Trance in Mayotte*. Cambridge: Cambridge University Press.

Myerhoff, Barbara G.
    1974   *The Peyote Hunt: The Sacred Journey of the Huichol Indians*. Ithaca, NY: Cornell University Press.

Schultes, Richard Evans, and Albert Hofmann
1979   *Plants of the Gods: Origins of Hallucinogenic Use.* NY: Alfred van der Marck Editions.

Tart, Charles T., ed.
1969   *Altered States of Consciousness: A Book of Readings.* NY: John Wiley.

Winkelman, Michael
1997   "Altered States of Consciousness and Religious Behavior" in Stephen Glazier, ed. *Anthropology of Religion: A Handbook of Method and Theory.* Westport, CN: Greenwood Press, pp. 393–428.

Zinberg, Norman E., ed.
1977   *Alternate States of Consciousness.* NY: Free Press.

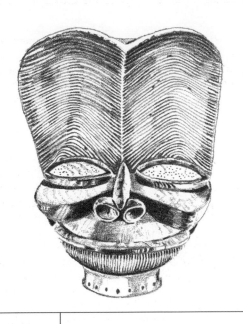

CHAPTER SIX

Ethnomedicine: Religion and Healing

Bacham dance mask from Cameroun.

If a single pervasive thought were to be singled out in this chapter, it would be the importance of culture in determining the etiology and treatment of disease and mental disorders. Just as humans have always suffered from disease, so, too, have we always responded to it, seeking ways to reduce its debilitating nature or, we hope, to banish it completely. All human societies have belief systems and practices that people turn to in order to identify disease and effect a cure. The integration of the study of these systems of beliefs and practices into the study of non-Western societies has created medical anthropology, the most recent addition to the discipline of anthropology (see Hahn 1995; Lindenbaum and Lock 1993; Mascie-Taylor 1993; Nichter 1992).

Explanations and cures of illnesses may be either natural or supernatural (a naturalistic response would not involve supernatural aid). As P. Stanley Yoder has clearly pointed out, one of the medical anthropologist's most important tasks is to distinguish between different types of causation and to understand the relationship between them, especially because "different types of causal explanations may be involved at different points during the process of diagnosis and treatment, or may characteristically demand differing treatments" (1982: 15). Moreover, because the range and variability of medical beliefs and practices among the peoples of the world are immense, there will be no easy explanation or simple generalization regarding causation and treatment of diseases. But always it will be possible to see the close relationship between medicine and religion, a cultural bonding that occurs in nonliterate, nonindustrialized cultures as well as in modern, technological cultures.

The importance of our understanding of ethnomedical systems is made clear by the fact that a great percentage of the non-Western world's population reside in areas that are little exposed to Western medical treatment. Primary among the concerns of such international groups as the World Health Organization is the role that improved health care can play in the socioeconomic development of Third World countries. The lack of implementation of modern medical care in these areas of the world is caused by a lack of both available funds and information. Partly in response to the dearth of funding, some health planners have proposed that the most effective way to expand modern primary care would be for

236

Western-trained practitioners to collaborate with traditional practitioners (Bichmann 1979: 175); however, lack of information is the greatest barrier to assessing the feasibility of such proposals in relation to national health goals and planning (Good 1977: 705). Because little substantive information concerning indigenous health care systems is available for non-Western countries, the identification and use of agents of change, such as local curers, to improve the quality of life in rural areas is extremely difficult.

It is noteworthy to point out also that intercultural contact seems to have caused an increase in both physical and psychological Western-based diseases among non-Western populations; the frustrations of not being able to cure these modern illnesses are liable to increase the use of traditional methods of healing. Other problems of contact also exist. Western-trained medical practitioners find little in traditional systems of health care they consider effective in either the physical or the mental realm. On the other hand, modern medical treatment is often rejected by those in the culture. For example, in rural contemporary Kenya, modern medical technology is not changing the pervasive "ancestor spirit-sorcery theory" of disease causation that has traditionally been used to account for all major misfortunes (Kramer and Thomas 1982: 169): As late as 1969 there was still no indication among the rural Kamba of Kenya that modern medicine had made prominent inroads at the level of prevention, either in effecting behavioral change or in modifying etiological beliefs, despite their long exposure to Western techniques.

Determining why the ill choose to accept or reject a system of treatment not only would define whom the people in the culture perceive as the proper healer but also would delineate their etiology of disease and their perception of appropriate treatment. What applied anthropologists are attempting to determine are the advantages and disadvantages of each of the health care systems— traditional and modern—in the eyes of the patients, as well as the nature of the knowledge healers and their clients draw upon in the process of selecting treatment. Unfortunately, previous research in traditional medical systems has essentially ignored the studied people's own explanations of these criteria, criteria that ordinarily include both natural and supernatural explanations.

Knowledge of the naturalistic treatments and ethnopharmacological systems of non-Western societies is also important, for much of the pharmacopoeia administered by traditional healers does work. (Societies everywhere possess naturalistic explanations and treatments. Cures derived from hundreds of wild plants were used by the North American Indians, for example, and techniques for the treatment of headaches and stomachaches, the setting of broken bones, bloodletting, lancing, cauterization, and other naturalistic skills are well known to the nonliterate world.) However, as the effectiveness of the traditional healer is dependent upon more than the use of proper chemical treatment, diagnosis is made not only at the empirical level but at the psychological and social levels as well. In speaking of Africa, for example, Wolfgang Bichmann notes that illness does not mean so much an individual event but a disturbance of social relations (1979: 177), and M. F. Lofchie points out that "African medical research has much to contribute to Western medicine: its wholism, emphasis on treatment of the entire family as well as the 'ill' person, and its encyclopedic lore of information about the curative properties of items available in nature—all of these principles are now working their way into Western medical vocabulary" (1982: vii).

For years it was widely believed that only "civilized" people were subject to mental illness, whereas the preliterates of the world led a blissful life free of neuroses and psychoses. It did not take anthropology long to prove that Rousseau's Noble Savage was just as susceptible to the major disorders of the mind as was the individual coping with life in the so-called civilized societies of the world. Anthropologists have sought answers to such important questions as whether mental illness rates differ cross-culturally; whether styles and types of illnesses vary; and whether it is more difficult to adjust to life in industrialized societies than in others. Anthropologists and others have shown, moreover, that traditional healers are particularly effective in the treatment of mental illness, and that their approaches to curing are beneficial to physical diseases as well. Not only are traditional healers' services readily available to the ill, for example, but their system of care is also nondisruptive to those in the culture, and the patient has the support of family members who are nearby or in actual attendance during the treatment. Beyond these advantages, and in contrast with the Western world, Third World countries frequently are much more accepting of those having mental illnesses. Sufferers of these disorders are often stigmatized in the West, and many attempt to hide their medical history.

A seven-year multicultural pilot study of severe mental illness by the World Health Organization reported in the magazine *Science '80* showed that relatively fast and complete recoveries from major psychoses are achieved in developing countries, such as Nigeria and India. In the United States and other Western countries, however, almost one-half of those who suffer psychotic breakdowns never recover. For example, whereas 58 percent of the Nigerians and 51 percent of the Indians studied had a single psychotic episode and were judged cured after treatment, the cure rate in the industrialized countries ranged from only 6 percent in Denmark to a high of 27 percent in China ("World Psychosis" 1980: 7). Certainly non-Western healing techniques are effective in the treatment of the mentally ill; however, the treatment of physiological diseases cannot match that of the West. The fact that many non-Western pharmaceuticals may be effective in one society and not in another demonstrates the important relationship of beliefs and cures—in particular, the interaction of the healer and the supernatural.

Throughout the world it is possible to place supernaturally caused illnesses into five categories: (1) sorcery, (2) breach of taboo, (3) intrusion of a disease object, (4) intrusion of a disease-causing spirit, and (5) loss of soul (Clements 1932: 252). It is important to note that these categories may not be recognized by certain societies. Indeed, it is a difficult task to determine the frequency and incidence of illnesses, especially mental illnesses, in non-Western, nonindustrialized countries. Native peoples may avoid seeking medical help from a modern health facility, for example, or, if they do seek treatment, there may be a question of accurate recordkeeping.

Anthropologists have correctly noted that the types of cures sought are based not only on the cause but also on the severity of the illness in terms of level of pain and difficulty of curing. Treatment based on cause and severity varies greatly; some non-Western groups maintain that most diseases are of natural origin, whereas others blame the supernatural realm for the misfortunes.

It is apparent that anthropologists must understand the integration of ethnomedical systems with the other areas of culture if they are successfully to conduct comparative studies. Ethnomedical systems are deeply ingrained in the structure of societies, functioning in ways that create a positive atmosphere for health care. No longer can we view non-biomedical medical methods as inferior; indeed, Western society owes much to traditional medicine, not the least of which is the support given to the patient by the family and the community.

The readings in this chapter, for the most part, deal with supernaturally caused diseases and mental illnesses and their etiology and treatment. Arthur C. Lehmann opens the chapter with an analysis of ethnomedicine among the Aka hunters and Ngando farmers. He stresses disease categories, disease etiology, treatment, and the role traditional healers (*ngangas*) play in interethnic contacts.

In the second article, L. A. Rebhum discusses anger and illness in northeast Brazil, where women use the term *swallowing frogs* to mean suppressing anger, hatred, or irritation and withstanding unfair treatment silently.

In the next article, William Wedenoja focuses on the role of women as curers in the Balm yards of Jamaica; he keys especially on the relationship between the Balm healers and their patients.

The final selection is an excerpt from the book *The Spirit Catches You and You Fall Down* by Anne Fadiman. Fadiman compassionately describes a Hmong family living in California, whose young daughter is diagnosed with epilepsy.

References

Bichmann, Wolfgang
   1979 "Primary Health Care and Traditional Medicine—Considering the Background of Changing Health Care Concepts in Africa." *Social Science and Medicine* 13B: 175–82.

Clements, Forrest E.
   1932 "Primitive Concepts of Disease." University of California *Publications in American Archaeology and Ethnology* 32 (2): 252.

Good, Charles M.
   1977 "Traditional Medicine: An Agenda for Medical Geography." *Social Science and Medicine* 11: 705–13.

Hahn, Robert A.
   1995 *Sickness and Healing: An Anthropological Perspective.* New Haven, Conn.: Yale University Press.

Kramer, Joyce, and Anthony Thomas
   1982 "The Modes of Maintaining Health in Ukambani, Kenya." In P. S. Yoder, ed., *African Health and Healing Systems: Proceedings of a Symposium,* pp. 159–98. Los Angeles: Crossroads Press, University of California.

Lindenbaum, Shirley, and Margaret Lock, eds.
   1993 *Knowledge, Power, and Practice: The Anthropology of Medicine and Everyday Life.* Berkeley: University of California Press.

Lofchie, M. F.
   1982 "Foreword." In P. Stanley Yoder, ed., *African Health and Healing Systems: Proceedings of a Symposium,* pp. vii–ix. Los Angeles: Crossroads Press, University of California.

Mascie-Taylor, C. G. N., ed.
   1993 *The Anthropology of Disease.* New York: Oxford University Press.

Nichter, Mark, ed.
   1992 *Anthropological Approaches to the Study of Ethnomedicine.* Philadelphia: Gordon and Breach.

"World Psychosis." *Science '80* 1 (6): 7.

Yoder, P. Stanley
   1982 "Issues in the Study of Ethnomedical Systems in Africa." In P. Stanley Yoder, ed., *African Health and Healing Systems: Proceedings of a Symposium,* pp. 1–20. Los Angeles: Crossroads Press, University of California.

29

Eyes of the *Ngangas:* Ethnomedicine and Power in Central African Republic

Arthur C. Lehmann

People of the Third World have a variety of therapies available for combating diseases but, because of cost, availability, and cultural bias, most rely on ethnomedical, or traditional, treatment rather than "biomedical," or Western, therapies. Dr. Lehmann's field research focuses on the importance of ngangas (traditional healers) as a source of primary health care for both the Aka Pygmy hunters and their horticultural neighbors, the Ngando of Central African Republic. Tracing the basis and locus of the ngangas' mystical diagnostic and healing powers, he shows that they are particularly effective with treatments for mental illness and, to an unknown extent, with herbal treatment of physical illnesses. The powers of the Aka ngangas, however, are also used to reduce the tensions between themselves and their patrons and to punish those Ngando who have caused the hunters harm. Lehmann points out the necessity of recognizing and treating the social as well as the biological aspects of illness and appeals to health care planners to establish counterpart systems that mobilize popular and biomedical specialists to improve primary health care in the Third World.

Ethnomedicine (also referred to as folk, traditional, or popular medicine) is the term used to describe the primary health care system of indigenous people whose medical expertise lies outside "biomedicine," the "modern" medicine of Western societies. Biomedicine does exist in the Third World, but it is unavailable to the masses of inhabitants for a number of reasons. Conversely, although popular medicine has largely been supplanted by biomedicine in the Western world, it still exists and is revived from time to time by waves of dissatisfaction with modern medicine and with the high cost of health care, by the health food movement, and by a variety of other reasons. The point is, all countries have pluralistic systems of health care, but for many members of society the

combat against the diseases that have plagued mankind is restricted to the arena of popular medicine.

This is particularly true in the developing nations, such as those of the sub-Saharan regions of Africa, where over 80 percent of the population live in rural areas with a dearth of modern medical help (Bichmann 1979; Green 1980). Between 1984 and the present, I have made six field trips to one such rural area (the most recent in 1994) to study the primary health care practices of Aka Pygmy hunter-gatherers and their horticultural neighbors, the Ngando of Central African Republic (C.A.R.).

The Aka and the Ngando

Several groups of the Pygmies live in a broad strip of forested territory stretching east and west across the center of Equatorial Africa. The two largest societies

This selection was written especially for this volume.

are the Mbuti of the Inturi Forest of Zaire and the Aka, who live in the Southern Rainforest that extends from the Lobaye River in Central African Republic into the People's Republic of the Congo and into Cameroun (Cavalli-Sforza 1971). Like the Mbuti, the Aka are long-time residents of their region. It is on the edge of the Southern Rainforest in and near the village of Bagandu that the Aka Pygmies and the Ngando come into the most frequent contact. The proximity, particularly during the dry season from December to April, allows for comparisons of health care systems that would be difficult otherwise, for the Aka move deep into the forest and are relatively inaccessible for a good portion of the year.

Since Turnbull described the symbiotic relationship between Mbuti Pygmies and villagers in Zaire (1965), questions remain as to why Pygmy hunters continue their association with their sedentary neighbors. Bahuchet's work shows that the relationship between the Aka and the Ngando of C.A.R. is one of voluntary mutual dependence in which both groups benefit; indeed, the Aka consider the villagers responsible for their well-being (1985: 549). Aka provide the Ngando with labor, meat, and forest materials while the Ngando pay the Aka with plantation foods, clothes, salt, cigarettes, axes and knives, alcohol, and infrequently, money.

This mutual dependence extends to the health care practices of both societies. Ngando patrons take seriously ill Aka to the dispensary for treatment; Aka consider this service a form of payment that may be withheld by the villagers as a type of punishment. On the other hand, Aka *ngangas* (traditional healers) are called upon to diagnose and treat Ngando illnesses. The powers believed to be held by the *ngangas* are impressive, and few, particularly rural residents question these powers or the roles they play in everyday life in Central African Republic.

Eyes of the *Ngangas*

The people believe that the *ngangas* intervene on their behalf with the supernatural world to combat malevolent forces and also use herbal expertise to protect them from the myriad of tropical diseases. Elisabeth Motte (1980) has recorded an extensive list of medicines extracted by the *ngangas* from the environment to counter both natural and supernatural illnesses; 80 percent are derived from plants and the remaining 20 percent from animals and minerals.

Both Aka and Ngando *ngangas* acquire their power to diagnose and cure through an extensive apprenticeship ordinarily served under the direction of their fathers, who are practicing healers themselves. This system of inheritance is based on primogeniture, although other than first sons may be chosen to become *ngangas*. Although Ngando *ngangas* may be either male or female, the vast majority are males; all Aka *ngangas* are males. In the absence of the father or if a younger son has the calling to become a healer, he may study under a *nganga* outside the immediate family.

During my six trips to the field, *ngangas* permitted me to question them on their training and initiation into the craft; it became apparent that important consistencies existed. First, almost all male *ngangas* are first sons. Second, fathers expect first sons to become *ngangas;* as they said, "It is natural." Third, the apprenticeship continues from boyhood until the son is himself a *nganga,* at which time he trains his own son. Fourth, every *nganga* expresses firm belief in the powers of his teacher to cure and, it follows, in his own as well. As is the case with healers around the world, despite the trickery sometimes deemed necessary to convince clients of the effectiveness of the cure, the *ngangas* are convinced that their healing techniques will work unless interrupted by stronger powers. Fifth, every *nganga* interviewed maintained strongly that other *ngangas* who were either envious or have a destructive spirit can destroy or weaken the power of a healer, causing him to fail. Sixth, and last, the origin and locus of the *ngangas'* power is believed to be in their eyes.

Over and over I was told that during the final stages of initiation the master *nganga* had vaccinated the initiate's eyes and placed "medicine" in the wound, thus giving the new *nganga* power to divine and effectively treat illnesses. At first I interpreted the term *vaccination* to mean simply the placement of "medicine" in the eyes, but I was wrong. Using a double-edged razor blade and sometimes a needle, the master *nganga* may cut his apprentice's lower eyelids, the exterior corners of the eyes, or below the eyes (although making marks below the eyes is now considered "antique," I was told); he concludes the ceremony by placing magical medicine in the cuts. At this moment, the student is no longer an apprentice; he has achieved the status of an *nganga* and the ability to diagnose illnesses with the newly acquired power of his eyes.

Not until my last field trip in 1994 did I witness a master *nganga* actually cut the whites of his apprentice's eyes. At the end of an hour-long interview with an *nganga,* which focused on my eliciting his concept of disease etiology in treatment of illness, I casually posed the question I had asked other *ngangas* many times before: "Do you vaccinate your apprentice's eyes?" The *nganga* beckoned his apprentice seated nearby, and, to my amazement, the apprentice immediately placed his head on the master's lap. I quickly retrieved my camcorder which I had just put away! The master removed a razor blade from a match box, spread the student's eyelids apart, deftly made five cuts on the whites of each eye, and squeezed the juice of a leaf (the "medicine") into the wounds. This astounding procedure performed on perhaps the most sensitive of all human parts took less than a total of three minutes and did not appear to cause the apprentice any degree of pain, albeit his eyes were red and his tears profuse.

During the career of an *nganga,* his eyes will be vaccinated many times, thus, it is believed, rejuvenating the power of the eyes to correctly diagnose illness and ensure proper therapy. It is clear that the multiple powers of *ngangas* to cure and to protect members of their band from both physical and mental illnesses as well as from a variety of types of supernatural attacks reside in their eyes.

It follows that the actual divinatory act involves a variety of techniques, particular to each *nganga,* that allows him to use his powers to "see" the cause of the illness and determine its treatment. Some burn a clear, rocklike amber resin called *paka* found deep in the rain forest, staring into the flames to learn the mystery of illness and the appropriate therapy. Some stare into the rays of the sun during diagnosis or gaze into small mirrors to unlock the secret powers of the ancestors in curing. Others concentrate on plates filled with water or large, brilliant chunks of glass. The most common but certainly the most incongruous method of acquiring a vision by both Aka and Ngando *nganga*s today is staring into a light bulb. These are simply stuck into the ground in front of the *nganga* or, as is the case among many village healers, the light bulb is floated in a glass of water during consultation. The appearance of a light bulb surfacing from an Aka *nganga*'s healing paraphernalia in the middle of a rain forest is, to say the least, unique. Western methods of divining—of knowing

the unknown—were not, and to some degree are not now, significantly different from the techniques of the *ngangas*. Our ways of "seeing," involving gazing at and "reading" tea leaves, crystal balls, cards, palms, and stars, are still considered appropriate techniques by many.

Therapy Choices and Therapy Managers

A wide variety of therapies coexist in contemporary Africa, and the situation in the village of Bagandu is no exception. The major sources of treatment are Aka *ngangas*, Ngando *ngangas*, kinship therapy (family councils called to resolve illness-causing conflicts between kin), home remedies, Islamic healers (marabouts), and the local nurse at the government dispensary, who is called "doctor" by villagers and hunters alike. In addition, faith healers, herbalists, and local specialists (referred to as "fetishers") all attempt, in varying degrees, to treat mental or physical illness in Bagundu. Intermittently Westerners, such as missionaries, personnel from the U.S. Agency for International Development, and anthropologists also treat physical ailments. Bagandu is a large village of approximately 3,400 inhabitants; however, most communities are much smaller and have little access to modern treatment. And, as Cavalli-Sforza has noted,

> If the chances of receiving Western medical help for Africans living in remote villages are very limited, those of Pygmies are practically nonexistent. They are even further removed from hospitals. African health agents usually do not treat Pygmies. Medical help comes exceptionally and almost always from rare visiting foreigners. (Cavalli-Sforza 1986: 421)

Residents of Bagandu are fortunate in having both a government dispensary and a pharmacy run by the Catholic church, but prescriptions are extremely costly relative to income, and ready cash is scarce. A more pressing problem is the availability of drugs. Frequently the "doctor" has only enough to treat the simplest ailments such as headaches and small cuts; he must refer thirty to forty patients daily to the Catholic pharmacy, which has more drugs than the dispensary but still is often unable to fill prescriptions for the most frequently prescribed drugs such as penicillin, medicine to counteract parasites, and antibiotic salves. Although the doctor does the best he can under these conditions, patients must often resort only to popular medical treatment—in spite of the fact that family members, the therapy managers, have assessed the illness as one best treated by biomedicine. In spite, too, of the regular unavailability of medicine, the doctor's diagnosis and advice is still sought out—"although many people will consent to go to the dispensary only after having exhausted the resources of traditional medicine" (Motte 1980: 311).

Popular, ethnomedical treatment is administered by kin, *ngangas* (among both the Aka and Ngando villagers), other specialists noted for treatment of specific maladies, and Islamic marabouts, who are recent immigrants from Chad. According to both Aka and Ngando informants, the heaviest burden for health care falls to these ethnomedical systems. Ngando commonly utilize home, kin remedies for minor illnesses, but almost 100 percent indicated that for more serious illnesses they consulted either the doctor or *ngangas* (Aka, Ngando, or both); to a lesser extent they visited specialists. The choice of treatment, made by the family therapy managers, rests not only on the cause and severity of the illness, but also on the availability of therapists expert in the disease or problem, their cost, and their proximity to the patient. Rarely do the residents of Bagandu seek the aid of the marabouts, for example, in part because of the relatively high cost of consultation. Clearly, both popular and biomedical explanations for illness play important roles in the maintenance of health among Bagandu villagers, although popular medicine is the most important therapy resource available. Popular medicine is especially vital for the Aka hunters, whose relative isolation and inferior status (in the eyes of the Ngando) have resulted in less opportunity for biomedical treatment. Yet even they seek out modern medicine for illnesses.

Whatever the system of treatment chosen, it is important to understand that "the management of illness and therapy by a set of close kin is a central aspect of the medical scene in central Africa. . . . The therapy managing group . . . exercises a brokerage function between the sufferer and the specialist" (Janzen 1978: 4). It is the kingroup that determines which therapy is to be used.

Explanations of Illness

The choice of therapy in Bagandu is determined by etiology and severity, as in the West. Unlike Western medicine, however, African ethnomedicine is not restricted to an etiology of only natural causation. Both the Aka and the Ngando spend a great deal of time, energy, and money (or other forms of payments) treating illnesses perceived as being the result of social and cultural imbalances, often described in supernatural terms. Aka and Ngando nosology has accommodated biomedicine without difficulty, but traditional etiology has not become less important to the members of these societies. Frequent supernatural explanations of illness by Aka and Ngando informants inevitably led me to the investigation of witchcraft, curses, spells, or the intervention of ancestors and nameless spirits, all of which were viewed as being responsible for poor health and misfortune. The Aka maintain, for example, that the fourth leading cause of death in Bagandu is witchcraft (diarrhea is the principal cause; measles, second, and convulsions, third [Hewlett 1986: 56]). During my research, it became apparent that a dual model of disease explanation exists among the Aka and Ngando: first, a naturalistic model that fits its Western biomedical counterpart well, and second, a supernaturalistic explanation.

Interviews with village and Pygmy *ngangas* indicated that their medical systems are not significantly different. Indeed, both groups agree that their respective categories of illness etiology are identical. Further, the categories are not mutually exclusive: an illness may be viewed as being natural, but it may be exacerbated by supernatural forces such as witchcraft and spells. Likewise, this phenomenon can be reversed: an illness episode may be caused by supernatural agents but progress into a form that is treatable through biomedical techniques. For example, my relatively educated and ambitious young field assistant, a villager, was cut on the lower leg by a piece of stone while working on a new addition to his house. The wound, eventually becoming infected, caused swelling throughout the leg and groin. As was the case in some of his children's illnesses, the explanation for the wound was witchcraft. It was clear to him that the witch was a neighbor who envied his possessions and his employment by a foreigner. Although the original cut was caused by a supernatural agent, the resulting infection fitted the biomedical model. Treatment by a single injection of penicillin quickly brought the infection under control, although my assistant believed that had the witch been stronger the medicine would not have worked. Here is a case in which, "in addition to the patient's physical signs and social relationships," the passage of time is also crucial to "the unfolding of therapeutic action" (Feierman 1985: 77). As the character of an illness changes with time as the illness runs its course, the therapy manager's decisions may change, because the perceived etiology can shift as a result of a variety of signs, such as a slow-healing wound or open conflict in the patient's social group (Janzen 1978: 9).

Studies on disease etiologies among select African societies (Bibeau 1979; Janzen 1978; Warren 1974) reported that most illnesses had natural causes, and this finding holds for the Ngando villagers as well. At first glance, these data would seem to reduce the importance of ngangas and of popular medicine generally, but it is necessary to recognize that ngangas treat both natural and supernatural illnesses utilizing both medical and mystical techniques. The question posed by Feierman, "Is popular medicine effective?" (1985: 5), is vital to the evaluation of ngangas as healers. Surely some traditional medicines used by these cures must in many cases work, and work regularly enough to earn the sustained support of the general public.

Illnesses of God and Illnesses of Man

Both the Ngando and Aka explanations for natural illnesses lack clarity. Some ngangas refer to them as "illnesses of God"; others simply identify them as "natural"; and still others frequently use both classifications, regularly assigning each label to specific ailments. Hewlett maintains that the Aka sometimes labeled unknown maladies as illnesses of God (1986: personal communication). On the other hand, the Bakongo of neighboring Zaire defined illnesses of God as those "generally, mild conditions which respond readily to therapy when no particular disturbance exists in the immediate social relationships of the sufferer. . . . The notion of 'god' does not imply divine intervention or retribution but simply that the cause is an affliction in the order of things unrelated to human intentions" (Janzen 1978: 9).

Both Janzen's and Hewlett's data are accurate, but my field data show as well that the explanations of natural illnesses among the Ngando and Aka not only refer to normal mild diseases and sometimes unknown ones but also to specific illnesses named by the ngangas and the residents of Bagandu. The confusion surrounding these mixed explanations of disease causation is an important topic for future ethnosemantic or other techniques of emic inquiry by ethnographers.

Residents of Bagandu and both Aka and Ngando ngangas categorized sickness caused by witchcraft, magic, curses, spells, and spirits as "illnesses of man." This is the second major disease category. Witchcraft, for example, while not the main cause of death, is the most frequently named cause of illness in Bagandu. Informants in Bagandu cite the frequency of witchcraft accusations as proof of their viewpoint. Antisocial or troublesome neighbors are frequently accused of being witches and are jailed if the charge is proven. Maladies of all sorts, such as sterility among females, are also commonly attributed to the innate and malevolent power of witches. These types of explanations are not unusual in rural Africa. What is surprising are reports of new illnesses in the village caused by witches.

All Ngando informants claimed, furthermore, that the problem of witchcraft has not diminished over time; on the contrary, it has increased. The thinking is logical: because witchcraft is believed to be inherited, any increase in population is seen also as an inevitable increase in the number of witches in the village. Population figures in the region of the Southern Rainforest have increased somewhat in the past few decades despite epidemics such as measles; accordingly, the incidence of maladies attributed to witches has increased. One informant from Bagandu strongly insisted that witches are not only more numerous but also much more powerful today than before. Offiong (1983) reported a marked increase of witchcraft in Nigeria and adjacent states in West Africa, caused not by inflation of population but by the social strain precipitated by the frustration accompanying lack of achievement after the departure of colonial powers.

Insanity is not a major problem among the Ngando. When it does occur, it is believed to be caused by witchcraft, clan or social problems, evil spirits, and breaking taboos. Faith healers, marabouts, and ngangas are seen as effective in the treatment of mental illness due to witchcraft or other causes. The role of faith healers is particularly important in the lives of members of the Prophetical Christian Church in Bagandu. They have strong faith in the healing sessions and maintain that the therapy successfully treats the victims of spirits' attacks. Informants also claim the therapy lasts a long time.

The curse is a common method of venting anger in Bagandu, used by both male and female witches. Informants stated that women use curses more than men and that the subjects of their attacks are often males. The curses of witches are counted as being extremely dangerous in the intended victim. One villager accused the elderly of using the curse as a weapon most frequently. Spell-casting is also common in the area, and males often use spells as a method of seduction.

Most, if not all, residents of Bagandu use charms, portable "fetishes," and various types of magical objects placed in and around their houses for protection. Some of these objects are counter-magical: they simultaneously protect the intended victim and turn the danger away from the victim to the attackers. Counter-magic is not always immediate; results may take years to appear. Charms, fetishes, and other forms of protection are purchased from *ngangas*, marabouts, and other specialists such as herbalists. For example, the Aka and Ngando alike believe that wearing a mole's tooth on a bracelet is the most powerful protection from attacks by witches.

To a lesser extent, spirits are also believed to cause illness. It is problematic whether or not this source of illness deserves a separate category of disease causation. Bahuchet thinks not; rather, he holds that spirit-caused illnesses should be labeled illnesses of God (1986: personal communication). It is interesting to note that in addition to charms and other items put to use in Bagandu, residents supplicate ancestors for aid in times of difficulty. If the ancestors do not respond, and if the victim of the misfortune practices Christianity, he or she will seek the aid of God. Non-Christians and Christians alike commonly ask diviners the cause of their problem, after which they seek the aid of the proper specialist. Revenge for real or imagined attacks on oneself or on loved ones is common. One method is to point a claw of a mole at the wrongdoer. Ngando informants maintain the victim dies soon after. Simple possession of a claw, if discovered, means jail for the owner.

My initial survey of Aka and Ngando *ngangas* in 1984 brought out other origins of illness. Two *ngangas* in Bagandu specifically cited the devil, rather than unnamed evil spirits, as a cause for disease. The higher exposure of villagers to Christianity may account for this attribution: seven denominations are currently represented in the churches of Bagandu. Urban *ngangas* questioned in Bangui, the capital, stressed the use of poison as a cause of illness and death. Although poisonings do not figure prominently as a cause of death among the Aka and Ngando, it is common belief that *ngangas* and others do use poison.

Finally, while not a cause for illness, informants maintained that envious *ngangas* have the power to retard or halt the progress of a cure administered by another. All *ngangas* interviewed in 1984 and 1985 confirmed not only that they have the power to interrupt the healing process of a patient but also that they frequently invoke it. Interestingly, *ngangas* share this awesome power with witches, who are also believed by members of both societies to be able to spoil the "medicine" of healers. This kind of perception of the *ngangas'* power accounts, in part, for their dual character: primarily beneficial to the public, they can also be dangerous.

While the numerical differences in the frequency of physiologically and psychologically rooted illnesses in Bagandu are unknown, Ngando respondents in a small sample were able to list a number of supernaturally caused illnesses that are treatable by *ngangas*, but only a few naturally caused ones. Among the naturalistic illnesses were illnesses of the spleen; *katungba*, deformation of the back; and *Kongo*, "illness of the rainbow." According to Hewlett (1986: 53), *Kongo* causes paralysis of the legs (and sometimes of the arms) and death after the victim steps on a dangerous mushroom growing on a damp spot in the forest where a rainbow-colored snake has rested. Had the Ngando sample been more exhaustive, it is probable that the list of natural diseases would have been greater, although perhaps not as high as the twenty natural illnesses the *ngangas* said they could treat successfully. That impressive list includes malaria, hernia, diarrhea, stomach illness, pregnancy problems, dysentery, influenza, abscesses, general fatigue, traumas (snake bite, miscellaneous wounds, and poisoning), and general and specific bodily pain (spleen, liver, ribs, head, and uterus).

Powers of the *Ngangas*

The powers of the *ngangas* are not limited to controlling and defeating supernatural or natural diseases alone. In the village of Bagandu and in the adjacent Southern Rainforest where the Ngando and Aka hunters come into frequent contact, tensions exist due to the patron-client relationship, which by its very economic nature is negative. These tensions are magnified by ethnic animosity. Without the Akas' mystical power, their economic and social inferiority would result in an even more difficult relationship with the Ngando. Here the powers of the Pygmy *ngangas* play an important part in leveling, to bearable limits, the overshadowing dominance of the Ngando, and it is here that the *ngangas* demonstrate their leadership outside the realm of health care. Each Aka has some form of supernatural protection provided by the *nganga* of his camp to use while in the village. Still, the need exists for the extraordinary powers of the *nganga* himself for those moments of high tension when Aka are confronted by what they consider the most menacing segments of the village population: the police, the mayor, and adolescent males, all of whom, as perceived by the Aka, are dangerous to their personal safety while in the village.

In the summer of 1986, I began to study the attitudes of village patrons toward their Aka clients and, conversely, the attitudes of the so-called wayward servants (Turnbull's term for the Mbuti Pygmy of Zaire, 1965) toward the villagers. Participant observation and selective interviews of patrons, on the one hand, and of hunters, on the other, disclosed other important tangents of power of the Aka in general and of their *ngangas* in particular. First, the Aka often have visible sources of power such as scarification, cords worn on the wrist and neck, and bracelets strung with powerful charms for protection against village witches. These protective devices are provided the Aka by their *ngangas*. Second, and more powerful still, are the hidden powers of the Aka in general, bolstered by the specific powers of the *ngangas*. Although the villagers believe the hunters' power is strongest in the forest, and therefore weaker in the village setting, Aka power commands the respect of the farmers. Third, the villagers acknowledge the Aka expertise in the art of producing a variety of deadly poisons, such as *sepi*, which may be used to punish farmers capable of the most

serious crimes against the Pygmies. The obvious functions of these means of protection and retribution, taken from the standpoint of the Aka, are positive. Clearly these powers reduce the tension of the Aka while in the village, but they also control behavior of villagers toward the hunters to some undefinable degree.

Villagers interpret the variety of punishments which the Aka are capable of meting out to wrongdoers as originating in their control of mystical or magical powers. Interestingly, even poisonings are viewed in this way by villagers because of the difficulty of proving that poison rather than mystical power caused illness or death. Although the use of poison is rare, it is used and the threat remains. Georges Guille-Escuret, a French ethnohistorian working in Bagandu in 1985, reported to me that prior to my arrival in the field that year three members of the same household had died on the same day. The head of the family had been accused of repeated thefts of game from the traps and from the camp of an Aka hunter. When confronted with the evidence—a shirt the villager had left at the scene of the thefts—the family rejected the demands of the hunter for compensation for the stolen meat. Soon thereafter, the thief, his wife, and his mother died on the same day. Villagers, who knew of the accusations of theft, interpreted the deaths as the result of poisoning or the mystical powers of the hunter.

Stories of Aka revenge are not uncommon, nor are the Akas' accusations of wrongdoing leveled against the villagers. To the Ngando farmers, the powers of the Aka *ngangas* include the ability to cause death through the use of fetishes, to cause illness to the culprit's eyes, and to direct lightning to strike the perpetrator. These and other impressive powers to punish are seen as real threats to villagers—but the power of the *ngangas* to cure is even more impressive.

Attempts in my research to delineate the strengths and weaknesses of the *ngangas* and other health care specialists discovered a number of qualities/characteristics widely held to be associated with each. First, each specialist is known for specific medical abilities; that is, Aka and Ngando *ngangas* recognize the therapeutic expertise of others in a variety of cures. A *nganga* from Bangui maintained that Aka *ngangas* were generally superior to the village healers in curing. This view is shared by a number of villagers interviewed, who maintained that the power of Aka *ngangas* is greater than that of their own specialists.

The Aka strongly agree with this view, and in a sense the Aka are more propertied in the realm of curing than are the villagers. There is no question that the Aka are better hunters. Despite the Ngandos' greater political and economic power in the area and the social superiority inherent in their patron status, the Ngando need the Aka. All these elements help balance the relationship between the two societies, although the supernatural and curative powers of Aka *ngangas* have not previously been considered to be ingredients in the so-called symbiotic relationship between Pygmy hunters and their horticultural neighbors.

Second, *ngangas* noted for their ability to cure particular illnesses are often called upon for treatment by other *ngangas* who have contracted the disease. Third, with one exception, all the *ngangas* interviewed agree that European drugs, particularly those contained in hypodermic syringes and in pills, are effective in the treatment of natural diseases. One dissenting informant from the capital disdained biomedicine altogether because, as he said, "White men don't believe in us." Fourth, of the fourteen Aka and Ngando *ngangas* interviewed in 1985, only five felt that it was possible for a *nganga* to work successfully with the local doctor (male nurse) who directed the dispensary in Bagandu. All five of these *ngangas* said that if such cooperation did come about, their special contribution would be the treatment of patients having illnesses of man, including mental illness resulting from witchcraft, from magical and spiritual attacks, and from breaking taboos. None of the *ngangas* interviewed had been summoned to work in concert with the doctor. Fifth, as a group, the *ngangas* held that biomedical practitioners are unable to successfully treat mental illnesses and other illnesses resulting from attacks of supernatural agents. In this the general population of the village agree. This is a vitally important reason for the sustained confidence in popular therapy in the region—a confidence that is further strengthened by the belief that the *ngangas* can treat natural illnesses as well. Sixth, the village doctor recognized that the *ngangas* and marabouts do have more success in the treatment of mental illnesses than he does. Although the doctor confided that he has called in a village *nganga* for consultation in a case of witchcraft, he also disclosed that on

frequent occasions he had to remedy the treatment administered by popular specialists for natural diseases. It is important to recognize that unlike biomedical specialists in the capital, the local doctor does appreciate the talents of traditional therapists who successfully practice ethnopsychiatry.

All respondents to this survey recognized the value of biomedicine in the community, and little variation in the types of cures the doctor could effect was brought out. No doubts were raised regarding the necessity of both biomedicine and popular therapy to the proper maintenance of public health. The spheres of influence and expertise of both types of practitioners, while generally agreed on by participants of the Ngando survey, did show some variation, but these were no more serious than our own estimates of the abilities of our physicians in the West. In short, all informants utilized both systems of therapy when necessary and if possible.

The continuation of supernatural explanations of illness by both the Ngando and the Aka results in part from tradition, in combination with their lack of knowledge of scientific disease etiology, and in part because of the hidden positive functions of such explanations. Accusations of witchcraft and the use of curses and malevolent magic function to express the anxiety, frustrations, and social disruptions in these societies. These are traditional explanations of disease, with more than a single focus, for they focus upon both the physical illness and its sociological cause. "Witchcraft (and by extension other supernatural explanations for illness and disaster) provides an indispensable component in many philosophies of misfortune. It is the friend rather than the foe of mortality" (Lewis 1986: 16). Beyond this rationale, reliance upon practitioners of popular medicine assures the patient that medicine is available for treatment in the absence of Western drugs.

The Role of Ethnomedicine

Among the Aka and Ngando and elsewhere, systems of popular medicine have sustained African societies for centuries. The evolution of popular medicine has guaranteed its good fit to the cultures that have produced it; even as disruptive an element of the system as witchcraft can claim manifest and latent functions that contribute to social control and the promotion of proper behavior.

Unlike Western drug therapies, no quantifiable measure exists for the effectiveness of popular medicine. Good evidence from World Health Organization studies can be brought forth, however, to illustrate the relatively high percentage of success of psychotherapeutic treatment through ethnomedicine in the Third World compared to that achieved in the West. The results of my research in Bagandu also demonstrate the strong preference of villagers for popular medicine in cases involving mental illness and supernaturally caused mental problems. At the same time, the doctor is the preferred source of therapy for the many types of natural disease, while *ngangas* and other specialists still have the confidence of the public in treating other maladies, referred to as illnesses of man and some illnesses of God. Whatever the perceived etiology by kingroup therapy managers, both popular and biomedical therapists treat natural illnesses. It is in this realm of treatment that it is most important to ask, "What parts of popular medicine work?" rather than, "Does popular medicine work?" Because evidence has shown that psychotherapy is more successful in the hands of traditional curers, it is therefore most important to question the effectiveness of popular therapy in handling natural illnesses. Currently, the effectiveness of traditional drugs used for natural diseases is unknown; however, the continued support of popular therapists by both rural and urban Africans indicates a strength in the system. The effectiveness of the *ngangas* may be both psychological and pharmaceutical, and if the ecological niche does provide drugs that do cure natural illnesses, it is vital that these be determined and manufactured commercially in their countries of origin. If we can assume that some traditional drugs are effective, governments must utilize the expertise of healers in identifying these.

It is unrealistic to attempt to train popular therapists in all aspects of biomedicine, just as it is unrealistic to train biomedical specialists in the supernatural treatments applied by popular practitioners. However, neither type of therapist, nor the public, will benefit from the expertise of the other if they remain apart. The task is to make both more effective by incorporating the best of each into a counterpart system that focuses on a basic training of healers in biomedicine. This combination must certainly be a more logical and economic choice than attempting to supply biomedical specialists to every community in Central African Republic, a task too formidable for any country north or south of the Sahara. The significance of this proposal is magnified by the massive numbers for whom biomedicine is unavailable, those who must rely only upon ethnomedicine.

Even if available to all, biomedicine alone is not the final answer to disease control in the Third World. Hepburn succinctly presents strong arguments against total reliance upon the biomedical approach:

> Biomedicine is widely believed to be effective in the cure of sickness. A corollary of this is the belief that if adequate facilities could be provided in the Third World and "native" irrationalities and cultural obstacles could be overcome, the health problems of the people would largely be eliminated. However, this belief is not true, because the effectiveness of biomedicine is limited in three ways. First, many conditions within the accepted defining properties of biomedicine (i.e., physical diseases) cannot be treated effectively. Second, by concentrating on the purely physical, biomedicine simply cannot treat the social aspects of sickness (i.e., illness). Third, cures can only be achieved under favorable environmental and political conditions: if these are not present, biomedicine will be ineffective (1988: 68).

The problems facing societies in Africa are not new. These same issues faced Westerners in the past, and our partial solutions, under unbelievably better conditions, took immense time and effort to achieve. If primary health care in the non-Western world is to improve, the evolutionary process must be quickened by the utilization of existing popular medical systems as a counterpart of biomedicine, by the expansion of biomedical systems, and by the cooperation of international funding agencies with African policymakers, who themselves must erase their antagonism toward ethnomedicine.

30

Swallowing Frogs: Anger and Illness in Northeast Brazil

L. A. Rebhun

In northeast Brazil, women use the term swallowing frogs *to mean suppressing anger, hatred, or irritation, and withstanding unfair treatment silently. In connection with "swallowing frogs," women in L. A. Rebhun's field research also complained of such folk illnesses as* nervos *("nerves"),* susto *(shock sickness),* blood-boiling bruises, mao olhado *(evil eye), and* peito aberto *(open chest). All of these illnesses are discussed by Rebhun in this selection, each of which she argues is as much an emotional syndrome as a folk medical syndrome and should be seen as an embodiment of distress in which physical symptoms and psychological experiences are identical. Thus, physical, social, and personal aspects of a situation all serve as evidence about whose bad behavior is making the individual sick. Rebhun also suggests that, through the women's use of emotional folk medical vocabulary, combined with culturally recognized behavioral symptoms, these folk medical syndromes can serve as powerful tactics for controlling and manipulating others.*

Coração do pobre não bate, apanha.
The hearts of the poor do not beat, they are beaten.

—Brazilian proverb

In Latin American folk medicine, emotion is recognized as a powerful force that can cause sickness. In addition, certain emotions, especially strong or unpleasant ones, can become sicknesses in themselves. In Northeast Brazil, both men and women suffer from emotion syndromes and the effects of suppressing strong sentiment, but the spectrum of allowed emotion is different for men and for women, as are the moral connotations of particular emotions; men and women also have different permitted means of expressing particular sentiments. While conducting

"Swallowing Frogs: Anger and Illness in Northeast Brazil" by L. A. Rebhun from MEDICAL ANTHROPOLOGY QUARTERLY, December 1, 1994. Copyright © 1994, American Anthropological Association. Reprinted by permission. [Endnotes and some references have been omitted for the present volume.]

fieldwork in Northeast Brazil, I often heard women say that they had to "swallow frogs" *(engolir sapos)* in particular situations. They used the term to mean both suppressing anger, hatred, or irritation, and putting up with unfair treatment silently.

In connection with "swallowing frogs," women also frequently complained of folk illnesses like *nervos* ("nerves"), *susto* (shock sickness), blood-boiling bruises, *mal olhado* (evil eye), and *peito aberto* (open chest). These syndromes constitute an interrelated group of emotion-based ailments, generally typical of women, which form part of sociomoral discourse on the proprieties of social interaction.

They may also be seen as symptoms of the pain of bridging gaps between cultural expectation and personal experience in emotion, a process neither easy nor simple. Often, several similar folk medical complaints are interrelated, as in the Northeast Brazilian versions of "nerves," susto, evil eye (cf. Scheper-Hughes 1992: 173) and peito aberto. A patient may be diagnosed with any or all of these, and the diagnosis reflects more opinion about the patient's personality and personal situation than the details of her symptoms. All of these complaints have in common strong sentiments such as anxiety, shock, envy, hatred, and anger, which are both common and disturbing in women who are generally expected to be self-sacrificing, loving, and generous. Diagnosis of one or more of these ailments reflects opinions on the appropriateness of a woman's experience of negative emotions.

These ailments are as much emotional as folk medical. As Finkler has shown, the idea that these kinds of syndromes are body metaphors for psychological distress is too Cartesian; they are better seen as embodiments of distress in which body symptom and psychological experience are one and the same (1989: 82). The physical and psychological also combine in social aspects of folk medical diagnosis. To say that one is suffering from "nerves," for example, is to describe both a set of symptoms and a psychosocial situation.

Individuals use emotional folk medical vocabulary as one aspect of self-presentation. Speakers combine behavioral symptoms (trembling, limping, and so forth), gossip about social situations, and such emotional indicators as facial expression, other body language, and voice inflection with folk medical vocabulary to create evidence for moral interpretations of their situations. Physical, social, and personal experiential aspects of their situation all combine as evidence for the truths of their moral assertions about whose bad behavior is making them sick. Because of embedded moral discourses, emotional folk medical syndromes can become powerful tactics in the struggle to control and manipulate friends, neighbors, and family members.

Emotion and Folk Illness

Over the last two decades, cross-cultural research has revealed how deeply culture and emotion are interwoven, how sentiments are shaped by the very disparate vocabularies of different languages, how cultural expectations shape emotional expression in particular circumstances, how intellect and emotion are indistinguishable in many cultural settings, and how medical and emotional concepts are intertwined in the folk medicine of many cultures.

Some folk medical vocabularies incorporate folk theories of emotion, as in the Andean *pena* in which

suffering, seen as inevitable, is believed to slowly turn the heart into stone, causing chest pains, sadness, erratic thinking, and, in extreme cases, rage attacks (Toussignant 1984: 387). Others express sociomoral concepts as when evil eye is attributed to the emotions of envy, jealousy, and anger, thought to be wicked and therefore destructive. Emotional folk medical complaints may also reflect ethnicity or group membership, constitute tactics in attempts at social manipulation, or embody distress not otherwise expressable. Such complaints may constitute what happens when people are not able to live up to the emotional expectations of their cultures, or when emotional expectations are contradictory, convoluted, or in flux.

"Nerves," susto, evil-eye sickness, and analogues of open chest have been described in other Latin American settings, often as separate syndromes, each with its own etiology and symptoms. They have been called culture-bound or culturally mediated syndromes and seen either as embodied expressions of psychosocial distress or as local variations of universal human psychiatric diseases.

Variations of such syndromes as evil eye and "nerves" can be found throughout the Mediterranean, North Africa, Latin America, and parts of Great Britain, as well as in some areas of North America. The great variety in diverse forms of such syndromes as evil eye, for example, has led some to posit that it is not one but rather several different syndromes while others insist that it constitutes a related cluster of variations on the same themes. In either case, both evil eye and "nerves" are complex, multivocal, multimeaning syndromes, so that different interpretations and significances may attach to them in dissimilar cultural settings or even in distinct circumstances within one cultural setting.

Field Site and Methods

From December 1988 to December 1990, I conducted research on emotion, family relations, and folk ailments in the context of Brazil's shifting economy. I worked in the Northeast Brazilian city of Caruaru, Pernambuco (population 200,000), and neighboring villages, using a combination of methods in my research, including both direct and participant observation, survey of archival sources and prior research on the region, interviews with local politicians and other officials about the legal framework of marriage, domestic violence, and child custody, and 120 interviews with local residents.

Because I was interested in extended networks of kin, friends, and neighbors, I used a snowball sampling method that has been shown to be effective in studies of small populations (Bernard 1994: 97–98). Interviews addressed demographic issues (age, marital status, birthplace, and so forth) and the meanings of words comprising emotional vocabulary, including what is called *sentimento* (sentiment) in local parlance as well as words used to describe body states considered part of sentimento. In addition, I asked informants to tell me their life stories and to comment on things that had happened to them and those they knew, for thematic analysis. I also interviewed religious healers and their patients about emotion-related folk medical complaints.

Brazil's Northeast is its most impoverished region, characterized by monetary instability, extremes of social inequality, low life expectancy, and very high infant mortality (IGBE/UNICEF 1986; Nations and Amaral 1991: 208). The past 30 years have seen the largest rural-to-urban migration in Brazil's history: one in five Brazilians migrated to cities between 1960 and 1970 (Perlman 1976: 5), and by 1980 55 percent of the Northeast's population was urban (de Araujo 1987: 167). Caruaru is the first urban stop for many former rural residents. Economic disarray has intensified reliance on social networks of friends and relatives. The region's population, struggling with new economic patterns in the midst of abject poverty, endemic disease, and an unstable economy, is deeply dependent on relatives and friends for the goods, services, and connections they need to survive. However, unable to trust old solidarities in the face of new, urban opportunities, they are frequently wracked by anger, resentment, and envy, all of which find expression in folk medical complaints.

Despite its relatively large population, Caruaru is organized like a series of villages pushed together. Residents know their immediate neighbors very well, and city blocks are often inhabited by single extended families. But few people have friends living more than a few blocks away, and many neighborhoods are inhabited by members of no more than two or three large extended families. Often, these families also have members in any of several small towns within about an hour's commute by bus of Caruaru. Economic and social ties to these out-of-town relatives are often stronger than ties to fellow Caruaruenses from different neighborhoods.

The Northeast is a semiarid region, subject to periodic droughts but lacking the reservoirs, irrigation, and piping technologies that would make it fully habitable. To the poor, life is a *luta* or struggle in which people survive through a combination of astute manipulation of opportunity and the capacity to endure suffering.

In Caruaru, economic opportunities include work in its famous markets, blue jeans factories, and the burgeoning tourist trade, centered on the sale of little clay figurines. My informants were drawn largely from the lower working class, including housewives, market vendors, blue jeans pieceworkers, factory workers, bakers, seamstresses, maids, baby-sitters, and laundresses as well as their auto mechanic, artisan, and factory-worker male companions. In addition, I interviewed a number of local school teachers and some farmers and field workers from the rural zone. They ranged in age from 14 to 78, with most in their 30s and 40s. Most were at least nominally Catholic, although about a third were Seventh-Day Adventist or other Protestant.

Power, Interpretation, and Vocabulary in Emotional Folk Ailments

Both the study of folk medical systems and that of emotion cross-culturally have been influenced by Foucault's emancipation of the concept of power from strict confinement in the political sphere to something immanent in all social bonds, ascending from the micropolitics of interpersonal relations, through local institutions, to national and international establishments (Foucault 1986: 229–235). As the interpretive nature of both medical diagnoses and emotional labeling has become clearer, so has the power struggle underlying interpretation. Lutz's point that emotion is a "cultural and interpersonal process of naming, justifying, and persuading by people in relationship to each other" (1988: 5) is equally valid for folk medical diagnoses.

Especially with emotion-related folk syndromes, the questions of whether, when, and how to be sick are important elements of social stratagems. As

Crandon asserts in a study of susto in Bolivia, the folk-illness label constitutes a social judgment about the situation of the sufferer. Crandon suggests that researchers ask not "what is susto," but rather "why is susto diagnosed in any particular case," since the same constellation of symptoms can also be diagnosed as indicating any of several other folk syndromes (Crandon 1983: 154). The same question can be asked of "nerves," peito aberto, and evil eye. What do these diagnoses mean, how are they interrelated, and how do they fit into the micropolitics of power in families and local communities?

One of the ways these diagnoses fit the micropolitics of family power is in their gendered nature. Men and women become angry at different things, and express their anger differently. In addition, the moral connotations of angry behavior are different for men and for women. A man, for example, may drink himself to unconsciousness or beat his wife and children regularly with little serious social consequence from his point of view, while women are more likely to express despair through folk medical syndromes. While both men and women see poor people as suffering strugglers, the religious veneration of suffering as a key social value is greater for women than for men. Women's suffering is both a consequence of their powerlessness vis-à-vis men and an image used to manipulate men through guilt (Rebhun 1993). While both men and women see themselves as oppressed by the opposite sex, there is also general agreement that women suffer more because of men than men do because of women.

Swallowing Frogs: The Cultural Context of Anger

The folk syndromes of "nerves," evil eye, peito aberto, and susto are interrelated through their relation to strong emotions, especially anger. Despite an infectious public joyousness and open sensuality, Northeast Brazilians tend to display a profound distrust of particular strong emotions, especially envy, anger, and certain forms of grief, which are seen as socially disruptive because of their very intensity (Nations and Rebhun 1988; Scheper-Hughes 1992). At the same time, people encounter many reasons to feel these, from the anguish of frequent bereavement, to the frustrating humiliations of trying to get basic services from an uncaring government bureaucracy, to the injustices of poverty, to the many betrayals perpetrated by those who are supposed to love one another.

My informants spoke of evil eye, "nerves," peito aberto, and susto as the result of their own and others' anger (raiva, cólera), hatred (ódio), fear (medo), envy (inveja), and worry (preocupação). Sadness (tristeza), grief (pena), and depression (depressão, abatimento) also figured into the experience of these ailments. Commonly, it was not the expression but rather the suppression of these emotions that was seen as causing sickness.

The word my informants most frequently used to refer to anger was raiva, from the Latin rabia, meaning madness. Raiva also refers to the disease rabies. Brazilian dictionaries tend to define raiva by using the word ódio (from the Latin odi, "I hate"), although bilingual dictionaries give "raiva" as "anger," and "ódio" as "hatred." The Brazilian Dicionário Aurélio lists as its second definition of raiva (after the disease) "the violent sentiment of hatred [sentimento violento de ódio]." Unlike the English, where anger, anxiety, and strangulation are etymologically associated, in Brazilian Portuguese, anger, hatred, violence, and the disease of mad dogs are associated.

Emotions have associated scenarios; that is, any given sentiment is bounded by beliefs about what situations properly inspire it, how it ought to be expressed or not expressed, and what the consequences of its experience should be, both for the individual and for the group. In Brazilian Portuguese, anger is violent, powerful, and associated with a dangerous disease. Its associated scenarios include furious action, attacks, fighting, and the possibility of death. It is no wonder that so many Northeast Brazilian women find it a particularly frightening, dangerous emotion to experience and to inspire in others.

Emotion also constitutes a moral idiom, it is a moral reaction to a particular perception of events. The moral statements implied through emotions are complex for several reasons. For one, they depend on shared understandings of the presumptions underlying them, and these understandings may not be as similar as people assume.

In Northeast Brazil, disagreements about who has wronged whom are common. Through gossip and argument, the legitimacy of the participants' emotions and their response to those emotions as well as the facts of any given case are analyzed and reanalyzed by the social group (cf. Crandon 1983, who describes a similar process in Bolivia). By communicating sentiment either in words or symptoms, people make moral arguments for their point of view on each others' behavior. Emotion-related folk ailments become statements in the ongoing struggle to control one another's behavior through moral suasion. Because the facts of any given case may be ambiguous and because the implications of any given emotion are also ambiguous, multiple interpretations may attach to any given case (cf. White 1990: 51). Emotional life becomes a series of battles over interpretation and consequences of moral behavior.

This process is particularly acute in the cases of anger, hatred, and envy in Northeast Brazil. Averill (1982), in a discussion of emotion in the United States, posits that the emotions of anger, envy, and jealousy vary neither in their experience nor in their expression but rather in the nature of the perceived moral wrong that inspires them: anger is a reaction to a perceived injustice to oneself or one's group, jealousy regards one's loss to another as unjust, and envy sees the good fortune of another as an unacceptable threat to one's own situation. All three involve resentment of the power or the primacy of another over self (1982: 11). This analysis can also be applied to Northeast Brazil, where anger, jealousy, and envy are incompatible with the female obligation to be compassionate and selfless.

The Heat of Anger: Blood-Boiling Bruises

My informants did not see emotions as concepts but rather as a kind of energy that is physically present, taking up space inside their bodies, leaping the divide between bodies, and acting according to the same physical properties as water (cf. Solomon 1984). Anger was described as being like steam, rising from the boiling of its heat and hurting with its pressure unless expressed. Women described their unexpressed anger as suffocating, unrelieved pressure.

Women often showed me small bruises on their thighs and arms, which they attributed to the force of their blood boiling in their veins with anger. *Preto* (black) is used as a synonym for rage as in the phrase *fiquei preto* ("I was furious [black]"). Bruises may occur in conjunction with sick headaches, in which

pounding, shooting pains in the forehead and neck combine with nausea and dizziness.

> It feels like someone tied a rope around my head and stayed twisting it and tightening it, and I go vomiting and dying of anger, and I have to go lie down or I'll faint.

Despite the presence of hot, suffocating rage, women often described themselves as unable to express their strong emotions openly.

> Once my husband said to me, "Tonight I'm going to take you out." So I went, got my nails done, my hair done, new dress, put makeup on, and I waited, waited, waited. He did not come home that night. I was so angry, my stomach hurt with anger [raiva], I had bruises on my thighs, you know, my blood boiling, vomiting with hatred [ódio]. But I never said anything to him, undressed, went to bed. The next day, it was like it never happened. I never mentioned it, he never mentioned it. . . . I don't know why. I never forgot it, my stomach hurt for days. But I never said anything.

One reason for silence is fear of open conflict, especially given anger's violent associations.

> I want to say everything that I feel, you know, that I suffer, but I don't say in order to not cause problems. Understand, I'm like this, my daughter, I suffer in my nerves because I keep things inside of me. I can't express, I don't want to bother anyone, and I can't say what I want to say.

The unexpressed emotion does not go away; instead, it stays as a suffocating, sickening presence inside the body.

> When I am angry at a person, I stay with a suffocation imprisoned inside of me. . . . I stay shut up. I continue vibrating.

There are a number of reasons for this inability to express anger. In some cases, the woman is afraid that her emotion will overpower her self-control, leading her to actions she will later regret.

> I am a very aggressive person, when I am angry, I really lose control. I'm afraid of myself sometimes.

In other cases, the anger is diverted onto easier targets, especially children. The woman feels such an accumulation of outrage that small irritations like childish pranks become too much to tolerate and she explodes in violence.

Ave Maria! Too nervous! Ave Maria! I swear a lot, fight too much with my kids, I want to beat them, to kill them in that moment, but then afterwards I cry, I repent, I see in myself that it isn't a normal thing, you know? That I am very nervous. Whatever little thing, it's enough if I tidy the house and then my little girl drops something on the floor, Ave Maria! I'm ready to die. The children have a damned fear of me because I'm, My Virgin Mary! Explosive. It's anger.

Women may also be constrained by economic dependence and fear, especially women in physically and emotionally abusive relationships. For example, one informant I shall call Rejanne was unable to escape an abusive boyfriend for ten years. Married at age 12, at 13 she had been kicked out by her husband because of rumors of infidelity, and none of her small-town neighbors would take her in or give her work. Desperate to avoid being forced into taking up residence as a prostitute at a local bordello, she went to live with a man who offered her a home in return for sex and housework. He brought her far away to São Paulo and kept her locked in their apartment, beating her if he suspected her of talking to anyone other than himself. Socially isolated, economically dependent, physically and emotionally battered, young and alone in her desperation, she was terrified to leave him and unable to assert herself within their relationship.

I always had to swallow frogs, you know, because I was totally dependent on him. . . . Even when I knew I was right and he was unjust, I had to swallow it, I had to obey. I had to apologize, I had to humble myself and submit, and even thank him for mistreating me, in fear of my life.

Only when he brought her back to her hometown after ten years away was she able to escape him with the help of her parents, who had forgiven her youthful escapades in the intervening years.

Rejanne's story, while dramatic, was not unusual. Domestic violence is common, and legal penalties are few for abusive husbands. While some women leave men who beat them, resist, or fight back, many feel trapped by fear, family pressure, economic dependence, and/or fear of scandal.

Despite attempts to diminish the importance of anger, women feel strongly. Like bereaved mothers of infants who consciously suppress their grief

(Nations and Rebhun 1988: 162), angry women use specific techniques to calm themselves when they are angry, like slow breathing, clenching their teeth to avoid speech, drinking herbal teas, taking tranquilizers, lying down, praying, or leaving the area until they feel composed.

When I have a problem with anger, I only get better if I leave and walk because if I stay in the house I will get even angrier . . . if not we will come to blows, so I prefer to leave a little bit. I get a cigarette and go into the world, disappearing.

For others, "swallowing frogs" is so habitual that they do it without thinking. Infuriating events simply leave them speechless.

My neighbor arrived saying [my husband] was betraying me with another woman. I was all shut up, I shut up, my daughter, I didn't have any voice, I said nothing, I don't like to fight, I don't like to quarrel, to exchange words, I only like peace, I like unity in my house, understand. . . . I do everything to have peace inside my house, but it is a torment for a mother to rule over [dominar] all these people, to have lots of kids and not to have problems with arguments. . . . We get angry at something and our nerves get tired, isn't it just like that?

Anger is seen as a force or energy that can enter people's bodies, causing harm. It is especially dangerous to the weakest.

Did you see Dona Maria passing by here with that crippled daughter of hers? Because when she was seven months' pregnant, her mother-in-law made her so angry, she fainted with anger boiling inside her, and it burst the baby's head so she was born like that, can't walk, can't talk, all stiff. A pregnant woman can't get angry, shouldn't even be in a place where other people are angry.

Infants are often seen as suffering the effects of other people's anger, either directly in the form of blows struck in anger, or because some adult quarrel spilled over and hit them with the force of adult emotion. A fetus is vulnerable to any shock, anger, or stress its mother may feel while pregnant, and infants and small children are vulnerable to an atmosphere of resentment, or anger, envy, or hatred directed at their adult relatives. Depending on the strength of the emotion, it can kill or physically harm a baby, or, as it does with adults, it can leave the baby with a nervous temperament.

The Rezadeira

Although folk diagnoses are not specifically part of Catholic doctrine, they are most likely to be diagnosed by folk Catholic faith healers, called *rezadeiras* if female and *rezadores* if male. Folk Catholic faith healers use prayers, rituals, advice, herbs, and pharmaceuticals in their treatments of common ailments. The folk medical systems used by popular and religious practitioners do not make Western biomedicine's sharp distinction between diseases of the body or mind and other types of misfortunes. These healers are as likely to be consulted for a run of bad luck as for a physical complaint.

Of rural origin, rezadeiras now flourish in cities where crowding and poor sanitation increase sickness. Whereas rural Catholic healers are as likely to be men as women, in cities, most are women and the majority of their patients are also women. Rezadeiras treat patients with prayers mixed with rhymes specific to particular ailments.

Some ailments, such as fallen fontanelle, are unique to infants, whereas others, such as peito aberto, are typical of adults. Even when adults and infants are diagnosed as having the same syndrome, the symptoms are different. Such labels as evil eye or susto refer to irritability, frequent crying, or physical symptoms like diarrhea in infants; in adults they describe embodied emotional distress (see also Crandon 1983: 159–60).

"Nerves": Daily Anxiety

Illnesses called "nerves" have been described throughout Europe and the Americas (Low 1989). Like many other aspects of European and New World folk medicine, they can be traced back to ancient Greek medicine. Both Hippocrates and Galen posited the existence of physical structures in the body that translated the desires of the mind into the actions of the body. They called these "nerves" (Davis and Whitten 1988). In Northeast Brazilian folk medicine, the nerves are seen as little strings that control the muscles and transmit tension. They can get worn out by too much use in the form of worry and tension or by the accumulation of shocks. When that happens, the person becomes *nervoso*, or nervous, a permanent state.

The nervoso person frequently experiences headaches, trembling, dizziness, fatigue, belly aches, and sometimes partial paralysis, tingling of the extremities, and appetite disturbances. But the hallmark of the condition of nervoso is the inability to tolerate or control stressful emotions. Through constant exposure to the shocks of painful emotion, the "nerves" sufferer has become too sensitive to life's emotional hardships. Nervosa women described themselves as "uncontrolled" *(descontrolada),* prone to attacks of rage or bouts of crying (Rebhun 1993: 138–40).

Nervos is perhaps more an idiom of daily life than a medical complaint per se.

> It gets me in the nerves, this difficult life, that I bear it, bear it, bear it, bear it, but also I don't have patience, it gives me that hatred [ódio] inside of me, it stays that, that [thing] locked inside. I stay with too much anger.

Both men and women can be nervoso (Duarte 1986), but the symptoms of the condition have different connotations. To the extent that *nervosismo* (nervousness) is a state of victimization, a constant vulnerability in which the person has lost her ability to withstand emotional shocks, it is feminine. However, some of the behaviors associated with a nervoso individual, irritability, bouts of rage, and violent outbursts, are considered normal in men but unacceptable in women (cf. Dunk 1989: 38), whereas fits of uncontrollable crying or moments of intense, paralyzing terror are more acceptable as feminine symptoms. Nervosismo is not only more typical of women, but because women's emotional repertoire is less constrained than men's, they can adapt it to a wider range of situations and plumb it for a greater number of meanings than can men.

Nervosismo is a chronic state, often described as either an innate or an acquired personality trait. It is related to evil eye and susto because either of those can cause it and because, along with them, it forms part of a discourse on anger. The presence of too much anger inside the body frazzles the nerves, leaving them unable to stand even mild negative emotions.

Open Chest: Sickness and Emotional Vulnerability

Anger can either be the person's own suppressed rage, or it can be other people's anger that enters a body not properly closed. This state of dangerous emotional openness is called peito aberto (open chest). It is said to be caused by carrying too much weight, which makes the heart expand, opening the chest, and allowing evil influences to enter. Rezadeiras diagnose open chest by measuring a string twice against the patient's forearm and then looping it around the chest. If the measured length does not close securely around the chest (and it never does), a diagnosis of open chest is made. It is treated by tying the string around the chest, praying while making the sign of the cross over the chest, and pushing inward on the chest and breasts. Then the string is measured again and again looped over the chest. This time, it fits, and the rezadeira declares the chest properly closed.

I have argued elsewhere (Rebhun 1994) that the "weight" (peso) in open chest is a metaphor: the emotional weight of unshed tears, unspoken fury, unexpressed hatred. Women speak of these sentiments as taking up space inside their bodies, pressing against the inside of the face, the chest, or the belly, and having to be restrained with a physical effort. When the emotional weight becomes too heavy to carry, it bursts out, leaving openings where it left the body. Other people's anger and envy can enter these openings in the form of evil eye.

The expansion of the chest in peito aberto is related to the idea that a woman's heart is large and grows each time she comes to care about another person. When the "weight" of caring for and worrying about others becomes too great, the woman's heart expands too much and pushes her chest open. The condition of being open is generally seen as associated with women, because their genitals are seen as physically open in form and because their hearts are thought emotionally open. Openness has a specifically sexual connotation; the word fechada (closed) can be used to mean "virgin." Defloration, pregnancy, childbirth, and the accumulated weight of emotional troubles open women's bodies even more, while men remain with closed bodies and emotionally closed hearts that evil influences cannot enter as easily (cf. Robben 1988: 115).

Peito aberto is tied to evil eye because it is through evil eye that anger and envy enter the opened body. Rezadeiras' treatments for evil eye usually start with peito aberto, in an effort to close the body, and then proceed to remove any existing evil eye. Relief is thought to be immediate but temporary because the situations that give rise to peito aberto and evil eye are recurrent.

Evil Eye: The Sickness of Others' Anger

References to evil eye and attempts to deflect it are ubiquitous in Northeast Brazil. People often follow compliments with "but I don't give evil eye" or write the phrase "o seu olho gordo é cego p'ra mim [your evil eye is blind to me]" on truck bumpers or the walls of stores, restaurants, and booths in the marketplace. In addition, people ward off evil eye with amulets such as figas and tiny glass eyes (often blue), as well as small figures of Buddha, placed in corners or on windowsills with their backs to any potential watchers and with a small plate of coins or water nearby.

Evil eye is designated by a number of words in Brazilian Portuguese including olhado (gaze), olho gordo (fat eye), and olho grande (big eye). Mau olhado (bad gaze) is the most common of these terms. The Northeastern Brazilian evil-eye belief is similar to the belief that some people can cause harm by gazing while experiencing envy or anger found in northern Africa, the Mediterranean, and nonindigenous Latin America (Dundes 1980; Roberts 1976). In Northeast Brazil, as in these areas, the belief occurs in two forms that are not clearly distinguished; in one, evil eye is deliberately used by the evil hearted to cause harm; in the other it is inadvertent. Evil-eye beliefs have been explained as a consequence of the notion that one person's gain is another's loss (Dundes 1980; Foster 1965, 1972), part of the psychodynamics of patronage (Garrison and Arensberg 1976), and fear of loss of vital fluids (Dundes 1980).

Many Northeast Brazilian customs forestall any possible envy and therefore prevent evil eye. For example, guests are typically offered water, coffee, and food upon entering homes, at least in part so that their hunger will not lead to envy of the household's food. Evil eye beliefs also show up in responses to compliments and in any other situations that may involve envy or anger. The standard response to a compliment is to offer the object of admiration to the admirer, who is honor bound to refuse it. Infants are believed especially vulnerable to evil eye, partly because they are weak, and partly because they are so highly desired, inviting envy by the childless (cf. Dundes 1980). Babies are kept indoors as much as possible, and when carried outside, they are carefully hidden from view with elaborate clothing. The whole baby bundle is then shaded from the glare of the sun and the view of passersby under a shawl for transport outside the home.

Mothers also pin amulets to babies' clothing as a protection against evil eye (cf. Cosminsky 1967: 167). Anyone who admires the baby will be jokingly importuned to adopt it. In addition, childless women who enter homes may be told to take one or more of the children. This forces them to explicitly deny any desire for or envy of the children, deflecting any evil eye they might have cast.

Rezadeiras treat evil eye with Catholic prayers mixed with charms specific to the ailment. As one healer explained, to treat evil eye:

> I pray the Lord's Prayer, the Apostle's Creed, the Hail Mary, the Hail Holy Queen, then for olhado I pray like this: "with two you were put on," it's the two eyes, isn't it? "With three I take you off," [that is] with the powers of the three people of the Holy Trinity. Pray three times and the olhado heals.

Evil eye can cause infertility and bad luck, make cattle stop giving milk, or cause dishes to break, crops to fail, plants to die, and house walls to crack. It is also said to cause a number of physical complaints.

Like other folk illnesses, evil-eye sickness affects infants differently from adults (cf. Crandon 1983). In infants, evil eye is said to cause recurrent problems such as frequent ear infection, fever, or nagging cough, and also diarrhea and symptoms of dehydration. It can lead to death. In older children and adults, evil eye can cause any wound to delay healing, any recurrent or persistent symptom, diarrhea, or fever. It can also cause dry, frizzy hair, split ends, and hair loss. Evil eye also describes illness related to family tensions, as in the case of Nezinha, described below.

Nezinha: A Case of Evil Eye

One thirty-five-year-old woman from Caruaru I shall call Nezinha sought treatment from rezadeira Dona Maria for insomnia, headache, body aches,

and general distress. After praying a general blessing in her front room where five or six other women gossiped about their symptoms while awaiting treatment, Dona Maria invited Nezinha and me to share a Coca-Cola in the kitchen. This provided the opportunity for a more private consultation during which the healer questioned her patient at length about her personal situation while providing me with explanatory asides. Nezinha said that she had run away with a boyfriend at a young age. During the eight years she lived with him, she had three children. When her marriage broke up, she moved to her parents' house. Because of difficulties in the early years of her parents' marriage, Nezinha (the firstborn) had been raised by her grandmother. This was the first time she had lived for any length of time at her parents' house. At the time she moved back, her brother had been planning to marry his longtime fiancée and to live with her in the second story of the house, but the addition of Nezinha, her three children, her maid, and the maid's children to the household destroyed that plan. The wedding was put off indefinitely, and the household reluctantly set about absorbing the new members.

The maid and her young daughter earned their keep with household labor, but Nezinha was unable to find work until her brother's fiancée got her a job at the fiancée's place of work. The job was enormously important to Nezinha's self-esteem and her desire for independence. She longed to earn enough to establish her own household. The fiancée wanted to help Nezinha because she could marry only if Nezinha were out of the household.

Old resentments caused tension between Nezinha and her mother: her parents had never gotten along well; her brother resented her presence; and she suspected that the maid was having an affair with her father as she had years earlier with Nezinha's husband. Nezinha stated that all of these tensions had frazzled her nerves, leaving her permanently nervosa, with trembling and heart palpitations. Then something else happened that drove her over the edge.

> It happens that my brother had an affair with a friend of mine. So my mother liked it a lot, because she doesn't like his fiancée and she hoped he would leave her. So she told the fiancée about the affair in hopes they would break up. But he left my friend. So then my mother was angry at me about something and said to the fiancée that I was the one

who arranged everything for the affair, who introduced them, you know, but I didn't, it's a lie. So the fiancée had a fight with my brother. So now my brother is angry at me, thinking that I told his fiancée, but I didn't tell her; my mother did. The fiancée hates me because she believes my mother's untrue story. My friend is angry with me because she's angry with my brother and the whole family, and she also thinks I told, but I didn't. My mother is mad at me because, because, well because she's always mad at me! I didn't do anything! Everybody is mad at me. Whenever there's tension in the house the kids start fussing and hanging on me and I hate that and then I yell at them and I feel bad. And I am here without being able to sleep, with a headache, constantly sick.

The rezadeira diagnosed evil eye and open chest. She performed the requisite blessings and sold Nezinha a candle, telling her to place her anger at her mother in the candle, scratch her mother's name on its side, and burn it in the cathedral. In addition, she prescribed an herbal tea to be taken before bedtime and told Nezinha to invite the fiancée to go to a movie and ask her advice on how to treat headaches. She further advised that Nezinha should take the children to play on a ferris wheel set up for a forthcoming town festival to distract them from the family tension and work on trying to stay out of her mother's way. Dona Maria explained to us that Nezinha's friends and relatives do not mean to make her sick, and she had to help them help her get better. With the protection of the prayer to "close" her body to evil influences and the removal of her own anger to be burned up by the candle, they could not hurt her.

The herbal tea (chamomile) was to help her feel calm enough to sleep. By asking the fiancée's advice, Nezinha would communicate her friendship and also let the fiancée know that she was suffering from the situation. The fiancée would be obligated to help Nezinha in order to avoid feeling guilty, and helping her would restore the two women's friendship on which Nezinha's job depended. Dona Maria continued her interpretation of Nezinha's situation:

> Some people think that evil eye is a supernatural thing, but it isn't. It's that no one likes it when others are angry or jealous. And we always sense the feelings of others in the same way that we can see and hear. So we stay nervous, thinking of what could happen. Everyone is afraid to be abandoned or attacked. So the fear, the anger, and the anxiety combine, and the person stays sick. So you have to protect with the powers of God, calm, and also improve the situation for the person to get better.

Dona Maria's explanation of evil eye was not unusual. Although a few rezadeiras described evil eye as a supernatural force, most described it in naturalistic terms, as a kind of "energy" or, like Dona Maria, as a consequence of emotional interactions. Several rezadeiras described evil eye as a "superstition of the people," explaining that it is really a kind of tension caused by the awareness of other people's anger and envy. In choosing to diagnose evil eye, Dona Maria was making a statement about Nezinha's personal situation.

Susto: Fear and Violence

Variants of folk ailments called *susto* (fright sickness) or *espanto* (the sickness of fright from seeing a ghost) have been widely described in Latin America and among U.S. Latinos (Clark 1978; Crandon 1983; Foster and Anderson 1978; Gillen 1948; Madsen 1964; Rubel 1964; Toussignant 1979). There are four major theoretical explanations for susto beliefs. They have been interpreted as forms of depression, anxiety, or hysteria. Alternatively, they have been seen as socially defined sick roles, which afflicted individuals use to deal with stress by eliciting community attention, moral support, and temporary respite from obligations.

Susto has been described as a cultural label for physiological syndromes such as hypoglycemia (Bolton 1981) and certain kinds of diarrhea in infants (Crandon 1983; Nations 1982). Crandon, in a study of Bolivian villagers, posits that when the label susto is applied to adults, it constitutes a communal statement about the situation of the patient. She sees the diagnosis of susto as a claim of vulnerability, deprivation, and disenfranchisement (1983: 161–64). A similar interpretation can be made in Northeast Brazil, where susto can cause the sufferer to become nervoso, losing the ability to withstand emotional or physical strain calmly.

Susto also carries implications of mistreatment in Northeast Brazil. Although descriptions of susto from other areas have emphasized the role of ghost encounters and soul loss, my informants used it to refer primarily to three kinds of shock: the trauma of a sudden death; the anguish of discovering sexual betrayal; and the impact of violent blows. In some cases, two or more of these types of shock are viewed as causing susto.

> When my mother died, I was in the 22nd day of confinement after the birth of a child. I fainted . . . because I can't under any circumstances have a fright. And after that I kept on getting nervos . . . and then I suffered a terrible grief with my husband because he was with another woman. I was one day away from giving birth, wanting to give him a son, and he was with this woman. So I was very disgusted with this. So the two sustos together gave me this problem with my nerves. Sometimes I have a great anger that I can't avenge, it's like I'm crying with anger, it's locked inside of me. I get revolted, disgusted, any little thing happens and I can't stand it any more, I get hurt. It's nervos, is what it is.

The term susto also came up frequently in interviews when I asked about the cause of the death of a child. Saying a child died of susto was often a reference either to the child having been killed violently or to a miscarriage attributed to a strong blow to the belly of a pregnant woman.

> My mother had six children, three died and three stayed [with us]. They died because of susto, because my father, he beat my mother, so the cause of the deaths of my siblings was my father and the susto he gave. . . . I remember that my mother was pregnant with a baby that her name was going to be Taxa. My mother was preparing the bottle for my little sister Paxa, so Papa came up behind her and kicked her in the back so that her belly hit the stove, and the hot gruel fell on top of her belly. Later that day she started to hemorrhage and lost the baby, because of the susto.

Some women described their own nervosismo as due to the susto from beatings that also killed their unborn children. For example, one 34-year-old woman had lost 6 of her 13 pregnancies after beatings by her husband. Paula described each of these miscarriages as having been due to susto.

> They died of susto. It was like, I lost my second child because of susto. *Oxente!* Because my husband really passed the limits with me, grabbed me by my feet and swung me upside down, he hit my head over there on the chairs, and I was all—I hit my head there on the corner of the wardrobe, and I was dizzy. . . . I was in agony, he was drunk you know. . . . And I was pregnant, and then he knocked me down and he gave me a punch in the

belly, so I started to lose the baby, so I picked up my daughter, you know she was 8 months old, and I went running to Papa's house.

But like Rejanne, Paula was not on good terms with her family. Her father was furious about what he considered to be her husband's disgraceful behavior. Her husband had convinced Paula's father to let her marry him despite his reputation as a drunk, by declaring himself cured and proving it by remaining sober over the course of a year of engagement. But the night before the wedding he went out drinking with his friends.

> So when it was getting to be about 5 o'clock, the steer was arriving [a reference to the marriage cart], I received notice that he was sick at his mother's house. So we went to find him with my father, and so when we arrived he didn't know anybody, even his bride he didn't recognize, and the stink of rum on him! . . . He seemed to be possessed by a demon [*endemoniado*]. . . . I was afraid to approach him. And because of this my father was disgusted with him, that his eldest daughter was getting married and the groom would behave this way on the day of the wedding! He said it was an insult to his honor, a disgrace to his daughter. But I married him anyway, because I loved him.

Her father's rage was so great that he disowned Paula, saying that if she wanted to marry a disgraceful man like that, she would have to bear the consequences. While fleeing the beating in panic, she remembered her father's words and fearful of being turned away, doubled over in pain, she stopped along the way.

> And then in the middle of the road, I was squatting and hemorrhaging, I met my mother-in-law . . . and she said, "A fight between husband and wife you resolve at home" and she brought me crying and miscarrying back. So I lost that baby because of the susto, and the other ones later, and it got me in my nerves, that I just lived trembling all the time.

Paula did not think it was possible to leave her husband because she had nowhere to go and no one to help her raise her seven children. She also stated that although she did not love her husband anymore, she had pity (*pena*) for him, and she hoped that someday he would stop drinking. Believing that he was basically a good man, she regarded his drinking as a kind of demonic possession rather than an aspect of his character, as her father did.

She had suffered from nervos for many years until she had a profound religious experience while speaking with a Jehovah's Witness missionary who came to her door. She stated that the personal relationship she now felt with Jesus had enabled her to replace anger with loving compassion and thereby to bear her burdens without sickness. During the year and a half that I knew her, she did not report any symptoms of "nerves."

Folk Ailments and the Suppression of Anger

Emotion is a supremely social phenomenon. It is the idiom in which social bonds are negotiated and maintained, the substance of which social tactics are made. As a personal experience, emotion is rooted in the body and suffuses the psyche; as a social experience, emotion responds to interpretations of the actions of others and moral connotations of social situations. As a moral statement, it has a uniquely evocative potency, making it ideal for social manipulation. It frequently finds expression in the form of folk medical syndromes.

In Northeast Brazil, nervos, peito aberto, evil eye, and susto together form a discourse on the sickening power of anger. Although each of these syndromes has similar symptoms, they connote different things about the sufferer. Susto is a state of emotional vulnerability caused by one or more shocking events. It can lead to nervos, or the frazzling of a person's ability to remain calm through repeated worry, grief, anger, and sadness. Peito aberto occurs when a woman's heart expands to encompass all those for whom she feels compassion and, combined with the seething of her own suppressed anger, pushes open her chest, allowing negative influences to enter. Evil eye is caused by the envy and anger of others, victimizing the sufferer.

The folk models of these syndromes allow individuals to use them as claims about themselves and the actions and motives of those they blame for their condition (cf. Migliore 1983: 8). Susto and nervos are statements about the impossibility of withstanding stress, shocks, and violence. Peito aberto is a comment on the challenges of opening one's heart to love while protecting oneself from hurt. Evil eye is a condemnation of those who are supposed to love but instead envy. Through these folk illnesses, Northeast Brazilian women and men discuss their traumas, weaknesses, and victimization, and negotiate social relations.

31

Mothering and the Practice of "Balm" in Jamaica

William Wedenoja

William Wedenoja has conducted field research in Jamaica since 1972, specializing in, among other interests, Afro-Jamaican religious cultism and folk healing. In this article, he centers on the gender of healers, a subject rarely treated in anthropological literature. In particular, Wedenoja aims his research at women who practice Balm, an Afro-American folk healing tradition in Jamaica that, he maintains, brings about maternal transference, encourages patients' dependency and regression, and appears to be a ritualized extension of mothering. Traditional therapy in Jamaica can be complex at first glance, but the author makes a clear distinction among Balm healers, obeah men (sorcerers), and scientists (who provide their clients good luck charms) and demonstrates the relationship of these specialists to Myalist healing cults, Revivalism, and Pentecostalism.

Wedenoja explains the incompatibility of so-called biomedical (modern) practitioners with the majority of Jamaicans whose disease etiology is not restricted to Western explanations of illness but includes ghosts (duppies), attacks by obeah men, fallen angels, demons, ancestor spirits, and the devil himself. The charismatic Mother Jones typifies Balm healers in Jamaica, and Wedenoja's description of her shows the importance of her strength and powers in primarily combating spiritual afflictions. The characterization of Mother Jones and others who practice Balm goes far in explaining why the author feels the feminine powers of women are vital to successful curing. Wedenoja's discussion of diagnostic divination ("concentration") is reminiscent of Lehmann's article, "Eyes of the Ngangas," in this chapter and suggests that healing, in all its forms, represents the strongest remnants of African culture in Jamaica.

Jamaican peasants show great concern for illness. It is a very common topic of discussion and a source of constant anxiety. There is, however, little understanding of the scientific theory of disease. Illnesses are blamed on drafts and exposure to cold temperature or imbalances of blood or bile in the body (M. F. Mitchell 1980: 28). They are also, perhaps more often, attributed to spiritual causes.

According to one Balm healer, the majority of illnesses are "chastisements" from God for "disobedience" to His ways. However, another said that "most sickness coming from nigromancy," which refers to Obeah (sorcery), and this is the most common belief. In the behavioral or perceived environment of Jamaican peasants, there are four types of malevolent spirits that can cause suffering: *duppies* (ghosts), fallen angels, demons, and the devil. In addition, ancestor spirits may punish their descendants. Jamaican peasants also worry that neighbors and relatives will turn, in envy or spite, to an *obeahman* (sorcerer), who has the supernatural

Reprinted from Carol Shepherd McClain, ed., WOMEN AS HEALERS, CROSS-CULTURAL PERSPECTIVES (New Brunswick and London, 1989), pp. 76–97, by permission.

power to manipulate spirits and use them to do harm.

The first resort in cases of illness is, of course, self-medication. Though Jamaica has a lengthy and extensive tradition of folk cures, it is dying out and rapidly being replaced by over-the-counter drugs. If an illness persists for several days, help may be sought from a private doctor or a government medical clinic, but there is widespread dissatisfaction with them. A sophisticated comparison of ninety-seven patients of healers and doctors in Jamaica by Long (1973: 217–32) showed that Balm healers are better liked, spend significantly more time with patients, and give more satisfying diagnoses than doctors.

The expense of a doctor's examination and prescription drugs is a serious drain on the financial resources of the average Jamaican, and seeing a doctor often involves significant travel and a long wait at the office. The greatest problem with the doctor-patient relationship, however, is communication, which is inhibited by cultural and class differences.

Doctors and patients normally come from separate subcultures of Jamaican society; they use different terms to describe symptoms and label diseases and they hold different beliefs about etiology and treatment. Consequently, a doctor may find it difficult to elicit diagnostically meaningful symptoms from a patient, and a patient may not understand a doctor's diagnosis or the purpose of prescribed medication. In addition, a patient may regard diagnostic inquiry as a sign of incompetence, because it is the custom of Balm healers to divine an illness before speaking with a patient. These factors undermine a patient's faith in a doctor and his expectation of successful treatment.

In general, rural Jamaicans are dissatisfied with the treatment they receive from doctors and have little faith in their effectiveness. Moreover, they believe doctors are incapable of dealing with illnesses of a "spiritual" nature. Therefore, many turn to religion and folk healers for relief.

A patient may consult an obeahman or a "scientist," but these magical practitioners are not generally viewed as healers. Obeahmen are widely feared for their power to curse others and control ghosts. People turn to scientists principally for good-luck charms like rings and bracelets, which are used to avoid accidents or to bring success.

Balm, which has been practiced for over one hundred years in Jamaica, is closely associated with an indigenous religious cult called Revival. Although Jamaicans regard Revivalism as a Christian faith, it is actually a syncretic, Afro-Christian religion that relies heavily on the intervention of spirits, often through dreams and "trance" states. Revival cults are descended from Myalist healing cults, which emerged in the late eighteenth century to counter Obeah (Wedenoja 1988). Many Revivalist ceremonies and practices are concerned with the prevention or alleviation of illness and misfortune, and about half of all Revival cults offer treatment for outsiders as well as members. Some Revivalists operate *balmyards* devoted entirely to the practice of healing. These healing centers employ Revivalist beliefs and practices but are not Revival cult centers.

Healing in Balmyards and Revival Cults

Jamaican peasant culture makes a distinction between the sacred and the profane, referred to indigenously as the "spiritual" and the "temporal." Revivalism is commonly called "the spiritual work" and Balm is often called "spiritual science," because they deal with spirits, treat spiritual afflictions, and rely on trance states. Although God is held to be the source of their healing power, the power is delivered to them through angels by means of the Holy Spirit. In contrast, Obeah is called "temporal science" because it can be learned and is not a gift. Moreover, Revivalists and balmists routinely rely on visions, dreams, precognition, glossolalia, and ceremonial possession trance, whereas the obeahman depends on magic and does not use altered states of consciousness.

The Balm healer is essentially a shaman, a person who has received—generally during a severe illness—a spiritual "calling to heal the nation" and the "spiritual gifts" of divination and healing. The balmist's power to heal is based on spirit mediumship; she works with angel familiars who advise her in diagnosis and treatment.

Patients are called out of a healing service, one at a time, to a shed where they are bathed in water that herbs have been boiled in. This bath is normally accompanied by the recitation of psalms. After being bathed, the patient is led to a private room for a consultation with the healer.

In order to diagnose an affliction, a Balm healer will perform a spiritual divination or "reading," which psychologically is an institutionalized form of empathy. There are several ways to read a patient, but in all cases symptoms are never elicited from the patient prior to a reading. The balmist must demonstrate her gift of healing by telling the patient what his or her problems are. One of the more common methods of divination is called "concentration": typically, the healer will gaze intently at a silver coin or a plant leaf in a glass of water until a "message" from an angel is received in her mind. Other forms of reading include interpreting the movement of the flame of a candle, reading a patient's tongue, card cutting, passing hands over the body of a patient, interpretation of dreams, and palm reading. Very powerful healers may be able to read patients simply by looking at them.

Balm healers deal with every conceivable form of human suffering except serious wounds and broken bones, but the most common complaint is pain in any part of the body. Another frequent problem is a vague syndrome called "bad feeling," which is generally characterized by sudden onset, "feeling out of self," losing self-control, feeling weak and fearful, profuse sweating, and fainting. Other popular problems include weakness, indigestion, headaches, and a feeling of "heaviness" or "beating" in the head. Every healer sees some cases of paralysis, blindness, crippled limbs, deafness, and dumbness. Mental disorders are almost always blamed on spirits, and they are frequently treated by healers. Patients also complain of problems in living such as excessive worry or "fretting," difficulties in raising children, and conflicts with family members, boyfriends, girlfriends, or spouses. Many patients believe that neighbors or relatives are trying to "kill" them—that is, using sorcery on them. Some are filled with hate and want to harm others supernaturally.

Balm healers specialize in spiritual afflictions. Although they usually provide or prescribe herbal remedies and common drugs, they also use rituals and magical items to counteract spiritual forces. Balmists routinely tell their patients to burn candles or frankincense and myrrh, recite prayers, and read psalms. They often anoint patients with lavender oil and perfumes or tell them to fast to "build up the spirit." Sometimes they will open and close a pair of scissors over the head of a patient to "cut"—that is, to exorcise—a spirit or use a padlock to "lock" a spirit.

A belief that conversion to Christianity and the living of a Christian life will protect one from Obeah and ghosts has been prevalent in Jamaica since the eighteenth century. Revivalism had its origin in antisorcery movements, and many of its ceremonies involve ritual combat with ghosts. . . .

Portrait of a Balm Healer

Ethnographic fieldwork is a fortuitous enterprise. By chance rather than by design, the hamlet I chose to live in had a very successful Revival cult led by a popular healer, who made me her "godson" on my first visit with her. During the following year and a half we spent a great deal of time together, and I came to know her as well as I have ever known anyone.

The Reverend Martha Jones, generally called "Mother" Jones (these are pseudonyms), is a stocky sixty-four-year-old black woman who stands about five feet five inches tall and weighs about 140 pounds. She lives with about thirty followers and children in a large house next to her church, which she founded in 1950.

Mother Jones was born in the community where she now lives, and spent her first twelve years there. Her father, who died in 1953, made his living as a painter and was also a leader in the local Missionary Alliance church, where she was baptized. She describes him as a quiet, strict, stern, sober, and hardworking man, who was close to her. Her mother, who died in 1937, was a housewife who gave birth to ten children, four of whom are still living. She too was quiet, strict, and home-loving.

Mother Jones was sickly throughout childhood and worried constantly about getting ill or hurt. She contracted malaria and typhoid fever, and lost her hair. Because she was their youngest child and so sickly, her parents were very protective, even keeping her from school, and gave her a great deal of attention.

At the age of twelve Mother Jones went to Kingston to live with an older sister, and she worked there as a maid for eighteen years. She married a black American sailor when she was twenty-two but never had any children. In her late twenties she had a number of "spiritual experiences"—epileptiform states and visions—and went to a Balm woman who told her she had a "spiritual gift."

Mother Jones moved to Washington, D.C., when she was thirty to work as a parlormaid for the British ambassador, but she became "crippled" during her first year there and received a vision telling her to return to Jamaica and start a healing ministry. After another year in Kingston, she and her husband moved to her home town and started a "work." Her husband, however, left in the following year, and she has not seen or heard from him since.

Mother Jones was ordained in the National Baptist church in 1960 and appointed "overseer" for four or five churches in the area. They eventually broke away, and she changed her membership to another American sect. Over the past twenty-five years, every moment of her life has been devoted to her church and healing. She once remarked to me, "my task is not an easy one, my time is not my own. I couldn't tell the day when I am able to rest my head on the pillow." Every Monday she holds a healing service and sees from ten to thirty patients. Throughout the week other patients come individually to her. And her church holds a variety of services and classes almost every day or night of the week.

The people in her community have great respect for Mother Jones, and she has many devoted followers throughout the island and among Jamaican communities in England, Canada, and the United States. No one doubts her integrity and devotion. Everyone refers to her as "Mother" and relates to her as a mother. She shows concern not only for her patients and followers but for the entire community and society as well. She likes children and they are attracted to her. About twenty children live with her: some are ill or handicapped and others have been left with her for discipline or because their mothers are unable to care adequately for them.

Mother Jones says that people come to her for healing when a doctor fails to find anything wrong with them and they think it must be a spiritual, not a physical, problem. She sends her patients to a doctor if she thinks they need one and, for her protection, usually insists that they see a doctor before coming under her care; otherwise she could be liable for prosecution. She does not normally treat someone who is on medication, because "you can't mix the spiritual and the temporal."

Mother Jones tells her patients that "the Lord will help them and they will be healed just through faith, if they believe." But, she laments, "Some people want more. . . . They want something to take way with them. . . . They seem to think it is someone's bad

intents. . . . They don't believe prayer and God will be able to keep them. . . . They feel they have to pay a lot of money . . . and get some superstitious something, or they are unsatisfied." Unlike some Jamaican healers, who blame many problems on Obeah and duppies and provide "guards" (protective amulets), Mother Jones often rebukes these patients by telling them "their thoughts are not right."

Mother Jones told me she wanted to be a preacher rather than a healer, but healing was the gift she received through the Holy Spirit. Although she says that spiritual healing is not a gift one can learn or teach, she does have pamphlets on gospel healing and an ancient book on anatomy, and she listens to radio talk shows on health problems.

One of Mother Jones's "spiritual gifts" is an ability to feel a patient's pain while she is "in the spirit." She also uses "concentration" to "read" a patient by staring at a glass of water with a leaf in it and asking the patient to drop a silver coin in "as a love offering" to an angel. Like most Balm healers, she does not ask patients to describe their symptoms, because she is supposed to be able to "read" them. But after giving a rather general diagnosis, she will question the patient and discuss the problem in detail before prescribing treatment.

All of the patients at a Monday healing service receive a glass of consecrated water and an herbal bath before seeing Mother Jones. In her private consultations with patients she often assigns them specific chapters of Scripture to read and gives them a "healing prayer" to wear next to the place of their illness. The latter is a sheet of "spirit writing," a propitiation to God written in cabalistic script while in a state of trance. She gives her patients "bush medicine" or herbs, prescriptions for vitamins and over-the-counter drugs, and offers advice on living. But she attributes her healing ability largely to her gift for spiritually absorbing a patient's suffering into her own body: "If you take their condition, you draw it off, the people goes free." She constantly complains about the suffering she bears for others, and says her gift might kill her if she entered a hospital.

A Healer's Personality

Mother Jones's roles as religious leader and healer appear to meet most of her personality needs well. They give her autonomy and dominance over others and gain her love, affection, and admiration. As a surrogate mother for many people, she can identify with her own mother, which gives her a strong sense of identity and relieves her of guilt. Healing provides her with a defense mechanism, undoing, which disguises her hostility toward others. It offers opportunities to criticize others and impose her strong sense of morality on those she dislikes. It is also, by means of projection, a way to satisfy her own need for nurturance. Mother Jones's ritual roles provide frequent and sanctioned outlets for her dissociative tendencies in the form of visions, trance, and ceremonial possession states. And her entire life is governed by such a narrow range of role expectations that she is seldom threatened and finds predictability and security in them. This restrictiveness is, however, something of a problem too: Mother Jones is always, in a sense, "on stage" and performing roles, which limits her personality and makes her lonely.

In order to have a successful balmyard or Revival cult, healing or leadership roles must be gratifying to patients and followers as well as to the healer or leader. I found several individuals who had a strong desire to become healers or leaders and had tried many times to establish a Balm practice or Revival cult, but had always failed to attract a clientele or devotees. They were not lacking in spiritual knowledge, but they did not meet the psychological needs of others. Given the renown and large following of Mother Jones, it is apparent that she not only meets her own needs but satisfies those of her patients and followers as well.

Mother Jones's characteristic optimism is encouraging to patients and raises their expectations for relief. Her sensitivity to the affective needs of others—that is, her warmth and concern—evokes feelings of love and security in her patients and allows her to establish rapport with a patient quickly. The psychological tests also show her to be a very creative and intuitive person, someone who thinks in a holistic manner and can easily make convincing interpretations of a case on the basis of a few clues.

Scheff (1975, 1979) has emphasized both the need for emotional arousal in therapy and the importance of group support if therapeutic change is to persist, and these elements are amply present in Mother Jones's practice. Her healing services employ drums and tambourines, singing and dancing, histrionic preaching, and ecstatic behavior, all of which is emotionally rousing. She holds periodic "Patient Tables," which are lengthy and ecstatic ceremonies, to honor former patients. And her patients often become involved in the regular cycle of ceremonies of her church, at which members are expected to "testify" often to their salvation or personal rebirth; normally, this involves declarations of the important influence of Mother Jones on their lives. The changes she instigates in her patients are then reinforced by her presence and by the support of other followers.

Women and Balm

This association of women with healing is not restricted to Balm and Revivalism. The medical system relies heavily on nurses and midwives, too. In rural areas, babies are delivered by government midwives, traditional *nanas*, or resident nurses at community clinics. The day-to-day operation of a rural hospital is managed almost entirely by the Matron and her nurses, with doctors serving mainly as surgeons and consultants. Obeahmen and scientists are, however, to my knowledge always men.

This sexual division of labor may be due, in part, to considerations of wealth and prestige. The practice of Obeah or Science is reputedly very remunerative and a source of great influence. But the practice of Balm, though it may bring one honor and respect, usually offers little in the way of income or formal prestige and power. As in most societies, men monopolize public positions of wealth and power and leave the less lucrative positions to women.

The association of men with sorcery and women with healing may also be based on cultural stereotypes about the sexes. In interviews and TAT responses, men are generally depicted as violent, troublesome, unreliable, untrustworthy, sexually aggressive, deceitful, and exploitative. Obeahmen are feared because they work in secret, with malicious ghosts (duppies), and cause harm or misfortune. Women, in contrast, are portrayed as peaceful, benevolent, nurturing, caring, responsible, and trustworthy. Correspondingly, Balm and Revivalism are benign institutions; their purpose is to counteract Obeah and malicious ghosts or provide protection from them. Thus we have a simple semiotic equation of Obeah with men, aggression, harm, and evil, on the one hand, and Balm and Revivalism with women, protection, helping, and good, on the other.

Mothering and Balm

The relationship between Balm healers and patients is a ritualized version of the mother-child relationship, and this is openly recognized in Jamaican culture. Healers are referred to as "mothers" and they are expected to play a maternal role. They are idealized as supermothers and adopted as surrogate mothers. Moreover, healers often refer to patients as their "children."

Familial idioms are used extensively in Revivalism, and they are not merely metaphors. Cultists behave according to the familial roles associated with their positions. The social organization of Revival cults strongly reflects the mother-centered pattern of the family in Jamaica, and one of the attractions of Revival cults is that they are fictive family groups.

The "Mother" is usually the central figure in a cult, and everything revolves around her. The "Armor Bearer," Mother Jones's "right hand," is in charge of the day-to-day activities of the cult, a role resembling that of the eldest daughter in a large family. Other women are referred to as "sisters." Some of the younger sisters, who are known as the "workers," serve the Armor Bearer much as younger daughters work under the eldest daughter in a family.

In general, women have instrumental roles that involve a great deal of work but little recognition, whereas men are given expressive roles that have prestige but little responsibility. The "Father" or "Daddy" is sometimes the dominant but more often a removed but respected figure. Many of the men are deacons, and they seem to play the role of uncles. The pastor of Mother Jones's church, who was raised by Mother Jones, is a handsome and charming young public health inspector. His official duties are to preach sermons and perform weddings and funerals, but he also fills the familial role, common in Jamaican families, of a favorite son who is admired by all. Other men are referred to as "brothers." Mother Jones always called me "my son," and her followers referred to me as "Brother Bill."

Mother Jones is a mother not just to her patients and followers but to the entire community. She is its moral standard and conscience and, more generally, a symbol of the love, affection, and devotion of mothers. There is a great respect for mothers in Jamaica, and the mother-child tie is the strongest bond in the society. Children are often reluctant to leave home and mother when they reach adulthood, and the most traumatic event in the life cycle is the death of one's mother. Mothers have almost total responsibility for their children; the role of fathers is largely limited to punishment for severe offenses. In addition, mothers delegate many domestic tasks and child-care responsibilities to their daughters, while sons are free to roam and play. The needs of rural children are therefore met largely by women.

The cultural patterning of the healer-patient relationship on the mother-child bond encourages maternal transference, regression, and the development of a dependency relationship. This can give the Balm healer a great deal of influence over her patients, because it makes them more receptive and suggestible. Moreover, the mother-child bond probably has some effect on all other relationships, because it is usually the first and most influential relationship in life. Maternal transference can thus provide the healer with an opportunity to make some rather fundamental changes in the personality and behavior of her patients.

Maternal dependency can be very supportive for patients. The healer, as a surrogate mother, consoles them, looks after them, and takes control when things go wrong. She gives them attention, affection, nurturance, encouragement, and offers them direction and purpose. Through attachment to her, they can regain a childlike sense of protection and security.

Western therapists would regard the dependency aspect of the healer-patient relationship in Balm as a problem, but it is not seen as one in Jamaica. Jamaicans are very sociable and they do not place much value on independence and self-reliance. Dependency is not condemned or discouraged.

Illness and Emotional Needs

Jamaican Balm exemplifies what I believe to be a basic principle of psychological anthropology, that every culture produces a unique set of personality needs and conflicts and develops institutionalized means for their satisfaction or resolution. Balm is not simply a traditional medical system but also, and perhaps more importantly, a source of psychological support. The psychological processes involved in Balm are not just techniques that facilitate healing but ends in themselves. Patients come to healers not only to be cured of illnesses but to gratify affective needs as well.

One of the dominant concerns of Jamaicans is "love." Many older people remarked to me that Jamaicans were once very "loving," but they are too "selfish" today. The plague of violence that Kingston has experienced over the past two decades is generally blamed on lack of love. Church sermons often dwell on social disorder, and Christian love is put forward as the salvation of society. "Peace and love" and the need for brotherly love and unity are central themes in popular music and in the ideology of the messianic cult of Rastafarianism. Mother Jones is of the opinion that most illnesses are due to "stress" in general and "lack of love" in particular. She says Jamaicans are not close, they fear each other, and they cannot give love to others. So she offers them her love, and tries to teach them to love others, to "make them whole."

What Jamaicans mean by "love" is closeness, caring, and concern for others—unity, sharing, and cooperation. Family ties are strong, and they want community relations to be close and friendly as well. Although there has probably been some erosion of *gemeinschaft* and a weakening of kin ties over the past few decades, I cannot agree with Mother Jones that Jamaicans are unloving. They are at least as "loving" as Americans, but they have a much stronger need for affiliation and place a higher value on interpersonal relations (Jones and Zoppel 1979; Phillips 1973). "Love" is a cultural focus, part of the Jamaican ethos, and one of the principal functions of Balm and Revivalism is to gratify that need.

Women and Healing

As Spiro (1978: xvi–xvii) has noted, "The practitioner of anthropology as 'science,' placing the local setting in a theoretical context, is concerned with the local as a variant of—and therefore a means for understanding—the universal." According to my analysis, the relationship between healers and patients in Balm is modeled on the mother-child relationship, a very strong bond in Jamaican society, and the mothering behavior of maternal figures such as Mother Jones provides emotional support for distressed and demoralized individuals. To what extent can this interpretation be generalized to other cultures?

A pioneering article by Carl Rogers (1957) identified congruence (genuineness and personality integration), unconditional positive regard (warm acceptance and nonpossessive caring), and accurate empathy as personal qualities that a healer must communicate to a patient if psychotherapeutic change is to take place. Additional research has indicated that effective healers are also intelligent, responsible, creative, sincere, energetic, warm, tolerant, respectful, supportive, self-confident, keenly attentive, benign, concerned, reassuring, firm, persuasive, encouraging, credible, sensitive, gentle, and trustworthy (J. D. Frank 1974; Lambert, Shapiro, and Bergin 1986). It should be noted, however, that these conclusions are based on research on American psychotherapists and thus the characteristics may not be universal.

Many of the personal qualities noted above seem to apply to women more than men. Women are said to be more empathic and have more positive feelings about being close to others, to be more cooperative and altruistic, to share more, to be more accommodative and interested in social relationships, to be more vocal, personal, and superior at nonverbal communication (G. Mitchell 1981), "more sensitive to social cues and to the needs of others" (Draper, quoted in Quinn 1977: 198), and more nurturant or kind and supportive to others (Martin and Voorhies 1975). In a study of kibbutz children, Spiro (1979: 93) found that girls showed more "integrative behavior"—aid, assistance, sharing and cooperation—than boys, and regularly consoled victims of aggression.

These claims about universal differences in adult male and female "styles" of behavior have apparently not been put to the test of a systematic cross cultural study. However, there are excellent data on children aged three through eleven from the Six Cultures Study (Whiting and Whiting 1975), which found that girls are more intimate-dependent (touch and seek help) and nurturant (offer help and support) and that boys are more aggressive (assault, insult, horseplay) and dominant-dependent (seek dominance and attention).

Characteristics associated with women seem to be closely related to their role as mothers. Although this may reflect an innate predisposition to bond with and nurture infants (Rossi 1977), it can also be adequately explained by socialization practices. Women have the main responsibility for child care in every society, and they are prepared for that role in childhood. A well-known cross-cultural survey on sex differences in socialization concluded that there is "a widespread pattern of greater pressure toward nurturance, obedience, and responsibility in girls, and toward self-reliance and achievement striving in boys" (Barry, Bacon, and Child 1957: 332).

There is a close correspondence between the personal qualities of effective healers and women, and it seems to be due to strong similarities between the roles of healing and mothering. According to Kakar (1982: 59), many psychotherapists claim that "the 'feminine' powers of nurturance, warmth, concern, intuitive understanding, and relatedness . . . are essential in every healing encounter and for the success of the healing process."

If "feminine powers" are essential for healing, then women should, on average, be more effective at it than men. In fact, a review of research on the sex of psychotherapists concluded that "there appear to be some demonstrable trends, under certain circumstances, toward greater patient satisfaction or benefit from psychotherapy with female therapists and no studies showing such trends with male therapists" (Mogul 1982: 1–3).

It might also be reasonable to expect that the majority of healers in the world are, as in Jamaica, women. However, a cross-cultural survey of seventy-three societies by Whyte (1978) found that male shamans were more numerous or powerful in 54 percent; female shamans were more numerous or powerful in only 10 percent. This finding does not necessarily disprove the hypothesis that women generally make better healers. Personal qualities are only one factor in recruitment to a healing role and social, political, and economic factors can be important too. Given what we know about sexual inequality, it would not be surprising to find that women occupy healing roles when these roles are low in prestige or income, while men come to monopolize them when healing is high in prestige or income. It would be worthwhile to conduct a more extensive cross-cultural survey on the sex of healers in a study that would broaden the subject from shamans to include other types of healers and would attempt to identify social conditions associated with a preponderance of male or female healers.

Although "feminine powers" such as nurturance, warmth, and concern may, as Kakar suggests, be necessary for effective healing, they are probably not sufficient. Healers also seem to be firm and often domineering. For example, Raymond Prince (personal communication) notes that Nigerian healers, who are almost all male, are "abrupt, authoritarian, and sometimes punitive in their relations with patients, particularly psychotic ones."

It is probably more accurate to say that the personal qualities of effective healers are androgynous. Mother Jones is not only warm, empathic, caring, sensitive, and supportive with her patients but also firm, assertive, and domineering. Male shamans often dress in female clothing and assume female roles (Halifax 1979:24). I noticed that the husky voice of a Jamaican male healer changed to a high pitch when he entered a trance to treat his patients, and he became warmer and more empathic as well. Torrey (1972:103) described a male healer in Ethiopia as having a fatherly relationship with his patients and an "underlying warmth . . . partly masked by an authoritarian manner."

The personal qualities of an effective healer may vary with the degree of involvement of men and women in child care in a society. However, the maternal element of healing is probably more constant than the paternal element, because women are always heavily involved in child care and there is much greater variation in the involvement of men. The emphasis on mothering in Balm is a reflection of the strong degree of maternal dependency in Jamaican society, which is encouraged by a high rate of father-absence and a general lack of involvement of men in child rearing. In addition, the androgynous character of Jamaican healers seems to be due to the fact that Jamaican mothers often have to play maternal and paternal roles in child care and family life.

Healing relationship may also vary with, and reflect, the style of parenting in a society. Jamaican mothers tend to be very domineering, restrictive, nagging, scolding, punitive, directive, and even dictatorial with their children. I observed a popular Balm healer who matched this description when I was asked to drive two patients to a balmyard. She was very abrasive and publicly scolded her patients, and I was quite surprised to hear my companions extolling her on our journey home. When I asked them if they would like her for a mother, they enthusiastically replied that she would be splendid.

32

The Spirit Catches You and You Fall Down

Anne F. Fadiman

Divergent understandings of illness—what causes it and how to respond to it—are described in this account of a Hmong refugee family who came to the United States from Laos in 1980. When the Lee family sought help at the local hospital for their infant daughter's seizures, she was diagnosed with epilepsy. The Hmong understood her symptoms as evidence of soul-flight or "the spirit catches you and you fall down," and a sign of a special individual called to be a shaman. Author Anne Fadiman considers the Lees' experiences in the context of Hmong approaches to child rearing, Hmong experiences with Western medicine, and attitudes toward epilepsy among the Hmong as well as historically in the West. She also describes the economic and structural factors shaping health care delivery in Merced, California, where 12,000 Hmong-Americans settled between the late 1970s and late 1990s.

Anne Fadiman is a journalist whose investigation relied on techniques similar to those of ethnographers: extensive recorded interviews, lengthy participant-observation, and thorough reading of related scholarship. Since its publication in 1997, the award-winning book from which this material is excerpted has received considerable attention from students of anthropology, medical and public health professionals, and the general reading public.

When Lia was about three months old, her older sister Yer slammed the front door of the Lees' apartment. A few moments later, Lia's eyes rolled up, her arms jerked over her head, and she fainted. The Lees had little doubt what had happened. Despite the careful installation of Lia's soul during the *hu plig* ceremony, the noise of the door had been so profoundly frightening that her soul had fled her body and become lost. They recognized the resulting symptoms as *qaug dab peg*, which means "the spirit

From: The Spirit Catches You and You Fall Down: A Hmong Child, Her American Doctors, and the Collision of Two Cultures, NY: Farrar, Straus and Giroux, 1997.
Information on sources, including bibliography and interviews, appears on pages 296–97 of the original publication from which this excerpt is drawn.

catches you and you fall down." The spirit referred to in this phrase is a soul-stealing *dab; peg* means to catch or hit; and *qaug* means to fall over with one's roots still in the ground, as grain might be beaten down by wind or rain.

In Hmong-English dictionaries, *qaug dab peg* is generally translated as epilepsy. It is an illness well known to the Hmong, who regard it with ambivalence. On the one hand, it is acknowledged to be a serious and potentially dangerous condition. Tony Coelho, who was Merced's congressman from 1979 to 1989, is an epileptic. Coelho is a popular figure among the Hmong, and a few years ago, some local Hmong men were sufficiently concerned when they learned he suffered from *qaug dab peg* that they volunteered the services of a shaman, a *txiv neeb*, to perform a ceremony that would retrieve Coelho's errant soul. The Hmong leader to whom they made this proposition politely discouraged them, suspecting that Coelho, who is a Catholic of Portuguese descent, might not appreciate having chickens, and maybe a pig as well, sacrificed on his behalf.

On the other hand, the Hmong consider *qaug dab peg* to be an illness of some distinction. This fact might have surprised Tony Coelho no less than the dead chickens would have. Before he entered politics, Coelho planned to become a Jesuit priest, but was barred by a canon forbidding the ordination of epileptics. What was considered a disqualifying impairment by Coelho's church might have been seen by the Hmong as a sign that he was particularly fit for divine office. Hmong epileptics often become shamans. Their seizures are thought to be evidence that they have the power to perceive things other people cannot see, as well as facilitating their entry into trances, a prerequisite for their journeys into the realm of the unseen. The fact that they have been ill themselves gives them an intuitive sympathy for the suffering of others and lends them emotional credibility as healers. Becoming a *txiv neeb* is not a choice; it is a vocation. The calling is revealed when a person falls sick, either with *qaug dab peg* or with some other illness whose symptoms similarly include shivering and pain. An established *txiv neeb*, summoned to diagnose the problem, may conclude from these symptoms that the person (who is usually but not always male) has been chosen to be the host of a healing spirit, a *neeb*. (*Txiv neeb* means "person with a healing spirit.") It is an offer that the sick person cannot refuse, since if he rejects his vocation, he will die. In any case, few Hmong would choose to decline. Although shamanism is an arduous calling that requires years of training with a master in order to learn the ritual techniques and chants, it confers an enormous amount of social status in the community and publicly marks the *txiv neeb* as a person of high moral character, since a healing spirit would never choose a no-account host. Even if an epileptic turns out not to be elected to host a *neeb*, his illness, with its thrilling aura of the supramundane, singles him out as a person of consequence.

In their attitude toward Lia's seizures, the Lees reflected this mixture of concern and pride. The Hmong are known for the gentleness with which they treat their children. Hugo Adolf Bernatzik, a German ethnographer who lived with the Hmong of Thailand for several years during the 1930s, wrote that the Hmong he had studied regarded a child as "the most treasured possession a person can have." In Laos, a baby was never apart from its mother, sleeping in her arms all night and riding on her back all day. Small children were rarely abused; it was believed that a *dab* who witnessed mistreatment might take the child, assuming it was not wanted. The Hmong who live in the United States have continued to be unusually attentive parents. A study conducted at the University of Minnesota found Hmong infants in the first month of life to be less irritable and more securely attached to their mothers than Caucasian infants, a difference the researcher attributed to the fact that the Hmong mothers were, without exception, more sensitive, more accepting, and more responsive, as well as "exquisitely attuned" to their children's signals. Another study, conducted in Portland, Oregon, found that Hmong mothers held and touched their babies far more frequently than Caucasian mothers. In a third study, conducted at the Hennepin County Medical Center in Minnesota, a group of Hmong mothers of toddlers surpassed a group of Caucasian mothers of similar socioeconomic status in every one of fourteen categories selected from the Egeland Mother-Child Rating Scale, ranging from "Speed of Responsiveness to Fussing and Crying" to "Delight."

Foua and Nao Kao had nurtured Lia in typical Hmong fashion (on the Egeland Scale, they would have scored especially high in Delight), and they were naturally distressed to think that anything might compromise her health and happiness. They therefore hoped, at least most of the time, the *qaug dab peg* could be healed. Yet they also considered the illness an honor. Jeanine Hilt, a social worker who knew the Lees well, told me, "They felt Lia was kind of an anointed one, like a member of royalty. She was a very special person in their culture because she had these spirits in her and she might grow up to be a shaman, and so sometimes their thinking was that this was not so much a medical problem as it was a blessing." (Of the forty or so American doctors, nurses, and Merced County agency employees I spoke with who had dealt with Lia and her family, several had a vague idea that "spirits" were somehow involved, but Jeanine Hilt was the only one who had actually asked the Lees what they thought was the cause of their daughter's illness.)

Within the Lee family, in one of those unconscious processes of selection that are as mysterious as any other form of falling in love, it was obvious that Lia was her parents's favorite, the child they considered the most beautiful, the one who was most extravagantly hugged and kissed, the one who was dressed in the most exquisite garments (embroidered by Foua, wearing dime-store glasses to work her almost microscopic stitches). Whether Lia occupied this position from the moment of her birth, whether it was a result of her spiritually distiguished illness, or whether it came from the special tenderness any parent feels for a sick child, is not a matter Foua and Nao Kao wish, or are able, to analyze. One thing that is clear is that for many years the cost of that extra love was partially borne by her sister Yer. "They blamed Yer for slamming the door," said Jeanine Hilt. "I tried many times to explain that the door had nothing to do with it, but they didn't believe me. Lia's illness made them so sad that I think for a long time they treated Yer differently from their other children."

During the next few months of her life, Lia had at least twenty more seizures. On two occasions, Foua and Nao Kao were worried enough to carry her in their arms to the emergency room at Merced Community Medical Center, which was three bolcks from their apartment. Like most Hmong refugees, they had their doubts about the efficacy of Western medical techniques. However, when they were living in the Mae Jarim refugee camp in Thailand, their only surviving son, Cheng, and three of their six surviving daughters, Ge, May, and True, had been seriously ill. Ge died. They took Cheng, May, and True to the camp hospital; Cheng and May recovered rapidly, and True was sent to another, larger hospital, where she eventually recovered as well. (The Lees also concurrently addressed the possible spiritual origins of their children's illnesses by moving to a new hut. A dead person had been buried beneath their old one, and his soul might have wished to harm the new residents.) This experience did nothing to shake their faith in traditional Hmong beliefs about the causes and cures of illness, but it did convince them that on some occasions Western doctors could be of additional help, and that it would do no harm to hedge their bets.

County hospitals have a reputation for being crowded, dilapidated, and dingy. Merced's county hospital, with which the Lees would become all too familiar over the next few years, is none of these.

The MCMC complex includes a modern, 42,000-square-foot wing—it looks sort of like an art moderne ocean liner—that houses coronary care, intensive care, and transitional care units; 154 medical and surgical beds; medical and radiology laboratories outfitted with state-of-the-art diagnostic equipment; and a blood bank. The waiting rooms in the hospital and its attached clinic have unshredded magazines, unsmelly bathrooms, and floors that have been scrubbed to an aseptic gloss. MCMC is a teaching hospital, staffed in part by the faculty and residents of the Family Practice Residency, which is affiliated with the University of California at Davis. The residency program is nationally known, and receives at least 150 applications annually for its six first-year positions.

Like many other rural county hospitals, which were likely to feel the health care crunch before it reached urban hospitals, MCMC has been plagued with financial problems throughout the last twenty years. It accepts all patients, whether or not they can pay; only twenty percent are privately insured, with most of the rest receiving aid from California's Medi-Cal, Medicare, or Medically Indigent Adult programs, and a small (but to the hospital, costly) percentage neither insured nor covered by any federal or state program. The hospital receives reimbursements from the public programs, but many of those reimbursements have been lowered or restricted in recent years. Although the private patients are far more profitable, MCMC's efforts to attract what its administrator has called "an improved payer mix" have not been very successful. (Merced's wealthier residents often choose either a private Catholic hospital three miles north of MCMC or a larger hospital in a nearby city such as Fresno.) MCMC went through a particularly rough period during the late eighties, hitting bottom in 1988, when it had a $3.1 million deficit.

During this same period, MCMC also experienced an expensive change in its patient population. Starting in the late seventies, Southeast Asian refugees began to move to Merced in large numbers. The city of Merced, which has a population of about 61,000, now has just over 12,000 Hmong. That is to say, one in five residents of Merced is Hmong. Because many Hmong fear and shun the hospital, MCMC's patient rolls reflect a somewhat lower ratio, but on any given day there are still Hmong patients in almost every unit. Not only do the Hmong fail re-soundingly to improve the payer mix—more than eighty percent are on Medi-Cal—but they have proved even more costly than other indigent patients, because they generally require more time and attention, and because there are so many of them that MCMC has had to hire bilingual staff members to mediate between patients and providers.

There are no funds in the hospital budget specifically earmarked for interpreters, so the administration has detoured around that technicality by hiring Hmong lab assistants, nurse's aides, and transporters, who are called upon to translate in the scarce interstices between analyzing blood, emptying bedpans, and rolling postoperative patients around on gurneys. In 1991, a short-term federal grant enabled MCMC to put skilled interpreters on call around the clock, but the program expired the following year. Except during that brief hiatus, there have often been no Hmong-speaking employees of any kind present in the hospital at night. Obstetricians have had to obtain consent for cesarean sections or episiotomies using embarrassed teenaged sons, who have learned English in school, as translators. Ten-year-old girls have had to translate discussions of whether or not a dying family member should be resuscitated. Sometimes not even a child is available. Doctors on the late shift in the emergency room have often had no way of taking a patient's medical history, or of asking such questions as Where do you hurt? How long have you been hurting? What does it feel like? Have you had an accident? Have you vomitted? Have you had a fever? Have you lost consciousness? Are you pregnant? Have you taken any medications? Are you allergic to any medications? Have you recently eaten? (The last question is of great importance if emergency surgery is being contemplated, since anesthetized patients with full stomachs can aspirate the partially digested food into their lungs, and may die if they choke or if their bronchial linings are badly burned by stomach acid.) I asked one doctor what he did in such cases. He said, "Practice veterinary medicine."

One October 24, 1982, the first time that Foua and Nao Kao carried Lia to the emergency room, MCMC had not yet hired any interpreters, de jure or de facto, for any shift. At that time, the only hospital employee who sometimes translated for Hmong patients was a janitor, a Laotian immigrant fluent in his own language, Lao, which few Hmong understand; halting in Hmong; and even more halting in English. On that day either the janitor was unavailable or the emergency room staff didn't think of calling him. The resident on duty practiced veterinary medicine. Foua and Nao Kao had no way of explaining what had happened, since Lia's seizures had stopped by the time they reached the hospital. Her only obvious symptoms were a cough and a congested chest. The resident ordered an X ray, which led the radiologist to conclude that Lia had "early bronchiopneumonia or tracheobronchitis." As he had no way of knowing that the bronchial congestion was probably caused by aspiration of saliva or vomit during her seizure (a common problem for epileptics), she was routinely dismissed with a prescription for ampicillin, an antibiotic. Her emergency room Registration Record lists her father's last name as Yang, her mother's maiden name as Foua, and her "primary spoken language" as "Mong." When Lia was discharged, Nao Kao (who knows the alphabet but does not speak or read English) signed a piece of paper that said, "I hereby acknowledge receipt of the instructions indicated above," to wit: "Take ampicillin as directed. Vaporizer at cribside. Clinic reached as needed 383-7007 ten days." The "ten days" meant that Nao Kao was supposed to call the Family Practice Center in ten days for a follow-up appointment. Not surprisingly, since he had no idea what he had agreed to, he didn't. But when Lia had another bad seizure on November 11, he and Foua carried her to the emergency room again, where the same scene was repeated, and the same misdiagnosis made.

On March 3, 1983, Foua and Nao Kao carried Lia to the emergency room a third time. On this occasion, three circumstances were different: Lia was still seizing when they arrived, they were accompanied by a cousin who spoke some English, and one of the doctors on duty was a family practice resident named Dan Murphy. Of all the doctors who have worked at MCMC, Dan Murphy is generally acknowledged to be the one most interested in and knowledgeable about the Hmong. At that time, he had been living in Merced for only seven months, so his interest still exceeded his knowledge. When he and his wife, Cindy, moved to Merced, they had never heard the word "Hmong." Several years later, Cindy was teaching English to Hmong adults and

Dan was inviting Hmong leaders to the hospital to tell the residents about their experiences as refugees. Most important, the Murphys counted a Hmong family, the Xiongs, among their closest friends. When one of the Xiong daughters wanted to spend the summer working in Yosemite National Park, Chaly Xiong, her father, initially refused because he was afraid she might get eaten by a lion. Dan personally escorted Chaly to Yosemite to verify the absence of lions, and persuaded him the job would do his daughter good. Four months later, Chaly was killed in an automobile accident. Cindy Murphy arranged the funeral, calling around until she found a funeral parlor that was willing to accommodate three days of incense burning, drum beating, and *qeej* playing. She also bought several live chickens, which were sacrificed in the parking lot of the funeral parlor, as well as a calf and a pig, which were sacrificed elsewhere. When Dan first saw the Lees, he instantly registered that they were Hmong, and he thought to himself: "This won't be boring."

Many years later, Dan, who is a short, genial man with an Amishstyle beard and an incandescent smile, recalled the encounter. "I have this memory of Lia's parents standing just inside the door to the ER, holding a chubby little round-faced baby. She was having a generalized seizure. Her eyes were rolled back, she was unconscious, her arms and legs were kind of jerking back and forth, and she didn't breathe much—every once in a while, there would be no movement of the chest wall and you couldn't hear any breath sounds. That was definitely anxiety-producing. She was the youngest patient I had ever dealt with who was seizing. The parents seemed frightened, not terribly frightened though, not as frightened as I would have been if it was my kid. I thought it might be meningitis, so Lia had to have a spinal tap, and the parents were real resistant to that. I don't remember how I convinced them. I remember feeling very anxious because they had a real sick kid and I felt a big need to explain to these people, through their relative who was a not-very-good translator, what was going on, but I felt like I had no time, because we had to put an IV in her scalp with Valium to stop the seizures, but then Lia started seizing again and the IV went into the skin instead of the vein, and I had a hard time getting another one started. Later on, when I figured out what had happened, or not happened, on the earlier visits

to the ER, I felt good. It's kind of a thrill to find something someone else has missed, especially when you're a resident and you are looking for excuses to make yourself feel smarter than the other physicians."

Among Dan's notes in Lia's History and Physical Examination record were:

HISTORY OF PRESENT ILLNESS: The patient is an 8 month, Hmong female, whose family brought her to the emergency room after they had noticed her shaking and not breathing very well for a 20-minute period of time. According to the family the patient has had multiple like episodes in the past, but have never been able to communicate this to emergency room doctors on previous visits secondary to a language barrier. An english speaking relative available tonight, stated that the patient had had intermittent fever and cough for 2–3 days prior to being admitted.

FAMILY & SOCIAL HISTORY: Unobtainable secondary to language difficulties.

NEUROLOGICAL: The child was unresponsive to pain or sound. The head was held to the left with intermittent tonic-clonic [first rigid, then jerking] movements of the upper extremities. Respirations were suppressed during these periods of clonic movement. Grunting respirations persisted until the patient was given 3 mg. of Valium I.V.

Dan had no way of knowing that Foua and Nao Kao had already diagnosed their daughter's problem as the illness where the spirit catches you and you fall down. Foua and Nao Kao had no way of knowing that Dan had diagnosed it as epilepsy, the most common of all neurological disorders. Each had accurately noted the same symptoms, but Dan would have been surprised to hear that they were caused by soul loss, and Lia's parents would have been surprised to hear that they were caused by an electrochemical storm inside their daughter's head that had been stirred up by the misfiring of aberrant brain cells.

Dan had learned in medical school that epilepsy is a sporadic malfunction of the brain, sometimes mild and sometimes severe, sometimes progressive and sometimes self-limiting, which can be traced to oxygen deprivation during gestation, labor, or birth; a head injury; a tumor; an infection; a high fever; a stroke; a metabolic disturbance; a drug allergy; a toxic reaction to a poison. Sometimes the source is obvious—the patient had a brain tumor or swallowed strychnine or crashed through a windshield—but in about seven out of ten cases, the cause is never determined. During an epileptic episode, instead of following their usual orderly protocol, the damaged cells in the cerebral cortex transmit neural impulses simultaneously and chaotically. When only a small area of the brain is involved—in a "focal" seizure— an epileptic may hallucinate or twitch or tingle but retain consciousness. When the electrical disturbance extends to a wide area—in a "generalized" seizure—consciousness is lost, either for the brief episodes called petit mal or "absence" seizures, or for the full-blown attacks known as grand mal. Except through surgery, whose risks consign it to the category of last resort, epilepsy cannot be cured, but it can be completely or partially controlled in most cases by anticonvulsant drugs.

The Hmong are not the only people who might have good reason to feel ambivalent about suppressing the symptoms. The Greeks called epilepsy "the sacred disease." Dan Murphy's diagnosis added Lia Lee to a distinguished line of epileptics that has included Søren Kierkegaard, Vincent van Gogh, Gustave Flaubert, Lewis Carroll, and Fyodor Dostoyevsky, all of whom, like many Hmong shamans, experienced powerful senses of grandeur and spiritual passion during their seizures, and powerful creative urges in their wake. As Dostoyevsky's Prince Myshkin asked, "What if it is a disease? What does it matter that it is an abnormal tension, if the result, if the moment of sensation, remembered and analysed in a state of health, turns out to be harmony and beauty brought to their highest point of perfection, and gives a feeling, undivined and undreamt of till then, of completeness, proportion, reconciliation, and an ecstatic and prayerful fusion in the highest synthesis of life?"

Although the inklings Dan had gathered of the transcendental Hmong worldview seemed to him to possess both power and beauty, his own view of medicine in general, and of epilepsy in particular, was, like that of his colleagues at MCMC, essentially rationalist. Hippocrates' skeptical commentary on the nature of epilepsy, made around 400 B.C., pretty much sums up Dan's own frame of reference: "It seems to me that the disease is no more divine than any other. It has a natural cause just as other disease have. Men think it is divine merely because they

don't understand it. But if they called everything divine which they do not understand, why, there would be no end of divine things."*

Lia's seizure was a grand mal episode, and Dan had no desire to do anything but stop it. He admitted her to MCMC as an inpatient. Among the tests she had during the three days she spent there were a spinal tap, a CT scan, an EEG, a chest X ray, and extensive blood work. Foua and Nao Kao signed " Authorization for and Consent to Surgery or Special Diagnostic or Therapeutic Procedures" forms, each several hundred words long, for the first two of these. It is not known whether anyone attempted to translate them, or, if so, how "Your physician has requested a brain scan utilizing computerized tomography" was rendered in Hmong. None of the tests revealed any apparent cause for the seizures. The doctors classified Lia's epilepsy as "idiopathic": cause unknown. Lia was found to have consolidation in her right lung, which this time was correctly diagnosed as aspiration pneumonia resulting from the seizure. Foua and Nao Kao alternated nights at the hospital, sleeping in a cot next to Lia's bed. Among the Nurse's Notes for Lia's last night at the hospital were: "0001. Skin cool and

---

*Despite this early attempt by Hippocrates (or perhaps by one of the anonymous physicians whose writings are attributed to Hippocrates) to remove the "divine" label, epilepsy continued, more than any other disease, to be ascribed to supernatural causes. The medical historian Owsei Temkin has noted that epilepsy has held a key position historically in "the struggle between magic and the scientific conception." Many treatments for epilepsy have had occult associations. Greek magicians forbade epileptics to eat mint, garlic, and onion, as well as the flesh of goats, pigs, deer, dogs, cocks, turtledoves, bustards, mullets, and eels; to wear black garments and goatskins; and to cross their hands and feet: taboos that were all connected, in various ways, with chthonic deities. Roman epileptics were advised to swallow morsels cut from the livers of stabbed gladiators. During the Middle Ages, when epilepsy was attributed to demonic possession, treatment included prayer, fasting, wearing amulets, lighting candles, visiting the graves of saints, and writing the names of the Three Wise Men with blood taken from the patient's little finger. These spiritual remedies were far safer than the "medical" therapies of the time—still practiced as late as the seventeenth century—which included cauterizing the head with a hot iron and boring a hole in the skull to release peccant vapors.

dry to touch, color good & pink. Mom is with babe at this time & is breastfeeding. Mom informed to keep babe covered with a blanket for the babe is a little cool." "0400. Babe resting quietly with no acute distress noted. Mom breast feeds off & on." "0600. Sleeping." "0730. Awake, color good. Mother fed." "1200. Held by mother."

Lia was discharged on March 11, 1983. Her parents were instructed, via an English-speaking relative, to give her 250 milligrams of ampicillin twice a day, to clear up her aspiration pneumonia, and twenty milligrams of Dilantin elixir, an anticonvulsant, twice a day, to suppress any further grand mal seizures.

Suggested Readings

Crapanzano, Vincent
 1973   *The Hamadha: A Study in Moroccan Ethnopsychiatry.* Berkeley: University of California Press.

Csordas, Thomas J.
 1994   *The Sacred Self: A Cultural Phenomenology of Charismatic Healing.* Berkeley: University of California Press.

Danforth, Loring M.
 1989   *Firewalking and Religious Healing: The Anatenaria of Greece and the American Firewalking Movement.* Princeton, N.J.: Princeton University Press.

Nichter, Mark, ed.
 1992   *Anthropological Approaches to the Study of Ethnomedicine.* Yverdon, Switzerland and Langhorne, PA: Gordon and Breach Science Publishers.

Roseman, Marina
 1991   *Healing Sounds from the Malaysian Rainforest: Temiar Music and Medicine.* Berkeley: University of California Press.

Sargent, Carolyn F., and Thomas M. Johnson, eds.
 1996   *Medical Anthropology: Contemporary Theory and Method.* Westport, Conn.: Praeger.

CHAPTER SEVEN

Witchcraft, Sorcery, Divination, and Magic

Devil mask from the Tyrol.

All societies recognize the frailness of the human condition; wherever pain, illness, injury, and unjustness exist, so do culturally prescribed explanations. In many parts of the world, where opportunities for formal education are limited to a small elite, although their economic and political power may be considerable, explanations of phenomena are still rooted deeply in traditional interpretations passed from generation to generation by word of mouth. In rural Africa, for example, where 70 to 90 percent of the population is not covered by public health services (Shehu 1975: 29), mental and physical illness are often accounted for in terms of a formidable array of supernatural sources, including witchcraft, sorcery, magic, curses, spirits, or a combination of these. Whether explanations for illness are "scientific" or "mystical," all societies must have explanations for crises. Mental and physical illness cannot be permitted to go unchecked. Witchcraft, sorcery, divination, and magic are ways of dealing with the supernatural, explaining the unexplainable, attempting to control or manipulate what otherwise cannot be controlled.

In many parts of the world, a vast number of daily crises are attributed to witchcraft, particularly in sub-Saharan Africa, where the highest level of belief in witchcraft exists today. Here witchcraft explanations are logical—indeed, some say indispensable. In short, witchcraft is an integral part of traditional African belief systems, as are sorcery and magic, and it is considered by many anthropologists to be essential to African religions.

Lucy Mair, a British social anthropologist and a leading authority on African witchcraft, points out that the belief in witchcraft is universal. Around the world, greed and sexual motifs are commonly associated with witches, as is the "nightmare" witch that prowls at night and is distinguished from the everyday witch by nocturnal habits (1969: 36–37). Women are more often labeled witches than men, and societies frequently associate particular types of personalities with individuals who they feel have the highest probability of becoming witches. According to Mair (1969: 43), many of the qualities associated with being a poor neighbor, such as unsociability, isolation, stinginess, unfriendliness, and moroseness, are the same qualities ascribed to the everyday witch. Nothing compares in terms of sheer evil, however, to the nightmare witch, whose hatred of the most basic tenets of human decency earns it a special place of infamy.

Witches, wherever they exist, are the antithesis of proper behavior. Their antisocial acts, moreover, are uncontrollable. A final commonality of witch beliefs is that their powers are innate, unlike those of the sorcerer, whose powers are learned; the witch inherits the power for evil or is given the power by God.

To the beginning student in anthropology, witchcraft surely must appear to affect a society negatively; a careful analysis of belief systems demonstrates more positive than negative functions, however. In his analysis of the functions of witchcraft among the Navaho, Clyde Kluckhohn evaluated the belief more positively than negatively in terms of economic and social control and the psychological states of a group (1967; Kluckhohn and Leighton 1962). Beliefs in witchcraft level economic differences, for example. Among the Navaho, the rich are believed to have gained their wealth by secret supernatural techniques. The only way to quell this kind of rumor is through generosity, which may take the form of redistribution of wealth among relatives and friends (Kluckhohn and Leighton 1962: 247). Kluckhohn demonstrated that witchcraft beliefs help reinforce social values. For example, the belief that uncared-for elderly will turn into witches demands that the Navaho treat the aged with proper care. The worry that the death of a close relative may cast suspicion of witchcraft on survivors also reinforces their social values regarding obligations to kin. Ironically, because leaders are thought to be witches, people were hesitant to be disobedient for fear of supernatural retribution (1967: 113).

Kluckhohn maintained that at the psychological level witchcraft was an outlet for hostility because frustrated individuals used witches as scapegoats. Anxiety and neglect could also be accommodated through commonly held witchcraft beliefs, for people showing symptoms of witchcraft-caused illnesses would reaffirm their importance to kin and the group at the public curing ceremonies (1967: 83–84).

The terms *witchcraft* and *sorcery* are often used interchangeably to mean any kind of evil magic; however, E. E. Evans-Pritchard's (1937) analysis of Azande witchcraft and sorcery resulted in a distinction between the two terms that is accepted by most anthropologists today. Generally speaking, a sorcerer intentionally seeks to bring about harm. Sorcerers have learned how to cast spells and use certain formulas and objects to inflict evil. The sorcerer's methods are real, not psychic like those of the witch. Sorcery is conscious and an acquired skill, whereas witchcraft is unconscious and innate. Contrary to witchcraft, sorcery is not always antisocial or illegitimate and occurs with a higher frequency than does witchcraft.

Interestingly, some scholars believe that witchcraft does not, in truth, exist despite the strong beliefs of those in the culture. Witchcraft, they argue, exists only in the minds of the people, whereas sorcery is proven by the presence of paraphernalia, medicines, and the identification of sorcerer specialists in the community. The point is, however, that witchcraft serves so many functions it is hard to believe its importance can be whittled away by the difficulties involved in trying to prove its existence or in distinguishing it from sorcery. Everywhere there is social conflict: People become angry, get insulted, or perhaps become jealous of someone's success; it is during such uncomfortable times that witches may be found at fault and sorcerers may be called upon for help.

When someone in North American culture thinks of witches and witchcraft, the usual association is with early modern European witchcraft and the Salem trials in New England in 1692. However, these European-based witch beliefs, including the Salem case, were quite different from those of the preliterate societies in which witchcraft occurs, where it functions as an everyday, socially acceptable way of managing tension, explaining the otherwise unexplainable, leveling disparities in wealth and status, and resolving social conflict. In contrast, early modern European witchcraft was a response to the strains of a time of profound change, marked by immense political and religious conflict. Although witch beliefs had been a feature of European culture since the Dark Ages, the Church managed to keep the situation under control until the turmoil of the sixteenth and seventeenth centuries, when the practice of labeling Church heretics as witches became popular and the witchhunt craze occurred. Naturally, the Salem witch-hunt of 1692 is of the greatest interest to Americans, but Salem's 200 arrests and 19 executions pale in comparison with the approximately 500,000 people who were executed in Europe during the fifteenth, sixteenth, and seventeenth centuries after having been convicted of witchcraft. At the end of this period, the witchcraze was coming to an end. "Cartesian and scientific thought had no room for witchcraft; ecclesiastical and civil authorities agreed that witch prosecutions had got out of hand; and European society was settling down to two centuries (1700–1900) of relative peace and prosperity" (Russell 1987: 196).

Ethnographic reports on witchcraft and sorcery dominate the literature, but other forces of evil are also responsible for much unjust suffering. One such power, but certainly not the only one, is the evil eye—widely known in the Middle East, parts of Europe, Central America, and Africa, areas characterized by Islamic and Judeo-Christian as well as so-called indigenous religious traditions. The evil eye was believed to be a voluntary power brought about by the malicious nature of the possessor, on the one hand, or an involuntary but still dangerous, uncontrolled power on the other. Strangers, dwarfs, old women, certain types of animals, menstruating women, and people with one eye have been often viewed as being particularly dangerous. Children and farm animals, the most precious of one's possessions, were thought most vulnerable to the evil eye, which could cause various disasters to occur immediately or in the future, particularly by asserting control over the victim. A variety of protective measures have been prescribed to ward off the evil eye. Glass evil eyes and variously shaped metal amulets, for example, are sold to tourists and residents alike in modern Greece. Plants, certain avoidance actions, colors, and magical words and gestures have also at different times and places been felt to be effective against the evil eye.

In addition to the evil eye, anguish can be created by malicious ghosts, spirit possession, attacks by enemy shamans, curses of the envious, and the spells of evil magicians and other specialists who have learned how to manipulate power to harm others. Each of these causes harms and creates fear in a community and as such is an index of social strain; however, each may also function positively by allowing individuals to blame supernatural agencies rather than kin and neighbors for illness or misfortunes that befall them.

Demons, spirits, ancestors, and gods all exist as realities in the human mind and possess the power to harm and harass the living. Good and evil are counterbalanced in every society through a variety of rituals and other forms of protection, yet this balance is inevitably broken by human weaknesses and transgressions that invite the evil nature of supernatural agents. The malicious acts of these agents inflict pain and anguish on the innocent as well as on those deserving of punishment. Although all supernaturals can possess an individual and cause an unending variety of harm, the most commonly known agent of possession is the demon. Demons may aid their human consorts from time to time, but generally they are seen as being responsible for diseases, injuries, or a myriad of major and minor personal and group disasters. More powerful than mere humans, they are also generally believed to be less powerful than gods and ancestral spirits (Collins 1978: 195).

Possession by demons is ordinarily considered dangerous, but this is not always the case. For the Aymara Indians of Bolivia, for example, possession results in serious consequences for the victims and their community, whereas among the Haitians it is actively sought at voodoo ceremonies in order to obtain the supernatural knowledge of the spirits. The acceptance or the actual seeking out of beneficent spirits and situating them in a medium where they can be called on when needed is termed "adorcism" by L. DeHeusch (1971). I. M. Lewis distinguishes between "central possession cults" and "peripheral possession cults." In the former, spirits, such as ancestors, most commonly possess men and sustain the moral order of society. In the latter, women and others having lesser status are possessed by malevolent spirits; possession of this type is often considered an illness and damages the social fabric of the group (1989). Haitians, however, conceive of both good and evil spirits, and all fear possession by the latter. "Possession, then, is a broad term referring to an integration of spirit and matter, force or power and corporeal reality, in a cosmos where the boundaries between an individual and her environment are acknowledged to be permeable, flexibly drawn, or at least negotiable" (Boddy 1994: 407).

The functions of possession commonly go unnoticed, overshadowed by the dramatic expressive actions of the possessed and those in attendance. Stanley and Ruth Freed (1964: 71) showed that spirit possession in a north Indian village functioned primarily to relieve the individual's intropsychic tensions while giving the victim the attention and sympathy of relatives and friends. The possession itself and its overt demonstration were only a vehicle for these functions. Even rules designed to avoid demons, such as the *jinns* of Islamic countries, can promote individual self-discipline and propriety in behavior, both as William Howells has pointed out, desirable qualities (1962: 202). The prohibitions promoted to avoid *jinns* do direct behavior toward socially approved goals, but, despite these positive functions, demons cause suffering and pain to members of both Western and non-Western societies and every society is forced to cope with their devious nature.

Exorcism—the driving away of evil spirits, such as demons, by chanting, praying, commanding, or other ritual means—occurs throughout the world and is invoked when an evil spirit has caused illness by entering a person's body. (A belief in exorcism assumes a related belief in the power of ritual to move an evil spirit from one place to another.) Although the idea that foreign objects can enter the body and cause illness has been widespread, it was especially prevalent among American Indians, where curers, shamans, and sometimes a specialist known as a "sucking doctor" had the ability to remove these materials by such techniques as rubbing and kneading the patient's body, gesturing over the diseased area, and directly sucking out the evil object. Shamans, because of the "trick" aspect of their rituals, are especially well versed in the intricacies of exorcism as a means of removal of disease-causing objects. Typically, a sleight-of-hand maneuver is used to show the patient that the harmful substance has been removed.

Howells (1962: 92–94) has described several techniques used around the world for exorcising evil spirits and diseases: using sweat-baths, cathartics, or emetics to flush out the offending spirits; trephining; manipulating and massaging the body; scraping or sponging the illness off the body; reciting magical spells, coaxing, or singing songs to lure the spirit away; tempting the spirit to evacuate the body by laying out a sumptuous meal for it; keeping the patient uncomfortable, sometimes by administering beatings, so the spirit will be discontented with the body and want to depart; building a fire under the patient to make it uncomfortably warm for the spirit; placing foul-smelling, overripe fruit near the patient; and scandalizing the demon by having the patient's naked wife jump over the patient.

Until the recent popularity of movies, television shows, and novels about possession by demons, the American public was largely unaware that exorcism has been practiced throughout the history of Western religions. Somewhat alarming to many Americans was the realization that the Catholic Church continued to approve exorcisms in twentieth-century America. The following seventeenth-century conjuration was recited by priests in order to exorcise evil spirits from troubled houses. The words may be different, as are the names for the supernatural beings referred to, but the intent of the conjuration is identical to incantations uttered by religious specialists in preliterate societies during exorcism rites for similar purposes:

> I adjure thee, O serpent of old, by the Judge of the living and the dead; by the Creator of the world who hath power to cast into hell, that thou depart forthwith from this house. He that commands thee, accursed demon, is He that commanded the winds and the sea and the storm. He that commands thee, is He that ordered thee to be hurled down from the height of heaven into the lower parts of the earth. He that commands thee is He that bade thee depart from Him. Hearken, then, Satan, and fear. Get thee gone, vanquished and cowed, when thou art bidden in the name of our Lord Jesus Christ who will come to judge the living and the dead and all the world by fire. Amen. (Crehan 1970: 873)

William James saw religion as the belief in an unseen order. If one important aspect of religion is helping believers come to know that unknown, it follows that divination is important to religion. *Divination* means learning about the future or about things that may be hidden. Although the word itself may be traced to *divinity*, which indicates its relationship to gods, the practice of divination belongs as much to magic as it does to religion proper. From the earliest times, human beings have wanted to know about such climatic changes as drought and heavy rainfall. Without scientific information to help predict natural events, early humans looked for "signs" in the flight of birds, the entrails of small animals, or perhaps the positions of coals in a fire or pebbles in a stream. To this day, the methods of divination in the world's cultures are far too varied and numerous to mention here.

Until recently, controversy has surrounded the definition of magic and religion by anthropologists. Only in the last few years have they come close to agreement that the dichotomy is a false one or that, if a dichotomy does exist, its ramifications are not significant to the study of the practitioners of each. Both magic and religion deal directly with the supernatural, and our understanding of the cultural applications of each provides deeper insights into the worldview of the people practicing them.

Magic is usually divided into types, depending on the techniques involved. For example, Sir James Frazer distinguished "imitative magic," in which the magician believes that the desired result can be achieved by imitation, from "contagious magic," in which materials or substances once in contact with the intended victim are used in the magical attack. Other scholars would include "sympathetic magic," a form of magic in which items associated with or symbolic of the intended victim are used to identify and carry out the spell. Obviously, sympathetic magic contains elements of both imitative and contagious magic.

These forms of magic, still in use today, have been important methods of reducing anxiety regarding problems that exceeded the ability of people to understand and control them, especially because of a lack of technological expertise. Divination, special formulas and incantations, spells and curses—all are considered magical, and all can be used for good or evil. Because these activities are learned, they should be differentiated from witchcraft, which is considered innate and, most believe, uncontrollable.

It is logical to assume that non-Western reliance on explanations of events in terms of magic, sorcery, and witchcraft is a natural outcome of a lack of scientific training. But it is equally important to note that Westerners also rely on religious beliefs, with faith playing a strong role in determining actions and behaviors in our daily lives. Our ethnocentrism still blinds us to the similarities between ourselves and our fellow humans throughout the world. The great questions concerning the human condition are asked by all peoples, and despite the disparate levels of technology our sameness is demonstrated by the universality of religion.

In the lead article of this chapter, James L. Brain employs a cross-cultural approach to witchcraft, emphasizing the near-universal image of woman as witch, and presents his theory that the mobility of nomadic societies, such as hunter-gatherers, accounts for the absence of witchcraft among those groups and its presence among the hunter's sedentary horticultural neighbors.

In the second article, Naomi M. McPherson investigates sorcery and concepts of deviance among the Kabana of Papua New Guinea. She shows the Kabana to be quite unusual in that, unlike most other groups, they do not always consider the practice of sorcery to be evil, and they believe that under certain conditions it can function positively in their society.

The third article is by T. M. Luhrmann; it describes typical contemporary witches and their rituals. Luhrmann's work is based on research with middle-class, urban witches in England in the 1980s.

In the fourth selection, E. E. Evans-Pritchard describes the Azande poison oracle *benge* and the beliefs surrounding its usage.

The Bronislaw Malinowski article is a classic work identifying circumstances in which magic is used, and it is based on the author's research in the Trobriand Islands of Melanesia. Rejecting the once-popular idea that primitive peoples are incapable of rational thought, Malinowski argues that Melanesians make use of an experience-based understanding of the world in a manner much like science, and they rely on magic only in situations of uncertainty.

In the last article, George Gmelch cleverly applies Malinowski's ideas on magic to baseball.

References

Boddy, Janice
1994 "Spirit Possession Revisited: Beyond Instrumentality." *Annual Reviews in Anthropology* 23: 407–34.

Collins, John J.
1978 *Primitive Religion.* Totowa, N.J.: Littlefield, Adams.

Crehan, J. H.
1970 "Exorcism." In Richard Cavendish, ed., *Man, Myth and Magic,* vol. 7, pp. 869–73. London: BPCC/Phoebus.

DeHeusch, L.
1971 *Why Marry Her? Society and Symbolic Structures.* Translated by J. Lloyd. Cambridge: Cambridge University Press.

Evans-Pritchard, E. E.
1937 *Witchcraft, Oracles and Magic Among the Azande.* Oxford: Clarendon Press.

Freed, Stanley A., and Ruth S. Freed
1964 "Spirit Possession as Illness in a North Indian Village." *Ethnology* 3: 152–71.

Howells, William
1962 *The Heathens.* Garden City, N.Y.: Doubleday.

Kluckhohn, Clyde
    1967 *Navaho Witchcraft*. Boston: Beacon Press (first published, 1944).

Kluckhohn, Clyde, and Dorothea Leighton
    1962 *The Navaho*. Cambridge, Mass.: Harvard University Press (first published 1946).

Lewis, I. M.
    1989 *Ecstatic Religion: A Study of Spirit Possession and Shamanism*. 2nd ed. London: Routledge.

Mair, Lucy
    1969 *Witchcraft*. New York: McGraw-Hill.

Russell, Jeffrey Burton
    1987 "Witchcraft." In Mircea Eliade, ed., *The Encyclopedia of Religion*, pp. 415–23. New York: Macmillan.

Shehu, U.
    1975 *Health Care in Rural Areas*. AFRO Technical Papers, no. 10.

33

An Anthropological Perspective on the Witchcraze

James L. Brain

At first glance, it would appear impossible that an anthropological investigation of the European witchcraze, so far removed from contemporary America, could shed light on current attitudes toward gender. In this article, however, James L. Brain demonstrates that the idea of the witch is closely related to the subversion of male authority, a reversal of patriarchal authority that Saint Paul asserted was divinely ordered. The denigration of women in European thought can, in part, be traced to Aristotle, who saw women's souls and bodies as being inferior. Weaknesses such as these, it was thought, predisposed women to be witches. Close on the heels of this came the idea of ritual pollution of men by women, female emissions being further evidence of women's inferiority.

The image of women as witches is widespread, but it was not until witchcraft was linked to the devil that it was considered heresy, a crime punishable by death. It is not difficult to link these historical attitudes toward women with the present. In fact, Brain maintains that "the witchcraze ended, but misogyny and gynophobia are still alive and well at the end of the twentieth century."

In addition to the issue of gender and witchcraft, Brain addresses the question of why witches are believed to exist in some societies and not others. Here the author's "mobility theory," based on the nomadic lifestyle of hunter-gatherers, offers a provocative explanation for the absence of witchcraft among these peoples but its presence among sedentary horticultural societies.

Our understanding of historical attitudes toward gender may be illuminated by a comparative cross-cultural approach to witchcraft. Two issues are especially important: the reason for the near universality of the image of woman as witch, and the idea that geographic and spatial mobility may be an important and overlooked factor in the absence of witchcraft accusations and in the decline of their frequency.

Reprinted from Jean R. Brink, Allison P. Coudert, and Maryanne C. Horowitz, eds., THE POLITICS OF GENDER IN EARLY MODERN EUROPE (Kirksville, Mo.: Sixteenth Century Journal Publishers, Inc., 1989), pp. 15–27. By permission of the publisher. The article's citations, originally numbered footnotes, have been interpolated into the text in this volume for consistency of presentation.

The Image of the Witch

Anthropological and historical evidence shows that the specific details of beliefs about witches and their behavior will vary according to the concerns of a particular society. There are, however, two universal constants about witch beliefs that cut across cultures: witches represent people's deepest fears about themselves and society, and they represent a reversal of all that is considered normal behavior in a particular society. This has been documented for small-scale societies (Wilson 1951; Mair 1969), but the situation in Europe needs to be examined. Norman Cohn discusses the European witchcraze in terms of "collective fantasies," "obsessive fears," and "unacknowledged desires" in the minds of sixteenth- and seventeenth-century men and women (Cohn 1975: 258–63). Margaret Murray and, to a certain extent, Carlo Ginzburg locate the origins of European witchcraft beliefs in pre-Christian religions (Ginzburg 1983; Murray 1931/1970).

It would be unfortunate if we were to revive Murray's hypothesis. The beliefs about witches can be explained without reference to pre-Christian religions, if we assume that witch-like behavior is a simple reversal of normal and socially accepted behavior. In Catholic Europe, the Church demanded attendance at mass in the daytime on Sundays; the predominant color there was white. By reversing this, one can easily predict that witches will celebrate their own sabbath at night, and that black will be the predominant color in their community or congregation—hence the term "black mass." Reversal also predicts that whatever ritual or service is performed will be a reversal of the Christian mass—the recitation of prayers backwards, the reversed cross, and worship of some form of Antichrist. The Church demanded acceptance of the doctrine of the Trinity, in which subliminally one can perceive that Mary is made pregnant by her own son in the shape of the Holy Ghost; the reversal of this doctrine makes profane incest an attribute of witches. If there was a sacred act of ritual cannibalism in Holy Communion, then witches could be expected to take part in some blasphemous form of cannibalism. The belief in Jesus' conquest of death and decay manifested itself in the idea that the bodies of saints do not decay at death; in witch beliefs, this finds its reversal in the belief in vampires that do not decay. If heterosexuality is the extolled norm, then homosexuality will be seen as witch-like, and if chastity is the ultimate condition of holiness then obviously one should expect witches to engage in sexual orgies.

This point can be carried even further: if patriarchal authority is divinely ordained, as Saint Paul insisted, then any attempt by women to subvert or to assume that authority can be seen as an illicit reversal and hence as witch-like behavior. The first example of the subversion of divine authority, of course, is attributed to Eve in her disobedience. Both Protestants and Catholics were concerned with issues of authority and women. Martin de Castañega's treatise on superstition and witchcraft (1529) answers the question of why women are more prone to be witches than men thus: "The first reason is because

Christ forbade them to administer the sacraments and therefore the devil gives them the authority to do it with his execrations" (Darst 1979: 298–322). Here we see not only the reversal of normal, i.e., God-given authority, but also the idea of the administration of blasphemous, heretical sacraments. Additional reversals occur in his explanations of how and why witches, like angels and Christ, can fly; how and why they, like Christ can walk on water; and how and why they, like Christ and the devil, can become invisible or change their shape (Darst 1979: 306). In the pattern of inheritance D. H. Darst records another reversal. Instead of passing on inheritance from father to son, witches inherit their discipleship to the devil from mother to daughter, from aunt to niece, or from grandmother to granddaughter.

To the issue of authority, feminist anthropological scholarship offers very cogent insights (Rosaldo 1974: 1–42). Authority is always legitimate; power may be, but often is not. Where women are denied authority, they inevitably seek their ends by the manipulation of the power they possess: by denying sex, food or nurture; by failing to perform household tasks, by outright disobedience, or by passive resistance in the form of sulking, scolding, and gossiping. All of these possibilities subvert legitimate male authority and can, therefore, be seen as evidence of witchcraft. One can conceive of a sliding scale: the less authority—or responsibility—women possess, the more manipulation of power will occur, and vice versa. Thus we can confidently expect to find the paradox that women are often extremely powerful in societies in which they are denied any authority; in these social organizations they develop strategies to attain their ends outside the legitimate parameters of authority.

This paradigm has great relevance to women in Renaissance Europe in terms of the generation of misogyny. As Lamphere demonstrates, the image of women in patrilineal and patrilocal societies is invariably negative: women are believed to be deceitful, untrustworthy and manipulative (Lamphere 1974: 97–112). This negative image is a direct result of marriage practices: the men are all related by blood; the women, because of rules of clan exogamy, are all strangers both to the men and to each other. In a large extended family, the men will have the solidarity of kinship; the women will lack any solidarity. In such societies the only possible way for a woman to achieve her goals is for her to manipulate those who possess legitimate authority—her husband and her sons. Lamphere contrasts this inevitably negative image of women with the very positive image enjoyed by Navajo women. In that matrilineal society marriage is often matrilocal, so that it is the husband who moves to his wife's family. Here he is the one surrounded by strangers and must depend on his wife to negotiate concessions for him. Under these circumstances women are viewed as competent managers and good negotiators. This shows that the locality of marriage is crucial in determining the image of women. While it is true that in northern European societies bilateral descent was the norm, most marriages probably have demanded that women move to join their husbands. If manipulation of power is the only available route a woman can follow to achieve her ends then inevitably her image will be that of a manipulative bitch—as the *Malleus Maleficarum* makes abundantly clear.

There is little doubt that a contributing factor to the denigration of women in European thought was the legacy of Aristotle by way, particularly, of Augustine. "Conceiving of the soul as possessing nutritive, sensitive or appetitive and reasonable faculties, Aristotle saw women's souls as deficient in all three aspects, but especially in the faculty of reason" (Robertson n.d.). Acceptance of this idea leads inexorably to the dicta of the *Malleus* about the predisposition of women to be witches because of their manifold weaknesses (Question 4) (Kramer and Sprenger 1971).

Not only was the woman's soul seen as inferior; her body was too. "In Aristotelian and Galenic terms, woman is less fully developed than man. Because of lack of heat in germination, her sexual organs have remained internal, she is incomplete, colder and moister in dominant humors. She has less body heat and thus less courage, liberality, moral strength" (Robertson n.d.). That these ideas may appear absurd to us has to be tempered by their legacy and persistence in more recent times. Darwin believed that women were less evolved than men because of their childlike skins and softness (Dykstra 1986: 167–73), and the Freudian doctrine of penis-envy surely owes something to them.

The denigration of the body leads into another area germane to the witch stereotype and one that has been much explored by anthropology. The ques-

tion of ritual pollution is used widely to "prove" that women are inferior, and doubtless has much to do with latter-day disputes about the ordination of women. All bodily emissions are considered polluting or, in our modern idiom, disgusting. Among others, Mary Douglas seeks an explanation for this attitude (Douglas 1966). In her opinion, all such substances are considered threatening because they are liminal, because they have "traversed the boundary of the body" and are thus of the body but yet not of the body, and thus do not fit our standard categories. While I do not dispute this point, I have argued elsewhere that what makes these substances so deeply threatening is that they remind us of death (Brain 1977b: 371–84). It is no coincidence that they are often sought for and used in magic intended to bring about the death of the victim. Of course, both men and women produce polluting emissions, but only women menstruate, give birth messily, and lactate. Customarily women take care of small babies who, like animals, are uncontrolled in their excretions, and the association with babies makes women additionally polluting. The issue of pollution throws additional light on why midwives were disproportionately often accused of witchcraft. Because they assisted at birth, they inevitably became contaminated with polluting substances. It should also be recalled that midwives traditionally laid out the dead and were contaminated by death, the ultimate pollutant.

Women's very physiology therefore makes them appear more polluted and polluting than men. Even in regard to the sexual act itself, a man can more easily be cleansed since his genitals are external and can be readily washed. A woman cannot be so readily cleansed, since her own polluting bodily fluids have been augmented by the deposition of the man's semen. Pollution alone would not make a witch, yet the *Malleus* makes clear that pollution is a primary aspect of sexuality. Sexuality is allied to temptation, and the Devil is the great tempter. Nowhere is this more powerfully demonstrated than through the medium of lust for women—"though the devil tempted Eve to sin, yet Eve seduced Adam" (*Malleus:* Part 1, Question 6).

Although the *Malleus* is obsessive in its misogyny and loathing of sex, it seems to deal only indirectly with one sexual matter—the nature of semen. Literary references of the Shakespearian period show that this was a subject that exercised men's minds. In some ways, this belief is still widely held as part of folk beliefs even today in the United States. The basic assumption of this belief is that marrow and semen are the same substance; the skull is the largest bone in the body and the brain is its marrow. Therefore any emission of semen depletes a man's life force and intelligence. "As the main storehouse of bone marrow, the brain is the source of semen, via the spinal cord. The supply is limited. . . . Loss of manhood, power, and ultimate life itself results from the 'spending' of the life force, which is a finite capital" (La Barre 1984: 130). Francis Bacon wrote in 1626 that "The skull has Braines, as a kind of Marrow, within it"; and even Leonardo da Vinci apparently believed in a duct connecting the brain to the penis via the spinal cord (La Barre 1984: 115–18). Understanding the belief that semen and marrow were one and the same gives point to the many references in literature to the danger of expending a man's marrow. If we grasp this unfounded fear, we can well understand yet another aspect of the witch image: that of the succubus and its terrifyingly debilitating potential.

Claude Lévi-Strauss suggested that the primary pair of oppositions is that of nature versus culture (Leach 1970: 35). Sherry B. Ortner claims that universally women are perceived as being, if not *part of* nature, at least as *closer to* nature than men, who are perceived as the generators of culture (Ortner 1974: 67–87). This position has been challenged (McCormack and Strathern 1980), but it is convincing. It generates the following sets of oppositions (always unequal in value):

> Nature—Culture
> Women—Men
> Darkness—Light
> Left—Right
> Disorder—Order
> Death—Life

It is significant that in many languages the word for left is synonymous with female and right with male (Brain 1977a: 180–92). One should note that "right" as in side or hand and "right" as in correct or "the right to" are not merely homonymous. The same is true of "droit" or "recht." Perceptually, witches are always believed to do and to be everything that is the reverse of normal and right. Similarly, all the

other characteristics in the left column are applicable to the witch stereotype.

The link between women and nature suggested by Ortner was hardly an unfamiliar one in Renaissance Europe. Bacon in particular took the view that the mission of science was the subjugation of nature. Moreover, he participated in the "rhetoric that conjoins the domination of nature with the insistent image of nature as female" (Fox-Keller 1983: 116).

That the image of witch as woman (or vice versa) is extremely widespread in the world is beyond doubt. Elsewhere in the world, and in Europe before the association of witchcraft with heresy, witchcraft was considered bad but of minor importance. During the witchcraze a new doctrine emerged that linked witchcraft with devil worship and hence with heresy. This change in doctrine made the image of woman as witch lethal to women. The change did not occur in a vacuum, and there are many powerful reasons why the witchcraze occurred. The witchcraze ended, but misogyny and gynophobia are still alive and well at the end of the twentieth century.

Mobility as a Factor in the Nonexistence or Decline of Witchcraft Beliefs

Examining non-Western small-scale societies, one discovers a rather startling fact. Societies with the simplest technologies of all—hunter-gatherers such as the San of the Kalahari, the Mbuti pygmies of the Ituri Forest, and the Hadza of northwest Tanzania— are quite unconcerned about witchcraft and do not think that it occurs in their societies (Marshall 1962: 221–52; Turnbull 1968: 132–37; Woodburn 1968: 49–55). They do, however, impute it to their sedentary agricultural neighbors (Turnbull 1961: 228; Woodburn 1982a: 431–51; Lee 1976: 127–29). When they themselves are forced into a sedentary way of life, "witchcraft fears are rampant" (Woodburn 1982b: 187–210). Why fears of witchcraft are unimportant to such peoples is described by several authors. Of the San peoples, L. Marshall writes, "the composition of a band is fluid—marriage takes individuals from one band to another, and whole families move from one band to another; bands split and disband completely" (Marshall 1976: 180). Similarly, Richard Lee notes that "hunters have a great deal of latitude to vote with their feet, to walk out of an unpleasant situation" (Lee 1972: 182). In J. Woodburn's description of conflict resolution in these societies lies the key to the absence of witchcraft beliefs. When conflict arises, people move, giving an ecological reason. Thus, "they solve disputes simply by refusing to acknowledge them" (Woodburn 1968: 156; 1979: 244–60).

It is significant that all these African hunter-gatherers possess negligible property and practice bilateral descent. The situation is very different in societies that practice unilineal descent. In his essay, Meyer Fortes suggests that unilineal descent is characteristic of societies in which property rights are acknowledged (Fortes 1953: 17–41). Such societies invariably subscribe to a belief in sorcery or witchcraft or both. Unlike their African counterparts, Australian hunter-gatherers practice unilineal descent. They claim ownership over totemic sites and believe in evil magic, as evidenced by accounts of "bone-pointing" (Thomas 1906; Spencer and Gillen 1904: 462–63; Spencer and Gillen 1899/1938: 533; Elkin 1938: 203–05; Meggitt 1962: 139, 176). All the accounts emphasize, however, that only men are involved; that the practice is thought to be rare. It is also believed that "the professional worker of magic is always to be found in another tribe" (Elkin 1938: 203). Woodburn suggests that the crucial factor that differentiates African from Australian hunter-gatherers is "the relatively tight control which men exercise over women" among the Australians (Woodburn 1979: 258). This point has relevance to the European witchcraze. It is also important that Woodburn describes the African hunter-gatherers as having an "immediate return system" of economics, whereas the Australians, more like sedentary peoples, have "delayed return systems" (Woodburn 1982a: 258). A comparable people, the Ona (or Selk'nam) of Tierra del Fuego, are a hunting-gathering people. Anne Chapman describes them as inegalitarian, oppressive to women (unlike the African hunter-gatherers). They put an "emphasis on patrilineality, and patrilocality [and] the preeminence of territoriality" (Chapman 1984: 63). Like the Australians, they change campsites frequently; like them they believe in sorcerers; like them they claim that sorcerers belong to another tribe (Bridges 1949: 213, 373).

If we turn to the nomadic pastoral peoples, we should, according to my hypothesis, find a situation similar to that found among the Australians and the Ona/Selk'nam, since all pastoralists practice patrilineal descent, and own property, but move fairly frequently. This proves to be the case. There is no mention of witchcraft among the Fulani (Peuls) of the Sahel region of West Africa (Stenning 1959, 1965), while among the pastoral Somali "magic, witchcraft and sorcery play a small part" (Lewis 1965). The same is true of the Turkana and Dodos of Northern Kenya (Gulliver and Gulliver 1953: 86), and the Karamojong of Northern Uganda (Dyson-Hudson 1966: 40), where "in theory, witches are never found in one's own settlement but always in a different group from one's own" (Gulliver and Gulliver 1953: 49). The closely related Jie, their neighbors, have adopted a partially sedentary mode of existence. They diagnose witchcraft as the cause for a sequence of misfortunes, and their "normal procedure [then] is to move to a new homestead to avoid the evil influence" (Gulliver 1955: 104). Similarly, the nomadic pastoral Maasai of Kenya and Tanzania believe that one can learn the techniques of sorcery, but "they have no conventional category of supernatural 'witches' . . . and they often make fun of their Bantu neighbors who they know do possess such beliefs" (Jacobs 1985). Their linguistically and ethnically similar sedentary neighbors, the Arusha (il Arusa), on the other hand, are very concerned about witchcraft (Gulliver 1963: 21). The same holds true for the closely related agricultural Nandi and Kipsigis in Kenya (Peristiany 1939: 94–95; Langley 1979: 10, 62), and for the related Lango and Teso of Uganda (Driberg 1923: 241ff; Lawrence 1957: 182; Gulliver and Gulliver 1953: 26). The ethnically different, click-speaking Sandawe, not far away, who were probably formerly hunter-gatherers, now practice agriculture. Predictably, G. W. B. Huntingford says of them that "witchcraft is prevalent and illness and death are attributed either to it or to the anger of ancestral spirits" (Huntingford 1953: 137–38).

The ethnographic data show that in societies with total mobility and little attachment to property and with consequently little development of hierarchy and authority, there are no fears about witchcraft. Where there is considerable mobility but some attachment to property—often expressed by the presence of unilineal descent—we can expect to find a belief that witchcraft exists. The assumption is, however, that it is located in some other group and can easily be avoided by the move of a homestead. As dwellings are temporary huts in a thorn corral or something similar, this is not considered a particularly serious matter. When we turn to the sedentary peoples of the non-industrial world, however, we can expect always to find beliefs in witchcraft. The details of the beliefs may vary, but, as I have already mentioned, there is a remarkable consistency about aspects of the beliefs.

At the same time, it is manifest that particular forms of social organization or socio-political situations can generate more or less acute fears of witchcraft. Siegfried Frederick Nadel shows convincingly that two peoples that are almost identical ethnically, linguistically, and culturally can demonstrate radically different attitudes to witchcraft (Nadel 1952: 18–29). One society was rife with fears and accusations; the other had none. The only difference between the two societies is that the former has three age grades; the latter six. To move into the next higher grade, men had to forego the privileges of the age group they were relinquishing. Where there are six grades this presents no problem; where there are only three, suspicions and accusations proliferate between the young men and those in the middle grade—who are understandably reluctant to assume the mantle of old age and to eschew sexual activity and other privileges. Comparably, J. C. Mitchell shows that even in the circumstances of a modern tobacco estate in Zimbabwe (then Rhodesia), relatively well-educated permanent staff members constantly suspected their colleagues of evil magic directed against them (Mitchell 1965: 196). Uneducated casual laborers on the same estate who in their home areas might well have been anxious about witchcraft were quite unconcerned during their temporary sojourn on the estate. The more highly educated workers were in constant contact with one another and were always in competition for the favors of the white management.

. . . That virtually everywhere people believed in witchcraft from time immemorial until the eighteenth century is well established (Trevor-Roper 1969: 91). Why, then, was there the enormous surge of accusations during the Renaissance period? And why did the craze draw to a close? As Thomas notes of the decline in belief and the acceptance of a more rational viewpoint, "the ultimate origins of this faith in unaided human capacity remain mysterious."

Thomas accepts that "the decline of magic coincided with a marked improvement in the extent to which the environment became amenable to control" (Thomas 1971: 650, 663). Better food supplies and conditions of health, the cessation of plague (Midelfort 1972: 194), better communications and banking services, insurance, better fire-fighting—all these factors undoubtedly contributed to a greater sense of security. While it is true that the human impulse to seek scapegoats remains with us in the twentieth century, we have, in the main, abandoned the idea of personal malice as a cause for misfortune. In contemporary small-scale societies this personal view of misfortune persists, as numerous anthropological studies show.

It is quite clear to anyone who has worked in countries where there is still a general belief in witchcraft that education alone, even at university level, does not destroy the belief. It is quite easy to graft a theory of witchcraft onto a scientific theory of causation such as the germ theory (Offiong 1985: 107–24), and thus to assume that even a microorganism can attack one person rather than another because some person used evil magic. Moreover, most rational scientific observers would admit that psychological factors are important in reducing immunity. The reality of psychosomatic afflictions, however, is rather different from imputing each misfortune to the malevolence of one's kin or neighbors. If we look at the history of Europe it is only too evident that education per se was not the major reason for the waning of the craze; indeed, as Joseph Klaits notes, "the educated were in the forefront of the witch hunts" (Klaits 1985: 1–2). The rebirth of ideas after the medieval period should, one would think, have signalled the end of belief, yet Trevor-Roper observes, "There can be no doubt that the witch-craze grew, and grew terribly, after the Renaissance" (Trevor-Roper 1969: 91).

The skeptics who had the courage to challenge the prevailing orthodoxy about witches did not dispute the existence of witchcraft. Not to believe in witches was often seen as tantamount to being an atheist, as Sir Thomas Browne pointed out (Browne 1964: 29). What Weyer and Scot in the sixteenth century objected to was the injustice of accusing the wrong people. Bekker in the seventeenth century based his challenge on a fundamentalist piece of theology: if the devil on his fall from heaven was locked up in hell, how then could he be involved with witches here on earth (Trevor-Roper 1969: 174).

Precisely what caused the change from the relatively benign attitude toward witches in the Middle Ages to the hysterical attitude characteristic of the *Malleus Maleficarum* (Midelfort 1972: 193–94) is the subject of an ongoing debate. Cross-cultural study may contribute to our understanding of what caused the end of the witchcraze. One reason may be the only conceivable aspect that our social organization shares with that of the African hunter-gatherers: our mobility.

Humanity is by its nature a mass of contradictions. Impulses for conformity war with those for individualism. Tension develops and somehow has to be resolved. Where it is possible physically to remove oneself from those with whom one is in conflict, the tension disappears. Where this is not possible and where it is socially unacceptable to admit to tension arising from feelings of hate toward close kin, spouses, affines or neighbors, the human imagination seems to build up a whole edifice of fantasy about witches based on childish fears and imaginings. This holds especially true for societies where childrearing practices are harsh. While the details of beliefs may vary according to cultural prescription, the broad outlines are remarkably similar worldwide. They retain their fascination even in our skeptical, secular world, as Bruno Bettelheim has reminded us (Bettelheim 1977).

It is Thomas's contention that the surge in witchcraft accusations in the late sixteenth and early seventeenth centuries was not generated by any fundamental change in folk beliefs, but by a change in the structure of society. He speaks of the "increasingly individualistic forms of behavior which accompanied the economic changes" (Thomas 1971: 561). Cross-culturally one might draw a parallel with present-day Africa, where scholars have universally reported the widespread belief that the practice of evil magic has proliferated (Middleton and Winter 1963: 25). In Europe the change was from a feudal society with its well-understood certitudes about class and status; in Africa from a tribal form of social organization in which status was largely ascribed to the emerging societies, in which status can be achieved through education, wage employment, cash-cropping, entrepreneurial, political and religious activities; class divisions have begun to appear and become institutionalized (Gluckman 1965).

During the sixteenth and seventeenth centuries there was enormous social, political, economic, and religious ferment in Europe. This led initially to feelings of deep insecurity in all these arenas of human activity, exacerbated by the Copernican revolution; it also led to unrivaled opportunities for the acquisition of wealth, power, and social status. All this activity generated great divisions in society, as well as powerful emotions such as envy, jealousy, hostility, self-questioning, and guilt. This is entirely consistent with the large number of witchcraft accusations in the Tudor and early Stuart periods. A similar phenomenon—though not on quite so lethal a scale—is taking place in Africa today. . . .

34

Sorcery and Concepts of Deviance Among the Kabana, West New Britain

Naomi M. McPherson

*Most beginning students of comparative religion picture sorcerers as practitioners of evil with few, if any, positive functions in their societies. Contrary to this general view, Naomi McPherson's data demonstrate that, depending on the circumstances that initiate the attack, sorcery may or may not be considered by the Kabana as a criminal act. She writes (*Anthropologica, *vol. 33, no. 1–2, 1991, p. 127):*

> *For the Kabana of New Britain, deviant behavior is essentially the advancement of self-interest untempered by self-regulation such that the individual infringes on the ability of others to pursue their own self-interest. Social labeling is applied to deviant behaviors, but no permanent stigma attaches to individuals. Reactions to deviance include shame, gossip and ridicule, proceedings before the village magistrate, and sorcery. The performance of sorcery, a major cause of death, is a complex and ambiguous event, insofar as a sorcerer's threat may both inhibit deviance and mediate conflict, but the actual enactment of the threat is itself a deviant act. In cases where a victim's illness is attributed to sorcery, a moot may be held to discern the motives of sorcery and identify the sorcerer. In a particular case, which is examined at length here, failure clearly to identify the sorcerer was followed by the victim's death.*

Deaths resulting from sorcery are always classified as "bad deaths" by the Kabana.

In the study of what we now recognize as "deviance" in Pacific societies, the work of Malinowski is central. Vincent considers his treatment of sorcery, in particular, to be "pathbreaking." In the Trobriands, sorcery was *both* a criminal practice and a method of administering justice. Which it was in any particular case depended on who was practising it on whom and when he was doing it. On the one hand, sorcery was

> the main criminal agency (Malinowski 1926: 85); on the other, the Trobriand chief used sorcery to punish offenders. . . . Thus he concluded that where there was no *formal* code or administration of justice, it was very difficult to draw a line between the "quasi-legal" and the "quasi-criminal." (Vincent 1990: 165–66)

The line was usually drawn in some public arena.

"Sorcery and Concepts of Deviance Among the Kabana, West New Britain" reprinted with permission from ANTHROPOLOGICA, Vol. 33, No. 1–2, 1991, pp. 127–43.

In this early view, sorcery may be either deviance per se, or it may be the *control* of deviance. This treatment is compatible with the labelling theory of deviance that has developed since Malinowski wrote, especially in its focus on reactions to deviance rather than deviance itself. Indeed, the earliest statement of labelling theory by Becker (1963: 10–11) included a lengthy citation of one of Malinowski's cases from *Crime and Custom in Savage Society* (Malinowski 1967). Becker used this quote to differentiate between the relatively common commission of an act and the rare adjudication of the same act as *deviant by virtue of the reaction to it.*

In this paper, a similar analysis is applied to the Kabana of West New Britain, Papua New Guinea. Labelling theory is used to call attention to the multiple levels of political negotiation that go into a decision about whether an act of sorcery is—or is not—deviant. In the process, the analysis leads us to an examination of the organizational complexity of labelling. In order to provide context for the analysis, I begin with a discussion of Kabana morality and then move to a discussion of lower, "pre-sorcery" levels of social control among the Kabana, and, finally, I examine Kabana notions of sorcery as a social sanction. With this background established, the paper then moves to an extended analysis of a particular case of alleged sorcery and the political negotiation that took place, when villagers tried to decide whether the sorcery was deviance or had been used as a means to *control* deviance. The case is a provocative and rich one, because the outcome of the negotiation was indeterminate. The line between sorcery as deviance and sorcery as control of deviance could not be drawn, and the case entered Kabana history as backdrop for some dispute that would arise later.

Kabana Morality

Among the Kabana of West New Britain, Papua New Guinea, the framework of ideal social values and morals is grounded in concepts of human nature and the obligations inherent in the structure of human relations. It is this ethic of morality which provides a guide for individual action, and against which actions are judged. In this non-literate society, where the locus of individual experience is social, relations among individuals and groups do not exist in the abstract but always and only in connection with some-

one or something else. Given the extensive and overlapping network of Kabana social relations, there is an equally extensive range of behaviour that can be perceived as deviant to some degree and can elicit varying degrees of response from a particular audience. What constitutes deviant behaviour thus depends on whether relevant others perceive a certain act as a threat to the basic tenets of Kabana social life, that is, to the moral obligations which structure human relations.

Offended persons may select from a hierarchy of responses of increasing complexity to restore and restructure their interpersonal relations. Ultimately, social conformity derives from a fundamental principle of reciprocal self-interest which is based upon two related concepts: self-regulation and self-help. Self-regulation entails that all individuals are deemed to be in control of their own existence and, therefore, are accountable to, and responsible for, others. Self-help is the principle whereby individuals who perceive their rights to have been infringed upon may rightfully take retaliatory action against those who have infringed upon them (cf. Lawrence 1984: 161). The interrelated concepts of self-help and self-regulation are, in turn, based on the Kabana belief in personal autonomy, that is, that all individuals have the freedom to empower their existence as a basic human right. For the Kabana, deviant behaviour is essentially the advancement of self-interest untempered by self-regulation such that the individual infringes on the ability of others to pursue their own self-interest.

The Kabana label behaviour but not individuals as deviant, and the imposition of negative sanctions in no way implies an intent to permanently discriminate against or stigmatize an offender. The aim of any sanction is to provide the culprit with the opportunity for expiation thereby limiting the consequences of the transgression to that single event. There is no intentional discrimination against, and no stigma applied to, offenders, for to stigmatize persons is to set aside and mark them permanently as incorrigibly different, thus denying them the opportunity to redress the imbalance in social relations caused by their offenses. By not allowing a person to rectify wrongful behaviour, others arbitrarily rescind that individual's personal autonomy, integrity and right to self-help, thus effectively reducing the individual to a non-social (and, therefore, non-human) being. To label an individual permanently as deviant is to place him or her outside the pale of human relations as a social pariah. Ultimately, such action is tantamount to a death sentence, because in societies of this nature, no one can exist outside the context of social relations. The only options left to the stigmatized individual would be exile or suicide (cf. Counts and Counts 1984; Lawrence 1984: 132).

Most reactions to deviance occur at the level of personal relations, though they may involve whole families. On occasion, however, reactions to deviance can be escalated to levels that involve multiple families within villages, and may even include whole villages. Sorcery events also involve their own levels of organization and styles of political negotiation.

After briefly delineating the range of responses to lower levels of deviance, I focus on a traditional village "court" proceeding which was convened in reaction to a particular sorcery event. Sorcery is the most pervasive and powerful regulatory device that the Kabana have for dealing with deviant behaviour. The practice of sorcery is not unambiguously right or wrong. As a negative sanction, sorcery is a legitimate form of social control, both an expected and accepted consequence of a breach of morality. Since sorcery is always potentially lethal, however, any act of sorcery, regardless of the circumstances, can be construed as a deviant act and thus be subject to negative social sanctions itself. The case history presented here demonstrates how the community reacted to the ambiguous nature of sorcery, when they attempted to determine whether or not one woman's imminent death by sorcery was a legitimate form of social control or a case of homicide, which, in turn, would require control.

Lower Levels of Social Control

All Kabana relationships are face-to-face relations and everyone is known to, and knows about, everyone else. Anonymity is impossible and no behaviour, albeit good, bad or indifferent, goes undiscovered. For the most part, a perceived breach of the ideal of reciprocal self-interest is couched in terms of positive criticism. Someone who ignores the rules of reciprocity is advised or reminded of the potentially negative consequences that could be experienced as a result of the impropriety. For example, a youth who avoids assisting his kin in cutting and hauling trees to make a garden fence may be criticized for his laziness and warned that when he needs the aid of these same kin in some venture of his own, such as the amassing of his bride-wealth, help may not be forthcoming. Continued failure to observe proper behaviour reduces a person's chances for success in other desired achievements, and, since it is in their own best interests to do so, most people adjust their behaviour in response to the pressure exerted on them to conform.

The Kabana do not equate simple non-conformity with deviance. Idiosyncratic personality types are marked, for example, by teasing or nicknaming. They may become the butt of jokes, be lampooned, criticized or otherwise disparaged, but there is no stigma imposed on them. When a person is recognized as having social or physical disabilities, others compensate for the idiosyncratic personality by lowering their expectations. Acknowledging individual differences defines the attributes of individuals who comprise a relationship, but the relationship itself remains unaffected, operating according to the level of expectations of all involved. Within the framework of lowered expectations, the idiosyncratic personality is recognized but not stigmatized in the sense of being negatively stereotyped or marginalized.

Shaming, gossip and ridicule are extremely effective means of sanctioning deviant behaviour. The power of shame as an overt negative sanction derives from the discomfort of "an intrusion of one's private self into public awareness and the reciprocal invasion of the self by public scrutiny" (Jorgensen 1983–84: 123). Shaming and gossip expose the inadequacies of the individual and exert pressure on the target to behave according to commonly held values and to repair the imbalance in social relations. The balance between public and private, self and other, is restored through a process of negotiations and settled when the culprit presents a gift of wealth to those who have gossiped about or shamed the victim. The gift of wealth both relieves the culprit of the sense of shame and obliges the recipients to curtail their slander or risk censure themselves for perpetuating a situation that has been resolved satisfactorily.

At a higher level of response, theft, physical violence and adultery often result in the perpetrator being brought before the village magistrate by the injured party. More often than not, in communities of this type, "the culprit is condemned on the basis of ideal social values even by those who have been guilty of the same offense in the past" (Lawrence 1984: 132). Again, since the Kabana label only behaviour, not individuals, as deviant, any sanction imposed by the public court allows the culprit the opportunity for expiation and limits the consequences of the transgression to a single event. Once reparation is made, usually in the form of a compensation payment, the incident is forgiven, although rarely forgotten, and the culprit resumes his or her usual place in the community. There is no intentional discrimination against, and no permanent stigma applied to, the offender.

For the Kabana, observation of the moral obligations that structure and organize normal relations can be, ultimately, a life-and-death matter. Persons who survive to an extreme old age are by definition those persons who have lived a morally correct life. Death from old age is a good death (cf. Counts and Counts 1976–77), a death which is the result of, and performs closure on, a socially correct and moral life span. The Kabana observe, however, that human nature being what it is, very few people survive to the culturally defined life span that culminates in a good death. With few exceptions, most people die a bad death as victims of sorcery (see Scaletta 1985).

Sorcery as Social Sanction and as Deviance

Sorcery can be defined as a form of esoteric knowledge bestowing personal power which the adept can use willfully to realize desired ends. While not everyone could or would acquire the knowledge and skill to become a sorcerer, all have access to sorcery as a mode of self-help by purchasing the services of a known sorcerer. Awareness of the fact that others can choose to exercise their right to self-help through sorcery serves to define sorcery as the primary deterrent to deviant behaviour. Victims of sorcery are assumed to be persons who have violated social mores and values thereby infringing on the rights of others. Because sorcery is notoriously difficult to control once unleashed, both the decision to sorcerize and the execution of that decision should result from corporate deliberation and follow certain other procedural rules. The injured party should discuss any intention to instigate redressive action in the form of sorcery with his or her kin. If one's kin are not in

agreement with such measures, the whole matter is dropped or deferred. If there is sufficient agreement to warrant action, however, usually because others have complaints against the intended victim or because the offence is such that sorcery is the only appropriate form of punishment, then the services of a sorcerer are solicited. Sorcery is a male prerogative acquired through apprenticeship and arranged in the *lum*, "men's house." Once the sorcerer has been approached and all the details have been worked out, the sorcerer and his clients exchange equal lengths of the most highly valued category of shell-money, *bula misi*. This exchange of wealth "buys" both the sorcerer's services and the silence and complicity of those employing him. Since the men's house is a semi-public domain, there is no question that the business of soliciting a sorcerer has been witnessed by other men in or near the building, and the whole episode becomes a topic for discreet gossip, a public secret, and moves into a wider area of involvement.

The sorcerer's role may also be construed as that of a mediator hired to resolve a conflict between two parties. Acting on behalf of his client, the sorcerer leaves a "calling card" (Zelenietz 1981: 105) which alerts the recipient that some action on his or her part has offended another party, thus jeopardizing their relationship. The calling cards of Kabana sorcerers can take a number of forms: a large basket, of the type only sorcerers carry, lodged in the rafters of the victim's house; a gutted frog pinioned on the footpath the victim travels to the gardens; a bundle of croton leaves tied in a particular way and placed conspicuously where the victim will find it, and so on.

Kabana sorcerers also send calling cards in the form of ensorcelled stones that they throw onto or into the victim's house. The stone called *pamododonga* carries a form of sorcery that causes the victim to become ill for an indefinite period or time. It is generally assumed that, during the illness, victims will examine their consciences, review their actions and deduce for themselves the nature of their transgressions. They can then take steps to rectify the situation by approaching those with whom they are in conflict and trying to negotiate a resolution to the difficulty. If a resolution is reached, they pay the sorcerer to rescind his spell. If they are unable to identify the locus of conflict, the sorcerer might approach them, inform them why they have been ill, remove the spell and restore health. It is more common, however, because sorcery is a non-confrontational social act, for spells to be removed as stealthily as they were applied. Then, a second stone, *angual*, is thrown on the victim's house. Sorcery of this type puts transgressors on notice that they should discover the source of the conflict and repair the rift in their relationships, before they develop into open confrontation.

Although sorcery is an expected negative sanction for breach of expected behaviour, the actual implementation of sorcery as a form of self-help is, in itself, a deviant act. Evidence of sorcery indicates that someone has succeeded in a private act of collusion. When sorcery is suspected, "the contradiction between autonomy and control is flagrantly exposed and every villager is witness to his or her own vulnerability" (Weiner 1976: 223). Sorcery takes away from the victim all that the Kabana define as human rights: the right to self-help, personal autonomy and control over one's existence. To be a victim of sorcery is to be threatened with death, for one's "personal autonomy has collapsed" (Weiner 1976: 219). It is for this reason that death by sorcery is a bad death. It is a bad death not just because of the manner in which it occurred, but also because of the manner in which it was incurred. Death by sorcery entails a negative judgment upon the behaviour of the victim by relevant others, but does not allow the culprit to amend the situation in his or her own best interests. Personal autonomy is negated and the target becomes a victim of the power that others wield in pursuit of their own self-interest. Death by sorcery is a moral issue, and those who practise it are themselves subject to public disapprobation: "Individual power, the cause of all death, demands the display of group power" (Weiner 1976: 226).

A Case of Sorcery

Jean had been seriously ill for three months. During this time, attempts to cure her had proved fruitless. Treatments at the local hospital and by local healers, and the attempts of a sorcerer-curer to heal her by extracting foreign substances from her body were all ineffective. From the beginning of her illness, Jean was convinced that she had been sorcerized, a conviction reinforced when all attempts to cure her

failed. Only the sorcerer who inflicts the spell has the correct formula for rescinding it and restoring the victim to health. As her illness progressed, Jean became more and more incapacitated. She became a non-participant in the myriad conceptual and social minutiae that make life worth living. As an invalid, her social interactions were essentially passive. She was dependent on others to care for her, and she resented being powerless, the victim of someone's ill-will. There was no question in anyone's mind, least of all Jean's, that she was dying. Her family refused, however, to open the magic bundle containing her vital essence, *tautau*, and kept it in contact with her body to prevent her death. The final indignity, from Jean's perspective, was that she was denied the right to take control of the situation and end her own life. (See Scaletta 1985 for a detailed discussion of these events.)

Given that illness or death caused by sorcery are the result of specifically inflicted punishment for a breach of socially expected behaviour on the part of the victim (or her family), Jean's condition created a climate of heightened awareness of a variety of social relations. Relations between Jean and other individuals, between her family and other family groups, between her hamlet and the other three hamlets in the village, and between her village as a unit and other villages, particularly the two villages where the majority of her cognatic kin lived, were all minutely scrutinized. There was constant re-evaluation and discussion of past events, interpersonal and intergroup interactions, in order to determine why, and by whom, she was sorcerized. Jean's personal crisis as an individual escalated to the level of an intervillage social crisis.

Jean added to the escalating tensions by making specific charges of sorcery against three men in the village. She accused Ken, her deceased husband's brother. His motive, she said, was revenge: Ken and his kin group were avenging the death of their brother by attacking his wife. The second man she accused was Lari. She had no specific reason for accusing him, except that he had renown as a powerful sorcerer, and was, at the time, under suspicion by everybody in the area as the individual responsible for the current drought. She argued that if Lari would create hardship in the whole area in his efforts to destroy a rival, then it was reasonable that he should attack her for no motive other than that it was in the nature of his disposition to do so. The third man she accused was Tomi, her sister's husband. Tomi was obsessively jealous of his wife and resented the time she spent in Jean's company. By eliminating her, Jean reasoned, Tomi was eliminating a major competitor for his wife's affection.

In all these accusations, Jean portrayed herself as an innocent victim. At no time did she name anyone who may have had reason to resort to sorcery in retaliation for some misdeed on her part. In proclaiming her innocence, she was implying that sorcery was being practised arbitrarily and, therefore, that everyone was vulnerable unless it could be stopped. Jean's steady decline, the general unease generated by the active presence of sorcery in their midst, the increasing strain between her cognatic and affinal kin and the intervillage tensions arising from Jean's accusations coalesced one morning with the arrival of a delegation of Jean's male kin from her natal village. They came both to express their anger that someone was "killing" their sister and to demand that a meeting be convened to "break the talk," to expose and punish the sorcerer.

Breaking the Talk

To "break the talk" means to cut through the multitude of conjecture and gossip about why a person has been sorcerized and by whom. When the "talk is broken," it is exposed to public scrutiny so that its veracity can be analyzed and a logical sequence of events leading up to the illness or death can be reconstructed. When the nature of the victim's offence has been determined, thereby identifying those who had reason to sorcerize her, witnesses can either refute or confirm the charges of culpability. The meeting to "break the talk" also provides a forum where persons who are associated with the illness or death, because of past disputes with the victim, can proclaim their innocence and clear their names, thereby avoiding the possibility that they might be sorcerized by the victim's avenging kin group. Ideally, this procedure culminates in a solid case of circumstantial evidence identifying the protagonists in the conflict, and leaves no doubt as to who caused the victim to become ill or to die. Any doubt as to the identity of the sorcerer is dispelled when those who witnessed the meeting between the sorcerer and the persons who employed him produce the length of

shell-money they were given to "buy" their silence. Ultimately, the "talk is broken" when the silence surrounding the act of collusion is broken, thus publicly exposing those who participated in the decision to sorcerize.

A meeting to "break the talk" is a highly charged public confrontation and represents the most complex level of the adjudication of deviance in Kabana culture. At such meetings in the past, it is said, the end came with a fight and the killing of the exposed sorcerer. The sorcerer's death was considered compensation for the death of the victim, and obviated (in theory, if not always in practice) the need for retributive sorcery by balancing the losses on both sides of the conflict. The death of the sorcerer was a public statement to those who sought control over others that homicidal sorcery was an amoral act so heinous that death was the only appropriate social response.

On the day of the meeting, all the adult males from the four concerned villages convened in the plaza in front of the "men's house." There were no women (except myself) or children visibly present. It was dangerous for them to be there. The meeting lasted for five hours, during which the discussion ranged widely. Several young men professed their lack of knowledge of sorcery, and called on their senior male relatives to attest to the fact that they had not instructed them in the ways and means of sorcery. Another man acknowledged that he had disputed with Jean and her sister over the ownership of certain sago palms, but said they had settled the problem, and that the altercation could not, therefore, be construed as a motive for sorcery on his part. Much of the meeting proceeded in this manner, the underlying premise being that unchallenged, public denials of guilt or involvement are sufficient to prove innocence. The most important contributions came from the three men specifically accused by Jean, and from Jean's brother.

The three accused took the opportunity to refute Jean's charges against them. Tomi, Jean's sister's husband, stated that he did not and could not know sorcery because he was associated with women (a consequence of his jealous obsession with his wife). This was common knowledge, he went on, for did not everyone refer to him as "first woman"? Sorcery is the business of men, and a man who spends his time with women would not have occasion to learn the art. Even if he did, his powers would be diminished by his contact with females, who are "different" (Tok Pisin: *narapela kain*) from men. It was true, he admitted, that he had tried to purchase rain magic (a form of sorcery) from an old man in another village, but he had been refused. Tomi had given valid reasons why he could not know sorcery, and why, even if he did have some skill as a sorcerer, this skill would be minimal. He had admitted to being in the company of a sorcerer, given reasons for being there and revealed the outcome of the meeting, thus forestalling any misconstruction of his behaviour by others who might have witnessed the meeting. No one challenged what he had to say.

Ken, Jean's husband's brother, also denied her accusations against him. He pointed out that when she first became ill, she had come to him on her own initiative and asked him to use his skills to cure her. He had assumed she was suffering from the effects of "bad blood," a problem peculiar to post-menopausal women. He had prepared the appropriate cure, which proved ineffective. Because of this and her worsening condition, she became fearful and accused him of sorcerizing rather than curing her. He also noted that she, and perhaps other members of her family, thought he might have attacked her in revenge for the death of his brother, Jean's husband. He denied the credibility of such speculations on the grounds that he was a member of the Catholic Church which forbade the practice of sorcery. He further denied the fact of sorcery, saying that sickness and death were not caused by human actors, but by God, as divine punishment for sins committed. Jean was dying, he concluded, because God was punishing her as a sinner.

The third man accused by Jean was Lari. As the person considered responsible for the drought and a self-acknowledged sorcerer, Lari defended himself on both counts. He argued that no one could claim they had actually seen him practising weather magic. Even though he had all the paraphernalia, which he then produced for all to see, without eyewitnesses, all the talk about him was nothing but air, insubstantial and without truth value. Did people think, he demanded, that he or a member of his family would be so "insane" (Kabana: *mangamanga*) as to attack this woman and run the risk of retaliation from her kin? They must look to the woman herself, he admonished, for the origin of her problem. From the time of their ancestors, he continued, there were

two reasons why females were attacked by sorcery. They were sorcerized for being foul-tempered, malicious gossips, and for repulsing the sexual advances of males, or conversely, for engaging in illicit love affairs. (The seeming paradox of this situation is more apparent than real, but a detailed discussion is beyond the scope of the task at hand.)

Lari's point here was to prompt people to examine Jean's behaviour rather than continuing to look for wrongdoing on the part of others. He was, in effect, both denying the validity of the scenario that Jean had created in which she played the role of innocent victim, and situating the whole episode within the accepted explanatory framework—people are sorcerized for breach of social norms. It then came out that during the weeks of Jean's illness, there had been a great deal of discussion about her reputation for maligning others, particularly two senior women who were highly respected. There was also talk of her affair with a married man who was also a person of some renown. It was further reported that she had accepted a proposal of marriage, and the shell money that accompanied it, from a man in the Kove district. She had later reneged on her promise to marry him, claiming that she wanted to remain a widow and live near her children, but had failed to return the shell money. The rejected man thus had motive—the loss of his shell money, not the broken promise—and the wherewithal to attack her, the Kove being notorious sorcerers. All agreed that any one of the foregoing was a likely origin of her illness and, if so, that (1) she had gotten only what she deserved, and (2) that, if the sorcery originated with the Kove man, her chances of recovery were slim because no one knew either the Kove techniques, or, consequently, the specific counter spell to effect a cure.

Discussion turned to the possibility that Jean was part of a long-standing vendetta to eliminate all the members of her family. In the past five years, sorcery had claimed the lives of Jean's father, her 20-year-old son, a classificatory son and her eldest son's wife. Everyone knew that her father had died of *mosi* "privately owned designs." Without permission or payment, he had used the traditional totemic designs of another kin group on a set of spirit masks of his own group. Death by sorcery was the expected and accepted response to such a serious crime; hence, there had been no "talk" or retaliation, and the incident was closed. Perhaps, however, the issue was not closed, and Jean was the most recent casualty of the offended group's unrequited anger for her father's transgression against them.

These observations focussed attention on indigenous ancestral laws, and Lari began a forceful harangue about the loss of traditional customs. In the past, he began, this meeting would have taken place inside the men's house, not in the open plaza. Now the men's house stood abandoned, and young men no longer gathered there to learn from their elders. Now men slept, not in the men's house, but with their wives and children in the women's houses. Even the practice of sorcery was no longer done according to tradition. In the time of their grandfathers, sorcery was always undertaken by two or three men with the sanction of their kin group. With these several people involved, it was possible to "break the talk," discover who worked the sorcery and why, and thus permit resolution of the situation. This was no longer possible because sorcery was being practised on an individual basis, making it impossible to expose and control the practice of sorcery.

Jean's elder brother Karl, located at the outer perimeter of the assembly, had stood quietly throughout the foregoing, awaiting his opportunity to speak. When he had everyone's attention, he began by reprimanding people for listening to Jean's accusations. The ravings of a sick person should not be given credibility. Such talk is *mangamanga*, "hysterical," and based on fear. He went on to point out that those who brought up his father's death by sorcery were wrong to revive this incident, for it implied that he, or a member of his family, had avenged their father's death and that Jean's illness was retaliation for that second death. When their father died, he and his brothers had "put on the grass skirt" worn by women. Metaphorically, he was arguing that they had become like women, and thus did not know or engage in sorcery. The death of their father had nothing to do with his sister's dying, and such talk must cease, he emphasized, so that old animosities were not revived. He reiterated that they must look to Jean's own behaviour as the cause of her dying, and, having nicely set the mood, he went on to elaborate what, in his opinion, that behaviour might have been.

Some years before, Jean and her husband had contracted a marriage between one of their sons and the daughter of Rio and Sandra, a couple who have considerable prestige in the area. During a ceremonial feast at another village, Jean's son had an affair with another woman. The young people were discovered, and, when confronted with the options of either paying fines to "buy their shame," or with getting married, the two said they wished to be married. With this public declaration of intent, they were married *de facto*, and the betrothal previously arranged by the young man's parents was nullified.

When the jilted girl's parents heard this, they were furious and confronted Jean and her husband. While venting her anger, the girl's mother assumed the stylistic stance associated with throwing spears during battle, and called down the name of her personal protective spirit upon Jean's head, an effective and sometimes deadly curse. She berated Jean for breaking the marriage contract, thereby shaming both her and her daughter. Jean claimed she had nothing to do with the situation, and had heard of her son's behaviour and marriage only after the fact.

Two days after this confrontation, Jean sat on some wood shavings on her verandah, and, several days later, her legs became swollen. It was assumed that Jean had been sorcerized by the offended parents through the medium of wood shavings. She was treated by a curer familiar with that type of sorcery, and the condition was removed. It now appeared that the sorcery had not been neutralized, but had lain dormant in her body these past years, and was only now manifesting itself as her current illness.

Karl's speech was extremely effective. He had discredited Jean's accusations against others as the ravings of a sick and frightened person, thus soothing the anxieties of the accused; he had denied that her illness was a continuation of the conflict that resulted in their father's death, thus avoiding the possibility of old animosities resurfacing, and he had described a specific breach of moral obligation—the breaking of a marriage contract. At the same time, he had left it an open question whether or not Jean was responsible for the breach. (Everybody knew that nowadays children made up their own minds about whom they would or would not marry.) His suggestion that specific, known events and individuals might be responsible for Jean's illness helped defuse the tensions that had built up around people's fears that sorcery was being practised arbitrarily. The individuals implicated had been away from the village for the past year, living in urban centres, and so were not on hand to give their interpretation or to defend themselves. No one else present hurried to defend them either, possibly because one of them was already considered responsible for other recent, and unresolved, sorcery related incidents. At the conclusion of his speech, the meeting was brought to a close. Karl had provided an acceptable explanatory framework for Jean's condition, thus redressing the "threat of disorderliness" that a motiveless death implies (Zelenietz 1981: 9). The consensus was, however, that the meeting had not been totally satisfactory. They had been unable to "break the talk" and prove conclusively the validity of the reconstruction. No one had come forth to bear witness against the sorcerer whose behaviour threatened Jean's life and the moral infrastructure of social order. Because the situation was not totally resolved, there was little hope that Jean could be cured.

Three weeks later, Jean died. When the funeral rites and period of mourning were finished, life in the village reverted to the status quo ante; the crisis created by Jean's dying and death might never have occurred. When I inquired of my informants what steps, if any, would be taken to avenge her death or punish the sorcerer, I was advised that we ought not to discuss such matters. Others might hear of our talk, assume we are plotting vengeance and take steps to protect themselves by striking first; we could be sorcerized. Circumstances surrounding her death are not forgotten. The entire experience will be woven into the fabric of ongoing personal and social relations where it will affect people's motives and behaviour in the future.

Conclusion

This analysis of sorcery and deviant behaviour in Kabana society shows that the generic processes noted in labelling theory can be applied to the cross-cultural study of deviance, even in a society in which deviants are not specifically "labelled." Certain kinds of behaviour, under certain conditions, are reacted to as deviant in Kabana society, and there are rules about what constitutes a socially acceptable response to deviant behaviour. The Kabana data show that, regardless of the level of community involvement, the reaction to deviant behaviour does not result in the typing of individuals as permanently

deviant, or in the differentiation of people into groups defined as "normals" and "deviants." Given the egalitarian ideology and lack of stratification in Kabana society, the creation of a class of deviants is unlikely, and, in Kabana terms, philosophically untenable. Rather, deviance is a highly negotiated, highly complex phenomenon which occurs in an interpersonal network. Sorcery is an interesting case in point. While it is inherently neither deviant nor a normative sanction for the social control of deviance, it may be negotiated as *either* according to the specifics of any particular case. It may begin with individual relations and end there; it may rise to the familial level and end there or escalate to even more complex levels before it is publicly mooted. In the moot, sorcery may be judged to be a device for the legitimate control of deviance, deviance in and of itself, or the problem of what it is may prove to be insoluble. *Whatever* the outcome, the case remains in the cultural memory of the groups involved and forms part of relevant knowledge that will be brought to bear in subsequent cases of sorcery or other trouble.

Afterword

The events described above took place in early 1983. When I returned to the village in 1985, one of the first pieces of news that I was given was that Ken, Jean's husband's brother, had been ill for some months and was currently at the local health clinic for medical treatment. The public explanation for his illness was that he "had no blood" (acute anaemia, possibly leukaemia?); the *very* private explanation was that he had been sorcerized. In response to my queries about who had sorcerized him and why, people referred to the case of Jean and her accusations against her brother-in-law. I was also advised not to pursue this matter with "certain other people," lest those people infer that my inquiries were informed by the (malicious) speculation of the people who spent time with me, thus placing them at risk. It was clear that Ken's lingering illness was linked to Jean's death by sorcery, but people preferred not to make this connection a matter of public record or public moot. The feeling was that, if ignored, the attacks and counterattacks of sorcery would cease, and order and well-being would prevail. I respected these views and did not pursue the matter further. Ken died in 1986 after a prolonged and painful dying process.

35

The Goat and the Gazelle: Witchcraft

T. M. Luhrmann

The following material is an excerpt from the author's book-length study of contemporary witches in England, based on fieldwork in London beginning in 1983. Luhrmann traces the modern revival of witchcraft to the influential writings of Gerald Gardner in the 1940s. However, from the point of view of present-day participants, nature-centered, or earth-centered, witchcraft is the most ancient of all religions, honoring goddess figures as personifications of nature. Its rituals relate to seasons and the natural world and are based on participants' reconstructions of pagan, or pre-Christian, religious practices. The author describes typical contemporary witches and their motivations for involvement, as well as their covens, including the one into which Luhrmann herself was initiated. She describes witches' rituals as typically involving chanting; the reading of texts; the use of magical circles, altars, and candles; and the symbolic offering of fruits.

Luhrmann's ethnography raises questions central to the anthropological consideration of magic, be it in England, Africa, or elsewhere (Luhrmann 1989: 7–8): Why do people find magic persuasive? How is it that some people, more than others, come to accept or "believe in" what is irrational and unacceptable to others? The witches documented by Luhrmann are ordinary people, well educated and usually middle-class, not mentally ill or in economic desperation (ibid.). The author documents the process by which emotional patterns and intellectual strategies change as participants come to accept the reality of magic. Such processes are at work, Luhrmann argues, in any circumstances in which specialized knowledge is acquired. What she discovers about contemporary witches holds intriguing parallels for us all, as we acquire the knowledge necessary to carry out our jobs or other roles in adult life.

Full moon, November 1984. In a witches' coven in northeast London, members have gathered from as far away as Bath, Leicester and Scotland to attend the meeting at the full moon. We drink tea until nine—in London, most rituals follow tea—and then change and go into the other room. The sitting room has been transformed. The furniture has been removed, and a twelve foot chalk circle drawn on the carpet. It will be brushed out in the morning. Four candlesticks stake out the corners of the room, casting shadows from the stag's antlers on the wall. The antlers sit next to a sheaf of wheat, subtle sexual symbolism. In spring and summer there are flowers everywhere. The altar in the centre of the circle is a chest which seems ancient. On top an equally ancient box holds incense in different drawers. On it, flowers and herbs surround a carved wooden Pan; a Minoan goddess figure sits on the altar itself amid a litter of ritual knives and tools.

The high priestess begins by drawing the magic circle in the air above the chalk, which she does with piety, saying "let this be a boundary between the world of gods and that of men." This imaginary circle is then treated as real throughout the evening. To leave the circle you slash it in the air and redraw it when you return. The chalk circle is always drawn with the ritual knife; the cakes, wine and the dancing always move in a clockwise direction. These rules are part of what makes it a witches' circle and they are scrupulously observed. On this evening a coven member wanted us to "do" something for a friend's sick baby. Someone made a model of the baby and put it on the altar, at the Minoan goddess' feet. We held hands in a circle around the altar and then began to run, chanting a set phrase. When the circle was running at its peak the high priestess suddenly stopped. Everyone shut their eyes, raised their hands, and visualized the prearranged image: in this case it was Mary, the woman who wanted the spell, the "link" between us and the unknown child. We could have "worked" without the model baby, but it served as a "focus" for the concentration. Witches of folklore made clay and waxen effigies over which they uttered imprecations—so we made effigies and kept a packet of plasticene in the altar for the purpose. By springtime, Mary reported, the child had recovered, and she thanked us for the help.

Modern witchcraft was essentially created in the forties—at least in its current form—by a civil servant, Gerald Gardner, who was probably inspired by Margaret Murray's historical account of witchcraft as an organized pre-Christian fertility religion branded devil-worship by the demonologists, and more generally by the rise of interest in anthropology and folklore. Gardner had met Aleister Crowley, knew of the Golden Dawn, and may have been a Freemason. (Indeed his rituals show Crowleyian and Masonic influence.) In the early fifties, Gardner published fictitious ethnographies of supposedly contemporaneous witches who practised the ancient, secret rites of their agrarian ancestors and worshipped the earth goddess and her consort in ceremonies beneath the full moon. He claimed to have

been initiated into one of these groups, hidden from watchful authorities since the "burning times." In his eyes, witchcraft was an ancient magico-religious cult, secretly practised, peculiarly suited to the Celtic race. Witches had ancient knowledge and powers, handed down through the generations. And unlike the rest of an alienated society, they were happy and content. This paragraph gives the flavour of his romanticism:

> Instead of the great sabbats with perhaps a thousand or more attendents [the coven] became a small meeting in private houses, probably a dozen or so according to the size of the room. The numbers being few, they were no longer able to gain power, to rise to the hyperaesthetic state by means of hundreds of wild dancers shrieking wildly, and they had to use other secret methods to induce this state. This came easily to the descendants of the heath, but not to the people of non-Celtic race. Some knowledge and power had survived, as many of the families had intermarried, and in time their powers grew, and in out of the way places the cult survived. The fact that they were happy gave them a reason to struggle on. It is from these people that the surviving witch families probably descend. They know that their fathers and grandfathers belonged, and had spoken to them of meetings about the time of Waterloo, when it was an old cult, thought to exist from all time. Though the persecution had died down from want of fuel, they realized that their only chance to be left alone was to remain unknown and this is as true today as it was five hundred years ago.

The invention of tradition is an intriguing topic: why is it that history should grant such authority, even in so rational an age? Witches speak of a secretive tradition, hidden for centuries from the Church's fierce eye, passed down in families until the present generation. There is no reason that such claims could not be true, but there is very little evidence to support them. The most sympathetic scholarship that speaks of an organized, pre-Christian witchcraft has very shaky foundations—although there is more recently work that suggests that there were at least shared fantasies about membership in witch-related societies. But those accused of witchcraft in early modern Europe were very likely innocent of any practice.

Witches have ambivalent attitudes towards their history, as a later chapter details. They share, however, a common vision of their past, differing only on whether this past is myth or legend. Many of them say that the truth of the vision is unimportant: it is the vision itself, with its evocative pull, that matters. The basic account—given by someone who describes it as a myth—is this:

Witchcraft is a religion that dates back to paleolithic times, to the worship of the god of the hunt and the goddess of fertility. One can see remnants of it in cave paintings and in the figurines of goddesses that are many thousands of years old. This early religion was universal. The names changed from place to place but the basic deities were the same.

When Christianity came to Europe, its inroads were slow. Kings and nobles were converted first, but many folk continued to worship in both religions. Dwellers in rural areas, the 'Pagans' and 'Heathens', kept to the old ways. Churches were built on the sacred sites of the old religion. The names of the festivals were changed but the dates were kept. The old rites continued in folk festivals, and for many centuries Christian policy was one of slow cooptation.

During the times of persecution the Church took the god of the Old Religion and—as is the habit with conquerors—turned him into the Christian devil. The Old Religion was forced underground, its only records set forth, in distorted form, by its enemies. Small families kept the religion alive and in 1951, after the Witchcraft Laws in England were repealed, it began to surface again.

It is indeed an evocative tale, with secrecy and martyrdom and hidden powers, and whether or not witches describe it as actual history they are moved by its affect.

Witchcraft is meant to be a revival, or re-emergence, of an ancient nature-religion, the most ancient of religions, in which the earth was worshipped as a woman under different names and guises throughout the inhabited world. She was Astarte, Inanna, Isis, Cerridwen—names that ring echoes in archaeological texts. She was the Great Goddess whose rites Frazer and Neumann—and Apuleius—recorded in rich detail. Witches are people who read their books and try to create, for themselves, the tone and feeling of an early humanity, worshipping a nature they understand as vital, powerful and mysterious. They visit the stone circles and pre-Christian

sites, and become amateur scholars of the pagan traditions behind the Easter egg and the Yule log.

Above all, witches try to "connect" with the world around them. Witchcraft, they say, is about the tactile, intuitive understanding of the turn of the seasons, the song of the birds; it is the awareness of all things as holy, and that, as is said, there is no part of us that is not of the gods.[1] One witch suggests a simple exercise to begin to glimpse the nature of the practice:

Perhaps the best way to begin to understand the power behind the simple word *witch* is to enter the circle . . . Do it, perhaps, on a full moon, in a park or in the clearing of a wood. You don't need any of the tools you will read about in books on the Craft. You need no special clothes, or lack of them. Perhaps you might make up a chant, a string of names of gods and goddesses who were loved or familiar to you from childhood myths, a simple string of names for earth and moon and stars, easily repeatable like a mantra.

And perhaps, as you say those familiar names and feel the earth and the air, the moon appears a bit closer, and perhaps the wind rustling the leaves suddenly seems in rhythm with your own breathing. Or perhaps the chant seems louder and all the other sounds far away. Or perhaps the woods seem strangely noisy. Or unspeakably still. And perhaps the clear line that separates you from bird and tree and small lizards seems to melt. Whatever else, your relationship to the world of living nature changes. The Witch is the change of definitions and relationships.

The Goddess, the personification of nature, is witchcraft's central concept. Each witch has an individual understanding of the Goddess, which changes considerably over time. However, simply to orient the reader I will summarize the accounts which I have heard and have read in the literature. The Goddess is multi-faceted, ever-changing—nature and nature's transformations. She is Artemis, virgin huntress, the crescent moon and the morning's freshness; Selene, Aphrodite and Demeter, in the full bloom of the earth's fertility; Hecate and axe-bearing Cerridwen, the crone who destroys, the dying forests which make

---

1. This is a phrase taken from Crowley's Gnostic Mass. It sometimes appears in witchcraft rituals or in writings about the practice.

room for new growth. The constant theme of the God-dess is cyclicity and transformation: the spinning Fates, the weaving spider, Aphrodite who each year arises virgin from the sea, Isis who swells and floods and diminishes as the Nile. Every face of the Goddess is a different goddess, and yet also the same, in a different aspect, and there are different goddesses for different years and seasons of one's life.

The Goddess is very different from the Judaeo-Christian god. She is in the world, of the world, the very being of the world. "People often ask me whether I *believe* in the Goddess. I reply, 'Do you believe in rocks?'" Yet she is also an entity, a metaphor for nature to whom one can talk. "I relate to the Goddess, every day, in one way or another. I have a little chitchat with Mommy." Witches have talked to me about the "duality" of their religious understanding, that on the one hand the Goddess merely personifies the natural world in myth and imagery, and that on the other hand the Goddess is there as someone to guide you, punish you, reward you, someone who becomes the central figure in your private universe. I suspect that for practitioners there is a natural slippage from metaphor to extant being, that it is difficult—particularly in a Judaeo-Christian society—genuinely to treat a deity-figure as only a metaphor, regardless of how the religion is rationalized. The figure becomes a deity, who cares for you.

Gardner began initiating people into groups called "covens" which were run by women called "high priestesses." Covens bred other covens; people wandered into the bookstore, bought his books and then others, and created their own covens. By now there are many types of witchcraft: Gardnerian, Alexandrian, feminist, "traditional" and so forth, named for their founders or their political ideals. Feminist covens usually only initiate women and they usually think of themselves as involved with a particularly female type of spirituality. Groups stemming from Gardner are called "Gardnerian." Alexandrian witchcraft derives from Alex Sanders' more ceremonial version of Gardnerian witchcraft. Sanders was a charismatic man who deliberately attracted the attention of the gutterpress and became a public figure in the late sixties. Some of those who read the sensationalistic exposés and watched the television interviews were drawn to witchcraft, and

Sanders initiated hundreds of applicants, sometimes on the evening they applied. Traditional witches supposedly carry on the age-old traditions of their families: whether by chance or otherwise, I met none who could substantiate their claim to an inherited ritual practice.

Covens vary widely in their style and custom, but there is a common core of practice. They meet on (or near) days dictated by the sky: the solstices and equinoxes and the "quarter days" between them, most of them fire-festivals in the Frazerian past: Beltane (1 May), Lammas (1 August), Halloween (31 October), Candlemas (2 February). These are the days to perform seasonal rituals, in which witches celebrate the passage of the longest days and the summer's harvest. Covens also meet on the full moons—most witches are quite aware of the moon's phases—on which they perform spells, rituals with a specific intention, to cure Jane's cold or to get Richard a job. Seasonal ritual meetings are called "sabbats," the full moon meetings, "esbats."[2] Membership usually ranges between three and thirteen members, and members think of themselves—or ideally think of themselves—as "family." In my experience, it usually took about a year of casual acquaintance before someone would be initiated. The process took so long because people felt it important that a group should be socially very comfortable with each other, and—crucially—that one could trust all members of the group. As a result, covens tended to be somewhat socially homogeneous. In the more "traditional" covens, there are three "degrees." First degree initiates are novices, and in their initiation they were anointed "witch" and shown the witches' weapons. Second degree initiates usually take their new status after a year. The initiation gives them the authority to start their own coven. It consists in "meeting" death—the initiate acts the part of death if he is male; if she is female, she meets death and accepts him. The intended lesson of the ritual is that the willingness to lose the self gives one control over it, and over the transformations of life

---

2. The terms are probably drawn from Margaret Murray, although *esbat* appears in a sixteenth-century French manuscript (Le Roy Ladurie 1987: 7). *Sabbat* is a standard demonologist's term.

and death. Third degree initiation is not taken for years. It is essentially a rite of mystical sexuality, though it is sometimes "symbolic" rather than "actual." It is always performed in privacy, with only the two initiates present. Behind the initiation lies the idea that one becomes the Goddess or God in one of their most powerful manifestations, the two dynamic elements of the duality that creates the world.

Witchcraft is a secretive otherworld, and more than other magical practices it is rich in symbolic, special items. Initiates have dark-handled knives they call "athames," which are the principal tools and symbols of their powers: they have special cups and platters and incense burners, sometimes even special whips to "purify" each other before the rite begins. There is always an altar, usually strewn with herbs and incense, with a statue of the Goddess, and there are always candles at the four directions, for in all magical practice the four directions (east, south, west, north) represent the four ancient elements (air, fire, water, earth) which in turn represent different sorts of "energies" (thought; will power; emotion; material stability). Then, another symbol of the secrecy and violation of convention, most covens work in the nude. This is ostensibly a sign of freedom, but probably stems from the evocative association of witchcraft and sexuality, and a utopian vision of a paradisial past. There are no orgies, little eroticism, and in fact little behaviour that would be different if clothes were being worn. That witches dance around in the nude probably is part of the attractive fantasy that draws outsiders into the practice, but the fantasy is a piece with the paganism and not the source of salacious sexuality. Or at least, that seemed to be the case with the five covens I met.

I was initiated into the oldest of these witches' groups, a coven which has remained intact for more than forty years. It was once Gardner's own coven, the coven in which he participated, and three of the current members were initiated under his care. It pleases the anthropologist's heart that there are traces of ancestor worship: the pentacle, the magical platter which holds the communion "mooncakes," was Gardner's own, and we used his goddess statue in the circle.

The coven had thirteen members while I was there. Four of them (three men and one woman) had been initiated over twenty-five years ago and were in their fifties: an ex-Cambridge computer consultant, who flew around the world lecturing to computer professionals; a computer software analyst, high priest for the last twenty years; a teacher; an ex-Oxford university lecturer. The high priestess was initiated twenty years ago and was a professional psychologist. Another woman, in her forties, had been initiated some ten years previously. She joined the group when her own coven disbanded; another man in his fifties also came from that coven. He was an electronic engineer in the music industry. By the time I had been in the group several months, Helga and Eliot's coven had disbanded (this was the coven associated with the Glittering Sword) and Helga at any rate preferred to think of herself as a Nordic Volva rather than as a Celtic witch. So she abandoned witchcraft altogether, though she became deeply engaged in the other magical practice, and Eliot and another member of his coven, the young Austrian who was also in the Glittering Sword, joined the group. The rest of the younger generation included a woman in her thirties who was a professional artist but spent most of her time then raising a young child. Another member was a middle-level manager of a large business. He was in his late thirties and was my "psychic twin": we were both initiated into the group on the same night. Another man, thirtyish, managed a large housing estate. The computer consultant and the teacher had been married twenty-five years, the high priest and high priestess had lived together for twenty. Four other members had partners who did not belong to the group, but two of them belonged to other magical groups. Three members of the group were married to or closely related to university lecturers—but this was an unusually intellectual group.

This coven, then, had a wide age range and was primarily composed of middle-class intellectuals, many of whose lovers were not members of the group. This was not particularly standard: another coven with whom this group had contact had nine members, all of whom were within ten years of age, and it included three married couples and three single individuals. A Cambridge coven had a similarly great age span, and as wide a range of professions. But one in Clapham was entirely upper working class, and its members were within about fifteen years of age. For the meetings, the group relied upon a standard ritual text. Gardner (with the help of Doreen Valiente, now an elder stateswoman in what is called the "Craft") had created a handbook of ritual practice called the "Book of Shadows," which had supposedly been copied by each initiate through the ages. ('Beltane special objects: jug of wine, earthenware chalice, wreaths of ivy . . . High priestess in east, high priest at altar with jug of wine and earthenware chalice . . .') The group performed these rites as written, year in and year out: they were fully aware that Gardner had written them (with help) but felt that as the original coven, they had a responsibility to tradition. In fact, some of them had been re-written by the high priest, because Gardner's versions were so simple: he felt, however, that he should treat them as Gardner's, and never mentioned the authorship.

The seasonal rituals were remarkable because in them, the priestess is meant to incarnate the Goddess. This is done through a ritual commonly known as "drawing down the moon." The high priestess' ritual partner is called the "high priest," and he stands opposite her in the circle and invokes her as the Goddess; and as Goddess, she delivers what is known as the "Charge," the closest parallel to a liturgy within the Craft. Gardner's Book of Shadows has been published and annotated by two witches, and it includes this text.

The high priest: *Listen to the words of the great Mother; she who of old was called among men Artemis, Astarte, Athene, Dione, Melusine, Aphrodite, Cerridwen, Dana, Arianhod, Isis, Bride, and by many other names.*

The high priestess: *Whenever ye have need of anything, once in the month, and better it be when the moon is full, then shall ye assemble in some secret place and adore the spirit of me, who am Queen of all witches. There shall ye assemble, ye who are fain to learn all sorcery, yet who have not won its deepest secrets; to these will I teach things that are yet unknown. And ye shall be free from slavery; and as a sign that ye be really free, ye shall be naked in your rites; and ye shall dance, sing, feast make music and love, all in my praise. For mine is the ecstacy of the spirit, and mine is also joy on earth; for my law is love unto all beings. Keep pure your highest ideal; strive ever towards it; let naught stop you or turn you aside. For mine is the secret door which opens up the Land of Youth, and mine is the cup of the wine of life, and the Cauldron of Cerridwen, which is the Holy Grail of im-*

mortality. I am the gracious Goddess, who gives the gift of joy unto the heart of man. Upon earth, I give the knowledge of the spirit eternal; and beyond death, I give peace, and freedom, and reunion with those who have gone before. Nor do I demand sacrifice; for behold, I am the mother of all living, and my love is poured out upon the earth.

The high priest: *Hear ye the words of the Star Goddess; she in the dust of whose feet are the hosts of heaven, and whose body encircles the universe.*

The high priestess: *I who am the beauty of the green earth, and the white Moon among the stars, and the mystery of the waters, and the desire of the heart of man, call unto thy soul. Arise and come unto me. For I am the soul of nature, who gives life to the universe. From me all things proceed, and unto me all things must return; and before my face, beloved of Gods and men, let thine innermost divine self be enfolded in the rapture of the infinite. Let me worship be with the heart that rejoiceth; for behold all acts of love and pleasure are my rituals. And therefore let there be beauty and strength, power and compassion, honour and humility, mirth and reverence within you. And thou who thinkest to seek for me, know that seeking and yearning shall avail thee not unless thou knowest the mystery; that if that which thou seekest thou findest not within thee, thou wilt never find it without thee. For behold, I have been with thee from the beginning; and I am that which is attained at the end of desire.*

The nature-imagery, the romantic poetry, the freedom—this is the style of language commonly heard within these ritual circles. The point of this speech is that every woman can be Goddess. Every man, too, can be god. In some Gardnerian rituals—like Halloween—the high priestess invokes the stag god in her priest, and he gives similar speeches.

When the coven I joined performed spells, no ritual form was prescribed because no spell was identical to any other. The idea behind the spell was that a coven could raise energy by calling on their members' own power, and that this energy could be concentrated within the magical circle, as a "cone of power," and directed towards its source by collective imagination. The first step in a spell was always to chant or meditate in order to change the state of consciousness and so have access to one's own power, and then to focus the imagination on some real or imagined visual representation of the power's goal. The most common technique was to run in a circle, hands held, all eyes on the central altar candle, chanting what was supposedly an old Basque witches' chant:

Eko, eko, azarak
Eko, eko, zamilak
Eko, eko, Cernunnos
Eko, eko, Aradia

Then, the circle running at its peak, the group suddenly stopped, held its linked hands high, shut its eyes and concentrated on a pre-arranged image.

Sometimes we prefixed the evening with a longer chant, the "Witches' Rune:"

Darksome night and shining moon
East, then South, then West, then North;
Hearken to the Witches' Rune—
Here we come to call ye forth!
Earth and water, air and fire,
Wand and pentacle and sword,
Work ye unto our desire,
Hearken ye unto our word!
Cords and censer, scourge and knife,
Powers of the witch's blade—
Waken all ye unto life,
Come ye as the charm is made!
Queen of Heaven, Queen of Hell,
Horned hunter of the night—
Lend your power unto the spell,
And work our will by magic rite!
By all the power of land and sea,
By all the might of moon and sun—
As we do will, so mote it be;
Chant the spell, and be it done!

The tone of the poem captures much about witchcraft; the special "weapons" with special powers, the earthly power and goddess power used within the spell, the dependence of the spell upon the witches' will.

Most of the coven meetings I attended in England—in all I saw the rituals of some six Gardnerian-inspired groups—were similar in style. However, there were also feminist covens, a type of witchcraft relatively rare in England but quite important in the States. Witchcraft appeals to feminists for a number of reasons. Witches are meant to worship a female deity rather than a male patriarch, and to worship her as she was worshipped by all people before the monotheistic religions held sway: as the moon, the earth, the sheaf of wheat. Members of feminist covens talk about witchcraft and its understanding

of cyclic transformation, of birth, growth and decay, as a "woman's spirituality," and the only spirituality in which women are proud to menstruate, to make love, and to give birth. These women (and sometimes also men) are often also compelled by the desire to reclaim the word "witch," which they see as the male's fearful rejection of a woman too beautiful, too sexual, or past the years of fertility. The witches of European witch-craze fantasies were either beautiful young temptresses or hags.

Feminist covens emphasize creativity and collectivity, values commonly found in that political perspective, and their rituals are often quite different from those in Gardnerian groups. Perhaps I could offer an example, although in this example the women did not explicitly describe themselves as "witches" but as participating in "women's mysteries."

On Halloween 1983 I joined a group of some fifteen women on top of a barrow in Kent. One of the women had been delegated to draw up a rough outline of the ritual, and before we left for the barrow she held a meeting in which she announced that she had "cobbled together something from Starhawk and Z Budapest [two feminist witchcraft manual authors]." (Someone shouted, "don't put yourself down.") She explained the structure of the rite as it stood and then asked for suggestions. Someone had brought a pot of red ochre and patchouli oil which she wanted to use, and someone else suggested that we use it to purify each other. Then it was suggested that we "do" the elements first, and people volunteered for each directional quarter. The person who had chosen earth asked if the hostess had any maize flour which she could use. We talked about the purpose of the rite. The meeting was like many other feminist organization meetings: long on equality, emotional honesty and earthiness, short on speed.

When we arrived on the barrow some hours later, we walked round in a circle. Four women invoked the elements, at the different directions, with their own spontaneously chosen words. It was an impressive midnight: leafless trees stark against a dark sky, some wind, an empty countryside with a bull in the nearby field. Then one woman took the pot of red ochre and drew a circle on the cheek of the woman to her left, saying, "may this protect you on Halloween night," and the pot passed around the circle. Then the woman who had drafted the ritual read an invocation to Hecate more or less taken from Starhawk, copied out in a looseleaf binder with a pentacle laminated on the front:

> This is the night when the veil that divides the worlds is thin. It is the New Year in the time of the year's death, when the harvest is gathered and the fields lie fallow. The gates of life and death are opened; the dead walk, and to the living is revealed the Mystery: that every ending is but a new beginning. We meet in time out of time, everywhere and nowhere, here and there, to greet the Death which is also Life, and the triple Goddess who is the cycle of rebirth.

Someone lit a fire in a dustbin lid (the cauldron was too heavy to carry from London) and each of us then invited the women that we knew, living or dead, to be present. We then chanted, the chant also taken from Starhawk, in which we passed around incense and each person said, "x lives, x passes, x dies"—x being anger, failure, blindness, and so forth. The chorus was: "it is the cold of the night, it is the dark." Then someone held up a pomegranate (this was found in both Starhawk and Z Budapest) and said, "behold, I show you the fruit of life." She stabbed it and said, "which is death" and passed it around the circle, and each woman put a seed in the mouth of the woman to her left, saying, "taste of the seeds of death." Then that woman held up an apple—"I show you the fruit of death and lo"—here she sliced it sideways, to show the five pointed star at its centre—"it contains the five pointed star of life." The apple was passed around the circle, each woman feeding her neighbour as before and saying, "taste of the fruit of life." Then we passed a chalice of wine and some bread, saying "may you never be hungry," pulled out masks and sparklers, and danced around and over the fire. Many of these actions required unrehearsed, unpremeditated participation from all members present, unlike the Gardnerian coven, where those not doing the ritual simply watch until they are called to worship or to take communion (members often take turns in performing the rituals, though). There was also the sense that the group had written some of the ritual together, and that some of the ritual was spontaneous.

There are also "solo" witches, individuals who call themselves witches even though they have never been initiated and have no formal tie to a coven. I met a number of these women (they were always women). One had an organization she called "Spook Enterprises" and sold candles shaped like cats and like Isis. Another called herself a witch but had never been initiated, although she was well-established in the pagan world. Another, the speaker at the 1983 Quest conference, gave talks on "village witchcraft": on inquiry, it appeared that she had been born in Kent, and was an ex-Girtonian.[3]

Mick, the woman of this sort whom I knew best, owned a Jacobean cottage where she lived alone on the edge of the Fens, the desolate drained farmland outside Cambridge. She managed a chicken farm. She told me that she discovered her powers at the age of ten, when she "cursed" her math teacher and he promptly broke his leg in two places. It was clear that witchcraft was integral to her sense of self, and she took it seriously, albeit with theatre. She called her cottage "Broomstick Cottage," kept ten cats and had a cast iron cauldron near the fire place. In the corner of the cottage she had a small statue of Pan on an altar, alongside a ritual knife stained with her own blood. Many of the villagers knew her and in Cambridge I heard of the "Fen witch" from at least four different sources. Once, when I was sitting in her garden (her Elizabethan herb garden), two little boys cycled past. One shouted to the other, "*that's* where the witch lives!" Mick got "collected" for her personality, she told me: people seem to think it exotic to have a witch to supper. And this may have been one of the reasons she cherished her claims. She was a very funny, sociable woman, always the centre of a party, but a bit lonely, I think, and a bit romantic: witchcraft served a different function for her than fervent Christianity might have done, but like all religions, the witchcraft reduced the loneliness, lent charm to the bleak landscape, and gave her a social role.

There is a certain feel to witchcraft, a humour and an enthusiasm, often missing in other groups. Witchcraft combines the ideal and the mundane. It blends spiritual intensity and romanticism with the lovable, paunchy flaws of the flesh. Fantasies of elfin unicorns side comfortably with bawdy Pans. The high priest of the coven I joined described this as "the goat and the gazelle": "all witches have a little of each." Part of this is the practice itself. People can

---

3. Girton is the oldest women's college at Cambridge.

look slightly ridiculous standing around naked in someone's living room. One needs a sense of humour in order to tolerate the practice, as well as enough romanticism to take it seriously. And witches are perhaps the only magicians who incorporate humour into their practice. Their central invocation, the declamation of the priestess-turned-goddess, calls for "mirth and reverence." Laughter often rings within the circle, though rarely in the rites. One high priestess spontaneously explained to me that "being alive is really rather funny. Wicca [another name for witchcraft] is the only religion that captures this."

36

Consulting the Poison Oracle Among the Azande

E. E. Evans-Pritchard

If one important aspect of religion is helping believers come to know the unknown, it follows that div-
ination is important to religion. Divination *means learning about the future or about things that*
may be hidden. Although the word itself can be traced to divinity, *which indicates its relationship to*
gods, the practice of divination belongs as much to magic as it does to religion proper. In this selec-
tion, E. E. Evans-Pritchard describes the Zande poison oracle benge, *a substance related to strych-*
nine, and the myriad sociocultural beliefs surrounding its usage. Anthropological literature has long
confirmed the great importance of divination to the Azande; it is a practice that cuts across every as-
pect of their culture. Azande diviners frequently divine with rubbing boards and termite sticks, but
for the most important decisions they consult benge *by "reading" its effect on chickens. Control over*
the poison oracle by older men assures them power over young men and all women. More impor-
tantly, control of benge *in all legal cases provides Zande princes with enormous power. Indeed, the*
entire legal system of the Zande rests with divination-based decisions.

E. E. Evans-Pritchard (1902–1973) was one of the most outstanding ethnographers of Africa in
the first half of the 20th century, and his writings on the Azande and the Nuer are classics in an-
thropology. His work epitomized the British structural functional approach, which emphasized syn-
chronic analyses and the study of social organization.

The usual place for a consultation is on the edge of cultivations far removed from homesteads. Any place in the bush screened by high grasses and brushwood is suitable. Or they may choose the corner of a clearing at the edge of the bush where crops will later be sown, since this is not so damp as in the bush itself. The object in going so far is to ensure secrecy, to avoid pollution by people who have not observed the taboos, and to escape witchcraft, which is less likely to corrupt the oracle in the bush than in a homestead.

Excerpted from Part III, Chapter 3: "Consulting the Poison Oracle," pp. 281–312 from WITCHCRAFT, ORACLES AND MAGIC AMONG THE AZANDE (1963) by E. E. Evans-Pritchard. Reprinted by permission of Oxford University Press.

Oracle poison is useless unless a man possesses fowls upon which to test it, for the oracle speaks through fowls. In every Zande household there is a fowl house, and fowls are kept mainly with the object of subjecting them to oracular tests. As a rule they are only killed for food (and then only cocks or old hens) when an important visitor comes to the homestead, perhaps a prince's son or perhaps a father-in-law. Eggs are not eaten but are left to hens to hatch out. Generally a Zande, unless he is a wealthy man, will not possess more than half a dozen grown fowls at the most, and many people possess none at all or perhaps a single hen which someone has given to them.

Small chickens, only two or three days old, may be used for the poison oracle, but Azande prefer them older. However, one sees fowls of all sizes at oracle consultations, from tiny chickens to half-grown cockerels and pullets. When it is possible to tell the sex of fowls Azande use only cockerels, unless they have none and a consultation is necessary at once. The hens are spared for breeding purposes. Generally a man tells one of his younger sons to catch the fowls the night before a séance. Otherwise they catch them when the door of the fowl house is opened shortly after sunrise, but it is better to catch them and put them in a basket at night when they are roosting.

Old men say that fully grown birds ought not to be used in oracle consultations because they are too susceptible to the poison and have a habit of dying straight away before the poison has had time to consider the matter placed before it or even to hear a full statement of the problem. On the other hand a chicken remains for a long time under the influence of the poison before it recovers or expires, so that the oracle has time to hear all the relevant details concerning the problem placed before it and to give a well-considered judgment.

Any male may take part in the proceedings. However, the oracle is costly, and the questions put to it concern adult occupations. Therefore boys are only present when they operate the oracle. Normally these are boys who are observing taboos of mourning for the death of a relative. Adults also consider that it would be very unwise to allow any boys other than these to come near their poison because boys cannot be relied upon to observe the taboos on meats and vegetables.

An unmarried man will seldom be present at a séance. If he has any problems his father or uncle can act on his behalf. Moreover, only a married householder is wealthy enough to possess fowls and to acquire poison and has the experience to conduct a séance properly. Senior men also say that youths are generally engaged in some illicit love affair and would probably pollute the poison if they came near it. It is particularly the province of married men with households of their own to consult the poison oracle and no occupation gives them greater pleasure. It is not merely that they are able to solve their personal problems; but also they are dealing with matters of public importance, witchcraft, sorcery, and adultery, in which their names will be associated as witnesses of the oracle's decisions. A middle-aged Zande is happy when he has some poison and a few fowls

and the company of one or two trusted friends of his own age, and he can sit down to a long séance to discover all about the infidelities of his wives, his health and the health of his children, his marriage plans, his hunting and agricultural prospects, the advisability of changing his homestead, and so forth.

Poor men who do not possess poison or fowls but who are compelled for one reason or another to consult the oracle will persuade a kinsman, blood-brother, relative-in-law, or prince's deputy to consult it on their behalf. This is one of the main duties of social relationships.

Control over the poison oracle by the older men gives them great power over their juniors and it is one of the main sources of their prestige. It is possible for the older men to place the names of the youths before the poison oracle and on its declarations to bring accusations of adultery against them. Moreover, a man who is not able to afford poison is not a fully independent householder, since he is unable to initiate any important undertaking and is dependent on the good will of others to inform him about everything that concerns his health and welfare. In their dealings with youths older men are backed always by the authority of the oracle on any question that concerns their juniors, who have no means of directly consulting it themselves.

Women are debarred not only from operating the poison oracle but from having anything to do with it. They are not expected even to speak of it, and a man who mentions the oracle in the presence of women uses some circumlocutory expression. When a man is going to consult the poison oracle he says to his wife that he is going to look at his cultivations or makes a similar excuse. She understands well enough what he is going to do but says nothing.

The poison oracle is a male prerogative and is one of the principal mechanisms of male control and an expression of sex antagonism. For men say that women are capable of any deceit to defy a husband and please a lover, but men at least have the advantage that their oracle poison will reveal secret embraces. If it were not for the oracle it would be of little use to pay bridewealth, for the most jealous watch will not prevent a woman from committing adultery if she has a mind to do so. And what woman has not? The only thing which women fear is the poison oracle; for if they can escape the eyes of men they cannot escape the eyes of the oracle. Hence it is said that women hate the oracle, and that if a woman finds some of the poison in the bush she will destroy its power by urinating on it. I once asked a Zande why he so carefully collected the leaves used in operating the oracle and threw them some distance away from the bush, and he replied that it was to prevent women from finding them and polluting them, for if they pollute the leaves then the poison which has been removed to its hiding place will lose its power.

Occasionally very old women of good social position have been known to operate the poison oracle, or at least to consult it. A well-known character of the present day, the mother of Prince Ngere, consults the poison oracle, but such persons are rare exceptions and are always august persons.

When we consider to what extent social life is regulated by the poison oracle we shall at once appreciate how great an advantage men have over women in their ability to use it, and how being cut off from the main means of establishing contact with the mystical forces that so deeply affect human welfare degrades a woman's position in Zande society. I have little hesitation in affirming that the customary exclusion of women from any dealings with the poison oracle is the most evident symptom of their inferior social position and means of maintaining it.

Great experience is necessary to conduct a séance in the correct manner and to know how to interpret the findings of the oracle. One must know how many doses of poison to administer, whether the oracle is working properly, in what order to take the questions, whether to put them in a positive or negative form, how long a fowl is to be held between the toes or in the hand while a question is being put to the oracle, when it ought to be jerked to stir up the poison, and when it is time to throw it on the ground for final inspection. One must know how to observe not only whether the fowl lives or dies, but also the exact manner in which the poison affects it, for while it is under the influence of the oracle its every movement is significant to the experienced eye. Also one must know the phraseology of address in order to put the questions clearly to the oracle without error or ambiguity, and this is no easy task when a single question may be asked in a harangue lasting as long as five or ten minutes.

Everyone knows what happens at a consultation of the poison oracle. Even women are aware of the procedure. But not every man is proficient in the art, though most adults can prepare and question the oracle if necessary. Those who as boys have often prepared the poison for their fathers and uncles, and who are members of families which frequent the court and constantly consult the oracle, are the most competent. When I have asked boys whether they can prepare the poison and administer it to fowls they have often replied that they are ignorant of the art. Some men are very expert at questioning the oracle, and those who wish to consult it like to be accompanied by such a man.

Any man who is invited by the owner of the oracle poison may attend the séance, but he will be expected to keep clear of the oracle if he has had relations with his wife or eaten any of the prohibited foods within the last few days. It is imperative that the man who actually prepares the poison shall have observed these taboos, and for this reason the owner of the poison, referred to in this account as the owner, generally asks a boy or man who is under taboos of mourning to operate the oracle, since there can be no doubt that he has kept the taboos, because they are the same for mourning as for oracles. Such a man is always employed when as in a case of sudden sickness, it is necessary to consult the oracle without warning so that there is no time for a man to prepare himself by observation of taboos. I shall refer to the man or boy who actually prepares the poison and administers it to fowls as the "operator." When I speak of the "questioner" I refer to the man who sits opposite to the oracle and addresses it and calls upon it for judgments. As he sits a few feet from the oracle he ought also to have observed all the taboos. It is possible for a man to be owner, operator, and questioner at the same time by conducting the consultation of the oracle by himself, but this rarely, if ever, occurs. Usually there is no difficulty in obtaining the services of an operator, since a man knows which of his neighbors are observing the taboos associated with death and vengeance. One of his companions who has not eaten tabooed food or had sexual relations with women for a day or two before the consultation acts as questioner. If a man is unclean he can address the oracle from a distance. It is better to take these precautions because contact of an unclean person with the oracle is certain to destroy its potency, and even the close proximity of an unclean person may have this result.

The owner does not pay the operator and questioner for their services. The questioner is almost invariably either the owner himself or one of his friends who also wishes to put questions to the oracle and has brought fowls with him for the purpose. It is usual to reward the operator, if he is an adult, by giving him a fowl during the séance so that he can place one of his own problems before the oracle. Since he is generally a man who wears a girdle of mourning and vengeance he will often ask the oracle when the vengeance magic is going to strike its victim.

To guard against pollution a man generally hides his poison in the thatched roof of a hut, on the inner side, if possible, in a hut which women do not use, but this is not essential, for a woman does not know that there is poison hidden in the roof and is unlikely to come into contact with it. The owner of the poison must have kept the taboos if he wishes to take it down from the roof himself, and if he is unclean he will bring the man or boy who is to operate the oracle into the hut and indicate to him at a distance where the poison is hidden in the thatch. So good a hiding place is the thatched roof of a hut for a small packet of poison that it is often difficult for its owner himself to find it. No one may smoke hemp in a hut which lodges oracle poison. However, there is always a danger of pollution and of witchcraft if the poison is kept in a homestead, and some men prefer to hide it in a hole in a tree in the bush, or even to build a small shelter and to lay it on the ground beneath. This shelter is far removed from human dwellings, and were a man to come across it in the bush he would not disturb it lest it cover some kind of lethal medicine. It is very improbable that witchcraft will discover oracle poison hidden in the bush. I have never seen oracle poison under a shelter in the bush, but I was told that it is frequently housed in this manner.

Oracle poison when not in use is kept wrapped in leaves, and at the end of a séance used poison is placed in a separate leaf-wrapping from unused poison. The poison may be used two or three times and sometimes fresh poison is added to it to make it more potent. When its action shows that it has lost its strength they throw it away.

Special care is taken to protect a prince's oracle poison from witchcraft and pollution because a prince's oracles reveal matters of tribal importance, judge criminal and civil cases, and determine whether vengeance has been exacted for death. A prince has two or three official operators who supervise his poison oracle. These men must be thoroughly reliable since the fate of their master and the purity of law are in their hands. If they break a taboo the whole legal system may become corrupted and the innocent be judged guilty and the guilty be judged innocent. Moreover, a prince is at frequent pains to discover witchcraft or sorcery among his wives and retainers which might do him an injury, so that his life is endangered if the oracle is not working properly.

Control of the poison oracle in all legal cases gave the princes enormous power. No death or adultery could be legally avenged without a verdict from their oracles, so that the court was the sole medium of legal action and the king or his representative the sole source of law. Although the procedure was a mystical one it was carried out in the king's name and he was vested with judicial authority as completely as if a more common-sense system of justice had obtained.

Azande are very secretive about oracle séances and wish no one to be present when they are inquiring about private matters unless he is a trusted friend. They do not tell any one except trusted friends that they are going to consult the oracle, and they say nothing about the consultation on their return. It frequently happens when a man is about to set out from his homestead to the place of the oracle that he is visited by someone whom he does not wish to acquaint with his business. He does not tell the unwelcome visitor that he must hurry off to consult the oracle, but uses any pretext to get rid of him, and prefers to abandon the consultation rather than confess his intentions.

After this short introduction I will describe the manner in which poison is administered to fowls. The operator goes ahead of the rest of the party in order to prepare for the test. He takes with him a small gourdful of water. He clears a space by treading down the grasses. Afterwards he scrapes a hole in the earth into which he places a large leaf as a basin for the oracle poison. From *bingba* grass he fashions a small brush to administer the poison, and from leaves he makes a filter to pour the liquid poison into the beaks of the fowls; and from other leaves he makes a cup to transfer water from the gourd to the poison when it needs to be moistened. Finally, he tears off some branches of nearby shrubs and extracts their bast to be used as cord for attaching to the legs of fowls which have survived the test so that they can be easily retrieved from the grass when the business of the day is finished. The operator does not moisten the poison till the rest of the party arrive.

There may be only one man or there may be several who have questions to put to the oracle. Each brings his fowls with him in an open-wove basket. As it has been agreed beforehand where the oracle consultation is to take place they know where to foregather. As each person arrives he hands over his basket of fowls to the operator who places it on the ground near him. A man who is used to acting as questioner sits opposite to it, a few feet away if he has observed the taboos, but several yards away if he has not observed them. Other men who have not kept the taboos remain at a greater distance.

When every one is seated they discuss in low tones whose fowl they will take first and how the question shall be framed. Meanwhile the operator pours some water from the gourd at his side into his leaf cup and from the cup on to the poison, which then effervesces. He mixes the poison and water with his finger tips into a paste of the right consistency and, when instructed by the questioner, takes one of the fowls and draws down its wings over its legs and pins them between and under his toes. He is seated with the fowl facing him. He takes his grass brush, twirls it round in the poison, and folds it in the leaf filter. He holds open the beak of the fowl and tips the end of the filter into it and squeezes the filter so that the liquid runs out of the paste into the throat of the fowl. He bobs the head of the fowl up and down to compel it to swallow the poison.

At this point the questioner, having previously been instructed by the owner of the fowl on the facts which he is to put before the oracle, commences to address the poison inside the fowl. He continues to address it for about a couple of minutes, when a second dose of poison is usually administered. If it is a very small chicken two doses will suffice, but a larger fowl will receive three doses, and I have known a fowl to receive a fourth dose, but never more than four. The questioner does not cease his address to the oracle, but puts his questions again and again in different forms, though always with the same refrain, "If such is the case, poison oracle kill the fowl," or "If such is the case, poison oracle spare the fowl." From time to time he interrupts his flow of oratory to give a technical order to the operator. He may tell him to give the fowl another dose of poison or to jerk it between his toes by raising and lowering his foot (this stirs up the poison inside the fowl). When the last dose of poison has been administered and he has further addressed it, he tells the operator to raise the fowl. The operator takes it in his hand and, holding its legs between his fingers so that it faces him, gives it an occasional jerk backwards and forwards. The questioner redoubles his oratory as though the verdict depended upon his forensic efforts, and if the fowl is not already dead he then, after a further bout of oratory, tells the operator to put it on the ground. He continues to address the poison inside the fowl while they watch its movements on the ground.

The poison affects fowls in many ways. Occasionally it kills them immediately after the first dose, while they are still on the ground. This seldom happens, for normally a fowl is not seriously affected till it is removed from the ground and jerked backwards and forwards in the hand. Then, if it is going to die, it goes through spasmodic stretchings of the body and closing of the wings and vomits. After several such spasms it vomits and expires in a final seizure. Some fowls appear quite unaffected by the poison, and when, after being jerked backwards and forwards for a while, they are flung to the ground peck around unconcernedly. Those fowls which are unaffected by the poison generally excrete as soon as they are put to earth. Some fowls appear little affected by the poison till put to earth, when they suddenly collapse and die.

One generally knows what the verdict is going to be after the fowl has been held in the hand for a couple of minutes. If it appears certain to recover the operator ties bast to its leg and throws it to the ground. If it appears certain to die he does not trouble to tie bast to its leg, but lays it on the earth to die. Often when a fowl has died they draw its corpse in a semicircle round the poison to show it to the poison. They then cut off a wing to use as evidence and cover the body with grass. Those fowls which survive are taken home and let loose. A fowl is never used twice on the same day.

The main duty of the questioner is to see that the oracle fully understands the question put to it and is acquainted with all facts relevant to the problem it is asked to solve. They address it with all the care for detail that one observes in court cases before a prince. This means beginning a long way back and noting over a considerable period of time every detail which might elucidate the case, linking up facts into a consistent picture of events, and the marshalling of arguments, as Azande can so brilliantly do, into a logical and closely knit web of sequences and interrelations of facts and inference. Also the questioner is careful to mention to the oracle again and again the name of the man who is consulting it, and he points him out to the oracle with his out-stretched arm. He mentions also the name of his father, perhaps the name of his clan, and the name of the place where he resides, and he gives similar details of other people mentioned in the address.

An address consists usually of alternate directions. The first sentences outline the question in terms demanding an affirmative answer and end with the command, "Poison oracle kill the fowl." The next sentences outline the question in terms demanding a negative answer and end with the command, "Poison oracle spare the fowl." The consulter then takes up the question again in terms asking an affirmative answer; and so on. If a bystander considers that a relevant point has been left out he interrupts the questioner, who then makes this point.

The questioner has a switch in his hand, and while questioning the oracle beats the ground, as he sits cross-legged, in front of it. He continues to beat the ground till the end of his address. Often he will gesticulate as he makes his points, in the same manner as a man making a case in court. He sometimes plucks grass and shows it to the poison and, after explaining that there is something he does not wish it to consider, throws it behind him. Thus he tells the oracle that he does not wish it to consider the question of witchcraft but only of sorcery. Witchcraft is *wingi,* something irrelevant, and he casts it behind him.

While the fowl is undergoing its ordeal men are attentive to their behavior. A man must tighten and spread out his bark-cloth loin-covering lest he expose his genitals, as when he is sitting in the presence of a prince or parent-in-law. Men speak in a low voice as they do in the presence of superiors. Indeed, all conversation is avoided unless it directly concerns the procedure of consultation. If anyone desires to leave before the proceedings are finished he takes a leaf and spits on it and places it where he has been sitting. I have seen a man who rose for a few moments only to catch a fowl which had escaped from its basket place a blade of grass on the stone upon which he had been sitting. Spears must be laid on the ground and not planted upright in the presence of the poison oracle. Azande are very serious during a séance, for they are asking questions of vital importance to their lives and happiness.

37

Rational Mastery by Man of His Surroundings

Bronislaw Malinowski

Rare is the anthropology course that sometime during the semester is not directed to the thought and writings of Bronislaw Malinowski (1884–1942). This world-famous Polish anthropologist was trained in mathematics but shifted his interests to anthropology after reading Sir James Frazer's The Golden Bough. *Malinowski's fieldwork in the Trobriand Islands of Melanesia influenced the direction of anthropology as an academic discipline. He is recognized as the founder of functionalism, an anthropological approach to the study of culture that believes each institution in a society fulfills a definite function in the maintenance of human needs. His major works include* Crime and Customs in Savage Society *(1926),* The Sexual Life of Savages *(1929), and* Coral Gardens and Their Magic *(1935). Malinowski was professor of anthropology at the University of London from 1927 until his death in 1942.*

In this classic article, originally published in 1925, Malinowski asks two important questions: Do preliterate people have any rational mastery of their surroundings and can primitive knowledge be regarded as a beginning or rudimentary type of science, or is it merely a crude hodgepodge devoid of logic and accuracy? Although the author's use of the word savage *is considered a pejorative by anthropologists today, in Malinowski's time it was commonplace.*

The problem of primitive knowledge has been singularly neglected by anthropology. Studies on savage psychology were exclusively confined to early religion, magic, and mythology. Only recently the work of several English, German, and French writers, notably the daring and brilliant speculations of Professor Lévy-Bruhl, gave an impetus to the student's interest in what the savage does in his more sober moods. The results were startling indeed: Professor Lévy-Bruhl tells us, to put it in a nutshell, that primitive man has no sober moods at all, that he is hopelessly and completely immersed in a mystical frame of mind. Incapable of dispassionate and consistent observation, devoid of the power of abstraction, hampered by "a decided aversion towards reasoning," he is unable to draw any benefit from experience, to construct or comprehend even the most elementary laws of nature. "For minds thus orientated there is no fact purely physical." Nor can there exist for them any clear idea of substance and attribute, cause and effect, identity and contradiction. Their outlook is that of confused superstition, "prelogical," made of mystic "participations" and "exclusions." I have here summarized a body of opinion, of which the brilliant French sociologist is the most decided and the most competent spokesman, but which numbers besides, many anthropologists and philosophers of renown.

Reprinted from MAGIC, SCIENCE AND RELIGION (New York: Doubleday, 1955), pp. 25–35, by permission of the Society for Promoting Christian Knowledge.

But there are dissenting voices. When a scholar and anthropologist of the measure of Professor J. L. Myres entitles an article in *Notes and Queries* "Natural Science," and when we read there that the savage's "knowledge based on observation is distinct and accurate," we must surely pause before accepting primitive man's irrationality as a dogma. Another highly competent writer, Dr. A. A. Goldenweiser, speaking about primitive "discoveries, inventions and improvements"—which could hardly be attributed to any preempirical or prelogical mind—affirms that "it would be unwise to ascribe to the primitive mechanic merely a passive part in the origination of inventions. Many a happy thought must have crossed his mind, nor was he wholly unfamiliar with the thrill that comes from an idea effective in action." Here we see the savage endowed with an attitude of mind wholly akin to that of a modern man of science!

To bridge over the wide gap between the two extreme opinions current on the subject of primitive man's reason, it will be best to resolve the problem into two questions.

First, has the savage any rational outlook, any rational mastery of his surroundings, or is he, as M. Lévy-Bruhl and his school maintain, entirely "mystical"? The answer will be that every primitive community is in possession of a considerable store of knowledge, based on experience and fashioned by reason.

The second question then opens: Can this primitive knowledge be regarded as a rudimentary form of science or is it, on the contrary, radically different, a crude body of practical and technical abilities, rules of thumb and rules of art having no theoretical value? This second question, epistemological rather than belonging to the study of man, will be barely touched upon at the end of this section and a tentative answer only will be given.

In dealing with the first question, we shall have to examine the "profane" side of life, the arts, crafts and economic pursuits, and we shall attempt to disentangle in it a type of behavior, clearly marked off from magic and religion, based on empirical knowledge and on the confidence in logic. We shall try to find whether the lines of such behavior are defined by traditional rules, known, perhaps even discussed sometimes, and tested. We shall have to inquire whether the sociological setting of the rational and empirical behavior differs from that of ritual and cult. Above all we shall ask, do the natives distinguish the two domains and keep them apart, or is the field of knowledge constantly swamped by superstition, ritualism, magic or religion?

Since in the matter under discussion there is an appalling lack of relevant and reliable observations, I shall have largely to draw upon my own material, most unpublished, collected during a few years' field work among the Melanesian and Papuo-Melanesian tribes of Eastern New Guinea and the surrounding archipelagoes. As the Melanesians are reputed, however, to be specially magic-ridden, they will furnish an acid test of the existence of empirical and rational knowledge among savages living in the age of polished stone.

These natives, and I am speaking mainly of the Melanesians who inhabit the coral atolls to the N.E. of the main island, the Trobriand Archipelago and the adjoining groups, are expert fishermen, industrious manufacturers and traders, but they rely mainly on gardening for their subsistence. With the most rudimentary implements, a pointed digging-stick and a small axe, they are able to raise crops sufficient to maintain a dense population and even yielding a surplus, which in olden days was allowed to rot unconsumed, and which at present is exported to feed plantation hands. The success in their agriculture depends—besides the excellent natural conditions with which they are favored—upon their extensive knowledge of the classes of the soil, of the various cultivated plants, of the mutual adaptation of these two factors, and, last not least, upon their knowledge of the importance of accurate and hard work. They have to select the soil and the seedlings, they have appropriately to fix the times for clearing and burning the scrub, for planting and weeding, for training the vines of the yam plants. In all this they are guided by a clear knowledge of weather and seasons, plants and pests, soil and tubers, and by a conviction that this knowledge is true and reliable, that it can be counted upon and must be scrupulously obeyed.

Yet mixed with all their activities there is to be found magic, a series of rites performed every year over the gardens in rigorous sequence and order. Since the leadership in garden work is in the hands of the magician, and since ritual and practical work are intimately associated, a superficial observer might be led to assume that the mystic and the rational behavior are mixed up, that their effects are not distinguished by the natives and not distinguishable in scientific analysis. Is this so really?

Magic is undoubtedly regarded by the natives as absolutely indispensable to the welfare of the gardens. What would happen without it no one can exactly tell, for no native garden has ever been made without its ritual, in spite of some thirty years of European rule and missionary influence and well over a century's contact with white traders. But certainly various kinds of disaster, blight, unseasonable droughts, rains, bush-pigs and locusts would destroy the unhallowed garden made without magic.

Does this mean, however, that the natives attribute all the good results to magic? Certainly not. If you were to suggest to a native that he should make his garden mainly by magic and scamp his work, he would simply smile on your simplicity. He knows as well as you do that there are natural conditions and causes, and by his observations he knows also that he is able to control these natural forces by mental and physical effort. His knowledge is limited, no doubt, but as far as it goes it is sound and proof against mysticism. If the fences are broken down, if the seed is destroyed or has been dried or washed away, he will have recourse not to magic, but to work, guided by knowledge and reason. His experience has taught him also, on the other hand, that in spite of all his forethought and beyond all his efforts there are agencies and forces which one year bestow unwonted and unearned benefits of fertility, making everything run smooth and well, rain and sun appear at the right moment, noxious insects remain in abeyance, the harvest yields a superabundant crop; and another year again the same agencies bring ill luck and bad chance, pursue him from beginning till end and thwart all his most strenuous efforts and his best-founded knowledge. To control these influences and these only he employs magic.

Thus there is a clear-cut division: there is first the well-known set of conditions, the natural course of growth, as well as the ordinary pests and dangers to be warded off by fencing and weeding. On the other hand there is the domain of the unaccountable and adverse influences, as well as the great unearned increment of fortunate coincidence. The first conditions are coped with by knowledge and work, the second by magic.

This line of division can also be traced in the social setting of work and ritual respectively. Though the garden magician is, as a rule, also the leader in practical activities, these two functions are kept strictly apart. Every magical ceremony has its distinctive name, its appropriate time and its place in the scheme of work, and it stands out of the ordinary course of activities completely. Some of them are ceremonial and have to be attended by the whole community, all are public in that it is known when they are going to happen and anyone can attend them. They are performed on selected plots within the gardens and on a special corner of this plot. Work is always tabooed on such occasions, sometimes only while the ceremony lasts, sometimes for a day or two. In his lay character the leader and magician directs the work, fixes the dates for starting, harangues and exhorts slack or careless gardeners. But the two roles never overlap or interfere: they are always clear, and any native will inform you without hesitation whether the man acts as magician or as leader in garden work.

What has been said about gardens can be paralleled from any one of the many other activities in which work and magic run side by side without ever mixing. Thus in canoe building empirical knowledge of material, of technology, and of certain principles of stability and hydrodynamics, function in company and close association with magic, each yet uncontaminated by the other.

For example, they understand perfectly well that the wider the span of the outrigger the greater the stability yet the smaller the resistance against strain. They can clearly explain why they have to give this span a certain traditional width, measured in fractions of the length of the dugout. They can also explain, in rudimentary but clearly mechanical terms, how they have to behave in a sudden gale, why the outrigger must be always on the weather side, why the one type of canoe can and the other cannot beat. They have, in fact, a whole system of principles of sailing, embodied in a complex and rich terminology, traditionally handed on and obeyed as rationally and consistently as is modern science by modern sailors. How could they sail otherwise under eminently dangerous conditions in their frail primitive craft?

But even with all their systematic knowledge, methodically applied, they are still at the mercy of powerful and incalculable tides, sudden gales during the monsoon season and unknown reefs. And here comes in their magic, performed over the canoe during its construction, carried out at the beginning and in the course of expeditions and resorted to in moments of real danger. If the modern seaman, entrenched in science and reason, provided with all sorts of safety appliances, sailing on steel-built steamers, if even he has a singular tendency to superstition—which does not rob him of his knowledge or reason, nor make him altogether prelogical—can we wonder that his savage colleague, under much more precarious conditions, holds fast to the safety and comfort of magic?

An interesting and crucial test is provided by fishing in the Trobriand Islands and its magic. While in the villages on the inner lagoon fishing is done in an easy and absolutely reliable manner by the method of poisoning, yielding abundant results without danger and uncertainty, there are on the shores of the open sea dangerous modes of fishing and also certain types in which the yield greatly varies according to whether shoals of fish appear beforehand or not. It is most significant that in the lagoon fishing, where man can rely completely upon his knowledge and skill, magic does not exist, while in the open-sea fishing, full of danger and uncertainty, there is extensive magical ritual to secure safety and good results.

Again, in warfare the natives know that strength, courage, and agility play a decisive part. Yet here also they practice magic to master the elements of chance and luck.

Nowhere is the duality of natural and supernatural causes divided by a line so thin and intricate, yet, if carefully followed up, so well marked, decisive, and instructive, as in the two most fateful forces of human destiny: health and death. Health to the Melanesians is a natural state of affairs and, unless tampered with, the human body will remain in perfect order. But the natives know perfectly well that there are natural means which can affect health and even destroy the body. Poisons, wounds, burns, falls are known to cause disablement or death in a natural way. And this is not a matter of private opinion of this or that individual, but it is laid down in traditional lore and even in belief, for there are considered to be different ways to the nether world for those who died by sorcery and those who met "natural" death. Again, it is recognized that cold, heat,

overstrain, too much sun, overeating can all cause minor ailments, which are treated by natural remedies such as massage, steaming, warming at a fire and certain potions. Old age is known to lead to bodily decay and the explanation is given by the natives that very old people grow weak, their esophagus closes up, and therefore they must die.

But besides these natural causes there is the enormous domain of sorcery and by far the most cases of illness and death are ascribed to this. The line of distinction between sorcery and the other causes is clear in theory and in most cases of practice, but it must be realized that it is subject to what could be called the personal perspective. That is, the more closely a case has to do with the person who considers it, the less will it be "natural," the more "magical." Thus a very old man, whose pending death will be considered natural by the other members of the community, will be afraid only of sorcery and never think of his natural fate. A fairly sick person will diagnose sorcery in his own case, while all the others might speak of too much betel nut or overeating or some other indulgence.

But who of us really believes that his own bodily infirmities and the approaching death is a purely natural occurrence, just an insignificant event in the infinite chain of causes? To the most rational civilized men health, disease, the threat of death, float in a hazy emotional mist, which seems to become denser and more impenetrable as the fateful forms approach. It is indeed astonishing that "savages" can achieve such a sober, dispassionate outlook in these matters as they actually do.

Thus in his relation to nature and destiny, whether he tries to exploit the first or to dodge the second, primitive man recognized both the natural and the supernatural forces and agencies, and he tries to use them both for his benefit. Whenever he has been taught by experience that effort guided by knowledge is of some avail, he never spares the one or ignores the other. He knows that a plant cannot grow by magic alone, or a canoe sail or float without being properly constructed and managed, or a fight be won without skill and daring. He never relies on magic alone, while, on the contrary, he sometimes dispenses with it completely, as in fire-making and in a number of crafts and pursuits. But he clings to it, whenever he has to recognize the impotence of his knowledge and of his rational technique.

I have given my reasons why in this argument I had to rely principally on the material collected in the classical land of magic, Melanesia. But the facts discussed are so fundamental, the conclusions drawn of such a general nature, that it will be easy to check them on any modern detailed ethnographic record. Comparing agricultural work and magic, the building of canoes, the art of healing by magic and by natural remedies, the ideas about the causes of death in other regions, the universal validity of what has been established here could easily be proved. Only, since no observations have methodically been made with reference to the problem of primitive knowledge, the data from other writers could be gleaned only piecemeal and their testimony though clear would be indirect.

I have chosen to face the question of primitive man's rational knowledge directly: watching him at his principal occupations, seeing him pass from work to magic and back again, entering into his mind, listening to his opinions. The whole problem might have been approached through the avenue of language, but this would have led us too far into questions of logic, semasiology, and theory of primitive languages. Words which serve to express general ideas such as *existence, substance,* and *attribute, cause* and *effect,* the *fundamental* and the *secondary;* words and expressions used in complicated pursuits like sailing, construction, measuring and checking; numerals and quantitative descriptions, correct and detailed classifications of natural phenomena, plants and animals—all this would lead us exactly to the same conclusion: that primitive man can observe and think, and that he possesses, embodied in his language, systems of methodical though rudimentary knowledge.

Similar conclusions could be drawn from an examination of those mental schemes and physical contrivances which could be described as diagrams or formulas. Methods of indicating the main points of the compass, arrangements of stars into constellations, co-ordination of these with the seasons, naming of moons in the year, of quarters in the moon—all these accomplishments are known to the simplest savages. Also they are all able to draw diagrammatic maps in the sand or dust, indicate arrangements by placing small stones, shells, or sticks on the ground, plan expeditions or raids on such rudimentary charts. By co-ordinating space and time they are able to arrange big tribal gatherings and to combine vast tribal movements over extensive areas. The use of leaves, notched sticks, and similar aids to memory is well known and seems to be almost universal. All such "diagrams" are means of reducing a complex and unwieldly bit of reality to a simple and handy form. They give man a relatively easy mental control over it. As such are they not—in a very rudimentary form no doubt—fundamentally akin to developed scientific formulas and "models," which are also simple and handy paraphrases of a complex or abstract reality, giving the civilized physicist mental control over it?

This brings us to the second question: Can we regard primitive knowledge, which, as we found, is both empirical and rational, as a rudimentary stage of science, or is it not at all related to it? If by science be understood a body of rules and conceptions, based on experience and derived from it by logical inference, embodied in material achievements and in a fixed form of tradition and carried on by some sort of social organization—then there is no doubt that even the lowest savage communities have the beginning of science, however rudimentary.

Most epistemologists would not, however, be satisfied with such a "minimum definition" of science, for it might apply to the rules of an art or craft as well. They would maintain that the rules of science must be laid down explicitly, open to control by experiment and critique by reason. They must not only be rules of practical behavior, but theoretical laws of knowledge. Even accepting this stricture, however, there is hardly any doubt that many of the principles of savage knowledge are scientific in this sense. The native shipwright knows not only practically of buoyancy, leverage, equilibrium, he has to obey these laws not only on water, but while making the canoe he must have the principles in his mind. He instructs his helpers in them. He gives them the traditional rules, and in a crude and simple manner, using his hands, pieces of wood, and a limited technical vocabulary, he explains some general laws of hydrodynamics and equilibrium. Science is not detached from the craft, that is certainly true, it is only a means to an end, it is crude, rudimentary, and inchoate, but with all that it is the matrix from which the higher developments must have sprung.

If we applied another criterion yet, that of the really scientific attitude, the disinterested search for knowledge and for the understanding of causes and reasons, the answer would certainly not be in a direct negative. There is, of course, no widespread thirst for knowledge in a savage community, new things such as European topics bore them frankly and their whole interest is largely encompassed by the traditional world of their culture. But within this there is both the antiquarian mind passionately interested in myths, stories, details of customs, pedigrees, and ancient happenings, and there is also to be found the naturalist, patient and painstaking in his observations, capable of generalization and of connecting long chains of events in the life of animals, and in the marine world or in the jungle. It is enough to realize how much European naturalists have often learned from their savage colleagues to appreciate this interest found in the native for nature. There is finally among the primitives, as every field worker well knows, the sociologist, the ideal informant, capable with marvelous accuracy and insight to give the *raison d'être,* the function and the organization of many a simpler institution in his tribe.

Science, of course, does not exist in any uncivilized community as a driving power, criticizing, renewing, constructing. Science is never consciously made. But on this criterion, neither is there law, nor religion, nor government among savages.

38

Baseball Magic

George Gmelch

In the preceding article, Malinowski observed that in the Trobriand Islands magic did not occur when the natives fished in the safe lagoons but when they ventured out into the open seas: then the danger and uncertainty caused them to perform extensive magical rituals. In the following article, anthropologist George Gmelch demonstrates that America's favorite pastime is an excellent place to put the test to Malinowski's hypothesis about magic. Anyone who has watched baseball, either at a ballpark or in front of a television set, is aware of some of the more obvious rituals performed by the players, but Gmelch, drawing upon his previous experience as a professional baseball player, provides an insider's view of the rituals, taboos, and fetishes involved in the sport. (The following is a 2007 revision of Gmelch's original article.)

On each pitching day for the first three months of a winning season, Dennis Grossini, a pitcher on a Detroit Tiger farm team, arose from bed at exactly 10:00 A.M. At 1:00 P.M. he went to the nearest restaurant for two glasses of iced tea and a tuna fish sandwich. When he got to the ballpark at 3:00 P.M., he put on the sweatshirt and jock he wore during his last winning game; one hour before the game he chewed a wad of Beech-Nut chewing tobacco. After each pitch during the game he touched the letters on his uniform and straightened his cap after each ball. Before the start of each inning he replaced the pitcher's rosin bag next to the spot where it was the inning before. And after every inning in which he gave up a run, he washed his hands.

When I asked which part of his ritual was most important, he said, "You can't really tell what's most important so it all becomes important. I'd be afraid to change anything. As long as I'm winning, I do everything the same."

Trobriand Islanders, according to anthropologist Bronislaw Malinowski, felt the same way about their fishing magic. Trobrianders fished in two different settings: in the *inner lagoon* where fish were plentiful and there was little danger, and on the *open sea* where fishing was dangerous and yields varied widely. Malinowski found that magic was not used in lagoon fishing, where men could rely solely on their knowledge and skill. But when fishing on the open sea, Trobrianders used a great deal of magical ritual to ensure safety and increase their catch.

Baseball, America's national pastime, is an arena in which players behave remarkably like Malinowski's Trobriand fishermen. To professional ballplayers, baseball is more than just a game, it is an occupation. Since their livelihoods depend on how well they perform, many use magic in an attempt to control the chance that is built into baseball. There are three essential activities of the game—pitching, hitting, and fielding. In the first two, chance can play a surprisingly important role. The pitcher is the player least able to control the outcome of his efforts. He may feel great and have good stuff warming up in the bullpen and then get in the game and get clobbered. He may make a bad pitch and see the batter miss it for a strike or see it hit hard but right into the hands of a fielder for an out. Conversely, his best pitch may be blooped for a base hit. He may limit the opposing team to just a few hits yet lose the game, and he may give up many hits and win. And the good and bad luck don't always average out over the course of a

Revised from the original article that appeared in TRANSACTION, vol. 8, no. 8 (1971), pp. 39–41, 54. Reprinted by permission of the author, George Gmelch.

season. For instance, this past season (2007) [Matt Cain/Jeriome Robertson] gave up 1.4 more runs per game than his teammate [Noah Lowry/Tim Redding] but only won 7 games while losing 16. Lowry won 14 games and only lost 8. Robertson went 15-9, while Redding was only 10–14. Both pitched for the same team—[the San Francisco Giants/the Houston Astros]—which meant they had the same fielders behind them. By chance, when Cain pitched the Giants scored few runs while his teammate Lowry enjoyed considerable run support. Regardless of how well a pitcher performs, the outcome of the game also also depends upon the proficiency of his teammates, the ineptitude of the opposition, and luck.

Hitting, which many observers call the single most difficult task in the world of sports, is also full of uncertainty. Unless it's a home run, no matter how hard the batter hits the ball, fate determines whether it will go into a waiting glove or find a gap between the fielders. The uncertainty is compounded by the low success rate of hitting: the average hitter gets only one hit in every four trips to the plate, while the very best hitters average only one hit in every three trips. Fielding, which we will return to later, is the one part of baseball where chance does not play much of a role.

How does the risk and uncertainty in pitching and hitting affect players? How do they try to control the outcomes of their performance? These are questions that I first became interested in many years ago both as a ballplayer and as an anthropology student. I had devoted much of my youth to baseball and played professionally as a first baseman in the Detroit Tiger organization in the 1960s. It was shortly after the end of one baseball season that I took an anthropology course called "Magic, Religion, and Witchcraft." As I listened to my professor describe the magical rituals of the Trobriand Islanders, it occurred to me that what these so-called primitive people did wasn't all that different from what my teammates and I did for luck and confidence at the ballpark.

Routines and Rituals

The most common way players attempt to reduce chance and their feelings of uncertainty is to develop a daily routine—a course of action which is regularly followed. Talking about the routines of ballplayers, Pittsburgh Pirates coach Rich Donnelly said:

> They're like trained animals. They come out here [ballpark] and everything has to be the same, they don't like anything that knocks them off their routine. Just look at the dugout and you'll see every guy sitting in the same spot every night. It's amazing, everybody in the same spot. And don't you dare take someone's seat. If a guy comes up from the minors and sits here, they'll say, "Hey, Jim sits here, find another seat." You watch the pitcher warm up and he'll do the same thing every time. . . . You got a routine and you adhere to it and you don't want anybody knocking you off it.

Routines are comforting; they bring order into a world in which players have little control. The varied elements in routines can produce the tangible benefit of helping the player concentrate. All ballplayers know that it is difficult to think and hit at the same time, and that following a routine can keep them from thinking too much. And sometimes practical elements in routines produce tangible benefits, such as helping the player concentrate. But often some of what players do goes beyond mere routine. These actions become what anthropologists define as *ritual*—prescribed behaviors in which there is no empirical connection between the means (e.g., tapping home plate three times) and the desired end (e.g., getting a base hit). Because there is no real connection between the two, rituals are not rational. Sometimes they are quite irrational. Similar to rituals are the nonrational beliefs that form the basis of taboos and fetishes, which players also use to bring luck to their side. But first let's take a close look at rituals.

Baseball rituals are infinitely varied. Most are personal, and are performed by individuals rather than by a team or group. Most are done in a private and unemotional manner, in much the same way players apply pine tar and rosin to their bats to improve the grip or dab eye black on their upper cheeks to reduce the sun's glare. A ballplayer may ritualize any activity that he considers important or somehow linked to good performance. Recall the variety of things that Dennis Grossini does, from specific times for waking and eating to foods and dress. White Sox pitcher Jason Bere listens to the same song on his iPod on the day he is scheduled to start. Atlanta Brave Denny Neagle goes to a movie on days he is scheduled to start. Pitcher Al Holland always played with two dollar bills in his back pocket. The Oriole's Glenn Davis used to chew the same gum every day during hitting streaks, saving it under his cap. Astros' infielder Julio Gotay always played with a cheese sandwich in his back pocket (he had a big appetite, so there might also have been a measure of practicality here). Red Soxer third baseman Wade Boggs ate chicken before every game during his career, and that was just one of many elements in his pre- and postgamepost game routine, which also included leaving his house for the ballpark at precisely the same time each day (1:47 for a 7:05 night game), running wind sprints at 7:17 for a 7:35 start, and drawing a chai, the Hebrew symbol for life, upon entering the batter's box.

Many hitters go through a series of preparatory rituals before stepping into the batter's box. These include tugging on their caps, touching their uniform letters or medallions, crossing themselves, and swinging, tapping, or bouncing the bat on the plate a prescribed number of times. Consider the Cubs Dodger's shortstop Nomar Garciaparra. After each pitch he steps out of the batter's box, kicks the dirt with each toe, adjusts his right batting glove, adjusts his left batting glove, and touches his helmet before getting back into the box. He insists that it is a routine, not superstition. "I'm just doing it to get everything tight. I like everything tight, that's all it is, really." Mike Hargrove, former Cleveland Indian first baseman, had so many time-consuming elements in his batting ritual that he was nicknamed "the human rain delay." Both players believe their batting rituals helped them regain their concentration after each pitch. But others wondered if the two had become prisoners of their elaborate superstitions.

Another ritual associated with hitting is tagging a base when leaving and returning to the dugout between innings. Some players don't feel right unless they tag a specific base on each trip between dugout and field. One of my teammates added some complexity to his ritual by tagging third base on his way to the dugout only after the third, sixth, and ninth innings.

Players who have too many or particularly bizarre rituals risk being labeled as flakes, and not just by teammates but by fans and the media as well. For example, ex-Mets pitcher Turk Wendell's eccentric rituals, which include chewing black licorice while pitching, only to spit it out, brush his teeth and

reload the candy between innings, and wearing a necklace of teeth from animals he has killed, made him a cover story subject in the *New York Times Sunday Magazine.*

Baseball fans observe a lot of this ritual behavior, such as pitchers smoothing the dirt on the mound before each new batter and position players tagging a base when leaving and returning to the dugout between innings, never realizing its importance to the player. The one ritual many fans do recognize, largely because it's a favorite of TV cameramen, is the "rally cap"—players in the dugout folding their caps and wearing them bill up in hopes of sparking a rally.

Most rituals grow out of exceptionally good performances. When a player does well, he seldom attributes his success to skill alone; he knows that his skills don't change much from day to day. So, then, what was different about today that can explain his three hits? He makes a correlation. That is, he attributes his success, in part, to an object, a food he ate, not having shaved, a new shirt he bought that day, or just about any behavior out of the ordinary. By repeating those behaviors, the player seeks to gain control over his performance, to bring more good luck. Outfielder John White explained how one of his rituals started:

> I was jogging out to centerfield after the national anthem when I picked up a scrap of paper. I got some good hits that night and I guess I decided that the paper had something to do with it. The next night I picked up a gum wrapper and had another good night at the plate . . . I've been picking up paper every night since.

When outfielder Ron Wright played for the Calgary Cannons he shaved his arms once a week. It all began two years before when he shaved his arm after an injury so it could be taped, and then hit three homers. Now he not only has one of the smoothest swings in the minor leagues, but two of the smoothest forearms. Wade Boggs's routine of eating chicken before every game began when he was a rookie in 1982 and noticed a correlation between multiple-hit games and poultry plates (his wife has 40 chicken recipes). One of Montreal Expo farmhand Mike Saccocio's rituals also concerned food: "I got three hits one night after eating at Long John Silver's. After that when we'd pull into town, my first question would be, "Do you have a Long John Silver's?" Unlike Boggs,

Saccocio abandoned his ritual and looked for a new one when he stopped hitting well.

During one game New York Yankee manager Joe Torre stood on the dugout steps instead of sitting on the bench when his team was batting. The Yankees scored a few runs, so he decided to keep on doing it. As the Yankees won nine games in a row, Torre kept standing. Torre explained, "I have a little routine going now. . . . As long as we score, I'll be doing the same thing."

When in a slump, most players make a deliberate effort to change their routines and rituals in an attempt to shake off their bad luck. One player tried taking different routes to the ballpark, another tried sitting in a different place in the dugout, another shaved his head, and several reported changing what they ate before the game. Years ago, some of my teammates rubbed their hands along the handles of the bats protruding from the bat bin in hopes of picking up some power or luck from the bats of others. I had one manager who would rattle the bat bin when the team was not hitting well, as if the bats were in a stupor and could be aroused by a good shaking. Diamondbacks left fielder Luis Gonzalez sometimes places his bats in the room where Baseball Chapel—a Sunday church service—is about to get underway. Gonzales hopes his bats will benefit, though he doesn't usually attend the service himself.

Taboo

Taboos (the word comes from a Polynesian term meaning prohibition) are the opposite of rituals. These are things you shouldn't do. Breaking a taboo, players believe, leads to undesirable consequences or bad luck. Most players observe at least a few taboos, such as never stepping on the chalk foul lines. A few, like Nomar Garciaparra, leap over the entire base path. One teammate of mine would never watch a movie on a game day, despite our playing nearly every day from April to September. Another teammate refused to read anything before a game because he believed it weakened his batting eye.

Many taboos take place off the field, out of public view. On the day a pitcher is scheduled to start, he is likely to avoid activities he believes will sap his strength and detract from his effectiveness. On the day they are to start, some pitchers avoid shaving, eating certain foods and even having sex (this nostrum is probably based on an 18th-century belief about preserving vital body fluids, but experts now agree there is no ill effect and there may actually be a small benefit). Others will not shave on the day of a game and refuse to shave again as long as they are winning. Early in one season Oakland's Dave Stewart had six consecutive victories and a beard by the time he lost.

Taboos usually grow out of exceptionally poor performances, which players, in search of a reason, attribute to a particular behavior. During my first season of pro ball I ate pancakes before a game in which I struck out three times. A few weeks later I had another terrible game, again after eating pancakes. The result was a pancake taboo: I never again ate pancakes during the season. (Conversely, after some success, Orioles pitcher Jim Palmer, insisted on eating pancakes before each of his starts.) Pitcher Jason Bere has a taboo that makes more sense in dietary terms: after eating a meatball sandwich and not pitching well, he swore them off for the rest of the season.

While most taboos are idiosyncratic, there are a few that all ballplayers hold and that do not develop out of individual experience or misfortune. These form part of the culture of baseball, and are sometimes learned as early as Little League. Mentioning a no-hitter while one is in progress is a well-known example. The origins of such shared beliefs are lost in time, though some scholars have proposed theories. For example, the taboo against stepping on the chalk foul lines when running onto or off the field between innings suggests National Baseball Hall of Fame research director Tim Wiles may be rooted in the children's superstition, "step on a crack, break your mother's back."

Fetishes

Fetishes are charms, material objects believed to embody supernatural power that can aid or protect the owner. Good-luck charms are standard equipment for some ballplayers. These include a wide assortment of objects from coins, chains, and crucifixes to a favorite baseball hat. The fetishized object may be a new possession or something a player found that coincided with the start of a streak and which he holds responsible for his good fortune. While playing in the Pacific Coast League, Alan Foster forgot his baseball shoes on a road trip and borrowed a pair from a teammate. That night he pitched a no-hitter, which he attributed to the shoes. Afterward he bought them from his teammate and they became a fetish. Expo farmhand Mark LaRosa's rock has a different origin and use:

> I found it on the field in Elmira after I had gotten bombed. It's unusual, perfectly round, and it caught my attention. I keep it to remind me of how important it is to concentrate. When I am going well I look at the rock and remember to keep my focus. The rock reminds me of what can happen when I lose my concentration.

For one season Marge Schott, former owner of the Cincinnati Reds, insisted that her field manager rub her St. Bernard "Schotzie" for good luck before each game. When the Reds were on the road, Schott would sometimes send a bag of the dog's hair to the field manager's hotel room. Religious medallions, which many Latino players wear around their necks and sometimes touch before going to the plate or mound, are also fetishes, though tied to their Roman Catholicism. Also relating to their religion, some players make the sign of the cross or bless themselves before every at bat (a few like Pudge Rodriguez do so before every pitch), and a few point or blow a kiss to the heavens after hitting a home run.

Some players regard certain uniform numbers as lucky. When Ricky Henderson came to the Blue Jays in 1993, he paid teammate Turner Ward $25,000 for the right to wear number 24. Don Sutton got off cheaper. When he joined the Dodgers he convinced teammate Bruce Boche to give up number 20 in exchange for a new set of golf clubs. Oddly enough, there is no consensus about the effect of wearing number 13. Some players shun it, while a few request it. When Jason Giambi joined the Oakland A's his favorite number 7 was already taken, so he settled for 16 (the two numbers add up to 7). When he signed with the Yankees, number 7 (Mickey Mantle's old number) was retired and 16 was taken, so he settled for 25 (again, the numbers add up to 7).

Number preferences emerge in different ways. A young player may request the number of a former star, sometimes hoping that it will bring him the same success. Or he may request a number he associates with good luck. Colorado Rockies' Larry Walker's fixation with the number 3 has become well known to baseball fans. Besides wearing 33, he takes three prac-

tice swings before stepping into the box, he showers from the third nozzle, he sets his alarm for three minutes past the hour, and he was wed on November 3 at 3:33 P.M. Fans in ballparks all across American rise from their seats for the seventh-inning stretch before the home club comes to bat because the number 7 is lucky, although the specific origin of this tradition has been lost.

Clothing, both the choice and the order in which it is put on, combines elements of both ritual and fetish. Some players put on each part of their uniform in a particular order. Expos farmhand Jim Austin always puts on his left sleeve, left pants leg, and left shoe before the right. Most players, however, single out one or two lucky articles or quirks of dress for ritual elaboration. After hitting two home runs in a game, for example, ex-Giant infielder Jim Davenport discovered that he had missed a buttonhole while dressing for the game. For the remainder of his career he left the same button undone. Phillies' Len Dykstra would discard his batting gloves if he failed to get a hit in a single at-bat. In a hitless game, he might go through four pair of gloves. For outfielder Brian Hunter the focus is shoes: "I have a pair of high tops and a pair of low tops. Whichever shoes don't get a hit that game, I switch to the other pair." At the time of our interview, he was struggling at the plate and switching shoes almost every day. For Birmingham Baron pitcher Bo Kennedy the arrangement of the different pairs of baseball shoes in his locker is critical:

> I tell the clubbies [clubhouse boys] when you hang stuff in my locker don't touch my shoes. If you bump them move them back. I want the Ponys in front, the turfs to the right, and I want them nice and neat with each pair touching each other. . . . Everyone on the team knows not to mess with my shoes when I pitch.

During hitting or winning streaks players may wear the same clothes day after day. Once I changed sweatshirts midway through the game for seven consecutive nights to keep a hitting streak going. Clothing rituals, however, can become impractical. Catcher Matt Allen was wearing a long sleeve turtleneck shirt on a cool evening in the New York-Penn League when he had a three-hit game. "I kept wearing the shirt and had a good week," he explained. "Then the weather got hot as hell, 85 degrees and muggy, but I would not take that shirt off. I wore it for another ten days—catching—and people thought I was crazy." Former Phillies, Expos, Twins, and Angels manager Gene Mauch never washed his underwear or uniform after a win. Perhaps taking a ritual to the extreme, Leo Durocher, managing the Brooklyn Dodgers to a pennant in 1941, spent three and a half weeks in the same gray slacks, blue coat, and knitted blue tie.

Former Oakland A's manager Art Howe often wouldn't wash his socks after the A's were victorious; and he would also write the lineup card with the same pen and tape the pregame radio show in the same place on the field. In the words of one veteran, "It all comes down to the philosophy of not messing with success—or deliberately messing with failure." Losing can produce the opposite effect, such as the Oakland A's players who went out and bought new street clothes in an attempt to break a 14-game losing streak.

Like most everything else, baseball's superstitions, change over time. Many of the rituals and beliefs of early baseball are no longer observed. In the 1920s-30s sportswriters reported that a player who tripped en route to the field would often retrace his steps and carefully walk over the stumbling block for "insurance." A century ago players spent time on and off the field intently looking for items that would bring them luck. To find a hairpin on the street, for example, assured a batter of hitting safely in that day's game. A few managers were known to strategically place a hairpin on the ground where a slumping player would be sure to find it. Today few women wear hairpins—a good reason the belief has died out. In the same era, Philadelphia Athletics manager Connie Mack hoped to ward off bad luck by employing a hunchback as a mascot. Hall of Famer Ty Cobb took on a young black boy as a good luck charm, even taking him on the road during the 1908 season. It was not uncommon then for players to rub the head of a black child for good luck.

To catch sight of a white horse or a wagonload of barrels was also a good omen. In 1904 the manager of the New York Giants, John McGraw, hired a driver with a team of white horses to drive past the Polo Grounds around the time his players were arriving at the ballpark. He knew that if his players saw white horses, they would have more confidence and that could only help them during the game. Belief in the power of white horses survived in a few backwaters until the 1960s. A gray-haired manager of a team I played for in Drummondville, Quebec, would drive around the countryside before important games and during the playoffs looking for a white horse. When he was successful, he would announce it to everyone in the clubhouse.

One belief that appears to have died out recently is a taboo about crossed bats. Some of my Latino teammates in the 1960s took it seriously. I still recall one Dominican player becoming agitated when another player tossed a bat from the batting cage and it landed on top of his bat. He believed that the top bat might steal hits from the lower one. In his view, bats contained a finite number of hits. It was once commonly believed that when the hits in a bat were used up, no amount of good hitting would produce any more. Hall of Famer Honus Wagner believed each bat contained only 100 hits. Regardless of the quality of the bat, he would discard it after its 100th hit. This belief would have little relevance today, in the era of light bats with thin handles—so thin that the typical modern bat is lucky to survive a dozen hits without being broken. Other superstitions about bats do survive, however. Position players on the Class A Asheville Tourists would not let pitchers touch or swing their bats, not even to warm up. Poor-hitting players, as most pitchers are, were said to pollute or weaken the bats.

While the elements in many rituals have changed over time, the reliance of players on them has not. Moreover, that reliance seems fairly impervious to advances in education.

Way back in the 1890s, in an article I found in the archives of the National Baseball Hall of Fame, one observer predicted that the current influx of better educated players into the game and the "gradual weeding out of bummers and thugs" would raise the intellectual standard of the game and reduce baseball's rampant superstitions. It didn't. I first researched baseball magic in the late 1960s; when I returned 30 years later to study the culture of baseball, I expected to find less superstition. After all, I reasoned, unlike in my playing days most of today's players have had some college. I did find that today's players are less willing to admit to having superstitions, but when I asked instead about their "routines" they described rituals and fetishes little different from my teammates in the '60s.

Uncertainty and Magic

The best evidence that players turn to rituals, taboos, and fetishes to control chance and uncertainty is found in their uneven application. They are associated mainly with pitching and hitting—the activities with the highest degree of chance—and not fielding. I met only one player who had any ritual in connection with fielding, and he was an error-prone shortstop. Unlike hitting and pitching, a fielder has almost complete control over the outcome of his performance. Once a ball has been hit in his direction, no one can intervene and ruin his chances of catching it for an out (except in the unlikely event of two fielders colliding). Compared with the pitcher or the hitter, the fielder has little to worry about. He knows that in better than 9.7 times out of 10 he will execute his task flawlessly. With odds like that there is little need for ritual.

Clearly, the rituals of American ballplayers are not unlike those of the Trobriand Islanders studied by Malinowski many years ago. In professional baseball, fielding is the equivalent of the inner lagoon while hitting and pitching are like the open sea.

While Malinowski helps us understand how ballplayers respond to chance and uncertainty, behavioral psychologist B. F. Skinner sheds light on why personal rituals get established in the first place. With a few grains of seed Skinner could get pigeons to do anything he wanted. He merely waited for the desired behavior (e.g., pecking) and then rewarded it with some food. Skinner then decided to see what would happen if pigeons were rewarded with food pellets regularly, every fifteen seconds, regardless of what they did. He found that the birds associate the arrival of the food with a particular action, such as tucking their head under a wing or walking in clockwise circles. About ten seconds after the arrival of the last pellet, a bird would begin doing whatever it associated with getting the food and keep doing it until the next pellet arrived. In short, the pigeons behaved as if their actions made the food appear. They learned to associate particular behaviors with the reward of being given seed.

Ballplayers also associate a reward—successful performance—with prior behavior. If a player touches his crucifix and then gets a hit, he may decide the gesture was responsible for his good fortune and touch his crucifix the next time he comes to the plate. Unlike pigeons, however, most ballplayers are quicker to change their rituals once they no longer seem to work. Skinner found that once a pigeon associated one of its actions with the arrival of food or water, only sporadic rewards were necessary to keep the ritual going. One pigeon, believing that hopping from side to side brought pellets into its feeding cup, hopped ten thousand times without a pellet before finally giving up. But, then, didn't Wade Boggs eat chicken before every game, through slumps and good times, for seventeen years?

Obviously the rituals and superstitions of baseball do not make a pitch travel faster or a batted ball find the gaps between the fielders, nor do the Trobriand rituals calm the seas or bring fish. What both do, however, is give their practitioners a sense of control, and with that, added confidence. And we all know how important that is. If you really believe eating chicken or hopping over the foul lines will make you a better hitter, it probably will.

Suggested Readings

Bowen, Elenore Smith [Laura Bohannan]
   1964   *Return to Laughter.* Garden City, N.Y.: Doubleday.

Colby, Benjamin N., and Lore M. Colby
   1981   *The Daykeeper: The Life and Discourse of an Ixil Diviner.* Cambridge, Mass.: Harvard University Press.

Douglas, Mary, ed.
   1970   *Witchcraft Confessions and Accusations.* London: Tavistock.

Kapferer, Bruce
 1997   *The Feast of the Sorcerer: Practices of Consciousness and Power.* Chicago: University of Chicago Press.

Orion, Loretta
 1995   *Never Again the Burning Times: Paganism Revived.* Prospect Heights, Ill.: Waveland Press.

Peek, Philip, ed.
 1991   *African Divination Systems: Ways of Knowing.* Bloomington: Indiana University Press.

Winkelman, Michael and Philip M. Peek, eds.
 2004   *Divination and Healing: Potent Vision.* Tucson: University of Arizona Press.

CHAPTER EIGHT

Ghosts, Souls, and Ancestors: Power of the Dead

Ivory pendant mask from Benin, Nigeria.

Religions universally promise believers that there is life after death. Although the worship of ancestors is not universal, a belief in the immortality of the dead occurs in all cultures. There is variation among cultures in the degree of interaction between the living and the dead, however, as well as in the intensity and concern a people may have for the deceased. Eskimos are never free of anxieties about ghosts, whereas Pueblo Indians are seldom bothered by them; the Plains Indians of North America constructed elaborate ghost beliefs, whereas the Siriono of South America, although believing in ghosts, paid little attention to them.

Perhaps humans have some basic need that causes us to believe in ghosts and to worship ancestors: to seek verification that, although the mortal body may die, the soul survives after death. The nineteenth-century sociologist Herbert Spencer speculated that the beginnings of religion were in ancestor worship—the need for the living to continue an emotional relationship with their dead relatives. A major problem with Spencer's argument is that many societies at the hunting-and-gathering level do not practice ancestor worship. The Arunta of Australia, for example, worshipped their totemic plants and animals, but not their human ancestors. This objection to Spencer's belief notwithstanding, ancestor worship does remind the living of a vital continuing link between the living and the dead. "Ritually, the most important category of animistic beings was the ancestors of the band, village, and clan or other kinship groups whose members believed they were bonded by common descent" (Harris 1989: 399).

One writer has pointed out that two major attitudes are widely held about the dead: that they either have left the society or remain as active members (Malefijt 1968: 156–59). In societies that separate the dead from the living social group, any possibility of the dead returning is regarded as undesirable because they could disrupt the social order and the daily routine of life. In such cultures, Annemarie de Waal Malefijt believes, the dead are likely to be greatly feared, and an elaborate belief system—a cult of the dead—is constructed and practiced in order to separate them from the living. The primary function of cults of the dead is to aid the survivors in overcoming the grief they may feel about the dead. Such cults are not found in societies where the dead are seen as active members of the group; instead, funeral ceremonies are undertaken with the hope the deceased will return to society in their new status. These beliefs, according to Malefijt, result in the development of ancestor cults instead of cults of the dead. S. C. Humphreys's *Comparative Perspectives on Death* (1981) sets out the great variety of belief concerning the fate of the dead, as does M. Bloch and J. Parry's work *Death and the Regeneration of Life* (1982).

Ancestor cults and the ritual that surrounds them may also be seen as an elaboration of cults of the dead. The Bantu of Africa, for example, outline distinct ancestral deities for each lineage and clan. All of these ancestral gods are gods to their living relatives, but not to individuals who belong to other kinship organizations. Further elaboration of Bantu ancestor worship may be seen in Bantu beliefs about the supernatural beings believed to head their royal clans. Gods of such royal clans are worshipped by the entire kingdom, not just the royal clan itself.

The study of ancestor worship conducted by American and British anthropologists has emphasized the connection between the identity and behavioral characteristics of the dead, on one hand, and the distribution and nature of their authority in both domestic and political domains of the society, on the other (Bradbury 1966: 127). Although the belief in ghosts of ancestors is universal, the functions ancestors play vary greatly among societies. It is also clear that variations in ancestor worship are directly related to social structure and that this relationship is not based on mere common religious interests alone: rather, the structure of the kin group and the relationships of those within it serve as the model of ancestor worship (Bradbury 1966: 128). Among the Sisala of Ghana, for example, only a select number of Sisala elders, based on their particular status and power within the group, can effectively communicate with the ghosts of ancestors (Mendonsa 1976: 63–64). In many other parts of the non-Western world, non-elder ritual specialists, such as heads of households, are responsible for contacting the ancestors. A cross-cultural study of fifty societies found that, where important decisions are made by the kin group, ancestor worship is a high probability (Swanson 1964: 97–108).

Many, but certainly not all, non-Western societies believe ancestors play a strong and positive role in the security and prosperity of their group, and anthropological data offer many of these kinds of examples. It is important, however, to recognize that ancestors are but one of several categories of spirits whose actions directly affect society. John S. Mbiti's study of East and Central Africa shows that the status of spirits may change through time. Ancestor spirits, the "living dead," are those whose memory still exists in the minds of their kin and who are primarily beneficial to the surviving relatives. When the living dead are forgotten in the memory of their group and dropped from the genealogy as a result of the passing of time (four or five generations), they are believed to be transformed into "nameless spirits," non-ancestors, characterized as malicious vehicles for misfortune of all kinds (1970). In keeping with Mbiti's model, the Lugbara of Uganda recognize two types of dead. The first group, simply called "ancestors," comprises nameless, all deceased relatives; these are secondary in importance to the recently deceased, called "ancestor spirits" or "ghosts," who can be invoked by the living to cause misfortune to befall those whose acts threaten the solidarity of the kin group (Middleton 1971: 488).

Clearly spirits, ghosts, and ancestors are often given unique statuses in the afterlife and are viewed as having different functions and effects on the living. In many respects, the relationship of fear and responsibility of elders toward ancestors is mirrored by the son-father relationship among the living. The ancestral world in many cases is an extension or a model of the real world. The supernatural status of the ancestors exhibits major differences, for, although one can argue to a point with an elder, no one questions the wisdom and authority of an ancestor.

The power of the dead is an important aspect of religion and social control. If, for example, a Lugbara man threatens the solidarity of the clan or lineage in any of a number of ways, the elder may invoke ghosts to punish the troublemaker (Middleton 1971: 488–92). Without doubt this veneration of the ancestors and the fear of their power help control many societies. Interestingly, ancestor worship also contributes to the conservative nature of those cultures where it is practiced. Typically, dead ancestors do not smile on any kind of change in the cultures of their living relatives. Because ghosts are capable of severely punishing an earthly mortal desirous of change, the force for conformity is strong.

Not all societies assign power to ancestors. In many cultures, North America included, a high god (monotheism) or gods (polytheism) exert authority over the living, punishing those who violate religious tenets, rules that often are duplicated in civil law and serve as the bases of appropriate social behavior. In these groups, ancestor cults and worship of the deceased are not found, although the spiritual nature of ancestors and belief in the afterlife persevere.

Among people where the deceased are believed to take an active role in society, the living are understandably concerned with the welfare of ancestors. Customs are established to assure the comfort of the dead in their life after death. Most commonly, rituals carried out at funerals, burials, and in some cases reburial or cremation, ensure that loved ones arrive safely at what the living believe is the proper abode of the dead. The care taken in preparing the deceased for the afterlife is an important reinforcement of the society's customs and an expression of unity among its members. Participation helps ensure that the same care can be expected to be given at the time of one's own death. Beyond this motivation, however, the power to rain down misfortunes is a major reason for carefully following customs surrounding the preparation, interment, and propitiation of the dead. No one wants to be subjected to supernatural punishment by vengeful and angry ghosts.

To most people in Western culture the word *ghost* brings forth an image of a disembodied spirit of a dead person swooping through dark halls, hovering frighteningly over a grave, or perhaps roaming aimlessly through damp woods. Typically, the ghost is observed wearing white sheets—an image that undoubtedly arises from the shroud or winding sheet used to wrap the corpse for its placement in the grave. There is a wide variety of shapes available to would-be ghosts, however. Some are transparent; some are lifelike apparitions of their former selves; others appear with horribly gaunt, empty faces, devoid of eyes and lips. Not all ghosts take a human or even vaguely human shape: horses frequently appear in phantom form, as do dogs and large birds, and ghost lore is full of accounts of ghost trains, stagecoaches, and, of course, such phantom ships as the Flying Dutchman.

Very few cultures do not support the idea of a separate spirit world—a land of the dead. It is to this other world that souls will travel and, once there, will rest in eternal peace. At some point in history, however, the notion arose that not all souls deserve an easy trip to a blissful spiritual world. Murderers, miscreants, and evil people, for example, might become ghosts doomed to wander the earthly world. Inadequate funerals also might give rise to restless ghosts, thus explaining the attention paid by cultures everywhere to meticulously preparing and dressing the corpse for burial and to placing gifts, food, and weapons in the grave or at the gravesite to enhance the spirit's journey to the place of eternal rest.

In the first selection, Paul Barber vividly illustrates the fear with which eighteenth-century Europeans regarded vampires.

Karen McCarthy Brown examines the practice of Vodou in Haiti, pointing out that, despite the distorted popular version we see all too frequently in the mass media, it is a legitimate religious practice of 80 to 90 percent of Haitians.

In the third selection, Peter A. Metcalf compares American and Berawan funeral rites. As Metcalf learned to see Berawan funerary customs as natural, American treatment of the dead began to seem exotic.

In the final article, Stanley Brandes describes the cross-cultural complexities arising from the death of an immigrant Guatemalan living in the United States and the individual's subsequent cremation. Brandes notes that the cremation was an unthinkable end for a deceased person in the individual's home village in Guatemala.

References

Bloch, M., and J. Parry, eds.
1982 *Death and Regeneration of Life.* Cambridge: Cambridge University Press.

Bradbury, R. E.
1966 "Fathers, Elders, and Ghosts in Edo Religion." In Michael Banton, ed., *Anthropological Approaches to the Supernatural*, pp. 127–53. London: Tavistock.

Harris, Marvin
1989 *Our Kind.* New York: Harper and Row.

Humphreys, S. C.
1981 *Comparative Perspectives on Death.* New York: Academic Press.

Malefijt, Annemarie de Waal
1968 *Religion and Culture: An Introduction to Anthropology of Religion.* New York: Macmillan.

Mbiti, John S.
1970 *African Religions and Philosophies.* Garden City, N.Y.: Doubleday.

Mendonsa, Eugene L.
1976 "Elders, Office-Holders and Ancestors Among the Sisala of Northern Ghana." *Africa* 46: 57–64.

Middleton, John
1971 "The Cult of the Dead: Ancestors and Ghosts." In William A. Lessa and Evon Z. Vogt, eds., *Reader in Comparative Religion: An Anthropological Approach*, 3rd ed., pp. 488–92. New York: Harper and Row.

Swanson, Guy A.
1964 *The Birth of the Gods.* Ann Arbor: University of Michigan Press.

39

The Real Vampire

Paul Barber

Tales of the undead in eighteenth-century Europe were preeminent in establishing the folklore of the vampire, a figure whose bloodlust struck stark terror into the hearts of believers of that day. Images of evil of such magnitude die hard. Bram Stoker's novel introduced the horrors of vampiric attack to the rest of the world through the character of Count Dracula, later immortalized on the American screen in the 1930s by Bela Lugosi. However, to many eighteenth-century Europeans, vampires were not fictional; they were real and accounted for deaths due to contagion in a world that had no theory of communicable disease. Paul Barber's forensic evidence provides a physiological basis for the belief that the dead could return from the grave, for Europeans then believed that any corpse having what they considered an abnormal or peculiar condition was most certainly a vampire. But the sociological explanations for the existence of vampires and the techniques for protecting themselves from them are equally provocative. One protective measure was the act of consuming the blood of a vampire, thereby invoking the elementary concept of similia similiis curantur *(similar things are cured by similar things), a rationale commonly found in folklore.*

Personal characteristics attributed to those with the potential to become vampires are amazing, like the characteristics of those accused of witchcraft today—for example, in Africa. Like the witches of Africa, vampires of Europe had the ability to leave the body and attack their victims unseen and, like witches, vampires were responsible for a wide variety of everyday, rather pedestrian misfortunes. Clearly, the human propensity to create monstrous mental images, such as vampires, responsible for misfortunes of such an extreme caliber as death, was and is common and functions as an explanation of the unexplainable. The negative effects on society, however, of the dysfunctional aspects of fear and accusation resulting from these mystical types of explanations cannot be discounted.

I saw the Count lying within the box upon the earth, some of which the rude falling from the cart had scattered over him. He was deathly pale, just like a waxen image, and the red eyes glared with the horrible vindictive look which I knew too well. . . .

The eyes saw the sinking sun, and the look of hate in them turned to triumph.

But, on the instant, came the sweep and flash of Jonathan's great knife. I shrieked as I saw it shear through the throat; whilst at the same moment Mr. Morris's bowie knife plunged into the heart.

It was like a miracle; but before our very eyes, and almost in the drawing of a breath, the whole body crumbled into dust and passed from our sight.

—Bram Stoker, *Dracula*

If a typical vampire of folklore were to come to your house this Halloween, you might open the door to encounter a plump Slavic fellow with long finger-nails and a stubbly beard, his mouth and left eye open, his face ruddy and swollen. He would wear informal attire—a linen shroud—and he would look for all the world like a disheveled peasant.

If you did not recognize him, it would be because you expected to see—as would most people today—a tall, elegant gentleman in a black cloak. But that would be the vampire of fiction—the count, the villain of Bram Stoker's novel and countless modern movies, based more or less on Vlad Tepes, a figure in Romanian history who was a prince, not a count; ruled in Walachia, not Transylvania; and was never viewed by the local populace as a vampire. Nor would he be recognized as one, bearing so little resemblance to the original Slavic revenant (one who returns from the dead)—the one actually called *upir* or *vampir.* But in folklore, the undead are seemingly everywhere in the world, in a variety of disparate cultures. They are people who, having died before their time, are believed to return to life to bring death to their friends and neighbors.

We know the European version of the vampire best and have a number of eyewitness accounts telling of the "killing" of bodies believed to be vampires. When we read these reports carefully and compare their findings with what is now known about forensic pathology, we can see why people believed that corpses came to life and returned to wreak havoc on the local population.

Europeans of the early 1700s showed a great deal of interest in the subject of the vampire. According to the *Oxford English Dictionary*, the word itself entered the English language in 1734, at a time when many books were being written on the subject, especially in Germany.

One reason for all the excitement was the Treaty of Passarowitz (1718), by which parts of Serbia and Walachia were turned over to Austria. The occupying forces, which remained there until 1739, began to notice, and file reports on, a peculiar local practice: exhuming bodies and "killing" them. Literate outsiders began to attend such exhumations. The vampire craze was an early "media event," in which educated Europeans became aware of practices that were by no means of recent origin.

In the early 1730s, a group of Austrian medical officers were sent to the Serbian village of Medvegia to investigate some very strange accounts. A number of

people in the village had died recently, and the villagers blamed the deaths on vampires. The first of these vampires, they said, had been a man named Arnold Paole, who had died some years before (by falling off a hay wagon) and had come back to haunt the living.

To the villagers, Paole's vampirism was clear: When they dug up his corpse, "they found that he was quite complete and undecayed, and that fresh blood had flowed from his eyes, nose, mouth, and ears; that the shirt, the covering, and the coffin were completely bloody; that the old nails on his hands and feet, along with the skin, had fallen off, and that new ones had grown; and since they saw from this that he was a true vampire, they drove a stake through his heart, according to their custom, whereby he gave an audible groan and bled copiously."

This new offensive by the vampires—the one that drew the medical officers to Medvegia—included an attack on a woman named Stanacka, who "lay down to sleep fifteen days ago, fresh and healthy, but at midnight she started up out of her sleep with a terrible cry, fearful and trembling, and complained that she had been throttled by the son of a Haiduk by the name of Milloe, who had died nine weeks earlier, whereupon she had experienced a great pain in the chest and became worse hour by hour, until finally she died on the third day."

In their report, *Visum et Repertum* (Seen and Discovered), the officers told not only what they had heard from the villagers but also, in admirable clinical detail, what they themselves had seen when they exhumed and dissected the bodies of the supposed victims of the vampire. Of one corpse, the authors observed, "After the opening of the body there was found in the *cavitate pectoris* a quantity of fresh extravascular blood. The *vasa* [vessels] of the *arteriae* and *venae*, like the *ventriculis cordis*, were not, as is usual, filled with coagulated blood, and the whole *viscera*, that is, the *pulmo* [lung], *hepar* [liver], *stomachus, lien* [spleen], *et intestina* were quite fresh as they would be in a healthy person." But while baffled by the events, the medical officers did not venture opinions as to their meaning.

Modern scholars generally disregard such accounts—and we have many of them—because they invariably contain "facts" that are not believable, such as the claim that the dead Arnold Paole, exhumed forty days after his burial, groaned when a stake was driven into him. If that is untrue—and it surely seems self-evident that it must be untrue—then the rest of the account seems suspect.

Yet these stories invariably contain detail that could only be known by someone who had exhumed a decomposing body. The flaking away of the skin described in the account of Arnold Paole is a phenomenon that forensic pathologists refer to as "skin slippage." Also, pathologists say that it is no surprise that Paole's "nails had fallen away," for that too is a normal event. (The Egyptians knew this and dealt with it either by tying the nails onto the mummified corpse or by attaching them with little golden thimbles.) The reference to "new nails" is presumably the interpretation of the glossy nail bed underneath the old nails.

Such observations are inconvenient if the vampire lore is considered as something made up out of whole cloth. But since the exhumations actually took place, then the question must be, how did our sources come to the conclusions they came to? That issue is obscured by two centuries of fictional vampires, who are much better known than the folkloric variety. A few distinctions are in order.

The folklore of the vampire comes from peasant cultures across most of Europe. As it happens, the best evidence of actual exhumations is from Eastern Europe, where the Eastern Orthodox church showed a greater tolerance for pagan traditions than the Catholic church in Western Europe.

The fictional vampire, owing to the massive influence of Bram Stoker's *Dracula*, moved away from its humble origin. (Imagine Count Dracula—in formal evening wear—undergoing his first death by falling off a hay wagon.)

Most fiction shows only one means of achieving the state of vampirism: people become vampires by being bitten by one. Typically, the vampire looms over the victim dramatically, then bites into the neck to suck blood. When vampires and revenants in European folklore suck blood—and many do not—they bite their victims somewhere on the thorax. Among the Kashubes, a Slavic people of northern Europe, vampires chose the area of the left breast; among the Russians, they left a small wound in the area of the heart; and in Danzing (now Gdansk), they bit the victim's nipples.

People commonly believed that those who were different, unpopular, or great sinners returned from the dead. Accounts from Russia tell of people who were unearthed merely because while alive they were alcoholics. A more universal category is the suicide. Partly because of their potential for returning from the dead or for drawing their nearest and dearest into the grave after them, suicides were refused burial in churchyards.

One author lists the categories of revenants by disposition as "the godless [people of different faiths are included], evildoers, suicides, sorcerers, witches, and werewolves; among the Bulgarians the group is expanded by robbers, highwaymen, arsonists, prostitutes, deceitful and treacherous barmaids and other dishonorable people."

A very common belief, reported not only from Eastern Europe but also from China, holds that a person may become a revenant when an animal jumps over him. In Romania there is a belief that a bat can transform a corpse into a vampire by flying over it. This circumstance deserves remark if only because of its rarity, for as important as bats are in the fiction of vampires, they are generally unimportant in the folklore. Bats came into vampire fiction by a circuitous route: the vampire bat of Central and South America was named after the vampire of folklore, because it sucks (or rather laps up) blood after biting its victim. The bat was then assimilated into the fiction: the modern (fictional) vampire is apt to transform himself into a bat and fly off to seek his victims.

Potential revenants could often be identified at birth, usually by some defect, as when (among the Poles of Upper Silesia and the Kashubes) a child was born with teeth or a split lower lip or features viewed as somehow bestial—for example, hair or a taillike extension of the spine. A child born with a red caul, or amniotic membrane, covering its head was regarded as a potential vampire.

The color red is related to the undead. Decomposing corpses often acquire a ruddy color, and this was generally taken for evidence of vampirism. Thus, the folkloric vampire is never pale, as one would expect of a corpse; his face is commonly described as florid or of a healthy color or dark, and this may be attributed to his habit of drinking blood. (The Serbians, referring to a redfaced, hard-drinking man, assert that he is "blood red as a vampire.")

In various parts of Europe, vampires, or revenants, were held responsible for any number of untoward events. They tipped over Gypsy caravans in Serbia, made loud noises on the frozen sod roofs of houses in Iceland (supposedly by beating their heels against them), caused epidemics, cast spells on crops, brought on rain and hail, and made cows go dry. All these activities attributed to vampires do occur: storms and scourges come and go, crops don't always thrive, cows do go dry. Indeed, the vampire's crimes are persistently "real-life" events. The issue often is not whether an event occurred but why it was attributed to the machinations of the vampire, an often invisible villain.

Bodies continue to be active long after death, but we moderns distinguish between two types of activity: that which we bring about by our will (in life) and that which is caused by other entities, such as microorganisms (in death). Because we regard only the former as "our" activity, the body's posthumous movements, changes in dimension, or the like are not real for us, since we do not will them. For the most part, however, our ancestors made no such distinction. To them, if after death the body changed in color, moved, bled, and so on (as it does), then it continued to experience a kind of life. Our view of death has made it difficult for us to understand earlier views, which are often quite pragmatic.

Much of what a corpse "does" results from misunderstood processes of decomposition. Only in detective novels does this process proceed at a predictable rate. So when a body that had seemingly failed to decompose came to the attention of the populace, theories explaining the apparent anomaly were likely to spring into being. (Note that when a saint's body failed to decompose it was a miracle, but when the body of an unpopular person failed to decompose it was because he was a vampire.) But while those who exhumed the bodies of suspected vampires invariably noted what they believed was the lack of decomposition, they almost always presented evidence that the body really was decomposing. In the literature, I have so far found only two instances of exhumations that failed to yield a "vampire." (With so many options, the body almost certainly will do something unexpected, hence scary, such as showing blood at the lips.) Our natural bias, then as now, is for the dramatic and the exotic, so that an exhumation that did not yield a vampire could be expected to be an early dropout from the folklore and hence the literature.

But however mythical the vampire was, the corpses that were taken for vampires were very real. And many of the mysteries of vampire lore clear up when we examine the legal and medical evidence surrounding these exhumations. "Not without astonishment," says an observer at the exhumation of a Serbian vampire in 1725, "I saw some fresh blood in his mouth, which, according to the common observation, he had sucked from the people killed by him." Similarly, in *Visum et Repertum*, we are told that the people exhuming one body were surprised by a "plumpness" they asserted had come to the corpse in the grave. Our sources deduced a cause-and-effect relationship from these two observations. The vampire was larger than he was because he was full to bursting with the fresh blood of his victims.

The observations are clinically accurate: as a corpse decomposes, it normally bloats (from the gases given off by decomposition), while the pressure from the bloating causes blood from the lungs to emerge at the mouth. The blood is real, it just didn't come from "victims" of the deceased.

But how was it that Arnold Paole, exhumed forty days after his death, groaned when his exhumers drove a stake into him? The peasants of Medvegia assumed that if the corpse groaned, it must still be alive. But a corpse does emit sounds, even when it is only moved, let alone if a stake were driven into it. This is because the compression of the chest cavity forces air past the glottis, causing a sound similar in quality and origin to the groan or cry of a living person. Pathologists shown such accounts point out that a corpse that did not emit such sounds when a stake was driven into it would be unusual.

To vampire killers who are digging up a corpse, anything unexpected is taken for evidence of vampirism. Calmet, an eighteenth-century French ecclesiastic, described people digging up corpses "to see if they can find any of the usual marks which leads them to conjecture that they are the parties who molest the living, as the mobility and suppleness of the limbs, the fluidity of the blood, and the flesh remaining uncorrupted." A vampire, in other words, is a corpse that lacks rigor mortis, has fluid blood, and has not decomposed. As it happens, these distinctions do not narrow the field very much: Rigor mortis is a temporary condition, liquid blood is not at all unusual in a corpse (hence the "copious bleeding" mentioned in the account of Arnold Paole), and burial slows down decomposition drastically (by a factor of eight, according to a standard textbook on forensic pathology). This being the case, exhumations often yielded a corpse that nicely fit the local model of what a vampire was.

None of this explains yet another phenomenon of the vampire lore—the attack itself. To get to his victim, the vampire is often said to emerge at night from a tiny hole in the grave, in a form that is invisible to most people (sorcerers have made a good living tracking down and killing such vampires). The modern reader may reject out of hand the hypothesis that a dead man, visible or not, crawled out of his grave and attacked the young woman Stanacka as related in *Visum et Repertum*. Yet in other respects, these accounts have been quite accurate.

Note the sequence of events: Stanacka is asleep, the attack takes place, and she wakes up. Since Stanacka was asleep during the attack, we can only conclude that we are looking at a culturally conditioned interpretation of a nightmare—a real event with a fanciful interpretation.

The vampire does have two forms: one of them the body in the grave; the other—and this is the mobile one—the image, or "double," which here appears as a dream. While we interpret this as an event that takes place within the mind of the dreamer, in nonliterate cultures the dream is more commonly viewed as either an invasion by the spirits of whatever is dreamed about (and these can include the dead) or evidence that the dreamer's soul is taking a nocturnal journey.

In many cultures, the soul is only rather casually attached to its body, as is demonstrated by its habit of leaving the body entirely during sleep or unconsciousness or death. The changes that occur during such conditions—the lack of responsiveness, the cessation or slowing of breathing and pulse—are attributed to the soul's departure. When the soul is identified with the image of the body, it may make periodic forays into the minds of others when they dream. The image is the essence of the person, and its presence in the mind of another is evidence that body and soul are separated. Thus, one reason that the dead are believed to live on is that their image can appear in people's dreams and memories even after death. For this reason some cultures consider it unwise to awaken someone suddenly: he may be dreaming, and his soul may not have a chance to

return before he awakens, in which case he will die. In European folklore, the dream was viewed as a visit from the person dreamed about. (The vampire is not the only personification of the dream: the Slavic *mora* is a living being whose soul goes out of the body at night, leaving it as if dead. The *mora* first puts men to sleep, and then frightens them with dreams, chokes them, and sucks their blood. Etymologically, *mora* is cognate with the *mare* of nightmare, with German *Mahr*, and with the second syllable of the French *cauchemar*.)

When Stanacka claimed she was attacked by Milloe, she was neither lying nor even making an especially startling accusation. Her subsequent death (probably from some form of epidemic disease; others in the village were dying too) was sufficient proof to her friends and relatives that she had in fact been attacked by a dead man, just as she had said.

This is why our sources tell us seemingly contradictory facts about the vampire. His body does not have to leave the grave to attack the living, yet the evidence of the attack—the blood he has sucked from his victims—is to be seen on the body. At one and the same time he can be both in the grave in his physical form and out of it in his spirit form. Like the fictional vampire, the vampire of folklore must remain in his grave part of the time—during the day—but with few exceptions, folkloric vampires do not travel far from their home towns.

And while the fictional vampire disintegrates once staked, the folkloric vampire can prove much more troublesome. One account tells that "in order to free themselves from this plague, the people dug the body up, drove a consecrated nail into its head and a stake through its heart. Nonetheless, that did not help: the murdered man came back each night." In many of these cases, vampires were cremated as well as staked.

In Eastern Europe the fear of being killed by a vampire was quite real, and the people devised ways to protect themselves from attacks. One of the sources of protection was the blood of the supposed vampire, which was baked in bread, painted on the potential victim, or even mixed with brandy and drunk. (According to *Visum et Repertum*, Arnold Paole had once smeared himself with the blood of a vampire—that is, a corpse—for protection.) The rationale behind this is a common one in folklore, expressed in the saying "similia similiis curantur" (similar things are cured by similar things). Even so, it is a bit of a shock to find that our best evidence suggests that it was the human beings who drank the blood of the "vampires," and not the other way around.

Perhaps foremost among the reasons for the urgency with which vampires were sought—and found—was sheer terror. To understand its intensity we need only recall the realities that faced our informants. Around them people were dying in clusters, by agencies that they did not understand. As they were well aware, death could be extremely contagious: if a neighbor died, they might be next. They were afraid of nothing less than death itself. For among many cultures it was death that was thought to be passed around, not viruses and bacteria. Contagion was meaningful and deliberate, and its patterns were based on values and vendettas, not on genetic predisposition or the domestic accommodations of the plague-spreading rat fleas. Death came from the dead who, through jealousy, anger, or longing, sought to bring the living into their realm. And to prevent this, the living attempted to neutralize or propitiate the dead until the dead became powerless—not only when they stopped entering dreams but also when their bodies stopped changing and were reduced to inert bones. This whole phenomenon is hard for us to understand because although death is as inescapable today as it was then, we no longer personify its causes.

In recent history, the closest parallel to this situation may be seen in the AIDS epidemic, which has caused a great deal of fear, even panic, among people who, for the time being at least, know little about the nature of the disease. In California, for instance, there was an attempt to pass a law requiring the quarantine of AIDS victims. Doubtless the fear will die down if we gain control over the disease—but what would it be like to live in a civilization in which all diseases were just as mysterious? Presumably one would learn—as was done in Europe in past centuries—to shun the dead as potential bearers of death.

40

Vodou

Karen McCarthy Brown

It is likely that no other topic in this book is as misunderstood as the religious practices of Haiti known as Vodou. Sensationalized popular culture and travelers' accounts have been merciless in delivering to the public a highly distorted picture of Haitian religious life. In this article, Karen McCarthy Brown explains that Vodou, often misspelled as Voodoo, is an African-based religion that serves several categories of spiritual beings through elaborate ceremonies and a loosely organized priesthood of both men and women. The country's dominant Roman Catholicism co-exists with Vodou, and a majority of Haitians comfortably follow both religions. Several prominent Haitian political leaders of the 20th century have been known for their strong involvement with Vodou, and as Brown explains here, Vodou plays a vital role in the large Haitian immigrant communities of North America.

Haiti, Vodou, and other examples of African-based culture in the Americas have received lively attention from anthropologists. Exemplary ethnographic works include E. Wade Davis's account of secret Vodou societies, The Serpent and the Rainbow *(1985), and Karen McCarthy Brown's own study of an individual healer-priestess in New York,* Mama Lola: A Vodou Priestess in Brooklyn *(1991, 2001).*

Vodou is a sometimes misleading, but nevertheless common, name for the religious practices of the majority of Haitians. Outsiders have given the name Vodou to the complex web of traditional religious practices followed in Haiti. Only recently, and still to a limited extent, have Haitians come to use the term as others do. Haitians prefer a verb to identify their religion: they speak of "serving the spirits."

A mountainous, poverty-stricken, largely agricultural country of approximately eight million people, Haiti has a land area of 10,700 square miles and occupies the western third of the island of Hispaniola, which it shares with the Dominican Republic.

This is where Caribbean Vodou began, but Haiti is not the only place Vodou is practiced. Vodou is also a central part of everyday life in Haitian diaspora communities in New Orleans and Santiago, Cuba, both products of the upheaval caused by the Haitian Revolution (1791–1804). More recent political and economic struggles in Haiti have also led to Vodou communities in New York City, Miami, Montreal, and Paris.

In Haiti, *vodou* originally referred to one ritual style among many in their syncretic religious system, the style most closely connected to Dahomey and the Fon language. The word *vodou* is derived from the Fon *vodun*, which means "god" or "spirit." *Hoodoo* is a related term from the same Fon word, yet, in the United States, it is almost always used as a derogatory term that focuses on black magic spells and charms.

Sensationalized novels and films, as well as spurious travelers' accounts, have painted a negative picture of Haitian religion. Vodou has been depicted as primitive and ignorant. Vodou rituals have been described as arenas for uncontrolled orgiastic behavior, and even cannibalism. The same writers stir up fear of Vodou and suggest that if whites get too close to a Vodou ceremony terrible things could happen. These distortions are attributable to the fear that the Haitian slave revolution sparked in whites. Haiti achieved independence in 1804, and thus became the first black republic in the Western Hemisphere at a time when the colonial economy was still heavily dependent on slave labor.

In Vodou there are three (not always clearly distinguished) categories of spiritual beings: *lemò*, *lemistè*, and *lemarasa* (respectively, "the dead," "the mysteries," and "the sacred twins"). While certain Vodou prayers, songs, and invocations preserve fragments of West African languages, Haitian Creole is the primary language of Vodou. Creole is the first and only language of more than one half the population of Haiti. It has a grammatical structure familiar to speakers of West African languages and an eighteenth-century French vocabulary mixed with a smattering of English words and expressions.

Although individuals and families regularly serve the Vodou spirits without recourse to religious professionals, throughout most of Haiti there is a loosely organized priesthood open to both men and women. The male priest is known as an *oungan* and the female priest is a *manbo*. There is a wide spectrum of Vodou ritualizing. There are individual acts of piety, such as lighting candles to petition particular spirits, and elaborate feasts, sometimes lasting days and including the sacrifice of several animals as part of the meals offered to the spirits. Energetic singing, dancing, and polyrhythmic drumming accompany the larger rituals. In the countryside, rituals often take place outdoors, on family land set aside for the spirits, and there is often a small cult house on that land where the family's altars are kept. Urban Vodou rituals tend to take place in an *ounfò* ("temple"). Urban altars, dense with sacrificial food and drink, sacred stones, and chromolithographs of the Catholic saints and other images, are maintained in *jèvo* ("altar rooms") off the central dancing and ritualizing space of the temple, the *peristyl*. In the cities, those who serve the spirits also tend to keep more modest altars in their own homes.

The goal of Vodou drumming, singing, and dancing is to *chofè*, to "heat up," the situation sufficiently to bring on possession by the spirits. As a particular spirit is summoned, a devotee enters a trance and becomes that spirit's *chwal* ("horse"), thus providing the means for direct communication between human beings and the spirits. The spirit is said to ride the *chwal*. Using the person's body and voice, the spirit sings, dances, and eats with the people and also deals out advice and chastisement. The people in turn offer the spirit a wide variety of gifts and acts of obeisance, the goal being to placate the spirit and ensure his or her continuing protection.

There are marked differences in Vodou as it is practiced throughout Haiti, but the single most important distinction is that between urban and rural Vodou. Haitian society is primarily agricultural, and the manner in which peasants serve the spirits is determined by questions of land tenure and ancestral inheritance. Urban Vodou is not tied to specific plots of land, but the family connection persists in another form. Urban temple communities become substitutes for the extended families of the countryside. The priests are called "papa" and "mama"; the initiates, who are called "children of the house" or "little leaves" refer to one another as "brother" and "sister." In general, urban Vodou is more institutionalized and often more elaborate in its rituals than its rural counterpart.

African Influence

Haiti's slave population was built up in the eighteenth century, a period in which Haiti supplied a large percentage of the sugar consumed in Western Europe. Vodou was born on sugar, sisal, cotton and coffee plantations out of the interaction among slaves who brought with them a variety of African religious traditions, but due to inadequate records, little is known about this formative period in Vodou's history. It has been argued by Haitian scholars such as Michel-Rolph Trouillot that the religion did not coalesce until after the revolution, but others suggest it had an effective presence, particularly in northern Haiti, during the latter part of the eighteenth century. James G. Leyburn in *The Haitian People* (1941) and Carolyn Fick in *The Making of Haiti* (1990) argue that Vodou played a key role in the organization of the slave revolt.

Among the African ethnic groups brought to Haiti as slave laborers, the most influential in shaping Haitian culture, including Vodou, were the Fon,

Mahi, and Nago from old Dahomey (the present Republic of Benin), those who came to be known as the Yoruba (Nigeria), and Kongo peoples (Angola, and the Democratic Republic of the Congo). Many of the names of Vodou spirits are easily traceable to their African counterparts; however, the spirits have undergone change in the context of Haiti's social and economic history. For example, Ogun among the Yoruba is a spirit of ironsmithing and other activities associated with metal, such as hunting, warfare, and modern technology. Neither hunting nor modern technology plays much of a role in the lives of Haitians. Haiti, however, does have a long and complex military history. Thus, the Haitian spirit Ogou is first and foremost a soldier whose rituals, iconography, and possession-performance explore both the constructive and destructive uses of military power, as well as its analogues with human relations—anger, self-assertion, and willfulness.

Africa itself is a powerful concept in Vodou. Haitians speak of Ginen ("Guinea") both as their ancestral home, the Guinea coast of West Africa, and as the watery subterranean home of the Vodou spirits. Calling a spirit *franginen* ("fully and completely African") is a way of indicating that the spirit is good, ancient, and proper. The manner in which an individual or a group serves the spirits may also be called *franginen,* with similar connotations of approval and propriety.

Roman Catholic Influence

For the most part, the slaveholders were Catholics and baptism for slaves was mandatory by French law. Many have argued that slaves used a veneer of Catholicism to hide their traditional religious practices from the authorities. While Catholicism may well have functioned in this utilitarian way for slaves on plantations, it is also true that the religions of West Africa from which Vodou was derived, already had a tradition of borrowing the deities of neighbors and enemies alike. Whatever Catholicism represented in the slave world, it was most likely also used as a means to expand Vodou's ritual vocabulary and iconography, thus helping captive laborers function in a nominally Catholic world. In 1804, immediately after Haiti declared its liberation, the Catholic Church withdrew all of its clergy from the new republic. Yet Catholicism survived in Haiti

for fifty years without contact with Rome and it did so through the imitative ritualizing of a Vodou figure known as *prêtsavan* ("bush priest") as well as the competitive market for healing charms and talismans that was kept going by defrocked Catholic priests and the self-appointed "clergy" who ended up in Haiti in the early nineteenth century.

Catholicism has had the greatest influence on the traditional religion of Haiti at the level of rite and image rather than theology. This influence works in two ways. First, those who serve the spirits call themselves Catholic, attend Mass, and undergo baptism and first communion. Because these Catholic rituals at times function as integral parts of larger Vodou rites, they can be even directed to participate by their Vodou spirits. Second, Catholic prayers, rites, images, and saints' names are integrated into the common ritualizing of Vodou temples. The prêtsavan is an active figure in Vodou. He achieves his title by knowing the proper, that is the Latin or French, form of Catholic prayers.

Over the years, a system of parallels has been developed between the Vodou spirits and the Catholic saints. For example, Dambala, the ancient and venerable snake deity of the Fon people, is venerated in Haiti both as Dambala and as St. Patrick, who is pictured in the popular chromolithograph with snakes clustered around his feet. In addition, the Catholic liturgical calendar dominates in much Vodou ritualizing. Thus the Vodou spirit Ogou is honored in Haiti and in the Haitian diaspora on July 25, the feast day of his Catholic counterpart.

Bondye, "the good God" is identified with the Christian God, and is said to be the highest, indeed the only, god. The spirits are said to have been angels in Lucifer's army whom God sent out of heaven and down to Ginen. Although the Vodou spirits may exhibit capricious behavior, they are not evil. Rather, they are seen as intermediaries between the people and the high god, a role identical to the one played by the so-called lesser deities in the religions of the Yoruba and Fon. Bondye is remote and unknowable. Although evoked daily in ordinary speech (almost all plans are made with the disclaimer *si dye vle* ("if God wills"), Bondye's intervention is not sought for help with life's problems. That is the work of the spirits.

Both the Catholic Church in Haiti and the government of Haiti have participated energetically in the persecution of those who serve the Vodou spirits. The last "antisuperstition campaign" was in the 1940s, but clerical and upperclass disdain for the religion has persisted much longer. In the twentieth century, Catholic clergy routinely preached against serving the spirits, and those who served them remarked, "That is the way priests talk." Many Catholic holy days have a Vodou dimension that church officials routinely manage to ignore.

For years Catholicism was the only religion in Haiti with official approval. Thus, the degree to which Vodou has been attacked, oppressed, tolerated, or even encouraged through the years has been largely a function of local politics. Presidents Dumarsais Estime (1946–1950) and Francois Duvalier (1957–1971) stand out from other Haitian heads of state because of their sympathy with Vodou. Jean-Bertrand Aristide, who was first elected president in 1990, was also a supporter of Vodou; in fact he changed the balance of religious power. On April 5, 2003, President Aristide fully recognized and fully empowered Vodou as a Haitian religion that could legally exercise its influence throughout Haiti according to the constitution and the laws of the republic.

Vodou Spirits

The Vodou spirits are known by various names: *lwa*, a common name with an uncertain origin; *sen*, "saints"; *mistè*, "mysteries"; *envizib*, "invisibles"; and more rarely, *zanj*, "angels." At some point in the development of Vodou the spirits were sorted into *nanchon*, "nations." The nanchon at an early point in their development appear to have functioned primarily as ethnic slave categories. The majority of the nation names are easily traceable to places in Africa: Rada, Ibo, Nago, Kongo. Later, however, these so-called nations became religious categories, diverse ritual styles of drumming, dancing, and honoring the Vodou spirits.

The Rada spirits (named after the Dahomean principality Allada, once a busy slave depot) comprise a collection of ancient, sweet-tempered, wise, and usually patient *lwa*. Then there are the fiery and powerful Petwo spirits. The origin of the name "Petwo" is contested, but the strong Kongo influence is not. The home of the Ogou, also hot spirits, is the Nago *nanchon*, a Dahomean name for Ketu Yoruba. Most big feasts end with the playful Gede, inveterate

rule breakers, who insist they are a *fami* ("family"), not a *nanchon*. In rural Vodou, a person may inherit responsibilities to one or more of these *nanchon* through maternal or paternal kin. Familial connections to the land, where the *lwa* are said to reside in trees, springs, and wells, may determine which particular spirits are served. In urban Vodou, there are a few important spirit *nanchon* that make their appearance, according to seniority and importance, in most major rituals. In Port-au-Prince, two *nanchon*, the Rada and the Petwo, have emerged as dominant largely by absorbing other *nanchon*. Rada and Petwo spirits contrast sharply. The Rada are *dous*, "sweet," and the Petwo, *cho*, "hot." When an individual, family, or temple is described as ritualizing in a mode that is *Rada net* ("straight Rada"), a great deal is being said about how that person or group functions socially as well as ritualistically. Each spirit has drum rhythms, dances, and food preferences that relate to its identifying characteristics. For example, Danbala, the gentle Rada snake spirit, is said to love *orja*, thick sugary almond syrup. His devotees perform a graceful spine-rippling dance called *yanvalu*. By contrast, the Petwo rhythm played for rum-drinking spirits is energetic and pounding, and the accompanying dance is characterized by fast, strong body movements.

The Vodou View of Person

In Vodou teachings the human being is composed of various parts: the body, that is, the gross physical dimension of the person who perishes after death, in addition to two to four souls, of which the most widely acknowledged are the *gwo bonanj*, and *ti bonanj*. The *gwo bonanj* ("big guardian angel") is roughly equivalent to consciousness or personality. When a person dies the *gwo bonanj* lingers, and immediately after death it must be protected because it is most vulnerable to capture and misuse by sorcerers. During possession, it is the *gwo bonanj* who is displaced by the spirit and sent to wander away from the body, as it does routinely during sleep. The *ti bonanj* ("little guardian angel") may be thought of as the spiritual energy reserve of a living person and, at times, as the ghost of a dead person.

Each person has one special *lwa* who is their *mèt-tet*, "master of the head." (The top of the head and the back of the neck are places where spirits may enter and leave.) The *mèt-tet* is the most important *lwa* served by a particular person and it reflects that person's personality to some degree. A Haitian whose family serves the spirits may inherit spiritual responsibilities to a deceased family member's *mèt-tet*. That is a big responsibility, but there are also things that can be gained. If the *mèt-tet* is conscientiously fed and honored, good luck and protection from both ancestor and *lwa* will be gained. In addition to the so-called masters of the head, most people who serve the spirits have a small number of other *lwa* with whom similar reciprocity has been established.

Unlike Catholic saints who are usually known through formulaic hagiography, Vodou *lwa* have richly developed histories, personalities, needs, desires, character strengths, and flaws, and even taste in food and drink. Because the *lwa* are fully developed characters and interact so intimately with *vivan-yo*, "the living," the practice of Vodou also functions as a system for categorizing and analyzing human behavior, in the individual and in the group. One of the characteristics of virtually all Caribbean African-based religions is the great amount of care given to analyzing social behavior and dealing with the results of that behavior.

Vodou and the Dead

Cemeteries are major ritual centers in both urban and rural Haiti. The first male buried in any cemetery is known as Bawon Samidi. Bawon's wife (or sister) is Gran Brijit, the first woman buried in the cemetery. Most cemeteries have a cross for Bawon either in the center of the cemetery or near its gate. Lakwa Bawon ("Bawon's Cross") marks the site's ritual center. Lighted candles and food offerings are left at the base of this cross. People stand with their hands on the cross praying aloud. Rituals for healing, love, or luck performed in rural cult houses or urban temples are not considered complete until physical remnants of the "work" are deposited at crossroads or at Bawon's Cross, which is itself a kind of crossroads marking the intersection of the land of the living and the land of the dead.

Haitians who serve the *lwa* usually make a clear distinction between the dead and the spirits. Yet a few of the ancestors, particularly if they were exceptional people when alive, actually evolve into spirits or *lwa*. Jean-Jacques Dessalines, Toussaint L'Ouverture, and John Kennedy have all been reported making cameo appearances through possession in Vodou ceremonies. The group of spirits, known as the Gede, have Bawon as their leader and are spirits of the dead as might be expected, but they are not ancestral spirits. Instead, they stand in for the entire community of human beings now deceased and in this context, Gede's crude comic performances make some sense. They are designed to bring the naughty to their knees and convince them that in the end, human beings all face the same fate. The Gede are inclusive, with no limits, and therefore almost any image will work on a Gede altar. Statues of the Buddha, Lao Tzu, King Kong, St. Gerard, and Elvis Presley have all been sighted on Vodou altars. In and around Port-au-Prince, the capital of Haiti and its largest city, the Gede are the object of elaborate ritualizing in the cemeteries and Vodou temples during the season of the Feast of All Souls, Halloween.

The Gede are not only spirits of death but also boosters of human sexuality, protectors of children, and irrepressible social satirists. Dances for Gede tend to be boisterous affairs, and new Gede spirits appear every year. The satirical, and often explicitly sexual, humor of the Gede levels social pretense. The Gede use humor to deal with new social roles and to challenge alienating social structures. Through possession-performance, they not only appear as auto mechanics and doctors, they also critique government bureaucrats, military figures, and Protestant missionaries.

Vodou Ceremonies

In some parts of rural Haiti, the ideal Vodou ceremony is one that serves the spirits as simply as possible because simplicity is said to reflect discrete but strong spiritual power, the African way of doing things (Larose, 1977). In practice, rural ritualizing tends to follow the fortunes of extended families. Bad times are often attributed to the displeasure of family spirits. When it is no longer possible to satisfy the spirits with small conciliatory offerings, the family will hold a large drumming and dancing feast that includes animal sacrifice. Urban Vodou, by contrast, has a more routine ritualizing calendar, and events tend to be larger and more elaborate. Ceremonies in honor of major spirits take place annually on or around the feast days of their Catholic counterparts and usually include sacrifice of an appropriate animal—most frequently a chicken, a goat, or a cow.

In both rural and urban settings, a rich variety of ceremonies meet specific individual and community needs: For example, healing rites, dedications of new temples and new ritual regalia, and spirit marriages in which a devotee is wed to a spirit usually of the opposite sex and must pledge sexual restraint one night each week, when he or she receives that spirit in dreams. There is also a cycle of initiation rituals that has both public segments and segments reserved for initiates. The latter include the *kanzo* rituals, which mark the first stage of initiation into Vodou, and those in which the adept takes the *ason,* the beaded gourd rattle symbolizing Vodou priesthood. Certain rituals performed during the initiation cycle, such as the *bule zen* ("burning the pots") and the *chirè ayzan* ("shredding the palm leaf") may also be used in other ritual contexts. Death rituals include the *desounen,* in which the soul is removed from the corpse and sent under the waters of Ginen, which is followed by the *wète mò nan dlo* ("bringing the dead from the waters"), a ritual that can occur only after a person has been dead for one year and one day. Herbal good-luck baths are routinely administered during the Christmas and New Year season. Elizabeth McAlister's 2002 book on Rara has convinced scholars, in the habit of dismissing Rara as an entertaining aspect of Carnival, of the deeply religious character of these irreverent parades that pour from the Vodou temples into the cemeteries and streets during the Catholic Lent.

Annual pilgrimages draw thousands of urban and rural followers of Vodou. The focal point of these Catholic-Vodou events is often a church situated near some striking feature of the natural landscape that is sacred to the *lwa.* The two largest pilgrimages are one held for Ezili Danto (Our Lady of Mount Carmel) in mid-July in the small town of Saut d'Eau, named for its spectacular waterfall, and one held for Ogou (St. James the Elder) in the latter part of July in the northern town of Plain du Nord, where a shallow, muddy pool adjacent to the Catholic church is dedicated to Ogou.

Vodou and Magic

Serge Larose (1977) has demonstrated that magic is not only a stereotypic label that outsiders have applied to Vodou, but also a differential term internal to the religion. Thus an in-group among the followers of Vodou identifies its own ritualizing as "African" while labeling the work of the out-group as *maji* ("magic"). Generally speaking, this perspective provides a helpful way to grasp the concept of magic within Vodou. There are, however, those individuals who, in search of power and wealth, self-consciously identify themselves with traditions of what Haitians would call "the work of the left hand." This includes people who deal in *pwen achte* ("purchased power points"), which means spirits or powers that have been bought rather than inherited, and people who deal in *zonbi.* A *zonbi* may be either the disembodied soul of a dead person whose powers are captured and used for magical purposes, or a soulless body that has been raised from the grave to do drone labor in the fields. Also included in the category of the left hand are secret societies known by such names as Champwel, Zobop, Bizango, and Zanglando. In urban settings in the late twentieth century secret societies began to operate as if they were a branch of the Mafia, but their deep history is quite different: They once represented religiously enforced rural law and order. The secret societies were groups of elders who used their power not for personal gains but to enforce social sanctions. For example, Wade Davis (1985) says that *zonbi* laborers were created by secret society tribunals who voted to use *zonbi* powder against a sociopath in their community.

The "work of the left hand" should not be confused with more ordinary Vodou ritualizing that can have a magical flavor, such as divination, herbal healing, and the manufacture of *wanga,* charms for love, luck, or health, or for the protection of the home, land, or person. Much of the work of Vodou priests is at the level of individual client-practitioner interactions. Theirs is a healing system that treats problems of love, health, family, and work. Unless a problem is understood as coming from God, in which case the Vodou priest can do nothing, the priest will treat it as one caused by a spirit or by a disruption in human relationships, including relations with the dead. Generally speaking, Vodou cures come about through ritual adjustment of relational systems.

Vodou in the Haitian Diaspora

Drought and soil erosion, poverty, high urban unemployment, and political oppression have led to massive emigrations from Haiti in the last half-century. Vodou has gone along with the Haitians who, in search of a better life, have come to major urban centers of North America. In New York, Miami, and Montreal, the cities with the greatest concentrations of Haitian immigrants, Vodou ceremonies are carried on in storefronts, rented rooms, high-rise apartments, and basement storage areas. North American rituals are often somewhat truncated versions of their Haitian counterparts. There may be no drums, and the only animals sacrificed may be chickens.

However it is possible to consult a manbo or oungan in immigrant communities with ease, and the full repertoire of rituals can be followed there, in one form or another. Even the pilgrimages are duplicated. On 16 July, rather than going to the mountain town of Saut d'Eau to honor Ezili Danto, New York Vodou practitioners take the subway to the Italian-American Church of Our Lady of Mount Carmel in East Harlem.

41

Death Be Not Strange

Peter A. Metcalf

In this article, Peter A. Metcalf compares American and Berawan funeral and mortuary rites and shows why Western practices so shocked the Berawan. To the Berawan, we trap the deceased in a suspended condition between life and death, producing evil, not beneficent spirits. "For the Berawan, America is a land carpeted with potential zombies." Metcalf's fieldwork not only explains the fate of the Berawan dead and demonstrates their beliefs to be as coherent and reasonable as any but also draws attention to the exotic nature of American funerary practices. His comparison reminds us that our level of ethnocentrism both leads us to view the beliefs of others as illogical and sometimes reprehensible and causes us to ignore our own death rituals and practices.

The popular view of anthropology is that it is concerned with faraway places, strange peoples, and odd customs. This notion was neatly captured by a nineteenth-century wit who described the field as "the pursuit of the exotic by the eccentric." In recent decades many anthropologists have tried to shake this image. They see the exotic as dangerously close to the sensational and, therefore, a threat to the respectability of a serious academic discipline. They argue that anthropology has solid theoretical bases, and that some anthropologists routinely work in cities right here in America. And they are right. Nevertheless, anthropologists are as much involved with the exotic as ever, and I think that this concern actually works to scholarship's advantage.

This continuing involvement is a result of the characteristic *modus operandi* of anthropologists. First, we seek out the exotic, in the sense of something originating in another country or something "strikingly or excitingly different," as my *Webster's* puts it. Second, we try to fit this alien item—culture trait, custom, piece of behavior—into its social and cultural context, thereby reducing it to a logical, sensible,

even necessary element. Having done that, we feel that we can understand why people do or say or think something instead of being divorced from them by what they say, think, or do.

Sir James Frazer, whose classic study of primitive religions, *The Golden Bough*, was first published in 1890, provides an excellent example of the eccentric in pursuit of the exotic. For him, the process of reducing the mysterious to the commonplace was the very hallmark of scientific progress. Like many anthropologists of his time, Frazer assumed that some societies were superior and others inferior, and that anthropology's main task was to describe how the latter had evolved into the former. To Frazer, Europe's technological achievements were proof of social, intellectual, and moral superiority. The dominance of the West represented the triumph of science, which in Frazer's evolutionary schema, superseded even the most rational of world religions. Science's clear light was to shine far and wide, driving superstition, the supernatural, and even God himself back into shadows and dimly lit corners.

But Frazer might have found a second aspect of the anthropological *modus operandi* less to his taste. In the course of making sense of someone else's behavior or ideas, we frequently begin to observe our own customs from a new angle. Indeed, this reflexive objectivity is often acclaimed as one of the great

"Death Be Not Strange" by Peter A. Metcalf reprinted from NATURAL HISTORY, June–July 1978, pp. 6–12; copyright © Natural History Magazine, Inc., 1978.

advantages of our methods and cited as a major justification for the long, expensive physical and psychic journeys that we make, seeking out societies far removed from our own cultural traditions. Less often remarked upon, however, is that the exotic possesses its own reflexive quality. As we learn to think of other people's ways as natural, we simultaneously begin to see our own as strange. In this sense, anthropologists import the exotic, and that, I suppose, puts us on the side of the angels.

An incident that occurred about four years ago during my field work in north-central Borneo brought home to me the depth and subtlety of anthropologists' involvement with the exotic. I was working with the Berawan, a small tribe comprising four communities, each made up of several hundred people living in a massive wooden longhouse. The four longhouses stand beside the great rivers that are the only routes into the interior of Borneo. Berawan communities live on fish and on rice planted in clearings cut anew in the rain forest each year. In the late nineteenth century, which was a stormy period of tribal warfare, each longhouse was a fortress as well as a home, and the Berawan look back with pride on the military traditions of that era.

Among the things that interested me about the Berawan were their funeral rites, which involve what anthropologists call "secondary burial," although the Berawan do not usually bury the dead at all. Full rites consist of four stages: the first and third involve ritual preparation of the corpse; the second and fourth make up steps in storage of the remains. The first stage, lasting two to ten days, consists of rites performed immediately after death. During the second stage, the bereaved family stores the corpse in the longhouse or on a simple platform in the graveyard. This storage lasts at least eight months and sometimes for several years if the close kin cannot immediately afford to complete the expensive final stages. Third, if the corpse has been in the graveyard, the family brings it back to the longhouse, where it is kept for six to ten days, while the family lavishly entertains guests who have been summoned from far and wide. Finally, the remains are removed to a final resting place, an impressively proportioned mausoleum.

Within this four-part plan, details of the corpse's treatment vary considerably. During the first storage stage, the family may place the corpse in a large earthenware jar or in a massive coffin hewn from a single tree trunk. For secondary storage, the family may use a valuable glazed jar or the coffin left over from the first stage. During the third-stage rites, the family may take out the bones of the deceased and clean them. As the corpse decomposes, its secretions may be collected in a special vessel. Some neighbors of the Berawan reportedly consume liquids of decomposition mixed with rice—a variety of endocannibalism.

For anthropologists, this intimate interaction with the corpse is certainly exotic. For Americans not professionally trained in the niceties of cultural relativism, Berawan burial is no doubt disgusting: keeping corpses around the house, shuttling them between the graveyard and the longhouse, storing them above ground instead of burying them, manipulating the bones, and, to Western eyes, paying macabre attention to the process of decay itself. My Berawan informants were aware that some phases of their ritual bothered Europeans. They soon learned, moreover, that I had a lot of questions about their funerals. One of the pleasures of working in Borneo is that people soon begin to cross-examine their interviewer. They are as curious about the stranger as he or she is about them. So before long, they began to quiz me about the death ways of my country.

On one memorable occasion, during a lull in ritual activity, I responded to one of these questions by outlining American embalming practices—the treatment of the corpse with preservative fluids and its display in an open coffin. I was well into my story, concentrating on finding the right words to describe this unfamiliar topic, when I became aware that a sudden silence had fallen over my audience. They asked a number of hesitant questions just to be sure that they had understood me correctly and drew away from me in disgust when they found that they had. So shocked were they that I had to backtrack rapidly and change my story. The topic was never broached again.

At the time, I did not understand why American embalming practices had so unnerved the Berawan. Now, having thought about the meaning of Berawan death rituals, I think that I do understand.

The death rituals of central Borneo early attracted the interest of explorers and ethnologists. In 1907, Robert Hertz, a young student of French sociologist Emile Durkheim, wrote an essay about these rites that has become a classic. Never having set foot in Borneo, Hertz relied on the accounts of travelers. Had he not been killed during the First World War, he might well have undertaken firsthand research himself. Nevertheless, his analysis is still routinely cited in discussions and comparisons of funeral customs. Yet, oddly, Hertz's central thesis has received very little attention. Hertz hypothesized that peoples who practice secondary burial have certain beliefs about the afterlife, namely, that the fate of the body provides a model for the fate of the soul.

Since Hertz did not know of the Berawan, they provided me with an appropriate test case for his hypothesis. I collected data on everything related to Berawan death rites: the people involved, mourning practices, related rituals, myths and beliefs, and so on. I also pressed my informants for interpretations of rituals. All the material I accumulated revealed a consistent set of ideas very similar to those described by Hertz. The Berawan believe that after death the soul is divorced from the body and cannot reanimate the already decaying corpse. However, the soul cannot enter the land of the dead because it is not yet a perfect spirit. To become one of the truly dead, it must undergo a metamorphosis. As the body rots away to leave dry bones, so the soul is transformed slowly into spirit form. As the corpse is formless and repulsive until putrefaction is completed, so the soul is homeless. It lurks miserably on the fringes of human habitation and, in its discomfort, may affect the living with illness. The third stage of the mortuary sequence, which Hertz called the "great feast," marks the end of this miserable period. The soul finally passes to the land of the dead, and the mortal remains of the deceased join those of its ancestors in the tomb.

But before this happy conclusion is reached, the hovering soul is feared because it may cause more death. Even more dread surrounds the body itself, caused not by the process of rotting, for that releases the soul of the deceased from the bonds of the flesh, but by the possibility that some malignant spirit of nonhuman origin will succeed in reanimating the corpse. Should this occur, the result will be a monster of nightmarish mien, invulnerable to the weapons of men, since it is already dead.

I once witnessed an incident that dramatically demonstrated how real is the Berawan fear of reanimated corpses. Toward sunset, a group of mourners

and guests were chatting casually beside a coffin that was being displayed on the longhouse veranda in preparation for primary storage. Suddenly there was a tapping sound, apparently from inside the coffin. The noise could have come from the house timbers, contracting in the cool of the evening, but the people present saw a different explanation. After a moment of shock, the women fled, carrying their children. Some panic-stricken men grabbed up what weapons were handy, while others tied up the coffin lid with yet more bands of rattan. Calm was not restored until later in the evening when a shaman investigated and declared that nothing was amiss.

We can now see why American mortuary practices so shock the Berawan. By delaying the decomposition of corpses, we commit a most unnatural act. First, we seem to be trying to trap our nearest and dearest in the unhappiest condition possible, neither alive nor in the radiant land of the dead. Second, and even more perverse and terrifying, we keep an army of undecomposed corpses, each and every one subject to reanimation by a host of evil spirits. For the Berawan, America is a land carpeted with potential zombies.

After a couple of years of field work, and an application of the ideas of Hertz and others, I can offer a relatively full account of Berawan death ways: what they express about Berawan notions of life and death; how they are manipulated by influential men in their struggles for power; how they relate to their sense of identity, art forms, and oral history. Meanwhile, I have also explored the literature on American death ways—and have found it wanting. For the most part, it is restricted to consideration of psychological variables—how people react to death, either the possibility of their own or that of close relatives and friends. None of these studies begins to explain why American funerals are the way they are; why they differ from British funerals, for instance.

Jessica Mitford, author of *The American Way of Death*, tried to explain the form that American funerals take by arguing that they are a product of the death industry's political power. But Mitford's theory does not explain the tacit support that Americans give to this institution, why successive immigrant groups have adopted it, or why reform movements have failed.

I have tried to relate American practices to popular ideas about the nature of a fulfilling life and a proper death. Despite these intellectual efforts, I am left with a prickly sense of estrangement. For, in fact, I had spared my Berawan friends the more gruesome details of embalming: replacement of the blood with perfumed formaldehyde and other chemicals; removal of the soft organs of the chest and abdomen via a long hollow needle attached to a vacuum pump; injection of inert materials. I did not mention the American undertaker's elaborate restorative techniques: the stitching up of mutilated corpses, plumping out of emaciated corpses with extra injections of waxes, or careful cosmetic care of hands and face. Nor did I tell the Berawan about the padded coffins, grave clothes ranging in style from business suits to negligees, and other funeral paraphernalia. Had I explained all this, their shock might have been transformed into curiosity, and they might have reversed our roles of social scientist and informant.

In the meantime, something of their reaction has rubbed off on me. I have reduced the celebrated mortuary rites of remote and mysterious Borneo to a kind of workaday straightforwardness, only to be struck by the exotic character of an institution in our very midst.

42

The Cremated Catholic:
The Ends of a Deceased
Guatemalan

Stanley Brandes

In this selection, Stanley Brandes describes the cross-cultural complexities arising from the accidental death of an immigrant Guatemalan living in the San Francisco Bay Area. The deceased, given the pseudonym "Axel Flores" by Brandes, could be buried in the Bay Area, cremated with the ashes disposed locally, or cremated with the ashes shipped to Guatemala. The most expensive option was to send the corpse back home for burial. Axel's father in Guatemala immediately rejected cremation, believing it was necessary to have his son's recognizable presence at the wake. A disintegrated body was unthinkable. The father insisted that his son's corpse be returned home and given the traditional ceremonies of his native village and those sanctioned by the Catholic Church. The story quickly became further complicated when Axel's sister, living in San Francisco, discovered not only that the San Mateo county coroner had confused her brother's body with that of another recently deceased man but also that the body had been sent to a funeral home and cremated. Because of his knowledge of Latino cultures, Professor Brandes was hired as a researcher and consultant by the lawyer representing Axel's family. Brandes discusses the ensuing legal suit by Axel's family against San Mateo County and the funeral home, observing that the complex legal proceedings demonstrate the globalization of liability claims and the monetary value of a mishandled corpse. As part of his research on the case, Brandes visited Axel's village in Guatemala and learned why the family so strongly resented cremation, noting especially the family's concern over the deceased's destiny in the afterlife and their own status within the village. Further complications discussed by Brandes involve the differing beliefs about cremation held by Roman Catholic teachings, the Guatemalan Catholic clergy, and village parishioners.

Stories about the commodification of dead bodies are generally sad and this one is no exception. The body in question belongs to a 31-year-old Latino

Stanley Brandes, "The Cremated Catholic: The Ends of a Deceased Guatemalan," *BODY AND SOCIETY, vol. 7 (2–3), 2001, pp. 111–20. Reprinted by permission of Sage Publications, Incorporated.*

migrant to the San Francisco Bay Area. On the night of 11 December 1994, in the city of Brisbane and for still unclear motives, the man strolled onto a busy highway, where he was hit by a car and instantly killed. His body was brought to the San Mateo County Morgue and was identified as that of Axel Flores, my pseudonym for this Guatemalan, who had come to the USA, among other reasons, to escape from dangers presented him by the civil war then raging in his native land. At the time of his death, Axel had already established a police record in northern California, a circumstance which facilitated his ready identification through fingerprints.

Axel's sister, residing in San Francisco, was immediately notified of the accident. She consulted with her parish priest, who reviewed her options and informed her that cremation was the least expensive choice. She then telephoned her father in Nahualtenango—the name I give to the small village near the southwest coast of Guatemala, where most of Axel's family still resides—to explain the alternatives to him and find out how he wanted her to dispose of the body. Axel could be buried in the San Francisco Bay Area, cremated with the remains shipped to Guatemala for burial, or cremated and the ashes disposed of locally. By far the most expensive alternative was to send Axel's corpse to Nahualtenango for burial.

When presented these alternatives, Axel's father immediately rejected cremation as utterly unthinkable. Despite the enormous cost, he insisted that the corpse should be returned to Nahualtenango intact so that his son could undergo the proper mortuary ceremonies—that is, ceremonies traditional to Nahualtenango and those commonly believed to be sanctioned by the Church. In order to follow through on this decision, Axel's father mortgaged his simple house and borrowed money at high interest from a moneylender in order to secure the necessary funds on short notice. Back in San Francisco, Axel's sister arranged to collect the body from the morgue and ship it to Guatemala. When she arrived to identify the body, however, she was presented first with one, then another cadaver, neither of which was Axel's. Investigation revealed that the County Coroner had confused Axel's body with that of another recently deceased man. (The Coroner's office explained feebly that both men were heavy and dark-skinned.) Axel's body, released to a funeral parlor several days earlier under the incorrect name, was accidentally cremated before the error could be detected. A thoroughly irreversible mistake had occurred. This case precipitated a legal suit by Axel's family against both San Mateo County and the funeral parlor. The funeral parlor settled with the family out of court. The complaint against San Mateo County, however, remains unresolved because the US embassy has refused to issue visas to the deceased's family to

travel to California for deposition. Until Axel's aggrieved relatives can make their depositions, the case can come to no final resolution.

The lawsuit of Axel's family against a funeral parlor and a California county morgue demonstrates globalization of liability claims as well as the potential monetary value of a mishandled corpse. US lawyers representing the family have asked for a total of $300,000 from the two defendant agencies. The plaintiffs' mediation brief states that:

> Under California law, a decedent's family and heirs have sole authority over the disposition of the remains following a death. Plaintiffs' authority in this regard was violated through a chain of errors, oversight and insufficient safeguards. . . . Beyond a doubt, the law holds that persons situated such as plaintiffs have standing to assert a claim for damages due to the mishandling of a corpse. Quesada v. Oak Hill Improvement Co. (1989) . . . establishes that individuals, entities and businesses engaged in the practice of handling a decedent's remains owe a duty to persons such as plaintiffs, and can be held liable for the negligent mishandling of a decedent's remains.

The monetary claims of Axel's family are, nonetheless, somewhat unusual. As the plaintiffs' mediation brief itself explains, "We are presented with a situation that is relatively rare in our practice—a case where the sole damages are for emotional distress."

The plaintiffs, Axel's father and siblings, claim that his accidental cremation has caused undue hardship and suffering. They harbor two interrelated concerns: first, Axel's destiny in the afterlife, and, second, their own status within Nahualtenango. Consider first Axel's presumed destiny. In Guatemala, say family members, the very idea of cremation is repulsive. "It's the way you treat a dog," states Axel's older brother, Genaro. Moreover, it is "a sin," says one of Axel's sisters; it is sinful not only for those who carried out the deed, but also for Axel himself, despite his innocence in the matter. There is no doubt in the minds of Axel's entire family that he will be barred forever from heaven. *Está sufriendo el alma*—"His soul is suffering," they claim. In the body's cremated state, the soul can never find release. Cremation itself is sufficient to prevent salvation.

The family adheres strongly to this belief, even though it controverts Roman Catholic teachings. In fact, since the Second Vatican Council in the mid-1960s, cremation has been permitted. It is also fair to say, however, that it has never been encouraged. The extreme infrequency of cremation in Latin America perhaps explains why clergy themselves are uncertain about its legitimacy. When Axel's family approached their parish priest with the confidential news that he had been cremated, the priest was stymied and forced to display his ignorance of Church policy. Catholic law requires that a *misa del cuerpo presente*—a Mass of the Present Body—be celebrated the day after a person dies. But, in the absence of the intact body, could the Mass of the Present Body be recited? The family had held a wake in Axel's father's home. However, it was a highly unconventional wake, taking place several weeks after death had occurred and in the absence of a corpse. Unwilling to risk making a decision contrary to Church teachings, the parish priest decided against celebrating the Mass of the Present Body. Subsequently, however, he did celebrate two additional customary Masses: one commemorating 40 days after death, the other commemorating the first anniversary of the death.

As a researcher on this legal case, I consulted with the two parish priests of Santo Tomás in nearby Chichicastenango, who agreed that, despite the concerns of Axel's family, cremation would not automatically bar the deceased from entering heaven. One of them replied matter-of-factly, "How can we ever know who will enter heaven and who not?" Nor had the priests heard of a single instance of cremation in all of Guatemala, despite the incontrovertible presence of crematoriums. In fact, crematoriums, a recent introduction into the country, advertise on Guatemalan television and radio. To promote business, they use the airwaves to combat popular claims that the Catholic Church opposes cremation.

Padre Alberto, the older of the two Chichicastenango priests, vigorously denounced these commercials as false advertising. At the beginning of our interview, he steadfastly maintained that the Church always has and still does oppose cremation. Only after being challenged by Padre Rodolfo, his younger, more learned colleague, did he waver. "As far as I know," said Padre Alberto, "the Church neither opposes nor approves of cremation. It has never said anything about the matter." Padre Roberto is well informed about Church policy; as we sit here today he is in Rome, probably being groomed for a high-level Church post. Even he, however, is beset by uncertainty. For example, he was wrong about his estimation of when cremation became legal. "Surely it came in with the present Pope," he said. Nor can he define authoritatively proper mortuary proceedings in a case like Axel's. He would only speculate that, when cremation occurs, the Mass of the Present Body should be celebrated prior to actual incineration.

If this interview indicates the general state of affairs in provincial Guatemala, is it any wonder that Axel's family flatly rejects cremation? In 1997—exactly 34 years after the Vatican legitimized cremation—the Guatemalan clergy still shows utter unfamiliarity with how the cremated body should be treated. This circumstance clearly undermines the time-honored anthropological distinction between religious orthodoxy and popular belief (Badone, 1990). A "two-tiered" approach to religion (Brown, 1981), in which the unreflective beliefs of the superstitious but devout masses are distinguished from the religious teachings of an erudite clergy, is entirely inapplicable to the case. With regard to cremation, the Guatemalan clergy seem as ignorant about procedure as do their poorly educated parishioners.

But, according to Axel's family, his destiny in the afterlife depends upon more than adherence to proper ritual. The very disintegration of his body, that his body has lost its wholeness, is equally threatening. During my brief visit to Nahualtenango, Axel's brother Genaro reiterated numerous times the statement from the Creed, which is recited in every Mass: "*Se levantarán los muertos,*" "The dead shall rise again." Genaro shrugs his shoulders and throws out his arms in despair as he asks, "How can Axel be resurrected if there is no body?" Genaro is not alone in his desperation. The anxiety provoked by the material discontinuity of the body is a familiar theme in Roman Catholic tradition, a tradition in which venerated body parts—foreskins and fingernails and strands of hair—nonetheless populate churches throughout Christendom.

Practically from the time of Saint Augustine, says Caroline Walker Bynum, "Scholastic theologians worried not about whether body was crucial to human nature, but about how part related to whole—that is, how bits could and would be reintegrated after scattering and decay" (Bynum, 1992: 253–54). In the 2nd and 3rd centuries, Christians fretted over the power of God to reinstate the divided body so that it could be properly resurrected (Bynum, 1992: 267–68). Although educated writers expressed confidence that the maimed bodies of saints would achieve salvation, "Ordinary believers . . . often went to extraordinary lengths to collect and reassemble the dismembered pieces of the martyrs for burial" (Bynum, 1992: 268). By the Middle Ages, states Bynum (1992: 272), "So highly charged was bodily partition that torturers were forbidden to effect it; they were permitted to squeeze and twist and stretch in excruciating ways, but not to sever or divide." Bodily fragmentation was so horrifying that theologians opposed cremation and physicans 'tried to preserve corpses forever from crumbling and putrefaction' (1992: 280). "Drawing and quartering, or burning (that is reduction to the smallest possible particles: ashes), were punishments reserved for treason, witchcraft and heresy" (1992: 276). Remarkably, these concerns endure to the present day. They are what inform contemporary Guatemalan mortuary beliefs and are the cause of Axel's family unremitting suffering.

But the family is tormented about more than Axel's fate. Concerned about their social status within Nahualtenango, they have struggled to keep Axel's shameful cremation a secret. Even I was implicated in this ultimately futile effort. While watching a soccer match one Sunday morning, Axel's brother introduced me to the village pharmacist, his closest friend and confidant in Nahualtenango. When the pharmacist asked why I had come so far, I almost confessed my true mission: to gather information on behalf of the lawyer representing Axel's family. Stopping short in my reply, I simply stated that I knew Axel's sister in California and she suggested that on my visit to Guatemala I stop at Nahualtenango personally to convey her greetings. By hiding my real motive, I was attempting to protect the family reputation. Only later did I discover that the pharmacist also knows about the cremation and was disguising his knowledge. A former neighbor and close friend of the family is informed too, and has been sworn to secrecy. One can only guess the extent to which the community at large is aware of what happened to their native son, Axel, during his self-imposed California exile. In recounting the reaction of the community to Axel's death, Genaro claims that everyone asked the family, "And the body? Where is the body? When will it arrive?" The family had recourse to only one excuse: they could not afford the expense of bringing Axel home. To make such an admission, in the context of Nahualtenango, is itself

shameful. And yet the family saw no alternative. The cremated remains might have been transported easily and inexpensively to Guatemala for burial. But this is an option that neither the family nor the community would find even minimally acceptable. A disintegrated body, in their view, is not only unworthy of Christian burial, it is unidentifiable. "How would we know that those ashes are Axel's?," the family asked. Their skepticism is entirely understandable. After all, if rich, powerful Californians could be so careless as to cremate the wrong corpse, there is little hope that they can properly sort human ashes.

To understand why cremation is an unacceptable alternative to the people of Nahualtenango, more than religious conviction and social status must be taken into account. After all, the family admits, with some reluctance but unmistakable certainty, that even without cremation, Axel might never have entered heaven. He had lived in an unmarried state with several women, two of whom gave birth to his children. This circumstance is sufficient to have compromised his destiny. The real crime of the San Mateo County Morgue is to have deprived his surviving relatives of his bodily presence. His recognizable presence was needed at the wake, during which villagers would have gathered at his home to help the family mourn the loss. His recognizable presence was needed for the Mass of the Present Body and for the burial that would have followed. His recognizable presence was even more urgently necessary for his mother, ailing at home in Nahualtenango in an advanced state of cancerous decay. When she died, only a few months after Axel, her quick demise was attributed to the fact that she never got to view Axel's corpse, rather than to her son's passing. For those who have survived the loss of mother and son, the greatest agony of all is Axel's absence from the village cemetery. Without his bodily presence, there is no way of relieving one's grief by visiting his grave and praying for his eternal soul. In Nahualtenango, visits to deceased relatives are normal on three occasions: 40 days after the death, a year after the death, and annually during All Souls and All Saints days, on 1 and 2 November. It is primarily in order to celebrate these occasions, to be near his son, that Axel's father was willing to go to such financial sacrifice to return the body to its proper resting place.

It is 20 July 1997, two and a half years after Axel's death. I walk with Axel's father, with his common-law son, with his siblings and their respective families from one end of the village to the other until we arrive at the Nahualtenango cemetery. As we enter holy ground, Axel's brother stops short, looks at me with penetrating eyes, and says, "*Esta es nuestra última morada. Aquí es donde venimos a parar todos [los del pueblo]. Esten donde esten, aquí vienen a parar*"—"This is our final abode. Here is where all of us from the village come to rest. Wherever we may be, here we come to rest." Indeed, the cemetery has the aspect of a miniature village, filled with hundreds of small houses decorated with miniature towers and gables. The graves stretch out in long, evenly spaced, parallel rows, a virtual replica of the grid plan town of the living residents of Nahualtenango. The graves themselves are brightly colored crypts, painted in the vivid purples, yellows, blues, oranges and maroons of the village houses themselves. The deceased lie, not below ground, but in cement sepulchers, many of them piled on top of one another, resting adjacent to one another, like so many cramped living quarters, in the fashion of pueblo houses. Nahualtenango tombs are reminiscent of small apartment buildings, where deceased members of a family congregate in eternal companionship. They bear nothing of the somber quality of most graves in Europe and the USA.

Axel's brother walks me to his mother's lonely grave, a low-lying concrete structure painted sky blue. Poking up out of each corner are tall steel construction poles, evidence that yet another crypt is meant to lie on top of this one. "Axel would have been here," says the brother, pointing to his mother's tomb. "She's dead," he says, "but at least she is here. We can come to visit her." His following statement is disarming. "*Esta panteón es alegría*"—"This cemetery is happiness."

At that moment, Robert Hertz's (1960) classic insights assumed immediate significance. Death does not occur when the heart stops beating; rather, the deceased retains a presence among the living for years after the actual physical demise. In Nahualtenango, the intact corpse is an enduring presence, a being that enjoys its own happy home in holy ground, forever accompanied by loving relatives, both dead and alive. Cremation, the drastic fragmentation of the body into its most minimal parts, deprives both the deceased and the survivors of everlasting companionship. The dead body which retains its wholeness remains connected to others, integrated within society. Societal integrity depends upon the integrity of the cadaver. It is the cremated body that is doomed forever to exist alone and that

provokes a tragic separation from the survivors. This irremediable loneliness constitutes the true agony of Axel and his family. It is the reason why, years after his death, there seems no sign of solace, nor is solace likely soon to come.

There is no doubt that Axel's death has exacted a steep emotional price from his family. And yet, it produced an immediate economic impact as well. Axel fathered a son by a woman from whom he is separated and whom he never legally married. With neither parent able to care for the child, Axel placed the boy in his father's care. The father, himself recently widowed, received regular payments from Axel, which he used to sustain both the boy and himself. These payments terminated abruptly upon Axel's death, thereby leaving the father with the responsibility of caring for his grandson but without adequate means to do so. "The situation doesn't allow me to support the son," says Axel's father gravely. Not only did Axel's father suddenly cease to receive remittances from abroad, in order to adhere to his community's religious guidelines, he was also forced to sacrifice his limited assets in order to bring Axel's body home. On the day we first met, he stated to me:

> When this terrible news [of Axel's death] arrived, I was filled with pain [from his wife's mortal illness]. . . . Well, there was no longer any money, señor. I mortgaged my house, because I desperately wanted to bring him home. . . . I had to put myself in debt, míster, I had to put myself in debt in order to wait for my son's arrival. I had to find the way to borrow money, Axel's mother was gravely ill.

To add to these financial problems, Axel's father became gravely ill. The cause for this illness is no doubt complex. It is safe to say, however, that the stress of his wife and son's almost simultaneous deaths must have aggravated his already poor state of health. At least he is convinced that Axel's death has had an adverse effect. As proof of his frailty, within minutes of meeting me he pulled out a large bag of medicine and counted the items one by one: 22 cardboard boxes, glass bottles and plastic containers in all. "This medicine costs a lot of money as well," he said.

Axel's death therefore exacted a high price from his Guatemalan relatives. The cremated corpse would cause eternal suffering for Axel's soul, forever unable to find heavenly peace. It would produce shame beyond anyone's imagining for Axel's family, unable to explain to the community of Nahualtenango the corpse's mysterious disappearance. Also, knowledge of the cremation was held responsible for hastening the mother's departure from this world. But Axel's cremated body, precisely because it received treatment contrary to the family's wishes, might justify the kind of monetary compensation that instantaneously would confer fabulous wealth upon any member of the family, in local terms. Indeed, the family might reasonably expect financial compensation. In recent years, in the San Francisco Bay Area alone, at least 62 people have won between $10,000 and $250,000 in lawsuits involving the careless mixing of ashes in local crematoriums (Anonymous, 1996; Holding, 1996). According to a newspaper report:

> The plaintiffs claimed that Pleasant Hill [Cemetery Inc.] had caused them severe emotional distress by cremating their relatives' bodies with those of others, dumping remains in existing graves and failing to return all the ashes. They also accused the cemetery of trying to hide its mistakes. (Holding, 1996: A12)

In one case alone—*Hansell v. Pleasant Hill Cemetery*—plaintiffs' attorney Kevin McInerney was reported to seek more than $2.5 million in fees. "You do these cases, and you hope to make a lot of money," stated McInerney, whose earnings in class action suits against crematoriums already amount to $25 million (Fried, 1998). In further cases, disclosure was made in 1997 of a small aircraft company in northern California which failed to honor hundreds of contracts with deceased clients and their relatives to scatter ashes over sea and countryside. According to one report, two hikers in Amador County, California accidentally stumbled across the unidentified bones of some 5,000 people.

> Turned out the bones were part of the cremated remains that a pilot named B.J. Elkin was supposed to scatter over the Sierra and elsewhere. But

instead of doing the job he was paid to do, he had merely dumped the remains onto his property. (Elias, 1997)

The resulting lawsuit involved dozens of crematoriums and mortuaries in settlements exceeding $32 million. According to reporter Paul Elias, this case "exposed a new and lucrative area for plaintiffs' lawyers to mine" (1997). It seems that burnt bodies are big business in California.

The California lawsuits against mortuary parlors and crematoriums revolve mainly around the disposal of remains. In all these instances, cremation was at least the families' preferred way to treat their relatives' corpses. In Axel's case, however, the family issued an explicit order not to cremate. The accidental cremation undoubtedly has caused terrible suffering for Axel's family—even, depending on one's religious beliefs, to Axel's soul. And yet the cremated body, abomination though it might be in terms of religious beliefs and community standing, might more than compensate the father for the loss of meagre remittances which the son provided while alive. The cremated body also has potential financial value to the rest of his relatives in Nahualtenango, who have suffered the social and emotional consequences of what they believe to be a sacrilegious treatment of his corpse.

Though Axel's cremated body might well leave his soul beyond heavenly salvation, it has become in some sense the hope for earthly salvation for his family. At first (and still) a sinful aberration, a horrific deviation from sacred norms, Axel's ashes have suddenly attained extravagant monetary value. In the hands of the US legal system, they have been converted into a commodity, a chip on the bargaining table, the hope for financial security for his family—and a source of income for lawyers and anthropologist alike.

Suggested Readings

Ahern, Emily M.
    1973   *The Cult of the Dead in a Chinese Village.* Stanford, Calif.: Stanford University Press.

Danforth, Loring M.
    1982   *The Death Rituals of Rural Greece.* Princeton, N.J.: Princeton University Press.

Green, James W.
  2008   *Beyond the Good Death: The Anthropology of Modern Dying.* Philadelphia: University of
          Pennsylvania Press.

Huntington, Richard, and Peter Metcalf
  1979   *Celebrations of Death: The Anthropology of Mortuary Ritual.* Cambridge: Cambridge
          University Press.

Kopytoff, Igor
  1971   "Ancestors and Elders in Africa." *Africa* 43 (2): 129–42.

Meyer, Richard E.
  1992   *Cemeteries and Gravemarkers: Voices of American Culture.* Logan: Utah State University Press.

Robben, Antonius C. G. M., ed.
  2004   *Death, Mourning, and Burial: A Cross-Cultural Reader.* Malden, MA: Blackwell Publishers.

Santino, Jack, ed.
  1994   *Halloween and Other Festivals of Death and Life.* Knoxville: University of Tennessee Press.

Vitebsky, Piers
  1993   *Dialogues with the Dead: The Discussion of Mortality Among the Sora of Eastern India.*
          Cambridge: Cambridge University Press.

CHAPTER NINE

Old and New Religions: The Changing Spiritual Landscape

Protective mask from the Sepik River region, New Guinea.

Anthropologists agree that all cultures experience continuous change. However, in the past, anthropology often emphasized cultural stasis among non-Western peoples and addressed change only as acculturation—the process by which populations adjust to life under a dominant power, usually colonial and Western. By the late 20th century, however, anthropologists had increasingly acknowledged cultural change as a continuous and universal process. Such change has accelerated and intensified on a global scale since the dawn of the industrial era, due to expanding economic structures, rapid innovations in technology, worldwide movements of populations, and new ways of relating to the natural environment. The end of the colonial era, around the mid 20th century for many countries, marked shifts in patterns of power as formerly colonized people gained political, though frequently not economic, independence. For the anthropologist interested in religion, these often interconnected social, economic, and environmental changes yield a wealth of fascinating subjects. This chapter includes articles addressing religious change and stability primarily within the confines of specific societies or communities.

Religion both shapes and is affected by larger changes, in a number of ways. As the articles here illustrate, in some cases religious practices are profoundly altered by radical, top-down transformations in politics, or the domination of one society by another (for example, in response to intrusive control by the state or under the persuasive influence of missionaries). In other cases, religion is a conservative force, such as when communities strive to maintain a lifestyle based on the past, validated by religious beliefs, or seek to reestablish a perceived golden age from the culture's past. Michael Lambek (2002) notes this contradictory pull of religious changes, commenting that, while the state and other powerful institutions may attempt to shape religion for their own ends, individuals and communities may use religion as a way to exercise power and control in their own lives; this may occur through intensified religious commitment—perhaps fundamentalism—or through various forms of ethical engagement, such as the human rights movement or environmentalism (p. 511).

One of the most dramatic examples of how a social group might actively attempt to transform its life through religious means is what, in a classic anthropological contribution, Anthony F. C. Wallace termed a revitalization movement: "a deliberate, organized, conscious effort by members of society to construct a more satisfying culture by rapid acceptance of a pattern of multiple innovations" (1956: 265). Wallace (1956) outlined several major types of revitalization movements that are clearly religious in nature and can coexist within a given society at any time. Key to the idea of revitalization movements is that they challenge what participants perceive as unacceptable conditions, such as poverty, disease, oppression, or, most commonly, the disruptive impact of a dominant, power-holding group. In Wallace's view, revitalization movements intially spring up around the inspiration of charismatic leaders but, under the right conditions, may become established, routinized religions.

Wallace's categories and definitions have been broadly accepted. Nativistic movements are characterized by a strong emphasis on the elimination of alien persons, customs, values, and material from the "mazeway," which Wallace defined as the mental image an individual has of the society and its culture, as well as of his or her own body and its behavior regularities, in order to act in ways to reduce stress at all levels of the system. Revivalistic movements emphasize the readoption of customs, values, and even aspects of nature in the mazeway of previous generations. Cargo cults emphasize the importation of alien values, customs and material into the mazeway, these being expected to arrive, metaphorically, as a ship's cargo. Vitalistic movements also emphasize the importation of alien elements into the mazeway, although not via a cargo mechanism. Millenarian movements emphasize changes in the mazeway through an apocalyptic world transformation engineered by the supernatural. Messianic movements emphasize the actual participation of a divine savior in human flesh in bringing about desired changes in the mazeway (1956: 267). (This categorization of revitalization movements, however, is only one of many schemes used by ethnographers, and, as John Collins has noted, "Any such scheme, basically, is merely a device to initiate thought and comparison" [1978: 137].)

The religious nature of revitalization in the non-Western world, particularly in Melanesia, is made clear not only by the expectation of a messiah and the millennium in some of the movements but also by the very structure of movement phenomena, in which prophets play an indispensable role. I. C. Jarvie maintains that the religious character of these movements can be explained by the fact that traditional institutions are not able to adopt and respond to social changes, and that the only new organizational system offered these societies by European colonialists is Christianity. Melanesians, for example, have learned more about organization from religion than from any other foreign institution, and it is logical for them to mold revitalization movements in religious form in order to accommodate, indeed combat, the impact of European society (1970: 412–13).

Revitalization in the broad sense of bringing new vigor and happiness to society is certainly not restricted to traditional groups or to the religious realm. Edward Sapir (1924), for example, spoke of cultures "genuine" and "spurious": in the former, individuals felt well integrated into their culture, and in the latter they experienced alienation from the mainstream of society. Examples of attempts to change Western cultures abound. Political and economic conditions have frequently moved modern prophets to seek power to change, sometimes radically, the institutional structure and goals of society.

Throughout the readings in this chapter, reference is frequently made to *churches*, *cults*, and *sects*. These terms have been used by scholars as well as the lay public to describe particular types of religious organizations, particularly in the context of Christianity. Typically, the word *church* is applied to the larger community's view of the acceptable type of religious organization, whereas the term *sect* is used to refer to a protest group. Sects represent dissent from the established or mainstream form of a religion, and they generally involve smaller numbers of people. The word *cult* is not as clearly defined as *sect* and *church* and appears to refer to a more casual, loosely organized group. Cults seem to have a fluctuating membership whose allegiance can be shared with other religious organizations. Of the three, *cult* has taken on such a perjorative character that the term is almost useless (Barkun 1994: 43). What is a church to one person may be viewed as a sect or cult by outsiders.

During the last few decades, there has been an immense growth in the number of religious groups in the United States; many of these groups have received substantial attention in the media. The Children of God, the Hare Krishna movement, the followers of Bhagwan Shree Rajneesh, and the Reverend Sun Myung Moon's Unification Church are a few examples of groups that have attracted thousands of adherents who apparently were disenchanted with more traditional religious options. Even within Christianity—the dominant religion of North America—countless organizations have arisen independently or splintered off from more established denominations, ranging from neighborhood storefront churches to such large, public relations– and media-savvy organizations as Vineyard Christian Fellowships and Promisekeepers. World history is replete with examples of new religious groups springing to life as people who are spiritually, politically, or economically dissatisfied seek alternatives to traditional religious organizations.

What is the appeal of these movements? What social forces underlie the development and rapid growth of religious movements? Many sociological and psychological analyses have attempted to answer these important questions (see especially Glock and Stark 1965; Eister 1972; Talmon 1969; Zaretsky and Leone 1974). Briefly, these studies draw a picture of people who have become attracted to new movements because of such lures as love, security, acceptance, and improved personal status.

Charles Y. Glock (1964) has listed five types of deprivation that may result in the establishment of a new sect or that may lead individuals to join one: (1) *economic deprivation*, which is suffered by people who make less money, have fewer material goods, and are financially beholden to others; (2) *organismic deprivation*, which applies to those who may exhibit physical, mental, and nutritional problems; (3) *ethical deprivation*, which grows out of a perceived discrepancy between the real and the ideal; (4) *psychic deprivation*, which can result in the search for meaning and new values (and which is related to the search for closure and simplicity); and (5) *social deprivation*, which results from a society's valuation of some individuals and their attributes over others. Established religions have tremendous staying power, and "it is certainly premature to conclude that religions as forces in the world and as forces in individual lives are a thing of the past" (Reynolds and Tanner 1994: 44). This is not to say that the so-called great faiths (such as Islam, Christianity, and Judaism) do not lose followers; they do. "It seems to be mainly in the northwest of Europe, in Scandinavia, and in parts of the United States that religion remains in the doldrums" (Reynolds and Tanner 1994: 44).

In the opening article, Anthony F. C. Wallace builds on his earlier analysis of revitalization movements, here emphasizing five distinct stages of such movements and some of the psychological aspects of participation.

The next two articles provide intriguing examples of revitalization movements. Alice Beck Kehoe discusses a short-lived movement that drew together Native Americans and others during a time of profound hardship. Peter M. Worsley describes a form of revitalization movement found in the Pacific region. Such cults blossomed in response to the rapid intrusion of foreign military installations during World War II.

Just as revitalization movements can be interpreted as responses to oppression and deprivation, more established religious movements can also be forms of protest. Focusing on three men in Kingston, Jamaica, William F. Lewis brings to life some of the beliefs and practices of Rastafari, a faith that voices dissent against the status quo, including racial inequality.

The fifth article emphasizes the relationship between language and religion, as Susan F. Harding painstakingly examines her encounter with an evangelical preacher during the 1980s, when fundamentalist Christianity was moving into political and public view in the United States.

In the sixth article, Carolyn Fluehr-Lobban introduces Islamic law, emphasizing changes and reinterpretations over time.

References

Barkun, Michael
  1994 "Reflections After Waco: Millennialists and the State." In James R. Lewis, ed., *From the Ashes: Making Sense of Waco,* pp. 41–49. Lanham, Md.: Rowman and Littlefield.

Collins, John J.
  1978 *Primitive Religion.* Totowa, N.J.: Rowman and Littlefield.

Eister, Allen
  1972 "An Outline of a Structural Theory of Cults." *Journal for the Scientific Study of Religion* 11: 319–33.

Glock, Charles Y.
  1964 "The Role of Deprivation in the Origin and Evolution of Religious Groups." In R. Lee and M. E. Marty, eds., *Religion and Social Conflict.* New York: Oxford University Press.

Glock, Charles, Y., and Rodney Stark
  1965 *Religion and Society in Tension.* Chicago: Rand McNally.

Jarvie, I. C.
  1970 "Cargo Cults." In Richard Cavendish, ed., *Man, Myth and Magic,* pp. 409–12. New York: Marshall Cavendish.

Lambek, Michael, ed.
  2002 *A Reader in the Anthropology of Religion.* Boston: Blackwell.

Reynolds, Vernon, and Ralph Tanner
  1994 *The Social Ecology of Religion.* New York: Oxford University Press.

Sapir, E.
  1924 "Culture, Genuine and Spurious." *American Journal of Sociology* 29: 401–29.

Talmon, Yonina
  1969 "Pursuit of the Millennium: The Relation Between Religious and Social Change." In Norman Birnbaum and Gertrude Lenzer, eds., *Sociology and Religion: A Book of Readings.* Englewood Cliffs, N.J.: Prentice Hall.

Wallace, A. F. C.
  1956 "Revitalization Movements." *American Anthropologist* 58: 264–81.

Zaretsky, Irving S., and Mark P. Leone, eds.
  1974 *Religious Movements in Contemporary America.* Princeton, N.J.: Princeton University Press.

43

Revitalization Movements

Anthony F. C. Wallace

Wallace's article shows how people use religious principles to cope with a cultural crisis that has prevented them from achieving a more satisfying culture. Revitalization movements have been witnessed frequently in diverse geographic regions, and each displays variation of expression that may be explained by the culturally specific conditions under which they are formed. As a social process, they have the goal of reconstituting a way of life that has been destroyed for one reason or another. Wallace helps us understand the phenomenon of revitalization by describing five overlapping but distinct stages. A revitalization movement, unlike cultural evolution and historical change, is a relatively abrupt culture change that frequently completes itself in the span of a few years.

During the middle decades of the 20th century, Wallace was one of the most prominent anthropologists working in the areas of cognition and psychology. He was particularly interested in the psychological effects of acculturation and rapid technological change. These interests are clearly apparent in the present article when he discusses "mazeway resynthesis" and "hysterical conversion," concepts that highlight the psychological aspects of abrupt social change. Wallace (b. 1923) has been a prolific author. His most acclaimed book is Rockdale: The Growth of an American Village in the Industrial Revolution *(New York: Knopf, 1978).*

During periods of stable moving equilibrium, the sociocultural system is subject to mild but measurable oscillations in degree of organization. From time to time, however, most societies undergo more violent fluctuations in this regard. Such fluctuation is of peculiar importance in culture change because it often culminates in relatively sudden change in cultural *Gestalt*. We refer, here, to revitalization movements, which we define as deliberate and organized attempts by some members of a society to construct a more satisfying culture by rapid acceptance of a pattern of multiple innovations (Wallace 1956b; Mead 1956).

The severe disorganization of a sociocultural system may be caused by the impact of any one or combination of a variety of forces that push the system

Reprinted from Anthony F. C. Wallace, CULTURE AND PERSONALITY, 2nd ed. (New York: Random House, 1970), pp. 188–99, by permission of the publisher and the author.

beyond the limits of equilibrium. Some of these forces are climatic or faunal changes, which destroy the economic basis of its existence; epidemic disease, which grossly alters the population structure; wars, which exhaust the society's resources of manpower or result in defeat or invasion; internal conflict among interest groups, which results in extreme disadvantage for at least one group; and, very commonly, a position of perceived subordination and inferiority with respect to an adjacent society. The latter, by the use of more or less coercion (or even no coercion at all, as in situations where the mere example set by the dominant society raises too-high levels of aspiration), brings about uncoordinated cultural changes. Under conditions of disorganization, the system, from the standpoint of at least some of its members, is unable to make possible the reliable satisfaction of certain values that are held to be essential to continued well-being and self-respect. The mazeway of a culturally disillusioned person, accordingly, is an image of a world that is unpredictable, or barren in its simplicity, or both, and is apt to contain severe identity conflict. His mood (depending on the precise nature of the disorganization) will be one of panic-stricken anxiety, shame, guilt, depression, or apathy.

An example of the kind of disorganization to which we refer is given by the two thousand or so Seneca Indians of New York at the close of the eighteenth century. Among these people, a supreme value is attached to the conception of the absolutely free and autonomous individual, unconstrained by and indifferent to his own and alien others' pain and hardship. This individual was capable of free indulgence of emotional impulses but, in crisis, freely subordinated his own wishes to the needs of his community. Among the men, especially, this ego-ideal was central in personality organization. Men defined the roles of hunting, of warfare, and of statesmanship as the conditions of achievement of this value; thus the stereotypes of "the good hunter," "the brave warrior," and "the forest statesman" were the images of masculine success. But the forty-three years from 1754, when the French and Indian War began, to 1797, when the Seneca sold their last hunting grounds and became largely confined to tiny, isolated reservations, brought with them changes in their situation that made achievement of these ideals virtually impossible. The good hunter could no longer hunt: the game was scarce, and it was almost suicidally dangerous to stray far from the reservation among the numerous hostile white men. The brave warrior could no longer fight, being undersupplied, abandoned by his allies, and his women and children threatened by growing military might of the United States. The forest statesman was an object of contempt, and this disillusionment was perhaps more shattering than the rest. The Iroquois chiefs, for nearly a century, had been able to play off British and French, then Americans and British, against one another, extorting supplies and guarantees of territorial immunity from both sides. They had maintained an extensive system of alliances and hegemonies among surrounding tribal groups. Suddenly they were shorn of their power. White men no longer spoke of the League of the Iroquois with respect; their western Indian dependents and allies regarded them as cowards for having made peace with the Americans.

The initial Seneca response to the progress of sociocultural disorganization was quasipathological: many became drunkards; the fear of witches increased; squabbling factions were unable to achieve a common policy. But a revitalization movement developed in 1799, based on the religious revelations reported by one of the disillusioned forest statesmen, one Handsome Lake, who preached a code of patterned religious and cultural reform. The drinking of whiskey was proscribed; witchcraft was to be stamped out; various outmoded rituals and prevalent sins were to be abandoned. In addition, various syncretic cultural reforms, amounting to a reorientation of the socioeconomic system, were to be undertaken, including the adoption of agriculture (hitherto a feminine calling) by the men, and the focusing of kinship responsibilities within the nuclear family (rather than in the clan and lineage). The general acceptance of Handsome Lake's Code, within a few years, wrought seemingly miraculous changes. A group of sober, devout, partly literate, and technologically up-to-date farming communities suddenly replaced the demoralized slums in the wilderness (Wallace 1970).

Such dramatic transformations are, as a matter of historical fact, very common in human history, and probably have been the medium of as much culture change as the slower equilibrium processes. Furthermore, because they compress into such a short space of time such extensive changes in pattern, they are somewhat easier to record than the quiet serial changes during periods of equilibrium. In general, revitalization processes share a common process structure that can be conceptualized as a pattern of temporally overlapping, but functionally distinct, stages:

I. *Steady State.* This is a period of moving equilibrium of the kind discussed in the preceding section. Culture change occurs during the steady state, but is of the relatively slow and chainlike kind. Stress levels vary among interest groups, and there is some oscillation in organization level, but disorganization and stress remain within limits tolerable to most individuals. Occasional incidents of intolerable stress may stimulate a limited "correction" of the system, but some incidence of individual ill-health and criminality are accepted as a price society must pay.

II. *The Period of Increased Individual Stress.* The sociocultural system is being "pushed" progressively out of equilibrium by the forces described earlier: climatic and biotic change, epidemic disease, war and conquest, social subordination, acculturation, internally generated decay, and so forth. Increasingly large numbers of individuals are placed under what is to them intolerable stress by the failure of the system to accommodate the satisfaction of their needs. Anomie and disillusionment become widespread, as the culture is perceived to be disorganized and inadequate; crime and illness increase sharply in frequency as individualistic asocial responses. But the situation is still generally defined as one of fluctuation within the steady state.

III. *The Period of Cultural Distortion.* Some members of the society attempt, piecemeal and ineffectively, to restore personal equilibrium by adopting socially dysfunctional expedients. Alcoholism, venality in public officials, the "black market," breaches of sexual and kinship mores, hoarding, gambling for gain, "scapegoating," and similar behaviors that, in the preceding period, were still defined as individual deviances, in effect become institutionalized efforts to circumvent the evil effects of "the system." Interest groups, losing confidence in the advantages of maintaining mutually acceptable interrelationships, may resort to violence in order to coerce others into unilaterally advantageous behavior. Because of the malcoordination of cultural changes during this period, they are rarely able to reduce the impact of the forces that have pushed the society out of equilibrium, and in fact lead to a continuous decline in organization.

IV. *The Period of Revitalization.* Once severe cultural distortion has occurred, the society can with difficulty return to steady state without the institution of a revitalization process. Without revitalization, indeed, the society is apt to disintegrate as a system: the population will either die off, splinter into autonomous groups, or be absorbed into another, more stable, society. Revitalization depends on the successful completion of the following functions:

1. Formulation of a code. An individual, or a group of individuals, constructs a new, utopian image of sociocultural organization. This model is a blueprint of an ideal society or "goal culture." Contrasted with the goal culture is the existing culture, which is presented as inadequate or evil in certain respects. Connecting the existing culture and the goal culture is a transfer culture: a system of operations that, if faithfully carried out, will transform the existing culture into the goal culture. Failure to institute the transfer operations will, according to the code, result in either the perpetuation of the existing misery or the ultimate destruction of the society (if not of the whole world). Not infrequently in primitive societies the code, or the core of it, is formulated by one individual in the course of a hallucinatory revelation; such prophetic experiences are apt to launch religiously oriented movements, since the source of the revelation is apt to be regarded as a supernatural being. Nonhallucinatory formulations usually are found in politically oriented movements. In either case, the formulation of the code constitutes a reformulation of the author's own mazeway and often brings to him a renewed confidence in the future and a remission of the complaints he experienced before. It may be suggested that such mazeway resynthesis processes are merely extreme forms of the reorganizing dream processes that seem to be associated with REM (rapid-eye-movement) sleep, which are necessary to normal health.

2. Communication. The formulators of the code preach the code to other people in an evangelistic spirit. The aim of the communication is to make converts. The code is offered as the means of spiritual salvation for the individual and of cultural salvation for the society. Promises of benefit to the target population need not be immediate or materialistic, for the basis of the code's appeal is the attractiveness of identification with a more highly organized system, with all that this implies in the way of self-respect. Indeed, in view of the extensiveness of the changes in values often implicit in such codes, appeal to currently held values would often be pointless. Religious codes offer spiritual salvation, identification with God, elect status; political codes offer honor, fame, the respect of society for sacrifices made in its interest. But refusal to accept the code is usually defined as placing the listener in immediate spiritual, as well as material, peril with respect to his existing values. In small societies, the target population may be the entire community; but in more complex societies, the message may be aimed only at certain

groups deemed eligible for participation in the transfer and goal cultures.

3. Organization. The code attracts converts. The motivations that are satisfied by conversion, and the psychodynamics of the conversion experience itself, are likely to be highly diverse, ranging from the mazeway resynthesis characteristic of the prophet, and the hysterical conviction of the "true believer," to the calculating expediency of the opportunist. As the group of converts expands, it differentiates into two parts: a set of disciples and a set of mass followers. The disciples increasingly become the executive organization, responsible for administering the evangelistic program, protecting the formulator, combatting heresy, and so on. In this role, the disciples increasingly become full-time specialists in the work of the movement. The tri-cornered relationship between the formulators, the disciples, and the mass followers is given an authoritarian structure, even without the formalities of older organizations, by the charismatic quality of the formulator's image. The formulator is regarded as a man to whom, from a supernatural being or from some other source of wisdom unavailable to the mass, a superior knowledge and authority has been vouchsafed that justifies his claim to unquestioned belief and obedience from his followers.

In the modern world, with the advantages of rapid transportation and ready communication, the simple charismatic model of cult organization is not always adequate to describe many social and religious movements. In such programs as Pentecostalism, Black Power, and the New Left, there is typically a considerable number of local or special issue groups loosely joined in what Luther Gerlach has called an "acephalous, segmentary, reticulate organization" (1968). Each segment may be, in effect, a separate revitalization organization of the simple kind described above; the individual groups differ in details of code, in emotional style, in appeal to different social classes; and, since the movement as a whole has no single leader, it is relatively immune to repression, the collapse of one or several segments in no way invalidating the whole. This type of movement organization is singularly well adapted to predatory expansion; but it may eventually fall under the domination of one cult or party (as was the case, for instance, in Germany when the SS took over the fragmented Nazi party, which in turn was heir to a large number of nationalist groups, and as is the case when a Communist party apparatus assumes control of a revolutionary popular front).

4. Adaptation. Because the movement is a revolutionary organization (however benevolent and humane the ultimate values to which it subscribes), it threatens the interests of any group that obtains advantage, or believes it obtains advantage, from maintaining or only moderately reforming the status quo. Furthermore, the code is never complete; new inadequacies are constantly being found in the existing culture, and new inconsistencies, predicative failures, and ambiguities discovered in the code itself (some of the latter being pointed out by the opposition). The response of the code formulators and disciples is to rework the code, and, if necessary, to defend the movement by political and diplomatic maneuver, and, ultimately, by force. The general tendency is for codes to harden gradually, and for the tone of the movement to become increasingly nativistic and hostile both toward nonparticipating fellow members of society, who will ultimately be defined as "traitors," and toward "national enemies."

True revolutions, as distinguished from mere coups d'état, which change personnel without changing the structure, require that the revitalization movement of which they are the instrument add to its code a morality sanctioning subversion or even violence. The leadership must also be sophisticated in its knowledge of how to mobilize an increasingly large part of the population to their side, and of how to interfere with the mobilization of the population by the establishment. The student of such processes can do no better than to turn to the works of contemporary practitioners such as Che Guevara and Mao Tse Tung for authoritative explications and examples of the revolutionary aspect of revitalization.

5. Cultural transformation. If the movement is able to capture both the adherence of a substantial proportion of a local population and, in complex societies, of the functionally crucial apparatus (such as power and communications networks, water supply, transport systems, and military establishment), the transfer culture and, in some cases, the goal culture itself, can be put into operation. The revitalization, if successful, will be attended by the drastic decline of the quasi-pathological individual symptoms of anomie and by the disappearance of the cultural distortions. For such a revitalization to be

accomplished, however, the movement must be able to maintain its boundaries from outside invasion, must be able to obtain internal social conformity without destructive coercion, and must have a successful economic system.

6. Routinization. If the preceding functions are satisfactorily completed, the functional reasons for the movement's existence as an innovative force disappear. The transfer culture, if not the goal culture, is operating of necessity with the participation of a large proportion of the community. Although the movement's leaders may resist the realization of the fact, the movement's function shifts from the role of innovation to the role of maintenance. If the movement was heavily religious in orientation, its legacy is a cult or church that preserves and reworks the code, and maintains, through ritual and myth, the public awareness of the history and values that brought forth the new culture. If the movement was primarily political, its organization is routinized into various stable decision-making and morale-and-order-maintaining functions (such as administrative offices, police, and military bodies). Charisma can, to a degree, be routinized, but its intensity diminishes as its functional necessity becomes, with increasing obviousness, outmoded.

V. *The New Steady State.* With the routinization of the movement, a new steady state may be said to exist. Steady-state processes of culture change continue; many of them are in areas where the movement has made further change likely. In particular, changes in the value structure of the culture may lay the basis for long-continuing changes (such as the train of economic and technological consequences of the dissemination of the Protestant ethic after the Protestant Reformation). Thus in addition to the changes that the movement accomplishes during its active phase, it may control the direction of the subsequent equilibrium processes by shifting the values that define the cultural focus. The record of the movement itself, over time, gradually is subject to distortion, and eventually is enshrined in myths and rituals which elevate the events that occurred, and persons who acted, into quasi- or literally divine status.

Two psychological mechanisms seem to be of peculiar importance in the revitalization process:

mazeway resynthesis (Wallace 1956a) and hysterical conversion. The resynthesis is most dramatically exemplified in the career of the prophet who formulates a new religious code during a hallucinatory trance. Typically, such persons, after suffering increasing depreciation of self-esteem as the result of their inadequacy to achieve the culturally ideal standards, reach a point of either physical or drug-induced exhaustion, during which a resynthesis of values and beliefs occurs. The resynthesis is, like other innovations, a recombination of preexisting configurations; the uniqueness of this particular process is the suddenness of conviction, the trance-like state of the subject, and the emotionally central nature of the subject matter. There is some reason to suspect that such dramatic resyntheses depend on a special biochemical milieu, accompanying the "stage of exhaustion" of the stress (in Selye's sense) syndrome, or on a similar milieu induced by drugs. But comparable resyntheses are, of course, sometimes accomplished more slowly, without the catalytic aid of extreme stress or drugs. This kind of resynthesis produces, apparently, a permanent alteration of mazeway: the new stable cognitive configuration, is, as it were, constructed out of the materials of earlier configurations, which, once rearranged, cannot readily reassemble into the older forms.

The hysterical conversion is more typical of the mass follower who is repeatedly subjected to suggestion by a charismatic leader and an excited crowd. The convert of this type may, during conversion display various dissociative behaviors (rage, speaking in tongues, rolling on the ground, weeping, and so on). After conversion, his overt behavior may be in complete conformity with the code to which he has been exposed. But his behavior has changed not because of a radical resynthesis, but because of the adoption under suggestion of an additional social personality which temporarily replaces, but does not destroy, the earlier. He remains, in a sense, a case of multiple personality and is liable, if removed from reinforcing symbols, to lapse into an earlier social personality. The participant in the lynch mob or in the camp meeting revival is a familiar example of this type of convert. But persons can be maintained in this state of hysterical conversion for months or years, if the "trance" is continuously maintained by the symbolic environment (flags, statues, portraits, songs, and so on) and continuous suggestions (speeches, rallies, and so on). The most familiar contemporary example is the German under Hitler who participated in the Nazi genocide program, but reverted to *Gemütlichkeit* when the war ended. The difference between the resynthesized person and the converted one does not lie in the nature of the codes to which they subscribe (they may be the same), but in the blandness and readiness of the hysterical convert to revert, as compared to the almost paranoid intensity and stability of the resynthesized prophet. A successful movement, by virtue of its ability to maintain suggestion continuously for years, is able to hold the hysterical convert indefinitely, or even to work a real resynthesis by repeatedly forcing him, after hysterical conversion, to reexamine his older values and beliefs and to work through to valid resynthesis, sometimes under considerable stress. The Chinese Communists, for instance, apparently have become disillusioned by hysterical conversions and have used various techniques, some coercive and some not, but all commonly lumped together as "brain-washing" in Western literature, to induce valid resynthesis. The aim of these communist techniques, like those of the established religions, is, literally, to produce a "new man."

It is impossible to exaggerate the importance of these two psychological processes for culture change, for they make possible the rapid substitution of a new cultural *Gestalt* for an old, and thus the rapid cultural transformation of whole populations. Without this mechanism, the cultural transformation of the 600,000,000 people of China by the Communists could not have occurred; nor the Communist-led revitalization and expansion of the USSR; nor the American Revolution; nor the Protestant Reformation; nor the rise and spread of Christianity, Mohammedanism, and Buddhism. In the written historical record, revitalization movements begin with Ikhnaton's ultimately disastrous attempt to establish a new, monotheistic religion in Egypt; they are found, continent by continent, in the history of all human societies, occurring with frequency proportional to the pressures to which the society is subjected. For small tribal societies, in chronically extreme situations, movements may develop every ten or fifteen years; in stable complex cultures, the rate of a societywide movement may be one every two or three hundred years.

In view of the frequency and geographical diversity of revitalization movements it can be expected that their content will be extremely varied, corresponding to the diversity of situational contexts and cultural backgrounds in which they develop. Major culture areas are, over extended periods of time, associated with particular types: New Guinea and Melanesia, during the latter part of the nineteenth and the twentieth centuries, have been the home of the well-known "cargo cults." The most prominent feature of these cults is the expectation that the ancestors soon will arrive in a steamship, bearing a cargo of the white man's goods, and will lead a nativistic revolution culminating in the ejection of European masters. The Indians of the eastern half of South America for centuries after the conquest set off on migrations for the *terre sans mal* where a utopian way of life, free of Spaniards and Portuguese, would be found; North American Indians of the eighteenth and nineteenth centuries were prone to revivalistic movements such as the Ghost Dance, whose adherents believed that appropriate ritual and the abandonment of the sins of the white man would bring a return of the golden age before contact; South Africa has been the home of the hundreds of small, enthusiastic, separatist churches that have broken free of the missionary organizations. As might be expected, a congruence evidently exists between the cultural *Anlage* and the content of movement, which, together with processes of direct and stimulus diffusion, accounts for the tendency for movements to fall into areal types (Burridge 1960).

44

The Ghost Dance Religion

Alice Beck Kehoe

During the late 1860s, a Northern Paiute Indian named Wodziwob ("white hair") experienced several visions telling him to create the Ghost Dance religion. By following Wodziwob's vision-revealed instructions, the Indians would hasten the day when white people would disappear, dead Indians would live again, and the old Indian way of life would return. The movement experienced early success and quickly expanded from the Great Basin area into California and Oregon but eventually faltered. In 1889, years after Wodziwob's religion had died, a second and more extensive Ghost Dance movement began, this time led by another Paiute Indian, Jack Wilson, or, in the Paiute language, Wovoka ("the woodcutter"). In this selection, Alice Beck Kehoe describes Wovoka's early life with David Wilson, an Anglo rancher, and his family, as well as his preaching as a young adult and his 1889 vision that resulted in his becoming a prophet. Kehoe believes that the Ghost Dance religion was a complete religion and that its basic message, though aimed primarily at Indians, was applicable to all people of goodwill. Wovoka's gospel was especially appealing to the Indians, who in 1889 were suffering from persecution by the whites, epidemics, loss of their economic resources and lands, and continuing attempts to eradicate their customs and beliefs. The Ghost Dance religion spread to the tribes of the Northwest, eventually reaching the plains from Oklahoma to Canada. The religion came to a violent end for the Sioux in late December 1890, with the killing of 370 Indians at Wounded Knee.

New Year's Day, 1892. Nevada.

A wagon jounces over a maze of cattle trails crisscrossing a snowy valley floor. In the wagon, James Mooney, from the Smithsonian Institution in far-away Washington, D.C., is looking for the Indian messiah, Wovoka, blamed for riling up the Sioux, nearly three hundred of whom now lie buried by Wounded Knee Creek in South Dakota. The men in the wagon see a man with a gun over his shoulder walking in the distance.

"I believe that's Jack now!" exclaims one of Mooney's guides. "Jack Wilson," he calls to the messiah, whose Paiute name is Wovoka. Mooney's other guide, Charley Sheep, Wovoka's uncle, shouts to his nephew in the Paiute language. The hunter comes over to the wagon.

"I saw that he was a young man," Mooney recorded, "a dark full-blood, compactly built, and taller than the Paiute generally, being nearly 6 feet in height. He was well dressed in white man's clothes, with the broad-brimmed white felt hat common in the west, secured on his head by means of a beaded ribbon under the chin. . . . He wore a good pair of boots. His hair was cut off square on a line below the base of the ears, after the manner of his tribe. His countenance was open and expressive of firmness and decision" (Mooney [1896] 1973: 768–69).

That evening, James Mooney formally interviewed Jack Wilson in his home, a circular lodge ten feet in diameter, built of bundles of tule reeds tied to a pole frame. In the middle of the lodge, a bright fire of sagebrush stalks sent sparks flying out of the wide smoke hole. Several other Paiutes were with Jack, his wife, baby, and little son when Mooney arrived with a guide and an interpreter. Mooney noticed that although all the Paiutes dressed in "white man's" clothes, they preferred to live in traditional wicki-ups. Only Paiute baskets furnished Jack Wilson's home; no beds, no storage trunks, no pots or pans, nothing of alien manufacture except the hunting gun and knife lay in the wickiup, though the family could have bought the invaders' goods. Jack had steady employment as a ranch laborer, and from his wages he could have constructed a cabin and lived in it, sitting on chairs and eating bread and beef from metal utensils. Instead, Jack and Mary, his wife, wanted to follow the ways of their people as well as they could in a valley overrun with Euro-American settlement. The couple hunted, fished, and gathered pine nuts and other seeds and wild plants. They practiced their Paiute religion rather than the Presbyterian Christianity Jack's employer insisted on teaching them. Mooney was forced to bring a Euro-American settler, Edward Dyer, to interpret for him because Jack would speak only his native Paiute, though he had some familiarity with English. This was Mason Valley, in the heart of Paiute territory, and for Jack and Mary it was still Paiute.

Jack Wilson told Mooney that he had been born four years before the well-remembered battle between Paiutes and American invaders at Pyramid Lake. The battle had been touched off by miners seizing two Paiute women. The men of the Paiute community managed to rescue the two women. No harm was done to the miners, but they claimed they were victims of an "Indian outrage," raised a large party of their fellows, and set off to massacre the Paiutes. Expecting trouble, the Paiute men ambushed the mob of miners at a narrow pass, and although armed mostly with only bows and arrows, killed nearly fifty of the mob, routing the rest and saving the families in the Indian camp. Jack Wilson's father, Tavibo, was a leader of the Paiute community at that time. He was recognized as spiritually blessed—gifted and trained to communicate with invisible powers. By means of this gift, carefully cultivated, Tavibo was said to be able to control the weather.

Tavibo left the community when his son Wovoka was in his early teens, and the boy was taken on by David Wilson, a Euro-American rancher with sons of his own close in age to the Paiute youth. Though employed as a ranch hand, Wovoka was strongly encouraged to join the Wilson family in daily prayers and Bible reading, and Jack, as he came to be called, became good friends with the Wilson boys. Through these years with the Wilsons, Jack's loyalty to, and pride in, his own Paiute people never wavered. When he was about twenty, he married a Paiute woman who shared his commitment to the Paiute way of life. With his wages from the ranch, Jack and Mary bought the hunting gun and ammunition, good-quality "white man's" clothes, and ornaments suited to their dignity as a respected younger couple in the Mason Valley community.

As a young adult, Jack Wilson began to develop a reputation as a weather doctor like his father. Paiute believe that a young person lacks the maturity and inner strength to function as a spiritual agent, but Jack was showing the self-discipline, sound judgment, and concern for others that marked Indians gifted as doctors in the native tradition. Jack led the circle dances through which Paiute opened themselves to spiritual influence. Moving always along the path of the sun—clockwise to the left—men, women, and children joined hands in a symbol of the community's living through the circle of the days. As they danced they listened to Jack Wilson's songs celebrating the Almighty and Its wondrous manifestations: the mountains, the clouds, snow, stars, trees, antelope. Between dances, the people sat at Jack's feet, listening to him preach faith in universal love.

The climax of Jack's personal growth came during a dramatic total eclipse of the sun on January 1, 1889. He was lying in his wickiup very ill with a fever. Paiute around him saw the sky darkening although it was midday. Some monstrous force was overcoming the sun! People shot off guns at the apparition, they yelled, some wailed as at a death. Jack Wilson felt himself losing consciousness. It seemed to him he was taken up to heaven and brought before God. God gave him a message to the people of earth, a gospel of peace and right living. Then he and the sun regained their normal life.

Jack Wilson was now a prophet. Tall, handsome, with a commanding presence, Jack already was respected for his weather control power. (The unusual snow blanketing Mason Valley when James Mooney visited was said to be Jack's doing.) Confidence in his God-given mission further enhanced Jack

Wilson's reputation. Indians came from other districts to hear him, and even Mormon settlers in Nevada joined his audiences. To carry out his mission, Jack Wilson went to the regional Indian agency at Pyramid Lake and asked one of the employees to prepare and mail a letter to the President of the United States, explaining the Paiute doctor's holy mission and suggesting that if the United States government would send him a small regular salary, he would convey God's message to all the people of Nevada and, into the bargain, make it rain whenever they wished. The agency employee never sent the letter. It was agency policy to "silently ignore" Indians' efforts toward "notoriety." The agent would not even deign to meet the prophet.

Jack Wilson did not need the support of officials. His deep sincerity and utter conviction of his mission quickly persuaded every open-minded hearer of its importance. Indians came on pilgrimages to Mason Valley, some out of curiosity, others seeking guidance and healing in that time of afflictions besetting their peoples. Mormons came too, debating whether Jack Wilson was the fulfillment of a prophecy of their founder, Joseph Smith, Jr., that the Messiah would appear in human form in 1890. Jack Wilson himself consistently explained that he was *a* messiah *like* Jesus but not the Christ of the Christians. Both Indians and Euro-Americans tended to ignore Jack's protestations and to identify him as "the Christ." Word spread that the Son of God was preaching in western Nevada.

Throughout 1889 and 1890, railroads carried delegates from a number of Indian nations east of the Rockies to investigate the messiah in Mason Valley. Visitors found ceremonial grounds maintained beside the Paiute settlements, flat cleared areas with low willow-frame shelters around the open dancing space. Paiutes gathered periodically to dance and pray for four days and nights, ending on the fifth morning shaking their blankets and shawls to symbolize driving out evil. In Mason Valley itself, Jack Wilson would attend the dances, repeating his holy message and, from time to time, trembling and passing into a trance to confirm the revelations. Delegates from other reservations were sent back home with tokens of Jack Wilson's holy power: bricks of ground red ocher dug from Mount Grant south of Mason Valley, the Mount Sinai of Northern Paiute religion; the strikingly marked feathers of the magpie;

pine nuts, the "daily bread" of the Paiutes; and robes of woven strips of rabbit fur, the Paiutes' traditional covering. James Mooney's respectful interest in the prophet's teachings earned him the privilege of carrying such tokens to his friends on the Cheyenne and Arapaho reservations east of the mountains.

Jack Wilson told Mooney that when "the sun died" that winter day in 1889 and, dying with it, he was taken up to heaven,

> he saw God, with all the people who had died long ago engaged in their oldtime sports and occupations, all happy and forever young. It was a pleasant land and full of game. After showing him all, God told him he must go back and tell his people they must be good and love one another, have no quarreling, and live in peace with the whites; that they must work, and not lie or steal; that they must put away all the old practices that savored of war; that if they faithfully obeyed his instructions they would at last be reunited with their friends in this other world, where there would be no more death or sickness or old age. He was then given the dance which he was commanded to bring back to his people. By performing this dance at intervals, for five consecutive days each time, they would secure this happiness to themselves and hasten the event. Finally God gave him control over the elements so that he could make it rain or snow or be dry at will, and appointed him his deputy to take charge of affairs in the west, while "Governor Harrison" [President of the United States at the time] would attend to matters in the east, and he, God, would look after the world above. He then returned to earth and began to preach as he was directed, convincing the people by exercising the wonderful powers that had been given him. (Mooney [1896] 1973: 771–72)

Before Mooney's visit, Jack Wilson had repeated his gospel, in August 1891, to a literate young Arapaho man who had journeyed with other Arapaho and Cheyenne to discover the truth about this fabled messiah. Jack instructed his visitors, according to the Arapaho's notes:

> When you get home you make dance, and will give you the same. . . . He likes you folk, you give him good, many things, he heart been sitting feel good. After you get home, will give good cloud, and give you chance to make you feel good. and he give you good spirit. and he give you all a good paint. . . .

Grandfather said when he die never no cry. no hurt anybody. no fight, good behave always, it will give you satisfaction, this young man, he is a good Father and mother, dont tell no white man. Jueses [Jesus?] was on ground, he just like cloud. Everybody is alive agin, I dont know when they will [be] here, may be this fall or in spring.

Everybody never get sick, be young again,— (if young fellow no sick any more,) work for white men never trouble with him until you leave, when it shake the earth dont be afraid no harm any body.

You make dance for six weeks night, and put you foot [food?] in dance to eat for every body and wash in the water. that is all to tell, I am in to you. and you will received a good words from him some time, Dont tell lie. (Mooney [1896] 1973:780–81)

Seeing the red ocher paint, the magpie feathers, the pine nuts, and the rabbit skin robes from the messiah, his Arapaho friends shared this message with James Mooney. Jack Wilson himself had trusted this white man. Thanks to this Arapaho document, we know that Jack Wilson himself obeyed his injunction, "Dont tell lie": he had confided to the Smithsonian anthropologist the same gospel he brought to his Indian disciples.

"A clean, honest life" is the core of Jack Wilson's guidance, summed up seventy years later by a Dakota Sioux who had grown up in the Ghost Dance religion. The circling dance of the congregations following Jack Wilson's gospel symbolized the ingathering of all people in the embrace of Our Father, God, and in his earthly deputy Jack Wilson. As the people move in harmony in the dance around the path of the sun, leftward, so they must live and work in harmony. Jack Wilson was convinced that if every Indian would dance this belief, the great expression of faith and love would sweep evil from the earth, renewing its goodness in every form, from youth and health to abundant food.

This was a complete religion. It had a transcendental origin in the prophet's visit to God, and a continuing power rooted in the eternal Father. Its message of earthly renewal was universalistic, although Jack Wilson felt it was useless to preach it to those Euro-Americans who were heedlessly persecuting the Indian peoples. That Jack shared his gospel with those non-Indians who came to him as pilgrims demonstrates that it was basically applicable to all people of goodwill. The gospel outlined personal behavior and provided the means to unite individuals into congregations to help one another. Its principal ceremony, the circling dance, pleased and satisfied the senses of the participants, and through the trances easily induced during the long ritual, it offered opportunities to experience profound emotional catharsis. Men and women, persons of all ages and capabilities, were welcomed into a faith of hope for the future, consolation and assistance in the present, and honor to the Indians who had passed into the afterlife. It was a marvelous message for people suffering, as the Indians of the West were in 1889, terrible epidemics; loss of their lands, their economic resources, and their political autonomy; malnourishment and wretched housing; and a campaign of cultural genocide aimed at eradicating their languages, their customs, and their beliefs.

Jack Wilson's religion was immediately taken up by his own people, the Northern Paiute, by other Paiute groups, by the Utes, the Shoshoni, and the Washo in western Nevada. It was carried westward across the Sierra Nevada and espoused by many of the Indians of California. To the south, the religion was accepted by the western Arizona Mohave, Cohonino, and Pai, but not by most other peoples of the American Southwest. East of the Rockies, the religion spread through the Shoshoni and Arapaho in Wyoming to other Arapaho, Cheyenne, Assiniboin, Gros Ventre (Atsina), Mandan, Arikara, Pawnee, Caddo, Kichai, Wichita, Kiowa, Kiowa-Apache, Comanche, Delaware (living by this time in Oklahoma), Oto, and the western Sioux, especially the Teton bands. The mechanism by which this religion spread was usually a person visiting another tribe, observing the new ceremonial dance and becoming inspired by its gospel, and returning home to urge relatives and friends to try the new faith. Leaders of these evangelists' communities would often appoint respected persons to travel to Nevada to investigate this claim of a new messiah. The delegates frequently returned as converts, testifying to the truth of the faith and firing the enthusiasm of their communities. Those who remained skeptics did not always succeed in defusing the flame of faith in others.

Never an organized church, Jack Wilson's religion thus spread by independent converts from California through Oklahoma. Not all the communities who took it up continued to practice it, when months or years passed without the hoped-for earth renewal. Much of Jack Wilson's religion has persisted, however, and has been incorporated into the regular religious life of Indian groups, especially on Oklahoma reservations. To merge into a complex of beliefs and rituals rather than be an exclusive religion was entirely in accordance with Jack Wilson's respect for traditional Indian religions, which he saw reinforced, not supplanted, by his revelations. Though the Sioux generally dropped the Ghost Dance religion after their military defeats following their initial acceptance of the ritual, older people among the Sioux could be heard occasionally singing Ghost Dance songs in the 1930s. The last real congregation of adherents to Jack Wilson's gospel continued to worship together into the 1960s, and at least one who survived into the 1980s never abandoned the faith. There were sporadic attempts to revive the Ghost Dance religion in the 1970s, though these failed to kindle the enthusiasm met by the original proselytizers.

"Ghost Dance" is the name usually applied to Jack Wilson's religion, because the prophet foresaw the resurrection of the recently dead with the hoped-for renewal of the earth. Paiute themselves simply called their practice of the faith "dance in a circle," Shoshoni called it "everybody dragging" (speaking of people pulling others along as they circled), Comanche called it "the Father's Dance," Kiowa, "dance with clasped hands," and Caddo, "prayer of all to the Father" or "my [Father's] children's dance." The Sioux and Arapaho did use the term "spirit [ghost] dance," and the English name seems to have come from translation of the Sioux. The last active congregation, however, referred to their religion as the New Tidings, stressing its parallel to Jesus' gospel.

To his last days in 1932, Jack Wilson served as Father to believers. He counseled them, in person and by letters, and he gave them holy red ocher paint, symbolizing life, packed into rinsed-out tomato cans (the red labels indicated the contents). With his followers, he was saddened that not enough Indians danced the new faith to create the surge of spiritual power that could have renewed the earth, but resurrection was only a hope. The heart of his religion was his creed, the knowledge that a "clean, honest life" is the only good life.

45

Cargo Cults

Peter M. Worsley

A cargo cult, one of the several varieties of revitalization movements, is an intentional effort on the part of the members of society to create a more satisfying culture. Characteristic of revitalization movements in Melanesia, but not restricted to that area, cargo cults bring scattered groups together into a wider religious and political unity. These movements are the result of widespread dissatisfaction, oppression, insecurity, and the hope for fulfillment of prophecies of good times and abundance soon to come. Exposure to the cultures and material goods of the Western world, combinations of native myth with Christian teachings of the coming of a messiah, and belief in the white man's magic— all contributed to the New Guinean's faith that the "cargo" would soon arrive, bringing with it the end of the present order and the beginning of a blissful paradise. Peter M. Worsley's article depicts a movement that often was so organized and persistent as to bring government work to a halt.

Patrols of the Australian government venturing into the "uncontrolled" central highlands of New Guinea in 1946 found the primitive people there swept up in a wave of religious excitement. Prophecy was being fulfilled: The arrival of the Whites was the sign that the end of the world was at hand. The natives proceeded to butcher all of their pigs—animals that were not only a principal source of subsistence but also symbols of social status and ritual preeminence in their culture. They killed these valued animals in expression of the belief that after three days of darkness "Great Pigs" would appear from the sky. Food, firewood, and other necessities had to be stockpiled to see the people through to the arrival of the Great Pigs. Mock wireless antennae of bamboo and rope had been erected to receive in advance the news of the millennium. Many believed that with the great event they would exchange their black skins for white ones.

This bizarre episode is by no means the single event of its kind in the murky history of the collision of European civilization with the indigenous cultures of the southwest Pacific. For more than one hundred years traders and missionaries have been reporting similar disturbances among the peoples of Melanesia, the group of Negro-inhabited islands (including New Guinea, Fiji, the Solomons, and the New Hebrides) lying between Australia and the open Pacific Ocean. Though their technologies were based largely upon stone and wood, these peoples had highly developed cultures, as measured by the standards of maritime and agricultural ingenuity, the complexity of their varied social organizations, and the elaboration of religious belief and ritual. They were nonetheless ill prepared for the shock of the encounter with the Whites, a people so radically different from themselves and so infinitely more powerful. The sudden transition from the society of the ceremonial stone ax to the society of sailing ships and now of airplanes has not been easy to make.

After four centuries of Western expansion, the densely populated central highlands of New Guinea remain one of the few regions where the people still carry on their primitive existence in complete independence of the world outside. Yet as the agents of the Australian Government penetrate into ever more remote mountain valleys, they find these backwaters of antiquity already deeply disturbed by contact with the ideas and artifacts of European civilization. For "cargo"—Pidgin English for trade goods—has long flowed along the indigenous channels of communication from the seacoast into the wilderness. With it has traveled the frightening knowledge of the white man's magical power. No small element in the white man's magic is the hopeful message sent abroad by his missionaries: the news that a Messiah will come and that the present order of Creation will end.

The people of the central highlands of New Guinea are only the latest to be gripped in the recurrent religious frenzy of the "cargo cults." However variously embellished with details from native myth the Christian belief, these cults all advance the same central theme: the world is about to end in a terrible cataclysm. Thereafter God, the ancestors, or some local culture hero will appear and inaugurate a blissful paradise on earth. Death, old age, illness, and evil will be unknown. The riches of the white man will accrue to the Melanesians.

Although the news of such a movement in one area has doubtless often inspired similar movements in other areas, the evidence indicates that these cults have arisen independently in many places as parallel responses to the same enormous social stress and strain. Among the movements best known to students of Melanesia are the "Taro Cult" of New Guinea, the "Vailala Madness" of Papua, the "Naked Cult" of Espiritu Santo, the "John Frum Movement" of the New Hebrides, and the "Tuka Cult" of the Fiji Islands.

At times the cults have been so well organized and fanatically persistent that they have brought the work of government to a standstill. The outbreaks have often taken the authorities completely by surprise and have confronted them with mass opposition of an alarming kind. In the 1930s, for example, villagers in the vicinity of Wewak, New Guinea, were stirred by a succession of "Black King" movements. The prophets announced that the Europeans would soon leave the island, abandoning their property to the natives, and urged their followers to cease paying taxes, since the government station was about to disappear into the sea in a great earthquake. To the tiny community of Whites in charge of the region, such talk was dangerous. The authorities jailed

four of the prophets and exiled three others. In yet another movement, that sprang up in declared opposition to the local Christian mission, the cult leader took Satan as his god.

Troops on both sides in World War II found their arrival in Melanesia heralded as a sign of the Apocalypse. The G.I.s who landed in the New Hebrides, moving up for the bloody fighting on Guadalcanal, found the natives furiously at work preparing airfields, roads and docks for the magic ships and planes that they believed were coming from "Rusefel" (Roosevelt), the friendly king of America.

The Japanese also encountered millenarian visionaries during their southward march to Guadalcanal. Indeed, one of the strangest minor military actions of World War II occurred in Dutch New Guinea, when Japanese forces had to be turned against the local Papuan inhabitants of the Geelvink Bay region. The Japanese had at first been received with great joy, not because their "Greater East Asia Co-Prosperity Sphere" propaganda had made any great impact upon the Papuans, but because the natives regarded them as harbingers of the new world that was dawning, the flight of the Dutch having already given the first sign. Mansren, creator of the islands and their peoples, would now return, bringing with him the ancestral dead. All this had been known, the cult leaders declared, to the crafty Dutch, who had torn out the first page of the Bible where these truths were inscribed. When Mansren returned, the existing world order would be entirely overturned. White men would turn black like Papuans, Papuans would become Whites; root crops would grow in trees, and coconuts and fruits would grow like tubers. Some of the islanders now began to draw together into large "towns"; others took Biblical names such as "Jericho" and "Galilee" for their villages. Soon they adopted military uniforms and began drilling. The Japanese, by now highly unpopular, tried to disarm and disperse the Papuans; resistance inevitably developed. The climax of this tragedy came when several canoe-loads of fanatics sailed out to attack Japanese warships, believing themselves to be invulnerable by virtue of the holy water with which they had sprinkled themselves. But the bullets of the Japanese did not turn to water, and the attackers were mowed down by machine-gun fire.

Behind this incident lay a long history. As long ago as 1857 missionaries in the Geelvink Bay region had made note of the story of Mansren. It is typical of many Melanesian myths that became confounded with Christian doctrine to form the ideological basis of the movements. The legend tells how long ago there lived an old man named Manamakeri ("he who itches"), whose body was covered with sores. Manamakeri was extremely fond of palm wine, and used to climb a huge tree every day to tap the liquid from the flowers. He soon found that someone was getting there before him and removing the liquid. Eventually he trapped the thief, who turned out to be none other than the Morning Star. In return for his freedom, the Star gave the old man a wand that would produce as much fish as he liked, a magic tree and a magic staff. If he drew in the sand and stamped his foot, the drawing would become real. Manamakeri, aged as he was, now magically impregnated a young maiden; the child of this union was a miracle-child who spoke as soon as he was born. But the maiden's parents were horrified, and banished her, the child, and the old man. The trio sailed off in a canoe created by Mansren ("The Lord"), as the old man now became known. On this journey Mansren rejuvenated himself by stepping into a fire and flaking off his scaly skin, which changed into valuables. He then sailed around Geelvink Bay, creating islands where he stopped, and peopling them with the ancestors of the present-day Papuans.

The Mansren myth is plainly a creation myth full of symbolic ideas relating to fertility and rebirth. Comparative evidence—especially the shedding of his scaly skin—confirms the suspicion that the old man is, in fact, the Snake in another guise. Psychoanalytic writers argue that the snake occupies such a prominent part in mythology the world over because it stands for the penis, another fertility symbol. This may be so, but its symbolic significance is surely more complex than this. It is the "rebirth" of the hero, whether Mansren or the Snake, that exercises such universal fascination over men's minds.

The nineteenth-century missionaries thought that the Mansren story would make the introduction of Christianity easier, since the concept of "resurrection," not to mention that of the "virgin birth" and the "second coming," was already there. By 1867, however,

the first cult organized around the Mansren legend was reported.

Though such myths were widespread in Melanesia, and may have sparked occasional movements even in the pre-White era, they took on a new significance in the late nineteenth century, once the European powers had finished parceling out the Melanesian region among themselves. In many coastal areas the long history of "blackbirding"—the seizure of islanders for work on the plantations of Australia and Fiji—had built up a reservoir of hostility to Europeans. In other areas, however, the arrival of the Whites was accepted, even welcomed, for it meant access to bully beef and cigarettes, shirts and paraffin lamps, whisky and bicycles. It also meant access to the knowledge behind these material goods, for the Europeans brought missions and schools as well as cargo.

Practically the only teaching the natives received about European life came from the missions, which emphasized the central significance of religion in European society. The Melanesians already believed that man's activities—whether gardening, sailing canoes, or bearing children—needed magical assistance. Ritual without human effort was not enough. But neither was human effort on its own. This outlook was reinforced by mission teaching.

The initial enthusiasm for European rule, however, was speedily dispelled. The rapid growth of the plantation economy removed the bulk of the able-bodied men from the villages, leaving women, children, and old men to carry on as best they could. The splendid vision of the equality of all Christians began to seem a pious deception in face of the realities of the color bar, the multiplicity of rival Christian missions and the open irreligion of many Whites.

For a long time the natives accepted the European mission as the means by which the "cargo" would eventually be made available to them. But they found that acceptance of Christianity did not bring the cargo any nearer. They grew disillusioned. The story now began to be put about that it was not the Whites who made the cargo, but the dead ancestors. To people completely ignorant of factory production, this made good sense. White men did not work; they merely wrote secret signs on scraps of paper, for which they were given shiploads of goods. On the other hand, the Melanesians labored week after week for pitiful wages. Plainly the goods must be made for Melanesians somewhere, perhaps in the Land of the Dead. The Whites, who possessed the secret of the cargo, were intercepting it and keeping it from the hands of the islanders, to whom it was really consigned. In the Madang district of New Guinea, after some forty years' experience of the missions, the natives went in a body one day with a petition demanding that the cargo secret should now be revealed to them, for they had been very patient.

So strong is this belief in the existence of a "secret" that the cargo cults generally contain some ritual in imitation of the mysterious European customs which are held to be the clue to the white man's extraordinary power over goods and men. The believers sit around tables with bottles of flowers in front of them, dressed in European clothes, waiting for the cargo ship or airplane to materialize; other cultists feature magic pieces of paper and cabalistic writing. Many of them deliberately turn their backs on the past by destroying secret ritual objects, or exposing them to the gaze of uninitiated youths and women, for whom formerly even a glimpse of the sacred objects would have meant the severest penalties, even death. The belief that they were the chosen people is further reinforced by their reading of the Bible, for the lives and customs of the people in the Old Testament resemble their own lives rather than those of the Europeans. In the New Testament they find the Apocalypse, with its prophecies of destruction and resurrection, particularly attractive.

Missions that stress the imminence of the Second Coming, like those of the Seventh Day Adventists, are often accused of stimulating millenarian cults among the islanders. In reality, however, the Melanesians themselves rework the doctrines the missionaries teach them, selecting from the Bible what they themselves find particularly congenial in it. Such movements have occurred in areas where missions of quite different types have been dominant, from Roman Catholic to Seventh Day Adventist. The reasons for the emergence of these cults, of course, lie far deeper in the life-experience of the people.

The economy of most of the islands is very backward. Native agriculture produces little for the world market, and even the European plantations and mines export only a few primary products and raw materials: copra, rubber, gold. Melanesians are quite unable to understand why copra, for example, fetches thirty pounds sterling per ton one month and but five pounds a few months later. With no notion of the workings of world-commodity markets, the natives see only the sudden closing of plantations, reduced wages and unemployment, and are inclined to attribute their insecurity to the whim or evil in the nature of individual planters.

Such shocks have not been confined to the economic order. Governments, too, have come and gone, especially during the two world wars: German, Dutch, British, and French administrations melted overnight. Then came the Japanese, only to be ousted in turn largely by the previously unknown Americans. And among these Americans the Melanesians saw Negroes like themselves, living lives of luxury on equal terms with white G.I.'s. The sight of these Negroes seemed like a fulfillment of the old prophecies to many cargo cult leaders. Nor must we forget the sheer scale of this invasion. Around a million U.S. troops passed through the Admiralty Islands, completely swamping the inhabitants. It was a world of meaningless and chaotic changes, in which anything was possible. New ideas were imported and given local twists. Thus in the Loyalty Islands people expected the French Communist Party to bring the millennium. There is no real evidence, however, of any Communist influence in these movements, despite the rather hysterical belief among Solomon Island planters that the name of the local "Masinga Rule" movement was derived from the word "Marxian"! In reality the name comes from a Solomon Island tongue, and means "brotherhood."

Europeans who have witnessed outbreaks inspired by the cargo cults are usually at a loss to understand what they behold. The islanders throw away their money, break their most sacred taboos, abandon their gardens, and destroy their precious livestock; they indulge in sexual license, or, alternatively, rigidly separate men from women in huge communal establishments. Sometimes they spend days sitting gazing at the horizon for a glimpse of the long-awaited ship or airplane; sometimes they dance, pray and sing in mass congregations, becoming possessed and "speaking with tongues."

Observers have not hesitated to use such words as "madness," "mania," and "irrationality" to characterize the cults. But the cults reflect quite logical and rational attempts to make sense out of a social order that appears senseless and chaotic. Given the ignorance of the Melanesians about the wider European society, its economic organization and its highly developed technology, their reactions form a consistent and understandable pattern. They wrap up all their yearning and hope in an amalgam that combines the best counsel they can find in Christianity and their native belief. If the world is soon to end, gardening or fishing is unnecessary; everything will be provided. If the Melanesians are to be part of a much wider order, the taboos that prescribe their social conduct must now be lifted or broken in a newly prescribed way.

Of course the cargo never comes. The cults nonetheless live on. If the millennium does not arrive on schedule, then perhaps there is some failure in the magic, some error in the ritual. New breakaway groups organize around "purer" faith and ritual. The cult rarely disappears, so long as the social situation which brings it into being persists.

At this point it should be observed that cults of this general kind are not peculiar to Melanesia. Men who feel themselves oppressed and deceived have always been ready to pour their hopes and fears, their aspirations and frustrations, into dreams of a millennium to come or of a golden age to return. All parts of the world have had their counterparts of the cargo cults, from the American Indian Ghost Dance to the Communist-millenarist "reign of the saints" in Münster during the Reformation, from medieval European apocalyptic cults to African "witch-finding" movements and Chinese Buddhist heresies. In some situations men have been content to wait and pray; in others they have sought to hasten the day by using their strong right arms to do the Lord's work. And always the cults serve to bring together scattered groups, notably the peasants and urban plebeians of agrarian societies and the peoples of "stateless" societies where the cult unites separate (and often hostile) villages, clans, and tribes into a wider religio-political unity.

Once the people begin to develop secular political organizations, however, the sects tend to lose their importance as vehicles of protest. They begin to relegate the Second Coming to the distant future or to the next world. In Melanesia ordinary political bodies, trade unions and native councils are becoming the normal media through which the islanders express their aspirations. In recent years continued economic prosperity and political stability have taken some of the edge off their despair. It now seems unlikely that any major movement along cargo-cult lines will recur in areas where the transition to secular politics has been made, even if the insecurity of prewar times returned. I would predict that the embryonic nationalism represented by cargo cults is likely in future to take forms familiar in the history of other countries that have moved from subsistence agriculture to participation in the world economy.

46

Urban Rastas in Kingston, Jamaica

William F. Lewis

William F. Lewis's anthropological research and publications focused largely on religion and social movements, most recently with Rastafari culture. In this selection Professor Lewis describes in rich ethnographic detail the personalities and attributes of Nigel, Lion, and David, three urban Rastas living in Kingston, Jamaica. As Lewis describes his interviews with the three Rastas, the reader learns about Rastafarian beliefs, rituals, symbols, diet, and language, as well as other aspects of the people he refers to as "Soul Rebels."

Many Americans think of the Rastafarians as members of a deviant subculture, knowing only the reggae music of the Rastafarian song-prophet Bob Marley, or the Rasta "dreadlocks," or perhaps the Rastafarian reputation as prodigious ganja smokers. The Rastafarian movement began in Jamaica in the early 1930s. Rastas believe that Haile Ras Tafari Selassi I of Ethiopia is their black Messiah—the King of Kings and Lord of Lords—and that black true believers will some day dismiss their white oppressors and be repatriated to Ethiopia, their spiritual homeland. Although the largest number of Rastas live in Jamaica, there are also followers in the United States, England, Canada, Ethiopia, and other parts of the world.

Nigel

On a sultry day in downtown Kingston a weary walker might come upon Nigel lounging on his front steps, shirtless, with a towel draped around his shoulders as he carefully dries himself after one of his periodic splash baths. That is how I first met him. A careless observer might take Nigel to be mad, a stigma with which Jamaican society labels the solitary life free from the cares of family and the demands of social responsibility. However, Nigel is affable, courteous and willing to share his wisdom with sympathetic listeners. I was one of them.

Nigel's conversations with passers-by can become serious communications. He interprets such a

happy occasion as the result of a mutual consciousness that compels people to reason with him. True communication is never mere serendipity. Once a male stranger (Nigel seldom if ever converses seriously with a female) demonstrates that his interests are compatible with Nigel's, his scrutiny and suspicion change to a more relaxed and intimate tone. Then Nigel asks the visitor to remove his shoes, unburden himself of his baggage, and empty his pockets of money, tobacco, and combs, things Nigel finds polluting. He requires all to relieve themselves of these demonic influences before any can enter his mansion. I complied.

Nigel's mansion turns out to be the building that housed his formerly prosperous clothing boutique which catered to the sartorial demands of the Jamaican elite. The quarters are large, two stories high, with spacious rooms that are now bereft of furniture and decoration. Nigel's mansion is but a vestige of the glamour and prestige he enjoyed as one of the wealthiest tailors in Jamaica. The yellow clippings that hang willy-nilly from the flaking walls of the main room bear silent witness to Nigel's renunciation of both his business and family. The Jamaican media once celebrated him as a promising designer of clothes for both the wealthy and the celebrated. That was before his commitment to the principles of Rastafari.

Nigel explains his conversion to Rastafari as an odyssey, a passage that began shortly after his appendectomy operation. Then modern drugs and treatments were of no avail in restoring his energy, vitality and spirit. However, an encounter with a Rasta turned into meetings of mutual communication and disclosure. On the Rasta's advice, Nigel drank large amounts of ganja tea and smoked equally large amounts of marijuana. He recovered his health. From then on, he affiliated himself with the ways of Rastafari, and he too hallowed the herb as the healing of nations. Furthermore, he attributes the restoration and continuance of his health to his dedication to the Rasta principles of love, meditation, reasoning and *ital* (natural) foods of which marijuana is a part.

Nigel found peace when he embraced Rastafari. His fashion industry and family were the weapons he created to wage warfare on people. Thus, he divested himself of his career and married life.

Shortly after his conversion in 1981, Nigel began to send funds to Rastas in the rural interior. At that time, Jamaican businesses were recouping their losses suffered under the democratic socialism of the Manley government which had threatened their profits. Nigel recalls how the bank officials thought that he was donating funds to a subversive group in the interior. A popular rumor at the time was that Manley's allies had contingents ready in the country who would help Cuban communists infiltrate Jamaica. Nigel was under great suspicion. The bank refused to handle any of his transactions. The government harassed him on charges of tax evasion. His wife tried to commit him to a mental institution. Nigel muses: "Because I was becoming aware of my own identity, I had to go through this suffering. That's in the past, the price I paid. Now I am free."

Now Nigel is neither an entrepreneur nor an artist but an ascetic. He refuses to touch money, and only the free will offerings of others sustain him. His meatless diet consists only of fruits, vegetables and an occasional fish. He abhors the eating of animal meat because dead flesh will only cause sickness for the person who consumes it. Nor will he accept any fruit or vegetable whose natural appearance has been altered by any cutting, mashing or peeling. Nigel seems lanky and anorexic. However, his appearance belies his vigor and vitality which are evident in his darting about and enthusiastically engaging the visitor in philosophical discussion about the affairs of the world, the way to health and the meaning of sexuality.

An aroma of ganja smoke clings to Nigel's long, unkempt and natural dreads. This slovenliness too is deceptive because Nigel is particularly fastidious about the cleanliness of his body and he meticulously monitors its functions. This leads him to administer frequent purgatives to himself lest the accumulation of toxins within cause harm for the whole body. His frequent cleansings and purgations of the body as well as the avoidance of contact with any decaying matter, especially a dead body, are normative in Nigel's life. Were these norms violated, his spiritual and physical health would be imperiled.

Without his regimen, Nigel would be unable to find the strength to weave his philosophical reflections through his writings, his conversations and solitary moments of meditation. Esoteric writings and volumes are scattered throughout his quarters. He has amassed stacks of newspaper clippings and sundry writings whose relationship to the philosophy of Rastafari at first glance appears obscure. Nevertheless, Nigel can explain every metaphor and symbol in his literary collection and connect them to what he believes are the truths of Rastafari. Included in his assemblage of works are titles such as: "Dread Locks Judgement," "Anthropology: Races of Man," "Radical Vegetarianism," "Rasta Voice Magazine," "Economy and Business," "Women as Sex Object," and "Pan African Digest." His own essays range from glosses on Joseph Owens' *Dread* and Dennis Forsythe's *Healing of Nations* to highly idealistic writing on a new economic order. Among these pieces is correspondence from previous English and American visitors to Nigel's mansion.

Nigel's own writings have an intense and highly involuted style which gives them an arcane quality, a form somewhat reminiscent of James Joyce's stream of consciousness. Tolerance and patience are demanded of the reader who wishes to decipher Nigel's turn of phrase and novel transformation of words. Indeed, the uninitiated reader might wonder if the police are not correct in simply shrugging him off as a Rasta who has had too much ganja. His prose is obscure and agonistic, but, nevertheless, he can elicit sense from every syllable, word and line. Nigel's deftness in turning his twisted writings into an articulate message makes him a shaman and mythmaker of sorts, for his vocalizations about the revelation he bears have the rhythm, cadence and timbre of a person standing outside of the self.

The Upper Room

Nigel's "Upper Room" is on the second level of the building with two large windows opening to a view of eastern Kingston and allowing the cool breezes from the sea to circulate through the room. It is furnished with a few mats, a raggedy sleeping cot over to the side, a square table on which the herb is blessed, and shelves along the wall on which lie chillum pipes of various lengths. The chillum pipes are stored for other Rastas who might visit and join Nigel for reasoning. In his Upper Room Nigel undergoes his most intense experience with ganja and elaborates ecstatically on Rastafari. In accord with what he believes to be Rastas' tradition, he excludes women from these sessions.

When the brethren have gathered in the Upper Room, Nigel raises his arms toward the East in a grand gesture and blesses the herb with vocalizations resembling glossolalia. "Amharic," he says as an aside, "the Ethiopian language." The blessings are spontaneous and ecstatic, but on listening closely I detected a word that sounded like *mirrikat,* the Amharic word for blessing. Later Nigel mentioned that he learned some Amharic at the Ethiopian Orthodox Church in Kingston.

After the chillum is filled, and the herb is burning, Nigel is the first to draw deeply from the pipe. His chest expands as smoke fills his lungs. He exhales billows of smoke through his nostrils and mouth, and the whiffs frame his lionlike face with tendrils of plumes that seep through his long locks and beard. Through the clouds of smoke, Nigel stares at all in the room with a fierce look, regal, but cutting and penetrating. His demeanor demands a response.

"The conquering Lion of Judah shall break every chain," I acclaim.

Nigel seems pleased with this affirmation of his link with the Emperor Haile Selassie, the Lion of Judah.

Another's turn comes to partake of the chalice, and Nigel passes the pipe with a most respectful gesture. Kneeling before the next brother with his own head bowed low to the floor, his outstretched arms offer him the chillum. The brother accepts, draws from it, and proclaims, "Jah Rastafari."

The chillum moves from participant to participant, brother to brother, each honoring the other with gestures of deference but never permitting their flesh to meet. Bodily contact is assiduously avoided. Soon the participants assume unusual bodily postures. The effect is startling. Nigel takes the lead in displaying great physical agility and dexterity by twisting his body into yogalike positions. All the brethren follow suit. They throw their bodies into lionlike leaps. Nevertheless, their bodily deportments are undertaken with great concentration and awareness, for not once did their acrobatic feats threaten to harm anyone in the room.

"What is love?" asks one of the brothers.

"Love is where there are no starving people. As long as there are hungry people, hatred is in power. Caring and supporting . . ."

Their dance continues, and perhaps ten minutes passes.

"Sex is a performance, a duty."

"Women are for pickneys (babies)."

Another interval, and more of their dancing.

"Burn Babylon." Some begin chanting the familiar lyric.

"Why the police brutality and why youths beaten by Babylon? They steal because they are hungry and want to fill their bellies. No crime in taking food because you are hungry."

"Africa for the blacks, Europe for the whites, Jamaica for the Arawaks."

David and Lion

Tourists and Jamaicans alike must cross an unsteady, wooden pier in order to board the ferry that takes passengers from Kingston Harbor to the legendary Port Royal across the bay. Once celebrated as a haunt for pirates and a playground for debauchery, Port Royal now rests quietly on the bay, chastised forever, it seems, by the raging earthquake it suffered in the late seventeenth century. That cataclysm hurled much of the port into the Caribbean.

Near the ramp leading to the pier lazes David, a Rasta brother. He is attending his concession stand which is simply a large crate hoisted on a dolly for maneuverability. From the cart, David sells Red Stripe beer, D & G sodas, as well as Benson cigarettes by ones and twos, and, of course, raw sugar cane and coconut, the most popular items. A sampling from his assortment of refreshments often comes as welcome relief for the overheated traveler after the half-hour trip across the bay.

David and Lion live together in a hovel about twenty yards from their stand. The shack rests precariously on the side of the pier, supported in part by the hanging branches of a huge tree on which part of it also leans. The roof and sidings are constructed of huge pieces of cardboard and plastic sheeting. Nearby, a slipshod folding chair, unworthy of any task, clings to the pier's edge and marks out an area that serves as a reception space for guests. The sound of the rushing water against the piles, the squeaking of the rats, and the dust from the parched earth fill the place David and Lion call home with a romantic irony. They sit between two worlds, perhaps a sign of their liminality. From one viewpoint, Port Royal's outlines loom across the bay standing witness to wanton living long ago. From another angle stands the symbol of law and order, a police station, to which the Rastas pay no heed.

Lion and David eat *ital* food, a healthy low-salt, low-fat and low-cholesterol diet, that consists mainly of vegetables, plantains and the occasional red snapper, caught off the pier. At a clearing away from their hut, they prepare the food on an aluminum can cover some twenty-four inches in diameter. The fare is seasoned with hot pepper and served on tin plates. Sometimes a rat might boldly rush a dish at what appears to be an opportune moment in an effort to wrest a morsel from a distracted diner. The Rastas, however, are generous and share their food with any of their guests, human and animal alike.

When business is slow at their stand, Lion, David and other brethren hustle on the streets of Kingston, selling anything from boxed donuts to belts and tams (knitted headgear which they themselves have crafted). They are talkative entrepreneurs and quick to prevail upon a prospective customer, especially a white tourist, to purchase one of their handiworks or products.

Reasoning

Toward late afternoon on a hot July day, two brethren arrive at the pier and exchange greetings with David. David assures the visiting brethren that I, the white guest sitting near the hut, have respect and love for Rastafari. Lion emerges from below the rafters of the pier where he was resting and lends support to David's assurances that their white visitor is trustworthy.

When the group is ready, David places the Bible on the ground and marks off a few pages from which he will draw his inspiration. The spliffs are lit with a short grace: "Give thanks." At that moment, however, some youths happen on the scene, probably drawn by the whiff of ganja smoke overcoming the salty sea breezes. They ask for some herb. Lion rebukes the boys and says: "This is high reasoning, boys, and not play." They run off. The Rastas return to the matter at hand.

David mulls over the scriptural passage about the Nazarites and the proscription on the cutting of hair. "Love is the foundation of Rastafari. The covenant is the hair, the locks. This is Godly."

As a group of commuters disembarks from the ferry and hurries by the group, scarcely giving them a glance, Lion comments: "Jamaican people cannot see the truth. They have eyes, hands, feet, but don't use them properly for justice and love. They are blinded."

Rashi holds his spliff and remarks pensively: "Rastas are clever, living for truth. The weed is important. It is healing."

After reflecting a bit on the wisdom in the herb, the Rastas turn to excoriating the success of reggae musicians, a discussion that enlivens the group. Few endearing words are spent on reggae musicians who, the Rastas believe, preach the philosophy of Rastafari, give interviews to magazines, enrich themselves, but filter none of their profits into the creation of a stronger culture for the rest of the brethren.

"Look how they draw up around Nesta's place on New Hope, clean and shining. Burn reggae."

All agree.

Soon the brethren fall into a quiet, meditative mood. A few reflect in low voices on the similarity between the churches and reggae. This prompts David to take up a verse from the scriptures and freely elaborate on it. The verse is: "Let the dead bury the dead."

"The churches in Jamaica bury only dead people, and take people's money to build bigger church buildings, instead of providing work and industry for people. The Rasta never dies but has life eternal, as Christ promised. God cannot lie. To have life eternal one must follow the Rasta culture in the Bible. Rasta is a new name. It is the new Jerusalem that Isaiah promised in the prophecy."

David's words excite the group, and they all affirm the equality of people. They denounce the hypocrisy of organized religion, reggae and the government for manipulating the Bible and authority. The more their anger with society increases, so much the more does the spontaneity of the gathering quicken.

David takes the spliff from a Rasta reclining next to him. Holding it, he prays that the chalice be not a source of condemnation but a guardian of life eternal. He inhales deeply, holds the smoke within, and for almost a minute after exhalation he gazes intently on me, the white visitor sitting across from him. Then:

"Rasta is not the color of the skin. Blacks hate their fellow man, just like white man hates. Even some Rastas have words on their lips but not in their hearts."

As darkness draws closer, and fewer people queue up for the ferry, the Rastas become more vociferous.

"Living is for the Rastas. Moses and the prophets are not dead, but reign in Zion, a Kingdom that is better than the one here. I have life. I will never die but go to Zion with Ras Tafari Selassie I" [pronounced as "aye"].

Interspersed among their exultations of Selassie are monotone chantings expressing a yearning for repatriation to a land of freedom from which they have been exiled.

"Africa yes! But not the Africa of today because it is just as corrupt as Jamaica."

Silence. The spliffs are lit again, passed around and blessed. The mood changes. The brethren become serious and playful, ecstatic and earthly. Lion leads this flow of sensuousness. He rolls on the ground, smiles, laughs lightly while singing an improvisation on liberty, freedom and repatriation. He kisses the roots of a nearby tree and exclaims: "Jah Rastafari."

The others participate in his display with their own paeans on liberation and freedom. Soon they too tumble over the ground, enjoying themselves im-

mensely, and encouraging me to "ride the vibes and feel freedom."

At dusk, bright lights illumine the decks of a British warship that had docked in the harbor earlier in the day. The sharp relief of the ship in the distance prompts Lion to remark:

"War is against Rastafari. Rastas do what is right for life and live forever. Jamaican people love war too much. I don't know why."

David pursues the thought further. "I-n-I is never listened to. We are rejected. They have no culture. They steal, kill and shoot."

Lion snuggles closer to the roots of the tree which are bulging from the parched earth. He seems to caress them.

"I-n-I Rastafari are the love in the world. We are very peaceful, loving and don't eat poisonous things, no salt, no liver, no dead animals."

Rashi adds: "We want wholeness, fullness of justice, fullness of love."

When asked to identify the source of his power, Rashi responds:

"I-n-I is the bible in the heart. The true bible is yet to be written. I-n-I moves beyond the bible. It is a word that we must move beyond. I-n-I live naturally in the fullness of divinity, don't have to go to school. Truth is in the heart. I-n-I have to learn our flesh and blood. Then everybody gets food, shelter. This is the truth."

Popes and priests irritate them. "Burn the pope. Burn the pope man. The Church is a vampire with their cars and living in the hills [an area where the elite reside]. The pope is a vampire, wants our blood. Selassie I is the head. The pope is the devil."

The light fades. More silence. The bay water slaps against the pilings. A rat tears across the planks and startles me. I jump. Lion, however, admonishes me with a reminder that the rat is only a creature.

"The barber shop is the mark of the beast. Comb and razor conquer. The wealth of Jah is with locks, in fullness of his company."

All nod in agreement. I mention that my understanding is increasing.

"Be careful with words, brother," Lion says, "overstand not understand. I people are forward people not backward."

Another interjects: "It is a brand new way of life. The language of I-n-I is forward. I-n-I people will pay no more. For five hundred years, they built Babylon on us, but they will do it no more."

47

Speaking Is Believing

Susan Friend Harding

After decades of standing aside from political life in America, fundamentalist or born-again Protestants moved assertively into public view in the 1980s, in part through leaders such as Jerry Falwell. During that period, Susan Friend Harding did fieldwork with fundamentalist Christians in Lynchburg, Virginia, the home of Falwell's movement, with a keen focus on how language is used. In a religion without elaborate rituals or visual symbolism, Harding argues language plays an especially significant role for fundamentalist Christians, whether in sermons, speeches, or witnessing, that is, engaging in persuasive conversations intended to convert. Harding's understanding of her own role as ethnographer was challenged by the community's perception of her as unsaved, with interviews serving as opportunities for witnessing.

Interviewing-turned-witnessing is just what occurred when Harding spoke with the Reverend Melvin Campbell. In the following material, a chapter from her book-length ethnography, Harding does a close reading of her encounter with Reverend Campbell. While believers and non-believers might interpret Campbell's words differently, Harding's goal is to establish how and why his speech is rhetorically effective. Campbell employs textual features such as personal anecdotes, Biblical narratives, analogies, symbolism, and surface-level details of vocabulary and grammar, to tell stories in a way that persuades the listener of the veracity of the Christian experience.

Harding's analysis is an excellent example of the language-centered approach within anthropology, as well as an anthropological contribution to the documentation of evangelical Christianity in the contemporary United States. Susan Friend Harding is Professor of Anthropology at the University of California, Santa Cruz.

> *To be converted, to be regenerated, to receive grace, to experience religion, to gain assurance are so many phrases which denote the process, gradual or sudden, by which a self hitherto divided, and consciously wrong, inferior and unhappy, becomes unified and consciously right, superior and happy, in consequence of its firmer hold upon religious realities. This at least is what conversion signifies in general terms, whether or not we believe that direct divine operation is needed to bring such a moral change about.*
>
> *—William James, 1906*

Dusk had fallen by the time I left Jordan Baptist Church, but the light bothered my eyes as I looked

From: THE BOOK OF JERRY FALWELL: FUNDAMENTALIST LANGUAGE AND POLITICS. *Princeton and Oxford: Princeton University Press, pp. 33–60, 2000.*

around the parking lot for my car. It seemed as if everything had moved slightly. The church was on the outskirts of one of the poorer parts of Lynchburg, and I would have to zigzag across a half dozen big streets that bisect the city to get back to my motel. I knew I was in some kind of daze after my long talk with the Reverend Melvin Campbell. I usually am after an interview, and this one had been especially intense. Halfway across town, I stopped at a stop sign, then started into the intersection, and was very nearly smashed by a car that seemed to come upon me from nowhere very fast. I slammed on the brakes, sat stunned for a split second, and asked myself "What is God trying to tell me?"

It was my voice but not my language. I had been inhabited by the fundamental Baptist tongue I was investigating. As the Reverend Campbell might have put it, the Holy Spirit was dealing with me, speaking to my heart, bringing me under conviction. He was showing me that life is a passing thing, that death could take me in an instant, no matter how much control I fancied I had over my life, and that I should put my life in the Lord's hands before it was too late.

If we conceive of conversion as a process of acquiring a specific religious language or dialect, I was initiated into the first stage of fundamental Baptist conversion as I sat in my car that evening in Lynchburg, awash in apprehension and relief. The process starts when an unsaved listener begins to appropriate in his or her inner speech the saved speaker's language and its attendant view of the world. The speaker's language, now in the listener's voice, converts the listener's mind into a contested terrain, a divided self. At the moment of salvation, which may come quickly and easily, or much later after great inward turmoil, the listener becomes a speaker. The Christian tongue locks into some kind of central, controlling, dominant place; it has gone beyond the point of inhabiting the listener's mind to occupy the listener's identity. The Holy Spirit, the very Word of God, has come, as fundamental Baptists say, to indwell the heart of the believer, who may now publicly display in speech and action a personal, which is to say, conversational, relationship with God.

Conversion is an inner transformation which quickens the supernatural imagination as it places new believers within the central storied sequence of the Christian Bible and enables them to approach the Bible as a living reality. Conversion transfers narrative authority—the Holy Spirit—to the newly faithful as well as the wherewithal to narrate one's life in Christian terms. As we will see, the keys that unlock the Kingdom of God include Bible-based interpretive practices which Christians experience as the indwelling of the Holy Spirit.

Among fundamental Baptists, the gospel of Jesus Christ is the plan of salvation, the good news, God's gift to all mankind. Narrowly defined, the gospel is the story, the message, of Christ's death, burial, and resurrection. More broadly, it is the storied sequence that renders the Bible whole, unified. How does the language and performance of fundamental Baptist gospel preaching (and witnessing, testifying, evangelizing, spreading the Word) convict and convert the unsaved listener? How does it work as a rhetoric of conversion? Witnessing is rhetorical in two senses, namely, as an argument about the transformation of self that lost souls must undergo, and as a method of bringing about that change in those who listen to it. Fundamental Baptist witnessing is not just a monologue that constitutes its speaker as a culturally specific person; it is also a dialogue that reconstitutes its listeners. My focus is on this latter aspect, on witnessing as the practice, the rite and the rhetoric, of conversion.

William James speculated that those who experienced dramatic conversions might have been born with a "melancholy disposition," a chronically "divided" mind, or else they had drunk "too deep of the cup of bitterness." Contemporary social scientists have also investigated converts to born-again Christianity for some indication of why they convert. The notion is, apparently, that those who convert are somehow susceptible, vulnerable, in need of something, so the question becomes: "Why? What's wrong? What's unsettling them?" Or, "What's setting them up? How have they been predisposed to convert?" Social scientists scrutinize the external psychological and social conditions of converts looking for clues, patterns, and causes. They have found evidence in converts' lives of psychological and social stress (due to marriage problems, loss of a job, imprisonment, adolescence, dating, serious illness or accidents, encounters with death, "role" transitions, moving to a new city, going to college, and so on). They have argued that converts were predisposed by previous conditioning (religious upbringing, education, class, gender), and by patterns of interpersonal influence (by converted kin, friends, mentors). These correlations are not satisfying explanations, however, because, among other things, none of the circumstances have been found with enough regularity among converts, and the same circumstances have been found among nonconverts with too much regularity.

There is also considerable literature, both popular and academic, on how various ritual practices and psychological techniques trigger experiences that result in a conversion from one worldview, or mind-set, to another.[1] Distinct conversion methods (social seclusion, dramatic enactments, bodily markings, physical stress or pain, fasting, interrogation, chanting, silence, immobility, and so on) certainly pave the way for radical shifts in belief and commitment. However, this approach, at least when plied by those who see conversion as a kind of brainwashing, overlooks how persuasive in a quite unsensational way the recruiting rhetoric is. It overlooks the extent to which the language of conversion as such "divides" the mind and contributes to bringing about conversion. The presumption which I think accounts for this oversight, and which in more muted form also guides many social scientific studies, is that "nobody in their right mind would believe this stuff." Since "belief" is irrational, some sort of suspension of normal thinking must have taken place and caused the convert to lose his or her grip on reality.

Social scientists and professed unbelievers in general do not let themselves get close enough to "belief" to understand it, or, for that matter, even to see what it is. Men and women convert to fundamental Christianity because they become convinced that supernatural reality is a fact, that Christ is the literal Son of God, that he did rise from the dead and is alive today, that the Holy Spirit is speaking to them, that Jesus will enter their hearts if they acknowledge their sins, that they will have eternal life, that God is really real. To continue to think otherwise would be irrational; it is disbelief that is false and unthinking. The appropriate question then is: How does this supernatural order become real, known, experienced, and absolutely irrefutable?

Among conservative Protestants, and especially among fundamentalists, it is the Word, the gospel of Jesus Christ, written, spoken, heard, and read, that converts the unbeliever. The stresses, transitions, influences, conditioning, and techniques scrutinized by many social scientists do not in themselves "explain," do not "cause," conversion to Christ. All they

do is increase the likelihood that a person might listen to the gospel; they may open or "prepare a person's heart." It is the Word of God, the gospel, and, believers would add, the Holy Spirit, God himself, that converts, that changes the heart.[2] We cannot understand fundamental Baptist conversion by looking only at what causes a person to listen to the gospel; the causes are innumerable. Rather, we must listen to the gospel with an open ear, and we must explore the interpretive practices that enable us to understand and accept what we hear.

Witnessing and preaching are the two main situations in which believers speak the gospel most intensely. Preaching—the sermon—is a formal oration addressed to a body of believers and nonbelievers by an ordained or anointed speaker in church services and revivals. Sermons occur in the context of clear ritual format, of a collective, sanctifying scenario in which the mode of interpretation is enacted. Witnessing is more informal and often occurs in the course of what appears to be no more than a conversation between the witness, who is *saved*, and an *unsaved* listener. But it is no mere conversation. The witness and the unsaved "do not share a common understanding— either of the immediate situation or of reality more generally." Witnesses are "aware of this difference in understanding and self-consciously set out to change the views of those they address" and to create a "compelling religious reality completely at variance with their [listener's] experience."

Witnessing aims to separate novice listeners from their prior, given reality, to constitute a new, previously unperceived or indistinct reality, and to impress that reality upon them, make it felt, heard, seen, known, undeniably real. The reality, or *truth*,

---

1. Whitehead (1987) provides an excellent, critical review of this literature in her study of conversion among Scientologists.

2. Christian social scientists and theologians have studied the secular literature on conversion and generated their own. Elmer Towns, dean of Jerry Falwell's Liberty Baptist Seminary and a nationally known researcher in the "science of church growth," told me that the highest rate of conversion occurred among prisoners, the second highest among the bankrupt; he also emphasized the importance of personal networks and of reaching people while they are "in transition" of some kind. The difference between Towns and secular social scientists is that Towns would never suggest any of these factors really causes conversion; the Holy Spirit convicts sinners and Christ saves them.

constituted in witnessing is, in part, a linguistic one: the supernatural manifests itself as God's voice and his spirit is communicated and experienced through words. Much collective ritual among orthodox Protestants is likewise centered on words, on the Word. Especially among fundamentalists, church services and revivals are stripped of overt, imagistic, and sacramental material; relatively little happens visually, and spiritual realities are not communicated through sensuous, nonlinguistic means. In a way, witnessing is pure fundamentalist ritual, shorn of almost all distractions. It is the plainest, most concentrated method for revealing and transmitting the Word of God, one in which language is intensified, focused, and virtually shot at the unwashed listener.

Fundamentalists are by no means unique in their use of oratory to convert others. Their general techniques and some of the content of their conversion rhetoric are broadly shared among conservative Protestants. Indeed, the principal of conversion, of one person insinuating his or her mode of interpretation in the mind of another, informs all dialogue.[3] What distinguishes fundamental Baptists from others is the degree to which they have formalized rhetorical techniques for converting others, the precise and distinctly unconscious manner in which those techniques appropriate the listener's dialogic imagination, and the particular transformations of self evoked in the listener.

As I sat in that intersection contemplating my near collision, it was quite specifically the Reverend Campbell's language, his supernaturalizing mode of interpretation, that unfurled itself in my mind. I had intended to interview him that afternoon, but within the first few minutes of our talk, Campbell assumed control of the dialogue and reframed my appointment to interview him into his opportunity to witness to me for an hour and a half.

---

3. This is how Bakhtin described ordinary dialogue from the speaker's point of view: "The speaker strives to get a reading on his own word, and on his own conceptual system that determines this word, within the alien conceptual system of the understanding receiver; he enters into dialogical relationships with certain aspects of this system. The speaker breaks through the alien conceptual horizon of the listener, constructs his own utterance on alien territory, against his, the listener's, apperceptive background."

A witnessing session minimally includes the gospel story (an exegesis of the death, burial, and resurrection of Jesus Christ) and a confrontation between the witness and his or her listener in which the witness invites or exhorts the listener to receive Christ as his or her personal savior. Witnesses may also tell how they and others came to know the Lord as savior; they may testify (give accounts of encounters between themselves and God, and other narrative evidence of God's intervention in the natural world) and deliver other doctrinal exegeses (regarding, for example, heaven and hell, the origin and nature of sin, or the ways of Satan).

Witnessing, like evangelistic preaching, "is intended to create a spiritual crisis by calling to the fore one's desperate and lost conditions, which one may have been totally unaware of." This crisis is the onset of the conversion process, what fundamentalists call "coming under conviction," and is based on a direct experience of the divine. You *know* when the Holy Spirit convicts you of, or makes you see, your sins. Conviction effects a deep sensation of one's own impurity and separation from God, or one's sinfulness, one's sin nature. And it engenders a sense that something has to be done about it. We shall see that the inner speech of convicted sinners is transformed as they are alienated from their previous voices (the old self, natural man); cast into a limbo (lost, in need, searching), that is to say, somehow in a liminal state, a state of confusion and speechlessness; and begin to hear a new voice (an inaudible voice, the Holy Spirit).

It is a kind of inner rite of passage that is completed when sinners are saved, or born-again, regenerated, washed in the blood of Christ. Salvation is experienced as a release from the bondage of sin and a personal reconciliation with God. A new self, or the spiritual man, emerges and the supernatural imagination is cut loose as the newborn Christian accepts the meaning of the gospel and begins to speak the language of Christ. In the words of Benetta Jules-Rosette, who studied among, and joined, the Apostles of John Maranke in Africa, conversion is "a powerful clash resulting from the shift from one realm of thought and action to another, a moment of specific *shock*. Under this shock, the very terms of physical existence seem to alter."

The power of the Reverend Campbell's rhetoric to induce liminality was seconded in my case by several circumstances—I was on a number of margins. It was late in the afternoon, and his church was on the edge of town. We were in a corner of the church, his study, alone, on the edge of propriety. I was beginning my fieldwork. And Campbell seemed to me a peripheral character in my study. Having grown up with Jerry Falwell and trained to be a preacher at his Liberty Bible Institute, Campbell was in, but not quite of, Falwell's empire. His congregation appeared to consist largely of white, working-class or unemployed men and women and their children. Jordan Baptist Church was, in his words, "a solid work," with about 350 members, and it sustained a number of outreaches, but Campbell and his congregation were not engaged in any of the political or cultural activism that earned Jerry Falwell a national reputation.

Campbell was a tall, trim, muscular man, his silvery gray hair piled up from his forehead in waves an inch or two high. He sat at his desk, I in a side chair, and he looked me in the eye the entire time we talked. Later I realized that most people who sat in the chair I was sitting in came to Campbell for spiritual help. I also realized he was eager to have me tape-record our conversation so that I might listen to it again and again should I prove too hard-hearted that afternoon to receive the help he offered me.

Born-again believers say that unbelievers cannot understand their faith. Jeanne Favret-Saada came to a similar conclusion while studying witchcraft in the Bocage region of France. "For anyone who wants to understand the meaning of [witchcraft] discourse, there is no solution but to practice it oneself, to become one's informant." This is so, she tells us, because there are only two "positions" from which a person speaks or hears speech about witchcraft: bewitched and unwitcher; if you are neither, you will never hear others speaking the discourse. The situation is, of course, quite different among fundamentalists. Gospel talk is public and targets outsiders, nonbelievers, but, as in witchcraft, there is no such thing as a neutral position, no place for an ethnographer who seeks "information." Either you are lost, or you are saved.

When I went to Lynchburg, I was naive enough to think I could be detached, that I could participate in the culture I was observing without partaking of it. I could come and stay for months, talk mainly to church people, attempt to "learn the culture," ask questions based on respect and knowledge; and still remain outside, separate, obscure about what I believed and disbelieved. But there was no such ground. I might think there was, but the church people did not, no matter what I said. It was inconceivable to them that anyone with an appetite for the gospel as great as mine was simply "gathering information," was just there "to write a book." No, I was searching. *God works in mysterious ways.* In my case, he seemed to be letting me find my way to him through this book I said I was writing about them. Several people told me as much; others just seemed amused when I told them what I was doing and gave me a look that suggested they knew better. My story about what I was doing there, instead of protecting me from "going native," located me in their world: I was a lost soul on the brink of salvation. And the Reverend Campbell spoke to me accordingly.

I asked him first how he became a pastor, and he took fifteen minutes to answer me. I had expected to get something akin to "information" or "facts," and he gave me a long story of personal transformation, one that began with how he had been saved and had served the Lord before he was called to preach. He never acknowledged my academic project and seemed to speak to me as if I were what they call a "nominal Christian," someone who might think she was a Christian but who had never been saved. He could assume I was not born-again simply because I did not indicate I was, as believers do when they meet, if only by a turn of phrase. Certainly, he was aware of himself as witnessing to me, and he had been trained, formally and informally, in soul-winning techniques, but his manner and his method seemed to draw more on unconscious intuition than deliberate design.

There were at least five distinct rhetorical movements in Campbell's witnessing talk that afternoon. He equated his present listener—me—with the listeners in his stories. He fashioned her as lost. He fashioned the gospel speaker—himself and others—as saved. He transformed lost listeners in his stories into gospel speakers. And he invited me to undergo the same transformation, the same narrative rite of passage, and become a gospel speaker. I will trace these movements by exhibiting and expanding on sequential pieces of Campbell's speech, hoping to show you, as much as tell you, what conversion and belief are among fundamental Baptists. Unfortunately, in words flattened out on a page, we may hear only suggestions of his Southern, fundamental

Baptist accent, his peculiar cadence, intonation, pausing, pitch, and stress.

I was saved when I was fifteen years old. I was a member of a Methodist church all of my life as a child. At the age of fifteen I still had not heard the gospel story of Jesus Christ and how that he died for our sins. I was instructed as a child coming up in the Methodist movement just to live a good life, to be morally good and to maintain all of those particular statuses, and I would be okay. Now I was invited by a friend to visit a Baptist church. . . . And this was an independent fundamental Baptist church. And of course they had one of those hell-fire-and-damnation preachers in there, and he got down on my case that night. And I began to look at things and I realized there was something missing in my life. Because, though we've never seen God, we're still aware of the fact that he is present, we know he's there. And even though I wasn't saved I knew there was something bombarding my life that was beyond my power to see or really understand at the time. And I couldn't understand why I wasn't receiving what I needed in a Methodist church. So after attending about three of their services—and incidentally they were in revival that week—then the spirit of God began to convict me about my place in life and how that I was lost and had not yet turned my whole life over to Christ, so I was saved that week, I went forward and gave my heart to Christ. Now this is a process that some folks misconstrue along the highways of life. "I put all the nine yards in that really belongs there . . . ," they think often that this is all that's necessary. But I realized that night there was a need in my life and that need was met, and so much the spirit of God came to live in my heart. Now this is God's gift to every person that receives Christ. So I joined that particular church after about a month of visiting there. But I was first saved and then I followed Christ to baptism, which I hadn't been baptized before. Of course the Methodist church, they sprinkle, and I don't have any argument with them there, other than the fact that I believe the Bible teaches immersion. And then after this, my life began to grow and materialize into something that was real, something that I could really identify with. That emptiness that was there before was now being replaced by something that had meaning and purpose in it. And I began to sense the need of telling others about what had happened to me. And basically I think perhaps the change could be detected in my life, as the Bible declares, that when a person is saved, the old man, the old person, or the character that they were passes away, and then they become a new creation in Christ Jesus. That is to say, they might be a char-acter that may be drinking and cutting up and carrying on, and a variety of things that are ill toward God. All of these things began to dissolve away. I found that I had no desires for all these things, but then I began to abhor them. I actually began to hate them. And this was in accordance with the Scriptures, as I found out later. And then as my life began to mature in Christ I found that I too could win others to Christ the same way I was won: by simply telling them that there's a heaven to gain and a hell to shun.

In his conversion narrative, the Reverend Campbell defined being "lost" and being "saved" and how he moved from one position to the other. Lostness, he indicated, is a position from which you listen, and salvation is one from which you speak. Campbell began to pull me in and placed me into his narrative in the position of listener.

Numerous poetic and performance features teem on the surface of Campbell's speech. There are verse markers ("and" and "now"), special codes, figurative language, symbolic and metaphoric parallelism, and appeals to tradition. These features mark the text as an oral performance and indicate a special relationship between performer and listener. It is a relationship in which the performer assumes responsibility for a display of competence, indirectly instructs the listener about how to interpret messages, and invites, elicits, participation. These tactics bind the listener to the performer in a relationship of dependence and keep the listener caught up in the display.

Campbell also communicated my relationship to his speech more directly through his use of pronouns (emphasis added): *I still had not heard the gospel story of Jesus Christ and how that he died for our sins. . . . Because, though we've never seen God, we're still aware of the fact that he is present, we know he's there.* Campbell continued to place me in his narrative during the rest of the time we talked by using the cooptive "we," and he frequently shifted his pronouns and at times used "you" ambiguously, as a personal and impersonal pronoun. His listener by these means became the subject of a whole range of presuppositions posited in such a way that they were difficult to resist.

At one point in this initial speech and at several points subsequently Campbell quite overtly identified me with his narrative listeners. The central, repeated narrative structure in his witnessing was a dialogic encounter between person and God, or between a lost listener and a saved speaker. The context of his witnessing, of course, was also conversational: Campbell and I were engaged in a dialogue, one in which he, who was saved, was speaking, and I, who was not saved, was listening. Early in his conversion narrative, Campbell began to collapse these parallel levels of conversational structure and thereby place me in his stories, in his speech:

Now I was invited by a friend to visit a Baptist church . . . and of course this was an independent fundamental Baptist church. And of course they had one of those hell-fire-and-damnation preachers in there, and he got down on my case that night. In describing his context the night he was converted, Campbell called attention to our—his and my—context. He too was a hell-fire-and-damnation preacher, and I, in effect, was informed that he would be getting down on my case and that I might be converted that afternoon. This was no mere innuendo: Campbell was thus aligning me and my encounter with him with the listening persons and their encounters with God in his stories. Whenever a saved speaker addressed a wayward listener, the speaker would also be addressing me. I too would be transfigured, if only by degrees, by the very act of listening to the Reverend Campbell.

Campbell reminded me of my position in his narrative several times. I heard it faintly when he said, *I found that I too could win others to Christ the same way I was won: by simply telling them that there's a heaven to gain and a hell to shun.* He was more explicit later, when he told me how he was called to preach.

Now when I had my calling at age twenty-nine, I was operating a service station. And I was in the station one afternoon, working on a car. And God did not speak to me with an audible voice, but he spoke to my heart. And there was a conversation going on much like the one that's here. I'm doing the talking and you're listening. And God was doing the talking and I was listening. I was down under the car, changing the oil, and . . . God was just dealing with me about doing this. And I said, "I can't do that." And much like Moses when the Word called him to do something, he said, "I can't even talk." And God said, "Well, I'll send your brother Aaron to help you." So every excuse I would come up with, he would head me off by instructing me that he would do something to meet my shortcomings. So I finally surrendered in the sense of the word that afternoon.

If I had any doubt about where I belonged in Campbell's talk, this story dispelled it. God spoke to him under his car that afternoon just as Campbell was speaking to me in his office. I am the listener; he is the speaker; that which transpires in his narrated dia-

logues shall somehow transpire between us. Campbell also introduced and located me within another parallel level of dialogic structure, between God and biblical figures. I must listen to Campbell as long ago Moses, and much later Campbell, listened to God. Clues such as these inform or, rather, persuade the listener that the witness's words, though they appear to be about the witness and about other characters on the narrative surface, are on a deep level about the listener: you, too, are a character in these stories; these stories are about you.

Keeping in mind that much of what the Reverend Campbell said about himself as he came "under conviction" also applied to his listener, let us examine how he fashioned the lost soul, the sinner, the person in need of salvation.

Young Campbell realized there was something missing in his life. There was a need in his life. He was lost and had not yet turned his whole life over to Christ. He was cutting up and carrying on, and doing a variety of things that were ill toward God. He realized his life was empty and lacked meaning; it was not maturing and growing into something that was real. Yet he knew there was something bombarding his life beyond his power to see or really understand. Campbell was ostensibly describing himself here, but because he had put me in his narrative in his place, he was also describing me. Indeed, he was refashioning me.

Campbell's language emptied my life, my personality, and erased my past. I was primarily distinguished by what I lacked and, given my lacking, by what I needed. I stood for absence, for void, yet I was aware of something more, something missing, unseen, hidden. And I would come to need that, to desire it, having been launched on a quest for affirmation and revelation which may be achieved only through conversion. All this was accomplished in me by implication and presupposition, not by direct argument. My consent was not sought; I was implicated, already enlisted as a collaborator, in my own metamorphosis.

As well as constituting the listener as a lost soul, Campbell in his conversion story began to fashion the speaker, the saved soul, as he narratively moved himself, you could say converted himself, from lost listener to a saved speaker of the Word of God.

The hell-fire-and-damnation preacher who got down on Campbell's case shortly became the spirit of God convicting him about his place in life—that he was lost and had not yet given his whole life over to Christ. He was saved, and he went forward and gave his heart to Christ, and the spirit of God came to live in his heart. His need was met. His life began to grow and materialize in to something that was real, something that had meaning and purpose in it. His old character and its desires passed away. Then he began to sense the need of telling others about what had happened to him and found that he too could win others to Christ in the same way that he was won. The spirit of God first worked on Campbell and brought him under conviction, then entered and transformed him, and finally spoke through him to bring others under conviction.

God's spirit, the Holy Spirit, converts sinners, but he (the fundamental Baptist Holy Spirit is a male person) speaks through those who preach the gospel. Preachers speak the Word of God; God speaks through them. Campbell had started a church in a storefront after God called him, and on the first day of services, he wondered why anyone would come there to hear him preach. Later he realized *it was the Word of God they must come to hear, and not me. It's the Word of God that must cause the change.* The change is caused not by God as an external agent, but by the Word, the spirit, of God, which is internalized when a person accepts Christ. *By nature, Adam and Eve, you know, they caused the problem, but they invested into everyone of us that would be borned a similar nature. Now this nature can be wiped clean, it can be changed by once again instilling the spirit of God within us.* Here, according to Campbell, is how the Holy Spirit works his will.

Now I realize many times when I preach, the Bible says preaching is as of foolishness. But there is another agent working while I'm preaching. And he's the Holy Spirit. And he's the one that grips the heart. I could throw a rock at you and you could throw another one at me. But if I make a statement from the Word of God, and the Holy Spirit bears me up, and he begins to deal with your heart about it, then when we have parted company, he's still working, and I'm gone. Now until we're saved, he lives without us. But when we're saved, he comes to live within us, and this is what we mean by receiving the Lord into us. When he comes to live in us he comes in the form of the Holy Spirit. I've never seen him. But like a mother with a child, she's not seen her unborn baby, but she knows he's there. You say, "How does she know?" She feels life and movement within her. Now the spirit of God is like another voice, like another party. And he is not a figment of the imagination. But the Bible says, he's a real personality, a real person. And actually he can catch your next word and stop it, if you're sensitive to him. And if you're not, you put a piece of tape across his mouth, you can fold him back into the innermost rooms of your heart and give him no liberty. But if you let him, he becomes the tutor of your life, the instructor, the guide, the teacher. And he tells— now when I use the term "tells," he speaks to my heart and he gives me—you've seen the time when you would sense something and you couldn't really say another person was talking to you, but you sense you ought to do something. You were impressed to get up and go see somebody or something. All right, this is the way the Holy Spirit works with me. He impresses me. He moves upon my heart to do certain things. And sometimes he gives me spiritual discernment that's almost like reading another person's mind. Many times I've had people sit down to talk with me, and the Holy Spirit would almost link my mind up with theirs and tell me certain things. And I cannot explain it, but this is because he is a third part of the Godhead. In reality, it's God living within us. Now once he's in here, the things that I used to love to do—and I mean I had a real passion for some things before I got saved—and when he came to live within me, all of a sudden I found that I hated and despised those things. Well, it wasn't my flesh; it was Christ living within me that was despising those things because they were anti- and alien to his nature.

Fundamental Baptists, especially preachers, are acutely aware of the power of witnessing and of the gospel, of the rhetoric of conversion in general. They attribute its transforming power to the workings of the Holy Spirit, that is, to supernatural agencies, but when they describe how those agencies work, they invariably refer to words, to speaking and hearing and reading. In effect, in a coded way, they recognize language as a medium, even a subject, of religious experience, and they coach the unconverted in the linguistic dimension of conversion.

The Holy Spirit uses Campbell's speech, as it were, to remodel his listeners' inner speech. The Holy Spirit impresses on Campbell what to say and deals with the hearts of his listeners, bearing him up, after he's gone. The heart is contrasted with the head and seems to mark the difference between unconscious and conscious knowledge and belief. The Holy Spirit, the Word, works on the unconscious mind to bring the conscious mind under conviction. As listeners appropriate the gospel, the Holy Spirit penetrates the conscious mind and becomes another voice, a real person, who begins to recast their inner speech. After salvation, the voice of the Holy Spirit guides converts, gives them discernment, and seems to alter the very chemistry of desire.

The Reverend Campbell spelled out the moment of salvation elliptically in his own conversion narrative, and he elaborated it in his disquisition on the Holy Spirit. He also posited the moment of salvation in highly charged symbolic terms, in biblical exegeses on birth and death, flesh, spirit, blood, and sacrifice.

Campbell drew on well-established parallels in evangelical culture between narratives of Christ's death, or the gospel story, and conversion narratives, and between the cosmic order outlined in the Bible from the Garden of Eden to Calvary and the epic of each individual in the face of inevitable death. The gospel story defines the movement, the passage that all believers must endure, from suffering and dying (coming under conviction), to burial (silence, absence, void), and resurrection (converting, being reborn, eternal life). As God restored man to himself by sacrificing his son on the cross, so the unsaved may restore themselves to God by dying to their old selves and being born anew in Christ. All they need do is acknowledge their sin nature, accept that Christ died for their sins, and ask him into their hearts. It is these words, once genuinely spoken, that resurrect a dead soul, that instill in the newborn believer the Holy Spirit, the very voice of God.

Campbell began to elaborate the connection between the gospel story and salvation, as witnesses often do, by talking about Nicodemus, who came to visit Jesus one night and said to him, as Campbell put it, *Now you've got something that we've missed.*

Jesus said, "Nicodemus, I'm going to limit my words in talking to you. Listen carefully." He said, "Ye must be borned again. Ye must be borned again." And Nicodemus said, "How in the world can a man be born when he's old? Is it possible that I could enter again a second time into my mother's womb and be born?" Jesus said, "No, you didn't listen. I'm going to repeat one more time. . . . You must be borned again. . . . That which is

born of flesh is flesh. That which is born of spirit is spirit. Marvel not that I say, you've already had one birth, but you need more. You need the birth that's going to change you from the one you received from Adam, which is a sinful nature. You've already experienced that first birth and you're full of yourself. But now you need the second birth, the one that will give you this indwelling of the spirit of God."

Now when I was born, I was born physically of my mother. Jesus said, "You must be borned of the water first, of the spirit second." . . . When a child is about to be born, it's first enclosed in the mother's womb. Is that true? [Yes.] That water must be broke before the child can be born. Now this is a representation of the first birth. He said, "You must be born of the water first, Nicodemus. You've already been born, you're here." But then he said, "Now you must be born by the spirit." Your mother birthed you the first time. And your mother cannot give you this spiritual birth. So this must come from above. Now God gives this second birth. [I ask, "How does the second birth change a person?"]

Okay, Susan, you have the characteristics and the traits of your mother and your father. True? ["Yes."] All right. Now the second birth will give you the characteristics or the traits of the Father that birthed you. Now the first time when you were born, you couldn't help your mother. If your life had depended on it, you had to depend upon her strength to bring you into this world. True? ["Yes."] Now when we're saved, or borned again, this is absolutely and totally dependent upon God.

Now where did the birth take place at? It had to be a birth of such a caliber that it had to take care of the whole world. And this was a place called Calvary. Jesus, when he was dying, was shedding his blood, and the Old Testament says that without the shedding of blood there is no remission, there can be no forgiveness for sin. So blood—the innocent—and God typified this in the animal sacrifices of the Old Testament. When Adam and Eve sinned. Genesis 3:21 said he slew innocent animals. And he took the skin off these animals, and he covered their nakedness, which is the type of giving them a covering which is representative of righteousness, and the blood was used to atone for their sins. . . . Atonement means to cover, and the blood of the animals of the Old Testament typified one day that Christ would come, shed his blood, but then this blood, this blood being shed now, brings about redemption and not atonement, which is a temporal covering. For thousands of years, the Jews under the Mosaic economy offered up sacrifice of animals—you've probably read that—and they did this because this was representative of one day a coming Savior.

You remember the incident in Exodus [sic], *about how Abraham went to offer his son Isaac on Mount Moriah. And the Bible says that Isaac the son said, "Father"—he didn't know what was going on—he said, "Here's the altar, here's the wood, here's the knife, here's the fire, but where's the sacrifice? Where's the lamb?" And Abraham said, "My son, God himself shall provide a sacrifice. A lamb." Now we go down several thousand years into the future, and John the Baptist, when he saw Jesus Christ for the first time, he told the disciples that were with him, he said, "Behold, take a look. Here is the lamb of God that will take away the sins of the world." And the lamb of God was Jesus Christ. Of course, Isaac was not slain. There was a ram caught in the thicket which was a type of substitution. So Jesus Christ died in my place as a substitution for me.*

According to Billy Graham, "the conquest of death is the ultimate goal of Christianity," and victory is achieved when sinners are born again and the spirit of God is instilled in them. Rebirth is totally dependent upon the grace of God, as a baby is totally dependent on its mother for its birth. Symbolically, Campbell first moved his listener from the first birth, the mother, flesh, and water breaking, to the second birth, the Father, spirit, and blood shed. The second (spirit/male) birth takes over, subverts, and cancels out the consequences of the first (flesh/female) birth, releasing the sinner from the wages of sin, death. The womb of the second birth was the cross at Calvary. Christ mediated between the first (flesh/female) and second (spirit/male) birth and created the possibility of reconciliation with God.

After spelling out the contrast between the first and the second birth, Campbell moved deeper into a discussion of blood, of the innocent. The blood of animals sacrificed under the law of Moses was a temporal, or a temporary and earthly, covering (atonement). The blood of Christ provided eternal, heavenly remission from sin (redemption). Through animal sacrifice, humans asked God's forgiveness and might stay his judgment, but they were still condemned to die. Only the self-sacrifice of God himself could lift the curse of Adam and Eve and overturn the Mosaic economy. God gave to man that which he had not asked Abraham to give, his only son, his own flesh and blood, and so made available eternal life to those who would believe. God no longer asks the blood of animals from men and women. He asks for repentance and faith in the saving grace of Christ. A sacrifice is still due, namely, the flesh-bound self of the first birth, which is offered up in the act of believing.

Animal blood is linked to spiritual death; it can only cover sin (separation from God, death) and nakedness (meaninglessness, void); and it only represents, or typifies, righteousness (order, reunion with God) and a coming Savior. Christ's blood actually saves men and women from spiritual death; Christ's death substitutes for them and creates eternal life. Here Campbell was using the New Testament to overtake, subvert, and transform the Old Testament; he seemed to suggest that "Mosaic" sacrifice only approximated, or signaled to, God, while born-again sacrifice relates directly to and reunites one with God.

On a symbolic level, Campbell argued that it was Christ's blood that made this transition possible. But narratively, that is, looking at the form his argument took on the surface of his whole juxtaposition of stories, Campbell emphasized the importance of spoken language, of dialogue, in making the passage from one world to the next. He repeatedly relied on dialogue—between Jesus and Nicodemus, himself and me, Isaac and Abraham, John the Baptist and the disciples—to set up the dilemma of human choice. In this respect, he was speaking as much within Old as New Testament tradition. Old Testament writers used "narration-through-dialogue" to highlight "human will confronted with alternatives which it may choose on its own or submit to divine intervention. Articulated language provides the indispensable model for defining [the] rhythm of political or historical alternatives, question and response, creaturely uncertainty over against the Creator's intermittently revealed design, because in the biblical view of reality words underlie reality." And it is through spoken dialogue, through witnessing, that each sinner is confronted with and makes the choice to accept or reject Christ.

The Reverend Campbell concluded an hour of virtually uninterrupted talk with a veritable gospel poem that fully realized the complex, holistic meaning of blood as birth and death and emphasized the mutuality of the sacrifice and reconciliation between humans and God. Campbell's speech is strikingly biblical here—in fact, much of it is a rephrasing of several verses from the Old Testament Book of Ezekiel—though as elsewhere he converts the Hebrew text to New Testament ends.[4]

My birth, it belongs to God. God made me. And then Paul said, "When I've been saved, I've been bought with a price." What was that price? His life at Calvary. That's what he gave for me. He ransomed me out of the, you might say, the slave markets of sin and brought me into a right relationship. And when I was unworthy, the Bible said he loved me. When I was wretched and naked, when I was borned, the prophets said it was like I was thrown out onto the ground. I had not been washed in salt. I had not been suppled [washed in water]. I had not been bathed in olive oil. I was laying there in my own blood, dying. And when he saw me, there was nothing about me that really made me desirable. Yet he looked beyond all of my faults and saw my needs, and he come, and he loved me, and he died for me. And he even made it available so that I could know this, and when I come to that knowledge, I had no alternative but to want to run to the one that loved me. Because nobody had ever cared for me like Jesus. And that's about the size of the story. Nobody.

Campbell then turned to me and asked, *Now Susan, let me ask you a question. Do you know Christ as your personal savior?* He asked me several more questions. *Do you believe in God? What if you died today?* Then he told me a story of a man he buried a few weeks before who had choked to death on some food. *Had no idea he would be sent out into eternity. . . . Life is just an uncertain thing.* He inquired again into my faith. *Have you ever sensed the presence of God?* Then he told me about a man who, at forty, lamented that he'd been looking for a wife for so long. Campbell told him, *I think God has sent you the right woman, probably twenty times, and you turned her down.* He said the man had overlooked the orchid and all the other beautiful

flowers while looking for a rose. *Can you identify with that?*

Then Campbell brought his exhortation to a rather stunning conclusion.

Now if in this life, the Bible says, only we have hope, then we of all men are most miserable. But you see my life, my hope, is in the life to come, and I realize this life is a passing thing. Jeremiah says it's like a vapor. It appears but for a little while, and then vanishes. We know how uncertain life is. We're just not sure how long things are going to go. I went to work one morning. I had some work to do on a Saturday morning. And one of my sons was fourteen years old. And the other one was fifteen years old. And we got up that morning. And I went in, and I russled with my son and rassled him out of bed, the one that was fourteen. And we got up that morning and ate breakfast. We opened the Word of God. We read and we prayed together as a family, my wife, my two sons, and I. And I went on to do that work that morning. It was a Saturday. And I had something I wanted to move. And I was operating a crane. And I accidentally killed him that morning. And I looked at God, and I said, "Lord, you told me in your Word that all things work together for good to those that love you, especially those that are called according to your purpose." And I said, "I've served you faithfully. And I've loved you. And I've given you my heart, my life, my soul, given you everything about me. And now I can't understand this, why you've taken my son." And God didn't speak with a voice that I heard with my ear but he spoke to my heart. He said, "Melvin, you know maybe you don't understand what I've done at this particular time, but, can you accept it?" And I said, "yes sir, I can accept it." And Susan, when I made that statement, and I settled that in my own heart, and I said "Lord, I accept it though I don't understand it," I don't know where to say it came from other than that God gave it to me, but he gave me a peace in my soul. And I have not questioned it since.

Now I went and shared it with my wife. I said, "Shelby," I said, "God said all things would work together for the good to us because we loved him." And she said basically the same thing I did, "Well, I don't understand. This isn't good." But I said, "Yeah, but God said it is good." And I shared with her, and when I shared this with her, she came of the same opinion. And we watched them close the casket on that little fellow and my, he was just super. I mean, he was almost my heart throb, you know, that was my baby. And yet he died in my arms. And yet I looked at God and I said, "Lord, I'm going to love you if you take my other son. I'm going to love you if you take

---

4. Compare the Reverend Campbell's language here with these words, which God spoke to Ezekiel regarding the nation of Israel (16:4–6): "And as for thy nativity, in the day thou wast born thy navel was not cut, neither wast thou washed in water to supple thee; thou wast not salted at all, nor swaddled at all. None eye pitied thee, to do any of these unto thee, to have compassion upon thee, but thou wast cast out in the open field, to the loathing of thy person, in the day that thou wast born. And when I passed by thee, and saw thee polluted in thine own blood, I said unto thee when thou wast in thy own blood, Live; yea, I said unto thee, when thou wast in thy blood, Live."

my wife. I'm going to love you if you take my health, if you strip me of everything I've got, I'm going to love you."

Now I'm saying that because, Susan, he is real. This is not mythology. I'm forty-six years old, and I'm no fool. God is alive. And his son lives in my heart. And I'd love for him to live in your heart. Of all that I could give or think of ever giving over to you, I hope that what we've talked about here today will help you make that decision, to let him come into your heart, and then he will be your tutor. And he'll instruct you in things that perhaps I've stumbled over today. Sometimes the vocabulary may not be appropriate to really describe the depth and the detail of the things that need to be said. But this is where the Holy Spirit can make intercession for us. The Bible says with groanings and utterings that we just cannot utter. I may miss something, but he'll bring it out. I may present something, and you don't understand it. But he will reveal it to you. This is what the whole thing is about.

Campbell began his ultimate narrative on a note of wistful resignation. Life is a passing thing, a vapor; it's here for a little while and then vanishes. Without pause, he shifted into a homey story about getting his sons up one Saturday morning, opening and reading the Word of God, and going out to work in the yard. Then in a split second he delivered a narrative shock: *And I accidentally killed him that morning.* The sentence disrupts his story. It startles his listener. But before it is absorbed, Campbell shifts to the real point—his conversation with God. God asked Melvin Campbell to accept what he, God, had asked Abraham to accept and what he, God himself, was willing to give: his son's death. And Melvin obeyed: *Yes, sir. I can accept it.* This sentence, in a moment as extreme and extraordinary as the tragic death of his son by his own hand, is what God asked of him to restore order in himself and in the world. By speaking his obedience, his submission to God's will, they were reconciled, and Campbell received in return peace in his soul, an eager willingness to give still more. The same gifts, he concluded, awaited me, if only I too would accept Christ. *This is what the whole thing is about.*

The unborn-again listener wants to know more about Campbell and Campbell's son, not about God's son. How did the boy die? How did Campbell really feel about it? What about his pain? His sorrow? His guilt? How could he speak to a stranger about what could be the most tragic moment in his life with such spareness, such calm, such calcula-

tion? The dialogues with God and with his wife sound like cloaks concealing what he really must have felt. At best, they ring of reinterpretation, of a retrospective story Campbell tells—one that, as he himself suggests, renders him at peace with his loss. The unregenerate listener interrogates Campbell's story as if it were a system of verbal clues about something outside itself—about the tragic event, his raw experience, the unmediated emotions of the moment, or his subsequent effort to recover and reintegrate—and finds the story distinctly odd, choppy, suspiciously elusive.

In contrast, the born-again believer, or the unbeliever who is being born-again, listens to the cadence and phrasing of Campbell's words, to the esthetic shape of his story and the multidimensional biblical universe it presupposes, and hears nothing but the truth, that is, the world evoked, the world constituted, by the story. Campbell's tale sounds homespun, but its threads are thousands of years old. In the story's rich weave are echoes of the trials of Job, and paraphrasings of David's songs in Psalms and of Paul's letters to the Romans and the Phillippians. Many of the literary devices that distinguish Hebrew scripture are also audible—the strategic use of "now" and "and"; the laconic pace; the use of minimal detail to establish time, place, character, and relationships; the characteristic rush of biblical narrative toward an essential moment; auspicious shifts and gaps that engage interpretive attention; the privileging of dialogue over narration to reveal character; and the repetiton of key dialogue and the movement of action-response. Campbell's supple mastery of biblical conventions authorize him as a "man of God," a man who breathed life into God's Word and whom God's Word breathed to life. But what made his story truly captivating and potentially transformative was its placement at the end of a sequence of biblical stories which, looking back, fashioned a series of interlocking sacrificial altars, and, looking forward, fashioned one upon which a sacrifice was due. This sequence, the sacrificial passage, was formed in his disquisition on the Old Testament stories of Adam and Eve, and Abraham and Isaac, and on the New Testament story of Christ's death at Calvary.

Campbell summed up the narrative economy laid down by those stories: *Now here's the entire Bible and its economy coming together. For four thousand years of the Old Testament, they offered up blood sacrifices. Now all of this together, combined, typified one day a coming hope. They looked through the offering of the blood one day to Calvary. . . . They looked forward and believed that he would* [die for us], *and I look back and believed that he did, and we all focus at a place called Calvary and realize why he died.*

Campbell called attention here to the way in which Bible-believing Christians make connections among the storied events, both biblical and historical. The interpretive links between his juxtaposed stories—between the animal blood shed at Eden and Mount Moriah and the divine blood shed at Calvary, and between Christ's self-sacrifice and ours—were "typological," or "figural," links. Old Testament storied events "typify" the central story of the New Testament. The skins that covered Adam and Eve and the blood of animals slain in the Old Testament were a "type" of righteousness, of redemption. Earlier events are types of later events. That is, earlier events prefigure later events, and later events complete, or fulfill, earlier, incomplete events. In figural interpretation, "an event on earth signifies not only itself but at the same time another, which it predicts or confirms. . . . The connection between occurrences is not regarded as primarily a chronological or causal development but as a oneness within the divine plan, of which all occurrences are parts and reflections." There is no distinction between biblical and historical stories here. Both are "events on earth" related by figuration, enabling Christians to envision "the real world as formed by the sequence told by the biblical stories."

Adam's sin called forth a sacrifice of animals to cover him with their skins. Abraham's obedience called forth the ram to substitute for Isaac. Both stories, or events, are interpreted as incomplete. Animal sacrifice only atones, only provides a temporal covering, a substitute for the ultimate sacrifice—death—that is due. When Christ made the ultimate sacrifice upon the cross for all mankind, he completed, he filled the gaps in, all the prior stories. In the same instant, he opened a gap that must be closed. Christ's death raised a question that must be answered by all those who come after: Whom did Christ die for? In answering, "He died for me," and in sacrificing their old selves to Christ, Campbell and all believers close the gap; they fulfill or complete the story. Simultaneously, their self-sacrifice poses the question anew to all who have not sacrificed themselves.

Not long after his exposé of our right relationship to Calvary, Campbell inquired into my beliefs and found, mostly from what was not said, that I was unlikely to be convinced that afternoon that Christ died for me. From then on his talk led in a zigzagging but steady fashion toward his sacrificing his own son for me in order to strike home his message one last time. In doing so, he set up a figural sequence of sacrifice stories, from Abraham and Isaac, to Christ's passion, to his own terrible tale, a sequence that looked forward with hope to the next story, my own self-sacrifice of faith.

Campbell wanted his listener to understand that she, her life, bore the same relationship to the story of Christ's sacrifice that that story bore to the story of Abraham and Isaac. Her story would fulfill Christ's in the same way that Christ's fulfilled the Old Testament tale. The moment of salvation is precisely the moment when a lost soul realizes that Christ died for *you*. Suddenly, the story of Calvary, the Bible as a whole, becomes "relevant." The context in which biblical stories are meaningful and the context of one's personal life collapse into each other, and the fusion evokes a sense of great insight, of miracle. All of these stories are speaking to you. These stories are God speaking to you.

More specifically, you stand in the same relation to the ram as Isaac did. The ram died in his stead. The lamb, Christ, died in your stead. This connection between stories/events is established through a sense of incompleteness, of "something missing." Isaac fashioned the gap in the form of a question: "Where's the sacrifice?" According to Campbell, Christ answered that question, completed that story, as he became the sacrifice that was due. Campbell acknowledged the gap in Christ's story by answering the implicit question, *Why did Christ die? Christ died for us,* so that we might live forever. We "complete" the story of Christ, we determine the meaning of Christ's death.

Campbell's final story about his son's death replicated the biblical stories in the obvious thematic sense—a father sacrifices his son. But the connection was not merely allusive. It is also figural. Campbell's story fulfilled Christ's, which fulfilled Abraham's. Campbell, like Abraham, like God himself, was willing to sacrifice his son in accordance with God's plan. But like their stories, his too was incomplete. It evoked a haunting sense of something missing. Why did Campbell's son die? Or, more precisely given the typological sequence, for whom did Campbell's son die? The answer, of course, had already been provided as well by the previous stories. He died for me. The Reverend Campbell sacrificed his son, narratively speaking, for me.

Through the cumulative pattern of his Bible-based storytelling that afternoon, Campbell created a space for me to take responsibility, and feel responsible, for determining the meaning of his son's death. That I owed him something, and what it was, and what I would receive in turn, was one of the last things the Reverend Campbell made clear to me: *Of all that I could give you or think of ever giving over to you, I hope that what we've talked about here today will help you make that decision, to let him come into your heart, and then he will be your tutor.* Campbell had fashioned access to a divine pattern of history for me, and the only question remaining was, would I accept it?

If conversion is a process of acquiring a specific religious language and witnessing is a conservative Protestant rite of conversion, then, if you are willing to be witnessed to, if you are seriously willing to listen to the gospel, you have begun to convert. Listening to the gospel initiates lost souls into the Word, the language of God.

The single most important unconscious clue I gave Campbell that I was "susceptible" to conversion was that I was willing to listen to the gospel. Crises, transitions, and upbringing as such do not lead you to convert. They may make you more likely to listen, and anything that makes you more likely to listen, including the work of ethnography, is actually what makes you susceptible.

"Susceptible" implies passivity, but I was not passively listening to Campbell. I was struggling mightily against the grain of my ignorance and incredulity to make sense of what he was saying. His language was so intense and strange, yet deceptively plain and familiar, full of complex nuances and pushes and pulls, that I had no time, no spare inner speech, to interpret him consciously, to rework what he said into my own words as he talked. I just gripped my chair, as it were, and took his words in straight. I was willfully uncritical as well in the sense that I wanted to understand, as best I could, his words from his point of view, to assume his position, to make his speech mine.[5] It was not exactly what Campbell said that brought me under conviction; it is that I took it up, merely by listening to him actively and uncritically.[6]

The membrane between disbelief and belief is much thinner than we think. All I had to do was to listen to my witness and to struggle to understand him. Just doing so did not make me a fundamental Baptist born-again believer, but it drew me across that membrane in tiny ways so that I began to acquire the knowledge and vision and sensibilities, to share the experience, of a believer. Believers and disbelievers assert there is no middle ground: you are either one or the other. You cannot both believe and disbelieve. But that is precisely what it means to be "under conviction." You do not believe in the sense of public declarations, but you gradually come to respond to, interpret, and act in the world as if you were a believer. It is a state of unconscious belief, experienced with more or less turmoil and anxiety, depending on how strong your disbelieving voices are. It also depends for the ethnographer on how adamant your colleagues are about the "dangers" of doing "this kind of fieldwork." I was given to think my

5. In fact, the listener can never really make the speaker's speech his own. Here is how Bakhtin described the dialogue from the listener's point of view: "As a living, socio-ideological concrete thing, as heteroglot opinion, language, for the individual consciousness, lies on the borderline between oneself and the other. The word in language is half someone else's. It becomes 'one's own' only when the speaker [that is, the listener becoming a speaker] populates it with his own intention, his own accent, when he appropriates the word, adapting it to his own semantic and expressive intention. Prior to this moment of appropriation, the word does not exist in a neutral language . . . , but rather it exists in other people's mouths, in other people's contexts, serving other people's intentions: it is from there that one must take the word, and make it one's own. . . . Expropriating it, forcing it to submit to one's own intentions and accents, is a difficult and complicated process."
6. "It seems to me that to explain what is involved in [witchcraft] situations simply by talking of the effect of suggestion is not sufficient, for this is to do no more than to give a name to the very thing which is doubtful. . . . So the touchstone of witchcraft is not so much the simple realization of a prediction or malediction, as the fact that it is taken up by the bewitched, who becomes the unwilling agent of fate."

credibility depended on my resisting any experience of born-again belief. The irony is that this space between belief and disbelief, or rather the paradoxical space of overlap, is also the space of ethnography. We must enter it to do our work.[7]

Campbell's testimony was a hodgepodge of stories sewn together with the scarlet thread of redemption, not a series of "logical" or "empirical" arguments. He persuaded me narratively. Disbelief is a conscious refusal to accept a particular version of reality, and believing involves the conscious acceptance of "doctrines," of particular claims about reality and one's relationship to it. But disbelief is also, in the case of evangelical Christianity at least, an unconscious refusal to participate in a particular narrative mode of knowing reality. Likewise, belief also involves an unconscious willingness to join a narrative tradition, a way of knowing and being through Bible-based storytelling and listening. You cannot tell born-again stories, you cannot fashion them, without acknowledging belief, but you can hear them, you can absorb them, and that's how you "believe" when you are under conviction. You get caught up in the stories, no matter what your conscious beliefs and disbeliefs are.

I was caught up in the Reverend Campbell's stories—I had "caught" his language—enough to hear God speak to me when I almost collided with another car that afternoon. Indeed, the near-accident did not seem like an accident at all, for there is no such thing as a coincidence in born-again culture; God's hand is everywhere. Gospel talk casts in your subliminal mind, your heart, a Bible-based sense of options poised to trigger God's speech, given a context in which you seem to have a choice to submit to God's will or ply your own. Preachers construct such contexts verbally, and life presents them virtually every day—those gaps in the ordinary, when the seams split and you encounter the unknown, the unexpected, the uncontrollable, the irrational, the uncanny, the miraculous. These are moments ripe for supernatural harvesting, moments when fear or awe mutes your natural voices and God may speak, offering you the opportunity to speak back.

Coming under conviction (listening to gospel stories or voices) is easy compared to being saved (speaking, telling stories). When you come under conviction, you cross through a membrane into belief; when you get saved, you cross another membrane out of disbelief. This passage is more problematic for some lost souls, for what outsiders would say were reasons of education, class, or intellect, and insiders would say was hardness of the heart, pride, or the work of the devil. However you explain it getting saved among fundamental Baptists involves publicly giving up disbelief, not just suspending it, but disavowing it. It involves accepting born-again belief in the sense of acquiring new knowledge of reality that quickens the supernatural imagination and yields a conversational relationship to God. Born-again knowledge becomes the centering principle of your identity, your personal and public life, your view of human nature and history. And it involves joining a particular narrative tradition to which you willingly submit your past, present, and future as a speaker.

One more reason Campbell was a compelling witness was the extent to which, and eloquence with which, he gave his life, narratively speaking, to the language of Christ. This willingness to submit one's life to God, to narrate one's experience and fashion stories out of it in dialogue with God's will and biblical truths, makes God, and his Word, most real and known and irrefutable to oneself and to one's listener. Campbell understood this, at least intuitively, well enough to tell me about killing his son just before his final appeal on behalf of my soul. The story disarmed me because he said he had killed his own son, because he so crisply gave up his grief and his guilt to God, and because he was telling me, a stranger and an outsider, about it. He sacrificed his own son to his narrative tradition with a calm assurance, a peace of heart, that I still find difficult to accept. Often that afternoon

---

7. Perhaps, as William James concluded about the divine, the only certain evidence of the reality that preoccupies ethnographers, of shared unconscious knowledge, is experiential. Faye Ginsburg (personal communication) put it this way: "Anthropologists approach self-alteration as a mode of knowing. Our epistemology requires that we alter ourselves in order to know." And Barbara Myerhoff, in her last film, *In Her Own Time,* said, "This is what anthropologists are taught to do. You study what is happening to others by understanding what is going on in you, and you yourself become the data-gathering instrument. You come from a culture, and you step into a new culture, and how you respond to the new one tells you about them, and it tells you about the one you came from."

I found myself at a loss for words as Campbell narratively generated what for me were novel grounds for knowing and for speaking, but the story of his son's death struck me dumb. He might as well have gone up in a puff of smoke.

A cynic, second-guessing Campbell's motives, would say he was manipulative, that he used this painful story to "get to" his listener. But from within born-again culture, this telling was the ultimate evidence of belief, Campbell's moment of maximum authenticity. If he told me the story for effect, it was to effect the reality of God in me. What God said to him and he said to God in that tragic moment meant that God is absolutely real. This was his own conclusion: *Now I'm saying that, Susan, because he is real. This is not mythology. I'm forty-six years old, and I'm no fool. God is alive. And his son lives in my heart.*

Among fundamentalist Baptists, the Holy Spirit brings you under conviction by speaking to your heart. Once you are saved, the Holy Spirit assumes your voice, speaks through you, and begins to rephrase your life. Listening to the gospel enables you to experience belief, as it were, vicariously. But generative belief, belief that indisputably transfigures you and your reality, belief that becomes you, comes only through speech: speaking is believing.

48

Islamic Law: The Foundation of Muslim Practice and a Measure of Social and Political Change

Carolyn Fluehr-Lobban

Thanks to well-intentioned but de-contextualized popular media coverage, many non-Muslims in the West are likely to have been exposed to the topic of the following article only through sensational news accounts of stonings for adultery, hand amputations for burglary, or honor killings of women. This article demonstrates how the anthropological perspective—with attention to variation within and among countries and across time—helps us see beyond simplistic reductions. Rather than being an immutable medieval tradition, Islamic law has evolved over twelve centuries in response to intellectual developments and specific cultural and historical circumstances, including European colonization and post-independence politics.

Author Carolyn Fluehr-Lobban is an anthropologist specializing in the study of Islamic law and its implications and has conducted research in Tunisia, Egypt, and Sudan. Here, she introduces key areas in the study and application of Islamic law: Islamic concepts of justice and punishment; Islam's distinctive forms of banking and finance, which avoid interest; economic development; and family law. Family law and the rights of women have seen dramatic change and reinterpretation in many Muslim countries during the 20th century, changes the author relates to new patterns in family life, such as the entry of women into the salaried workforce and the promotion of family planning.

Carolyn Fluehr-Lobban is Professor of Anthropology at Rhode Island College. The chapter from which this text has been adapted includes case study material on Tunisia, Egypt, Sudan, and Malaysia, omitted here due to length.

Islamic law is based on the immutable holy sources of the Qur'an and Sunna and is therefore a religious law in theory—al-fiqh, or jurisprudence—and Shari'a, the law in practice. The Qur'an, as the revealed word of God, and the teachings and the practice of the Messenger of God, Muhammad, are fundamental

From: ISLAMIC SOCIETIES IN PRACTICES, *2nd ed. University Press of Florida, copyright by the Board of Regents of the State of Florida, pp. 163–76 and 192–96, 2004.*

sources that have been interpreted over the ages but cannot be altered. However, the various schools of jurisprudence that have developed since the introduction of Islam, primarily in the first century after the Hegira (seventh to eighth centuries C.E.), reveal that the law is not static or immutable. These schools include the Maliki, Hanafi, Hanbali, and Shafi', as well as others that are a bit more obscure, which had their origins and influence in various parts of the original core of the early Islamic world. For example, the Maliki school grew out of the customs in practice in Medina and Mecca and spread throughout North and West Africa, while the Hanafi school spread with the Ottoman Empire. The differences in interpretation between the different schools are, relatively speaking, rather minor and do not represent doctrinal or factional differences in Islamic law.

Shari'a, as a religious law, is comprehensive and theoretically applies to all legal matters that we would differentiate in the West as civil, criminal, and family law. There is even a system of economics, banking, and finance that has grown out of Islamic prescriptions. In practice, in the modern period, Islamic Shari'a was circumscribed by Ottoman rule, which secularized the law in commerce and trade and relegated the Shari'a more to a law governing personal status matters of Muslims. The colonial powers reinforced and amplified this model, introduced their own Western laws in civil and criminal areas, and left Islamic law to govern family matters almost exclusively. Thus the current movement by the Islamists to restore the comprehensive role of the Shari'a in Islamic society does have historical legitimacy. However, Western and Muslim critics have questioned the compatibility of Islamic law with the standards and demands of the modern state in terms of protecting the rights of non-Muslims and women. . . .

Each of the countries of the Arab-Muslim Middle East share Islamic culture, and they share, to varying degrees, Arabic language and culture. Most are nations with a background of European colonialism, French rule in the case of the Maghrib and the Levant, Italian rule in Libya, and British rule in the cases of the Nile Valley countries of the Sudan and Egypt, Jordan, Palestine, Iraq, and the oil nations of the Persian Gulf and Arabian Peninsula. Each country has been governed, since independence or the formation of a new nation, essentially by a monarchy or single party or military monopoly that has effectively excluded democratic elections or referenda on the subjects of family and social change or on any other matter.

Shari'a in Arabic means the "correct path," and in a religious sense it is quite clear that this means adhering to a correctly guided life that is upright and conforming to the teachings and practice of Islam. Living in a Shar'i way can be used to describe a proper home for a husband and wife, or living with one's family and assisting them rather than living alone in a flat, or to describe the revived form of Islamic dress that many young Muslim women are adopting. All are examples of proper conduct guided by the religion of Islam. From an Islamic point of view, there is little distinction between sacred and secular, and the different contextual use of terms like Shar'i and Shari'a is more noticeable to the Western non-Muslim than to the Muslim, for whom religion and society more comfortably commingle. The past development and future role of Islamic law in Muslim societies is a critical part of the contemporary debate regarding the "correct path" for Islamic nations to pursue into the twenty-first century.

For thirteen centuries, Islamic law has developed within Muslim communities and states comprehending civil, criminal, and family legal matters. Interpretations of the holy sources have developed through discussion and commentary relying upon the judgment of the jurists and scholars of the golden ages of Muslim caliphates—from Baghdad to Cordoba, from the Maghrib to central and south Asia. Great scholars such as al-Ghazali wrote detailed opinions upon multiple subjects relating to Muslim life, Islamic civil society, family relations, and relations with non-Muslims. These opinions are remarkable and worthy of greater weight than the Orientalist view of Max Weber that "Kadi justice" was no more than capricious decision making by Islamic judges who decided cases whimsically and not based on the more "logical" Western use of precedent.

For example, as early as the tenth century, Muslim jurists determined that since the Qur'an was silent on contraception birth control was permissible in Islamic society (Musallam 1986, 16). The method discussed was coitus interruptus, or male withdrawal. Medieval Arab medical texts also noted female techniques, such as vaginal suppositories or other barriers to the womb. "Spilling the seed," or male withdrawal, was forbidden in Jewish and Christian law, so this Islamic interpretation was novel and presaged developments in the twentieth century debates over theological and secular legal interpretations of birth control and the right to life. Al-Ghazali (1058–1111), one of the most influential of early jurists, argued that contraception for reasons of economy or to protect a wife from dangerous childbirth was lawful, but contraception to prevent the birth of daughters was not (Musallam 1986, 22). The right of a wife to sexual fulfillment in Muslim marriage intrigues and surprises Westerners accustomed to views of Eastern women as disempowered. . . . .

Slavery was acknowledged as part of existing social conditions when Islam began in the Hijaz and although it was not banned, legal opinion held that its practice was mollified by recommending kind treatment of slaves, including marriage, property, and inheritance rights, as well as heavenly reward for manumission, or freeing of slaves.

Interpretations regarding the treatment of non-Muslims living within Muslim states favored Kitabiyeen (Jews and Christians) over pagans, who were not endowed with the same rights as either Muslim or Kitabiyeen. The idea of a multireligious Islamic state may be viewed either as a contradiction in terms or as an idea to be developed further by Muslim reformers.

Islamic Law during Colonialism

More than twelve centuries of Islamic societies in local and state practice in Africa and Asia preceded the colonization of most of the Muslim world by European powers. Colonizing pressures from Europe threatened the Ottoman Empire and forced it into decline before its demise after World War I. Ottoman Hanafi law spread as official law throughout its empire, while local traditions favored Maliki traditions—especially in Africa—and Shafi'i traditions were favored in parts of Asia, while the Hanbali school was adopted by the Wahhabis in Arabia.

In 1798, with the Napoleonic invasion of Egypt, the era of European colonialism of "the Orient" began in earnest. Britain and France particularly vied for control of the trade routes and the natural resources. Lord Nelson's defeat of Napoleon secured Egypt for Britain, and for much of the nineteenth century Britain made strategic alliances with the Ottomans in their pursuit of empire. From Egypt they sought to control the Nile Valley, but met with resistance from the Sudanese Mahdi, Muhammad Ahmed, whose jihad against the foreign invader prevented British rule, beginning with the battle at Khartoum (1884–85). The Mahdi ruled much of the country until 1898, when the British returned in force under H. H. Kitchener with gunboats and gatling guns. They overcame Sudanese resistance, slaughtering over ten thousand one morning at the battle of Omdurman.

In 1885 the major European powers met in Berlin to divide up the African continent into spheres of influence. In Islamic Africa, British colonial rule was extended with and without resistance not only in Egypt and the Sudan but also in Uganda, Kenya, Tanganyika, South Africa, Rhodesia, Zambia, Nigeria, Ghana, and Sierre Leone. France, the political rival, colonized Algeia in 1830 and the rest of the Maghrib before the end of the century. The French secured Senegal, Ivory Coast, and the Sahelian countries of Mali, Niger, and Chad with their armies.

In Asia, the British secured India, Pakistan, Ceylon, Burma, and Thailand along with the major Muslim countries of Malaysia and Indonesia.

Colonial attitudes toward Shari'a were generalized and filtered through the indirect rule of the British, who used an English governor general and local rulers and officials as intermediaries, and the direct rule of the French, who placed themselves in official positions from the top down through the colonial hierarchy. Islamic law was treated as a form of "customary" law and relegated to personal status or family law matters. European-based law was imposed in the more politically important areas of property, civil, and criminal law. Certain Islamic institutions were retained or created—such as mosques, Islamic schools for training local imams, and "Mohammedan" courts with Muslim judges administering to family law needs. Emphasis was placed on controlling Islamic institutions and keeping them within the bounds of the colonial government without suppressing them altogether. However, monitoring the activities of the Muslim 'ulama under colonial rule was routine.

Lord Cromer, the architect of English colonialism in Egypt and the Sudan, wrote to the governor general of Sudan about how to handle the 'ulama at the Kadi School. Cromer wrote that he did not like the "tone" of the Grand Kadi's report, which desired the teaching of "pure Mohammedan law without alteration or amendment." "This is sheer nonsense," Cromer exclaimed. "Mohammedan law more than anything else is what is keeping the Mohammedans back. I am inclined to think that a Kadi who holds these views is not the man you want for the job, although I recognize that it is probably difficult to get anybody better. They are pretty well all of them alike, so I would advise keeping a careful watch over him, and not trusting him too far" (Cromer to

Wingate, 11 February 1907, Sudan Archives, University of Durham).

The Indian Penal Code was created by the English to introduce Western criminal law into the East and was adapted to multiples colonial holdings in the Islamic and other colonies. French Napoleonic law was applied in their colonies consistent with direct rule. In Egypt, Tunisia, Lebanon, and other former French colonies, the tradition was established of using three sitting judges in civil cases. (Although French occupation of Egypt only lasted from 1798 until 1803, this tradition continues to this day.) Local qadis administered personal status family law from Malaysia and Indonesia, to India, to British-controlled Middle East and North Africa, but they suffered less pay, lower status, poorer facilities, and political isolation from the central government and from their colleagues in the civil and criminal division of the judiciary. This imposed inferior status during colonialism was keenly felt such that when opportunities for enhanced status for Islamic governance and Muslim institutions appeared—such as with various Islamist political movements—qadis and members of the 'ulama class of religious scholars embraced these opportunities, even if they were not committed Islamists. This broader colonial historical background to understanding calls for the restoration or full implementation of Shari'a as state law is often ignored in Western discourse on the rise of Islamism. The Shari'a judges and members of the High Court with whom I worked told me of this inherited sense of inferiority as well as of their nearly universal celebration when Shari'a was made state law.

Punishment in Islam

Hadd (*hudud*, pl.) penalties—including flogging, amputation, and stoning for crimes of immorality, theft, fornication and adultery—are much discussed in the West as inhumane, uncivilized, or barbaric. Such penalties are Qur'anic, meaning they are mentioned specifically in the Holy Book, and as such are of such clear intent by God that their application is accepted. But over the centuries they have been the subject of much debate about their application because they are so severe.

> As for the thief, both male and female, cut off their hands.
> It is the reward of their own deeds, an exemplary punishment from Allah. (sura 5:38)

> But who so repents after his wrongdoing and amends, lo! Allah will relent toward him. Lo! Allah is Forgiving, Merciful. (sura 5:39, Pickthall translation)

The standard of proof of the crimes punishable by hudud penalties requires the admission of the guilty person or the testimony of four full witnesses (meaning four men or double the number of women). This requirement is so difficult to fulfill that the intent appears to be that hudud penalties should be used rarely, as examples. In Sudan since Shari'a became state law under Numeiri after 1983, and in the period of the rule of the National Islamic Front after 1989 when extremist interpretations prevailed, hundreds of amputations have been carried out by the Islamist Courts of Prompt Justice. Some of these amputees were not Muslims but were southerners displaced by the chronic civil war; it is not permissible to apply hadd punishments to non-Muslims. And many were poor men of the street, homeless vagrants accused or caught stealing, presumably from economic need. International human rights groups have criticized this application of hudud not only as cruel but as un-Islamic, since they were applied against non-Muslims and failed the stringent Islamic test of proof. The amputees in Sudan have organized themselves into mutual aid societies and are being assisted by Muslims who disapprove of the wrongful carrying out of these harsh penalties.

For example, in the case of adultery, both the man and the women are to receive hadd punishments.

> The adulterer and the adulteress, scourge ye each one of them [with] a hundred stripes. And let not pity for the two withhold you from obedience to Allah, if ye believe in Allah and Last Day. And let a party of believers witness their punishment. (sura 24:2)

> And those who accuse honorable women but bring not four witnesses, scourge them with eighty stripes, and never (afterward) accept their testimony—they indeed are evil doers. (sura 24:4)

> Save those who afterward repent and make amends. (For such) lo! Allah is Foregiving, Merciful. (sura 24:5, Pickthall translation)

In each case where the hadd punishment is mentioned, the Qur'an adds that repentance and amendment yield God's forgiveness and mercy. However, the contemporary sentencing and application of the hudus penalties seem to have held neither to the standard of proof nor to the invocation of God's mercy.

Studies of the application of hudud penalties in the past cannot as yet answer the question of the frequency of their application within the caliphates or Muslim empires, such as the Moghuls or Ottomans. However, in the context of politicized Islamist states, such as Sudan, Afghanistan under the Taliban, Saudi Arabia, or Nigeria, the application of hudud punishments has raised many religious, political, and human rights questions. Most common has been the application of flogging for "immoral" behavior and amputation for theft. Sentences of stoning for adultery have been handed down in Sudan and Nigeria, but have not been carried out.

Islamic criminal law and hudud penalties are legal in countries where a comprehensive Shari'a is applied: Iran, Pakistan, Saudi Arabia, Afghanistan under the Taliban, Sudan, and northern Nigeria. The hadd punishment of stoning for adultery has been applied not only in Sudan but also in northern Nigeria, where Islamism has been on the rise. In Sudan there was an international outcry because the penalty was levied against a Christian woman from the south who was a refugee in Khartoum from the civil war waged there. International human rights groups protested the application of Islamic law against a non-Muslim as well as the cruelty of the punishment. The Islamist government of Sudan backed down, as did the Nigerian government in the ruling by its Supreme Court in the case of Salfiya Hussaini, a Muslim woman from the northern city of Sokoto who had been convicted of having sex outside of wedlock and sentenced to death by stoning. She was the first of two women convicted since a dozen northern Nigerian states had instituted Shari'a as state law; the second was sentenced in Katsina state after President Olusegun Obasanjo declared beheadings, amputations, and stonings unconstitutional (*Providence Journal*, March 26, 2002). International pressure included the withdrawal of the Miss World Pageant from Nigeria, moving it to London in 2002 in protest of the government's failure to deal decisively with the stoning cases. Nigeria's delicate constitutional balance among its multiple ethnicities and between its Muslim north and Christian and animist south suggests that a major constitutional and political crisis would develop if a stoning sentence were carried out. Nigerian Muslim critics fear the intercommunal violence between Christians and Muslims that will spread if the sentence is applied, and they point out correctly that the Qur'an is clear about punishing both the man and the woman, not just the woman whose pregnancy clearly marks her.

The hudud punishments have been applied and executed in countries where Islamism (political Islam) or Wahhabism (conservative and puritanical interpretations) are in force using the apparatus of the state, such as in Sudan, northern Nigeria, or Saudi Arabia. Application of these severe punishments may be used to exhibit the unlimited power and Islamic character of the state, or they may be used to terrify their potential opponents. It is significant that they are not applied in Muslim countries that are officially secular states, such as in Indonesia or Egypt.

Contemporary Banking and Finance

The religious inspiration for an Islamic system of economics stems from the Qur'anic prohibition on usury, *riba,* which in itself derives from the fundamental principle of *tawheed,* the unity and oneness of God, and the relationship of cooperation and equity that is commanded between Muslims. *Riba* literally means "an increase" and was the subject of the last revelation of the Prophet; riba is usually interpreted as any form of direct interest charges upon money loaned or borrowed. Financial dealings that unite and provide support for the Umma have been favored. Waqf (awqaf, pl.) is a religiously inspired bequest of land or funding for the construction or maintenance of beneficial projects, such as the building of mosques, schools, and medical facilities that benefit the Muslim community. A waqf is a special testamentary bequest made in God's name that is permanent and cannot be sold or transferred without the intervention of local religious leaders. This explains why mosques built under waqf regulation centuries before the present are still standing and are maintained. A special family waqf could also be nominated to increase the share of inheritance to a needy Qur'anic heir, but could not be used to disinherit a proscribed relative in Muslim inheritance. Likewise, zakat—religious almsgiving and one of the five pillars—is a compulsory obligation to financially or materially assist the needy in the Muslim community. The Islamic states have imposed a zakat tax to enforce this religious obligation.

By analogy, that which divides the Muslim community, such as unjust economic practices involved in usury, is forbidden in Islam. The Qur'an specifically condemns the taking of interest on loans as a form of expropriation, since it claims more from a person's capital than its fair value. Likewise, it is commonly said that it is wrong to profit from another person's hardship, the assumption being that only a needy person would seek a loan.

Islam encourages commerce, trade, and economic growth. However, any financial dealings that involve charging interest are banned, as are trade and commerce in commodities that are forbidden, such as pork, alcohol, or drugs. The selling of products that are known to cause harm to humans, such as guns and tobacco, is considered by some religious scholars as *haram* (forbidden) or *makruh* (reprehensible). The sale of stolen property is also forbidden, although it is permitted in much of Western civil law.

The fundamental ban on interest charges led in the 1970s to the creation of new Islamic banks and institutions of investment. An interesting, but less well known, aspect to the current revival of Islam has been the creation of Islamic alternatives in the economic sphere. The Islamic banking and finance movement was synthesized by a combination of religious philosophy and practical need to meet the economic demands of Muslims engaging in local and international commerce. The Islamic banks were started with capital from Saudi Arabia, Dubai, and Bahrain, which have continued to play a dominant role in the ownership of these alternative financial institutions. Ironically, while the finance capital originates in the Gulf among some of its richest families (e.g., in the Faisal Islamic banks), most of the Islamic banks have been established in the poorer Arab states, chiefly Egypt, Sudan, and Jordan, where they have come to dominate smaller local banking needs. It is virtually impossible to separate the movement to promote Islamic economics from the movement to restore Islamic principles in government and society, thus Islamic banking is very much tied to Islamic revival. After 9/11, some Islamic banks were alleged to be funnels for funding al-Qaeda operatives; however, Western banks could just as well have been involved.

The rules regarding Islamic banking and investment, while common in theory, may vary in practice. The Islamic alternatives that have been devised to avoid charging interest emphasize partnership and profit-sharing in investment. A common type of loan from an Islamic bank is known as *mudarabah,* whereby the bank loans money to a client to finance a business venture in return for which the bank receives a specified percentage of the net profits of the business for a designated period. Share of the profits provides for repayment of the principal plus a profit for the bank to pass on to its depositors. Should a mudarabah enterprise lose money or fail to thrive, the bank, the borrower, and the bank's depositors all jointly absorb the loss. This puts into practice the basic Islamic principle that lenders and borrowers of capital should share risks and rewards.

Another commonly used technique is *murabahah,* whereby the bank purchases goods in its own name and takes title to these goods, and then sells them at an agreed-upon markup. The profit that the bank derives is justified in terms of the service rendered. This technique is frequently used for the financing of trade.

Trade and commerce must conform to Islamic teachings; commercial dealings with alcohol, drugs, pork products, pornography, and sexually exploitative material are forbidden. Some interpretations also forbid the sale of guns, ammunition, and any other deadly weapons. The Taliban in Afghanistan curtailed the drug trade during their years of rule; however, other Afghani governments observed no contradiction in the international trade in drugs, especially after 9/11 and the U.S. invasion that toppled the Taliban. Shortly after the end of the Taliban regime, the international drug trade resumed as a lucrative means of fueling various movements. Some scholars make a sharp distinction over the application of the rules of investment and trade between Muslims, where rules are essential, and with non-Muslims, where they are not.

To be clear, Islam does not condemn profit taking from legitimate businesses so long as the accumulation of wealth is not based on interest earned by loaning money. For example, loans made by the Islamic Development Bank to poorer Islamic countries using capital from the richer Arab-Muslim nations are interest-free. This stands in marked contrast to the interest-bearing loans made by the Western capitalist nations whose banking systems and economies are founded on loaning money at prescribed interest rates. Often poorer nations use their entire GNP to pay off the interest on loans from Western financial institutions like the World Bank or International Monetary Fund. While loans from the Islamic Development Bank may have other strings attached that make them less desirable, the element of long-term indebtedness is absent.

The Islamic banking movement reflects popular Islamist sentiment and propagandizes for it. In the Sudan, the Islamic banking movement is closely tied to the growth of the National Islamic Front and is largely responsible for funding it. Islamic banks have come to dominate all banking transactions under the current Islamist regime, having been favored by the government as being exempt from state regulation. The banks have offered opportunities to small and medium-sized business ventures that have aided in their mass appeal, and have served, to break the monopoly of some of the old merchant families that have dominated trade and commerce since colonial times. With 60 percent of the capital being foreign based, typically Saudi or other Gulf money, the stability of the banks depends on the maintenance of good ties with these nations. During the 1991 Gulf War, the Sudan sided with Iraq and thus incurred the wrath of Saudi Arabia, which in turn limited its flow of capital into the country. Sudan turned to Iran for economic and military assistance, which has also Islamized its banking system.

The Islamic banking and financial institutions have not always lived up to the high standards expected of them. In Egypt, for example, Islamic investment corporations established envious reputations for very high rates of return on money invested, sometimes as high as 20–25 percent. These high returns brought more capital to the Islamic alternative, not necessarily for religious motives. Standing outside of government regulation, some improprieties were inevitable. During the late 1980s, there was a scandal in Egypt involving corruption and misrepresentation of monies invested in several of the largest Islamic investment corporations, with the result that the government stepped in and imposed strict guidelines over what had been a laissez-faire economic situation.

The challenge presented by the very existence and dramatic growth of the Islamic banks is one that is faced by secular regimes, fearful of their ties to the Islamic revival movements but reluctant to restrain them for fear of popular resistance. The Islamic banks present an indigenous challenge to the Western financial institutions, like the English-based Barclay's Bank, the French Credit Lyonaise, or Citibank, which have been accustomed to controlling the movement of foreign capital in many Arab-Muslim nations; they may find that regional Islamic financial institutions will replace the international flow of capital among Muslim nations.

Likewise, an economic system that operates on totally different premises, such as the Islamic ban on charging interest, has a broad appeal among the debt-ridden nations of the world and poor people in general. In my own teaching about Islamic concepts, I find that many of my students, who are themselves struggling to make ends meet, are attracted to the ideas of Islamic economics. Even the more cynical among them, who see banking fees and service charges as a form of "interest" taken by the Islamic banks, yield the point that the system is more open to the poorer echelons of society and would have popular appeal. Some of my Muslim students point with pride to the economic alternatives that have sprung up within Muslim communities whereby mortgages on houses and car loans are made using Islamic principles that bypass the usurious loans made by American banks. These loans involve the joint purchase of the house, for example, by a group of Muslim investors who receive "rent" or "use" payments from the occupant of the home, who is also an investor; when the home is eventually sold and a profit presumably made, all of the investors share in the profit made from the sale of the home. Islamic investment corporations have been established in a number of U.S. and Canadian cities to handle these alternative economic transactions for Muslims seeking a banking method that conforms to their religious principles.

In a related vein, American Muslims are advised not to use VISA or MasterCard because they charge interest rates for the unpaid balance. It is, or has been, preferable to choose the American Express card, which charges an annual service fee instead of charging interest.

To many non-Muslim Americans, including the students I have taught over the years, many of these ideas make sense as a collective approach to solving what are otherwise individual financial problems. However, the social collectivity, based or religion or some other common bond, is difficult to create in Western society, which has been erected so fundamentally upon individualism.

Development Programs

A number of solutions to the dramatic regional economic imbalances between rich and poor Arab and Muslim states have been proposed, involving Western technology, Arab or Muslim capital, and indigenous labor. The potential partnership for purposes of economic development of Western technology purchased by Arab capital and managed by local labor has been more attractive in theory than in practice. Western technological ventures have been more interested in contract work than in a long-term commitment to development projects, while Arab capital has been less willing to risk long-term ventures.

Various Arab development funds have been organized for several decades on the principle that surplus Arab capital, generated in the oil-producing countries with their relatively small populations and limited agricultural resources, should be invested in the capital-poor nations with large labor pools and greater agricultural potential. In fact, the flow of Arab capital into poorer nations has been timid, due to politically generated risks of failure and elevated expectations of the recipient nations. Nationalistic considerations came into play when foreign investors, Arab and non-Arab, sought to buy into safer ventures, such as real estate.

The common bond of Islam between capital-rich and capital-poor nations in the region has engendered a religiously based system of financing and investment, with the creation of various alternate Islamic financial and investment institutions in the 1970s, including the Islamic Development Bank and private Islamic banks, such as the Faisal Islamic Bank, relying heavily on Saudi capital, the Baraka Group of Bahrain, and others. These financial groups and development banks employ the investment alternative of shared ventures, where the capital is provided by one partner and the labor and management of the project are provided by the other partner. Together they share the risks and profits in proportions agreed upon in advance of the undertaking.

As a religiously based alternative for economic investment, there is much to be admired in theory in Islamic investment. With their philosophy of sharing capital and labor, risk and profit, they have helped to mobilize indigenous small businesses that had been alienated and rejected by the power of traditional wealth concentrated in the hands of a few families. However, the Islamic banks have also acted as a funnel for controlled investment, such as financing Islamic Jihad, the al-Qaeda organization of Osama bin Laden, or the National Islamic Front in the Sudan, which have pursued a political agenda of Islamization and militant and violent actions against the rational economic interests of the nation and region as a whole. It is ironic that the religiously correct Islamic banks and financial groups operate primarily outside the Arabian Peninsula, while the major Western banks are favored within these oil-producing countries.

Family Law

Although different in the particulars of the historical development of family law matters, the laws of each country all derive from a common Islamic base of interpretation of the fundamental sources of Shari'a, the Qur'an and Sunna. Many predominantly Islamic states have religious and cultural minorities who have been historically exempted from Muslim family laws. Moreover, each country has been affected by recent revisions of Muslim family law, especially concerning marriage and divorce. Child betrothal has virtually disappeared, and the right of the woman, not her father, to choose her husband has been supported in the law. The previous unilateral right of the husband to divorce has been seriously undermined, with a corresponding rise in the legal interpretation and actual practice of the wife's right to judicial divorce. This began in North Africa as early as 1915 when the Ottoman Empire introduced judicial divorce for women; Sudan and Egypt later followed this example. This legal development was consistent with the Maliki religious interpretation that a woman should not be harmed in her marriage. Thus, the initial grounds that were recognized for women seeking divorce in court were injury or harm, at first interpreted as physical harm, such as beating, abandonment, or failure to support, but later incorporating notions of psychological abuse, such as insult. Change in the reform of the divorce laws is uneven and still ongoing, as women in Kuwait and Saudi Arabia lack this right and Jordan granted women the right to judicial divorce in 2002 after a government human rights commission recommended the change.

The right of a wife and the duty of a husband to support the family have been reinforced strongly in the recent decades of economic growth in some Arab-Muslim countries and relative stagnation in others. With massive labor migration from poorer to richer Arab countries, the stress placed on the family has been observed most acutely in the sharp rise in cases of nonsupport raised by wives against husbands who are labor migrants. One of the advantages of the Umma is the idea that national boundaries can be irrelevant in Islamic family law cases, such that Muslim courts of differing nations recognize the actions and decisions from other national Islamic courts.

Even though there are great commonalities in the religious law and practice of Muslim communities, each nation has its own unique political developments in relation to the larger issue of secularism versus Islamic revival. . . .

Changing Family Patterns and Implications for Muslim Family Law

From a social scientific perspective, the changes in family law are reflective of changes that have been taking place in Muslim societies for generations. These are especially dramatic with respect to the status of women, for whom major social change took place in the twentieth century, especially in the decades since the advent of independence.

Most impressive has been the entry of women into the workforce. Women represent significant numbers where the economic need is the greatest, but educated middle-class women have entered into the professions in ever-increasing numbers as well. Egypt and Tunisia have the greatest number (25 percent) of women undertaking salaried employment outside the home. Even in a country as traditionally conservative as the Sudan, the participation of women in the workforce has more than doubled in the past few decades, from 7 percent to 15 percent of all women. The percentage of women in the workforce in Iran increased in the 1980s. This may seem low by Western standards, where typically well over 50 percent of women work for wages. But similar economic and social forces are at work in the Arab-Muslim world and are occurring at a more rapid pace than in the West. Since such work by women may be considered shameful according to Arab and Islamic values, it is usually undertaken only under the worst of economic and social conditions. Historically, women driven to work by personal circumstances were looked upon as the most pitiable of humans. The idea that women might work in factories, in government or business offices, or in gender-mixed situations was unthinkable only a generation or two ago. But the shame is beginning to be replaced with a sense of dignity in work, and many women have entered professions seen as "male," such as engineering, medicine, or law.

Of course, women work, as do men, whether they reside in the urban centers or in the countryside. Apart from the domestic work, growing numbers of women are working in the informal economic sector as street vendors, maids and domestics, or in craft production (such as carpet weaving). This work, although described as self-employment, places women in highly dependent positions whereby their livelihood or supplement to family income depends upon their relations with economic middlemen or those who hire them unofficially. Needless to say, the transience, vulnerability, and lack of benefits that a person working in the informal sector receives represent hardships for these working women. Despite often difficult working conditions, the entry of women into the informal sector is an offshoot of the larger social transformation that has brought women into the formal working sector (see Lobban 1998).

This economic participation of women amounts to a social transformation in the postindependence period, and to be sure, it correlates highly with the era of secular politics and the state support for the emancipation of women. With Islamist agitation, the propriety of women in the workforce is under intense scrutiny. . . . . .

An interesting survey of five hundred Sudanese women with an average age of twenty-six and ten years of marriage was conducted under the auspices of the Ahfad University College for women (Grotberg and Washi 1991), a pioneer in women's education in the Sudan and in the Muslim world generally. Sixty percent of these women married traditionally, that is, they married their first cousins, usually their father's brother's son. Thirteen percent were salaried employees. Those who indicated that they exercised personal choice in the selection of their husbands had significantly lower fertility rates. These women had, on average, 3.5 children, while the general fertility rate for Muslim Sudanese women is 6.0 children. In contrast, the ideal "modern" family is described by these women as having two children. The average educational level of women in the sample was middle school, and their husbands were generally better educated, with some secondary school training.

Family Planning Movement

An untutored Western response to fundamentalism in the Muslim world projects onto that social reality the forces at work in one's own society. Thus, "fundamentalism" in the Islamic world might suggest a ban or hostility toward birth control and family planning, as that issue has divided liberal and conservative religion in the West. In fact, there has been no comparable right-to-life movement in the Muslim world, and family planning information has entered Islamic society without much rancorous theological or political struggle. The accepted religious interpretation of the beginning of life is at the time of "quickening," or the time when the mother feels life in her body. Thus abortion in the early stages of the development of the fetus is not a moral problem. However, if that abortion is linked to immoral and illicit sexual conduct, then the consequences are grave. Indeed, because sexual activity is so controlled and constrained in the Muslim world, the emphasis in birth control has been placed on preventing pregnancy within the context of a married woman's life. The idea that birth control information and devices should be made available to unmarried women is anathema to every basic value of Islamic society and sexuality.

The family planning movement has entered Arab-Muslim society, generally speaking, as a by-product of the movement for female emancipation, which in turn was linked to the nationalist movements. Family planning clinics initially were introduced with the idea that the full incorporation of women's labor and participation in the newly independent nation required smaller families.

In the case of the nations we have been examining, family planning movements were enthusiastically endorsed and promoted by the official women's organizations, such as the National Union of Tunisian Women, the Sudanese Women's Union, and the Egyptian Women's Union. To assist the working woman, accessible and inexpensive daycare centers were also established by these women's organizations. For urban, relatively better educated working women, family size did decrease. However, in Egypt, where family planning was embraced as government policy and the emphasis shifted to rural women reducing the number of pregnancies, the results were far less successful. Egypt became recognized as an exception to the rule that urbanization curtails family size; large numbers of Egyptian peasants were streaming into Egypt's cities and still fellahin women were bearing an average of seven children. Government propaganda and international financial aid for family planning programs instilled questions in the minds of many Egyptians as to motives, and the government got the message that the limited success and unenthusiastic response from people was a form of passive resistance. The programs then shifted to a more decentralized approach, involving local women cooperating with family planning clinics, without the apparent heavy hand of the government, and a greater success rate has been achieved.

Numerous studies have shown that the most effective way to reduce population is to promote education for women. There is a powerful and persuasive correlation between the number of years of a woman's education and the number of her children. The correlation is an inverse one: the greater the educational level, the fewer the children. In Grotberg and Washi's study of young married Sudanese women, lower fertility rates correlate not only with education but also with the following set of attitudes: (1) a man and a woman can be friends, (2) strict segregation of the sexes can be relaxed, (3) a woman can choose to work outside of the home, (4) women can be involved in politics, and (5) women and men are equally competent and should enjoy equal rights.

These attitudes are just beginning to emerge in many Middle Eastern Muslim states, and the rates of change are uneven in the various countries. However, on the matter of family planning, there has not been the resistance and social turbulence that has been witnessed in many Western nations, driven by a theological interpretation that life begins at conception and that reproduction is a legitimate matter for the state.

Economic Pressures on the Family

Despite rapid and massive urbanization in the Arab and Muslim worlds, much of traditional family structure remains intact. However, some cracks in the foundation of social life are becoming visible. Although the majority of people in the Middle Eastern nations now live in cities, the integrity of the extended family has generally been upheld. Elsewhere urbanization has had a devastating effect on the extended family, and it is likely to have profound effects on the Muslim extended family in the Middle East in the future. In other regions the nuclear family has come to replace the extended family, and in other places the nuclear family has broken down into matrifocal (single mother–headed household) units. Despite massive rural to urban migration and male out-migration from poorer nations to richer ones, the essential qualities of the extended family have held together. That is, family members speak of the larger extended family as a unit experiencing either good or bad times economically, and poor economies at home have brought about a necessary alliance between family members.

However, this is in the short term; in the long term the extended family may not fare so well in the absence of physical or residential unity to reinforce the ideology of family solidarity. In each of the three countries where I have conducted studies of Islamic family law, one of the major areas of concern is the failure of husbands/fathers who have migrated abroad for work to provide adequate economic support to those whom they are bound legally to support. Primarily, this affects the immediate nuclear family, and the majority of court cases have been suits brought by wives against husbands. But with most people still residing in some form of a communal-extended household, the impact is greater than on the nuclear family alone. These changes in the stability of family life may lead to even greater problems if present trends continue, especially if the economic imbalances in the region continue to foster massive rural to urban migration and expatriate migration.

Suggested Readings

Brown, Michael F.
   1997   *The Channeling Zone: American Spirituality in an Anxious Age.* Cambridge, Mass.: Harvard University Press.

Goldberg, Harvey E.
   1987   *Judaism Viewed from Within and from Without: Anthropological Studies.* Albany: State University of New York Press.

La Barre, Weston
   1970   *The Ghost Dance: Origins of Religion.* Garden City, N.Y.: Doubleday.

Mardin, S.
   1989   *Religion and Social Change in Modern Turkey: The Case of Bediuzzaman Said Nursi.* Albany: State University of New York Press.

Marty, Martin E., and R. Scott Appleby
   1991–95   *The Fundamentalism Project.* 5 vols. Chicago: University of Chicago Press.

Thrupp, Sylvia, ed.
   1970   *Millenial Dreams in Action: Studies in Revolutionary Religious Movements.* New York: Schocken Books.

Volkman, Toby Alice
   1985   *Feasts of Honor: Ritual and Change in the Toraja Highlands.* Urbana: University of Illinois Press.

CHAPTER TEN

Religion as Global Culture: Migration, Media, and Other Transnational Forces

Throughout much of the history of anthropology, anthropologists tended to view cultures as discrete and homogeneous units—as groups of people who are pretty much alike and live in communities that are bounded in some identifiable way. Many anthropologists emphasized contrasts between the West and elsewhere and presented non-Western cultures in static terms, either overlooking the changes that occur over time in all societies or viewing change as a one-way process, with Western powers imposing unidirectional change on passive, less developed communities. By the last decades of the 20th century, however, anthropologists had begun to pay more attention to complex and multidirectional interconnections between societies. Localized religious change was the main theme of Chapter 9. Our concluding chapter considers how religion shapes and is shaped by cultural phenomena on a global scale, spreading beyond the boundaries of particular human groups.

Examination of how societies affect one another, and how different groups within a society affect one another, has led anthropologists to a number of new areas of inquiry, many of which have profound significance for the study of religion and the supernatural. Like other aspects of culture, religion has come to be seen in relation to politics, the state, international economic structures, and the media. These have all been areas of intense recent interest for anthropology. With the discipline's traditional emphasis on cultural relativism, it has been natural for anthropologists to also take a strong interest in systems of power and inequality, including race and gender. Historical perspectives have been particularly important in such analyses; for example, areas of focus have included the relationship between religion and colonialism in Africa, the effects of missionaries on Native Americans and in the Pacific, and the ways in which women have resisted control by traditional modes of religious authority.

One of the most influential contemporary anthropologists to grapple with the reformulation of culture in a global context is Arjun Appadurai of Yale University. He has coined a set of five terms to describe the dimensions through which cultural materials flow around the world (Appadurai 1996: 33–37). By utilizing the suffix *-scape* rather than a more common term, Appadurai highlights what he calls the disjunctures among these five flows, all of which transcend boundaries of culture, society, and nation. The five "scapes" are building blocks that shape our imagined worlds, or the ways individuals and groups conceive of themselves and think about their place in the world—who they are and how they want to be.

1. *Ethnoscapes* are the moving groups of people in our world, such as tourists, immigrants, refugees, exiles, and guest workers. These humans move around, carrying goals, values, and ideas about themselves and others.

2. *Technoscapes* are the patterns by which all kinds of technology, high and low, move at high speeds across the world.

3. *Financescapes* refers to the distribution of capital and such nation-transcending phenomena as currency markets, stock exchanges, and commodity speculations.

4. *Mediascapes* are the images and the media themselves that disseminate information globally, such as newspapers, magazines, television, and electronic information sources. These profoundly influence how we perceive our lives and imagine the lives of people who live elsewhere.

5. *Ideoscapes* are frequently shaped by state ideologies. On all continents, components of many globally dispersed ideoscapes derived from the Enlightenment worldview and include such notions as *freedom, rights,* and *democracy*.

The point is that our modern-day cultures, or perhaps even past cultures, cannot be thought of as bounded, isomorphic entities, coherent in themselves. The relationships among Appadurai's five scapes are unpredictable, rapidly changing, and highly dependent on particular circumstances and contexts.

Such ways of thinking about culture and global interconnections offer a number of new avenues for understanding religion. A key question concerns the degree to which religion is a force for conformity and homogenization, especially in a global context. Is religion part of the McDonaldization of the world? In a recent book on religion and globalization, Hopkins et al. write:

> If religion is one of the most fundamental means of organizing human life, then the seeds of globalization may lie within religion itself. We cannot talk about globalization without talking about religion, and we cannot talk about religion without considering how it might have laid the foundations for globalization's inception and launching. Does religion prepare the ground, both culturally and socially, for globalization?... Might a dialectical tension exist between religion and globalization, a codependence and codetermination, manifesting in different modes of religious revitalization? Religion, in various contexts, may serve as an agent of homogenization or an agent of heterogenization. (2001: 4)

The term *globalization* itself is provocative and has swept through both scholarly and popular discussions to become one of the major concepts guiding our understanding of social processes. In its narrowest sense, *globalization* refers to the worldwide movement of finance capital but, in its more common, broader sense, it refers to the international spread of ideas, materials, technology, labor, and even people. Responses to globalization run the gamut from positive to negative. As examples of the negative impacts of globalization, one might point to deforestation; the spread of infectious diseases, such as HIV, ebola, and SARS; the extinction of local languages; and the exploitation of labor in the sweatshops of multinational manufacturers. On the other hand, globalization offers opportunities for the expansion of human rights and democracy; the growth of nongovernmental organizations (NGOs) to protect the environment; the emancipation of women; and the territory-less exchange of ideas on the Internet (Hopkins et al. 2001: 3). In terms of religion, processes of globalization at work for centuries have spread Christianity, Islam, and Buddhism far beyond their geographic points of origin, and today's information technologies allow anyone who uses the Web or watches TV to cruise the "spiritual marketplace," to use a term coined by journalist Donald Lattin (quoted in Batstone 2001: 228).

There are close connections among globalization (however one defines it), the spread of capitalism, and the consumer culture that goes along with capitalism. Because anthropologists are interested in how groups of people resist structures of power, many have turned their attention to religion as a form of anti-systemic protest (Robbins 1999). Some feel that the only groups around the world that actually seek to overthrow or replace the culture of capitalism are religious groups, including Liberation Theology Catholics in Latin America, Islamic fundamentalists in Arab and Southeast Asian countries, and some Protestant fundamentalists in the United States. The so-called fundamentalist movements that are offshoots of major world religions (especially Protestant Christianity and Islam) are markedly different in scope and organization from the smaller religious protest movements examined in Chapter 9, such as the Ghost Dance movement and cargo cults. However, contradictions abound. In one of the upcoming articles, Mark Juergensmeyer's survey of religious nationalist movements around the world highlights examples that are decidedly anti-capitalism and anti-globalization.

An ethnographic study by Simon Coleman (2000) exemplifies the anthropological approach to studying religion in relation to globalization and documents the interplay of people, technology, finance, media, and ideology noted by Appadurai. During the 1990s, Coleman studied conservative Protestant Christians in Uppsala, Sweden, and found that the spread of charismatic Christianity across national borders reveals much about how the global and the local shape one another. By talking with Swedish charismatic Christians, attending their worship services, and observing their use of television, video, and Internet technologies, Coleman came to understand how participants strike a complex balance between their immediate community, their national identity, and a sense of global belonging.

In the selections that follow, we have chosen to highlight only a small number of topics related to religion, globalization, and the spread of culture across national boundaries. We begin with an example of the movement of people, and its potential for increased understanding as well as intolerance. Homa Hoodfar's work on Muslim women's clothing addresses the historical effects of confrontational contact between Western and Middle Eastern peoples and includes a discussion of Muslim communities in North America. Hoodfar dispels the notion that modest Islamic women's dress is "traditional" and unchanging or is a sign of oppression. Given this background of misunderstanding, how will the participation of Muslims in Canadian universities and communities shape life in the 21st century?

The second article documents two rituals among Lao Buddhists living in the United States emphasizing how religion builds and asserts new forms of identity for immigrants.

Mark Juergensmeyer's article turns our attention to one of the more disturbing implications of globalized religious phenomena: the rise of violent activist movements advocating violence and terror. Juergensmeyer's work includes examples that readers will frequently find mentioned in the news.

The issue of how popular and entertainment-oriented media represent religion is significant, with rich potential for comparison across cultures. How are religious institutions depicted in the soap operas of Latin America? How are spiritual resources drawn on in the supernatural TV dramas of South and Southeast Asia? What happens when commercial entertainment is shaped strongly by a few capital-rich industry centers, such as the United

States, Japan, and India? Our concluding article takes a look at U.S. religion as depicted in the television show *The Simpsons*. What have the world's millions of viewers of *The Simpsons* learned from that show about religion in America?

References

Appadurai, Arjun
  1996 *Modernity at Large: Cultural Dimensions of Globalization.* Minneapolis: University of Minnesota Press.

Batstone, David
  2001 "Dancing to a Different Beat: Emerging Spiritualities in the Network Society." In Dwight N. Hopkins et al., *Religions/Globalizations: Theories and Cases,* pp. 226–42. Durham, N.C.: Duke University Press.

Coleman, Simon
  2000 *The Globalisation of Charismatic Christianity: Spreading the Gospel of Prosperity.* Cambridge: Cambridge University Press.

Hopkins, Dwight N., Lois Ann Lorentzen, Eduardo Mendieta, and David Batstone, eds.
  2001 *Religions/Globalizations: Theories and Cases.* Durham, N.C.: Duke University Press.

Robbins, Richard H.
  1999 *Global Problems and the Culture of Capitalism.* Boston: Allyn & Bacon.

49

The Veil in Their Minds and on Our Heads: Veiling Practices and Muslim Women

Homa Hoodfar

Anyone who has read a newspaper or magazine from the Western press in recent years is likely to recognize that their depictions of Islam and Muslim societies prominently feature women's dress. In many news photographs, women's head coverings signify the status of women or the modernity of a culture. Immigration, the global spread of faiths, and the international political and economic conflicts of recent years have made Muslim communities increasingly visible in North America and Europe. Western tradition has long equated the veil with oppression or ignorance, so Muslim women frequently bear the brunt of misunderstanding and intolerance, especially from well-intentioned non-Muslims who are concerned about women's rights. A goal of anthropology, however, is to look within cultures to discover meaning and significance, rather than to assume that the observer already knows what something means or to impose facile judgments.

Homa Hoodfar, a Canadian anthropologist of Iranian descent, here shows the malleability and complexity of veiling by paying careful attention to the experiences of Muslim women, arguing that many Western images of the veil are inaccurate and romanticized. To illustrate how Islamic women's dress has varied in response to changing social conditions, the author focuses on women's dress in Iran between the 1930s and the 1980s, including anecdotes from her own family. Finally, Hoodfar discusses her fieldwork among Muslim communities in Canada, highlighting difficulties faced by women who wear modest dress. Hoodfar argues that misconceptions about Muslim women are a form of racism that prevents Muslims and others from joining together to fight injustice.

The scholarly literature on women and Islam, including the role of dress, is voluminous. Interested students might wish to read In Search of Islamic Feminism *by Elizabeth Fernea (Doubleday, 1998) and* Beyond the Veil: Male-Female Dynamics in a Modern Muslim Society *by Fatima Mernissi (Saqi Books, rev. ed. 2003).*

Muslim women, and particularly Middle Eastern and North African women, for the past two centuries have been one of the most enduring subjects of discussion in the Western media. I can also assert without hesitation that the issue of the veil and the oppression of Muslim women has been the most frequent topic of conversation and discussion I have been engaged in, often reluctantly, during some twenty years of my life in the Western world (mostly in the UK and Canada). Whenever I meet a person of white/European descent, I regularly find that as soon as he or she ascertains that I am Muslim/Middle Eastern/Iranian, the veil very quickly emerges as the prominent topic of conversation. This scenario occurs everywhere: in trains, at the grocery store, at the launderette, on the university campus, at parties. The range of knowledge of these eager conversants varies: some honestly confess total ignorance of Islam and Islamic culture or Middle Eastern societies; others base their claims and opinions on their experiences in colonial armies in the Middle East, or on their travels through the Middle East to India during the 1960s; still others cite as reference films or novels. What I find remarkable is that, despite their admitted ignorance on the subject, almost all people I have met are, with considerable confidence, adamant that women have a particularly tough time in Muslim cultures. Occasionally Western non-Muslim women will tell me they are thankful that they were not born in a Muslim culture. Sometimes they go so far as to say that they are happy that I am living in their society rather than my own, since obviously my ways are more like theirs, and since now, having been exposed to Western ways, I could never return to the harem!

For years I went through much pain and frustration, trying to convey that many assumptions about Muslim women were false and based on the racism and biases of the colonial powers, yet without defending or denying the patriarchal barriers that Muslim women (like women in many other countries, including Western societies) face. I took pains to give examples of how Western biases against non-Western cultures abound. In research, for example, social scientists often fail to compare like with like. The situation of poor illiterate peasant women of the South is implicitly or explicitly compared with the experiences of educated upper-middle-class women of Western societies. Failing to adequately contextualize non-Western societies, many researchers simply assume that what is good for Western middle-class women should be good for all other women. It is frustrating that, in the majority of cases, while my conversants listen to me, they do not hear, and at the end of the conversation they reiterate their earlier views as if our discussion were irrelevant. In more recent years, they treat me as an Islamic apolo-

gist, which silences me in new ways that often preclude argument.

I had assumed that my experiences were unique and were the result of my moving in milieux that had little contact with or knowledge about Muslim communities and cultures. However, through my recent research on the integration of Muslim women in educational institutions and the labor market in Canada, which has brought me into contact with many young Muslim women, I have come to realize that these reactions on the part of the dominant group are much more prevalent than I had thought. Moreover, the Muslim community, and in particular veiled women, suffer the psychological and socioeconomic consequences of these views. This situation has created a high level of anger and frustration in response to the deliberate racism toward Muslims in Canada and the unwillingness, despite ample examples, to let go of old colonial images of passive Muslim women. The assumption that *veil* equals *ignorance* and *oppression* means that young Muslim women have to invest a considerable amount of energy to establish themselves as thinking, rational, literate students/individuals, both in their classrooms and outside.

In this essay, I draw on historical sources, my research data on young Muslim women in Canada, as well as my own experience as a nonveiled Muslim woman of Iranian descent. I argue that the veil, which since the nineteenth century has symbolized for the West the inferiority of Muslim cultures, remains a powerful symbol both for the West and for Muslim societies. While for Westerners its meaning has been static and unchanging, in Muslim cultures the veil's functions and social significance have varied tremendously, particularly during times of rapid social change. Veiling is a lived experience full of contradictions and multiple meanings. While it has clearly been a mechanism in the service of patriarchy, a means of regulating and controlling women's lives, women have used the same social institution to free themselves from the bonds of patriarchy. Muslim women, like all other women, are social actors, employing, reforming, and changing existing social institutions, often creatively, to their own ends. The static colonial image of the oppressed veiled Muslim woman thus often contrasts sharply with the lived experience of veiling. To deny this is also to deny Muslim women their agency.

The continuation of misconceptions and misinterpretations about the veil and veiled women has several consequences, not just for Muslim women but also for occidental women. The mostly man-made images of oriental Muslim women continue to be a mechanism by which Western dominant cultures re-create and perpetuate beliefs about their superiority. The persistence of colonial and racist responses to their societies has meant that Muslim communities and societies must continually struggle to protect their cultural and political identities, a situation that makes it harder for many Muslim women, who share the frustration of their community and society, to question the merits and uses of the veil within their own communities. Moreover, the negative images of Muslim women are continually presented as a reminder to European and North American women of their relative good fortune and as an implied warning to curb their "excessive" demands for social and legal equality. Yet all too often Western feminists uncritically participate in the dominant androcentric approaches to other cultures and fail to see how such participation is ultimately in the service of patriarchy. Significantly, Western feminists' failure to critically interrogate colonial, racist, and androcentric constructs of women of non-Western cultures forces Muslim women to choose between fighting sexism or racism. As Muslim feminists have often asked, must racism be used to fight sexism?

To illustrate the persistence of the social and ideological construction of the veil in colonial practices and discourses and its contrast to the lived experience of veiling, I first briefly review a history of the veil and its representation in the West. Then, by examining some of the consequences of both compulsory de-veiling and re-veiling in Iran, I demonstrate the costs to Iranian women of generalized and unsubstantiated assumptions that the veil is inherently oppressive and hence that its removal is automatically liberating. I then discuss some of my findings on the representation of the veil and its usage in the context of Canadian society and its consequences for young Muslim women in their communities and in their interaction with other women, particularly feminists. I point out how the androcentric images and stereotypes of occidental and oriental women inhibit women's learning about and from each other

and weakens our challenge to both patriarchy and Western imperialism.

The Origins of the Veil

The practice of veiling and seclusion of women is pre-Islamic and originates in non-Arab Middle Eastern and Mediterranean societies. The first reference to veiling is in an Assyrian legal text that dates from the thirteenth century B.C., which restricted the practice to respectable women and forbade prostitutes from veiling. Historically, veiling, especially when accompanied by seclusion, was a sign of status and was practiced by the elite in the ancient Greco-Roman, pre-Islamic Iranian, and Byzantine empires. Muslims adopted the veil and seclusion from conquered peoples, and today it is widely recognized, by Muslims and non-Muslims, as an Islamic phenomenon that is presumably sanctioned by the Qur'an. Contrary to this belief, veiling is nowhere specifically recommended or even discussed in the Qur'an. At the heart of the Qur'anic position on the question of the veil is the interpretation of two verses (Surah al-Nur, verses 30–31) that recommend women to cover their bosoms and jewelry; this has come to mean that women should cover themselves. Another verse recommends to the wives of the Prophet to wrap their cloak tightly around their bodies, so as to be recognized and not be bothered or molested in public (Surah al-Ahzab, verse 59). Modern commentators have rationalized that since the behavior of the wives of the Prophet is to be emulated, then all women should adopt this form of dress. In any case, it was not until the reign of the Safavids (1501–1722) in Iran and the Ottoman Empire (1357–1924), which extended to most of the area that today is known as the Middle East and North Africa, that the veil emerged as a widespread symbol of status among the Muslim ruling class and urban elite. Significantly, it is only since the nineteenth century, after the veil was promoted by the colonials as a prominent symbol of Muslim societies, that Muslims have justified it in the name of Islam, and not by reference to cultural practices.

Although the boundaries of veiling and seclusion have been blurred in many debates, and particularly in Western writing, the two phenomena are separate, and their consequences for Muslim women are vastly different. Seclusion, or what is sometimes known as *purdah,* is the idea that women should be protected, especially from males who are not relatives; thus they are often kept at home where their contact with the public is minimized. Seclusion may or may not be combined with the veiling that covers the whole body.

It has been argued that seclusion developed among Mediterranean and Middle Eastern societies because they prefer endogamous marriages; consequently they tend to develop social institutions that lend themselves to more control of young people, particularly women. The argument is made even more strongly for Muslim women because they inherit wealth and remain in control of their wealth after marriage. Although a daughter's inherited share is equal to half that of a son, it is also established, by religion, that a father does not have the power to disinherit his daughters. It is an irony of history that the more economic rights women have had, the more their sexuality has been subject to control through the development of complex social institutions. Nonetheless, outside the well-to-do social elites, seclusion was rarely practiced to any considerable degree, since women's economic as well as reproductive labor was essential for the survival of their households. In reality, the majority of social classes, particularly in rural settings, practiced segregation and sexual division of labor rather than seclusion. The exertion of these controls often created an obstacle but did not erase Muslim women's control of their wealth (if they had any), which they managed.

However, as the socioeconomic conditions changed and factory production and trade became the major sources of wealth and capital, elite women lost ground to their male counterparts. The ideology of seclusion prevented their easy access to the rapidly changing market and to information, thus limiting their economic possibilities. Consequently their socioeconomic position vis-à-vis their husbands deteriorated. Moreover, the informal social institutions, class alliances, and kin networks that had protected women to some extent were breaking down very rapidly. In the twentieth century, this context is an important, though often neglected, reason for women of the upper classes in the Middle East to become more radically involved in the women's movement. In Egypt, where the socioeconomic changes were most rapid, the women's movement developed into an organized and effective political force that other political groups could not afford to ignore. As for women in other social groups, the "modern" and "traditional" ideologies of domesticity often excluded women from better-paying jobs in the public sector, particularly if this involved traveling outside their neighborhoods and being in contact with unrelated males. Moreover, the early modern governments that sponsored the training of many citizens in fields such as commercial and international law, engineering, and commerce, following the European model, closed these options to women until a much later date, thereby reproducing and occasionally intensifying the gap already existing between men's and women's economic opportunities.

The veil refers to the clothing that covers and conceals the body from head to ankle, with the exception of the face, hands, and feet. Incidentally, this is also a very accurate description of the traditional male clothing of much of the Arab world, although in different historical periods authorities have tried, with varying degrees of success, to make the clothing more gender specific. The most drastic difference between male and female clothing worn among the Arab urban elite was created with the Westernization and colonization of Muslim societies in the Middle East and North Africa. Men, particularly, began to emulate European ways of dress much sooner and on a larger scale than women did.

Although in Western literature the veil and veiling are often presented as a unified and static practice that has not changed for more than a thousand years, the veil has been varied and subject to changing fashion throughout past and present history. Moreover, like other articles of clothing, the veil may be worn for multiple reasons. It may be worn to beautify the wearer, much as Western women wear makeup; to demonstrate respect for conventional values, or to hide the wearer's identity. In recent times, the most frequent type of veiling in most cities is a long, loosely fitted dress of any color combination, worn with a scarf wrapped (in various fashions) on the head so as to cover all the hair. Nonetheless, the imaginary veil that comes to the minds of most Westerners is an awkward black cloak that covers the whole body, including the face, and is designed to prevent women's mobility. Throughout history, however, apart from the elite, women's labor was necessary to the functioning of the household and the economy, and so they wore clothing that would not hamper their movement. Even a casual survey of clothing among most rural and urban areas in the Middle East and other Muslim cultures would indicate that these women's costumes, though all are considered Islamic, cover the body to different degrees. The tendency of Western scholars and the colonial powers to present a unidimensional Islam and a seamless society of Muslims has prevented them from exploring the socioeconomic significance of the existing variations that were readily available, sometimes in their own drawings and paintings. Similarly, scholarly study of Islamic beliefs and culture focused on Islamic texts and use of Islamic dialogues, while overlooking the variations in the way Islam was practiced in different Islamic cultures and by different classes.

Although clothing fulfills a basic need of human beings in most climates, it is also a significant social institution through which important ideological and nonverbal communication takes place. Clothing, in most aspects, is designed to indicate not only gender and stage of life cycle, but also to identify social group and geographic area. Moreover, in the Middle East, veiling has been intertwined with Islamic ethics, making it an even more complex institution. According to Muslims, women should cover their hair and body when they are in the presence of adult men who are not close relatives; thus when women put on or take off their veil, they are defining who may or may not be considered kin. Furthermore, since veiling defines sexuality, by observing or neglecting the veil, women may define who is a man and who is not. For instance, high-status women may not observe the veil in the presence of low-status men.

In the popular urban culture of Iran, in situations of conflict between men and women who are outside the family group, a very effective threat that women have is to drop their veil and thus indicate that they do not consider the contester to be a man. This is an irrevocable insult and causes men to be wary of getting into arguments with women. Similarly, by threatening to drop the veil and put on male clothing, women have at times manipulated men to comply with their wishes. One such example can be drawn from the Tobacco Movement of the late nineteenth century in Iran. In a meeting on devising resistance strategies against the tobacco monopoly and concessions given to Britain by the Iranian government, men expressed reluctance to engage in radical political action. Observing the men's hesitation, women nationalists who were participating in the meeting (from the women's section of the mosque) raised their voices and threatened that if the men failed to protect their country for the women and children, then the women had no alternative but to drop their veil and go to war themselves. Thus, the men were obliged to consider more radical forms of action.

The Making of the Veil in Their Minds

It was in the late eighteenth and early nineteenth century that the West's overwhelming preoccupation with the veil in Muslim cultures emerged. Travel accounts and observations from commentators prior to this time show little interest in Muslim women or the veil. The sexual segregation among all sects (Muslims, Christians, and Jews) in Mediterranean and Middle Eastern cultures was established knowledge and prior to the nineteenth century rarely attracted much attention from European travelers. Some pre-nineteenth-century accounts did report on oriental and Muslim women's lack of morality and shamelessness based on their revealing clothes and their free mobility. Others observed and commented on the extent of women's power within the domestic domain, an aspect totally overlooked in the latter part of the nineteenth century.

The representation of the Muslim orient by the Christian occident went through a fundamental change as the Ottoman Empire's power diminished and the Muslim orient fell deeper and deeper under European domination. The appearance and circulation of the earliest version of *A Thousand and One Nights* in the West coincided with the Turkish defeat. By the nineteenth century the focus of representation of the Muslim orient had changed from the male barbarian, constructed over centuries during the Crusades, to the "uncivilized" ignorant male whose masculinity relies on the mistreatment of women, primarily as sex slaves. In this manner images of Muslim women were used as a major building block for the construction of the orient's new imagery, an imagery that has been intrinsically linked to the hegemony of Western imperialism, particularly that of France and Britain.

Scholars of Muslim societies, including feminists, have recently begun to trace the entrenchment of the Western image of the oppressed Muslim woman. This informal knowledge about Muslim women seeped into numerous travel books and occasionally into historical and anthropological accounts of the region. In a century and a half, 1800 to 1950, an estimated sixty thousand books were published in the West on the Arab orient alone. The primary mission of these writings was to depict the colonized Arabs/Muslims as inferior/backward and urgently in need of progress offered to them by the colonial superiors. It is in this political context that the veil and the Muslim harem, as the world of women, emerged as a source of fascination, fantasy, and frustration for Western writers. Harems were supposed to be places where Muslim men imprisoned their wives, who had nothing to do except beautify themselves and cater to their husbands' huge sexual appetite. It is ironic that the word *harem*, which etymologically derives from a root that connotes *sacred* and *shrine*, has come to represent such a negative notion in the Western world. Women are invariably depicted as prisoners, frequently half-naked and unveiled and at times sitting at windows with bars, with little hope of ever being free. How these mostly male writers, painters, and photographers have found access to these presumably closed women's quarters/prisons is a question that has been raised only recently.

Western representations of the harem were inspired not only by the fantasies of *A Thousand and One Nights*, but also by the colonizers' mission of subjugation of the colonized, to the exclusion of the reality of the harems and the way women experienced them. Of little interest to Western readers was the fact that during the nineteenth century in most Middle Eastern societies over 85 percent of the population lived in rural areas, where women worked on the land and in the homes, with lives very different from the well-to-do urban elites (who, in any case, were a very small minority). When Western commentators of the nineteenth century came across a situation that contradicted their stereotype of the power structure in Muslim households, they simply dismissed it as exceptional.

It is important to bear in mind that the transformation in the representation of Muslim women during the nineteenth century did not occur in isolation from other changes taking place in the imperial land, as Mabro has pointed out. During the same period, the ideology of femininity and what later came to be known as the Victorian morality was developing in Britain, and variations on this theme were coming into existence in other areas of the Western world. Yet Western writers zealously described the oppression of Turkish and Muslim women, with little regard for the fact that many of these criticisms applied equally to their own society. Both Muslim oriental and Christian occidental women were thought to be in need of male protection and intellectually and biologically destined for the domestic domain. Moreover, in both the orient and occident women were expected to obey and honor their husbands. In his book *Sketches of Persia,* Sir John Malcolm reports a dialogue between himself and Meerza Aboo Talib in which he compares the unfavorable position of Persian women relative to European women. Aboo Talib makes the point that "we consider that loving and obeying their husbands, giving proper attention to their children, and their domestic duties, are the best occupations for females." Malcolm then replies that this made the women slaves to their husbands' pleasure and housework. That is, of course, quite correct, but, as Mabro has pointed out, Aboo Talib's comment on Persian women was an equally correct description of women's duty in most European societies, including Britain, at the time.

Neither did Western women traveler-writers draw parallels between the oppression of women in their own society and that of women in the orient. For instance, European women of the nineteenth century were hardly freer than their oriental counterparts in terms of mobility and traveling, a situation of which many European female expatriates repeatedly complained. Mobile Shaman, in her book *Through Algeria,* lamented that women were not able to travel unless accompanied by men. Western women travelers often wrote about the boredom of oriental women's lives. It often escaped them that in many cases it was precisely the boredom and the limitation of domestic life that had been the major motivating force behind many Western women's travels to the orient, an option no doubt open only to very few. Similarly, while Western writers of the nineteenth century wrote about the troubled situation of women in polygamous marriages and the double standard applied to men and women, they totally ignored the plight of "mistresses" in their own societies and the vast number of illegitimate children, who not only had no right to economic support but as "bastards" were also condemned to carry the stigma of the sin of their father for the rest of their life. Clearly, societies in the Muslim orient and the Christian occident both practiced a double standard as it applied to men and women. Both systems of patriarchy were developed to cater to men's whims and to perpetuate their privileges. But the social institutions and ethos of the orient and occident that have developed in order to ensure male prerogatives were/are different. The Western world embraced a monogamous ideology, overlooking the bleak life of a huge group of women and their illegitimate children. In the orient, at the cost of legitimization of polygynous marriages and institutionalizing the double standard, women and their children received at least a limited degree of protection and social legitimacy. Although the occident demonstrated little interest in the oriental images of the European world, numerous nineteenth-century documents indicate that oriental writers were conscious of the contradiction between the presentation of a civilized façade and the hideous and cruel reality of the Western world for many women and children.

Women in Qajar Iran were astonished by the clothing of Western women and the discomfort that women must feel in the heavy, tight garments; they felt that Western societies were unkind to their women by attempting to change the shape of their bodies, forcing them into horrendous corsets. A scenario quoted in Mabro has aptly captured the way oriental and occidental women viewed each other: "When Lady Mary Montague was pressed by the women in a Turkish bath to take off her clothes and join them, she undid her blouse to show them her corset. This led them to believe that she was imprisoned in a machine which could only be opened by her husband. Both groups of women could see each other as prisoners and of course they were right."

As the domination by Europe over the orient increased, it shattered Islamic societies' self-confidence as peoples and civilizations. Many, in their attempt to restore their nations' lost glory and independence, sought to Westernize their society by emulating Western ways and customs, including the clothing. The modernizers' call for women's formal education

was often linked with unveiling, as though the veil per se would prevent women from studying or intellectual activities. The reformers proposed a combination of unveiling and education in one package, which at least partly stemmed from their belief that the veil had become in the West a symbol of their society's "backwardness." In many Muslim societies, particularly among urban elites, patriarchal rulers had often enforced (and in some cases still do) the veil to curtail women's mobility and independence. The reformers' criticisms were mostly directed at the seclusion in the name of the veil, for clearly, seclusion and public education were incompatible. Nonetheless, given the connections between the veil and Islamic ethics in Muslim cultures, the reformers and modernizers made a strategic mistake in combining unveiling with formal education. Conservative forces, particularly some of the religious authorities, seized the opportunity to legitimize their opposition to the proposed changes in the name of religion and galvanized public resistance. Though education is recommended by Islam equally for males and female, in fact the public is largely opposed to unveiling.

Despite much opposition from religious and conservative forces, many elite reformists in the Middle East (both males and females) pressed for de-veiling. In Egypt, where feminist and women's organizations had emerged as important political forces vocally criticizing colonial power, it was the women activists who initiated and publicly removed the veil during a demonstration in Cairo in 1923. Egypt thus became the first Islamic country to de-veil without state intervention, a situation that provoked heated debates in Egypt and the rest of the Arab and Muslim world. Recent assessment of de-veiling has dismissed the importance of this historical event on the grounds that veiling only affected upper-class women. But, as I have argued elsewhere, "although Egyptian women of low-income classes never veiled their faces and wore more dresses which did not prevent movement, they nevertheless regarded the upper-class veil as an ideal. It was not ideology which prevented them from taking 'the veil,' rather it was the lack of economic possibilities." The de-veiling movement among upper-class Egyptian women questioned not only the ideology of the veil but also the seclusion of women in the name of the veil and Islam.

In other countries, such as Iran and Turkey, it was left to the state to outlaw the veil. Although the rhetoric of de-veiling was to liberate women so they could contribute to build a new modern nation, in reality women and their interests counted little. Rather, they had become the battlefield and the booty of the harsh and sometimes bloody struggle between the secularists and modernists on one side, and the religious authorities on the other. The modernist states, eager to alienate and defeat the religious authorities, who historically had shared the state's power and who generally opposed the trend toward secularization, outlawed the veil and enlisted the police forces to compel deveiling without considering the consequences of this action for women, particularly those outside the elite and middle classes of large urban centers. Ataturk (1923–38), who represented the secularist, nationalist movement in Turkey, outlawed the veil and in fact all traditional clothing including the fez; the Turks were to wear European-style clothing in a march toward modernity. Iran followed suit and introduced clothing reform, albeit a milder version, but the stress was put on de-veiling. Feminists and women activists in Iran were less organized than their counterparts in Egypt and Turkey. Debates on women's issues and the necessity of education were primarily championed by men and placed in the context of the modernization of Iran to regain its lost glory. In these discussions, women were primarily viewed as the mothers of the nation, who had to be educated in order to bring up educated and intelligent children, particularly sons. The veil was often singled out as the primary obstacle to women's education.

The Veil on Our Heads: Iran, a Case Study

De-veiling, particularly without any other legal and socioeconomic adjustments, can at best be a dubious measure of women's "liberation" and freedom of movement, and it can have many short- and long-term consequences. To illustrate this point, here I review the experiences of my own grandmother and her friends during the de-veiling movement in the 1930s, and then compare this with some of the trends that have developed with the introduction and strict enforcement of compulsory veiling under the current Islamic Republic of Iran.

In 1936, the shah's father, as part of his plan to modernize Iran, decided to outlaw the veil. The government passed a law that made it illegal for women to be in the street wearing the veil (or, as Iranians refer to it, the *chador*, which literally means *tent* and consists of a long cape-type clothing that covers from head to ankle but normally does not cover the face) or any other kind of head covering except a European hat. The police had strict orders to pull off and tear up any scarf or *chador* worn in public. This had grievous consequences for the majority of women, who were socialized to see the veil and veiling as legitimate and the only acceptable way of dressing. Nonetheless, it is important to note the impact of the compulsory de-veiling for rural and urban women, younger and older women, as well as women of different classes. As the state had little presence in the countryside and since most rural women dressed in their traditional clothing, the law had only a limited impact in the countryside. The women who were urban modern elites welcomed the change and took advantage of some of the educational and employment opportunities that the modern state offered them. Women of the more conservative and religious social groups experienced some inconvenience in the early years of compulsory de-veiling, but they had the means to employ others to run their outdoor errands. However, it was the urban lower middle classes and low-income social groups who bore the brunt of the problem. It is an example of these social groups that I present here.

Contrary to the assumptions and images prevalent in the West, women generally were not kept in harems. Most women of modest means who lived in urban households often did the shopping and established neighborly and community networks, which, in the absence of any economic and social support by the state, were a vital means of support during hard times. Many young unmarried women, including some of my aunts, went to carpet weaving workshops, an equivalent activity in many ways to attending school. Attending these workshops gave the young women legitimate reason to move about the city and socialize with women outside their circle of kin and immediate neighbors. Learning to weave carpets in this traditional urban culture was, however, fundamentally different from the crocheting and embroidery engaged in by Victorian ladies: carpet weaving was a readily marketable skill which enabled them to earn some independent income, however small, should they have need.

The introduction of the de-veiling law came at a time of rapid social change created by a national economy in turmoil. In search of employment, thousands of men, especially those with no assets or capital, had migrated to Tehran and other large cities, often leaving their families behind in the care of their wives or mothers, since among the poor, nuclear families were the prevalent form of household. Those men who did not migrate had to spend longer hours at their jobs, usually away from home, while leaving more household responsibilities to their wife. My grandmother, a mother of seven children, lived in Hamedan, an ancient city in the central part of Iran. By the time of de-veiling, her husband, whose modest income was insufficient to cover the day-to-day expenses of his family, had migrated to Tehran in the hope of finding a better job, and she carried sole responsibility for the public and private affairs of her household. According to her, this was by no means an exceptional situation but was in fact common for many women. Evidently this commonality encouraged closer ties between the women, who went about their affairs together and spent much time in each other's company.

Because the women would not go out in public without a head covering, the de-veiling law and its harsh enforcement compelled them to stay home and beg favors from their male relatives and friends' husbands and sons for the performance of the public tasks they normally carried out themselves. My grandmother bitterly recounted her first memory of the day a policeman chased her to take off her scarf, which she had put on as a compromise to the *chador*. She ran as the policeman ordered her to stop; he followed her, and as she approached the gate of her house he pulled off her scarf. She thought the policeman had deliberately allowed her to reach her home decently, because policemen had mothers and sisters who faced the same problem: neither they nor their male kin wanted them to go out "naked." For many women it was such an embarrassing situation that they just stayed home. Many independent women became dependent on men, while those who did not have a male present in the household suffered most because they had to beg favors from their

neighbors. "How could we go out with nothing on?" my grandmother asked us every time she talked about her experiences. Young women of modest income stopped going to the carpet weaving workshops. Households with sufficient means would sometimes set up a carpet frame at home if their daughters were skilled enough to weave without supervision. Gradually, however, the carpet traders started to provide the wool, the loom, and other necessary raw materials to the households with lesser means and, knowing that women had no other option, paid them even smaller wages than when they went to the workshops. Moreover, this meant that women lost the option of socializing with those outside their immediate kin and neighbors, thus young women were subject to stricter control by their family. Worse yet, male relatives began to assume the role of selling completed carpets or dealing with the male carpet traders, which meant women lost control over their wages, however small they were.

Apart from the economic impact, de-veiling had a very negative impact on the public, social, and leisure activities of urban women of modest means. For instance, historically, among urban Shi'ites, women frequently attended the mosque for prayer, other religious ceremonies, or simply for some peace and quiet or socializing with other women. They would periodically organize and pay a collective visit to the various shrines across town. The legitimacy of this social institution was so strong that even the strictest husbands and fathers would not oppose women's participation in these visits, although they might ask an older woman to accompany the younger ones. My grandmother, and women of her milieu, regretfully talked about how they missed being able to organize these visits for a long time, almost until World War II broke out. She often asserted that men raised few objections to these limitations, and said, "Why would they, since men always want to keep their women at home?"

One of the most pleasant and widespread female social institutions was the weekly visit to the public bath, of which there were only a few in the town. Consequently, the public bath was a vehicle for socialization outside the kin and neighbor network. Women would go at sunrise and return at noon, spending much time sharing news, complaining about misfortune, asking advice for dealing with business, family, and health problems, as well as finding suitors for their marriageable sons, daughters, kin, and neighbors. At midday, they would often have drinks and sweets. Such a ritualized bath was especially sanctioned within Muslim religious practices, which require men and women to bathe after sexual intercourse; bathing is also essential for women after menstruation before they resume the daily prayers. A long absence from the public bath would alarm the neighbors of a possible lapse in the religious practices of the absentee. Therefore they had to develop a strategy that would allow them to attend to their weekly ablutions without offending modesty by "going naked" in the street, as the de-veiling law would require them to do.

The strategies they developed varied from bribing the police officers to disappear from their route, to the less favored option of warming up enough water to bathe and rinse at home. Due to the cold climate in Hamedan, and the limited heating facilities available, this option was not practical during the many cold winter months. One neighbor had heard of women getting into big bags and then being carried to the public bath. So, women of the neighborhood organized to make some bags out of canvas. The women who were visiting the public bath would get into the bags, and their husbands, sons, or brothers would carry them in the bags over their shoulder, or in a donkey- or horse-driven cart to the public bath, where the attendant, advised in advance, would come and collect them. At lunch time the women would climb back in the bags and the men would return to carry them home.

Although this strategy demonstrates how far people will go to defy imposed and senseless worldviews and gender roles envisaged by the state, it is also clear that in the process women have lost much of their traditional independence for the extremely dubious goal of wearing European outfits. One can effectively argue that such outfits, in the existing social context, contributed to the exclusion of women of popular classes and pushed them toward seclusion, rather than laying the ground for their liberation. The de-veiling law caused many moderate families to resist allowing their daughters to attend school because of the social implication of not wearing a scarf in public. Furthermore, as illustrated above, women became even more dependent on men since

they now had to ask for men's collaboration in order to perform activities they had previously performed independently. This gave men a degree of control over women they had never before possessed. It also reinforced the idea that households without adult men were odd and abnormal. Moreover, not all men collaborated. As my grandmother observed, many men used this opportunity to deny their wives the weekly money with which women would pay their public bath fare and the occasional treat to consume with women friends. Yet other men used the opportunity to gain complete control over their household shopping, denying women any say in financial matters.

Wearing the *chador* remained illegal, although the government eventually relaxed the enforcement of the de-veiling law. In the official state ideology, the veil remained a symbol of backwardness, despite the fact that the majority of women, particularly those from low and moderate income groups and the women of the traditional middle classes in the urban centers, continued to observe various degrees of *hijab* (covering). The government, through its discriminatory policies, effectively denied veiled women access to employment in the government sector, which is the single most important national employer, particularly of women. The practice of excluding veiled women hit them particularly hard as they had few other options for employment. Historically, the traditional bazaar sector rarely employed female workers, and while the modern private sector employed some blue-collar workers who wore the traditional *chador,* rarely did they extend this policy to white-collar jobs. A blunt indication of this discrimination was clear in the policies covering the use of social facilities such as clubs for civil servants provided by most government agencies or even private hotels and some restaurants, which denied service to women who observed the *hijab.*

This undemocratic exclusion was a major source of veiled women's frustration. To demonstrate but a small aspect of the problem for women who observed the *hijab,* I give two examples from among my own acquaintances. In 1975 my father was paid a visit by an old family friend and her daughter to seek his advice. The family was deeply religious but very open-minded, and the mother was determined that her daughters should finish their schooling and seek employment before they marry. She argued that there is no contradiction between being a good Muslim and being educated and employed with an independent income of one's own. After much argument, the father agreed that if the oldest daughter, who had graduated from high school, could find a job in the government sector, he would not object to her working. Since, as a veiled woman, she had little chance of even obtaining an application, she asked an unveiled friend to go to the Ministry of Finance and fill out the application form. With the help of neighbors, the mother managed to arrange an interview for her. The dilemma was that, should she appear at the interview with *chador* or scarf on her head, she would never get the job and all their efforts would be wasted. It was finally agreed that she would wear a wig and a very modest dress and leave for the interview from a relative's house so that the neighbors would not see her. After a great deal of trouble, she finally was offered a position and convinced her father not to object to her wearing a scarf while at work. Thus she would leave her house wearing the *chador* and remove it, leaving just a scarf on her hair, before she arrived at work. To her colleagues, she explained that because she lived in a very traditional neighborhood, it would shame her family if she left the house without a *chador*.

A similar example can be drawn from the experience of a veiled woman I met at university in Iran. She came from a religious family with very modest means. She had struggled against a marriage arranged by her family, and managed to come to university always wearing her *chador*. She graduated with outstanding results from the Department of Economics and taught herself a good functional knowledge of English. She hoped, with her qualifications, to find a good job and help her family, who had accommodated her nontraditional views. To satisfy the modesty required by her own and her family's Islamic beliefs, and the need to be mobile and work, she designed for herself some loosely cut, but very smart, long dresses that included a hood or a scarf. But her attempt to find a job was fruitless, though she was often congratulated on her abilities. Knowing that she was losing her optimism, I asked her to come and apply for an opening at the Irano-Swedish company where I worked temporarily as assistant to the personnel manager. When she visited the office, the secretary refused to give her an ap-

plication form until I intervened. Later, my boss inquired about her and called me to his office. To my amazement, he said that it did not matter what her qualifications were, the company would never employ a veiled woman. I asked why, since the company had Armenians, Jews, Baha'is, and Muslims, including some very observant male Muslims, we could not also employ a practicing female Muslim, especially since we needed her skills. He dismissed this point, saying it was not the same thing; he then told the secretary not to give application forms to veiled women, as it would be a waste of paper. My friend, who had become quite disappointed, found a primary teaching job at an Islamic school at only an eighth of my salary, though we had similar credentials.

A few years prior to the Iranian revolution, a tendency toward questioning the relevance of Eurocentric gender roles as the model for Iranian society gained much ground among university students. During the early stages of the revolution this was manifested in street demonstrations, where many women, a considerable number of whom belonged to the nonveiled middle classes, put on the veil and symbolically rejected the state-sponsored gender ideology. Then, in 1980, after the downfall of the shah and the establishment of the Islamic Republic, the Islamic regime introduced compulsory veiling, using police and paramilitary police to enforce the new rule. Despite the popularity of the regime, it faced stiff resistance from women (including some veiled women) on the grounds that such a law compromised their democratic rights. The resistance led to some modification and a delay in the imposition of compulsory veiling. After more than a decade of compulsory veiling, however, the regime still is facing resistance and defiance on the part of women, despite its liberal use of public flogging, imprisonment, and monetary fines as measures of enforcement of the veil. The fact is that both rejection of the shah's Eurocentric vision and the resistance to the compulsory veil represents women's active resistance to the imposed gender role envisaged for women by the state.

The Islamic regime has no more interest in the fate of women per se than did the shah's modernist state. Women paid heavily, and their democratic rights and individual freedom once again were challenged. The Islamic regime, partly in celebration of its victory over the modernist state of the shah and partly as a means for realizing its vision of "Islamic" Iran, not only introduced a strict dress code for women but also revoked many half-hearted reforms in the Iranian Personal Law, which had provided women with a limited measure of protection in their marriage. The annulment meant wider legal recognition of temporary marriage, polygyny, and men's right to divorce at will. Return to the *shariah* (Muslim law) also meant women were prevented from becoming judges. The new gender vision was also used to exclude women from some fields of study in the universities. These new, unexpected changes created such hardship, insecurity, and disillusionment for many women, regardless of whether they had religious or secular tendencies, that they became politically active to try to improve their lot. However, strategies that women with religious and Islamic tendencies have adopted are very different from those of secular women's groups.

The impact of compulsory veiling has been varied. There is no doubt that many educated middle-class women, who were actually or potentially active in the labor market, either left their jobs (and a considerable number left the country) voluntarily or were excluded by the regime's policies. However, these women were replaced by women of other social groups and not by men. Labor market statistics indicate that, contrary to the general expectation of scholars, the general public, and the Islamic state itself, the rate of female employment in the formal sector has continued to increase in the 1980s even during the economic slump and increased general unemployment. Similarly, the participation of women in all levels of education, from adult literacy to university level, has continued to increase.

Significantly, whether women believe and adhere to the veiling ideology or not, they have remained active in the political arena, working from within and outside the state to improve the socioeconomic position of women. Iranian women's achievements in changing and redefining the state vision of women's rights in "Islam" in just over one and a half decades have been considerable. For instance, the present family protection law, which Muslim women activists lobbied for and Ayatollah Khomeini signed in 1987, offers women more actual protection than had been afforded by the shah's Family Code, introduced in 1969, since it entitles the wife to

half the wealth accumulated during the marriage. More recently, the Iranian parliament approved a law that entitles women to wages for housework, forcing the husbands to pay the entire sum in the event of divorce.

Although, as in most other societies, the situation of Iranian women is far from ideal or even reasonable, nonetheless the lack of interest or acknowledgment of Muslim women activists' achievements on the part of scholars and feminist activists from Europe and North America is remarkable. Such disregard, in a context where the "excesses" of the Islamic regime toward women continue to make headlines and Muslim women and religious revivalism in the Muslim world continue to be matters of wide interest, is an indicator of the persistence of orientalist and colonial attitudes toward Muslim cultures. Whenever unfolding events confirm Western stereotypes about Muslim women, researchers and journalists rush to spread the news of Muslim women's oppression. For instance, upon the announcement of compulsory veiling, Kate Millett, whose celebrated work *Sexual Politics* indicates her lack of commitment to and understanding of issues of race, ethnicity, and class (although she made use of Marxist writings on development of gender hierarchy), went to Iran supposedly in support of her Iranian sisters. In 1982 she published a book, *Going to Iran*, about her experiences there. Given the atmosphere of anti-imperialism and anger toward the American government's covert and overt policies in Iran and the Middle East, her widely publicized trip to Iran was effectively used to associate those who were organizing resistance to the compulsory veil with imperialist and pro-colonial elements. In this way her unwise and unwanted support and presence helped to weaken Iranian women's resistance. According to her book, Millett's intention in going to Iran, which is presented as a moment of great personal sacrifice, was not to understand why Iranian women for the first time had participated in such massive numbers in a revolution whose scale was unprecedented, nor was it to listen and find out what the majority of Iranian women wanted as women from this revolution. Rather, according to her own account, it was to lecture to her Iranian sisters on feminism and women's rights, as though her political ideas, life expectations, and experiences were universally applicable. This is symptomatic of ethnocentrism (if we don't call it racism) and the lingering, implicit or explicit assumption that the only way to "liberation" is to follow Western women's models and strategies for change; consequently, the views of third world women, and particularly Muslim women, are entirely ignored.

Veiled Women in the Western Context

The veiling and re-veiling movement in European and North American societies has to be understood in the context not only of continuing colonial images but also of thriving new forms of overt and covert chauvinism and racism against Islam and Muslims, particularly in these post–cold war times. Often, uncritical participation of feminists/activists from the core cultures of Western Europe and North America in these oppressive practices has created a particularly awkward relationship between them and feminists/activists from Muslim minorities both in the West and elsewhere. This context has important implications for Muslim women, who, like all other women of visible minorities, experience racism in all areas of their public life and interaction with the wider society, including with feminists and feminist institutions. Muslim women, faced with this unpleasant reality, feel they have to choose between fighting racism and fighting sexism. Their strategies have to take account of at least three interdependent and important dimensions: first, racism; second, how to accommodate and adapt their own cultural values and social institutions to those of the core and dominant cultures that are themselves changing very rapidly; and finally, how to devise ways of (formally and informally) resisting and challenging patriarchy within both their own community and that of the wider society without weakening their struggle against racism. In my ongoing research on young Muslim women in Montreal, I was impressed by how the persistence of the images of oppressed and victimized Muslim women, particularly veiled women, creates barriers for them, the majority of whom were brought up in Canada and feel a part of Canadian society. Consequently, many now do not even try to establish rapport with non-Muslim Québecoise and Anglo women. A college student, angered by my comment that "when all is said and done, women in Canada share many obstacles and must learn to share experiences and develop, if

not common, at least complementary strategies," explained to me:

> it is a waste of time and emotion. They [white Canadian women] neither want to understand nor can feel like a friend towards a Muslim. Whenever I try to point out their mistaken ideas, for instance by saying that Islam has given women the right to control their wealth, they act as if I am making these up just to make Islam look good, but if I complain about some of the practices of Muslim cultures in the name of Islam they are more than ready to jump on the bandwagon and lecture about the treatment of women in Islam. I wouldn't mind if at least they would bother to read about it and support their claims with some documentation or references. They are so sure of themselves and the superiority of their God that they don't think they need to be sure of their information! I cannot stand them any more.

Another veiled woman explained the reasons for her frustration in the following manner:

> I wouldn't mind if only the young students who know nothing except what they watch on television demonstrated negative attitudes to Islam, but sometimes our teachers are worse. For instance, I have always been a very good student, but always when I have a new teacher and I talk or participate in the class discussion the teachers invariably make comments about how they did not expect me to be intelligent and articulate. That I am unlike Muslim women. . . . What they really mean is that I do not fit their stereotype of a veiled woman, since they could hardly know more Muslim women than I do and I cannot say there is a distinctive model that Muslim women all fit into. Muslim women come from varieties of cultures, races, and historical backgrounds. They would consider me unsophisticated and criticize me if I told them that they did not act like a Canadian woman, because Canada, though small in terms of population, is socially and culturally very diverse.

Some Western feminists have such strong opinions about the veil that they are often incapable of seeing the women who wear them, much less their reasons for doing so. Writing in the student newspaper, one McGill student said that she could not decide whether it is harder to cope with the sexism and patriarchy of the Muslim community, or to tolerate the patronizing and often unkind behavior of white feminists. She then reported that her feminist housemate had asked her to leave the house and look for other accommodations because she couldn't stand the sight of the veil and because she was concerned about what her feminist friends would think of her living with a veiled woman, totally disregarding the fact that, though veiled, she was nonetheless an activist and a feminist.

The stereotypes of Muslim women are so deep-rooted and strong that even those who are very conscious and critical of not only blatant racism but of its more subtle manifestations in everyday life do not successfully avoid them. To the Western feminist eye, the image of the veiled woman obscures all else. One of my colleagues and I were discussing a veiled student who is a very active and articulate feminist. I made a comment about how intelligent and imaginative she was. While he admiringly agreed with me, he added (and I quote from my notes): "She is a bundle of contradictions. She first came to see me with her scarf tightly wrapped around her head . . . and appeared to me so lost that I wondered whether she would be capable of tackling the heavy course she had taken with me. . . . She, with her feminist ideas, and critical views on orientalism, and love of learning, never failed to amaze me every time she expressed her views. She does not at all act like a veiled woman." As a "bundle of contradictions" only because she wears the veil, consisting of a neat scarf, while otherwise dressed like most other students, she has to overcome significant credibility barriers. The fact that, at the age of nineteen, without language proficiency or contacts in Montreal, she came to Canada to start her university studies at McGill has not encouraged her associates to question their own assumption about "veiled women." Neither has anyone wondered why Muslim women, if by virtue of their religion they are so oppressed and deprived of basic rights, are permitted by their religious parents to travel and live alone in the Western world.

I had thought that part of the problem was that the veil has become such an important symbol of women's oppression that most people have difficulty reducing it to simply an article of clothing. However, I discovered that the reality is much more complicated than the veil's being simply a visible marker. For instance, a Québecoise who had converted to Islam and observed the veil for the past four years said she had no evidence that wearing the veil was a hindrance to a woman's professional and educational achievements in Canada. In support of

her claim she told me of her recent experience at work:

> When I was interviewed for my last job, in passing I said that I was a Muslim and since I wear the veil I thought they made note of it…. I was offered the job and I was working for almost nine months before I realized nobody seemed to be aware that I was a Muslim. One day, when I was complaining about the heat, one of my colleagues suggested that I take off my scarf. To which I answered that as a practicing Muslim I did not want to do that. At first he did not believe me, and when I insisted and asked him and others who had joined our conversation if they had seen me at all without the scarf, they replied, no, but that they had thought I was following a fashion!

She then added that while she is very religious and believes that religion should be an important and central aspect of any society, the reality is that Canada is a secular society and that for the most part people care little about what religious beliefs one has.

While her claim was confirmed to varying degrees by a number of other white Canadian veiled women, converts to Islam, my own experience, and that of other nonwhite, non-Anglo/French Canadian veiled women is markedly different. Here is a recent experience. Last year, my visit to a hairdresser ended in disastrously short hair. I was not accustomed to such short hair and for a couple of weeks I wore a scarf loosely on my head. While lecturing in my classes I observed much fidgeting and whispered discussions but could not determine the reason. Finally, after two weeks, a student approached me to ask if I had taken up the veil. Quite surprised, I said no and asked what caused her to ask such a question. She said it was because I was wearing a scarf; since I was always saying positive things about Islam they thought I had joined "them." "Them?" I asked. She said, "Yes, the veiled women." Perplexed, I realized that what I discuss in lectures is not evaluated on the merits of my argument and evidence alone, but also on the basis of the listener's assumption about my culture and background. My colorful scarf, however loosely and decoratively worn, appears to my students as the veil, while the more complete veil of a practicing but culturally and biologically "white" Muslim who had worn the veil every day to work is seen as fashion! The main conclusion that I draw from these incidents is that the veil by itself is not so significant, after all; rather, it is who wears the veil that matters. The veil of the visible minorities is used to confirm the outsider and marginal status of the wearer. Such incidents have made me realize why many young Muslim women are so angry and have decided against intermingling with Anglo/Québecoise women. After all, if I, as a professor in a position of authority in the classroom, cannot escape the reminder of being the "other," how could the young Muslim students escape it?

Many Muslim women who are outraged by the continuous construction of Islam as a lesser religion and the portrait of Muslims as "less developed" and "uncivilized" feel a strong need for the Muslim community to assert its presence as part of the fabric of Canadian society. Since the veil, in Canadian society, is the most significant visible symbol of Muslim identity, many Muslim women have taken up the veil not only from personal conviction but to assert the identity and existence of a confident Muslim community and to demand fuller social and political recognition.

In the context of Western societies, the veil can also play a very important role of mediation and adaptation, an aspect that, at least partly due to colonial images of the veil, has been totally overlooked by Western feminists. The veil allows Muslim women to participate in public life and the wider community without compromising their own cultural and religious values. Young Canadian Muslim women, particularly those who are first-generation immigrants to Canada, have sometimes seen the wearing of the veil as affording them an opportunity to separate Islam from some of their own culture's patriarchal values and cultural practices that have been enforced and legitimated in the name of religion. Aware of the social and economic consequences of wearing the veil in the Western world, taking it up is viewed by many Muslims as an important symbol of signifying a woman's commitment to her faith. Thus many veiled women are allowed far more liberty in questioning the Islamic foundation of many patriarchal customs perpetuated in the name of Islam. For instance, several veiled women in my sample had successfully resisted arranged marriages by establishing that Islam had given Muslim women the right to choose their own partners. In the process, not only did they secure their parents' and their communities' respect, but they also created an awareness and a model of resistance for other young women of their community.

Wearing the veil has helped many Muslim women in their effort to defuse their parents' and communities' resistance against young women going away to university, particularly when they had to leave home and live on their own in a different town. Some of the veiled women had argued successfully that Islam requires parents not to discriminate against their children and educate both male and female children equally; hence, if their brothers could go and live on their own to go to university, they should be given the same opportunities. The women in the study attributed much of their success to their wearing of the veil, since it indicated to the parents that these young women were not about to lose their cultural values and become "white Canadian"; rather, they were adopting essential and positive aspects of their Canadian and host society to blend with their own cultural values of origin.

Many Muslim women have become conscious of carrying a much larger burden of establishing their community's identity and moral values than their male counterparts, the great majority of whom wear Western clothes entirely and do not stand out as members of their community. Yet frequently, when Muslim women criticize some of the cultural practices of their own community and the double standards often legitimized in the name of Islam, they are accused by other elements in their community of behaving like Canadians and not like Muslims. Many women eager to challenge their family's and community's attitude toward women have found that wearing the veil often means they are given a voice to articulate their views and be heard in a way that nonveiled Muslims are not. Their critics cannot easily dismiss them as lost to the faith. However, in wearing the veil they often find that they are silenced and disarmed by the equally negative images of Muslim and Middle Eastern women held by white Anglo/Québecoise women, images that restrict the lives of both groups of women.

Conclusion

In this paper I have tried to demonstrate how the persistence of colonial images of Muslim women, with their ethnocentric and racist biases, has formed a major obstacle to understanding the social significance of the veil from the point of view of the women who live it. By reviewing the state-sponsored deveiling movement in the 1930s in Iran and its consequences for women of low-income urban strata, and the reemergence of veiling during the anti-shah movement as an indication of rejection of state Eurocentric gender ideology, I argued that veiling is a complex, dynamic, and changing cultural practice, invested with different and contradictory meanings for veiled and nonveiled women as well as men. Moreover, by looking at the reintroduction of compulsory veiling in the Islamic Republic of Iran under Khomeini and the voluntary veiling of Muslim women in Canada, I argued that while veiling has been used and enforced by the state and by men as means of regulating and controlling women's lives, women have used the same institution to loosen the bonds of patriarchy imposed on them.

Both de-veiling, as organized by the Egyptian feminist movement in the 1920s, and the current resistance to compulsory veiling in Iran are indications of defiance of patriarchy. But veiling, viewed as a lived experience, can also be a site of resistance, as in the case of the anti-shah movement in Iran. Similarly, many Muslim women in Canada used the veil and reference to Islam to resist cultural practices such as arranged marriages or to continue their education away from home without alienating their parents and communities. Many veiled Muslim women employ the veil as an instrument of mediation between Muslim minority cultures and host cultures. Paradoxically, Western responses to Muslim women, filtered through an orientalist and colonialist frame, effectively *limit* Muslim women's creative resistance to the regulation of their bodies and their lives.

The assumption that veiling is solely a static practice symbolizing the oppressive nature of patriarchy in Muslim societies has prevented social scientists and Western feminists from examining Muslim women's own accounts of their lives, hence perpetuating the racist stereotypes that are ultimately in the service of patriarchy in both societies. On the one hand, these mostly man-made images of the oriental Muslim women are used to tame women's demand for equality in the Western world by subtly reminding them how much better off they are than their Muslim counterparts. On the other hand, these oriental and negative stereotypes are mechanisms by which Western-dominant culture re-creates and perpetuates beliefs about its superiority and dominance. White North American feminists, by adopting a racist construction of the veil and taking part in daily racist incidents, force Muslim women to choose between fighting racism and fighting sexism. The question is, why should we be forced to choose?

50

Ritual and the Performance of Buddhist Identity Among Lao Buddhists in North America

Penny Van Esterik

In the following article, Penny Van Esterik considers two key rituals in the religious life of the Lao, both as refugees in North America and in late-20th century Lao People's Democratic Republic. Soukhouan rituals therapeutically strengthen an individual's morale and social bonds—enacted by tying strings to one's wrist—while the That Luang *festival celebrates an important pilgrimage site in Vientiane, the capital city of Laos. The author traces the shifting meanings of these rituals amidst political change in Laos, and considers the many ways in which they build community and assert new identities for Lao in North America. What emerges is a picture of religion as malleable, adaptive, and dynamic in response to social conditions.*

A documentary film entitled "Blue Collar and Buddha" (New York: Filmmakers Library, c1987) illustrates the challenges facing Lao refugees in Rockford, Illinois, in the 1980s, and includes footage of community life at the local Lao temple. Further ethnographic work on Laos appears in The Lao: Gender, Power, and Livelihood *by Carol Ireson-Doolittle and Geraldine Moreno-Black (Boulder, CO: Westview Press, 2004). Penny Van Esterik is Professor of Anthropology at York University and a widely published specialist on mainland Southeast Asia.*

The lowland Lao first entered North America as refugees around 1978 following the take-over of the Royal Lao government by the Pathet Lao and the establishment of the Lao People's Democratic Republic (Lao PDR). By 1985, 102,783 Lao had resettled in the United States and 12,793 in Canada. The Lao Lum or lowland Lao are the largest ethnic group in Lao PDR, and the majority practice Theravāda Buddhism.

This paper examines the transformation of a ritual act, *Soukhouan,* and the celebration of a ritually charged

From: AMERICIAN BUDDHISM: METHODS AND FINDINGS IN RECENT SCHOLARSHIP, *ed. Duncan Ryūken Williams and Christopher S. Queen (Surrey, Great Britain: Curzon Press), 1999, pp. 57–68.*

place, *That Luang,* Vientiane, the capital of Lao PDR. Both are key parts of performing Lao religious and ethnic identity in Lao PDR and in North America. Both these rituals reside more or less comfortably within Theravāda Buddhism. I first consider *Soukhouan* rituals, and then the celebrations surrounding *That Luang.* The paper concludes with some speculations with regard to Buddhism and the establishment of Lao national and ethnic identity in North America.

Soukhouan

Soukhouan rituals accompany Buddhist, community, and household celebrations and express the heart of Lao identity. Despite the disruption of war and socialist reconstruction and the changes in the lives of Lao refugees resettled in North America, this ritual celebrates social relatedness in a concrete and powerful way. *Soukhouan* reasserts and strengthens social bonds by helping individuals "pull themselves together" and by tying individuals to their communities.

Soukhouan rituals literally invite the thirty-two components of an individual's spirit essence, or *khouan*, to reside comfortably and permanently in the hair whorls on the crown of the head. If the *khouan* leaves the body for any length of time, physical or mental illness or even death might result. The prerevolutionary, or feudalist, form of *Soukhouan* was probably the most elaborate, although Ananda Rajah argues that this feudalist "traditional" image of the *Soukhouan* ceremony reflects a romanticized, idealized view.

Soukhouan ceremonies vary in complexity, with weddings and New Year's being the most elaborate. The basic *Soukhouan* structure includes a set of actions, objects, and words that accomplish a ritual task. That task is to strengthen an individual's morale by attracting and binding the wandering souls firmly into the individual's body.

Soukhouan rites celebrate rites of passage, such as marriage, pregnancy, birth, and ordination; mark the start of an undertaking, such as a trip or military service; celebrate someone's return to the community after an absence; strengthen someone suffering from a long or serious illness; dispel bad luck; and welcome officials or guests to a community or a celebration.

The term *Soukhouan* is in most general use; the term *baci* refers specifically to the conical tray-like structure for the "auspicious rice" used in the ritual. The Cambodian origin of the word hints at the more formal or royal context of the term *baci*, compared to the more informal term, *Soukhouan*. The *khouan* are attracted back to the body by the beauty of the words and by the flowers and offerings built up on a tree-like structure on a tray or in an offering bowl. Here, the talent, wealth, and imagination of the sponsors of the ritual can be fully displayed. Precut lengths of white string are draped from the branches of the *baci*. The structure is decorated with fresh flowers, and beneath the *baci* are dishes of rice, boiled eggs, bananas and other fruit, alcohol, and delicacies to attract a wandering soul.

The officiant is not a monk but a lay elder who probably spent some time in the monkhood. While relatives and friends surround the candidate to be honored, the officiant takes a few strings from the *baci* and recites prayers to entice the wandering souls back into the body of the candidate. These prayers include the Pali verses honoring the Buddha, Dhamma, and Sangha, the Invitation to the Deities (*Anchern Theweda*), and other prayers appropriate to the context.

Following these invocations, the cotton threads are carefully picked off the *baci* and used to bind, first, the wrist of the celebrant, and later, others participating in the *Soukhouan*. While the elders tie strings around the wrist of the celebrant, they recite a formulaic wish for long life, wealth, happiness, and the success of the current undertaking— ordination to the monkhood, a journey overseas, marriage, or school exams. Following the *Soukhouan* and the ceremony of which it forms a part, such as the ordination of a new monk, participants share a festive meal.

Soukhouan may also be performed in much less elaborate settings, as, for example, when a young man who finds he must leave his village suddenly goes to his elderly relatives for their blessings and good wishes for his safety and success. But he still carries with him the strings on his wrist for at least three days and nights to remind him of the strength of his family's concern and to boost his morale.

When the Pathet Lao established the Lao PDR in 1975, they were unable to purge all remnants of royalist ritual; including *Soukhouan*. The Pathet Lao, after their unsuccessful efforts to destroy religion altogether, are now skilled in pulling apart the strands of ethnic and religious identity to emphasize some and downplay others. Since there is no longer a Lao king, royal symbols have largely disappeared or been reinterpreted in Lao PDR.

In contemporary socialist Laos, *Soukhouan* ceremonies still form the basis of wedding ceremonies, along with government authorization for the marriage of its cadre. Martin Stuart-Fox notes that *Soukhouan* persist in the new regime as ceremonies of welcome or farewell for guests, to mark an auspicious occasion, or to prepare for an important event. Lao refugees leaving camps to be repatriated in Laos are given a *Soukhoun* ceremony to wish them luck on their return to Laos. Although some of the more magical or feudalistic language may be altered for officials, *Soukhouan* rituals are not described as needing to be purged from Lao culture. That is, they are not seen as superstitious, feudalistic remnants, but as expressions of egalitarian reciprocity and generosity. In fact, Mayoury Ngaosyvathn sees *Soukhouan* as strengthening the moral stance of the new regime by emphasizing marital fidelity and the respect of children for their parents. Less ostentatious and expensive ceremonies also enhance the equality-oriented policy of the new government.

Soukhouan rituals have also thrived in refugee camps and in Lao refugee communities in North America. They have been successfully adapted to meet new needs in new contexts. Their core meaning remains intact, although the acts are reinterpreted. Lao refugees from New England, for example, comment on constructing *baci*:

> Here in America we make the floral offerings with leaves and flowers that we gather. At home in Laos we used to arrange the flowers differently, just the buds in rows, stuck into a banana stock. Here we don't have banana stalks so we do it this way now . . . We arrange flowers in a beautiful silver bowl. On the leaves are many strings to bless our loved ones. You tie a string around the person's wrist and say a blessing for strength, health, and long life. There are different blessings for different people. When your wrists are tied in the *baci* ceremony you must keep the strings on for three days and nights.

In North America, the delicacies under the *baci* include cans of Coca Cola, Twinkles, and Oreo cookies, which are later eaten by children.

In North American communities, Lao continue to celebrate their ethnic identity with *Soukhouan*, particularly for weddings. During Buddhist services, parents may approach Buddhist monks to tie threads around the wrists of a sick child. Following a motorcycle accident, a very acculturated-looking young Lao couple requested the monk and elders to perform an abbreviated *Soukhouan* for them to rid them of bad luck. For these individuals, the strings tied by monks or elders around the wrist of the person for whom the ceremony is performed reestablish the psychological equilibrium of the individual, bring blessings, and promote good health.

As the strings help individuals "pull themselves together" in the face of challenges, so too the strings tie individuals more tightly into their communities. *Soukhouan*, as a joint social activity, affirms core Lao values of reciprocity and sociability. Ngaosyvathn writes that *Soukhouan*

> expresses traditional Lao values of avoidance of conflict and aims at promoting consensus within the social fabric and strengthening social ties. As a key element of Lao culture, the ritual is a microcosm of Lao values serving to integrate the individual both spiritually and socially. In these terms, the ritual may be seen as the quintessential expression of conceptualizations of Lao identity.

Soukhouan rituals present great analytical challenges for anthropologists because they require examination once again of the relations between different aspects of religious and cultural practice; *Soukhouan* encompasses animistic, Buddhist, and court Brahman concepts in a single ritual event.

The problem of where spirits and Hindu deities fit into Theravāda Buddhist practice is epitomized in *Soukhouan* rituals. To some extent, the potential contradictions are also resolved. For in the practice of *Soukhouan*, the strands are truly interwoven and bound together in the performative act. The question raised by scholars regarding whether *Soukhouan* is a Buddhist, animist, or court Brahman ritual is not raised by participants because it is not relevant to them. The act of performing a *Soukhouan* integrates and demonstrates the interdependence of all the strands of Lao religion.

The historical, textual, and contextual strands of Theravāda Buddhism, spirit worship, and court Brahmanism are all intertwined in *Soukhouan*. In different contexts, one strand predominates or provides the dominant symbol for religious activities. Currently, the symbols of court Brahmanism are effectively purged from the Lao religious scene. Kingship no longer exists as the pivotal reference point for ritual behavior as it still is in Thailand. Nevertheless, the more formal *baci* invoke the Hindu gods to observe and participate in the *Soukhouan*.

The greatest contradiction between the various strands in Lao religion concerns the person. Theravāda Buddhism is based on concepts of *anatta* (non-self) and *anicca* (impermanence). How can these concepts provide the basis for stable social and political hierarchies and institutions of some permanence? *Soukhouan* fixes the temporary manifestation we perceive as humans long enough to "tie down" this human illusion with all its suffering and imperfections and gives it a fixed bounded identity. Building on the insightful work of G. Condominas, we can use the concept of "enboîtment" to stress the importance of the body or person as the first "box," surrounded sequentially by the household, village, and *muang* (political realm, principality, or city). It is the body that is most immediately addressed in *Soukhouan* rituals.

Soukhouan, the most basic Lao ritual, stresses the integrity and identity of persons and offers ritual protection to keep mobile "souls" trapped within a person's body. Only then can a person act (morally or immorally) within a Buddhist social order. Lao Buddhists are not ambiguous about non-self and impermanence as guiding principles. They place priority on the integrity of the person as a social actor. Thus, they have been able to carry the ritual guaranteeing this integrity across revolutions and resettlement virtually unchanged.

The loss of "soul," vital essence or *khouan*, is a powerful metaphor for the experience of Lao Buddhists in North America, as individuals were separated from their homeland and loved ones and faced painful disruptions to every aspect of their lives. Like the wandering souls unable to return to their homes, refugees wander without homes, facing dangerous and unknown conditions. *Soukhouan* rituals are particularly necessary when the social order has been disrupted, as in the experience of refugee flight and resettlement. For Lao refugee communities throughout North America, it is the strength of these social bonds that can tie souls into bodies, and reintegrate individuals into new community settings in North American cities and, for repatriated Lao, into the transformed villages of the Lao PDR.

That Luang

The festival of *That Luang*, celebrated in late November or early December around the *stūpa* (reliquary) outside of Vientiane has been described as "the most important occasion in the Lao religious calendar." The *stūpa* housing Buddha relics was built around 1567 when the Lao capital was shifted to Vientiane. The French restored the monument after its burning in the 1870s. It has since become an important pilgrimage center. But without the Lao king, the ritual has become more of a "national ceremony" in Lao PDR as well as in North America.

More so than most Lao rituals, *That Luang* celebrates a place as well as an event. Since the ritual of *That Luang* is so intimately connected with the *stūpa* outside Vientiane, it is surprising that it has been transferred to North America so successfully. In the Kingdom of Laos, government officials used to pledge allegiance to the Lao king during *That Luang* rituals. However, the ritual of *That Luang* was secularized during the revolution and served as a central rallying ground for official post-liberation rallies in 1975. Its symbolic importance was further exploited when Lao PDR officials offered food and robes to the resident monks at the site in 1979. In 1995, a number of NGOs produced a calendar widely distributed in Vientiane. The cover showed two temples flanking a large rendering of *That Luang* with a procession of men and women from a number of different ethnic groups playing instruments and dancing together. This is particularly noteworthy, since the midland Khmu and upland Hmong head the procession beside the lowland Lao, who are not Buddhists. *That Luang* is clearly becoming a sign of national identity rather than religious identity.

Photographs of *That Luang* are prominently displayed in Lao homes and at Lao community events in North America. The festival of *That Luang* was first celebrated in Toronto as a Buddhist merit-making occasion in the late 1980s. Dominating these celebrations was a model of the *stūpa* at Vientiane built out of bright yellow-painted styrofoam. The model, standing about eight feet high, was decorated with Christmas tree lights and flowers. The model stood in the middle of the hall, with the laity sitting on all sides of the model, facing the monks on the stage at the front of the room.

A merit-making service preceded the celebration of *That Luang*. Following the monks' meal and final chants, community members and visitors from New York State joined in a procession around the model of *That Luang*. The procession formed behind four money trees (*Kalapra-pruk*), to the accompaniment of drums and cymbals, with guests and important male community leaders leading the procession in three clockwise circumambulations of the *stūpa*. As the procession passed the monks on the stage, the monks sprinkled holy water on the crowd. The demeanor of the chanting monks and the sedate male marchers— eyes downcast and hands folded in front of chests— contrasted strikingly with the joyous singing and dancing of the middle-aged women who broke out of the throng to dance, "hoot," sing, and entice participation from embarrassed teenage males sitting on the periphery of the room smirking or trying to ignore the antics of their mothers, sisters, and aunts. "You would think they were drunk," muttered one black leather-jacketed youth in English.

Following the procession, the merit accrued by participating in the ritual and giving generously was shared with others. Merit transference is stressed whenever there is a rupture in the social order, such as during funerals and ordinations; for refugees, the rupture in the social order is particularly obvious. Transferring merit is one of the ten traditional good deeds of Theravāda Buddhism. The sharing of merit with the gods and with the wandering ghosts (Pali: *peta*, the only non-humans who can acquire merit) is mentioned in Buddhist scriptures (*Anguttara-Nikāya, sutta* 50; *Dīgha-Nikāya, sutta* 16). In practice, the act of sharing merit is a very human response to the loss of loved ones and the uncertainty of their rebirth status. While the monks chant the verse to share merit with all sentient being, all present slowly pour water from a small bottle into pedestal bowls. By this act, those who perform meritorious acts generously wish that others—particularly their deceased relatives—could reap the benefits of their meritorious deeds. For the Lao, this wish is most intensively directed towards deceased parents in Lao PDR.

This act of generosity is particularly poignant for refugees who may have left their parents behind. For others, close relatives remain missing and presumed dead. Few refugees in North America can afford to return to Laos at short notice in time for their parents' funerals, which is why the act of transferring merit is more significant for Lao refugees than for Lao Buddhists in Laos. During a service at a temple in Vientiane, Laos, in July 1989, the act was performed very quickly with water poured onto plants and over cobblestones much more casually than at the Toronto services. There was not the emotional intensity and tension during the chanting that one feels among Lao refugees in Toronto.

This practice also reflects core Lao values regarding responsibilities to elders and parents. These responsibilities do not end with resettlement in a third country. In fact, they become more complex, as the Lao in North America must deal with missing parents, parents whose funerals and memorial services were incomplete, and caring for elderly relatives. For example, an unmarried Lao refugee in Toronto who could not support his elderly parents placed his parents in a subsidized seniors' apartment where neither he nor their grandchildren could stay overnight for a visit. The old couple felt imprisoned—isolated and useless because they were cut off from their relatives. Regulations in the apartments made it impossible for the unmarried son to fulfil his responsibilities to his parents.

Merit-making through water pouring (*Kruat nam*) is a metaphor of loss and death. It expresses one of the dominant ethical preoccupations of Lao refugees and exemplifies the kind of problems they face in adapting to their new home. With the loss of their parental and ancestral generations, they lose the direct continuity with their past that is at the core of Lao identity. For Lao Buddhists in North America, the practice of transferring merit to deceased relatives helps bridge the distance between Laos and North America, past and present, old and new responsibilities.

Following the *That Luang* ritual procession, the food offered to the monks is redistributed to the laity in the form of a communal meal. This is more than just the commensality of most Lao social occasions. For it is considered a particular blessing to share the food given to and accepted by the monks. Anyone participating in the ritual occasion is welcome and encouraged to join the groups of friends sitting around raised bamboo trays laden with special Lao food dishes. Even those who have not contributed food are actively encouraged to share the meal, as if the sharing of food may cause the intention to give generously to arise among all partaking of the meal. Leftover food is carefully wrapped and taken to those who were unable to attend the ceremony, so that they too may participate in the blessings created by the communal merit-making.

This shared meal of Buddhist merit-makers is a model of reciprocity, redistribution, and generosity and actually creates groups. The act of eating together and sharing each other's food constitutes a group, even if this group identity can only be maintained for a short period of time and must be reconstituted on the next ritual occasion. However, it is a concrete and reliable means of establishing a moral community where people know they can develop relations of trust with others and cooperate in joint activities within the domain of religion.

The centrality of food in Lao ceremonies cannot be overemphasized. Yet the relations between food and religious practice have been transformed in North America. On ritual occasions, there is an excess of food donated to the monks. This is in the form of cooked glutinous rice, unpeeled fruit, and special dishes such as curries and soups to be served with the rice. The rice and fruit are placed directly into the alms bowls of the monks. The other dishes are arranged on trays and presented to the monks. In fact, the monks take only a small amount from the dishes displayed on the trays, although they symbolically accept all the food presented. This excess of food is redistributed to the laity in the form of a communal meal following the service. This is an important social and political occasion in North America, as it is one of the few occasions when Lao from distant communities get together.

Adapting Buddhism

It is difficult to be a Lao in North America, difficult to form a Lao community, and difficult to be a Buddhist in a Judeo-Christian context. Lao who arrive in North American cities together may not have known each other in the camps in Thailand let alone in Laos. They share a national origin and the refugee experience, but little else. From this commonality, they must construct Lao identity and Lao community. Buddhist ritual occasions provide special opportunities for forming and strengthening groups. The problem of dealing with strangers is a problem of trust. Who is trustworthy? Who shares your personal standards of morality? Who is a true friend? Buddhist merit-making is an opportunity for displaying one's moral worth and demonstrating one's trustworthiness.

But focusing on Buddhist rituals emphasizes solidarity of ethnic communities rather than cleavages along class and religious lines. Buddhist temples are also sites of conflict over power, resources, and cultural change. Any Buddhist temple established in a North American city can no longer be the "hub" of community life; the physical space of the temple no longer dominates the landscape nor serves the multiple functions performed by a Lao temple in Laos. In Laos, the temple and Buddhist activities were totally integrated into everyday life. In North America, the temple loses: its centrality—spatially, cognitively, and socially—because of the dispersed population

and the economic effort Lao refugees need to expend to survive and prosper in North America.

The timing of communal celebrations in North America must be integrated with work weeks. Services are generally held on Sundays, when Buddhist and Christian services compete within the community. That is, it is not easy to participate in both ritual systems on a single weekend, However, in some communities, Buddhist services are held on Saturdays, freeing refugees to attend Christian services, often with their sponsors, on Sundays.

In North America, ritual events are condensed in time. Rituals that lasted three days in Laos take one day in North America. All-day rituals in Laos are condensed to two or three hours in North America. This is partly related to the shift in the use of the weekend, when there are other alternative ways to spend time. Rituals compete with sports and other leisure activities, carried out on weekends, where in Laos, ritual time replaced work time. In North America, other social, economic, and political activities are embedded within ritual time. Since there are only a limited number of occasions for widely dispersed Lao families to get together, Buddhist rituals are also occasions for visiting, matchmaking, selling cloth from Lao PDR, and exchanging information about available jobs and apartments. Religious identity becomes secondary to cultural identity, as temples become sites for cultural preservation through music, dance, and language classes. While public funds cannot be used to support religious initiatives, they can be used to support cultural centers and ethnic associations.

When monks are only available occasionally, ritual cycles change to accommodate their schedules. Seasonal rituals may be stressed or unstressed depending on the availability of monks. On the occasion of a single monk's visit to a community, a public ritual might be held on Sunday, a house blessing at a sponsor's home the next day, and a service to dispel bad luck at a third house. This opportunistic scheduling means that ritual acts which may normally never occur together in Laos will be put together in North America.

These changes in scheduling, condensation, and embeddedness in ritual time may be quite disorienting for elderly Lao familiar with the more leisurely pace of ritual time in Laos. However, since most Lao in North America experienced the disruptions of normal time during the war and the suspension of time while in refugee camps, they adapt readily to the temporal structures of future-oriented Westerners, even within their religious domain.

The Lao face particularly difficult problems resolving the meaning of Lao cultural identity outside of Laos. Rituals such as *Soukhouan* and *That Luang* provide raw materials from which individual Lao can begin to structure a new identity in North America. From these ritual acts they select those values which are central to their individual and collective identities as *Lao* rather than their identity as Buddhists.

Nevertheless, Buddhism is important to this task because it provides a framework for explaining suffering and for making sense out of an otherwise chaotic world. Buddhist temples also provide material as well as spiritual insurance against unforeseen needs, counseling, alternative healing techniques, crisis intervention, recreational activities, as well as spiritual resources. Buddhist rituals performed in new lands remain an important part of reconstituting identity.

51

Religious Terror and Global War

Mark Juergensmeyer

The late 20th and early 21st centuries have been characterized, Mark Juergensmeyer writes, by a globe-spanning war between culture-based ideologies and the secular state. Here, Juergensmeyer considers ideas about such warfare (which in truth is often not a war at all), emphasizing the role of religion and conflicting ideologies about the place of religion in modern life. He considers religious terror in a wide range of examples, including the World Trade Center attacks on September 11, 2001; the Oklahoma City bombing; Japan's Aum Shinrikyo; Hamas and the Palestinian conflict; and religiously based violence in India and Sri Lanka. The author explores why images of warfare seem to "work," providing justification for violence and credibility for causes, and ultimately prompting equally violent reactions.

Mark Juergensmeyer directs the Orfalea Center for Global and International Studies and is a professor of global and international studies, sociology, and religious studies at University of California, Santa Barbara. Among his numerous publications on religious violence is Terror in the Mind of God: The Global Rise of Religious Violence *(University of California Press, 2000). The present article first appeared in a collection of articles by scholars from numerous disciplines, in response to the September 11, 2001, tragedy.*

Though the horrific images of the aerial assaults on the World Trade Center and the Pentagon on September 11, 2001 were shocking, the headlines of American newspapers on September 12 contained another surprise: how quickly the rhetoric of warfare entered into public consciousness. "The world at war," pronounced one headline. "The first war of the twenty-first century," President George W. Bush proclaimed. The September 11, 2001 assaults were in fact the most spectacular of a decade-long series of attempts by Osama bin Laden's Al Qaeda network to bring the rest of the world into his view of

From: UNDERSTANDING SEPTEMBER, 11, *ed. Craig Calhoun, Paul Price, and Ashley Timmer. New York: The Free Press, pp. 27–40.*

global war. An earlier, less devastating attack on the World Trade Center in 1993 received scarcely a shrug from the American populace. But in 2001 he was more successful, both in the enormity of the event and in the change in America's mindset that it created.

Yet even though it seemed palpably to be an act of war, it was not clear what kind of war it was. The instant comparisons to Pearl Harbor seemed forced. The Japanese attack that signaled America's entry into World War II was, after all, the military act of a sovereign state. Osama bin Laden's Al Qaeda network was essentially a rogue band of transnational activists based in distant caves but spread throughout the world. What united them was neither a state-centered organization nor a political ideology, but the ties of a certain form of politicized religion and the riveting image of an evil secular foe.

The Al Qaeda network has not been alone in the religious assault on the secular state. In the last fifteen years of the post–Cold War world, religion seems to have been connected with violence everywhere: from the World Trade Center bombings to suicide attacks in Israel and Palestine; assassinations in India, Israel, Egypt, and Algeria; nerve gas in the Tokyo subways; abortion clinic killings in Florida; and the bombing of Oklahoma City's federal building. What unites these disparate acts of violence is their perpetrators' hatred of the global reach of the modern secular state.

Thus in many ways the September 11 attacks were part of a global confrontation. In the minds of many on both sides this confrontation is increasingly viewed as a war—though the enemies in this engagement are less like the axis of powers engaged in World War II than the ideological foes of the Cold War. Like the old Cold War, the confrontation between these new forms of culture-based politics and the secular state is global in its scope, binary in its opposition, occasionally violent, and essentially a difference of ideologies; and, like the old Cold War, each side tends to stereotype the other. The image of war mobilizes the animosities of both sides. The major differences between the old Cold War and the new one is that the present war is in a sense imaginary—it entails very little state support—and the various forms of religious opposition are scarcely united. Yet when they do lash out in acts of terrorism, as September 11 demonstrated, the results can be as awesome as they are destructive.

The Role of Religion

What is odd about this new global war is not only the difficulty in defining it and the non-state, transnational character of the opposition, but also the opponents' ascription to ideologies based on religion. The tradition of secular politics from the time of the Enlightenment has comfortably ignored religion, marginalized its role in public life, and frequently co-opted it for its own civil religion of public religiosity. No one in the secular world could have predicted that the first confrontations of the twenty-first century would involve, of all things, religion—secularism's old, long-banished foe.

Religious activists are puzzling anomalies in the secular world. Most religious people and their organizations are either firmly supportive of the secular state or quiescently uninterested in it. Osama bin Laden's Al Qaeda network, like most of the new religious activists, comprises a small group at the extreme end of a hostile subculture that itself is a small minority within the larger world of their religious cultures. Osama bin Laden is no more representative of Islam than Timothy McVeigh is of Christianity, or Japan's Shoko Asahara is of Buddhism.

Still, one cannot deny that the ideals and ideas of activists like bin Laden are authentically and thoroughly religious and could conceivably become popular among their religious compatriots. The authority of religion has given bin Laden's cadres the moral legitimacy of employing violence in their assault on the very symbol of global economic power. It has also provided the metaphor of cosmic war, an image of spiritual struggle that every religion has within its repository of symbols—the fight between good and bad, truth and evil. In this sense, then, the attack on the World Trade Center was very religious. It was meant to be catastrophic, an act of biblical proportions.

Though the World Trade Center assault and many other recent acts of religious terrorism have no obvious military goal, they are meant to make a powerful impact on the public consciousness. These are acts meant for television. They are a kind of perverse performance of power meant to ennoble the perpetrators' views of the world and to draw us into their notions of cosmic war. In my comparative study of cases of religious terrorism around the world I have found a strikingly familiar pattern. In all of these cases, concepts of cosmic war are accompanied by strong claims of moral justification and an enduring absolutism that transforms worldly struggles into sacred battles. It is not so much that religion has become politicized, but that politics have become religionized. Worldly struggles have been lifted into the high proscenium of sacred battle.

This is what makes religious warfare so difficult to combat. Its enemies have become satanized—one cannot negotiate with them or easily compromise. The rewards for those who fight for the cause are transtemporal, and the time lines of their struggles are vast. Most social and political struggles look for conclusions within the lifetimes of their participants, but religious struggles can take generations to succeed. When I pointed out to political leaders of the Hamas movement in Palestine that Israel's military force was such that a Palestinian military effort could never succeed, I was told that "Palestine was occupied before, for two hundred years." The Hamas official assured me that he and his Palestinian comrades "can wait again—at least that long," for the struggles of God can endure for eons. Ultimately, however, they knew they would succeed.

Insofar as the U.S. public and its leaders embraced the image of war following the September 11 attacks, America's view of this war was also prone to religionization. "God Bless America" became the country's unofficial national anthem. President George W. Bush spoke of the defense of America's "righteous cause," and the "absolute evil" of its enemies. Still, the U.S. military engagement in the months following September 11 was primarily a secular commitment to a definable goal and largely restricted to limited objectives in which civil liberties and moral rules of engagement, for the most part, still applied.

In purely religious battles, waged in divine time and with heaven's rewards, there is no need to compromise one's goals. There is no need, also, to contend with society's laws and limitations when one is obeying a higher authority. In spiritualizing violence, therefore, religion gives the resources of violence a remarkable power.

Ironically, the reverse is also true: Terrorism can give religion power. Although sporadic acts of terrorism do not lead to the establishment of new religious states, they make the political potency of religious ideology impossible to ignore. The first wave of religious activism, from the Islamic revolution in Iran in 1978 to the emergence of Hamas during the Palestine *intifada* in the early 1990s, was focused on religious nationalism and the vision of individual religious states. Increasingly, religious activism has a more global vision. Such disparate groups as the Christian militia, the Japanese Aum Shinrikyo, and the Al Qaeda network all target what their supporters regard as a repressive and secular form of global culture and control.

Global War

The September 11 attack and many other recent acts of religious terrorism are skirmishes in what their perpetrators conceive to be a global war. This battle is global in three senses. The choices of targets have often been transnational. The World Trade Center employees killed in the September 11 assault were citizens of 86 nations. The network of perpetrators was also transnational: The Al Qaeda network, which was implicated in the attack—though consisting mostly of Saudis—is also actively supported by Pakistanis, Egyptians, Palestinians, Sudanese, Algerians, Indonesians, Malaysians, Filipinos, and a smattering of British, French, Germans, Spanish, and Americans. The incident was global in its impact, in large part because of the worldwide and instantaneous coverage of transnational news media. This has been terrorism meant not only for television but for global news networks such as CNN—and especially for Al Jazeera, the Qatar-based news channel that beams its talk-show format throughout the Middle East.

Increasingly terrorism has been performed for a televised audience around the world. In that sense it has been as real a global event as the transnational activities of the global economy, and as vivid as the globalized forms of entertainment and information that crowd satellite television channels and the Internet. Ironically, terrorism has become a more efficient global force than the organized political efforts to control and contain it. No single entity, including the United Nations, possesses the military capability and intelligence-gathering capacities to deal with worldwide terrorism. Instead, consortia of nations have been formed to handle the information-sharing and joint operations required to deal with forces of violence on an international scale.

This global dimension of terrorism's organization and audience, and the transnational responses to it, give special significance to the understanding of terrorism as a public performance of violence—as a social event that has both real and symbolic aspects. As the late French sociologist Pierre Bourdieu observed, our public life is shaped by symbols as much as by institutions. For this reason, symbolic acts—the "rites of institution"—help to demarcate public space and indicate what is meaningful in the social world. In a striking imitation of such rites, terrorism has provided its own dramatic events. These rites of violence have signaled alternative views of public reality: not just a single society in transition, but a world challenged by strident religious visions of transforming change.

What is extraordinary about such performances is their success in bringing the rest of the world into their world view—specifically their view of the world at war. War is an enticing conceptual construct, an all-embracing view of the world that contains much more than the notion of forceful contestation. It points to a dichotomous opposition on an absolute scale. War suggests an all-or-nothing struggle against an enemy who is determined to destroy. No compromise is deemed possible. The very existence of the opponent is a threat, and until the enemy is either crushed or contained, one's own existence cannot be secure. What is striking about a martial attitude is the certainty of one's position and the willingness to defend it, or impose it on others, to the end.

Such certitude may be regarded as noble by those whose sympathies lie with it and dangerous by those who do not agree with it. But either way it is not civil. One of the first rules of conflict resolution is the willingness to accept the notion that there are flaws on one's own side as well as on the opponent's side. This is the sensible stand to take if one's goal is to get along with others and avoid violence. But often that is not the goal. In fact, a warring attitude implies that the one who holds it no longer thinks compromise is possible or—just as likely—does not want an accommodating solution to the conflict in the first place. In fact, if one's goals are not harmony but the empowerment that comes with using violence, it is in one's interest to be in a state of war. In such cases, war is not only the context for violence but also the excuse for it. This reasoning holds true even if the worldly issues that are at heart in the dispute do not seem to warrant such an extreme and ferocious position.

This logic may explain why acts of terrorism seem so puzzling to people outside the movements that perpetrate them and entirely understandable to those within them. The absolutism of war makes compromise unlikely, and those who suggest a negotiated settlement can be excoriated as the enemy. In the Palestinian situation, the extreme religious positions on both sides loathed the carefully negotiated compromise once promised by Israel's Yitzhak Rabin and Palestine's Yasir Arafat. "There is no such thing as coexistence," a Jewish activist in Israel told me, explaining that there was a biblical requirement for Jews to possess and live on biblical land. This was why he despised the Oslo and Wye River accords

and regarded Rabin and Benjamin Netanyahu as treasonous for signing them. Hamas leaders told me essentially the same thing about the necessity for Arab Muslims to occupy what they regarded as their homeland. They expressed anger toward their own secular leader—Yasir Arafat—for having entered into what both Jewish and Muslim extremists regarded as a dangerous and futile path toward an accommodation deemed by them to be impossible. The extremes on both sides preferred war over peace.

One of the reasons why a state of war is often preferable to peace is that it gives moral justification for acts of violence. Violence, in turn, offers the illusion of power. The idea of warfare implies more than an attitude; ultimately it is a world view and an assertion of identity. To live in a state of war is to live in a world in which individuals know who they are, why they have suffered, by whose hand they have been humiliated, and at what expense they have persevered. It provides cosmology, history, and eschatology, and offers the reins of political control. Perhaps most importantly, it holds out the hope of victory and the means to achieve it. In the images of religious war this victorious triumph is a grand moment of social and personal transformation, transcending all worldly limitations. One does not easily abandon such expectations. To be without such images of war is almost to be without hope itself.

The idea of warfare has had an eerie and intimate relationship with religion. History has been studded with overtly religious conflicts such as the Crusades, the Muslim conquests, and the Wars of Religion that dominated the politics of France in the sixteenth century. These have usually been characterized as wars in the name of religion, rather than wars conducted in a religious way. However, the historian Natalie Zemon Davis has uncovered what she calls "rites of violence" in her study of religious riots in sixteenth-century France. These constituted "a repertory of actions, derived from the Bible, from the liturgy, from the action of political authority, or from the traditions of popular folk practices, intended to purify the religious community and humiliate the enemy and thus make him less harmful." Davis observed that the violence was "aimed at defined targets and selected from a repertory of traditional punishments and forms of destruction." According to Davis, "even the extreme ways of defiling corpses—dragging bodies through the streets and throwing them to the dogs, dismembering genitalia and selling them in mock commerce—and desecrating religious objects," had what she called "perverse connections" with religious concepts of pollution and purification, heresy and blasphemy.

Anthropologist Stanley Tambiah showed how the same "rites of violence" were present in the religious riots of South Asia. In some instances innocent bystanders would be snatched up by a crowd and burned alive. According to Tambiah, these horrifying murders of defenseless and terrified victims were done in a ritual manner, in "mock imitation of both the self-immolation of conscientious objectors and the terminal rite of cremation." In a macabre way, the riotous battles described by Davis and Tambiah were religious events. But given the prominence of the rhetoric of warfare in religious vocabulary, both traditional and modern, one could also turn this point around and say that religious events often involve the invocation of violence. One could argue that the task of creating a vicarious experience of warfare—albeit one usually imagined as residing on a spiritual plane—is one of the main businesses of religion.

Virtually all cultural traditions have contained martial metaphors in their symbols, myths, and legendary histories. Ideas such as the Salvation Army in Christianity or a Dal Khalsa ("army of the faithful") in Sikhism characterize disciplined religious organizations. Images of spiritual warfare are even more common. The Muslim notion of jihad is the most notable example, but even in Buddhist legends great wars abound. In Sri Lankan culture, for instance, virtually canonical status is accorded the legendary history recorded in the Pali Chronicles, the Dipavamsa and the Mahavamsa, that related the triumphs of battles waged by Buddhist kings. In India, warfare contributes to the grandeur of the great epics, the Ramayana and the Mahabharata, which are tales of seemingly unending conflict and military intrigue. More than the Vedic rituals, these martial epics defined subsequent Hindu culture. Whole books of the Hebrew Bible are devoted to the military exploits of great kings, their contests related in gory detail. Though the New Testament does not take up the battle cry, the later history of the Church does, supplying Christianity with a bloody record of crusades and religious wars.

What is unusual about contemporary acts of terrorism is that the vision of religious war is not confined to history and symbols but is a contemporary reality. Politics have become religionized as struggles in the real world become baptized with the absolutism of religious fervor. Acts of violence are conducted not so much to wage a military campaign as to demonstrate the reality of the war to a unknowing public. In such cases, the message is the medium in which it is sent: The bombings provide moments of chaos, warfare, and victimage that the perpetrators want a slumbering society to experience. These acts make the point that war is at hand by providing a bloody scene of battle in one's own quiet neighborhoods and everyday urban streets.

What is buttressed in these acts of symbolic empowerment is not only the credibility of their cause. These acts, for the moment, place the perpetrators on a par with the leaders of governments that they target, and equate the legitimacy of the secular state with their own vision of religious social order. Through the currency of violence they draw attention to what they believe to be significant and true about the social arena around them. In the language of Bourdieu they create a perverse "habitus," a dark world of social reality, forcing everyone to take stock of their perception of the world. Thus the very act of performing violence in public is a political act: It announces that the power of the group is equal or superior to that of the state. In most cases this is exactly the message that the group wants to convey.

The establishment of political rule based on religious law has been the primary aim of many Muslim groups. Members of Hamas regarded this as the main difference between their organization and the secular ideology of Fateh and other groups associated with Yasir Arafat's Palestinian Authority. A similar argument has been made by activists associated with Egyptian groups. Mahmud Abouhalima told me that President Hosni Mubarak could not be a true Muslim because he did not make *shari'a*—Islamic law—the law of the land. A cleric in Cairo's conservative Al-Azhar theological school told me he resented his government's preference for Western law. "Why should we obey Western laws when Muslim laws are better?" he asked me. It is this position that has been assumed by many Muslim activists: that Western political institutions and the ideology on which they were based should be banished from their territories. They want to rebuild their societies on Islamic foundations.

Yet the images of political order that these activists yearn to create have been deliberately fuzzy. Sometimes the goals have appeared to be democratic, sometimes socialist, sometimes a sort of religious oligarchy. Sometimes the goals have been nationalist, at other times international in scope. A Hamas leader told me that what distinguished his organization from Yasir Arafat's Fateh movement was that Fateh was waging a "national struggle" whereas Hamas was "transnational." The Al Qaeda network of Osama bin Laden has been especially striking in its global reach and curious in its lack of a specific political program. It is as if the idea of global struggle is sufficient, its own reward. Although it is clear who the supporters of Al Qaeda hate, nowhere have they given a design for a political entity—Islamic or otherwise—that could actually administrate the results of a victory over American and secular rule and the emergence of a religious revolution, should they achieve it.

My conclusion is that acts of religious terrorism are largely devices for symbolic empowerment in wars that cannot be won and for goals that cannot be achieved. The very absence of thought about what the activists would do if they were victorious is sufficient indication that they do not expect to win, nor perhaps even want to do so. They illustrate a peculiar corollary to the advice of the French theorist, Frantz Fanon, during Algeria's war of independence some years ago, when he advocated terrorism as the Algerians' mobilizing weapon. Fanon reasoned that even a small display of violence could have immense symbolic power by jolting the masses into an awareness of their own potency. What Fanon did not realize was that for some activist groups the awareness of their potency would be all that they desired.

Yet these acts of symbolic empowerment have had an effect beyond whatever personal satisfaction and feelings of potency they have imparted to those who supported and conducted them. The very act of killing on behalf of a moral code is a political statement. Such acts break the state's monopoly on morally sanctioned killing. By putting the right to take life in their own hands, the perpetrators of religious violence have made a daring claim of power on behalf of the powerless, a basis of legitimacy for public order other than that upon which the secular state relies. In doing so, they have demonstrated to everyone how fragile public order actually is, and how fickle can be the populace's assent to the moral authority of power.

Empowering Religion

Such religious warfare not only gives individuals who have engaged in it the illusion of empowerment, but it also gives religious organizations and ideas a public attention and importance that they have not enjoyed for many years. In modern America and Europe, the recent warfare has given religion a prominence in public life that it has not held since before the Enlightenment, more than two centuries ago.

Although each of the violent religious movements around the world has its own distinctive culture and history, I have found that they have three things in common regarding their attitudes toward religion in society. First, they reject the compromises with liberal values and secular institutions that most mainstream religion has made, be it Christian, Muslim, Jewish, Hindu, Sikh, or Buddhist. Second, radical religious movements refuse to observe the boundaries that secular society has set around religion—keeping it private rather than allowing it to intrude into public spaces. And third, these movements try to create a new form of religiosity that rejects what they regard as weak modern substitutes for the more vibrant and demanding forms of religion that they imagine to be essential to their religion's origins.

During a prison interview, one of the men accused of bombing the World Trade Center in 1993 told me that the critical moment in his religious life came when he realized that he could not compromise his Islamic integrity with the easy vices offered by modern society. The convicted terrorist, Mahmud Abouhalima, claimed that the early part of his life was spent running away from himself. Although involved in radical Egyptian Islamic movements since his college years in Alexandria, he felt there was no place where he could settle down. He told me that the low point came when he was in Germany, trying to live the way that he imagined Europeans and Americans carried on: where the superficial comforts of sex and inebriates masked an internal emptiness and despair. Abouhalima said his return to Islam as the center of his life carried with it a renewed sense of obligation to make Islamic society truly Islamic—to "struggle against oppression and injustice" wherever it existed. What was now constant, Abouhalima said, was his family and his faith. Islam was both "a rock and a pillar of mercy." But it was not the Islam of liberal, modern Muslims: They, he felt, had compromised the tough and disciplined life the faith demanded. In Abouhalima's case, he wanted his religion to be hard, not soft like the humiliating, mind-numbing comforts of secular modernity. Activists such as Abouhalima—and, for that matter, Osama bin Laden—have imagined themselves to be defenders of ancient faiths. But in fact they have created new forms of religiosity: Like many present-day religious leaders they have used the language of traditional religion in order to build bulwarks around aspects of modernity that have threatened them, and to suggest ways out of the mindless humiliation of modern life. It is vital to their image of religion, however, that it be perceived as ancient.

The need for religion—a "hard" religion as Abouhalima called it—was a response to the soft treachery they had observed in the new societies around them. The modern secular world that Abouhalima and the others inhabited was a dangerous and chaotic sea, in which religion was a harbor of calm. At a deep level of their consciousnesses they sensed their lives slipping out of control, and they felt both responsible for the disarray and a victim of it. To be abandoned by religion in such a world would mean a loss of their own individual locations and identities. In fashioning a "traditional religion" of their own making, they exposed their concerns not so much with their religious, ethnic, or national communities, but with their own personal, perilous selves.

These intimate concerns have been prompted by the perceived failures of public institutions. As Pierre Bourdieu observed, social structures never have a disembodied reality; they are always negotiated by individuals in their own strategies for maintaining self-identity and success in life. Such institutions are legitimized by the "symbolic capital" they accrue through the collective trust of many individuals. When that symbolic capital is devalued, when political and religious institutions undergo what the German social philosopher Jurgen Habermas has called a "crisis of legitimacy," this devaluation of authority is experienced not only as a political problem but as an intensely personal one, as a loss of agency.

It is this sense of a personal loss of power in the face of chaotic political and religious authorities that

is common, and I believe critical, to Osama bin Laden's Al Qaeda group and most other movements for Christian, Muslim, Jewish, Sikh, Buddhist, and Hindu nationalism around the world. The syndrome begins with the perception that the public world has gone awry, and the suspicion that behind this social confusion lies a great spiritual and moral conflict, a cosmic battle between the forces of order and chaos, good and evil. The government—already delegitimized—is perceived to be in league with the forces of chaos and evil.

Secular government is easily labeled as the enemy of religion, because to some degree it is. By its nature, the secular state is opposed to the idea that religion should have a role in public life. From the time that modern secular nationalism emerged in the eighteenth century as a product of the European Enlightenment's political values, it did so with a distinctly antireligious, or at least anticlerical, posture. The ideas of John Locke about the origins of a civil community, and the "social contract" theories of Jean-Jacques Rousseau required very little commitment to religious belief. Although they allowed for a divine order that made the rights of humans possible, their ideas had the effect of taking religion-at least Church religion—out of public life. At the time, religious "enemies of the Enlightenment" protested religion's public demise. But their views were submerged in a wave of approval for a new view of social order in which secular nationalism was thought to be virtually a natural law, universally applicable and morally right.

Post-Enlightenment modernity proclaimed the death of religion. Modernity signaled not only the demise of the Church's institutional authority and clerical control, but also the loosening of religion's ideological and intellectual grip on society. Scientific reasoning and the moral claims of the secular social contract replaced theology and the Church as the bases for truth and social identity. The result of religion's devaluation has been "a general crisis of religious belief," as Bourdieu has put it.

In countering this disintegration, resurgent religious activists have proclaimed the death of secularism. They have dismissed the efforts of secular culture and its forms of nationalism to replace religion. They have challenged the notion that secular society and the modern nation-state are able to provide the moral fiber that unites national communities, or give it the ideological strength to sustain states buffeted by ethical, economic and military failures. Their message has been easy to believe and has been widely received, because the failures of the secular state have been so real.

The moral leadership of the secular state was increasingly challenged in the last decade of the twentieth century following the breakup of the Cold War and the rise of a global economy. The Cold War provided contesting models of moral politics—communism and democracy—that were replaced with a global market that weakened national sovereignty and was conspicuously devoid of political ideals. The global economy became controlled by transnational businesses accountable to no single governmental authority and with no clear ideological or moral standards of behavior. But while both Christian and Enlightenment values were left behind, transnational commerce did transport aspects of Westernized popular culture to the rest of the world. American and European music, videos, and films were beamed across national boundaries, where they threatened to obliterate local and traditional forms of artistic expression. Added to this social confusion were convulsive shifts in political power that followed the break-up of the Soviet Union and the collapse of Asian economies at the end of the twentieth century.

The public sense of insecurity that came in the wake of these cataclysmic global changes was felt not only in the societies of those nations that were economically devastated by them—especially countries in the former Soviet Union—but also in economically stronger industrialized societies. The United States, for example, saw a remarkable degree of disaffection with its political leaders and witnessed the rise of right-wing religious movements that fed on the public's perception of the inherent immorality of government.

Is the rise of religious terrorism related to these global changes? We know that some groups associated with violence in industrialized societies have had an antimodernist political agenda. At the extreme end of this religious rejection in the United States were members of the American antiabortion group Defensive Action; the Christian militia and Christian Identity movement; and isolated groups such as the Branch Davidian sect in Waco, Texas. Similar attitudes toward secular government emerged in Israel—the religious nationalist ideology of the Kach party was an extreme example—and, as the Aum Shinrikyo movement has demonstrated, in Japan. As in the United States, contentious groups within these countries were disillusioned about the ability of secular leaders to guide their countries' destinies. They identified government as the enemy.

The global shifts that have given rise to antimodernist movements have also affected less-developed nations. India's Jawaharlal Nehru, Egypt's Gamal Abdel Nasser, and Iran's Reza Shah Pahlavi once were committed to creating versions of America—or a kind of cross between America and the Soviet Union—in their own countries. But new generations of leaders no longer believe in the Westernized visions of Nehru, Nasser, or the Shah. Rather, they are eager to complete the process of decolonialization and build new, indigenous nationalisms.

When activists in Algeria who demonstrated against the crackdown against the Islamic Salvation Front in 1991 proclaimed that they were continuing the war of liberation against French colonialism, they had the ideological rather than political reach of European influence in mind. Religious activists such as the Algerian leaders, the Ayatollah Khomeini in Iran, Sheik Ahmed Yassin in Palestine, Sayyid Qutb and his disciple, Sheik Omar Abdul Rahman, in Egypt, L. K. Advani in India, and Sant Jarnail Singh Bhindranwale in India's Punjab have asserted the legitimacy of a postcolonial national identity based on traditional culture.

The result of this disaffection with the values of the modern West has been a "loss of faith" in the ideological form of that culture—secular nationalism, or the idea that the nation is rooted in a secular compact rather than religious or ethnic identity. Although a few years ago it would have been a startling notion, the idea has now become virtually commonplace that secular nationalism is in crisis. In many parts of the world it is seen as an alien cultural construction, one closely linked with what has been called "the project of modernity." In such cases, religious alternatives to secular ideologies have had extraordinary appeal.

This uncertainty about what constitutes a valid basis for national identity is a political form of postmodernism. In Iran it has resulted in the rejection of a modern Western political regime and the creation of a successful religious state. Increasingly, even secular scholars in the West have recognized that religious ideologies might offer an alternative to modernity in the political sphere. Yet, what lies beyond modernity is not necessarily a new form of political order, religious or not. In nations formerly under Soviet control, for example, the specter of the future beyond the socialist form of modernity has been one of cultural anarchism.

The Al Qaeda network associated with Osama bin Laden takes the challenge to secularism to yet another level. The implicit attack on global economic and political systems that are leveled by religious nationalists from Algeria to Indonesia are made explicit: America is the enemy. Moreover, it is a war waged not on a national plane but a transnational one. Their agenda is not for any specific form of religious nation-state, but an inchoate vision of a global rule of religious law. Rather than religious nationalists, transnational activists like bin Laden are guerrilla antiglobalists.

Postmodern Terror

Bin Laden and his vicious acts have a credibility in some quarters of the world because of the uncertainties of this moment in global history. The fear that there will be a spiritual as well as a political collapse at modernity's center has, in many parts of the world, led to terror. Both violence and religion have appeared at times when authority is in question, since they are both ways of challenging and replacing authority. One gains its power from force and the other from its claims to ultimate order. The combination of the two in acts of religious terrorism has been a potent assertion indeed. Regardless of whether the perpetrators consciously intend them to be political acts, all public acts of violence have political consequences. Insofar as they have been attempts to reshape the public order, these acts have been examples of what Jose Casanova has called the increasing "deprivatization" of religion. In various parts of the world where attempts have been made by defenders of religion to reclaim the center of public attention and authority, religious terrorism is often the violent face of these attempts.

The postmodern religious rebels such as those who rally to the side of Osama bin Laden are therefore neither anomalies nor anachronisms. From Algeria to Idaho, they are small but potent groups of violent activists who represent masses of potential supporters, and they exemplify currents of thinking and cultures of commitment that have risen to counter the prevailing modernism. The enemies of these groups have seemed to most people to be both benign and banal: such symbols of prosperity and authority as the World Trade Center. The logic of this kind of militant religiosity has therefore been difficult for many people to comprehend. Yet its challenge has been profound, for it has contained a fundamental critique of the world's post-Enlightenment secular culture and politics.

Acts of religious terrorism have thus been attempts to use violence to purchase public recognition of the legitimacy of this view of the world at war. Since religious authority can provide a ready-made replacement for secular leadership, it is no surprise that when secular authority has been deemed morally insufficient, the challenges to its legitimacy and the attempts to gain support for its rivals have often been based in religion. When the proponents of religion have asserted their claim to be the moral force undergirding public order, they sometimes have done so with the kind of power that even a confused society can graphically recognize: the force of terror.

What the perpetrators of such acts of terror expect—and indeed welcome—is a response as vicious as the acts themselves. By goading secular authorities into responding to terror with terror, they hope to accomplish two things. First, they want tangible evidence for their claim that the secular enemy is a monster. Second, they hope to bring to the surface the great war—a war that they have told their potential supporters was hidden, but real. When the American missiles began to fall in Afghanistan on October 7, less than a month after the September 11 attacks, the Al Qaeda forces must initially have been exhilarated, for the war they had anticipated for so long had finally arrived. Its outcome, however, likely gave them less satisfaction: Their bases were routed, their leadership demolished, and the Muslim world did not rise up in support in the numbers and enthusiasm they had expected. Yet the time line of religious warfare is long, and the remnant forces of Al Qaeda most likely still yearn for the final confrontation. They are assured that the glorious victory will ultimately be achieved, for they are certain that it is, after all, God's war, not theirs.

52

Homer the Heretic and Charlie Church: Parody, Piety, and Pluralism in *The Simpsons*

Lisle Dalton, Eric Michael Mazur, and Monica Siems

Although some might argue that watching TV is a form of ritual activity, actual depictions of religion are conspicuously absent from most television programs. To the horror of some critics, and to the delight of millions of viewers around the world, a significant exception is the animated comedy series created by Matt Groening, The Simpsons. *Authors Dalton, Mazur, and Siems draw examples from throughout the hundreds of episodes that have aired since 1990 to make their case that religion is one of the most prominent themes in the show. Self-consciously utilizing stereotypes and irony,* The Simpsons *holds a comic mirror to religion in contemporary America. As the present authors put it, the characters are "us" but "not us," exaggerated and distorted images of ourselves as we struggle with diverse forms of personal and noninstitutional religiosity. Through it all, the authors suggest, the show posits an underlying human goodness, exposing but not debunking the myths that order our values.*

Most of the family shows are namby-pamby sentimentality or smarmy innuendo. We stay away from that.

—Matt Groening

The story goes like this: Marge and Homer take some time for themselves and leave Bart, Lisa, and Maggie with Grandpa. Agents from child welfare discover the children running amok and place them into foster care with the neighbors. The new foster father, Ned Flanders, faints upon hearing that the children

have never been baptized, so he packs up the children and his own family and heads for the Springfield River. Homer, missing the point, panics because "in the eyes of God they'll be Flanderseses." At the river Homer pushes Bart out of "harm's way," and the baptismal water falls on his own head. When Bart asks him how he feels, Homer responds, in an uncharacteristically pious voice, "Oh, Bartholomew, I feel like St. Augustine of Hippo after his conversion by Ambrose of Milan." When Ned Flanders gasps, "Homer, what did you just say?" Homer replies nonchalantly, "I said shut your ugly face, Flanders!" The moment of spiritual inspiration has passed, and the children are back with their parents, unbaptized and safe ("Home Sweet Home-Diddily-Dum-Doodily").

The prominent role of religion and the attitude toward it are not unique to this episode. Once a week for nearly the past decade (and more in syndication) *The Simpsons* has proved itself unafraid to lampoon

Evangelicals, Hindus, Jews, and religion generally. The frequency of religious plots and subthemes would itself be enough to distinguish this show from other prime-time fare. Not since the Lutheran program *Davey and Goliath* has a cartoon addressed religion so forthrightly. But while that Sunday morning program carried moral lessons of faith, this Sunday evening program ridicules the pious, lampoons the religious, and questions traditional morality. Instead of sermonizing at the audience, this program speaks with them, and possibly for them as well.

This half-hour series emerged as one of the most popular shows of the 1990s, and it regularly addresses issues involving institutional religion—including representations of religious traditions, discussions of moral and religious themes, and portrayals of mythological figures—as well as that which is often labeled "spirituality." Regular characters include a Hindu convenience store manager, a Jewish entertainer, an Evangelical neighbor, and a Protestant minister. Evil, morality, sin, the soul, and other religious themes are openly discussed. In terms of the genres associated with the show—the situation comedy and the animated cartoon—*The Simpsons* represents quite a departure from traditional fare in which religion is rarely if ever addressed. The writers' treatment of religion might even be construed as a heresy of sorts. Yet it is often an insightful heresy, for although the program thrives on satire, caricature, and irony, it does so with a keen understanding of current trends in American religion. *The Simpsons* implicitly affirms an America in which institutional religion has lost its position of authority and where personal expressions of spirituality have come to dominate popular religious culture.

"Don't Have a Cow, Man!": Reactions to *The Simpsons*

The Simpsons were the brainchild of Matt Groening, who developed the characters in short cartoons on the *Tracey Ullman Show* in the late 1980s. When *The Simpsons* aired in January 1990, it was the first animated prime-time series on American television in more than two decades. An immediate success, within a year it was the highest rated show on its network and was often among the top ten shows on television. It occasionally outperformed *The Cosby Show,* a family-oriented situation comedy that dominated

the ratings in the late 1980s. Over time its weekly ratings have declined, but the program still consistently ranks as one of the network's top shows. Its success has continued in syndication, ranking first among reruns during the 1994–95 season (Freeman 1995, 14). The program has become so popular that it is able to attract popular cultural icons (including actors, comedians, musicians, athletes, and talk show hosts) as guest "voices."

The Simpsons has also been a merchandiser's dream. During its first season, more than a billion dollars' worth of licensed Simpsons merchandise was sold in the United States. In 1991, licensed manufacturers shipped up to a million T-shirts per week. In an example of a show's cultural impact, some school principals banned a shirt featuring Bart and the slogan "Underachiever and Proud of It" (Riddle 1994, A5), and unlicensed merchandise (including one with Bart depicted as an African American) is commonplace despite millions spent to enforce copyright (Lefton 1992, 16).

This popularity also brought in intense scrutiny from critics. Emerging amid the family values debates of early 1990s, *The Simpsons* has undergone close examination for its portrayal of family life. One famous jibe came from President George Bush in a 1992 speech before the National Religious Broadcasters Association, in which he called for "a nation closer to *The Waltons* than *The Simpsons*." Other critics have damned *The Simpsons* as a symptomatic expression of the contempt for traditional values that permeates American culture. In his critique of the entertainment industry, Michael Medved catalogs instances of religious characters portrayed as duplicitous, hypocritical, insincere, and even criminal (1992). He cites one scene from *The Simpsons* in which Bart utters an irreverent prayer ("Two Cars in Every Garage, Three Eyes on Every Fish") as proof of the industry's pattern of religious insensitivity. Another media critic, Josh Ozersky, places *The Simpsons* in a wider critique of "anti-families" that includes *Roseanne* and *Married . . . With Children,* noting that while "the playful suppression of unhappiness has always been one of TV's great strengths," this new breed of sitcom also deflects public concern away from social disintegration related to the decline of the family. As such, the irony and sarcastic humor of these shows—though he admits *The Simpsons* often tends toward "witty and valid social criticism"—serve to extend television's unhealthy influence over the American public's self-image. "TV," he laments, "has absorbed the American family's increasing sense of defeat and estrangement and presented it as an ironic in-joke." And while this mocking might temporarily placate the dysfunctional tendencies of our times, it does not "lift the spirits." Ozersky argues that the deployment of irony in the face of domestic discontents is an "assault on the family and on all human relationships" since it acts as the "antithesis of deep feeling," "discourages alarm at the decline of the family," and disparages the "earnest, often abject bonds of kin" that lie at the heart of family life. He urges readers to reject "the soullessness of TV's 'hip, bold,' anti-life world" (1991, 11–12, 14, 93).

Despite such condemnations, reactions to *The Simpsons* have not been entirely negative. Many writers (in secular and religious periodicals) praise the show's clever writing and, oddly enough— considering this is a cartoon—its realism. Danny Collum praises *The Simpsons* for "grasping the complexity and ambiguity of human life." He credits it for its insightful, even realistic portrayal of an American family that is frequently abrasive, argumentative, and beset by financial problems. Collum notes that the Simpsons are among the few TV families that go to church or consult a minister. And while he recognizes their religiosity tends toward "pretty lame K-mart evangelicalism," it merits consideration because it shows characters striving for a "moral anchor" and a "larger sense of meaning" in the midst of otherwise chaotic and aimless lives (1991, 38–39). Chiding religious groups and educators who have denounced the series as promoting bad behavior, Victoria Rebeck praises it as sharp satire that shows how parents are often ill equipped to cope with their children's (and their own) problems. For her, this comes as a welcome departure from the "pretentious misrepresentation of family life that one finds in the 'model family' shows" (1990, 622). Similarly, Frank McConnell notes that *The Simpsons* "deconstructs the myth of the happy family" and "leaves what is real and valuable about the myth unscathed. . . . They are caricatures not just of us, but of us in our national delusion that the life of the sitcom family is the way things are 'supposed' to be" (1990, 389). He praises the show's humanism and rapid-fire humor, which he considers "profoundly sane."

"Gabbin' About God": Scholarly Viewing of Religion and Television

That *The Simpsons* generates such divergent reactions from critics suggests that it has struck a sensitive nerve that lies close to the heart of the public debate over the portrayal of religious values in the media. In an ambitious 1994 study of religion on television, researchers conducted a five-week analysis of religious behaviors on prime-time shows. After cataloging the activities of 1,462 characters in one hundred episodes, the study found that religion was "a rather invisible institution" in prime time; fewer than 6 percent of the characters had an identifiable religious affiliation, and religiosity was rarely central to the plots or the characters. The report concluded that "television has fictionally 'delegitimized' religious institutions and traditions by symbolically eliminating them from our most pervasive form of popular culture" (Skill et al. 1994, 251–67, especially 265). The study may have been biased; other explanations for the "symbolic elimination" of religion in prime-time television range from skittishness about offending religious adherents to alleged irreligiosity within the entertainment industry. Nonetheless, as Medved claims, the result is programming that often seems an "affront [to] the religious sensibilities of ordinary Americans" (1992, 50).

On the other hand, other scholars argue that it is better to analyze television using broader conceptions of religion. For them, the very act of watching television serves as a religious event—a domestic ritual of devotion to stories that would function like religious narratives in other cultures and eras. Gregor Goethals, borrowing from sociologists Peter Berger and Thomas Luckmann, asserts that television provides a symbolic universe that serves as an overarching framework for ordering and interpreting experience (1981, 125; see also Greeley 1987). Hal Himmelstein analyzes television programming in terms of various persistent "myths," including "the sanctity of the ordinary American family," "the triumph of personal initiative over bureaucratic control," and "the celebration of celebrity." He further argues that these myths sustain the political and economic needs of various social institutions (1994, 3, 10).

These debates over religion on *The Simpsons* reflect what anthropologist Clifford Geertz called the "intrinsic double aspect" of cultural products that are both models *of* and models *for* reality. Does *The Simpsons* reflect our attitudes—particularly toward religion—or does it shape them? Does television act as mirror to show us ourselves as we really are, or as we ought to be? As the reactions to *The Simpsons* suggest, it is an important debate. Geertz argues that such cultural patterns "give meaning . . . to social and psychological reality both by shaping themselves to it and by shaping it to themselves" (1973, 93). The reaction to *The Simpsons,* mirroring broader debates about America's values and morality, suggests that the show serves as a model of contemporary belief and behavior in American life; the show is a microcosm of what Americans currently do and do not hold sacred. This picture of America delights some, and appalls others. And although *The Simpsons* targets many social institutions, myths, and presumptions, religion inspires some of the show's sharpest satire, and correspondingly some of its best insights into contemporary America.

"Home Sweet Home-Diddily-Dum-Doodily": Welcome to Springfield

It is the world of the Simpson family that feeds the recriminations and fears of those who despise it, while offering humor, irony, succor, and a subtle morality play for those who adore it. Through the television lens (or more appropriately, its mirror), viewers see the mundane lives of the Simpsons, and themselves in the reflection—an odd but often uncannily accurate portrait of Americana. The cast represents a cross section of ages, genders, races, and religions; it includes police officers, teachers, entertainers, clergy, bartenders, and janitors. The Simpson family includes Homer (a dim employee at a nuclear power plant), his wife Marge (a devoted but overworked housewife), and their children: Bart (a good-natured but mischievous boy), Lisa (a precocious, sensitive girl), and infant Maggie.

The fact that the characters are cartoons presents an interesting dynamic, separating the "reality" of our lives from the "pretend" world of the Simpsons. Even so, the family presents noble truths, painful realities, and ironic depths in a very "real" way, enabling viewers to identify with the sentiments and to

be altered by them. This two-way relationship invites viewers to enter the Everytown of Springfield, to visit the Simpsons' world and perhaps comprehend how it informs their own. While they rarely "mug" for the camera, the self-reflexive actions of the characters help by constantly acknowledging their television status. From the show's opening sequence that depicts the characters racing home to watch their own opening credits to the frequent sub-references to other television shows, networks, and personalities, viewers are reminded of television's importance in the lives of the Simpson family and—since we are watching them watch—our own. Indeed, as if to mock our own viewership, the Simpsons' television is often alluded to as the sixth (and most appreciated) member of the family. The Simpsons watch television and are conscious of its influence over their lives, while we watch them and ponder, fret, and complain about how they are reflecting and shaping our thoughts and attitudes.

In Springfield, representatives of religious communities are rendered as stereotypes, easily identifiable to viewers and easily objectionable to adherents. The only regularly appearing Jewish character, Herschel Schmuykl "Krusty the Klown" Krustofsky, is the star of Bart and Lisa's favorite television program. He is anything but devout. A gross caricature of a stereotypically secularized Jew corrupted by wealth and fame, Krusty is addicted to cigarettes, gambling, and pornography. He dislikes children, finances his lavish debt-ridden lifestyle by over-marketing his own image unabashedly, and fakes his own death to avoid paying taxes. In an episode that parodies *The Jazz Singer,* Krusty recites a Hebrew prayer while visiting the Simpsons and later admits that as a youth he disappointed his father by abandoning rabbinical studies to become a clown. The rest of the episode involves the attempts by Bart and Lisa to reconcile the estranged father and son. Using advice from various Jewish sources, they eventually succeed ("Like Father, Like Clown").

Another character, Apu Nehasapeemapetalan, is manager of the local "Kwik-E-Mart" and one of the few identifiable Hindus on network television. Apu practices vegetarianism, maintains an in-store shrine to the elephant-headed deity Ganesha (quite plausible insofar as Ganesha's connection to prosperity appeals to the ambitions of the Hindu diaspora), and marries according to Hindu ritual. In Springfield, however, Apu must endure the slights of his incredulous customers; Homer belittles Apu's diet, throws peanuts at the shrine, and suggests that Apu "must have been out taking a whiz when they were giving out gods" ("Homer the Heretic"). More problematic is the inference that South Asians manage all convenience stores; Homer joins Apu on a Himalayan pilgrimage to visit the high "guru" of Kwik-E-Marts, and during a visit to a seaside town, the Simpson family stops at a local convenience mart managed by another South Asian ("Homer and Apu"; "Summer of 4 ft. 2").

The subjects of the most mockery, however, are the Simpsons' evangelical Christian neighbors, the Flanders family. Exceedingly cheerful, Ned, his wife Maude, and their "goody-goody" children Rod and Todd provide the perfect foil to the Simpson family. They are polite, well-liked, righteous, generous, peaceful, and neighborly—all qualities the Simpsons seem to lack. They are also extraordinarily pious: spotting escaped zoo animals running through town, Ned exclaims that he has seen the elephants of the apocalypse. Maude reminds him that the Bible describes four horsemen, not elephants. "Gettin' closer," he replies ("Bart Gets an Elephant"). Bart uses a special microphone to fool Rod and Todd into thinking that God is communicating with them over the radio. On another occasion they bounce on a trampoline and exclaim, "Each bounce takes us closer to God," and "Catch me Lord, catch me," before crashing into each other ("Radio Bart"; "Homer Alone").

Stereotyping is not the only way institutional religion is lampooned; religious leadership is the butt of much of the program's humor. Though other religious figures appear on the program (most notably in an ecumenical radio program entitled "Gabbin' about God" with a minister, Krusty's father the rabbi, and a Catholic priest ["Like Father, Like Clown"]), there is no doubt that the Reverend Timothy Lovejoy represents all clergy—to their general misfortune. When ever-righteous Ned Flanders telephones Lovejoy upon learning that the Simpson children were never baptized, Lovejoy—clearly annoyed by Flanders's intrusion—suggests that Ned consider another religious tradition: "They're basically all the same," he notes before hanging up. When Marge asks if a particular activity is a sin, Lovejoy picks up the Bible and exclaims, "Have you read this thing lately, Marge? Everything's

a sin" ("Home Sweet Home-Diddily-Dum-Doodily"). He encourages Marge to seek a divorce during a weekend retreat she and Homer attend to fix their marriage ("War of the Simpsons"). And when a comet threatens to destroy Springfield—and immediately after Homer laments not being religious—Lovejoy is seen running down the street yelling, "It's all over, people, we don't have a prayer" ("Bart's Comet").

Lovejoy's anemic approach condemns all religious leadership and is part of a larger critique of religious traditions consistent with the other stereotypes and the actions of the regular characters. After eating potentially poisonous sushi, Homer prepares for death by spending his last moments listening to the Bible on tape. Unfortunately, the "begats" put him to sleep, causing him to miss the sunrise he had hoped to die watching ("One Fish, Two Fish, Blowfish, Blue Fish"). (He survives.) Bart responds to a request for grace with a somewhat irreverent prayer: "Dear God: We paid for all the stuff ourselves, so thanks for nothing" ("Two Cars").

The program also uses familiar supernatural religious figures for comic effects. Both Satan and God have appeared on the program, and their portrayals mix the sublime and demonic with the ridiculous, presenting them as much human as they are supernatural. Satan is a familiar visitor to Springfield; in various episodes he offers Homer a doughnut in exchange for his soul; holds appointments with Montgomery Burns, the devious owner of the local nuclear plant; and uses a personal computer to keeps tabs on lost souls. Satan manifests in different forms, and typical of the program's use of irony, he is portrayed in one episode by Ned Flanders ("Treehouse of Horror IV"). In contrast, God is a cross between Mel Brooks's "Two-thousand-year old man" character and Charlton Heston's aged Moses—a familiar stereotype with a humorous and not-too-blasphemous sting. As might be expected of an anthropomorphic God, however, certain divine attributes (omniscience, omnipresence) seem lacking; in a meeting with Homer, God inquires whether St. Louis still has a football team (at the time, it did not) and later excuses himself to appear on a tortilla in Mexico ("Homer the Heretic").

The depictions of God and Satan reinforce the morality play qualities of the Simpson characters. Homer, as Everyman, is a poorly educated working man. He is simple, well meaning, loving, and committed to his family, regardless of how much they annoy him. Marge, as Charity, is always doing for others, particularly her family, while neglecting herself. In the few cases where she is self-indulgent, she ends up plagued by guilt, and though tempted by vices, she always returns to care for her loved ones. The eldest child, Bart, as Temptation, is the animated Tom Sawyer. He is an irascible boy who never studies, serves detention, plays pranks, yet loves his sister, obeys his mother, and occasionally respects his father. The eldest daughter, Lisa, as Wisdom, is the smart student and teacher's pet, the child who dreams of Nobel prizes and presidential elections and who relies on her saxophone and the Blues to release her from her torment. The youngest child, Maggie, represents Hope, the embodiment of innocence and vulnerability.

Juxtaposed with the dubious portrayals of institutional religion are nuanced and intricate examples of admirable and noble behavior. Krusty, Apu, and Ned are volunteer fire fighters who help put out the burning Simpson home after Homer falls asleep on the couch smoking a cigar (and skipping church) ("Homer the Heretic"). Ned, despite Homer's frequent ribbing and abuse, adheres closely to the Christian ideals of turning the other cheek and practicing charity. He invites the Simpsons to his barbecues, shares football tickets with Homer, offers to donate organs (without solicitation), lets the town come into his family's bomb shelter to avoid a comet's destruction, and agrees to leave it and face near certain doom when it becomes too crowded ("Homer Loves Flanders"; "When Flanders Failed"; "Homer's Triple Bypass"; "Bart's Comet"). Even the Simpsons, "America's favorite dysfunctional family" (Rebeck 1990, 622) often overcome their John Bunyanesque characterizations. Marge and Homer reject opportunities to be unfaithful, attend a retreat to save their marriage, and drag the family to a seminar to improve their communication skills. Homer attempts to improve his relationship with his father, hunts down his half-brother, and tolerates his annoying sisters-in-law. Though constant rivals, Bart and Lisa share genuine affection and occasionally work together; when Lisa becomes the star goalie of Bart's rival ice hockey team, the two put down their sticks and exit the rink arm-in-arm rather than compete for their parents' love. Bart even solicits the

assistance of a Michael Jackson sound-alike to help write Lisa a birthday song ("Life on the Fast Lane"; "The Last Temptation of Homer"; "Colonel Homer"; "War of the Simpsons"; "Bart's Inner Child"; "One Fish, Two Fish"; "Grandpa vs. Sexual Inadequacy"; "Oh Brother, Where Art Thou?"; "Lisa on Ice"; "Stark Raving Dad").

The diverse attitudes toward religion come together in the episode titled "Homer the Heretic." Refusing to attend church, Homer embarks on a journey of personal spirituality, encounters Apu's Hinduism and Krusty's Judaism, and ultimately comes face to face with God. During a dream God grants Homer permission to miss church, and when he awakens he is a changed man: calm, peaceful, and able to commune directly with nature. The following week, while asleep on the couch, Homer sets the house alight, and the volunteer fire department (Krusty, Ned, and Apu, or as Reverend Lovejoy puts it, "the Jew, the Christian, and the miscellaneous") rushes to put it out. Homer questions the value of attending church, since the Flanderses' house is also on fire. "He's a regular Charlie Church," Homer notes, suggesting that religious faith did not protect the Flanderses' home. But just as Homer utters these words, a providential cloud forms over the Flanderses' home and rain extinguishes the blaze—but leaves the fire burning the Simpson home. Asked by Marge if he has learned anything, Homer notes that God is angry and vengeful. The Reverend Lovejoy replies that it is the charity of the pluralistic volunteer fire department and not God's anger that is the lesson to be learned. The house is saved, and so is Homer's faith—in humanity, if not in God.

And so, perhaps, is the viewers', if the focus shifts from the show's content to its context, to what is happening on *this* side of the glass. Reverend Lovejoy's sentiment—that "God was working in the hearts of your friends and neighbors when they came to your aid"—represents the sort of generic Christianity prevalent in today's mainline Protestant churches and in most television portrayals of religion. Against the backdrop of declining religious authority, increasing personal choice, and "flattening" of doctrines into more palatable themes, television presents revamped morality plays such as this in which personal piety, religious pluralism, and sincere goodness rate higher than denominational adherence and church attendance. The show's coda reinforces this point: having promised to be "front row center" in church the next Sunday, there is Homer, snoring through Lovejoy's sermon, dreaming of another tête-à-tête with God (in which God informs Homer not to be upset, since "nine out of ten religions fail in their first year").

"Send in the Clowns": Analyzing the Simpsons

It is helpful to take a step back and remember that this is (after all) a cartoon, written by comedy writers and drawn by comic artists. Several episodes feature gestures that highlight the characters' traditionally animated hands: three fingers and a thumb. Indeed, whatever "reality" is posited in the program is of the viewers' making. By working both sides of the reality mirror, the show engenders feelings of both identity and difference—the characters are both "us" and "not us." They are "us" in the sense that they are not ideal, but "not us" in the sense that—their cartoonishness aside—they fall far shorter of the mark than we think we do. The television mirror here is a funhouse one, which provides an exaggerated, distorted, yet still recognizable image of ourselves. Ozersky notes this and criticizes the show not only for failing to provide a positive model but for rewarding an attitude of superiority and ironic smugness in its viewers. Closer to the mark, however, might be Rebeck's observation that such critics "have missed the point. The Simpsons is satire," and as such its characters "are not telling people how to act" (1990, 622).

Interestingly, Rebeck illustrates her point with a religious-themed episode; she compares The Simpsons' detractors to a minor but recurring character in the show, the Sunday school teacher. Beleaguered by the children's questions about whether their pets will go to heaven—particularly Bart's inquiries about an amputee's leg and a robot with a human brain—she finally blurts out, "All these questions! Is a little blind faith too much to ask for?" ("The Telltale Head"). At best, some critics want proactive television that encourages viewers to maintain a level of "blind faith" in certain cherished ideals and values. At worst, they lambast The Simpsons because it fails to reinforce our society's "dominant ideology" with its cherished myths of eternal progress and traditional authority structures.

But exposing a myth to ridicule and debunking it are two different things. Recall that McConnell's highest praise for The Simpsons was that "it deconstructs the myth of the happy family wisely and miraculously leaves what is real and valuable about the myth unscathed" (1990, 390). Rebeck notes that the Simpsons are not characters to be emulated, but "if anything, they are giving people an outlet so they won't have to act out" (1990, 622). Herein lies another paradox; it is precisely *because* the program fails to offer us any sustained ideals of its own—least of all desirable ideals that challenge the majority—that it serves as a negative model for mainstream ideals of family and religion, if only by default, and offers instead a catharsis generated by a good laugh.

If many of television's early sitcoms were little more than thinly veiled presentations of the "American dream," The Simpsons and shows like it come much closer to actually representing "comedy" than most of its predecessors. Himmelstein notes that, to those having difficulty handling "the chaos of daily life," comedy represents "the logical order of the ideal" by revealing the "ludicrous and ridiculous aspects of our existence." It is most powerful, he concludes, "when it is possible for both the artist and the spectator to note the contradictions and value conflicts of society." Comedy shades into satire when it deals with what he calls "traditional and ever-present irritations which people know as evils but which they also find themselves powerless to eradicate" (1994, 77).

On The Simpsons, the disjunction between the way things are and the way they ought to be persists, and any bridge across that gap proves temporary and largely unrecognized by the supposedly victorious Simpsons themselves. At the end of an episode, the family often debates the "lesson" they've learned, with none of them seeming to get the point. Thus, if the inclusion of humor at the expense of institutional structures marks The Simpsons as satire, this recurring failure to offer true resolutions distinguishes it as irony. Defined by literary critic Alan Wilde, irony in our era is "a mode of consciousness, a perceptual response to a world without unity or cohesion" which nonetheless bears "the potential for affirmation" of both the world's absurdity and its "unfinished" nature (1981, 2, 6). Here it seems that the models "of" and "for" society coalesce. Rebeck notes, "The Simpsons show us . . . what it was about our upbringing that made us brats as kids and neurotic as adults" (1990, 622). They do not show us how to remedy those conditions, implying that they don't need fixing. In an imperfect world one fares best by behaving imperfectly.

Ozersky sees *The Simpsons* functioning this way, with profoundly negative implications for society. He argues that the show makes viewers "less inclined to object to the continuing presence of unsafe workplaces, vast corporations, the therapy racket, and all the other deserving targets of *The Simpsons'* harmless barbs" (1991, 92). But Ozersky fails to see another side to the "irony" coin. For segments of society who *cannot* object to those failings, *The Simpsons* reminds them that they are not *completely* powerless as long as they can laugh at the forces that oppress them. James Chesebro identifies irony as the "communication strategy" of the disenfranchised that reassures an audience because it presents characters who are "intellectually inferior and less able to control circumstances than is the audience" (Chesebro 1979; quoted in Himmelstein 1994, 79). In other words, the character's life is more absurd than the viewers'—a funhouse mirror. This is especially true in cases of what Chesebro calls "unknowing irony" in which the character's "ignorance and social powerlessness" are not feigned. Archie Bunker, the somewhat pitiable and perennially unredeemed bigot of *All in the Family,* is a perfect example of "unknowing irony" from the pre-*Simpsons* television era. In order for ironic programming to serve as a model "for" society, he had to remain unredeemed. Otherwise the show would have been something substantially different from what it was. As Himmelstein notes, self-knowledge and self-criticism in Archie would "sacrifice" the show's "unknowing irony" and turn it from "a biting artistic revelation of bigotry in a contemporary social milieu" to a "a popularized group-therapy session thrown in the audience's face" (1994, 125). And while *The Simpsons* contains far fewer "serious" moments than *All in the Family* did—Homer is clearly more absurd and less pitiable than Archie ever was—the two proceed in a decidedly "live and don't learn" manner.

Not surprisingly, Homer's lack of intellectual and moral progress is expressed most powerfully in the religious-themed episodes. The accidental baptism in the Springfield River mentioned earlier elicits in him only temporary piety. He becomes a messianic leader for the "Stonecutters" (a men's organization modeled on Freemasonry), but his attempts to get the members to dedicate themselves to charitable acts causes the group to disband ("Homer the Great"). In the "Homer the Heretic" episode, not even a face-to-face encounter with the Almighty can change Homer's character. At every turn the opportunity for redemption passes, and Homer is back where he started: marginal, powerless, and unenlightened. In all these episodes, it is not unbelief that is counseled, but rather belief in basic values (for example, charity, camaraderie, and support) in a different way—within the family rather than outside it. In the end, Homer realizes the folly of striving too hard to "belong," and instead ends most episodes proud and confident of who he is, warts and all. As Richard Corliss notes, "Homer isn't bright, but he loves his brood." He is also a faithful husband and father who "will do anything—go skateboarding off a cliff, defy his boss, buy Lisa a pony—if the tots scream loud enough and if Marge gives him a lecture" (1994, 77). In other words, Homer's progress (or lack thereof) in each episode reveals a character who can be counted on to do the right thing, if accidentally or begrudgingly. This conveys a sense of an underlying human goodness, however many layers of ineptitude one might have to penetrate to find it.

"All the World Loves a Clown": The Simpsons as Religious Archetypes

And thus we return to the notion of the Simpsons—especially Homer—as "us" and "not us." He has the same values and desires, but expresses them in a buffoonish style. This is the key to discerning the significance of *The Simpsons* not only as satire of religious phenomena, but also as a religious phenomenon in itself. The history of religions has many examples of clowns who convey messages to the faithful. Historian Don Handelman describes the linguistic connections between "buffoon" and "fool" and notes the "affinities" between the fool in medieval drama and the clown as religious performer. According to Handelman, "Clowns are ambiguous and ambivalent figures. . . . The clown in ritual is at once a character of solemnity and fun, of gravity and hilarity, of danger and absurdity, of wisdom and idiocy, and of the sacred and the profane" (1987).

A character such as Homer Simpson oscillates between knowing and not knowing, between knowing that he knows and not knowing that he knows. He approaches the divine but simultaneously defames it, and thus embodies the irony of a character who knows no real resolution.

In some religions, the identity and difference between clowns and their audiences is an immensely significant dialectic—that paradox of "us" but "not us." In the Hopi tradition, ritual clowns perform actions backward, upside down, or in an otherwise ridiculous fashion—for example, entering a plaza by climbing head-first down a ladder. They may engage in exaggerated simulated intercourse and perform other activities that violate Hopi social norms. Interpretations have stressed two aspects: entertainment value and the pedagogic value of illustrating the foolishness of misbehaving. In this sense, Hopi clowns foster a sense of superiority among the audience members who know more and are more sophisticated than the clowns. However, as Emory Sekaquaptewa notes, clowns, while parodies of the society, must be recognizable in order to have an effect. It may be a funhouse mirror, but it's still a mirror, and clowns show that the way *not* to behave is precisely the way we often behave in an imperfect world. As Sekaquaptewa explains, clowns show that people "have only their worldly ambition and aspirations by which to gain a spiritual world of eternity. . . . We cannot be perfect in this world after all and if we are reminded that we are clowns, maybe we can have, from time to time, introspection as a guide to lead us right" (1989, 151).

Thus sacred clowns, through their mockery of norms, serve to reinforce a tradition's values. They "contradict the laws of society to remind people of distinctions between the sacred and profane. They cross ordinary boundaries in order to define them" (Bastien 1987). *The Simpsons* represents both a model of and a model for contemporary American society, not only because it reveals contemporary attitudes about religious institutions, morality, and spirituality, but also because it functions in the time-honored way of religious satirists. As Joseph Bastien notes, "Traditionally, religions have employed humor and satire to bring people together and dissolve their differences. Clownish antics . . . [are] not intended to desecrate the sacred but to dispel some of the rigidity and pomposity of the church-goers" (1987). The targets of *The Simpsons'* ridicule are hardly malevolent forces but rather exponents of what Victoria Rebeck calls a "sincere but useless" form of religion, teaching us that the most ridiculous thing a person can do is take anything in life too seriously (1990, 622). "The laughter of fools," Bastien says, is "praise to a God who disdain[s] pride among his people" (1987). But surely such a God would permit us to be proud of ourselves for getting the joke.

Conclusion: "A Noble Spirit Embiggens the Smallest Man"

In a cartoon universe that thrives on irony, satire, and endless subversion there can be no heresy save an unreasonable dedication to convention. In Homer's world, and perhaps in our own, there is no longer a well-defined orthodoxy against which a meaningful heresy might be mounted. This does not diminish the fact that the Simpsons fulfill the important function of the sacred clowns—sustaining what is important by poking fun at religious conventions. What is important to believe and do, however, defies description. In keeping with the show's insight into the contemporary religious scene there is a persistent message of a loss of institutional authority (although institutional practice and loyalty linger) coupled with diverse forms of personal and noninstitutional religiosity. In this light the would-be "heretic" Homer fulfills the role of the American spiritual wanderer; though linked culturally (if unsteadily and unenthusiastically) to biblical tradition, he regularly engages a mosaic of other traditions, mythologies, and moral codes. In the face of these ever-shifting layers of meaning, he stumbles along, making the most of his limited understanding of their complexities. His comic antics remind us that the making of meaning (religious or otherwise) is ever an unfinished business and that humor and irony go a long way toward sweetening and sustaining the endeavor.

Suggested Readings

Coleman, Simon
  2000   *The Globalisation of Charismatic Christianity: Spreading the Gospel of Prosperity.* Cambridge: Cambridge University Press.

Coward, Harold, John R. Hinnell, and Raymond Brady Williams, eds.
  2000   *The South Asian Religious Diaspora in Britain, Canada, and the United States.* Albany: State University of New York Press.

Eickelman, Dale F., and Jon W. Anderson, eds.
  1999   *New Media in the Muslim World.* Bloomington: Indiana University Press.

Hefner, Robert
  1998   "Multiple Modernities: Christianity, Islam, and Hinduism in a Globalizing Age." *Annual Review of Anthropology* 27: 83–104.

Kinney, Jay
  1995   "Net Worth? Religion, Cyberspace, and the Future." *Futures* 27(7): 763–75.

Sylvan, Robin
  2002   *Traces of the Spirit: The Religious Dimensions of Popular Music.* Albany: State University of New York Press.

Veer, Peter van der, ed.
  1996   *Conversion to Modernities: The Globalization of Christianity.* New York: Routledge.

Glossary

acculturation: Culture change occurring under conditions of close contact between two societies. The weaker group tends to acquire cultural elements of the dominant group.

age-grade: An association that includes all the members of a group who are of a certain age and sex (for example, a warrior age-grade).

age-set: A group of individuals of the same sex and age who move through some or all of the stages of an age-grade together.

Al-fiqh: Islamic jurisprudence or legal theory.

ancestor worship: A religious practice involving the worship of the spirits of dead family and lineage members.

animatism: The attribution of life to inanimate objects.

animism: The belief in the existence of spiritual beings (Tylor's minimal definition of religion).

anthropomorphism: The attribution of human physical characteristics to objects not human.

anthropophagy: The consumption of human flesh (cannibalism).

apotropaic: Having the power to avert misfortune, bad luck, or evil.

associations: Organizations whose membership is based on the pursuit of special interests.

Aum Shinrikyo: A Japanese religious movement, whose followers were accused of releasing nerve gas in a Tokyo subway station in 1995.

avoidance rules: Regulations that define or restrict social interaction between certain relatives.

ayahuasca: From Quechua language, a psychoactive substance used for religious purposes by native peoples of the Amazon. Primary ingredient is the *Banisteriopsis* vine.

baci: A form of offering in Lao Buddhist rituals, often a conical or tree-shaped structure including flowers, foods, and sacred strings.

berdache: A French term for North American Indian transvestites who assume the cultural roles of women.

binary opposition: Contrasting pairs of items or concepts, such as male/female, heaven/hell, black/white. According to Claude Lévi-Strauss and the structuralist school, a fundamental characteristic of human thought.

bokors: A Haitian term for Vodou sorcerers who administer so-called zombie powder to their intended victims.

cannibalism: *See anthropophagy.*

Cartesian: Ideas attributed to philosopher René Descartes; specifically, the notion that the human mind and body are two separate entities.

ceremony: A formal act or set of acts established by custom as proper to a special occasion, such as a religious rite.

chador: In Iran, a long, capelike form of women's dress that usually does not cover the face. Literally means "tent."

charisma: Personal leadership qualities that endow an individual with the ability to attract followers. Often this quality of leadership is attributed to divine intervention.

455

Charismatic Renewal movement: Non-mainstream group within Roman Catholicism that incorporates features of charismatic or Pentecostal Protestant worship.

cicatrization: Ritual and cosmetic scarification.

clan: A unilineal descent group based on a fictive ancestor.

communitarianism: A secular or religious lifestyle in which groups share beliefs and material goods; these groups are ordinarily isolated from the general population.

cosmogony: Symbolic materials, such as myths, accounting for the origins of the universe.

cosmology: A theory or view of the nature of the universe, including humans' place in it.

couvade: Culturally prescribed behavior of a father during and after the birth of his child; for example, mimicking the mother's labor pains.

coven: An organization of witches with a membership traditionally set at thirteen.

creationism: The belief that the living world originated from a divine act of creation. In the United States, usually associated with acceptance of the biblical book of Genesis as literal truth, belief that the earth is relatively young, and belief that both the physical structures and the living species of the earth have not changed since creation.

cult: An imprecise term, generally used as a pejorative to describe an often loosely organized group possessing special religious beliefs and practices.

cultural relativism: The concept that any given culture must be evaluated in terms of its own belief system.

cultural universals: Aspects of culture believed to exist in all human societies.

culture: The integrated total of learned behavior that is characteristic of members of a society.

culture trait: A single unit of learned behavior or its product.

curse: An utterance calling upon supernatural forces to send evil or misfortune to a person.

dar al-Islam: Territory or land where Islamic law is practiced.

demon: A person, spirit, or thing regarded as evil.

descent: A recognized parent-child connection that defines relationships within larger family groups.

diaspora: The dispersion or scattering of a population. Today, peoples that have migrated in large numbers across the globe, but who retain some sense of community or common identity—for example, the African diaspora, the South Asian diaspora, and, historically, the Jewish diaspora.

diffusion: A process in which cultural elements of one group pass to another.

divination: The process of contacting the supernatural to find an answer to a question regarding the cause of an event or to foretell the future.

ecosystem: Plants and animals connected to one another and their environment through a flow of energy and materials.

embodiment theory: In anthropology, a perspective that views culture and the self in relation to the human body, for example, considering how emotion, pain, ritual, or violence are experienced by and produced by the body. Seeks to avoid mind/body dualism.

emic: Shared perceptions of phenomena and ideology by members of a society; insiders' views.

endocannibalism: The eating of the remains of kinsmen and/or members of one's own group.

ethnocentrism: A tendency to evaluate foreign beliefs and behaviors according to one's own cultural traditions.

ethnography: A detailed anthropological description of a culture.

ethnology: A comparison and analysis of the ethnographic data from various cultures.

ethnomedicine: Beliefs and practices relating to diseases of the indigenous peoples of traditional societies.

ethos: The characteristic and distinguishing attitudes of a people.

etic: An outside observer's viewpoint of a society's phenomena or ideology.

euhemerism: The belief that myths are inaccurate, primitive explanations of the natural world or distorted accounts of the historical past. Based on the name of the classical philosopher Euhemeros of Messene (330–260 BCE).

exogamy: A rule specifying marriage outside one's kin group or community.

exorcism: The driving away of evil spirits by ritual.

familiar: A spirit, demon, or animal that acts as an intimate servant.

fetish: An object that is worshipped because of its supernatural power.

folk medical syndrome: Illnesses that reflect a combination of emotional, cultural, and physical causes, usually associated with a particular culture or community.

folk model: A culturally based way of perceiving or understanding something, frequently in opposition to scientific or empirically based understandings.

folklore: The traditional beliefs, legends, myths, sayings, and customs of a people.

functionalism: An analytical approach that attempts to explain cultural traits in terms of the uses they serve within a society.

fundamentalism: A commitment to what are perceived as the original, core, and inerrant facets of a faith. May represent opposition to the status quo or to the current distribution of power within society or a religious group. In U.S. Protestantism, includes acceptance of the Bible as literal truth.

Ghost Dance: A nativistic movement among several tribes of North American Indians during the late nineteenth century.

ghosts: Spirits of the dead.

glossolalia: The verbalizing of utterances that depart from normal speech, such as the phenomenon of "speaking in tongues."

god: A supernatural being with great power over humans and nature.

gynophobia: An abnormal fear of women (also spelled *gynephobia*).

Hadd (pl. Hudud): Penalties in Islamic law.

hajj: The Muslim pilgrimage to Mecca.

hajji: Honorific title for Muslims who have made the pilgrimage to Mecca.

hallucinogen: Any of a number of hallucination-producing substances, such as LSD, peyote, ebene, and marijuana.

harem: The interior, domestic space of a Muslim home that observes seclusion of women. Usually includes women related through the extended family.

hijab: An Arabic word meaning "covering," used widely by Muslims across the world to refer to modest women's dress, which might take a variety of forms. Often interpreted in the West as "the veil."

holistic: In anthropology, the approach that emphasizes the study of a cultural and bioecological system in its entirety.

idolatry: Excessive devotion to or reverence for a person or thing.

imam: In Arabic language, prayer leader.

incest taboo: The prohibition of sexual relations between close relatives as defined by society.

intercessory prayer: A request to a god, calling for aid to others.

invocation: The act of conjuring, or calling forth, good or evil spirits.

jihad: In Arabic language, lit. "struggle." Broadly conceived, this may be either internal or external struggle. May describe acts of war or resistance, though the word is not limited to this meaning.

kaiko: Part of the ritual cycle of the Tsembaga of New Guinea; a festival involving the sacrificial butchering of pigs, dancing, and the hosting of guests.

karma: The Buddhist idea, connected to the belief in reincarnation, that one's present status in life is determined by one's actions in past lives. Accumulating spiritual merit through one's own actions, or on behalf of others, can affect karma.

legend: A folk narrative that relates an important event popularly believed to have a historical basis although not verifiable.

Liberation Theology: A school of thought within Roman Catholicism, particularly in Latin America, that emphasizes social justice and the eradication of poverty.

liturgy: Public rituals and services of the Christian Church.

madrasa: In Arabic language, school.

magic: A ritual practice believed to compel the supernatural to act in a desired way.

magic, contagious: A belief that associated objects can exert an influence on each other—for example, a spell cast using the intended victim's property.

magic, imitative: A belief that imitating a desired result will cause it to occur.

magic, sympathetic: A belief that an object can influence others that have an identity with it—for example, a bow symbolizes the intended victim.

mámas: Priests among the Kogi of Colombia.

mana: A sacred force inhabiting certain objects and people, giving them extraordinary power.

manioc: A nutritious, starchy, edible root grown in the tropics; also known as cassava.

mara'akáme: A religious leader or shaman among the Huichol.

mazeway: Anthony F. C. Wallace's term for an individual's cognitive map and positive and negative goals.

merit: In the Buddhist doctrine of karma, spiritual good that may accumulate or diminish, affecting the circumstances of one's rebirth.

monasticism: The institution or system of life associated with a monastery and its occupants.

monomyth: According to Joseph Campbell, the basic narrative that organizes all myths of the world.

monotheism: A belief that there is only one god.

moral injunction: A command, an order, or a prohibition regarding the right way to live.

Mudarabah: Type of loan offered by Islamic banks to avoid interest or usury.

mufti: Specialist in Islamic law, who is capable of making legal interpretations.

mysticism: A contemplative process whereby an individual seeks union with a spiritual being or force.

myth: A sacred narrative believed to be true by the people who tell it.

nationalism: The idea of, and advocacy of, independence and unity of a nation. Usually based on some aspect(s) of group identity, such as ethnicity, language, or shared history. May be combined with other words—for example, to distinguish nationalism based on religious ties (religious nationalism) or nationalism that ignores religious affiliations (secular nationalism).

necromancy: The ability to foretell the future by communicating with the dead.

neo-paganism: A range of contemporary nature-oriented religions that draw inspiration from folklore, mythology, academic sources, and popular culture. Includes contemporary witches and practitioners of Wicca.

neurosis: A mild psychological disorder.

New Age: A loosely used term describing a combination of spirituality and superstition, fad and farce, that supposedly helps believers gain knowledge of the unknown. Largely a North American phenomenon, the movement includes beliefs in psychic predictions, channeling, astrology, and the powers of crystals and pyramids.

novice: A person in training to become a priest.

oath: An appeal to a deity to witness the truth of what one says.

occult: Certain mystic arts or studies, such as magic, alchemy, and astrology.

orality: A term used by Walter J. Ong to refer to reliance on nonprint forms of communication technology.

ordeal: A ritual method to supernaturally determine guilt or innocence by subjecting the accused to a physical test.

organic unity: The idea that cultures are composed of integrated parts, balanced and functioning harmoniously.

orthodox: Being in line with the main teachings of a church or religious tradition; conforming to a standard doctrine.

otherworldly: Devoted to concerns beyond the present material world; in connection with spiritual concerns or the prospect of an afterlife.

pantheism: The belief that God is everything and everything is God; (also) the worship of all gods.

participant observation: An anthropological field technique in which the ethnographer is immersed in the day-to-day activities of the community being studied.

patrilineal: The rule of descent in which individuals are related through the father's line only.

Pentecostalism: A segment of Christianity that emphasizes involvement with the Holy Spirit (the third person of the holy trinity) through such experiences as divine healing, prophecy, and speaking in tongues.

petition prayer: A request to a god, calling for assistance or success for oneself.

peyote: A spineless cactus native to Mexico and Texas, scientific name *Lophophora williamsii*; sometimes referred to as peyotl (from Aztec or Nahuatl) or, mistakenly, as mescal. It is used ceremonially by indigenous peoples of Mexico, as well as the Native American Church, for its production of visual hallucinations.

peyote cult: A cult surrounding the ritual ingestion of peyote; commonly associated with certain Native American religious beliefs.

polygamy: Marriage to multiple partners.

polygyny: Marriage of one man to more than one woman.

polysemic: Having multiple meanings. A quality attributed to many symbols.

polytheism: See *pantheism*.

possession: A trance state in which malevolent or curative spirits enter a person's body.

primary source: Material coming from a source directly connected to a phenomenon. For example, texts authored by participants or newspaper stories published at the time of an event. Contrast to secondary sources, which are accounts, analyses, or interpretations written by later scholars or commentators.

primitive: A term used by anthropologists, especially in the past, to describe a culture lacking a written language; cultures also characterized by low-level technology, small numbers, few extra-societal contacts, and homogeneity (sometimes referred to as preliterate or nonliterate cultures).

profane: Not concerned with religion or the sacred; the ordinary.

prophet: A religious leader or teacher regarded as, or claiming to be, divinely inspired who speaks for a god.

propitiation: The act or acts of gaining the favor of spirits or deities.

psychosis: A psychological disorder sufficiently damaging that it may disrupt the work or activities of a person's life.

purdah: The seclusion of women as practiced by some Hindus and Muslims. From the Urdu language.

qadi: Judge in Islamic law or shari'a.

reciprocity: A system of repayment of goods, objects, actions, and sometimes money through which obligations are met and bonds created.

reincarnation: The belief that the soul reappears after death in another and different bodily form.

religion: A set of beliefs and practices pertaining to supernatural beings or forces.

revitalization movements: According to Anthony F. C. Wallace, a deliberate, organized, conscious effort by members of a society to construct a more satisfying culture.

rites of passage: Rituals associated with such critical changes in personal status as birth, puberty, marriage, and death.

ritual: A secular or sacred, formal, solemn act, observance, or procedure in accordance with prescribed rules or customs.

rumbim: A plant used ritually by the Tsembaga of New Guinea. Associated with a ritual period of obligations and prohibitions, at the termination of warfare.

sacred: Venerated objects and actions considered holy and entitled to reverence.

sacrifice: The ritualized offering of a person, a plant, or an animal as propitiation or in homage to the supernatural.

Santería: Cuban religion synthesizing elements from Yoruba religion in west Africa and Roman Catholicism.

sect: A small religious group with distinctive beliefs and practices that set it apart from other similar groups in the society.

secular: Not sacred or religious.

shaman: A religious specialist and healer with powers derived directly from supernatural sources.

shari'a: The body of law and legal decisions associated with Islam.

shaykh: In Arabic language, respected elder, teacher, head of tribe, or head of religious order.

society: A group of people sharing a territory, language, and culture.

sorcery: The use of magical paraphernalia by an individual to harness supernatural powers ordinarily to achieve evil ends.

soul: The immortal or spiritual part of a person believed to separate from the physical body at death.

Spiritism: A Christian movement based on the writings of Allan Kardec, in mid-19th century France, emphasizing the use of séances and mediums to communicate with the dead. Similar to English movement known as *Spiritualism*. Spiritism is currently practiced in several countries around the world, but the greatest number of adherents are in Brazil.

structuralism: An anthropological approach to the understanding of the deep, subconscious, unobservable structure of human realities that is believed to determine observable behavior (a leading exponent: Claude Lévi-Strauss).

supernatural: A force or an existence that transcends the natural.

Sutras: The sacred texts or scriptures of Buddhism.

symbol: An object, a gesture, a word, or another representation to which an arbitrary shared meaning is given.

syncretism: A process of culture change in which the traits and elements of one culture are given new meanings or new functions when they are adapted by another culture—for example, the combining of Catholicism and African religion to form Vodou.

taboo: A sacred prohibition put upon certain people, things, or acts that makes them untouchable, unmentionable, and so on (also *tabu, tabou, tapu*).

talisman: A sacred object worn to ensure good luck or to ward off evil. Also known as an amulet or a charm.

teleology: The process of being directed by an end or shaped by a purpose, especially in nature.

theocracy: Rule by religious specialists.

theology: Religious knowledge or belief; the study of god or religion, from the perspective of believers.

totem: An animal, a plant, or an object considered related to a kin group and viewed as sacred.

trance: An altered state of consciousness induced by religious fervor, fasting, repetitive movements and rhythms, drugs, and so on.

transcendence: The condition of being separate from or beyond the material world.

Txiv neeb: Hmong shaman.

'ulama: Muslim religious scholars.

'ummah: In Islam, the community of believers.

Vodou: A syncretic religion of Haiti that combines Catholicism and African religion; sometimes referred to as Tovodun or Vodun.

Wahhabism: A very conservative orientation within Islam, rejecting innovations or reinterpretations after the earliest period of the religion. Prominently associated with Saudi Arabia.

Waqf: In Islam, gift of resources for the construction or maintenance of projects beneficial to the Muslim community.

Witchcraft: An evil power inherent in certain individuals that permits them, without the use of magical charms or other paraphernalia, to do harm or cause misfortune to others.

Witnessing: In fundamentalist Christianity, engaging in persuasive conversations intended to convert others.

Zakat: In Islam, alms or charitable giving, a key obligation of the faith.

zombie: In Haiti, an individual believed to have been placed in a trancelike state through the administration of a psychotropic drug given secretly, thus bringing the victim under the control of another.

Bibliography

The following bibliography is a compilation of the lists of references or suggested readings that accompanied each article in its original publication. (In some cases, a list of references has been constructed from footnote citations in the original.) We have rendered the citations in as consistent a form as possible, but minor variations in form and content are inevitable because of the varied citation styles of the original publishers.

A few articles were not accompanied by references in their original publication and accordingly are not included here.

CHAPTER ONE
The Anthropological Study of Religion

Religion
Clifford Geertz

REFERENCES

Bettelheim, Bruno
    1954   *Symbolic Wounds: Puberty Rites and the Envious Male. Glencoe,* Ill.: Free Press.

Campbell, Joseph
    1949   *The Hero with a Thousand Faces.* New York: Pantheon.

Devereux, George
    1951   *Reality and Dream: Psychotherapy of a Plains Indian.* New York: International Universities Press.

Eliade, Mircea
    [1949] 1958   *Patterns in Comparative Religion.* New York: Sheed and Ward.

Erikson, Erik H.
    [1950] 1964   *Childhood and Society.* 2nd ed. New York: Norton.

Geertz, Clifford
    1966   "Religion as a Cultural System." In Michael Banton, ed., *Anthropological Approaches to the Study of Religion.* A.S.A.

Monograph No. 3. London: Tavistock Publications Limited.

Hallowell, A. Irving
    1955   *Culture and Experience.* Philadelphia: University of Pennsylvania Press.

Kardiner, Abram
    1945   *The Psychological Frontiers of Society.* New York: Columbia University Press.

Kluckhohn, Clyde
    1944   *Navaho Witchcraft.* Harvard University. Peabody Museum of American Archaeology and Ethnology Papers, vol. 22, no. 2. Cambridge, Mass.: The Museum.

Lang, Andrew
    [1898] 1900   *The Making of Religion.* 2nd ed. New York: Longmans.

Lessa, William A., and Evon Z. Vogt, eds.
    1965   *Reader in Comparative Religion: An Anthropological Approach.* 2nd ed. New York: Harper.

Lévi-Strauss, Claude
    [1958] 1963   *Structural Anthropology.* New York: Basic Books.
    [1962] 1966   *The Savage Mind.* University of Chicago Press.

Radcliffe-Brown, A. R.
    [1952] 1961   *Structure and Function in Primitive Societies: Essays and Addresses.* Glencoe, Ill.: Free Press.

Róheim, Geza
  1950   *Psychoanalysis and Anthropology: Culture,*
          Personality and the Unconscious. New
          York: International Universities Press.

Spier, Leslie
  1921   *The Sun Dance of the Plains Indians: Its*
          Development and Diffusion. American
          Museum of Natural History
          Anthropological Papers, vol. 16, part 7.
          New York: The Museum.

Whiting, John, and Irvin L. Child
  1953   *Child Training and Personality: A Cross-*
          Cultural Study. New York: Yale University
          Press.

Religious Perspectives in Anthropology
Dorothy Lee

REFERENCES

Barton, R. F.
  1946   *The Religion of the Ifugao.* In American
          Anthropological Association *Memoirs,*
          no. 65.

Black Elk
  1932   *Black Elk Speaks. Being the Life Story of a*
          Holy Man of the Oglala Sioux, as Told to
          John G. Neihardt (Flaming Rainbow). New
          York: William Morrow.

Brown, Joseph Epes
  1953   *The Sacred Pipe: Black Elk's Account of the*
          Seven Rites of the Oglala Sioux. Norman:
          University of Oklahoma Press.

Firth, Raymond
  1940   *The Work of the Gods in Tikopia.* London:
          Lund, Humphries.
  1950   *Primitive Polynesian Economy.* New York:
          Humanities Press.

Henry, Jules
  1941   *Jungle People.* New York: J. J. Augustin.

Redfield, Robert, and W. Lloyd Warner
  1940   "Cultural Anthropology and Modern
          Agriculture." In *Farmers in a Changing*
          World, 1940 Yearbook of Agriculture.
          Washington, D.C.: United States
          Government Printing Office.

Thompson, Laura
  1946   *The Hopi Crisis: Report to Administrators.*
          (Mimeographed.)

Vanoverbergh, Morice
  1936   *The Isneg Life Cycle.* Publication of the
          Catholic Anthropological Conference,
          vol. 3, no. 2.

Anthropologists Versus Missionaries: The Influence of Presuppositions
Claude E. Stipe

REFERENCES

Bennett, John W.
  1946   "The Interpretation of Pueblo Culture: A
          Question of Values." *Southwestern Journal*
          of Anthropology 2: 361–74.

Boutilier, James A., Daniel T. Hughes, and Sharon
          W. Tiffany, eds.
  1978   *Mission, Church, and sect in Oceania.*
          Ann Arbor: University of Michigan
          Press.

Burridge, Kenelm O.L.
  1978   "Introduction: Missionary Occasions."
          In J. A. Boutilier, D. T. Hughes, and
          S. Tiffany, eds., *Mission, Church, and Sect*
          in Oceania, pp. 1–30. Ann Arbor:
          University of Michigan Press.

Chagnon, Napoleon A.
  1967   "Yanomamö: The Fierce People." *Natural*
          History 78: 22–31.
  1974   *Studying the Yanomamö.* New York: Holt,
          Rinehart and Winston.

Codrington, R. H.
  1891   *The Melanesians: Studies in Their*
          Anthropology and Folklore. Oxford:
          Clarendon Press.

Colson, Elizabeth
  1976   "Culture and Progress." *American*
          Anthropologist 78: 261–71.

Ember, Carol R., and Melvin Ember
  1977   *Cultural Anthropology.* 2nd ed. Englewood
          Cliffs, N.J.: Prentice Hall.

Evans-Pritchard, E. E.
  1965   *Theories of Primitive Religion.* London:
          Oxford University Press.

1972   "Religion and the Anthropologists." *Practical Anthropology* 19: 193–206. (Originally published in *Blackfriars* 41 [April 1960]: 104–18.)

Forman, Charles W.
1978   "Foreign Missionaries in the Pacific Islands During the 20th Century." In J. A. Boutilier, D. T. Hughes, and S. Tiffany, eds., *Mission, Church, and Sect in Oceania*, p. 35–63. Ann Arbor: University of Michigan Press.

Fortune, Reo
1963   *Sorcerers of Dobu*, New York: Dutton.

Geertz, Clifford.
1966   "Religion as a Cultural System." In Michael Banton, ed., *Anthropological Approaches to the Study of Religion*, pp. 1–46. New York: Praeger.

Gluckman, Max
1962   "Les rites de passage." In Max Gluckman, ed., *Essays on the Ritual of Social Relations*, pp. 1–52. Manchester: University of Manchester Press.

Graburn, Nelson K. H.
1969   *Eskimos Without Igloos: Social and Economic Development in Sugluk*. New York: Little, Brown.

Hill, W. W.
1944   "The Navaho Indians and the Ghost Dance of 1890." *American Anthropologist* 46: 523–27.

Hippler, Arthur E.
1974   "Some Alternative Viewpoints on the Negative Results of Euro-American Contact with Non-Western Groups." *American Anthropologist* 76: 334–37.

Hogbin, Ian
1964   *A Guadalcanal Society: The Koaka-Speakers*. New York: Holt, Rinehart and Winston.

Horton, Robin
1971   "African Conversion." *Africa* 41: 85–108.

Hughes, Daniel T.
1978   "Mutual Biases of Anthropologists and Missionaries." In J. A. Boutilier, D. T. Hughes, and S. Tiffany, eds., *Mission, church, and Sect in Oceania*, pp. 65–82. Ann Arbor: University of Michigan Press.

Jocano, F. Landa
1969   *Growing Up in a Philippine Barrio*. New York: Holt, Rinehart and Winston.

Keesing, Roger M.
1976   *Cultural Anthropology: A Contemporary Perspective*. New York: Holt, Rinehart and Winston.

Kopytoff, Igor
1964   "Classifications of Religious Movements: Analytic and Synthetic." In June Helm, ed., *Symposium on New Approaches to the Study of Religion*, pp. 77–90. Seattle: University of Washington Press.

Latukefu, Sione
1978   "Conclusion: Retrospect and Prospect." In J. A. Boutilier, D. T. Hughes, and S. Tiffany, eds., *Mission, Church, and Sect in Oceania*, pp. 457–64. Ann Arbor: University of Michigan Press.

Lawrence, Peter
1964   *Road Belong Cargo: A Study of the Cargo Movement in the Southern Madang District of New Guinea*. Manchester: University of Manchester Press.
1970   "Daughter of Time." In T. G. Harding and B. J. Wallace, eds., *Cultures of the Pacific: Selected Readings*, pp. 267–84 New York: Free Press.

Leach, E. R.
1954   *Political Structures of Highland Burma: A Study of Kachin Social Structure*. London: G. Bell.

Lewis, Diane
1973   "Anthropology and Colonialism." *Current Anthropology* 14: 581–91.

Lowie, Robert H.
1963   "Religion in Human Life." *American Anthropologist* 65: 532–42.

Middleton, John
1970   *The Study of the Lugbara: Expectation and Paradox in Anthropological Research*. New York: Holt, Rinehart and Winston.

Miller, Elmer S.
1975   "Shamans, Power Symbols, and Change in Argentine Toba Culture." *American Ethnologist* 2; 477–96.

O'Brien, Denise, and Anton Ploeg
1964 "Acculturation Movements Among the Western Dani." *American Anthropologist* 66, no. 2, part 2: 281–92.

Osborne, Kenneth B.
1970 "A Christian Graveyard Cult in the New Guinea Highlands." *Practical Anthropology* 17: 10–15.

Peel, J. D. Y.
1968 *Aladura: A Religious Movement Among the Yoruba.* London: Oxford University Press.

Powdermaker, Hortense
1966 *Stranger and Friend: The Way of an Anthropologist.* New York: W. W. Norton.

Radcliffe-Brown, A. R.
1952 "Religion and Society." In A. R. Radcliffe-Brown, ed., *Structure and Function in Primitive Society,* pp. 153–77. New York: Free Press.

Ribeiro, René
1962 "Brazilian Messianic Movements." In S. L. Thrupp, ed., *Millennial Dreams in Action,* pp. 55–69. The Hague: Mouton.

Richards, Cara E.
1977 *People in Perspective: An Introduction to Cultural Anthropology.* 2nd ed. New York: Random House.

Richardson, Miles
1975 "Anthropologist—the Myth Teller." *American Ethnologist* 2: 517–33.

Salamone, Frank A.
1976 "Learning to Be a Christian: A Comparative Study." *Missiology* 4: 53–64.
1977 "Anthropologists and Missionaries: Competition or Reciprocity?" *Human Organization* 36: 407–12.
1979 "Epistemological Implications of Fieldwork and Their Consequences." *American Anthropologist* 81: 46–60.

Tiffany, Sharon W.
1978 "Introduction to Part 4: Indigenous Response." In J. A. Boutilier, D. T. Hughes, and S. Tiffany, eds., *Mission, Church, and Sect in Oceania,* pp. 301–5. Ann Arbor: University of Michigan Press.

Tonkinson, Robert
1974 *The Jigalong Mob: Aboriginal Victors of the Desert Crusade.* Menlo Park, Calif.: Cummings.

Turnbull, Colin
1961 *The Forest People: A Study of the Pygmies of the Congo.* Garden City, N.Y.: Doubleday.

Wallace, A. F. C.
1970 *The Death and Rebirth of the Seneca.* New York: Random House/Vintage Books.

Thai Buddhism and the Popularity of Amulets in Anthropological Perspective
Pamela Moro

REFERENCES

Asad, Talal
1993 "The Construction of Religion as an Anthropological Category." In *Geneaologies of Religion: Discipline and Reasons of Power in Christianity and Islam.* Baltimore: The Johns Hopkins University Press, pp. 27–54.

Bowie, Katherine Ann
1997 *Rituals of National Loyalty: An Anthropology of the State and the Village Scout Movement in Thailand.* NY: Columbia University Press.

Budge, E. A. Wallis
1961 *Amulets and Talismans.* New Hyde Park, NY: University Books. (Originally published in 1911.)

CIA World Factbook
2009 www.cia.gov/library/publications/the-world-factbook/index.html, accessed February 14.

Daniels, Inge Maria
2003 "Scooping, Raking, Beckoning Luck: Luck, Agency and the Interdependence of People and Things in Japan." *Journal of the Royal Anthropological Institute* 9(4):619–638.

Frazer, James
1922 *The Golden Bough: A Study in Magic and Religion.* NY: The Macmillan Company.

Gaster, Theodor H.
  2005 "Amulets and Talismans." In *Encyclopedia of Religion*, ed. Lindsay Jones. 2nd ed. Detroit: Thomson Gale, pp. 297–301.

GreenwichMeanTime.com
  2009 www.greenwichmeantime.com/ timezone/usa/websites/business/ franchise/7-eleven/accessed February 19.

Head, Jonathan
  2007 "Thailand's Frenzy for Amulets," BBC News. http://newsvote.bbc.co.uk/ mpapps/pagetools/print/news.bbc.co .uk/2/hi/asia-pacific/6976705.stm, March 3. Accessed January 24, 2009.

Japan News Review
  2007 "7-Eleven World's Largest Chain Store," July 12. www.webcitation.org/ 5dsuOCKUU, accessed February 19, 2009.

Klima, Alan
  2002 *The Funeral Casino: Meditation, Massacre, and Encounters with the Dead in Thailand*. Princeton: Princeton University Press.

Long, Carolyn Morrow
  2001 *Spiritual Merchants: Religion, Magic, and Commerce*. Knoxville: University of Tennessee Press.

Lopez, Donald S.
  1998 *Prisoners of Shangri-La: Tibetan Buddhism and the West*. Chicago: University of Chicago Press.

Morell, David, and Chai-ana, Samudavanija
  1981 *Political Conflict in Thailand: Reform, Reaction, and Revolution*. Cambridge, MA: Oelgeschlager, Gunn & Hain, Publishers.

Morris, Brian
  2006 *Religion and Anthropology: A Critical Introduction*. NY: Cambridge University Press.

Morris, Desmond
  1999 *Body Guards: Protective Amulets and Charms*. Shaftesbury, Dorset: Element.

Morris, Rosalind C.
  2000 *In the Place of Origins: Modernity and Its Mediums in Northern Thailand*. Duke, NC: Duke University Press.

Mulder, Niels
  1985 *Everyday Life in Thailand: An Interpretation*. 2nd ed. Bangkok: Editions Duang Kamol.

Paine, Sheila
  2004 *Amulets: Sacred Charms of Power and Protection*. Rochester, VT: Inner Traditions.

Rajadhon, Phya Anuman
  1968 "Thai Charms and Amulets." In *Essays on Thai Folklore*. Bangkok: Editions Duang Kamol, pp. 268–95.

Redfield, Robert
  1956 *Peasant Society and Culture*. Chicago: University of Chicago Press.

Singer, Milton
  1970 *When a Great Tradition Modernizes: An Anthropological Approach to Indian Civilization*. Chicago: University of Chicago Press.

Spiro, Melford E.
  1982 *Buddhism and Society: A Great Tradition and Its Burmese Vicissitudes*. 2nd ed. Berkeley: University of California Press. (First edition published in 1970.)

Tambiah, Stanley Jeyaraja
  1984 *The Buddhist Saints of the Forest and the Cult of Amulets*. Cambridge and NY: Cambridge University Press.

Taylor, James
  2008 *Buddhism and Postmodern Imaginings in Thailand: The Religiosity of Urban Space*. Burlington, VT: Ashgate.

Terwiel, B. J.
  1975 *Monks and Magic: An Analysis of Religious Ceremonies in Central Thailand*. Lund, Sweden: Studentlitteratur.

Wikipedia, the Free Encyclopedia
  2009 "7-Eleven." http://en.wikipedia.org/wiki/7-Eleven. Accessed February 17.

CHAPTER TWO
Myth, Symbolism, and Taboo

The Study of Mythology
Scott Leonard and Michael McClure

REFERENCES

Boas, Franz
  [1928] 1986 *Anthropology and Modern Life*. New York: Dover.

Bolen, Jean Shinoda
    1985   *Goddesses in Every Woman*. New York: Harper and Row.

Campbell, Joseph
    [1949] 1972   *The Hero with a Thousand Faces*. Princeton, N.J.: Princeton University Press.
    1959   *The Masks of God*. Vol. 1: *Primitive Mythology*. New York: Viking.
    1962   *The Masks of God*. Vol. 2: *Oriental Mythology*. New York: Viking.
    1964   *The Masks of God*. Vol. 3: *Occidental Mythology*. New York: Viking.
    1968   *The Masks of God*. Vol. 4: *Creative Mythology*. New York: Viking.
    1972   *Myths to Live By*. New York: Viking.

Campbell, Joseph, with Bill Moyers
    1985   *The Power of Myth*. New York: Doubleday.

Doniger, Wendy
    1998   *The Implied Spider: Politics and Theology in Myth*. New York: Columbia University Press.

Doty, William G.
    2000   *Mythography: The Study of Myths and Rituals*. 2nd ed. Tuscaloosa: University of Alabama Press.

Durkheim, Émile, and Marcell Mauss
    1963   *Primitive Classification*. Trans. Rodney Needham. Chicago: University of Chicago Press.

Eliade, Mircea
    1974   *Patterns in Comparative Religion*. New York: New American Library.
    1975   *Myth and Reality*. New York: Harper and Row.
    1975   *Myths, Dreams, and Mysteries*. New York: Harper and Row.
    1983   *The Sacred and the Profane*. Magnolia, Mass.: Peter Smith.
    1985   *Cosmos and History: The Myth of the Eternal Return*. New York: Garland.

Ellwood, Robert
    1999   *The Politics of Myth: A Study of C. G. Jung, Mircea Eliade, and Joseph Campbell*. Issues in the Study of Religion series. Albany: State University of New York.

Fontenrose, Joseph
    1971   *The Ritual Theory of Myth*. Berkeley: University of California Press.

Frazer, James George
    1922   *The Golden Bough*. Abridged ed. London: Macmillan.

Freud, Sigmund
    1900   *The Interpretation of Dreams*. London.
    1918   *Totem and Taboo*. New York.
    1953–66   *The Standard Edition of the Complete Psychological Works of Sigmund Freud*. London: Hogarth.

Jung, Carl Gustav
    [1959] 1980   *The Archetypes and the Collective Unconscious*. Bollingen Series 20. Princeton, N.J.: Princeton University Press.
    [1964] 1988   *Man and His Symbols*. New York: Doubleday.

Kirk, Geoffrey Stephen
    1970   *Myth: Its Meaning and Functions in Ancient and Other Cultures*. Berkeley: University of California Press.

Lévi-Strauss, Claude
    1979   *Myth and Meaning*. New York: Schocken/Pantheon.
    [1981] 1990   *The Naked Man*. Trans. John and Doreen Weightman. Chicago: University of Chicago Press.
    1990   *The Raw and the Cooked*. Trans. John and Doreen Weightman. Chicago: University of Chicago Press.

Lincoln, Bruce
    1999   *Theorizing Myth: Narrative, Ideology, and Scholarship*. Chicago: University of Chicago Press.

Malinowski, Bronislaw
    [1926] 1971   *Myth in Primitive Psychology*. Westport, Conn.: Negro Universities Press.

Propp, Vladimir
    [1968] 1990   *Morphology of the Folktale*. Trans. Laurence Scott. Austin: University of Texas Press.

Scholes, Robert
    1974   *Structuralism in Literature: An Introduction.*
            New Haven, Conn.: Yale University
            Press.

Segal, Robert A.
    1996   *Theories of Myth: From Ancient Israel and
            Greece to Freud, Jung, Campbell, and Lévi-
            Strauss.* Philosophy, Religious Studies,
            and Myth Series, vol. 3. New York:
            Garland Press.

The Virgin of Guadalupe: A Mexican National Symbol

Eric R. Wolf

REFERENCES

Amaya, Jesus
    1931   *La madre de Dios: genesis e historia de
            nuestra señora de Guadalupe,* p. 230.
            Mexico.

Bermúdez, María Elvira
    1955   *La vida familiar del mexicano,* chaps. 2, 3.
            Mexico.

Bushnell, John
    1955   "La Virgen de Guadalupe as Surrogate
            Mother in San Juan Atzingo," Paper read
            before the 54th Annual Meeting of the
            American Anthropological Association,
            18 November.

Chevalier, François
    1952   *La formation des grands domains au
            Mexique,* p. xii. Paris.

Echánove Trujillo, Carlos A.
    1948   *Sociologia mexicana,* p. 105. Mexico.

Gillin, John
    1952   "Ethos and Cultural Aspects of
            Personality." In Sol Tax, ed., *Heritage of
            Conquest,* pp. 193–212.

González y González, Luis
    1948   "El optimismo nacionalista como factor
            en la independencia de México." *Estudios
            de historiografia Americana,* p. 194. Mexico.

Gruening, Ernest
    1928   *Mexico and Its Heritage,* p. 235. New York.

Hewes, Gordon W.
    1954   "Mexicans in Search of the 'Mexican.'"
            In *American Journal of Economics and
            Sociology,* XIII, 209–223.

León, Nicolas
    1924   *Las castas del México colonial o Nueva
            España.* Mexico.

Mackay, John A.
    1933   *The Other Spanish Christ,* pp. 110–17.
            New York.

Mandelbaum, David G.
    1953   "On the Study of National Character."
            American Anthropologist, LVII, p. 185.

Marshall, C. E.
    1939   "The Birth of the Mestizo in New Spain."
            Hispanic American Historical Review, XIX,
            161–84.

de la Maza, Francisco
    1953   *El guadalupismo mexicano,* pp. 12–14, 30,
            33, 39–40, 41, 43–49, 64, 82, 143. Mexico.

Northrup, F. S. C.
    1953   *The Meeting of East and West,* p. 25.
            New York.

Paz, Octavio
    1947   *El laberinto de la soledad,* pp. 71–89.
            Mexico.

Pompa y Pompa, Antonio
    1938   *Album del IV centario guadalupano,* p. 173.
            Mexico.

Redfield, Robert, and Sol Tax
    1952   "General Characteristics of Present-Day
            Mesoamerican Indian Society." In Sol
            Tax, ed., *Heritage of Conquest,* pp. 31–39.
            Glencoe.

de Sahagún, Bernardino
    1938   *Historia general de las cosas de nueva españa,* I,
            lib. 6. Mexico.

Simpson, Lesley B.
    1953   "Mexico's Forgotten Century." *Pacific
            Historical Review,* XXII, 114, 115.

Tannanebaum, Frank
    1933   *Peace by Revolution,* p. 39. New York.

Torres Quintero
    1921   *México hacía el fin del virreinato español.*
            Mexico.

Villoro, Luis
    1950   *Los grandes momentos del indigenismo en México*, pp. 131–38. Mexico.

Wolf, Eric R.
    1955   "The Mexican Bajio in the Eighteenth Century." *Middle American Research Institute Publication* XVII, pp. 180–99.
    1956   "Aspects of Group Relations in a Complex Society: Mexico." *American Anthropologist*, LVII, 1065–78.
    "La formación de la nación." *Ciencias Sociales*, IV, 50–51, 103–106.

de Zamacois, Niceto
    1878–   *Historia de México,* VI, 253.
    82   Barcelona-Mexico.

Zavala, Silvio
    1947   *La filosofia en la conquista de America.* Mexico.

Taboo
Mary Douglas

REFERENCES

Douglas, Mary
    1966   *Purity and Danger.* New York: Frederick A. Praeger.

Steiner, Franz
    [1956] 1967   *Taboo.* London: Penguin.

CHAPTER THREE
Ritual

Betwixt and Between: The Liminal Period in *Rites de Passage*
Victor W. Turner

REFERENCES

Bettelheim, Bruno
    1954   *Symbolic Wounds, Puberty Rites and the Envious Male.* New York: Free Press.

Douglas, Mary
    1966   *Purity and Danger*. London: Routledge and Kegan Paul.

Elwin, Verrier
    1955   *The Religion of an Indian Tribe.* London: Geoffrey Cumberlege.

Harrison, Jane
    1903   *Prolegomena to the Study of Greek Religion.* London: Cambridge University Press.

Hocart, A. M.
    1952   *The Life-Giving Myth.* London: Methuen and Co.

James, William
    1918   *Principles of Psychology.* Vol. 1. New York: H. Holt.

Kuper, Hilda
    1947   *An African Aristocracy.* London: Oxford University Press.

McCulloch, J. A.
    1913   "Monsters," in *Hastings Encyclopaedia of Religion and Ethics.* Edinburgh: T. and T. Clark.

Richards, A.
    1956   *Chisungu.* London: Faber and Faber.

Turner, Victor
    1962   "Chihamba, the White Spirit." *Rhodes-Livingstone Papers*, no. 33. Manchester.

Warner, Lloyd
    1959   *The Living and the Dead: A Study of the Symbolic Life of Americans.* New Haven, Conn.: Yale University Press.

"I Bow My Head to the Ground": Creating Bodily Experience Through Initiation
Michael Atwood Mason

REFERENCES

Abrahams, Roger
    1977   "Toward an Enactment-Centered Theory of Folklore," in W. Bascom, ed., *Frontiers of Folklore*, pp. 79–120. Boulder: Westview Press.

Bascom, William
    1991   *Ifá Divination: Communication Between Gods and Men in West Africa.* Bloomington: Indiana University Press.

Bauman, Richard
  1977   *Verbal Art as Performance*. Prospect
          Heights, IL: Waveland Press.
  1986   *Story, Performance, and Event: Contextual
          Studies of Oral Narrative*. Cambridge:
          Cambridge University Press.

Bourdieu, Pierre
  1989   *Outline of a Theory of Practice*. Cambridge:
          Cambridge University Press. (Originally
          published 1977.)

Brandon, George
  1983   *The Dead Sell Memories*. Ann Arbor:
          University Microfilms International.

Brown, David
  1989   *Garden in the Machine: Afro-Cuban Sacred
          Art and Performance in Urban New Jersey
          and New York*. Ph.D. dissertation, Yale
          University.

Cabrera, Lydia
  1980   *Yemayá y Ochún*. Miami: Colección del
          Chicherekú en el exilio.

Carter, George
  1990   Telephone interview with the author,
          Bloomington, Ind., and Washington D.C.,
          7 December.

Comaroff, Jean
  1985   *Body of Power, Spirit of Resistance*. Chicago:
          University of Chicago Press.

Cowan, Jane
  1990   *Dance and the Body Politic in Northern Greece*.
          Princeton: Princeton University Press.

Douglas, Mary
  1978   *Implicit Meanings: Essays in Anthropology*.
          London: Routledge & Kegan Paul.

Ecún, Obá
  1985   *Oricha: Metodología de la religion Yoruba*.
          Miami: Editorial SIBI.

Ekman, Paul
  1977   "Biological and Cultural Contributions
          to Body and Facial Movement," in J.
          Blacking, ed., *Anthropology of the Body*,
          pp. 39–84. New York: Academic Press.

Feher, Michael
  1989   "Introduction to Fragments of
          a History of the Human Body."
          Zone 3:10–17.

Flores, Ysamur
  1990   "Fit for the Queen: A Consecration Outfit
          for Yemayá." *Folklore Forum* 23:47–56.

Friedman, Robert
  1982   Making an Abstract World Concrete:
          Knowledge Competence, and Structural
          Dimensions of Performance among Batá
          drummers in Santeria. Ph.D. dissertation,
          Indiana University.

Glassner, Barry
  1990   "Fit for Postmodern Selfhood." In H.
          Becker and M. McCall, eds., *Symbolic
          Interaction and Cultural Studies*, pp. 215–43.
          Chickgo: University of Chicago Press.

González, P.
  1992   Interview with the author, Hyattsville, Md.,
          13 December.

Gregory, S.
  1986   *Santería in New York City*. Ann Arbor:
          University Microfilms International.

Hanks, William
  1984   "Sanctification, Structure, and Experience
          in a Yucatec Ritual Event." *Journal of
          American Folklore* 97: 131–66.

Hymes, Dell
  1974   *Foundations in Sociolinguistics: An
          Ethnographic Approach*. Philadelphia:
          University of Pennsylvania Press.

Jackson, Michael
  1989   *Paths toward a Clearing: Radical
          Empiricism and Ethnographic Inquiry*.
          Bloomington: Indiana University
          Press.

MacAloon, John
  1984a   "Introduction." In J. MacAloon, ed., *Rite,
          Drama, Festival, Spectacle: Rehearsals
          toward a Theory of Cultural Performances*,
          pp. 1–18. Philadelphia: Institute for the
          Study of Human Issues.
  1984b   "Olympic Games and the Theory of
          Spectacle in Modern Societies." In
          J. MacAloon, ed., *Rite Drama, Festival,
          Spectacle: Rehearsals toward a Theory of
          Cultural Performances*, pp. 240–80.
          Philadelphia: Institute for the Study of
          Human Issues.

Mauss, Marcel
1973 "Techniques of the Body." *Economy and Society* 2:70–88.

McArthur, Phillip
1989 "Competence in Performance: A Critical Review." *Folklore Forum* 22:113–18.

Mead, George Herbert
1938 *The Philosophy of the Act*. Chicago: University of Chicago Press.

Munn, Nancy
1973 "Symbolism in a Ritual Context: Aspects of Symbolic Action." In J. Honigmann, ed., *The Handbook of Social and Cultural Anthropology*, pp. 579–612. Chicago: Rand McNally College Publishing.

Murphy, Joseph
1981 "Ritual Systems in Cuban Santería." Ph.D. dissertation, Temple University.
1988 *Santería: An African Religion in America*. Boston: Beacon Press.

Myerhoff, Barbara
1984 "A death in Due Time: Construction of Self and Culture in a Ritual Drama." In J. MacAloon, ed., *Rite, Drama, Festival Spectacle: Rehearsals toward a Theory of Cultural Performances*, pp. 149–78. Philadelphia: Institute for the Study of Human Issues.

Poole, Roger
1975 "Objective Sign and Subjective Meaning." In J. Benthall and J. Polhemus, eds., *The Body as a Medium of Expression*, pp. 74–106. London: Allen Lane.

Rappaport, Roy
1989 "Ritual." In E. Barnouw, ed., *International Encyclopedia of Communications*, vol. 3, pp. 467–73. New York: Oxford University Press.

Rogers, Andres
1973 *Los Caracoles*. Washington D.C.: RICO Publishing.

Stoeltje, Beverly
1988 "Gender Representations in Performance: The Cowgirl and the Hostess." *Journal of Folklore Research* 25:141–53.

Stoeltje, Beverly, and Richard Bauman
1989 "Community Festival and the Enactment of Modernity." In R. Walls and G. Schoemaker, eds., *The Old Traditional Way of Life: Essays in Honor of Warren Roberts*, pp. 159–71. Bloomington, Ind.: Trickster Press.

Turner, Bryan
1984 *The Body and Society*. Oxford: Basil Blackwell.

Turner, Victor
1967 *The Forest of Symbols*. Ithaca, NY: Cornell University Press.
1969 *The Ritual Process*: Structure and Anti-Structure. Ithaca, NY: Cornell University Press.

Van Gennep, Arnold
1909 *The Rites of Passage*. London: Routledge and Kegan Paul.

Wafer, Jim
1991 *The Taste of Blood: Spirit Possession in Brazilian Candomblé*. Philadelphia: University of Pennsylvania Press.

Return to Wirikuta: Ritual Reversal and Symbolic Continuity on the Peyote Hunt of the Huichol Indians
Barbara G. Myerhoff

REFERENCES

Eliade, Mircea
1960 "The Yearning for Paradise in Primitive Tradition." In H. A. Murray, ed., *Myth and Mythmaking*, pp. 61–75. New York: Braziller.
1962 *The Two and the One*. New York: Harper Torchbooks.
1964 *Shamanism: Archaic Techniques of Ecstasy*. Trans. W. R. Trask. Bollingen Series LXXVI. New York: Pantheon.

Graves, Robert, and Raphael Patai
1966 *Hebrew Myths: The Book of Genesis*. New York: McGraw-Hill.

Guillaumont, A., et al., trans.
1959 *The Gospel According to Thomas*. New York: Harper.

Middleton, John
　1960　*Lugbara Religion: Ritual and Authority Among an East African People*. London: Oxford University Press.
　1974　*Peyote Hunt: The Sacred Journey of the Huichol Indians*. Ithaca, N.Y.: Cornell University Press.

Neumann, Erich
　1954　*The Origins and History of Consciousness*. New York: Bollingen.

Watts, Alan W.
　1970　*The Two Hands of God: The Myths of Polarity*. New York: Collier.

Ritual Regulation of Environmental Regulations Among a New Guinea People
Roy A. Rappaport

REFERENCES

Berg, C.
　1948　"Protein Deficiency and Its Relation to Nutritional Anemia, Hypoproteinemia, Nutritional Edema, and Resistance to Infection." In M. Sahyun, ed., *Protein and Amino Acids in Nutrition*, pp. 290–317. New York: Reinhold.

Burton, B. T., ed.
　1959　*The Heinz Handbook of Nutrition*. New York: McGraw-Hill.

Elman, R.
　1951　*Surgical Care*. New York: Appleton-Century-Crofts.

Food and Agriculture Organization of the United Nations.
　1964　"Protein: At the Heart of the World Food Problem." *World Food Problems* 5. Rome: FAO.

Homans, G. C.
　1941　"Anxiety and Ritual: The Theories of Malinowski and Radcliffe-Brown." *American Anthropologist* 43: 164–72.

Houssay, B. A., et al.
　1955　*Human Physiology*. 2nd ed. New York: McGraw-Hill.

Large, A., and C. G. Johnston
　1948　"Proteins as Related to Burns." In M. Sahyun, ed., *Proteins and Amino Acids in Nutrition*, pp. 386–96. New York: Reinhold.

Lund, C. G., and S. M. Levenson
　1948　"Protein Nutrition in Surgical Patients." In M. Sahyun, ed., *Proteins and Amino Acids in Nutrition*, pp. 349–63. New York: Reinhold.

Moore, O. K.
　1957　"Divination—a New Perspective." *American Anthropologist* 59: 69–74.

National Research Council
　1963　*Evaluation of Protein Quality*. National Academy of Sciences—National Research Council Publication 1100. Washington, D.C.: NAS/NRC.

Vayda, A. P., A. Leeds, and D. B. Smith
　1961　"The Place of Pigs in Melanesian Subsistence." In V. E. Garfield, ed., *Proceedings of the 1961 Annual Spring Meeting of the American Ethnological Society*, pp. 69–77. Seattle: University of Washington Press.

Wayne-Edwards, V. C.
　1962　*Animal Dispersion in Relation to Social Behaviour*. Edinburgh and London: Oliver & Boyd.

Zintel, Harold A.
　1964　"Nutrition in the Care of the Surgical Patient." In M. G. Wohl and R. S. Goodhart, eds., *Modern Nutrition in Health and Disease*, 3rd ed. pp. 1043–64. Philadelphia: Lee & Febiger.

A Handmaid's Tale: The Rhetoric of Personhood in American and Japanese Healing of Abortions
Thomas J. Csordas

REFERENCES

Blacker, Carmen
　1989　"The Seer as Healer in Japan." In *The Seer in Celtic and Other Traditions*, ed. Hilda Ellis Davidson, pp. 116–23. Edinburgh: John Donald.

Csordas [Chordas], Thomas J.
1994   *The Sacred Self: A Cultural Phenomenology of Charismatic Healing.* Berkeley: University of California Press.
1977   *Language, Charisma, and Creativity: The Ritual Life of a Religious Movement.* Berkeley: University of California Press.

Dieterlin, Germaine
1971   "L'Image du Corps et les Compsantes de la Personne chez les Dogon." In *La Notion de Personne en Afrique Noir,* ed. Germaine Dieterlin, pp. 205–29. Paris: Editions du Centre National de la Recherche Scientifique.

Fogelson, Raymond D.
1982   "Person, Self, and Identity: Some Anthropological Retrospects, Circumspects and Prospects." In *Psychosocial Theories of the Self,* ed. Benjamin Lee, pp. 67–109. NY: Plenum Press.

Fortes, Meyer
1987   "The Concept of the Person." In *Religion, Morality, and the Person: Essays on Tallensi Religion,* ed. Meyer Fortes. Cambridge: Cambridge University Press.

Ginsburg, Faye
1989   *Contested Lives: The Abortion Debate in an American Community.* Berkeley: University of California Press.

LaFleur, William R.
1992   *Liquid Life: Abortion and Buddhism in Japan.* Princeton: Princeton University Press.

Layne, Linda
1992   "Of Fetuses and Angels: Fragmentation and Integration in Narratives of Pregnancy Loss." *Knowledge and Society* 9: 29–58.

Linn, Matthew, Dennis Linn, and Sheila Fabricant
1985   *Healing the Greatest Hurt.* NY: Paulist Press.

McCall, Kenneth
1982   *Healing the Family Tree.* London: Sheldon Press.

McGuire, Meredith
1982   *Pentecostal Catholics: Power, Charisma, and Order in a Religious Movement.* Philadelphia: Temple University Press.

1983   "Words of Power: Personal Empowerment and Healing." *Culture, Medicine, and Psychiatry* 7: 221–40.

Morgan, Lynn
1989   "When Does Life Begin: A Cross-cultural Perspective on the Personhood of Fetuses and Young Children." In *Abortion Rights and Fetal "Personhood,"* eds. Ed Doerr and James Prescott. NY: Centerline Press and American for Religious Liberty.

Picone, Mary J.
1986   "Buddhist Popular Manuals and the Contemporary Commercialization of Religion in Japan." In *Interpreting Japanese Society: Anthropological Approaches,* ed. Joy Hendry and Jonathen Webber, pp. 157–65. Oxford: Oxford University Press.

Scheper-Hughes, Nancy
1990   "Mother Love and Child Death in Northeast Brazil." In *Cultural Psychology: Essays on Comparative Human Development,* eds., J. Stigler, R. Shweder, and C. Herdt, pp. 542–65. Cambridge: Cambridge University Press.

Straus, Anne S.
1977   "Northern Cheyenne Ethnopsychology." *Ethos* 5(3): 326–57.

Werblowsky, R. J. Zwi
1991   "Mizuko Kuyo: Notulae on the Most Important 'New Religion' of Japan." *Japanese Journal of Religious Studies* 18: 295–354.

Body Ritual Among the Nacirema
Horace Miner

REFERENCES

Linton, Ralph
1936   *The Study of Man.* New York: D. Appleton-Century Co.

Malinowski, Bronislaw
1948   *Magic, Science, and Religion.* Glencoe: Free Press.

Murdock, George P.
    1949   *Social Structure*. New York: Macmillan.

CHAPTER FOUR
Shamans, Priests, and Prophets

Religious Specialists
Victor W. Turner

REFERENCES

Buber, Martin
    [1936] 1958   *I and Thou*. 2nd ed. New York: Scribner.

Callaway, Henry
    1885   *The Religious System of the Amazulu*. Folklore Society Publication No. 15. London: Trubner.

Durkheim, Emile
    [1893] 1960   *The Division of Labor in Society*. Glencoe, Ill.: Free Press.

Elwin, Verrier
    1955   *The Religion of an Indian Tribe*. Bombay: Oxford University Press.

Evans-Pritchard, E. E.
    [1949] 1954   *The Sanusi of Cyrenaica*. Oxford: Clarendon Press.
    [1956] 1962   *Nuer Religion*. Oxford: Clarendon Press.

Firth, R. W.
    1964a   "Shaman." In Julius Gould and William L. Kolb, eds., *A Dictionary of the Social Sciences*, pp. 638–39. New York: Free Press.
    1964b   "Spirit Mediumship." In Julius Gould and W. L. Kolb, eds., *Dictionary of the Social Sciences*, p. 689. New York: Free Press.

Gelfand, Michael
    1964   *Witch Doctor: Traditional Medicine Man of Rhodesia*. London: Harvill.

Herskovits, Melville J.
    1938   *Dahomey: An Ancient West African Kingdom*. 2 vols. New York: Harvill.

Howells, William W.
    1948   *The Heathens: Primitive Man and His Religions*. Garden City, N.Y.: Doubleday.

Knox, Ronald A.
    1950   *Enthusiasm: A Chapter in the History of Religion; With Special Reference to the XVII and XVIII Centuries*. New York: Oxford University Press.

Lessa, William A., and Evon Z. Vogt, eds.
    [1958] 1965   *Reader in Comparative Religion: An Anthropological Approach*. New York: Harper.

Lowie, Robert H.
    1954   *Indians of the Plains*. American Museum of Natural History, Anthropological Handbook No. 1. New York: McGraw-Hill.

Nadel, Siegfried F.
    1954   *Nupe Religion*. London: Routledge.

Parrinder, Edward G.
    1954   *African Traditional Religion*. London: Hutchinson's University Library.

Parsons, Talcott
    1963   "Introduction." In Max Weber, *The Sociology of Religion*. Boston: Beacon.

Piddington, Ralph
    1950   *Introduction to Social Anthropology*. 2 vols. New York: Fredrick A. Praeger.

Richards, Audrey I.
    [1940] 1961   "The Political System of the Bembe Tribe: Northeastern Rhodesia." In Meyer Fortes and E. E. Evans-Pritchard, eds., *African Political Systems*. New York: Oxford University Press.

Wach, Joachim
    1958   *The Comparative Study of Religions*. New York: Columbia University Press.

Weber, Max
    [1922] 1963   *The Sociology of Religion*. Boston: Beacon.

Worsley, P. M.
    1957a   "Millenarian Movements in Melanesia." *Rhodes-Livingstone Journal* 21: 18–31.

1957b *The Trumpet Shall Sound: A Study of "Cargo" Cults in Melanesia.* London: MacGibbon and Kee.

Shamanism
Piers Vitebsky

REFERENCES

Atkinson, J. M.
1989 *The Art and Politics of Wana Shamanship.* Berkeley: University of California Press.
1992 "Shamanisms Today." *Annual Review of Anthropology* 21: 307–30.

Balzer, M. M.
1990 *Shamanism: Soviet Studies of Traditional Religion in Siberia and Central Asia.* Armonk: M. E. Sharpe.

Castaneda, C.
1968 *The Teachings of Don Juan: A Yaqui Way of Knowledge.* Berkeley: University of California Press.

de Heusch, L.
1981 "Possession and Shamanism." In L. de Heusch, ed., *Why Marry Her? Society and Symbolic Structures.* Cambridge: Cambridge University Press.

Eliade, M.
1964 *Shamanism: Archaic Techniques of Ecstasy.* NY: Pantheon.

Halifax, J.
1979 *Shamanic Voices: A Survey of Visionary Narratives.* NY: Dutton.

Harner, M.
1982 *The Way of the Shaman.* NY: Bantam.

Hoppál, M., ed.
1984 *Shamanism in Eurasia.* Göttingen: Herodot.

Katz, R.
1982 *Boiling Energy: Community Healing among the Kalahari Kung.* Cambridge, MA: Harvard University Press.

Kendall, L.
1985 *Shamans, Housewives and Other Restless Spirits: Women in Korean Ritual Life.*

Honolulu: University of Hawaii Press.

Lewis, I. M.
1989 *Ecstatic Religion: A Study of Shamanism and Spirit Possession.* London and NY: Routledge.

Popov, A. A.
1936 "Tavgiytsy [The Tavgy]." In *Trudy Instituta Antropologii I Etnografii,* Vol. I, Pt. 5, Moscow and Leningrad.

Rasmussen, K.
1929 *The Intellectual Culture of the Kglulik Eskimos.* Copenhagen: Gyldendalske.

Reichel-Dolmatoff, G.
1975 *The Shaman and the Jaguar: A Study of Narcotic Drugs among the Indians of Colombia.* Philadelphia: Temple University Press.

Schultes, R. E., and A. Hofmann.
1979 *Plants of the Gods: Origins of Hallucinogenic Use.* London: Hutchinson.

Shirokogoroff, S. M.
1935 *The Psychomental Complex of the Tungus.* London: Kegan Paul.

Siikala, A. L.
1978 *The Rite Technique of the Siberian Shaman.* Helsinki: Academia Scientiarum Fennica.

Thomas, N., and C. Humphrey, eds.
1994 *Shamanism, History and the State.* Ann Arbor: University of Michigan Press.

Vitebsky, P.
1993 *Dialogues with the Dead: The Discussion of Mortality among the Sora of Eastern India.* Cambridge: Cambridge University Press.
1995a *The Shaman.* London: Macmillan; Boston: Little Brown.
1995b "From Cosmology to Environmentalism: Shamanism as Local Knowledge in a Global Setting." In R. Fardon, ed., *Counterworks.* London: Routledge.

Walsh, R. N.
1990 *The Spirit of Shamanism.* Los Angeles: Tarcher.

Training for the Priesthood Among the Kogi of Colombia
Gerardo Reichel-Dolmatoff

REFERENCES

Preuss, Konrad Theodor
1926– *Forschungsreise zu den Kágaba. Beobachtungen,*
1927 *Textaufnahmen und sprachliche Studien bei einem Indianerstamme in Kolumbien, Südamerika.* 2 vols. St. Gabriel-Mödling: Anthropos Verlag.

Reichel-Dolmatoff, Gerardo
1950 "Los Kogi: Una tribu indígena de la Sierra Nevada de Santa Marta, Colombia." Vol. 1. *Revista del Instituto Etnológico Nacional* (Bogota) 4: 1–320.
1951a *Datos histórico-culturales sobre las tribus de la antigua Governación de Santa Marta.* Bogota: Imprenta del Banco de la República.
1951b *Los Kogi: Una tribu indígena de la Sierra Nevada de Santa Marta, Colombia.* Vol. 2. Bogota: Editorial Iqueima.
1953 "Contactos y cambios culturales en la Sierra Nevada de Santa Marta." *Revista Colombiana de Antropología* (Bogota) 1: 17–122.
1974 "Funerary Customs and Religious Symbolism Among the Kogi." In Patricia J. Lyon, ed., *Native South Americans— Ethnology of the Least Known Continent.* Boston/Toronto: Little, Brown.

CHAPTER FIVE
Altered States of Consciousness and The Religious Use of Drugs

Trance, Possession, Shamanism, and Sex
I. M. Lewis

REFERENCES

Banyai, E. I.
1984 "On the Technique of Hypnosis and Ecstasy: An Exceptional Psychophysiological Approach." In M. Hoppal, ed. *Shamanism in Eurasia.* Gottingen: Edition Herodot.

Bargen, D. G.
1997 *A Woman's Weapon: Spirit Possession in the Tale of the Genji.* Honolulu: University of Hawaii Press.

Constantinides, P.
1977 "Ill at Ease and Sick of Heart: Symbolic Behaviour in a Sudanese Healing Cult." In J. M. Lewis, ed., *Symbols and Sentiments,* pp. 61–84. London.

Crapanzano, V.
1973 *The Hamadsha: A Study in Moroccan Ethnopsychiatry.* Berkeley: University of California Press.

Davis, W.
1980 *Magic and Exorcism in Modern Japan.* Stanford: Stanford University Press.

Devereux, G.
1974 "Trance and Orgasm in Euripides: Bakchai." In A. Angoff and D. Barth, eds., *Parapsychology and Anthropology,* pp. 36–52. New York: Parapsychology foundation.

Dodds, E. R.
1951 *The Greeks and the Irrational.* Berkeley: University of California Press.

Eliade, M.
1951 *Chamanisme et les Techniques Archaiques de l'Extase.* Paris: Payot.

Erwin, F. R., R. M. Palmour, B. E. P., Murphy, R. Prince, and R. C. Simons
1988 "The Psychobiology of Trance: Physiological and Endocrine Correlates." *Transcultural Psychiatric Research Review* 25: 267–284.

Fales, E.
1996 "Scientific Explanations of Mystical Experiences, Part I: The Case of St. Teresa." *Religious Studies* 32: 143–63.
1996 "Part II: The Challenge of Theism." *Religious Studies* 32: 299–313.

Gombrich, R. and Obeysekere, G.
1988 *Buddhism Transformed: Religious Change in Sri Lanka.* New Jersey: Princeton University Press.

Graham, H.
1976   "The Social Image of Pregnancy:
        Pregnancy as Spirit Possession." *The
        Sociological Review* 291–308.

Grof, S.
1977   "The Implications of Psychedelic Research
        for Anthropology: Observations from LSD
        Psychotherapy." In I. M. Lewis, ed.,
        Symbols and Sentiments, pp. 141–74.
        London: Academic Press.

Hamayon, R.
1996   "Pour en Finir avec la 'Transe' et l' 'Extase'
        dans l' 'Etude du Chamanisme." In
        M. I. Beffa and M. D. Even, eds. 2,
        Variations Chamaniques. Paris: University
        of Paris, X.

Heusch, L. de.
1962   "Cultes de Possession et Religions
        Initiatiques de Salut en Afrique." *Annales
        du Centre d'Etudes des Religions Brussels.*
1971   *Pourquoi l' Epouser?* Paris: Gallimard.
1997   "Pour en Revenir a la Transe" Paper
        presented to the IVth Conference,
        International Society for Shamanic
        Research, Chantilly.

Lewis, I. M.
1989   [1971] *Ecstatic Religion,* 2nd edition,
        London: Routledge.
1996   *Religion in Context*. Cambridge:
        Cambridge University Press.
1999   *Arguments with Ethnography*. London:
        Athlone Press.

Lewis, I. M., S. Hurreiz, and A. al-Safi, eds.
1991   *Women's Medicine: The Zar/Bori Cult in
        Africa and Beyond*. Edinburgh: Edinburgh
        University Press.

Lot-Falck, E.
1977   "A Propos du Terme Chamane." *Etudes
        Mongols et Siberiennes* 8, Nanterre.

Maffesoli, M.
1993   *The Shadow of Dionysus: A Contribution
        to the Sociology of the Orgy*. Albany:
        State University of New York.

Martino, E. de
1961   *La Terra del Rimorso*. Milan: Feltrinelli.

Mastromattei, R.
1988   *La Terra Reale*. Rome: Valerio Levi.

Maxfield, M.,
1990   "The Effects of Rhythmic Drumming on
        EEG and Subjective Experience." Ph. D.
        Unpublished dissertation, Institute of
        Trans personal Psychology. Melo Park,
        CA.

Metraux, A.
1952   *Voodoo in Haiti*. London: Deutsch.

Nabokov, I.
1997   "Expel the Lover, Recover and Wife:
        Symbolic Analysis of a South Indian
        Exorcism." *Journal Royal Anthropological
        Institute* 3(2).

Overton, J. A.
1998   "Shamanism and Clinical Hypnosis: A
        Brief Comparative Analysis." *Shaman*
        6(2): 117–50.

Pizza, G.
1997   "The Virgin and the Spider:
        Reconsidering Spirit Possession in
        Southern Europe." Paper presented to
        the IVth Conference, International
        Society for Shamanic Research,
        Chantilly.

Prince, R., ed.
1982   "Shamans and Endorphins." *Ethos* (special
        issue) 10.

Reichel-Dolmatoff, G.
1972   *Amazonian Cosmos*. Chicago: University
        of Chicago Press.

Rouget, G.
1985   *Music and Trance* (revised English edition).
        Chicago: University of Chicago Press.

Shirokogoroff, S. M.
1935   *Psychomental Complex of the Tungus*.
        London: Kegan Paul.

Siikala, A. L.
1978   "The Rite Technique of the Siberian
        Shaman." Helsinki, FF Communications
        39(220).

Stirrat, R. L.
1977   "Demonic Possession in Roman Catholic
        Sri Lanka." *Journal of Anthropological
        Research* 33(2): 133–57.

Zolla, E.
1986   *L'Amante Invisible: l'Erotica Sciamanica*.
        Venice: Marsillo Editori.

Hypnosis and Trance Induction in the Surgeries of Brazilian Spiritist Healer-Mediums

Sydney M. Greenfield

REFERENCES

Brown, Diana DeG.
1986 *Umbanda: Religion and Politics in Urban Brazil.* Ann Arbor: UMI Research Press.

Cavalcanti, M. L. C.
1983 *O Mundo Invisivel: Cosmologiá, Sistema Ritual e Noção de Pessoa no Espiritísmo.* Rio de Janeiro: Zahar Editôras.

Esdaile, James
1957 [1850] *Hypnosis in Medicine and Surgery.* New York: Julian Press.

Geisler, Patric, and Sidney M. Greenfield
1989 "Penetrating Symbols, Penetrating Knives: The Medical and Physiological Implications of Brazilian Spiritistic "Folk" Surgery for Clinical Hypnosis." Paper presented at the 31st Annual Scientific Meeting and Workshops of the American Society of Clinical Hypnosis, Nashville, TN, March 11–15, 1989.

Greenfield, Sidney M.
1972 "Charwomen, Cesspools and Road Building: An Examination of Patronage, Clientage and Political Power in Southestern Minas Gerais." In A. Strickon and S. M. Greenfield, eds. *Structure and Process in Latin America,* pp. 71–100. Albuquerque: University of New Mexico Press.
1977 "Patronage, Politics and the Articulation of Local Community and National Society in Pre-1968 Brazil." *Journal of Inter-American Studies and World Affairs* 19:139–72.
1979 "Domestic Crises, Schools and Patron-Clientage in Southeastern Minas Gerais." In M. L. Margolis and W. E. Carter, eds. *Brazil: Anthropologial Perspectives,* pp. 362–78. New York: Columbia University Press.

1987 "The Return of Dr. Fritz: Spiritist Healing and Patronage Networks in Urban, Industrial Brazil." *Social Science and Medicine* 24:12:1095–1108.
1990 "German Spirit Doctors in Spiritist Healing in Urban Brazil." In *Ethnobiology: Implications and Applications: Proceedings of the First International Congress of Ethnobiology* (Belem 1988), Vol. 2. D. A. Posey and W. L. Overal, Organizers, pp. 241–56. Belem, Brazil: SCT/PR, CNPq, Museu Paraense Emilio Goeldi.

Greenfield, Sidney M., and John Gray
1988 "The Return of Dr. Fritz: Healing by the Spirits in Brazil." Video Documentary Produced at the Educational Communications Department of the University of Wisconsin-Milwaukee.
1989 "José Carlos and His Spirits: The Ritual Initiation of a *Zelador dos Orixás.*" Video Documentary Produced at the Educational Communications Department of the University of Wisconsin-Milwaukee.

Greenfield, Sidney M., and Russell Prust
1990 "Popular Religion, Patronage, and Resource Distribution in Brazil: A Model of an Hypothesis for the Survival of the Economically Marginal." In M. E. Smith, ed. *Perspectives on the Informal Economy. Society for Economic Anthropology Monograph* No. 8. p. 123–46. Washington, D.C.: University Press of America.

Hilgard, E. E., and J. R. Hilgard
1975 *Hypnosis in the Relief of Pain.* Los Altos, CA: William Kaufmann.

Hutchinson, Bertram
1966 "The Patron-Dependant Relationship in Brazil: A Preliminary Examination." *Sociologia Ruralis* 6:3–30.

Kardec, Allan
1980 *The Gospel According to Allan Kardec.* Brooklyn, NY: T. Gaus.

Kardec, Allan
(A. Blackwell, trans.) n.d. *The Spirit's Book.* São Paulo: Livraria Allan Kardec.

McGregor, P.
  1967 *Jesus of the Spirits.* New York: Stein and Day.

Pressel, Esther J.
  1974 "Umbanda Trance and Possession in São Paulo, Brazil." In F. Goodman, J. Henney, and E. Pressel, eds., *Trance, Healing and Hallucination.* pp. 113–225. New York: John Wiley and Sons.

Renshaw, Park
  1969 "A Sociological Analysis of Spiritism in Brazil." Ph. D. dissertation, University of Florida.

Roniger, L.
  1981 "Clientelism and Patron-Client Relations: A Bibliography." In S. N. Eisenstadt and R. Lemarchand, eds., *Political Clientelism, Patronage, and Development.* London: Sage Publications.
  1987 "Caciquismo and Coronelismo: Contextual Dimensions of Patron Brokerage in Mexico and Brazil." *Latin American Research Review* 22:2:71–100.

Rossi, Ernest L.
  1986 *The Psychobiology of Mind-Body Healing: New Concepts of Therapeutic Hypnosis.* New York. W. W. Norton and Co.

Stephen, Michele
  1989 "Constructing Sacred Worlds and Autonomous Imaging in New Guinea." In G. Herdt and M. Stephen, eds., *The Religious Imagination in New Guinea*, pp. 211–36. New Brunswick and London: Rutgers University Press.

Strickon, Arnold, and Sidney M. Greenfield
  1972 "The Analysis of Patron-Client Systems: An Introduction." In A. Strickon and S. M. Greenfield, eds., *Structure and Process in Latin America*, pp. 1–7. Albuquerque, NM: The University of New Mexico Press.

Ritual Enemas
Peter T. Furst and Michael D. Coe

REFERENCES

Benson, Elizabeth P.
  1972 *The Maya World.* New York: Apollo.
  1975 *Death and the Afterlife in Pre-Columbian America.* Washington, D.C.: Dumbarton Oaks.

Coe, Michael D.
  1966 *The Maya.* New York: Frederick A. Praeger.
  1975 *Classic Maya Pottery at Dumbarton Oaks.* Washington, D.C.: Dumbarton Oaks.

Furst, Peter T.
  1972 *Flesh of the Gods: The Ritual Use of Hallucinogens.* New York: Frederick A. Praeger.
  1976 *Hallucinogens and Culture.* Corte Madera, Calif.: Chandler & Sharp Publishers.
  1977 "High States in Culture-Historical Perspective." In Norman E. Zinberg, ed., *Alternate States of Consciousness.* New York: Free Press.

Thompson, J. Eric
  1970 *Maya History and Religion.* Norman: University of Oklahoma Press.

The Sound of Rushing Water
Michael Harner

REFERENCES

Karsten, R.
  1935 "The Head-Hunters of Western Amazonas." In *Commentationes Humanarum Litteraru.* Finska Vetenskaps-Societeten 7(1). Helsingfors.

Stirling, M. W.
  1938 *Historical and Ethnographical Material on the Jivaro Indians.* U.S. Bureau of American Ethnology Bulletin 117. Washington, D.C.: Smithsonian Institution.

Up de Graff, F. W.
  1923 *Headhunters of the Amazon: Seven Years of Exploration and Adventure.* London: H. Jenkins.

Wilbert, Johannes
  1972 "Tobacco and Shamanistic Ecstasy Among the Warao Indians of Venezuela." In Peter J. Furst, ed., *Flesh of the Gods: The Ritual Use of Hallucinogens*, pp. 55–83. New York: Praeger.

The Rave: Spiritual Healing in Western Subcultures
Scott Hutson

REFERENCES

Appadurai, Arjun
1986   *The Social Life of Things: Commodities in Cultural Perspective.* Cambridge: Cambridge University Press.

Baudrillard, Jean
1988   *America.* London: Verso.

Bourdieu, Pierre
1977   *Outline of a Theory of Practice.* Cambridge: Cambridge University Press.
1984   *Distinction: A Social Critique of the Judgment of Taste.* Cambridge, MA: Harvard University Press.

Brown, Michael F.
1997   *The Channeling Zone: American Spirituality in an Anxious Age.* Cambridge, MA: Harvard University Press.

Bruner, Edward M.
1994   "Abraham Lincoln as Authentic Reproduction: A Critique of Postmodernism." *American Anthropologist* 96(2): 397–415.

Brushman, Richard, ed.
1970   *The Great Awakening: Documents on the Revival of Religion, 1740–45.* New York: Atheneum.

Calhoon, Robert
1994   "The Evangelical Persuasion." In R. Hoffman and P. Albert, eds., *Religion in a Revolutionary Age.* Charlottesville: University Press of Virginia.

Champion, Sarah
1998   "Fear and loathing in Wisconsin." In S. Redhead, ed., with D. Wynne and J. O'Connor. *The Clubcultures Reader.* Oxford: Blackwell.

Cole, Nathan
1970   [1741]. "Conversion: The spiritual travels of Nathan Cole." In R. Brushman, ed., *The Great Awakening: Documents on the Revival of Religion, 1740–1745.* New York: Atheneum.

Connor, Steve
1997   *Postmodernist Culture: An Introduction to Theories of the Contemporary,* 2d ed. London: Blackwell.

Csikszentmihalyi, Mihalyi
1975   *Play and Intrinsic Rewards. Journal of Humanistic Psychology* 15(3): 41–63.

Danforth, Loring
1989   *Firewalking and Religious Healing: The Anastenaria of Greece and the American Firewalking Movement.* Princeton, NJ: Princeton University Press.

Dery, Mark
1994   "Flame Wars." In M. Dery, ed. *Flame Wars: The Discourse of Cyberculture.* Durham, NC: Duke University Press.

Dibbell, Julian
1994   "A Rape in Cyberspace; or, How an Evil Clown, a Haitian Trickster Spirit, Two Wizards, and a Cast of Dozens Turned a Database into a Society." In M. Dery, ed. *Flame Wars: The Discourse of Cyberculture.* Durham, NC: Duke University Press.

Eliade, Mircea
1960   "The yearning for Paradise in Primitive Tradition." In H. A. Murray, ed. *Myth and Mythmaking,* New York: Braziller.
1964   *Shamanism: Archaic Techniques of Ecstasy.* Princeton, NJ: Princeton University Press.

Epstein, Jonathan S.
1998   "Introduction: Generation X, Youth Culture, and Identity." In J. Epstein, ed. *Youth Culture: Identity in a Postmodern world.* Oxford: Blackwell.

Fischer, Michael M. K.
1999   "Worlding Cyberspace: Toward a Critical Ethnography in Time, Space, and Theory." George E. Marcus, ed. *Critical anthropology Now: Unexpected contexts, shifting constituencies, changing agendas.* Santa Fe, NM: School of American Research Press.

Foster, Hal
1985   *Recodings.* Port Townsend WA: Bay Press.

Galanter, Marc
1989   *Cults: Faith, Healing, and Conversion.* New York: Oxford University Press.

Geertz, Clifford
1973   "Thick Description: Toward an Interpretive Theory of Culture." In *The Interpretation of Cultures*. New York: Basic Books.

Gotcher, J. Michael, and Ellen Kanervo
1997   "Perceptions and Uses of Electronic Mail." *Social Science Computer Review* 15(2): 145–58.

Greenhouse, Carol J.
1986   *Praying for Justice*. Ithaca, NY: Cornell University Press.

Hakken, David
1999   *Cyborg@Cyberspace?* New York: Routledge.

Harding, Susan F.
1987   "Convicted by the Holy Spirit: The Rhetoric of Fundamental Baptist Conversion." *American Ethnologist* 14(1): 167–81.

Harner, Michael
1990   *The Way of the Shaman*. New York: Harper and Row.

Hesmondhalgh, David
1995   "Technoprophecy: A Response to Tagg." *Popular Music* 14(2): 261–63.

Hexham, Irving and Karla Poewe
1986   *Understanding cults and new religions*. Grand Rapids, MI: William Beerdsman.

Jameson, Fredric
1984   "Postmodernism, or the Cultural Logic of Late Capitalism." *New Left Review* (196): 53–92.

Joralemon, Donald
1990   "The Selling of the Shaman and the Problem of Informant Legitimacy." *Journal of Anthropological Research* 46: 105–118.

Katz, Richard
1982   "Accepting 'Boiling Energy.'" *Ethos* 10(4): 344–368.

Lasch, Christopher
1979   *The Culture of Narcissism: American Life in an Age of Diminishing Expectations*, New York: W. W. Norton.

Lee, Richard
1967   "Trance Cure of the !Kung Bushman." *Natural History* 76(9): 31–7.

Marcus, George E. and Michael M. K. Fisher
1986   *Anthropology as Cultural Critique: An Experimental Moment in the Human Sciences.* Chicago, IL: University of Chicago Press.

Mckay, George
1996   *Senseless Acts of Beauty: Cultures of Resistance since the Sixties.* London: Verso.

McRobbie, Angela
1994   *Postmodernism and Popular Culture.* London: Routledge.

Melechi, Antonio
1993   "The ecstasy of disappearance." In *Rave off: Politics and deviance in contemporary youth culture*, ed. Steve Redhead. Aldershot: Avebury.

Myerhoff, Barbara
1974   *Peyote hunt: The sacred journey of the Huichol Indians*. Ithaca NY: Cornell University Press.

Neher, Andrew
1962   "A physiological explanation of unusual behavior in ceremonies involving drums." *Human Biology* 4: 151–160.

Niman, Michael I.
1997   *People of the rainbow: A nomadic utopia.* Knoxville: University of Tennessee Press.

Pearson, Anthony
1987   "The Grateful Dead phenomenon: An ethnomethodological approach." *Youth and Society* 18(4): 418–432.

Redhead, Steve
1993   "The Politics of Ecstatsy." In Steve Redhead, ed., *Rave Off: Politics and Deviance in Contemporary Youth Culture.* Aldershot: Avebury.

Reynolds, Simon
1998a   *Generation Ecstasy: Into the World of Techno and Rave Culture.* Boston, MA: Little, Brown and Company.
1998b   "Rave Culture: Living Dream or Living Death?" In Steve Redhead, ed., with D. Wynne and J. O'Connor, *The Clubcultures Reader.* Oxford: Blackwell.

Richard, Birgit, and Heinz Hermann Kruger
1998   "Ravers' Paradise?: German Youth Cultures in the 1960s." In Tracey Skelton and Gill Valentine ed., *Cool Places: Geographies of Youth cultures.* London: Routledge.

Rietveld, Hillegonda
   1993   "Living the dream." In Steve Redhead,
          ed., *Rave Off: Politics and Deviance in
          Contemporary Youth Culture*. Aldershot:
          Avebury.

Rouget, Gilbert
   1985   *Music and Trance*. Chicago, IL: University
          of Chicago Press.

Rushkoff, Douglas
   1994   *Cyberia: Life in the Trenches of Hyperspace*.
          New York: Harper Collins.

Russell, Kristian
   1993   "Lysergia Suburbia." In Steve Redhead,
          ed. *Rave Off: Politics and Deviance in
          Contemporary Youth Culture*. Aldershot:
          Avebury.

Saunders, Nicholas
   1995   *Ecstasy and the Dance Culture*. London:
          Turnaround.

Sardiello, Robert
   1994   "Secular Rituals in Popular Culture:
          A Case for Grateful Dead Concerts
          and Dead Head Identity." In Jonathan
          S. Epstein, ed., *Adolescents and their
          music*. New York: Garland Publishing.

Tagg, Philip
   1994   "From refrain to rave: the decline of
          figure and the rise of ground." *Popular
          Music* 13(2): 209–222.

Thornton, Sarah
   1995   *Club Cultures: Music Media and Subcultural
          Capital*. Cambridge: Polity Press.

Tomlinson, Lori
   1998   "This ain't no disco". . . or is it? Youth
          culture and the rave phenomenon." In
          J. Epstein, ed., *Youth Culture: Identity in a
          Postmodern World*. Oxford: Blackwell.

Turkie, Sherry
   1995   *Life on the Screen*. New York: Simon &
          Schuster.

Turner, Victor
   1967   *The Ritual Process: Structure and Anti-
          structure*. Chicago IL: Aldine.

Walter, V. J., and W. G. Walter
   1949   "The Central Effects of Rhythmic Sensory
          Stimulation." *Electroencephalography and
          Clinical Neurophysiology* 1: 57–86.

CHAPTER SIX
Ethnomedicine: Religion and Healing

Eyes of the *Ngangas:* Ethnomedicine and Power in Central African Republic
Arthur C. Lehmann

REFERENCES

Bahuchet, Serge
   1985   *Les Pygmées Aka et la Forêt Centrafricaine*.
          Paris: Bibliothèque de la Selaf.

Bibeau, Gillies
   1979   *De la maladie a la guerison. Essai d'analyse
          systematique de la medecine des Angbandi
          du Zaire*. Doctoral dissertation, Laval
          University.

Bichmann, Wolfgang
   1979   "Primary Health Care and Traditional
          Medicine—Considering the Background
          of Changing Health Care Concepts in
          Africa." *Social Science and Medicine* 13B:
          175–82.

Cavalli-Sforza, L. L.
   1971   "Pygmies: An Example of Hunters
          Gatherers, and Genetic Consequences
          for Man of Domestication of Plants and
          Animals." In J. de Grouchy, F. Ebling,
          and I. Henderson, eds., *Human Genetics:
          Proceedings of the Fourth International
          Congress of Human Genetics*, pp. 79–95.
          Amsterdam: Excerpta Medica.

Cavalli-Sforza, L. L., ed.
   1986   *African Pygmies*. New York: Academic
          Press.

Feierman, Steven
   1985   "Struggles for Control: The Social Roots
          of Health of Healing in Modern Africa."
          African Studies Review 28: 73–147.

Green, Edward
   1980   "Roles for African Traditional Healers in
          Mental Health Care." *Medical Anthropology*
          4(4): 490–522.

Hepburn, Sharon J.
   1988   "W. H. R. Rivers Prize Essay (1986):
          Western Minds, Foreign Bodies." *Medical

Anthropology Quarterly 2 (New Series): 59–74.

Hewlett, Barry S.
1986   "Causes of Death Among Aka Pygmies of the Central African Republic." In L. L. Cavalli-Sforza, ed., *African Pygmies*, pp. 45–63. New York: Academic Press.

Janzen, John M.
1978   *The Quest for Therapy: Medical Pluralism in Lower Zaire.* Los Angeles: University of California Press.

Lewis, I. M.
1986   *Religion in Context: Cults and Charisma.* Cambridge: Cambridge University Press.

Motte, Elisabeth
1980   *Les plantes chez les Pygmées Aka et les Monzombode la Lobaye.* Paris: Bibliothèque de la Selaf.

Offiong, Daniel
1983   "Witchcraft Among the Ibibio of Nigeria." *African Studies Review* 26(1): 107–24.

Turnbull, Colin
1965   *Wayward Servants.* New York: Natural History Press.

Warren, Dennis M.
1974   "Disease, Medicine, and Religion Among the Techinman-Bono of Ghana; A Study in Culture Change." Ph.D. dissertation, Indiana University.

Yoder, P. Stanley
1982   "Issues in the Study of Ethnomedical Systems in Africa." In P. Stanley Yoder, ed., *African Health and Healing Systems: Proceedings of a Symposium*, p. 120. Los Angeles: Crossroads Press, University of California.

Swallowing Frogs: Anger and Illness in Northeast Brazil

L. A. Rebhun

REFERENCES

Araujo, Tania Bacelar de
1987   "Nordeste: Diferenciais demográficos regionais seus determinantes—Cademos de Estudos sociais." *Recife* 3(3): 167–92.

Averill, James R.
1982   *Anger and Aggression: An Essay in Emotion.* New York: Springer.

Bernard, H. Russell
1994   *Research Methods in Anthropology: Qualitative and Quantitative Approaches.* 2nd ed. Thousand Oaks, Calif.: Sage.

Bolton, Ralph
1981   "Susto, Hostility, and Hypoglycemia." *Ethnology* 19: 261–76.

Camino, Linda
1989   "Nerves, Worriation, and Black Women: A Community Study in the American South." In D. L. Davis and S. Low, eds., *Gender, Health, and Illness: The Case of Nerves*, pp. 295–314. New York: Hemisphere.

Clark, Margaret
1978   "Three Cases of Folk Disorder Among Mexican-Americans: Implications for the Study of Culture Change." *Kroeber Anthropological Society Papers* 55/56 (University of California, Berkeley).

Cosminsky, Sheila
1967   "The Evil Eye in a Quiche Community." In C. Maloney, ed., *The Evil Eye*, pp. 163–74. New York: Columbia University Press.

Davis, Dona Lee
1989   "The Variable Character of Nerves in a Newfoundland Fishing Village." *Medical Anthropology* 11: 63–78.

Davis, D., and N. O. Whitten
1988   "Medical and Popular Traditions of Nerves." *Social Science and Medicine* 26(12): 1209–21.

Duarte, Luiz Fernando D.
1986   *Da vida nervosa nas clases trabalhadores urbanas.* Rio de Janeiro: Jorge Zahar Editor/CNPq.

Dunk, Pamela
1989   "Greek Women and Broken Nerves in Montreal." *Medical Anthropology* 11: 29–45.

Foster, George
1965   "Peasant Society and the Image of Limited Good." *American Anthropologist* 67: 293–315.

1972 "The Anatomy of Envy: A Study in
      Symbolic Behavior." *Current Anthropology*
      13: 165–202.

1976 "Disease Etiologies in Non-Western
      Medical Systems." *American
      Anthropologist* 78: 773–82.

Foster, George, and Barbara Anderson
1978 *Medical Anthropology.* New York: Wiley.

Foucault, Michel
1986 "Disciplinary Power and Subjection."
      In Steven Lukes, ed., *Power,* pp. 229–42.
      Oxford: Basil Blackwell.

Garrison, Vivian, and Conrad M. Arensberg
1976 "The Evil Eye: Envy or Risk of Seizure?
      Paranoia or Patronal Dependence?" In
      Clarence Maloney, ed., *The Evil Eye,*
      pp. 287–328. New York: Columbia
      University Press.

Gillen, J.
1945 *Mochel: A Peruvian Coastal Community.*
      Institute of Social Anthropology
      Publication 3. Washington, D.C.:
      Smithsonian Institution Press.

1948 "Magical Fright." *Psychiatry*
      11: 387–400.

Goebel, O.
1973 "El Susto: A Descriptive Analysis."
      International Journal of Social Psychiatry
      19: 38–43.

Guarnaccia, Peter J., Victor DeLaCancela, and
      Emilio Carrillo
1989 "The Multiple Meanings of Ataque
      de Nervios in the Latino
      Community." *Medical Anthropology*
      11: 47–62.

Herzfeld, Michael
1981 "Meaning and Morality: A Semiotic
      Approach to Evil Eye Accusations in a
      Greek Village." *American Ethnologist*
      8: 560–74.

1984 "The Horns of the Mediterraneanist
      Dilemma." *American Ethnologist*
      11: 439–54.

1986 "Closure as Cure: Tropes in the
      Exploration of Bodily and Social
      Disorder." *Current Anthropology*
      27(2): 107–20.

IGBE/UNICEF
1986 *Perfil estatistico de crianças e mães no Brasil:
      Aspectos socio-economicos da mortalidade
      infantil em areas urbanas.* Rio de Janeiro:
      UNICEF.

Kiev, Ari
1968 *Curanderismo: Mexican American Folk
      Psychiatry.* New York: Free Press.

1972 *Transcultural Psychiatry.* New York:
      Free Press.

Krieger, Laurie
1989 "Nerves and Psychosomatic Illness: The
      Case of Um Ramadan." In D. L. Davis
      and S. M. Low, eds., *Gender, Health, and
      Illness: The Case of Nerves,* pp. 181–93.
      New York: Hemisphere.

Logan, M.
1979 "Variations Regarding Susto Causality
      Among the Cakchiquel of Guatemala."
      Culture, Medicine, and Psychiatry 3:
      153–66.

Low, Setha
1989 "Health, Culture, and the Nature of
      Nerves: A Critique." *Medical
      Anthropology* 2: 91–95.

Madsen, William
1964 "Value Conflicts and Folk Psychiatry in
      South Texas." In Ari Kiev, ed., *Magic,
      Faith, and Healing,* pp. 420–40. New York:
      Free Press.

Migliore, Sam
1983 "Evil Eye or Delusions: On the
      Consistency of Folk Models." *Medical
      Anthropology Quarterly* 14(2): 4–9.

Nations, Marilyn
1982 "Illness of the Child: The Cultural
      Context of Childhood Diarrhea in
      Northeast Brazil." Ph.D. dissertation,
      Department of Anthropology,
      University of California,
      Berkeley.

Nations, Marilyn, and Mara Lucia Amaral
1991 "Flesh, Blood, Souls, and Households:
      Cultural Validity in Mortality Inquiry."
      Medical Anthropology Quarterly (n.s.) 5:
      204–20.

Nations, Marilyn, L. Camino, and F. Walker
1988   "'Nerves': Folk Idiom for Anxiety and Depression?" *Social Science and Medicine* 26: 1245–59.

O'Nell, C. W.
1975   "An Investigation of Reported 'Fright' as a Factor in the Etiology of Sustos." *Ethos* 3: 41–63.

O'Nell, C. W., and A. Rubel
1976   "The Meaning of Sustos." *Actas del Congreso Internacional de Americanistas* 3: 343–49.

Perlman, Janice
1976   *The Myth of Marginality.* Berkeley: University of California Press.

Rebhun, L. A.
1993   "Nerves and Emotional Play in Northeast Brazil." *Medical Anthropology Quarterly* (n.s.) 7: 131–51.

Robben, Antonius C. M. G.
1988   "Conflicting Gender Conceptions in a Pluriform Fishing Economy: A Hermeneutic Perspective on Conjugal Relationships in Brazil." In J. Nadel-Klein and D. L. Davis, eds., *To Work and to Weep: Women in Fishing Economies,* pp. 106–29. St. Johns, Newfoundland: Institute of Social and Economic Research.

Roberts, J.
1976   "Belief in the Evil Eye in Western Perspective." In Clarence Maloney, ed., *The Evil Eye,* pp. 223–78. New York: Columbia University Press.

Rubel, A.
1964   "The Epidemiology of a Folk Illness: Susto in Hispanic America." *Ethnology* 3: 268–83.

Sarbin, Theodore R.
1986   "Emotion and Act: Roles and Rhetoric." In Rom Harré, ed., *The Social Construction of Emotions,* pp. 83–97. Oxford: Basil Blackwell.

Toussignant, M.
1979   "Espanto: A Dialogue with the Gods." *Culture, Medicine, and Psychiatry* 3: 347–61.

Uzzell, D.
1974   "Susto Revisited: Illness a Strategic Role." *American Ethnologist* 1: 369–78.

Mothering and the Practice of "Balm" in Jamaica
William Wedenoja

REFERENCES

Barry, H., M. K. Bacon, and I. L. Child
1957   "A Cross-Cultural Survey of Some Sex Differences in Socialization." *Journal of Abnormal and Social Psychology* 55: 327–32.

Frank, J. D.
[1961] 1974   *Persuasion and Healing: A Comparative Study of Psychotherapy.* Rev. ed. New York: Schocken.

Halifax, J.
1979   *Shamanic Voices.* New York: E. P. Dutton.

Jones, E., and C. L. Zoppel
1979   "Personality Differences Among Blacks in Jamaica and the United States." *Journal of Cross-Cultural Psychology* 10: 435–56.

Kakar, S.
1982   *Shamans, Mystics, and Doctors: A Psychological Inquiry into India and Its Healing Traditions.* Boston: Beacon Press.

Lambert, M. J., D. A. Shapiro, and A. E. Bergin
1986   "The Effectiveness of Psychotherapy." In S. L. Garfield and A. E. Bergin, eds., *Handbook of Psychotherapy and Behavior Change.* 3rd ed. New York: John Wiley.

Long, J. K.
1973   "Jamaican Medicine: Choices Between Folk Healing and Modern Medicine." Ph.D. dissertation, Department of Anthropology, University of North Carolina.

Martin, K., and B. Voorhies
1975   *Female of the Species.* New York: Columbia University Press.

Mitchell, G.
1981   *Human Sex Differences: A Primatologist's Perspective.* New York: Van Nostrand Reinhold.

Mitchell, M. F.
1980   "Class, Therapeutic Roles, and Self-Medication in Jamaica." Ph.D.

dissertation, Medical Anthropology, University of California at Berkeley and San Francisco.

Mogul, K. M.
1982   "Overview: The Sex of the Therapist." *American Journal of Psychiatry* 139: 1–11.

Phillips, A. S.
1973   *Adolescence in Jamaica.* Kingston: Jamaica Publishing House.

Prince, Raymond
n.d.   *Personal communication.*

Quinn, N.
1977   "Anthropological Studies on Women's Status." *Annual Review of Anthropology* 6: 181–225. Palo Alto, Calif.: Annual Reviews.

Rogers, C. R.
1957   "The Necessary and Sufficient Conditions of Therapeutic Personality Change." *Journal of Consulting Psychology* 21(2): 95–102.

Rossi, A. S.
1977   "A Biosocial Perspective on Parenting." *Daedalus* 106(2): 1–32.

Scheff, T. J.
1975   "Labeling, Emotion, and Individual Change." In T. J. Scheff, ed., *Labeling Madness,* pp. 75–89. Englewood Cliffs, N.J.: Prentice Hall.
1979   *Catharsis in Healing, Ritual, and Drama.* Berkeley: University of California Press.

Spiro, M. E.
1978   *Burmese Supernaturalism.* Expanded ed. Philadelphia: Institute for the Study of Human Issues Press.
1979   *Gender and Culture: Kibbutz Women Revisited.* New York: Schocken.

Torrey, E. F.
1972   *The Mind Game.* New York: Bantam.

Wedenoja, W.
1988   "The Origins of Revival, a Creole Religion in Jamaica." In G. Saunders, ed., *Culture and Christianity: The Dialectics of Transformation.* Westport, Conn.: Greenwood.

Whiting, B. B., and J. M. Whiting
1975   *Children of Six Cultures: A Psycho-Cultural Analysis.* Cambridge, Mass.: Harvard University Press.

Whyte, M. K.
1978   *The Status of Women in Preindustrial Societies.* Princeton, N.J.: Princeton University Press.

CHAPTER SEVEN
Witchcraft, Sorcery, Divination, and Magic

An Anthropological Perspective on the Witchcraze

James L. Brain

REFERENCES

Bettlelheim, Bruno
1977   *The Uses of Enchantment.* New York: Random House.

Brain, James L.
1977a   "Handedness in Tanzania." *Anthropos* 72: 180–92.
1977b   "Sex, Incest and Death: Initiation Rites Reconsidered." *Current Anthropology* 18(2): 371–84.

Bridges, E. L.
1949   *The Uttermost Parts of the Earth.* New York: Dutton.

Browne, Thomas
1964   *Religio Medici and Other Works.* In L. C. Martin, ed. Oxford: Clarendon Press.

Chapman, Anne
1984   *Drama and Power in a Hunting Society.* Cambridge: Cambridge University Press.

Cohn, Norman
1975   *Europe's Inner Demons: An Inquiry Inspired by the Great Witch-Hunt.* New York: Basic Books.

Darst, D. H.
1979   "Witchcraft in Spain: The Testimony of Martin de Castenga's Treatise on Superstition and Witchcraft (1529)."

Proceedings of the American Philosophical Society 123(5): 298–322.

Douglas, Mary
  1966   *Purity and Danger.* London: Routledge and Kegan Paul.

Driberg, J. H.
  1923   *The Lango.* London: T. Fisher Unwin.

Dykstra, B.
  1986   *Idols of Perversity.* New York: Oxford University Press.

Dyson-Hudson, N.
  1966   *Karimojong Politics.* Oxford: Clarendon Press.

Elkin, Adolphus Peter
  1938   *Australian Aborigines.* Sydney: Angus and Robertson.

Fortes, Meyer
  1953   "The Structure of Unilineal Descent Groups." *American Anthropologist* 55: 17–41.

Fox-Keller, E.
  1983   "Feminism and Science." In E. Abel and E. K. Abel, eds., *The Signs Reader.* Chicago: University of Chicago Press.

Ginzburg, Carlo
  1983   *The Night Battles: Witchcraft and Agrarian Cults in the Sixteenth and Seventeenth Centuries.* Baltimore: Johns Hopkins University Press.

Gluckman, Max
  1965   *Politics, Law and Ritual in Tribal Society.* Oxford: Blackwell.

Gulliver, P.
  1955   *The Family Herds.* London: Routledge and Kegan Paul.
  1963   *Social Control in an African Society.* Boston: Boston University Press.

Gulliver, P., and P. H. Gulliver
  1953   *The Central Nilo-Hamites.* London: International African Institute.

Huntingford, G. W. B.
  1953   *The Southern Nilo-Hamites.* London: International African Institute.

Jacobs, Alan
  1985   *Personal communication.*

Klaits, Joseph
  1985   *Servants of Satan.* Bloomington: Indiana University Press.

Kramer, Heinrich, and Jakob Sprenger
  1971   *Malleus Maleficarum.* Translated by Montague Summers. New York: Dover.

La Barre, Weston
  1984   *Muelos: A Stone Age Superstition.* New York: Columbia University Press.

Lamphere, L.
  1974   "Strategies, Cooperation and Conflict Among Women in Domestic Groups." In Michelle Z. Rosaldo and L. Lamphere, eds., *Women, Culture and Society,* pp. 97–112. Stanford, Calif.: Stanford University Press.

Langley, Michael
  1979   *The Nandi of Kenya.* New York: St. Martin's Press.

Lawrence, J. T. D.
  1957   *The Iteso.* London: Oxford University Press.

Leach, Edmund Ronald
  1970   *Claude Lévi-Strauss.* Harmondsworth, UK: Penguin Books.

Lee, Richard B.
  1972   "Work Effort, Group Structure and Land Use Among Contemporary Hunter-Gatherers." In B. Ucko and R. Trimingham, eds., *Man, Settlement and Urbanism.* London: George Duckworth and Company.
  1976   *Kalahari Hunter-Gatherers.* Cambridge: Harvard University Press.

Lewis, I. M.
  1965   "Shaikhs and Warriors in Somaliland." In J. L. Gibbs, ed., *Peoples of Africa.* New York: Holt, Rinehart and Winston.

Mair, L.
  1969   *Witchcraft.* New York: McGraw-Hill.

Marshall, L.
  1962   "!Kung Bushmen Religious Beliefs." *Africa* 32(3): 221–52.
  1976   *The !Kung of Nyae.* Cambridge, Mass.: Harvard University Press.

McCormack, C., and M. Strathern, eds.
1980 *Nature, Culture and Gender.* Cambridge: Cambridge University Press.

Meggitt, M. J.
1962 *Desert People.* Chicago: University of Chicago Press.

Middleton, John, and E. Winter, eds.
1963 *Witchcraft, Sorcery and Magic in East Africa.* London: Routledge and Kegan Paul.

Midelfort, H. C. Erik
1972 *Witch Hunting in Southwestern Germany.* Stanford, Calif.: Stanford University Press.

Mitchell, J. C.
1965 "The Meaning of Misfortune for Urban Africans." In M. Fortes and G. Dieterlen, eds., *African Systems of Thought.* London: Oxford University Press.

Murray, Margaret
1970 *The God of the Witches.* New York: Oxford University Press. (First published by Sampson, Low, and Matson, 1931.)

Nadel, Siegfried Frederick
1952 "Witchcraft in Four African Societies: An Essay in Comparison." *American Anthropologist* 54: 18–29.

Offiong, D. A.
1985 "Witchcraft Among the Ibibio." *African Studies Review* 21(1): 107–24.

Ortner, Sherry B.
1974 "Is Female to Nature as Man Is to Culture?" In Michelle Z. Rosaldo and L. Lamphere, eds., *Woman, Culture and Society,* pp. 67–87. Stanford, Calif.: Stanford University Press.

Peristiany, J. G.
1939 *The Social Institutions of the Kipsigis.* London: George Routledge.

Robertson, E.
n.d. *An Anchorhold of Her Own.* Knoxville: University of Tennessee Press.

Rosaldo, Michelle Z.
1974 "Introduction and Overview." In Michelle Z. Rosaldo and L. Lamphere, eds., *Woman, Culture and Society,* pp. 1–42. Stanford, Calif.: Stanford University Press.

Spencer, B., and J. Gillen
[1899] 1938 *The Native Tribes of Central Australia.* London: Macmillan.
1904 *The Northern Tribes of Central Australia.* London: Macmillan.

Stenning, D.
1959 *Savannah Nomads.* London: Oxford University Press.
1965 "The Pastoral Fulani of Northern Nigeria." In J. L. Gibbs, ed., *Peoples of Africa.* New York: Holt, Rinehart and Winston.

Thomas, Keith
1971 *Religion and the Decline of Magic.* New York: Charles Scribner's Sons.

Thomas, N. W.
1906 *The Natives of Australia.* London: Archibald Constable.

Trevor-Roper, H. R.
1969 *The European Witch-Craze of the Sixteenth and Seventeenth Centuries and Other Essays.* New York: Harper and Row.

Turnbull, C.
1961 *The Forest People.* New York: Simon and Schuster.
1968 "The Importance of Flux in Two Hunting Societies." In Richard B. Lee and I. DeVore, eds., *Man the Hunter,* pp. 132–37. Chicago: Aldine.

Wilson, M.
1951 "Witch Beliefs and Social Structure." *American Journal of Sociology* 56: 307–13.

Woodburn, J.
1968 "An Introduction to Hadza Ecology." In Richard B. Lee and I. DeVore, eds., *Man the Hunter,* pp. 49–55.
1979 "Minimal Politics: The Political Organization of the Hadza of North Tanzania." In W. A. Shack and P. S. Cohen, eds., *Leadership: A Comparative Perspective,* pp. 244–60. Oxford: Clarendon Press.

1982a "Egalitarian Societies." *Man* 17: 431–51.

1982b "Social Dimensions of Death in Four African Hunting and Gathering Societies." In Maurice Bloch and Jonathan Parry, eds., *Death and the Regeneration of Life,* pp. 187–210. Cambridge: Cambridge University Press.

Sorcery and Concepts of Deviance Among the Kabana, West New Britain

Naomi M. McPherson

REFERENCES

Becker, H.
 1963 *Outsiders: Studies in the Sociology of Deviance.* New York: Free Press.

Counts, D. A., and D. R. Counts
 1976– "The Good Death in Kalisi." *Omega* 7(4):
 77 367–73.
 1984 "People Who Act Like Dogs: Adultery and Deviance in a Melanesian Community." Paper read at the conference Deviance in a Cross-Cultural Context. University of Waterloo, Waterloo, Ontario, June.

Jorgensen, D.
 1983– "The Clear and the Hidden: Person, Self,
 84 and Suicide Among the Telefolmi of Papua New Guinea." *Omega* 14(2): 113–26.

Lawrence, P.
 1984 *The Garia: An Ethnography of a Traditional Cosmic System in Papua New Guinea.* Carlton, Australia: Melbourne University Press.

Malinowski, B.
 [1926] 1967 *Crime and Custom in Savage Society.* C. K. Ogden, ed. Totowa, N.J.: Littlefield Adams.

Scaletta, N.
 1985 "Death by Sorcery: The Social Dynamics of Dying in Bariai, West New Britain." In D. A. Counts and D. R. Counts, eds. *Aging and Its Transformations: Moving Toward Death in Pacific Societies,* pp. 223–47. ASAO Monograph Series, no. 10. Lanham, Md.: University Press of America.

Vincent, Joan
 1990 *Anthropology and Politica: Visions, Traditions, and Trends.* Tucson: University of Arizona Press.

Weiner, A.
 1976 *Women of Value, Men of Renown: New Perspectives in Trobriand Exchange.* Austin: University of Texas Press.

Zelenietz, M.
 1981 "One Step Too Far: Sorcery and Social Control in Kilenge, West New Britain." *Social Analysis* 8: 101–18.

The Goat and the Gazelle: Witchcraft

T. M. Luhrmann

REFERENCES

Adler, M.
 1986 *Drawing Down the Moon,* pp. 45–46, 105. Boston: Beacon Press.

Crowley, A.
 [1929] 1976 *Magick in Theory and Practice,* pp. 345–61. New York: Dover.

Farrar, J., and S. Farrar
 1981 *Eight Sabbats for Witches,* pp. 17, 20, 42–43. London: Robert Hale.
 1984 *The Witches' Way.* London: Robert Hale.

Gardner, G. B.
 [1954] 1982 *Witchcraft Today,* p. 46. New York: Magickal Childe.

Le Roy Ladurie, E.
 1987 *Jasmin's Witch.* Aldershot, UK: Scholar Press.

Starhawk
 1979 *The Spiral Dance,* p. 77. New York: Harper and Row.

Rational Mastery by Man of His Surroundings

Bronislaw Malinowski

REFERENCES

Boas, F.
 1910 *The Mind of Primitive Man.*

Brinton, D. G.
 1899 *Religions of Primitive Peoples.*

Codrington, R. H.
  1891   *The Melanesians.*

Crawley, E.
  1902   *The Mystic Rose.*
  1905   *The Tree of Life.*

Durkheim, E.
  1912   *Les Formes elementaires de la Vie religieuse.*

Ehrenreich, P.
  1910   *Die Allgemeine Mythologie.*

Frazer, J. G.
  1910   *Totemism and Exogamy.* 4 vols.
  1911–   *The Golden Bough.* 3rd ed. 12 vols.
  14
  1913   *The Belief in Immortality and the Worship of the Dead.* 3 vols.
  1919   *Folklore in the Old Testament.* 3 vols.

Goldenweiser, A. A.

  1923   *Early Civilization.*

Harrison, J.
  1910–   *Themis.*
  12

Hastings, J.
  n.d.   *Encyclopedia of Religion and Ethics.*

Hobhouse, L. T.
  1915   *Morals in Evolution.* 2nd ed.

Hubert, H., and M. Mauss
  1909   *Melanges d'histoire des religions.*

King, I.
  1910   *The Development of Religion.*

Kroeber, A. L.
  1923   *Anthropology.*

Lang, A.
  1889   *The Making of Religion.*
  1901   *Magic and Religion.*

Lévy-Bruhl, M.
  1910   *Les Fonctions mentales dans les sociétés inférieures.*

Lowie, R. H.
  1920   *Primitive Society.*
  1925   *Primitive Religion.*

Malinowski, B.
  1915   *The Natives of Mailu.*
  1916   *"Baloma." Journal of the Royal Anthropological Institute.*
  1922   *Argonauts of the Western Pacific.*
  1923–   *Psyche.* Vols. III(2), IV(4),
  25   V(3).

Marett, R. R.
  1909   *The Threshold of Religion.*

McLennan, J. F.
  1886   *Studies in Ancient History.*

Preuss, K. Th.
  1904   *Der Ursprung der Religion und Kunst.*

Schmidt, W.
  1912   *Der Ursprung der Gottesidee.*

Seligman, C. G.
  1910   *The Melanesians of British New Guinea.*

Smith, W. Robertson
  1889   *Lectures on the Religion of the Semites.*

Thurnwald, R.
  1912   *Forschungen auf den Solominseln und Bismarckarchipel.*
  1921   *Die Gemeinde der Banaro.*
  1922   *"Psychologie des Primitiven Menschen."* In G. Kafka, ed., *Handbuch der Vergl. Psychol.*

Tylor, E. B.
  1903   *Primitive Culture.* 4th ed. 2 vols.

Van Gennep, A.
  1909   *Les Rites de Passage.*

Westermarck, E.
  1905   *The Origin and Development of the Moral Ideas.* 2 vols.

Wundt, Wilh.
  1904   *Volkerpsychologie.*

Baseball Magic
George Gmelch

REFERENCES

Gmelch, G.
  2001   *Inside Pitch: Life in Professional Baseball.* Washington, D.C.: Smithsonian Institution Press.

Malinowski, B.
  1948   *Magic, Science and Religion and Other Essays.* Glencoe, II: Free Press.

Skinner, B. F.
  1938   *Behavior of Organisms: An Experimental Analysis.* New York: D. Appleton-Century Co.

Skinner, B. F.
1953   *Science and Human Behavior.* New York: Macmillan.

Torrez, Danielle Gagnon
1983   *High Inside: Memoirs of a Baseball Wife.* New York: G. P. Putnam's Sons.

CHAPTER EIGHT
Ghosts, Souls, and Ancestors: Power of the Dead

Vodou
Karen McCarthy Brown

REFERENCES

Brown, Karen McCarthy
2001   *Mama Lola: A Vodou Priestess in Brooklyn.* Updated edition. Berkeley: University of California Press.

Cosentino, Donald
1995   *The Sacred Arts of Haitian Vodou.* Los Angeles: UCLA Fowler Museum of Cultural History.

Courlander, Harold
1960   *The Drum and the Hoe: Life and Lore of the Haitian People.* Berkeley: University of California Press.

David, Wade
1985   *The Serpent and the Rainbow.* New York: Simon & Schuster.
1988   *Passage of Darkness.* Chapel Hill: University of North Carolina Press.

Dayan, Joan
1998   *Haiti, History, and the Gods.* Berkeley: University of California Press.

Deren, Maya
1953   *Divine Horsemen: The Living Gods of Haiti.* New Paltz, N.Y. [Reprint 1983.]

Desmangles, Leslie G.
1993   *The Faces of the Gods: Vodou and Roman Catholicism in Haiti.* Chapel Hill: University of North Carolina Press.

Fick, Carolyn E.
1990   *The Making of Haiti: The San Domingue Revolution from Below.* Knoxville: University of Tennessee Press.

Greene, Anne
1993   *The Catholic Church in Haiti: Political and Social Change.* East Lansing: Michigan State University Press.

Herskovits, Melville J.
1937   *Life in a Haitian Village.* New York: Doubleday.

Larose, Serge
1977   "The Meaning of Africa in Haitian Vodu." In I. M. Lewis, ed., *Symbols and Sentiments: Cross-Cultural Studies in Symbolism.* London: Acedemic Press.

Leyburn, James G.
1941   *The Haitian People.* New Haven, Conn. [Revised edition 1966.]

McAlister, Elizabeth
2002   *Rara!: Vodou, Power, and Performance in Haiti and Its Diaspora.* Berkeley: University of California Press.

Metraux, Alfred
1959   *Voodoo in Haiti.* New York: Schocken.

Rey, Terry
1999   *Our Lady of Class Struggle: The Cult of the Virgin Mary in Haiti.* Trenton, N.J.: Africa World Press.

Thompson, Robert Farris
1981   *Flash of the Spirit: African and Afro-American Art and Philosophy.* New York: Vintage.

Trouillot, Michel-Rolph
1996   *Silencing the Past: Power and the Production of History.* Boston, Mass.: Beacon Press.

The Cremated Catholic: The Ends of a Deceased Guatemalan
Stanley Brandes

REFERENCES

Anonymous
1996   "Families Win Awards from Crematorium." *San Francisco Chronicle,* July 24, A15.

Badone, Ellen, ed.
  1990 *Religious Orthodoxy and Popular Faith in European Society.* Princeton, N.J.: Princeton University Press.

Brown, Peter
  1981 *The Cult of the Saints: Its Rise and Function in Latin Christianity.* Chicago: University of Chicago Press.

Bynum, Carolyn Walker
  1992 *Fragmentation and Redemption: Essays on Gender and the Human Body in Medieval Religion.* New York: Zone Books.

Fried, Rinat
  1998 "Fees at Issue in $20M Cremate Case." *The Recorder,* October 16.

Hertz, Robert
  1960 *Death and the Right Hand.* Glencoe, Ill.: Free Press.

Holding, Reynolds
  1996 "16 Win Damages in Crematorium Suits." *San Francisco Chronicle,* July 10, A12.

CHAPTER NINE
Old and New Religions: The Changing Spiritual Landscape

Revitalization Movements
Anthony F. C. Wallace

REFERENCES

Burridge, K.
  1960 *Mambu: A Melanesian Millennium.* New York: Humanities Press.

Gerlach, L. P.
  1968 "Five Factors Crucial to the Growth and Spread of a Modern Religious Movement." *Journal for the Scientific Study of Religion* 7: 23–40.

Mead, M.
  1956 *New Lives for Old.* New York: Morrow.

Wallace, A. F. C.
  1956a "Mazeway Resynthesis: A Bio-Cultural Theory of Religious Inspiration." *Transactions of the New York Academy of Sciences* 18: 626–38.
  1956b "Revitalization Movements." *American Anthropologist* 58: 264–81.
  1970 *The Death and Rebirth of the Seneca.* New York: Knopf.

The Ghost Dance Religion
Alice Beck Kehoe

REFERENCES

Mooney, James
  [1896] 1973 *The Ghost-Dance Religion and Wounded Knee.* New York: Dover Publications (Originally published as Part 2, *Fourteenth Annual Report 1892–93,* Bureau of Ethnology. Washington, D.C.: Government Printing Office.)

Cargo Cults
Peter M. Worsley

REFERENCES

Worsley, Peter
  1957 *The Trumpet Shall Sound: A Study of "Cargo" Cults in Melanesia.* London: MacGibbon & Kee.

Speaking Is Believing
Susan F. Harding

REFERENCES

Alter, Robert
  1981 *The Art of Biblical Narrative,* p. 69. New York: Basic Books.

Auerbach, Erich
   1953   *Mimesis: The Representation of Reality in
          Modern Literature,* p. 73. Princeton, NJ:
          Princeton University Press.

Bakhtin, M. M.
   1981   *"Discourse in the Novel"* pp. 282,
          293–94. In M. Holquist, ed., *The
          Dialogic Imagination: Four Essays
          by M. M. Bakhtin.* Austin: University
          of Texas Press.

Bauman, Richard
   1977   *Verbal Art as Performance,* pp. 15–24.
          Prospect Heights, IL: Waveland Press.

Borker, Ruth
   n.d.   *The Presentation of the Gospel in Everyday
          Life,* pp. 1, 3. Unpublished manuscript.

Favret-Saada, Jeanne
   1980   *Deadly Words: Witchcraft in the Bocage,*
          pp. 16, 22, 113–14. Cambridge, UK:
          University of Cambridge Press.

Frei, Hans
   1974   *The Eclipse of Biblical Narrative: A Study
          of Eighteenth and Nineteenth Century
          Hermeneutics,* p. 1. New Haven, CT: Yale
          University Press.

Graham, Billy
   1983   *Approaching Hoofbeats: The Four Horsemen
          of the Apocalypse,* p. 203. Waco, TX: Word
          Books.

Heirich, Max
   1977   *"A Change of Heart: A Test of Some
          Widely Held Theories of Religious
          Conversion." American Journal of
          Sociology* 83 (3): 653–80.

Hill, Samuel S.
   1985   *The South and the North in American
          Religion,* p. 26. Athens: University of
          Georgia Press.

James, William
   1906   *The Varieties of Religious Experience,*
          p. 158. New York: Collier Books.

Jules-Rosette, Benetta
   1976   *"The Conversion Experience: The
          Apostles of John Maranke,"* p. 135.
          Journal of Religion in Africa 7(2):
          132–64.

Islamic Law: The Foundation of Muslim Practice and a Measure of Social and Political Change

Carolyn Fluehr-Lobban

REFERENCES

Grotberg, Edith, and S. Washi
   1991   "Critical Factors in Women's Status
          Predictive of Fertility Rates in the
          Sudan." Paper presented at the eleventh
          annual conference of the Sudan Studies
          Association, Vassar College.

Lobban, Richard
   1982   "Class and Kinship in Sudanese Urban
          Communities." *Africa* 52(2): 51–76.

Musallam, Basim F.
   1986   *Sex and Society in Islam.* Cambridge:
          Cambridge University Press.

Pickthall, Muhammad M.
   1977   *The Meaning of the Glorious Qur'an.* New
          York: Muslim World League.

CHAPTER TEN
Religion as Global Culture: Migration, Media, and Other Transnational Forces

The Veil in Their Minds and on Our Heads: Veiling Practices and Muslim Women

Homa Hoodfar

REFERENCES

Ahmed, Leila
   1982   "Feminism and Feminist Movement
          in the Middle East." *Women's
          Studies International Forum*
          5(2): 153–68.

Alloula, Malek
   1986   *The Colonial Harem.* Minneapolis:
          University of Minnesota Press.

Atkinson, James
    1832   *Customs and Manners of Women of Persia and Their Domestic Superstitions.* New York: Burt Franklin.

Bedawi, Jamal A.
    n.d.   *The Muslim Woman's Dress According to the Qur'an and the Sunnah.* London: Ta-Ha.

Eberhardt, Isabelle
    1987   *The Passionate Nomad: The Diary of Isabelle Eberhardt.* Ed. and intro. by Rana Kabbani. London: Virago Press.

Esposito, John
    1988   *Islam: The Straight Path.* New York: Oxford University Press.

Fernea, Elizabeth Warnock
    1965   *Guests of the Sheikh.* New York: Doubleday.

Hoodfar, Homa
    1989   "A Background to the Feminist Movement in Egypt." *Bulletin of Simone de Beauvoir Institute* 9(2): 18–23.
    1991   "Return to the Veil: Personal Strategy and Public Participation in Egypt." In N. Redclift and M. T. Sinclair, eds., *Working Women: International Perspectives on Labour and Gender Ideology.* London: Routledge.
    1992   "Feminist Anthropology and Critical Pedagogy: The Anthropology of Classrooms' Excluded Voices." *Canadian Journal of Education* 17(3): 303–20.

Jalabi, Afra
    1992   "Veiled Oppression and Pointed Fingers." *McGill Daily,* September 28 (special issue on "Culture Fest").

Jayawardena, Kumari
    1986   *Feminism and Nationalism in the Third World.* London: Zed Press.

Kabbani, Rana
    1986   *Europe's Myths of the Orient.* Bloomington: Indiana University Press.

Kader, Soha Abdel
    1988   *Egyptian Women in Changing Society 1899–1987.* Boulder, Colo.: Reinner.

Keddie, Nikki R., and Beth Baron
    1991   *Women in Middle Eastern History: Shifting Boundaries in Sex and Gender.* New Haven, Conn.: Yale University Press.

Lazreg, M.
    1988   "Feminism and Difference: The Perils of Writing as a Woman on Women in Algeria." *Feminist Studies* 14(1): 81–107.

Mabro, Judy
    1982   *Veiled Half-Truths: Western Travellers' Perceptions of Middle Eastern Women.* London: I. B. Tauris.

MacLeod, Arlene Elowe
    1991   *Accommodating Protests: Working Women and the New Veiling in Cairo.* New York: Columbia University Press.

Malcolm, John
    1949   *Sketches of Persia from the Journals of a Traveler in the East.* London: J. Murray.

Mernissi, Fatima
    1991   *The Veil and the Male Elite: A Feminist Interpretation of Women's Rights in Islam.* New York: Addison-Wesley.

Millet, Kate
    1982   *Going to Iran.* New York: Coward, McCann and Geoghean.

Mir-Hosseini, Ziba
    1992   *Marriage on Trial: A Study of Islamic Law.* London: I. B. Tauris.

Nader, Laura
    1989   "Orientalism, Occidentalism and the Control of Women." *Cultural Dynamics* 2(3): 323–55.

Pastner, C. M.
    1978   "Englishmen in Arabia: Encounters with Middle Eastern Women." *Signs* 4(2): 309–23.

Rugh, Andrea
    1986   *Reveal and Conceal: Dress in Contemporary Egypt.* Syracuse, N.Y.: Syracuse University Press.

Said, Edward
    1978   *Orientalism.* London: Routledge and Kegan Paul.
    1993   *Culture and Imperialism.* New York: Knopf.

Suratgar, Olive Hepburn
    1951   *I Sing in the Wilderness: An Intimate Account of Persia and Persians.* London: Edward Stanford.

Tabari, Azar, and Nahid Yeganeh
1982   *In the Shadows of Islam: The Women's Movement in Iran.* London: Zed Press.

Tillon, Germaine
1983   *The Republic of Cousin: Women's Oppression in Mediterranean Society.* London: Al Saqi Books.

Wikan, Unni
1982   *Behind the Veil in Arabia.* Chicago: University of Chicago Press.

Ritual and the Performance of Buddhist Identity Among Lao Buddhists in North America
Penny Van Esterik

REFERENCES

Archaimbault, Charles
1971   *The New Year Ceremony at Basak (South Laos).* Trans. S. Boas. Ithaca, NY: Cornell University Southeast Asia Program.

Battisti, Rosemarie
1989   "Preserving the Spiritual and Cultural Heritage of Amerasian and Southeast Asian Families." In *Reasons for Living and Hoping: The Spiritual and Psycho-Social Needs of Southeast Asian Refugee Children and Youth Resettled in the United States.* Washington, D.C: The International Catholic Child Bureau, Inc.

Bernstein, S.
1989   'Reflections on What It Means to be an American Buddhist.' In *Reason for Living and Hoping: The Spiritual and Psycho-Social Needs of Southeast Asian Refugee Children and Youth Resettled in the United States.* Washington, D.C.: The International Catholic Child Bureau, Inc.

Berval, René de
1959   *Kingdom of Laos.* Limoges, France: A Bontemps Co., Ltd.

Bliatout, B. T., et al.
1985   "Mental Health and Preservation Activities Targeted to Southeast Asian Refugees." In T. Owen, ed., *Southeast Asian Mental Health: Treatment, Prevention, Services, Training and Research.* Washington, D.C.: National Institute of Mental Health.

Burford, G.
1981   "Lao Retrospectives: Religion in a Cultural Context." *Journal of Refugee Research* 1: 50–58.

Burwell, R. J., P. Hill, and J. F. Van Weklin
1986   "Religion and Refugee Resettlement in the United States: A Research Note." *Review of Religious Research* 27: 356–366.

Canda, Edward, and Thitya Phaobtong
1992   "Buddhism as a Support System for Southeast Asian Refugees." *Social Work* 37, no.1: 61–67.

Condominas, G.
1987   "In Search of a Vat: The Dai Lu in Internal and the Lao in External Exile." In *Proceedings of the International Conference on Thai Studies,* 445–56. Canberra: Australian National University.

Diamine, Arthur
1985   *Laos: Keystone of Indochina.* Boulder: Westview Press.

Evans, Grant
1990   *Lao Peasants under Socialism.* New Haven: Yale University Press.

Gombrich, R., and G. Obeyesekere
1988   *Buddhism Transformed,* p. 24. Princeton, NJ: Princeton University Press.

Gunn, G.
1982   "Theravadins and Commissars: The State and National Identity in Laos." In M. Stuart-Fox, ed., *Contemporary Laos,* 76–100. New York: St. Martin's Press.

Halpern, Joel, and Sam Pettengill
1987   *The Far World Comes Near: The Kingdom of Laos and Laotian Americans—An Exhibition of Laotian Arts and Culture.* Amherst, MA: Augusta Savage Gallery, University of Massachusetts, Amherst.

Hein, Jeremy
1995   *From Vietnam, Laos and Cambodia: Refugee Experience in the United States,* p. 8. New York: Twayne Publishers, 1995.

Kuamtou, S.
1981   "Lao In Kalihi." In T. Beng, ed., *New Immigrants*. New York: Pilgrim Press.

Lafont, P. B.
1982   "Buddhism in Contemporary Laos." In M. Stuart-Fox, ed., *Contemporary Laos*, 148–62. New York: St Martin's Press.

LeBar, F., and A. Suddard
1960   *Laos: Its People, Its Society, Its Culture*. New Haven: HRAF Press.

Lewis, R. E. M., W. Fraser, and P. J. Pecora.
1988   "Religiosity among Indochinese Refugees in Utah." *Journal for the Scientific Study of Religion* 27: 272–83.

McIntosh, W., and J. Alston
1981   *Religion and the New Immigrants: Initial Observations Concerning Lao Refugees in Houston, Texas*. Paper presented at the Annual Meeting of the Association for the Sociology of Religion, Toronto, Canada.

McLellan, Janet
1987   "The Role of Buddhism in Managing Ethnic Identity among Tibetans in Lindsay, Ontario." *Canadian Ethnic Studies* 19: 63–76.

Muecke, Marjorie
1987   "Resettled Refugees' Reconstruction of Identity. Lao in Seattle." *Urban Anthropology* 16, no. 3–4: 273–89

Ngaosyvathn, Mayoury
1990   "Individual Soul, National Identity: The *Baci*-Sou Khuan of the Lao." *Sojourn* 5: 283–07.

Rajah, Ananda
1990   'Orientalism, Commensurability and the Construction of Lao Identity: A Comment on the Notion of Lao Identity.' *Sojourn* 5: 308–33.

Stuart-Fox, Martin
1983   "Marxism and Theravada Buddhism: The Legitimation of Political Authority in Laos." *Pacific Affairs* 56: 428–54.

Stuart-Fox Martin, and Rod Bucknell
1982   "Politicization of the Buddhist *Sangha* in Laos." *Journal of Southeast Asian Studies* 13: 60–68.

Suksamran, Somboon
1977   *Political Buddhism in Southeast Asia*, London: C. Hurst and Company.

Tambiah, Stanley J.
1970   *Buddhism and the Spirit Cults of Northeast Thailand*. Cambridge: Cambridge University Press.

Van Esterik, John.
1985   "Lao" in D. Hines, ed., *Refugees in the United States*, 149–65. Westport, CT: Greenwood Press.

Van Esterik, Penny
1992   *Taking Refuge: Lao Buddhists in North America*. Tempe, AZ: Program for Southeast Asian Studies, Arizona State University.
1982   "Interpreting Cosmology: Guardian Spirits in Thai Buddhism." *Anthropos* 77: 1–15.
1981   "In-Home Sponsorship for Southeast Asian Refugees: A Preliminary Assessment." *Journal of Refugee Resettlement* 1, no. 2: 18–26.
1980   "Cultural Factors Affecting the Adjustment of Southeast Asian Refugees." In E. Tepper, ed., *Southeast Asian Exodus: From Tradition to Settlement*, 151–71. Ottawa: Canadian Asian Studies Association.

Religious Terror and Global War
Mark Juergensmeyer

REFERENCES

Abouhalima, Mahmud
1997   Author's interview with convicted codefendant in World Trade Center bombing. United States Penitentiary, Lompoc, CA, August 19, September 30.

Bourdieu, Pierre
1977   *Outline of a Theory of Practice*, p. 171–83. Trans. Richard Nice. Cambridge: Cambridge University Press.
1991   *Language and Symbolic Power*, pp. 72–76, 116, 117. Trans. Gino Raymond and Matthew Adamson. Cambridge, MA: Harvard University Press.

Bourdieu, Pierre and Loic J. D. Wacquant
  1992   *An Invitation to Reflexive Sociology*, p. 131
          Chicago: University of Chicago Press.

Casanova, José
  1994   *Public Relations in the Modern World*,
          p. 211. Chicago University of Chicago
          Press.

Chatterjee, Partha
  1993   *The Nation and Its Fragments: Colonial and
          Postcolonial Histories*. Princeton: Princeton
          University Press.

Fanon, Frantz
  1963   *The Wretched of the Earth*. New York:
          Grove Press.

Friedland, Roger
  1999   "When God Walks in History: The
          Institutional Politics of Religious
          Nationalism," *International Sociology*,
          September.

Habermas, Jurgen
  1975   *Legitimation Crisis*. Trans. Thomas
          McCarthy. Boston: Beacon Press.
  1987   "Modernity—An Incomplete Project,"
          p. 148, reprinted in Paul Rainbow and
          William M. Sullivan, eds., *Interpretive
          Social Science: A Second Look*. Berkeley:
          University of California Press.

McMahon, Darrin
  2000   *Enemies of the Enlightenment: The French
          Counter-Enlightenment and the Making of
          Modernity*. New York: Oxford University
          Press.

Ibraheem el-Geyoushi, Dr. Muhammad
  1990   Author's interview with Dean of the
          Faculty of Dawah, Al-Azhar University,
          Cairo, May 30.

Juergensmeyer, Mark
  1993   *The New Cold War? Religious Nationalism
          Confronts the Secular State*, 11–25.
          Berkeley: University of California Press.
  2000   *Terror in the Mind of God: The Global Rise of
          Religious Violence*. Berkeley: University of
          California Press.
  2002   *Gandhi's Way: A Handbook of Conflict
          Resolution*. Berkeley: University of
          California Press.

Lerner, Yoel
  1998   Author's interview with Director of the
          Sannhedrin Institute, Jerusalem. March 2.

McMahon, Darrin
  2001   *Enemies of the Enlightenment: The French
          Counter-Enlightenment and the Marking of
          Modernity*. New York: Oxford University
          Press.

Rantisi, Dr. Abdul Aziz
  1998   Author's interview with cofounder and
          political leader of Hamas, Khan Yunis,
          Gaza, March 1–2.

Tambiah, Stanley
  1996   *Leveling Grounds: Ethnonationalist
          Conflicts and Collective Violence in South
          Asia*, pp. 310–11. Berkeley: University of
          California Press.

Zemon Davis, Natalie
  1973   "The Rites of Violence: Religious Riots in
          Sixteenth-Century France." *Past and
          Present* 59 (May): 55–53, 81–82.

Homer the Heretic and Charlie Church: Parody, Piety, and Pluralism in *The Simpsons*

Lisle Dalton, Eric Michael Mazur, and Monica Siems

REFERENCES

Bastien, Joseph
  1987   "Humor and Satire." In Mircea Eliade,
          ed., *Encyclopedia of Religion*. New York:
          Macmillan.

Chesebro, James
  1979   "Communication, Values, and Popular
          Television Series: A Four-Year
          Assessment." In H. Newcomb, ed.,
          Television: The Critical View. 2nd ed.
          New York: Oxford University Press.

Collum, Danny Duncan
  1991   " . . . Because He Made So Many of
          Them." *Sojourners* 20 (November):
          38–39.

Corliss, Richard
  1994   "Simpsons Forever!" *Time*, May 2, p. 77.

Freeman, Michael
  1995 "The Official End (1994–95 Syndication Season Led by *The Simpsons*)." *Mediaweek*, September 18, p. 14.

Geertz, Clifford
  1973 "Religion as a Cultural System." In *The Interpretation of Cultures*, pp. 87–125. San Francisco: Basic Books.

Goethals, Gregor
  1981 *The TV Ritual.* Boston: Beacon Press.

Greeley, Andrew
  1987 "Today's Morality Play: The Sitcom." *New York Times*, May 17, pp. 1, 40 (Arts and Leisure).

Handelman, Don
  1987 "Clowns." In M. Eliade, ed., *Encyclopedia of Religion.* New York: Macmillan.

Himmelstein, Hal
  1994 *Television Myth and the American Mind.* 2nd ed. Westport, Conn.: Praeger.

Lefton, Terry
  1992 "Don't Tell Mom: Fox Looks to a Degenerate Clown and a Violent Cat-and-Mouse Duo to Revitalize *The Simpsons'* Merchandise Sales." *Brandweek*, August 10, pp. 16–17.

McConnell, Frank
  1990 " 'Real' Cartoon Characters: *The Simpsons*." *Commonweal*, June 15, pp. 389–90.

Medved, Michael
  1992 *Hollywood vs. America: Popular Culture and the War on Traditional Values.* New York: HarperCollins.

Olive, David
  1992 *Political Babble: The 1,000 Dumbest Things Ever Said by Politicians.* New York: Wiley.

Ozersky, Josh
  1991 "TV's Anti-Families: Married . . . with Malaise." *Tikkun* 6 (January–February): 11–14, 92–93.

"Prime-Time Religion."
  1992 *Christianity Today*, March 9, p. 60.

Rebeck, Victoria
  1990 "Recognizing Ourselves in *The Simpsons*." *Christian Century*, June 27, p. 622.

Richmond, Ray, and Antonia Coffman, eds.
  1997 *The Simpsons: A Complete Guide to Our Favorite Family.* New York: HarperCollins.

Riddle, Lyn
  1994 "A Rascal Cartoon Character Sets Off a Controversy in South Carolina." *Los Angeles Times*, Mary 1, p. A5.

Rosenthal, Andrew
  1992 "In a Speech, President Returns to Religious Themes." *New York Times*, January 18, p. A17.

Sekaquaptewa, Emory
  1989 "One More Smile for a Hopi Clown." In D. M. Dooling and P. Jordan-Smith, eds., *I Become Part of It: Sacred Dimensions in Native American Life.* San Francisco: HarperSan Francisco.

Skill, Thomas, et al.
  1994 "The Portrayal of Religion and Spirituality on Fictional Network Television." *Review of Religious Research* 35 (March): 251–67.

Wilde, Alan
  1981 *Horizon of Assent: Modernism, Postmodernism, and the Ironic Imagination.* Baltimore, Md.: Johns Hopkins University Press.

Index